THE PAPERS OF ULYSSES S. GRANT

THE PAPERS OF

ULYSSES S. GRANT

Volume 29:

October 1, 1878–September 30, 1880

Edited by John Y. Simon

ASSOCIATE EDITOR
Aaron M. Lisec

ASSISTANT EDITOR
Leigh Fought

TEXTUAL EDITOR
Cheryl R. Ragar

SOUTHERN ILLINOIS UNIVERSITY PRESS

CARBONDALE

Library of Congress Cataloging in Publication Data (Revised)

Grant, Ulysses Simpson, Pres. U.S., 1822–1885.
   The papers of Ulysses S. Grant.

   Prepared under the auspices of the Ulysses S. Grant Association.
   Bibliographical footnotes.
      CONTENTS: v. 1. 1837–1861.—v. 2. April–September 1861.—v. 3.
   October 1, 1861–January 7, 1862.—v. 4. January 8–March 31, 1862.—
   v. 5. April 1–August 31, 1862.—v. 6. September 1–December 8,
   1862.—v. 7. December 9, 1862–March 31, 1863.—v. 8. April 1–July 6,
   1863.—v. 9. July 7–December 31, 1863.—v. 10. January 1–May 31,
   1864.—v. 11. June 1–August 15, 1864.—v. 12. August 16–November 15,
   1864.—v. 13. November 16, 1864–February 20, 1865.—v. 14. February 21–April 30, 1865.—v. 15. May 1–December 31, 1865.—v. 16.
   1866.—v. 17. January 1–September 30, 1867.—v. 18. October 1, 1867–
   June 30, 1868.—v. 19. July 1, 1868–October 31, 1869.—v. 20. November 1, 1869–October 31, 1870.—v. 21. November 1, 1870–May 31,
   1871.—v. 22. June 1, 1871–January 31, 1872.—v. 23. February 1–December 31, 1872.—v. 24. 1873.—v. 25. 1874.—v. 26. 1875.—v. 27.
   January 1–October 31, 1876.—v. 28. November 1, 1876–September
   30, 1878.—v. 29. October 1, 1878–September 30, 1880.
      1. Grant, Ulysses Simpson, Pres. U.S., 1822–1885. 2. United
   States—History—Civil War, 1861–1865—Campaigns and battles—
   Sources. 3. United States—Politics and government—1869–1877—
   Sources. 4. Presidents—United States—Biography. 5. Generals—
   United States—Biography. I. Simon, John Y., ed. II. Ulysses S. Grant
   Association.
   E660.G756   1967   973.8'2'0924   67–10725
   ISBN-13: 978-0-8093-2775-1 (v. 29)
   ISBN-10: 0-8093-2775-9 (v. 29)

The paper used in this publication meets the minimum requirements of
American National Standard for Information Sciences—Permanence
of Paper for Printed Library Materials, ANSI Z39.48–1992. ⊚

Published with the assistance of a grant from the National Historical
Publications and Records Commission.

Contents

═══

Introduction

═══════

Ulysses S. Grant concluded his European travels during the final months of 1878. Leaving Paris, he toured Spain and Portugal and met the royal families in both countries. Spain had not impressed him. "There seems to be no satisfaction with existing affairs and I would not be surprised to hear of a revolution breaking out at any time." At Gibraltar, Grant visited the British governor and inspected the garrison. Back in Paris, Grant reflected on the trip thus far. "We have seen the Capitols and most of the principle towns, and the people, of every Country in Europe. I have not yet seen any to be jealous of."

Having decided to push eastward into Asia, Grant persuaded his son Frederick Dent Grant and close friend Adolph E. Borie to accompany him. They joined the Grants in France in January, 1879. John Russell Young, the *New York Herald* correspondent who had accompanied Grant through much of his previous travel, also joined the party, poised to chronicle Grant's journey.

Before he left for Asia, Grant made a hurried trip to Ireland. Irish nationalists, who remembered his snub of a Fenian delegation while president, protested the visit. Made an honorary citizen in Dublin, Grant joked that he intended to run for local office. "It strikes me you did not know rightly what you were doing when you made me a freeman of your city—that you did not know the trouble you were about getting into—for I am a troublesome candidate, and may trouble some of you here." Grant also toured the Protestant strongholds of Belfast and Londonderry, noting, "There are no more thrifty, self reliant & contented people in europe to-day than the people of north Ireland."

Back on the continent, Grant and his companions took a French steamer from Marseilles on January 23. The ship ran along the west coast of Italy and reached Alexandria, Egypt, in less than a week. The party then journeyed by land to the Suez Canal and boarded a British steamer bound for Bombay. During the voyage, Grant began a travel diary, in which he described a stop at Aden. "The natives are of a low order of savages; hair died—or colored from some process—red, curled into small corkscrew tufts. It is fortunate that enlightened nations take possession of such people and make them, and their soil, produce something for the advancement of civilization of the human race."

After a few days in Bombay, the party traversed the northern provinces of India, visiting the Taj Mahal and other tourist sites, riding elephants, and observing ancient farming practices. At the holy city of Benares, he observed Hindu mystics at prayer. "It is a grave question whether they should be disturbed in their faith. It teaches no cruelty to beast or man, and sets up a good system of morals for the guidance of its followers." Still, he supported British rule. "It would be a sad day for the people of India and for the commerce of the world if the English should withdraw." British Viceroy Edward Robert Bulwer-Lytton celebrated Grant's arrival in Calcutta with a state dinner and later played cards with his guest. Bulwer-Lytton's subsequent allegations of drunken and licentious behavior by Grant are impossible to credit.

From Calcutta, Grant and his party continued by sea to Burma, Malaysia, Singapore, Siam, and Hong Kong. In his diary, Grant compared the Burmese and Indian people. "But the first great difference that strikes the traveler is the greater prosperity of the Burmese, and their much better personal appearance. They like to dress—in gay colors—and all do wear clothing. The Indian covers but little of his person and cares but little about what portion is covered." By contrast, the Siamese appeared backward, but King

Chulalongkorn impressed his guest. "The ease and grace and high degree of civilization of the ruling class among a people who have made so little advance in civilization strikes one with amazement." Grant rewarded the king's hospitality with friendship and advice on diplomacy and commerce. At Macao, Grant looked in on "one of the licensed gambling houses." "We are now on the home stretch," he wrote from Hong Kong, "letters going much quicker to America by the East than by the West."

Grant reached Shanghai on May 17. In coastal trading areas, he found the Chinese dominated by European colonists. "They are patient enduring and of long suffering in their weakness. But once feeling themselves strong they are likely to become cruel overbearing and vindictive. They cannot be much blamed if this prediction comes true. At present their rights are scarsely respected in any open port where foreigners are admitted." At Peking, he advised Prince Kung. "You do not want the foreigner to come in and put you in debt by lending you money and then taking your country. That is not the progress that benefits mankind, and we desire no progress either for ourselves or for China that is not a benefit to mankind." Grant stressed the difference between American policy and European behavior. "There is no temptation to the United States to adventures outside of our own country." Grant encouraged Chinese education and economic development. He found the Chinese "a people of wonderful shrewdness and industry," and believed that in less than a half century "Europe will be complaining of the too rapid advance of China."

At Tientsin, Grant befriended the local viceroy, Li Hung-chang, chief promoter of China's modernization. Li and Prince Kung persuaded Grant to arbitrate a dispute between China and Japan over possession of the Ryukyu Islands. "War in itself is so great a calamity that it should only be invoked when there is no way of saving a nation from a greater." Grant's informal mediation in China and Japan, and his recommendation that special commissioners be appointed to continue negotiations, possibly prevented a war.

Grant left for Japan aboard the U.S.S. *Richmond* without Borie, who had left the party at Shanghai because of poor health.

Welcomed at Nagasaki, Grant continued to contrast United States and European practices. "America has much to gain in the east. No nation has greater interests at stake. But America has nothing to gain except what comes from the cheerful acquiescence of the eastern people, and insures them as much benefit as it does us. I should be ashamed of my country if its relations with other nations, and especially with these ancient and most interesting empires in the east, were based upon any other idea." Cholera outbreaks restricted touring in Japan, and Grant spent several weeks in Tokyo and environs. His audiences with the emperor and empress broke new ground in Japan's external relations. Parties and celebrations filled the final days of his stay. "My visit to Japan has been the most pleasant of all my travels. The country is beautifully cultivated, the scenery is grand, and the people, from the highest to the lowest, the most kindly & the most cleanly in the world." On September 3, Grant departed for San Francisco on the *City of Tokio.*

A thunderous reception greeted Grant upon his return to the United States on September 20. At receptions, parades, and other public gatherings, Grant assured his fellow citizens that overseas travel had not lessened his enthusiasm for his home country. Civil War veterans in San Francisco heard Grant expand on this theme. "If you had traveled around the world as I have for the past two or three years you would appreciate, like me, the value of our common country more completely than any man can who stays at home." To banqueting journalists, Grant said, "The good opinion of my countrymen is dearer to me than that of the whole world besides." Over the next weeks, Grant toured northern California, Oregon, and Washington Territory, returning to many places he had first seen as an army officer in the 1850s. A crowd of 4,000 in Portland heard Grant reflect. "It is a pleasure to be back again near the place I enjoyed so much 26 or 27 years ago. I am glad to note evidences of your prosperity, and I take it as only a beginning of the great improvement in the near future." Before heading east again, Grant told a San Francisco gathering, "I hope that another quarter of a century will not elapse before I shall be able to visit you again."

Along the Union Pacific Railroad, people clamored to see Grant at every city, town, and tiny station, and he spoke on many occasions when he would have preferred to pass through quietly or rest. At Virginia City, Nevada, Grant visited the Comstock Lode mines to check on his investments. At Ogden, Utah Territory, he said a few words even though in pain from a sprained back caused by a sudden lunge of his railroad car. At Schuyler, Nebraska, Grant responded to a state senator, "I am glad to see this prairie State growing as it appears to be." On November 5, Grant and his wife reached their home in Galena, but they soon left for Chicago, where hundreds of thousands paraded through the streets and veterans cheered Grant at the annual reunion of the Society of the Army of the Tennessee. Grant told his former soldiers that "it affords me heartfelt pleasure to again see you, my earliest comrades in arms in the great conflict for Nationality and the Union of all the States under one free and always-to-be-maintained Government." After a few quiet weeks in Galena, the pair returned to Philadelphia on December 16, triumphantly completing their circumnavigation of the globe. Again the recipient of adulation, Grant exclaimed, "It makes me feel very grateful to Philadelphians to be always so welcomed by them."

Unwilling to settle in Galena, searching for business opportunities that would bring financial security, and still restive, Grant planned a winter trip to Cuba and Mexico. He persuaded Lieutenant General Philip H. Sheridan and his wife to join the party, which also included Frederick Grant and his wife, Chicago newspaperman Byron Andrews, and illustrator Frank H. Taylor, who later published scenes from their travels. Venturing into Florida for the first time while on his way to Cuba, Grant commented on the cordiality he received from all southerners and the importance of national unity. He wrote to a friend, "This state has a great future before it. . . . It affords the best opening to be found in any country for young men of little means but full of energy, industry and patience." Grant found Cuba oppressively hot and accommodations primitive, and the visit was marred by news of Borie's death, "one of our best of friends & of Philadelphias noblest and most highly respected citizens." Mexico and its promising economic future interested Grant much more. "With proper encouragement for a time, the introduction of foreign capital and enterprise to put the people on their feet Mexico would become a rich country." En route from Vera Cruz to Galveston, the Grants encountered a severe storm that delayed their arrival and led to fears that their steamer had been lost. Grant later told a reporter "he had had the pleasure of reading his obituary in a Democratic paper, and commenting on it seemed rather pleased that his actions were attributed at least to honest motives."

Another procession of receptions and speeches ensued as Grant visited New Orleans and Mobile, then moved north through the Mississippi River valley. Calling for reconciliation and harmony, Grant found both at the hands of his hosts. At Vicksburg, a former Confederate colonel reminded Grant about "a time when your presence here was less welcome than it is to-day." Yet Grant made clear he had not lost sight of civil rights for blacks and the cause of public education. Black audiences from Galveston to Memphis heard him state his desire that all citizens reach their potential and obtain happiness. "I hope everything for the colored people, and may you make freedom a blessing to yourselves."

Behind the scenes, as he traveled north, friends pushed Grant to allow his name to be used at the Republican national convention set for early June in Chicago. Despite public and private denials, Grant was inevitably drawn into the contest. "I pay no attention to political letters. I am not half as much interested in that matter as my friends seem to be, nor a tenth as much as my enemies. I can submit without loss of rest to the verdict no matter what it may be." Events at the Republican convention sorely tested Grant's equanimity. Grant's adherents, dubbed "Stalwarts," deadlocked with delegates supporting U.S. Senator James G. Blaine of Maine and Secretary of the Treasury John Sherman. Famously "306" in number, the Stalwarts persisted through the thirty-sixth ballot when a compromise candidate, U.S. Representative James A. Garfield of Ohio, finally reached the necessary majority. Grant thanked his de facto floor leader, U.S. Senator Roscoe Conkling of New York.

"Individually, I am much relieved at the result, having grown weary of constant abuse—always disagreeable, and doubly so when it comes from former professed friends. I have no presentiment as to what is likely to be the result of the labors of the Convention, or the result of the election which is to follow, but I hope for the best to the country."

Leaving politics behind, Grant traveled west in July and August to examine mines in New Mexico Territory and Colorado. Leaving Julia at a mountain resort, Grant visited booming Leadville, and inspected remote mining camps by mule, delighting the miners. "While riding alongside the creek which empties into the lake, the General was informed that it was known as S-n o' a B---h creek, when he suggested it be changed to Carl Schurz creek." Grant returned to Galena and politics in September. Courted by Republican party officials, Grant agreed to campaign for the ticket, writing to vice presidential candidate Chester A. Arthur, "Sincerely believing that the Democratic Party, as now constituted and controlled, is not a fit party to trust with the control of the general Government, I believe it to the interest of all sections, South as well as North, that the Republican Party should succeed in November." Garfield's opponent, Major General Winfield S. Hancock, Grant initially characterized as a good man connected to a bad party. Now, in a lengthy and controversial interview, Grant condemned Hancock as "vain, selfish, weak, and easily flattered." In Warren, Ohio, Grant told a large political rally: "I am a Republican as the two great political parties are now divided, because the Republican Party is a national party seeking the greatest good for the greatest number of citizens." As the campaign entered its final month, Grant prepared to head east, determined to play his part.

Family provided relief from business and politics. Grant doted on his grandchildren, predicting that three-year-old Julia Grant "is going to be very pretty, and she is very smart." He also anticipated a visit from daughter Ellen Grant Sartoris and her son Algernon, when he and the boy could "have a good time fishing, driving fast horses, playing in the sand &c." The marriage of his youngest son added to the family circle.

Abroad and at home, Grant demonstrated a large and generous spirit as well as a profound love for the nation and its ideals. Travel broadened his perspectives. Energetic and in good health, Grant sought new enterprises and explored new avenues to earn money. Grant approached his sixtieth birthday looking forward to fresh challenges.

We are indebted to J. Dane Hartgrove and Howard H. Wehmann for assistance in searching the National Archives; to Harriet F. Simon for proofreading; and to Kimberly T. Dowd and John H. Killmaster, graduate students at Southern Illinois University, for research assistance.

Financial support for the period during which this volume was prepared came from Southern Illinois University, the National Endowment for the Humanities, and the National Historical Publications and Records Commission.

John Y. Simon

August 16, 2006

Editorial Procedure

1. Editorial Insertions

A.   Words or letters in roman type within brackets represent editorial reconstruction of parts of manuscripts torn, mutilated, or illegible.

B.   [. . .] or [— — —] within brackets represent lost material which cannot be reconstructed. The number of dots represents the approximate number of lost letters; dashes represent lost words.

C.   Words in *italic* type within brackets represent material such as dates which were not part of the original manuscript.

D.   Other material crossed out is indicated by ~~cancelled type~~.

E.   Material raised in manuscript, as "4th," has been brought in line, as "4th."

2. Symbols Used to Describe Manuscripts

AD	Autograph Document
ADS	Autograph Document Signed
ADf	Autograph Draft
ADfS	Autograph Draft Signed
AES	Autograph Endorsement Signed
AL	Autograph Letter
ALS	Autograph Letter Signed

ANS	Autograph Note Signed
D	Document
DS	Document Signed
Df	Draft
DfS	Draft Signed
ES	Endorsement Signed
LS	Letter Signed

3. *Military Terms and Abbreviations*

Act.	Acting
Adjt.	Adjutant
AG	Adjutant General
AGO	Adjutant General's Office
Art.	Artillery
Asst.	Assistant
Bvt.	Brevet
Brig.	Brigadier
Capt.	Captain
Cav.	Cavalry
Col.	Colonel
Co.	Company
C.S.A.	Confederate States of America
Dept.	Department
Div.	Division
Gen.	General
Hd. Qrs.	Headquarters
Inf.	Infantry
Lt.	Lieutenant
Maj.	Major
Q. M.	Quartermaster
Regt.	Regiment or regimental
Sgt.	Sergeant
USMA	United States Military Academy, West Point, N.Y.
Vols.	Volunteers

4. Short Titles and Abbreviations

ABPC	*American Book Prices Current* (New York, 1895–)
Badeau	Adam Badeau, *Grant in Peace. From Appomattox to Mount McGregor* (Hartford, Conn., 1887)
CG	*Congressional Globe.* Numbers following represent the Congress, session, and page.
J. G. Cramer	Jesse Grant Cramer, ed., *Letters of Ulysses S. Grant to his Father and his Youngest Sister, 1857–78* (New York and London, 1912)
DAB	*Dictionary of American Biography* (New York, 1928–36)
Foreign Relations	*Papers Relating to the Foreign Relations of the United States* (Washington, 1869–)
Garland	Hamlin Garland, *Ulysses S. Grant: His Life and Character* (New York, 1898)
Julia Grant	John Y. Simon, ed., *The Personal Memoirs of Julia Dent Grant* (New York, 1975)
HED	*House Executive Documents*
HMD	*House Miscellaneous Documents*
HRC	*House Reports of Committees.* Numbers following *HED, HMD,* or *HRC* represent the number of the Congress, the session, and the document.
Ill. AG Report	J. N. Reece, ed., *Report of the Adjutant General of the State of Illinois* (Springfield, 1900)
Johnson, Papers	LeRoy P. Graf and Ralph W. Haskins, eds., *The Papers of Andrew Johnson* (Knoxville, 1967–2000)
Lewis	Lloyd Lewis, *Captain Sam Grant* (Boston, 1950)
Lincoln, Works	Roy P. Basler, Marion Dolores Pratt, and Lloyd A. Dunlap, eds., *The Collected Works of Abraham Lincoln* (New Brunswick, 1953–55)
Memoirs	*Personal Memoirs of U. S. Grant* (New York, 1885–86)
Nevins, Fish	Allan Nevins, *Hamilton Fish: The Inner History of the Grant Administration* (New York, 1936)

O.R.	*The War of the Rebellion: A Compilation of the Official Records of the Union and Confederate Armies* (Washington, 1880–1901)
O.R. (Navy)	*Official Records of the Union and Confederate Navies in the War of the Rebellion* (Washington, 1894–1927). Roman numerals following *O.R.* or *O.R.* (Navy) represent the series and the volume.
PUSG	John Y. Simon, ed., *The Papers of Ulysses S. Grant* (Carbondale and Edwardsville, 1967–)
Richardson	Albert D. Richardson, *A Personal History of Ulysses S. Grant* (Hartford, Conn., 1868)
SED	*Senate Executive Documents*
SMD	*Senate Miscellaneous Documents*
SRC	*Senate Reports of Committees.* Numbers following *SED, SMD,* or *SRC* represent the number of the Congress, the session, and the document.
USGA Newsletter	*Ulysses S. Grant Association Newsletter*
Young	John Russell Young, *Around the World with General Grant* (New York, 1879)

5. Location Symbols

CLU	University of California at Los Angeles, Los Angeles, Calif.
CoHi	Colorado State Historical Society, Denver, Colo.
CSmH	Henry E. Huntington Library, San Marino, Calif.
CSt	Stanford University, Stanford, Calif.
CtY	Yale University, New Haven, Conn.
CU-B	Bancroft Library, University of California, Berkeley, Calif.
DLC	Library of Congress, Washington, D.C. Numbers following DLC-USG represent the series and volume of military records in the USG papers.
DNA	National Archives, Washington, D.C. Additional numbers identify record groups.

IaHA	Iowa State Department of History and Archives, Des Moines, Iowa.
I-ar	Illinois State Archives, Springfield, Ill.
IC	Chicago Public Library, Chicago, Ill.
ICarbS	Southern Illinois University, Carbondale, Ill.
ICHi	Chicago Historical Society, Chicago, Ill.
ICN	Newberry Library, Chicago, Ill.
ICU	University of Chicago, Chicago, Ill.
IHi	Illinois State Historical Library, Springfield, Ill.
In	Indiana State Library, Indianapolis, Ind.
InFtwL	Lincoln National Life Foundation, Fort Wayne, Ind.
InHi	Indiana Historical Society, Indianapolis, Ind.
InNd	University of Notre Dame, Notre Dame, Ind.
InU	Indiana University, Bloomington, Ind.
KHi	Kansas State Historical Society, Topeka, Kan.
MdAN	United States Naval Academy Museum, Annapolis, Md.
MeB	Bowdoin College, Brunswick, Me.
MH	Harvard University, Cambridge, Mass.
MHi	Massachusetts Historical Society, Boston, Mass.
MiD	Detroit Public Library, Detroit, Mich.
MiU-C	William L. Clements Library, University of Michigan, Ann Arbor, Mich.
MoSHi	Missouri Historical Society, St. Louis, Mo.
NHi	New-York Historical Society, New York, N.Y.
NIC	Cornell University, Ithaca, N.Y.
NjP	Princeton University, Princeton, N.J.
NjR	Rutgers University, New Brunswick, N.J.
NN	New York Public Library, New York, N.Y.
NNP	Pierpont Morgan Library, New York, N.Y.
NRU	University of Rochester, Rochester, N.Y.
OClWHi	Western Reserve Historical Society, Cleveland, Ohio.
OFH	Rutherford B. Hayes Library, Fremont, Ohio.
OHi	Ohio Historical Society, Columbus, Ohio.

OrHi	Oregon Historical Society, Portland, Ore.
PCarlA	U.S. Army Military History Institute, Carlisle Barracks, Pa.
PHi	Historical Society of Pennsylvania, Philadelphia, Pa.
PPRF	Rosenbach Foundation, Philadelphia, Pa.
RPB	Brown University, Providence, R.I.
TxHR	Rice University, Houston, Tex.
USG 3	Maj. Gen. Ulysses S. Grant 3rd, Clinton, N.Y.
USMA	United States Military Academy Library, West Point, N.Y.
ViHi	Virginia Historical Society, Richmond, Va.
ViU	University of Virginia, Charlottesville, Va.
WHi	State Historical Society of Wisconsin, Madison, Wis.
Wy-Ar	Wyoming State Archives and Historical Department, Cheyenne, Wyo.
WyU	University of Wyoming, Laramie, Wyo.

Chronology

October 1, 1878–September 30, 1880

═══

1878, Oct. 3.   In Paris, USG attended a dinner at the U.S. legation.

Oct. 12.   USG and party left Paris for Bordeaux.

Oct. 15–16.   At Vitoria, Spain, USG observed army maneuvers with King Alfonso XII.

Oct. 18–23.   USG toured Madrid museums and the nearby Escorial.

Oct. 24.   USG visited a sword factory and synagogue in Toledo.

Oct. 27–Nov. 1.   At Lisbon.

Nov. 3–12.   Back in Spain, USG visited Cordova, Seville, and Cadiz.

Nov. 12–18.   At Gibraltar, USG dined with the governor, Lord Napier, joined a fox hunt, and reviewed British troops.

Nov. 19–23.   USG and party visited Granada and Malaga.

Dec. 6–11.   At Pau, France, USG attended dinners and a fox hunt, then returned to Paris on Dec. 12.

1879, Jan. 3.   At Dublin, when USG was made an honorary citizen he noted that as president he had represented "more Irishmen and their descendants" than Queen Victoria.

Jan. 6–8.   At Londonderry and Belfast, nationalists protested USG's alleged snub of an Irish delegation in 1876.

Jan. 21.   USG left Paris for Marseilles with a party that included his son Frederick, Adolph E. Borie, and John Russell Young.

Jan. 23.   The Grant party sailed from Marseilles aboard a French steamer bound for Alexandria, Egypt.

Jan. 30.   From Alexandria, USG traveled overland to Suez and boarded a British steamer for Bombay.

FEB. 13–18. At Bombay, USG was fêted by his British hosts, met local Parsees, toured schools and the jewelry district, and attended horse races.

FEB. 19–20. While visiting Jabalpur, USG rode an elephant to a nearby quarry. "Was much pleased with the intelligence of these animals."

FEB. 23. After a stop at Allahabad, USG arrived at Agra and visited the Taj Mahal.

FEB. 25. USG witnessed ritual animal sacrifice in an ancient palace at Ulwar.

MAR. 1–4. USG saw ancient ruins, tombs, and deserted villages near Delhi, then toured positions of the 1857 siege with a British survivor.

MAR. 8. USG observed Hindu pilgrims in the holy city of Benares.

MAR. 10–16. While at Calcutta, USG dined with Viceroy Edward Robert Bulwer-Lytton.

MAR. 19–22. USG visited Rangoon and the golden pagoda of Shwedagon.

MAR. 29. At Penang, Chinese merchants asked USG to oppose legislation restricting Chinese immigration to the U.S.

APRIL 1–9. USG and party visited Singapore after stopping at Malacca.

APRIL 7. Vivien May Sartoris, granddaughter, born.

APRIL 13–18. At Bangkok, USG held talks with King Chulalongkorn.

APRIL 25–26. USG and party toured Saigon.

APRIL 30. At Hong Kong, USG visited his friend and former C.S.A. partisan ranger John S. Mosby.

MAY 6. USG visited the Chinese viceroy at Canton, after a procession witnessed by 200,000.

MAY 12. USG and party departed Hong Kong for Amoy.

MAY 17–23. At Shanghai, USG attended a ball and a torchlight parade and addressed U.S. Civil War veterans.

MAY 27–31. USG befriended Viceroy Li Hung-chang at Tientsin.

JUNE 3–10. At Peking, "this forsaken city," USG and party visited the Great Wall and the Temple of Heaven, which USG deemed "not worth the trouble of a visit."

JUNE 5–8. During talks with Prince Kung, USG agreed to mediate a dispute between China and Japan over the Ryukyu Islands.

JUNE 12–14. USG held talks with Li Hung-chang at Tientsin.

JUNE 15. USG and party boarded the U.S.S. *Richmond* off Tientsin.

JUNE 21–27.   While at Nagasaki, Japan, USG and Julia Grant planted a banyan tree in a park.

JUNE 28–JULY 2.   With travel hindered by a cholera outbreak, USG toured Japan's inland sea aboard the *Richmond.*

JULY 3.   USG arrived at Tokyo after landing at nearby Yokohama.

JULY 4.   USG met the Emperor and Empress and celebrated Independence Day with American residents.

JULY 7.   USG reviewed Japanese troops with Emperor Meiji.

JULY 8.   Tokyo honored USG with an evening lantern procession.

JULY 9.   USG attended a dinner at Yokohama.

JULY 10.   USG visited a Tokyo normal school and attended a university commencement.

JULY 16.   USG attended a Kabuki play staged in his honor at Tokyo's Shintomiza Theater. USG wrote: "The Japanese are altogether the superior people of the East."

JULY 19–28.   USG visited Nikkō and toured local shrines and scenic spots.

AUG. 4.   Back in Tokyo, USG learned that Japanese reactionaries had threatened to assassinate him and others.

AUG. 7.   USG telegraphed his willingness to lead a proposed Nicaragua canal project.

AUG. 10.   In an audience with Emperor Meiji, USG denounced the treatment of Asiatic nations by the Western powers.

AUG. 12–19.   USG visited the hot springs at Hakone.

AUG. 13.   In a letter to both parties, USG proposed a conference to settle the Ryukyu dispute.

AUG. 16.   U.S. newspapers published a false rumor that Nellie Grant Sartoris had died.

AUG. 20–SEPT. 2.   In Tokyo, USG visited a military school and the race track, attended a festival at Uyeno Park, and bade farewell to Emperor Meiji.

SEPT. 3.   USG and party departed on the *City of Tokio.*

SEPT. 20.   USG arrived at San Francisco to a tumultuous welcome.

SEPT. 25.   USG addressed veterans of both armies at Oakland.

SEPT. 27.   USG saw *HMS Pinafore* at San Francisco's California Theatre. Later, he attended a veterans' campfire.

SEPT. 29.   USG told thousands of children that only schools "can insure the permanency and perpetuity of our institutions."

OCT. 1–6.   USG and party toured Yosemite Valley by stagecoach and visited the giant sequoias.

OCT. 8. U.S. Senator William Sharon of Nev. hosted a dinner for USG and 2,000 guests at Belmont, his Calif. estate.

OCT. 13. At Astoria, Ore., USG recalled his first visit in 1852. On the same day, at Vancouver, Washington Territory, USG noted: "I lived a year on the spot on which I now stand."

OCT. 14. En route from Vancouver to Portland, Ore., USG's steamer briefly ran aground. USG teased his wife: "Julia, you ought to be satisfied now, we've gone to the bottom at last."

OCT. 15. At Portland, USG toured public schools and took a Columbia River excursion.

OCT. 16. USG visited Salem, Ore.

OCT. 22–23. At Sacramento, USG toured public schools and gave a lengthy interview about China and Japan.

OCT. 25. USG left San Francisco.

OCT. 27–29. USG spoke at Virginia City, Carson City, and Reno, Nev. Deep inside the Virginia Consolidated Mine, USG joked about leaving reporters and politicians there, "but there ain't room for all that ought to be put here."

OCT. 30. Before a speech at Ogden, Utah Territory, USG said he had grown accustomed to public speaking during his travels. "I think I am improving, for my knees don't knock together like they did at first."

OCT. 31. After stops in Wyoming Territory, USG entertained veterans aboard his train.

Nov. 1. USG noted rapid growth in Neb., with towns "as thick as blackberries."

Nov. 3–4. Crossing Iowa, USG addressed a veterans' banquet at Council Bluffs and spoke at the Burlington high school.

Nov. 5–11. At Galena, USG said: "I can take my quiet and ease here better than any-where else."

Nov. 12. Chicago greeted USG with a massive parade. Watching from his hotel balcony, USG met Samuel L. Clemens.

Nov. 13. USG told a Society of the Army of the Tennessee reunion: "Avoid quarreling among ourselves, and we need have no fear for the future."

Nov. 22. USG visited Platteville, Wis.

Nov. 29. The Grants hosted a reception for Galena friends.

DEC. 1. USG visited friends at Dubuque.

DEC. 4–8. At Chicago, USG met clergy at the home of Frederick Dent Grant and planted an elm tree in South Park.

Dec. 9.   USG spoke at Logansport, Ind., and at Indianapolis.

Dec. 10.   At Louisville, USG's reception "astonished" him.

Dec. 11.   USG addressed a large crowd at Cincinnati's Music Hall.

Dec. 12.   USG spoke to soldiers' orphans at Xenia, Ohio, and addressed a banquet at Columbus.

Dec. 13–14.   At Pittsburgh, USG addressed business and civic leaders at several appearances.

Dec. 15.   USG spoke before the governor's mansion in Harrisburg.

Dec. 16.   Completing his tour around the world, USG arrived at Philadelphia and reviewed a large parade in his honor.

Dec. 24.   USG visited his mother and sister at Jersey City.

Dec. 26.   At Philadelphia, USG addressed the Universal Peace Union and privately met President Rutherford B. Hayes.

Dec. 27–30.   At Washington, D.C., USG visited Edward F. Beale.

Dec. 31.   USG stopped at Columbia, S.C., and Augusta, Ga.

1880, Jan. 1.   USG addressed black militia at Beaufort, S.C.

Jan. 2–3.   USG spent the night at Savannah before boarding a steamer for Fla.

Jan. 8–14.   USG and party navigated the St. Johns and Oklawaha rivers.

Jan. 18.   From St. Augustine, USG wrote: "This state has a great future before it."

Jan. 21.   At Key West, USG said: "Cubans, or any other refugees in this country, would always find a free home with us."

Jan. 22–Feb. 13.   In Cuba, USG and party stayed at the governor's palace, witnessed carnival, and visited a tobacco and sugar plantation and hot springs.

Feb. 5.   Borie died at Philadelphia.

Feb. 18.   Matías Romero and other Mexican officials welcomed USG at Vera Cruz.

Feb. 23.   At Mexico City, USG and Lt. Gen. Philip H. Sheridan met President Porfirio Díaz.

Feb. 24.   USG visited Molino del Rey and recounted scenes from the Mexican War.

Mar. 4–8.   USG visited silver mines north of Mexico City.

Mar. 17.   USG promised to promote railroad-building in Mexico.

Mar. 19–23.   Between Vera Cruz and Galveston, a storm in the Gulf of Mexico delayed the *City of Mexico* and prompted rumors it had sunk.

Mar. 25.   USG spoke to black students in Galveston.

MAR. 26–29.   USG visited San Antonio and Houston.

MAR. 31–APRIL 8.   At New Orleans, USG addressed the legislature, visited black churches and schools, attended numerous banquets, and was made a duke by the Mardi Gras society.

APRIL 6.   USG inspected jetties at the mouth of the Mississippi River.

APRIL 9.   En route to Mobile, USG passed the home of Jefferson Davis in Biloxi, Miss.

APRIL 12.   A former Miss. col. welcomed USG to Vicksburg.

APRIL 13.   At Memphis, USG spoke at a downtown rally and a Beale Street church, then visited a black school.

APRIL 15.   USG visited Little Rock.

APRIL 16.   At Cairo, USG recalled when "your little city was a camp of bristling bayonets."

APRIL 19.   USG reached Galena after numerous stops to greet Ill. crowds.

MAY 5.   USG addressed a rally at Springfield, Ill.

MAY 6.   Republicans opposed to a third term for USG met at St. Louis.

MAY 26–28.   Young visited USG at Galena and wrote that "we knocked about the country together like a pair of boys on a holiday."

MAY 31.   USG spent the night with friends at Dubuque.

JUNE 2.   Republicans convened at Chicago.

JUNE 7.   Balloting began at Chicago.

JUNE 8.   James A. Garfield was nominated on the thirty-sixth ballot after delegates deadlocked between USG and James G. Blaine.

JUNE 9.   USG stopped briefly at Chicago to thank supporters.

JUNE 10.   At Milwaukee, USG addressed a national veterans' reunion. Privately, he declared himself "much relieved at the result" in Chicago.

JUNE 14.   USG spoke at Fond du Lac, Wis.

JUNE 17.   USG and Julia Grant returned to Galena.

JUNE 22.   USG declined the presidency of the Panama Canal Co.

JUNE 24.   At Cincinnati, Democrats nominated Maj. Gen. Winfield S. Hancock for president.

JULY 1.   USG spoke at Jacksonville, Ill.

JULY 2.   USG spoke at Merriam, Kan., and Kansas City.

JULY 3–4.   USG visited Fort Leavenworth, Kan.

JULY 7–16.   In New Mexico Territory, USG toured mines.

JULY 24.   USG addressed veterans at Leadville, Colo.

JULY 31–AUG. 10.   Traveling mostly by pack mule, USG toured mining camps near Gunnison, Colo.

AUG. 16.   At Denver, USG rode horseback in a parade to his hotel.

AUG. 21.   USG attended a banquet at Boulder.

AUG. 23.   USG spoke at Cheyenne, Wyoming Territory.

AUG. 27.   At Galena, USG addressed the Garfield and Arthur club.

SEPT. 6–8.   USG attended the Wis. State Fair at Madison.

SEPT. 15–16.   USG attended the Winnebago County Fair at Rockford, Ill.

SEPT. 21.   Interviewed at Galena, USG criticized Hancock's record in postwar La. and called him "a weak, vain man."

SEPT. 21.   Jesse Root Grant, Jr., married Elizabeth Chapman in San Francisco.

SEPT. 28.   USG addressed a large Republican rally at Warren, Ohio. Later, USG, U.S. Senator Roscoe Conkling, and others visited Garfield at nearby Mentor.

The Papers of Ulysses S. Grant
October 1, 1878–September 30, 1880

To John W. Mackay

Paris, France
Oct. 1st /78

J. W. MACKAY, ESQR
DEAR SIR:

[Before my] departur[e from Paris] last Ju[ne you were] kind en[ough to order for] me two [thousand shares] of Yellow [Jacket Silver] Mining [Stock—Since that] I have [not heard whether] the pur[chase was made or] if so a[t what figures, My] son U. [S-Grant Jr. who lives] in New [York City, holds whet] securitie[s I am possessed of] and I wrote to him of the purchase made, but not through what agency.¹ But [he] has been ready at all times [since to pay] the purchase [money if required or the banking rate of interest if the money is not required. Seeing that there has been a sudden run all along the lines of Nevada Mining stocks my special object in writing is to find out whether I own any of them, what they cost. I am the more interested because my stay] abroad is somewhat contingent upon the result. I will be under many obligations to you if you will drop me a line, care Drexel Harjes & Co. 31 Boulivard Haussmann, giving me the information asked.

Mrs. Grant & I enjoyed a most delightful summer in Northern Europe especially through Norway & Sweden The Scandinavian countries it seems to me present many more attractions to the American traveler than Switzerland or the usual summer routes selected by them. We have been but a few days in Paris and have not yet had the pleasure of seeing Mrs Mackay though we will call within a day or two.

Very Truly yours
U. S. GRANT

ALS (partial facsimile), Scott J. Winslow Associates, Inc., *Autographs and Americana*, April 14, 2006, no. 181. Born in 1831 in Ireland, John W. Mackay became wealthy through mining ventures in Calif. and Nev. and expanded his business activities into banking and real estate. See *New York Times*, July 21, 1902; Ethel Manter, *Rocket of the Comstock (The Story of John William Mackay)* (Caldwell, Idaho, 1950).

1. See *PUSG*, 28, 406–7.

To Adam Badeau

Paris, France
SOct. 3d /78

Dear General,

Your letter of the 1st is just at hand. I am sorry you are to unwell to come over before my departure. The latter part of next week we start on our trip through Spain & Portugal. As we will probably visit Algiers, and possibly some other points on the Mediterranean before returning to Paris, we may not return here before December.

I have no knowledge of an intention on the part of either Gov. Fish or Judge Davis to write a Civil history of my Civil Administration. If they should do so it would probably be confined chiefly to matters relating to the State Dept. foreign relations, &c. and would, in that event, be a great help to the preparation of the volume you propose to write.

I would not push the matter of back pay while holding, or wishing to hold, the Consul General ship. It would furnish a pretext for your removal. I think you ought to hurry up Volume II however and get advantage of the present desire to collect war reminiscences.

We are all well.

Very Truly yours
U. S. Grant

Gen. A. Badeau, Consul Gen.l &c.

ALS, Munson-Williams-Proctor Institute, Utica, N. Y. See *Badeau*, p. 507. On Oct. 16, 1878, Adam Badeau, consul gen., London, wrote to Orville E. Babcock that he decided to follow USG's advice concerning army back pay and had visited USG in Paris the previous week. "*Confidential . . .* He left for Spain on the 12th, goes also to Portugal &

Algiers; returns to Paris in December, and will probabl[y] spend the winter there. In the spring Mrs Grant wants to come to England, as Nellie expects to be confined. (You know how delicate the General is, so please dont let this become known.) I dont think he'll go home for another year. He says he may go to India, or remain in Europe. I took him all the first part of the March to the Sea, up to the time when it was finally determined on. He liked it very much, thought it very fair to Sherman, and wants me to send him the proofs. Before doing so I want to have your opinion and Porter's. I want to do Sherman every justice.—I find I cannot possibly finish the book in two volumes. . . . Everybody I see here, and that I saw in Paris, every body who writes me from home says one thing about Grant. If the communist movement continues, he must stand; and even Belmont and the Appletons will support him. But otherwise, on old issues, or simply on the anti greenback, can even he be elected? I dont want him to run and be defeated. Of course, no other Republican has a chance, but what chance has he? . . ." ALS, ICN.

To Edward F. Beale

Paris, France
Oct. 6th /78

MY DEAR GENERAL:

We have now been in Paris for nearly two weeks and are getting ready for our journeying again. This time we go to Spain, Portugal and a little of Africa bordering on the Mediterranean & Atlantic. This done we will settle down for the winter probably in Paris, though possibly in the south of France or Italy. I received your last letter some time ago, while in Vienna I think. I found Vienna one of the most beautiful cities in Europe. But every body retires so horribly early. After ten at night the streets are as silent as the grave.

I hope your diplomacy will prove successful in bringing the Arabian steed![1] I have heard nothing from him however. By accident we have not yet met Mrs. Bakhmitoff.[2] She did not learn of our arrival until we had been here a a week, and then when she did call both Mrs. Grant and myself were out. I believe she is well however and hope Mrs. Grant will see a good deal of her yet before we start.— The weather has been very fine since our last arrival in Paris, the first good weather I have ever seen here for any number of consecutive days. But I would like to swap off the balance of this week to be with you visiting the farm and looking at the colts. I hope the latter are doing well and that they will not disappoint you.

If you see Dan Ammen tell him that I have entirely abandoned the idea of going around the world. Certainly so unless I should conclude to remain absent another year, which I think entirely improbable. Mrs. Grant joins me in kindest regards to Mrs. Beale, Miss Emily and yourself.

Very Truly yours

U. S. GRANT

GN. ED F. BEALE.

ALS, DLC-Decatur House Papers.
    On Sept. 30, 1878, USG wrote to Edward T. Steel and William W. Justice, Pa. merchants. "General & Mrs. Grant accept with pleasure the invitation of Mr. Edward Steel and Mr. Wm W. Justice to dinner on Wednesday, Oct. 2d at seven O'clock." AN (facsimile), Daniel F. Kelleher Co., Inc., Oct. 18, 1997, no. 253.
    On Oct. 3, Edward F. Noyes, U.S. minister, Paris, held a dinner for USG at the legation. See John Russell Young diary, Oct. 3, 1878, DLC-John Russell Young; *New York Herald*, Oct. 4, 1878.

    1. See *PUSG*, 28, 353–57.
    2. Edward F. Beale's eldest daughter. See *ibid.*, p. 300.

To John W. Mackay

Paris, France

Oct. 6th /78.

J. W. MACKAY ESQR
DEAR SIR;

In my letter to you of the 1st of Oct. I neglected to say that if you had purchased two thousand shares of "Yellow Jacket" for me you are authorized to sell at your discretion or retain if you think proper. Whatever becomes of it I shall be entirely satisfied knowing that it is beyond human kind to judge with accuracy as to what lays hidden in the bowels of the earth. You are authorized—and if you feel inclined I wish you would—invest for me to the extent of $25,000. I have securities with my son, U S Grant, Jr 120 Broadway New York City upon which he can realize at any time. For any investm[ent] you have made for me, or do make, he can deposite the securities when you want, or realize on them and pay the [money. He is instructed to do so] if called upon.

Very Truly Yours

U. S. Grant

ALS (partial facsimile), Scott J. Winslow Associates, Inc., *Autographs and Americana*, April 14, 2006, no. 181. For John W. Mackay's unsuccessful speculation in the Yellow Jacket and other mines, see *New York Times*, Dec. 12, 1879.

To Elihu B. Washburne

Paris, France

Oct. 7th /78

My Dear Mr. Washburne:

I am just in receipt of your very welcome letter of the 23d of Sept. I have no recollection of receiving a letter from you written about the time of your departure from Paris.[1] I am sure I should have answered had such a letter reached me. The last communication I remember any thing of was either a letter or dispatch—the latter I think—received by me at Frankford, in answer to one stating the time I would remain there.[2] I was very sorry not to meet you there.

As you say it is bliss to be out of the United States just at a time when every bad element in the country are seemingly carrying every thing before them. It is to be hoped, and I think, confidantly to be relied upon, that all the isms will have run their course before /80. (It is incomprehensible that men—not to say a majority—could be found who are willing to upset the country financially just at a time when we have got so near to specie payments, when we have established the highest credit known among nations, and when general prosperity to the country is just dawning. The whole democratic party cried itself hoarse over the outrage upon the Constitution when the Nation, in its desperation adopted the "Legal Tender note." Every democratic Judge upon the Supreme Bench, I believe, gave a judicial opinion against the Constitutionality of the Act, and every republican member of the Court sustained it only on the ground of imperitive necessity, a means to save the nations life: on the ground of self defense and self preservation justifying the means. Now the whole party seems to be willing to issue an unlimited quantity of this money in spite of their previous declarations; in spite of the solemn promise that above a certain amount—400.000.000—should not be issued; in spite of the solemn obligation that those issued should be redeemed in coin, understood at the time to be gold coin. I believe I am right in this statement of the views of the Supreme Court on the money question.[3]

In the matter that I wrote you about I felt that I was doing right. The Wilsons have disappointed me more than any persons I ever reposed confidence in. The abuse Harry Wilson heaped upon Porter was worse than any thing he said about you, and at a time when he was not only holding a position which gave him and his family a support, directly from Porter but he was visiting him regularly, stopping for dinner often, occasionally staying all night, and some times borrowing money. I understand he has been quite as unsparing of me although I have recently received a letter from him which brands him as a liar if he has ever done so up to the date of his letter. I sent the letter to Buck and told him to preserve it,[4] but to show it to you if the opportunity presents itself.

We leave here in a few days for Spain & Portugal. When we have visited those two countries we will have been in every Country in Europe, and a little of Africa and Asia. I have enjoyed it all very much but often feel homesick to get back. If I should go back now however I would have no home to go to. In the Spring I would have my Long Branch house where I ~~could~~ can stay through the summer and make arrangements for the Winter. Mrs. Grant joins me in kindest regards to Mrs. Washburn and the children as well as to yourself. I will always be glad to hear ~~you~~ from you, and hope I shall not prove negligent in answering.

Remember both Mrs. Grant and myself to Jones[5] and family and to all our Galena friends now residing in Chicago.

Very Truly Yours

U. S. GRANT

P. S. We had letters from Fred & his wife recently speaking of a pleasant dinner party they enjoyed at your house. We embrace

them among our Galena friends, transplanted in Chicago, and desired our remembrance to be extended to them also.

ALS, IHi.
    On Sept. 22, 1878, USG, Ragatz, Switzerland, wrote to Herman Kreismann, con-
sul gen., Berlin. "In you next letter to our mutual friend, The Hon. E. B. Washburne,
please present my compliments and say that Mrs Grant and myself are well; have enjoyed our European trip very much and regret that we had not the pleasure of meeting
him before his return to the United States." Copy (embedded in Kreismann to [Elihu B.
Washburne], Oct. 16, 1878), DLC-Elihu B. Washburne. In his letter to "Dear friend,"
Kreismann added: ". . . In Switzerland I was most of the time at Ragatz and passed a
full week there with General Grant and wife—We were a great deal together and I was
much pleased to hear them both speak so well and kindly of you. The General, I became
convinced thinks you are estranged from him and very much wants to be on good terms
with you. I had asked him for an autograph for a friend and he handed me a letter which, I
think, I had better transcribe for you as follows: . . . Mrs Grant and the General looked in
first rate health. They went to Paris from Switzerland and are to visit Spain, Portugal &
Algiers yet this fall and then spend the winter at Florence & Rome. In the Spring they
expect to return to the United States; at least so the General says. As to the succession
in the Presidency, although they do not say so of course, they seem to feel perfectly sure
of it. As freely and kindly as the General talked of you he was most reserved and cool
respecting Russ Jones, and more strongly yet he seemed to feel against Harry Wilson.
The fact that the last with his brother Bluford had been to dinner at your house seemed
much to worry him. In Illinois he seems to sympathise with Logan. To me he was quite
friendly and I passed an agreeable week with him. Mrs Grant wants particularly to be
remembered to Mrs W. . . ." ALS, *ibid.* See letter to Elihu B. Washburne, Dec. 24, 1878.

    1. Washburne left Paris in late summer, 1877.
    2. See *PUSG*, 28, 241–42.
    3. For the Legal Tender Act of 1862, see Charles Fairman, *Reconstruction and Re-
union 1864–88* (New York, 1971), I, 677–775.
    4. See *PUSG*, 28, 468–74.
    5. J. Russell Jones remained in Chicago after failing to prevent his ouster as col-
lector of customs. See *ibid.*, 27, 265–67; Charles Richard Williams, ed., *Diary and Letters
of Rutherford Birchard Hayes* (Columbus, 1922–26), III, 433, 442, 451, 453; George R.
Jones, *Joseph Russell Jones* (Chicago, 1964), pp. 78–79.

To William S. Stokley et al.

BORDEAUX, France, Oct. 13, 1878.
Hon. WILLIAM S. STOKLEY, Mayor of Philadelphia; JOSEPH L. CAVEN,
President of Common Council, and GEORGE A. SMITH, President of
Select Council:—

    GENTLEMEN—The resolutions of the Select and Common Coun-
cils of Philadelphia that a joint special committee of nine members

from each chamber of Councils be appointed for the purpose of receiving me on my return to your city was duly received.

If I return to the United States by way of the Atlantic I shall surely go by the line of steamers running to Philadelphia, and will give your committee notice of the time of sailing and the probable time of arrival on other side.

With many thanks for the honor done me by the Councils and citizens of Philadelphia, I am, with highest respects, your obedient servant

U. S. GRANT.

New York Herald, Oct. 27, 1878. William S. Stokley, a Republican, served as Philadelphia mayor from 1872. He received USG's letter on Oct. 26, 1878. *Philadelphia Public Ledger*, Oct. 28, 1878. Joseph L. Caven, a lawyer with interests in real estate and insurance, ran unsuccessfully as the Democratic candidate for Philadelphia mayor in 1878. George A. Smith was elected president of the Select Council in 1876.

On Thursday, Oct. 10, 1878, John W. Forney had reported from Paris. "General Grant visited the balloon 'Captive' last Tuesday, and was escorted around the grounds. He did not ascend; but was curious about the whole organization. The projector, Gifford, left offended because the ex-President did not 'gush.' I was a little sorry, but then Grant is not very effusive, even to Frenchmen. . . ." *Philadelphia Press*, Oct. 31, 1878. See Gaston Tissandier, *Le Grand Ballon Captif: A Vapeur de M. Henry Giffard* (Paris, 1878); L. T. C. Rolt, *The Aeronauts: A History of Ballooning 1783–1903* (New York, 1966), pp. 149–52.

On Oct. 12, USG left Paris for Spain. On Oct. 13, John Russell Young wrote in his diary while stopped at Bordeaux. ". . . Dinner & we walked an hour in the moonlight, & the Gen. & I talked for two hours on many points, mainly his actions on the question of inflation." DLC-John Russell Young. See *Young*, I, 506–18.

To Adam Badeau

———

Lisbon, Portugal

Oct. 27th /78

DEAR BADEAU:

Your letter of the 17th come to hand in Madrid[1] when I was so busy that I did not get to write a letter to anyone. I can give no explanation of the dispatches you speak of from Spottsylvania, of 10th & 11th of May /64 to Meade directing him to be prepared in a certain event to move to Gordonsville. The only thing is that I had in mind the possibility, if things favored it, of moving by my

right flank instead of the left as we had been doing before. Gordonsville must have been put in without much reflection knowing
that if we did move to the right events would determine where we
would march to with any reference to the original orders.[2]

We arrived here this a. m. at five oclock having been in the cars
two nights and one day from Madrid, without getting out once by
the way for meals. Spain may contain much of interest to see but
the accomodations for travel are horrible.

Yours as ever

U. S. GRANT

ALS, Munson-Williams-Proctor Institute, Utica, N. Y. On Oct. 25, 1878, USG left Madrid for Portugal. See John Russell Young diary, Oct. 25–27, 1878, DLC-John Russell
Young. On Oct. 28, Young, Lisbon, wrote in his diary. "To-day wrote a good deal on
my notes of Gen. Grants conversation. In conversing with him, made several valuable
notes, more especially about the Southern isthmus canal.—Rode all over town, and
had a beautiful view of Lisbon from the fort on the top of the hill. Came back, dined &
went with the Gen. to walk & call on Mr. Moran. Remained an hou[r.]" *Ibid.* For further details on USG's visit to Portugal, see *ibid.*, Oct. 29–31, Nov. 1–2, 1878; *New York
Herald,* Nov. 8, 1878, Jan. 25, 1879; *Young,* I, 534–47; *Julia Grant,* pp. 256–57.

On Nov. 5, Benjamin Moran, U.S. minister, Lisbon, wrote to Secretary of State
William M. Evarts. ". . . General Grant arrived in this City, accompanied by Mrs
Grant, Mr John Russell Young and Senr da Cunha at an early hour on Sunday the
27th ultimo, and was cordially received at the Station by the American and Portugese
Officials. . . . General Grant describes this reception as characterized by exceptional
personal warmth and as peculiarly agreable to him. On the 31st he and his Suite attended the Opera by Royal invitation in honor of the King's birth day; and on the 1st instant they dined in State with the King and Royal Family at the Palace of the Ajuda. . . .
The General and Suite left for Cordova in Spain, on Saturday evening the 3d instant,
in a Saloon Car furnished by the Government, . . ." LS, DNA, RG 59, Diplomatic Despatches, Portugal. *Foreign Relations, 1878,* pp. 745–46. See *ibid.*, pp. 746–47.

On Nov. 14, Adam Badeau, consul gen., London, wrote to Gen. William T. Sherman. ". . . I have a recent letter from Gen Grant, at Lisbon. I saw him for a day or two
in Paris, when I took him some ~~proof~~ ms about the correspondence between himself
and and you, anterior to the March to the Sea. He said I had given the exact truth, and
he thought you would be pleased with it, and advised me to print it, and send you the
proofs, which I shall do. It would be a great thing to be able to say that both you and
he endorse my statement. What I have been especially anxious about—is to dispel the
notion afloat in some quarters, that there was any rivalry between you: I think I have
treated the theme in such a way as to accomplish this, and so far as I could—given
you each your own glory: enough, either, for any man. . . ." ALS, DLC-William T.
Sherman.

1. On Oct. 18, 9:00 A.M., USG had arrived in Madrid. On Oct. 19, Young wrote
in his diary. "Today Gen. Grant spent quietly. Mr. Lowell came and took him to the
palace to visit the Princess of Asturias. I remain home and write. In the [e]vening
there is a shower, but we [m]anage to see the Plaza Mayor, & to [a]rrive home not much

damaged. The General talked a good deal of Lincoln, and the last days he spent with him at City Point." DLC-John Russell Young. For USG in Madrid, see *ibid.*, Oct. 18, 20–23, 1878; *New York Herald*, Oct. 28, 1878. On Oct. 23, a Spanish official wrote to USG. "Allow me to hand you the enclosed circular order for all Agents of the Southern Railway Company: a saloon carriage will be prepared for you to morrow morning for Toledo and friday night for Lisbon." ANS, DLC-USG, IB. While in Toledo on Oct. 24, USG visited the sword factory and synagogue. See Young diary, Oct. 24, 1878, DLC-John Russell Young.

On Oct. 29, Tuesday, James Russell Lowell, U.S. minister, Madrid, wrote to Evarts. "I have the honor to inform you that General Grant arrived here on the morning of the 18th. . . . Though he arrived in Madrid on the day he originally fixed, he had entered Spain three days earlier than he intended in compliance with an invitation of the King (received through the Spanish Consul at Bordeaux) to be present at the autumn manoeuvres near Vitoria. General Grant while there was presented to the King, dined with him and rode by his side during one of the reviews. He spoke in very warm terms of the excellent quality, appearance and discipline of the Spanish troops. During his stay here he visited the various museums, the Escorial and Toledo. . . ." LS, DNA, RG 59, Diplomatic Despatches, Spain. *Foreign Relations, 1878*, pp. 803–4. See *New York Herald*, Dec. 30, 1878, Jan. 6, 13, 1879; *Young*, I, 518–33; *Julia Grant*, pp. 256–57. For Lowell's private view of USG, see Charles Eliot Norton, ed., *Letters of James Russell Lowell* (New York, 1894), II, 232–33. See also *ibid.*, pp. 7, 27, 56; letter to Daniel Ammen, Nov. 15, 1878; Lowell to Young, Nov. 19, 1878, DLC-John Russell Young; Young, *Men and Memories* (New York, 1901), II, 279–85, 288; Mrs. Thomas Bailey Aldrich, *Crowding Memories* (Boston, 1920), pp. 227–28; Martin Duberman, *James Russell Lowell* (Boston, 1966), pp. 281–82, 293.

On Oct. 16, Jacques Hartog, Vitoria, had written to King Alfonso XII of Spain. "I find myself in Spain with his Excellency General Grant, and am ~~glad~~ pleased to be here under your 'Majesty's' reign. I am anxious to carry with me some souvenir of your Majesty, and would be honoured if your ~~Majesty~~ gave me a decoration in one of your majestys' orders. I have no claim for such a distinction except that I am General Grant Secretary, and have been one of his Suite during his residence in Europe. I am Sure a compliment of this kind to me, would not be distastfull to the General. Otherwise I would not trouble your Majesty. with this letter" ALS, DLC-USG, IB. Hartog's request caused diplomatic difficulties. See Young, *Men and Memories*, II, 285–87.

2. See *Badeau*, p. 508; *PUSG*, 10, 418.

To Frederick Dent Grant

Gibralter, Nov. 14th /78

Dear ~~Buck~~Fred,

We have now been at this place two days; have dined with the Gov. Gen.[1] go on a Fox hunt to-morrow with the officers of the garrison; dine with them on our return in the evening, and leave here sunday[2] for Malaga & Grenada. We changed our plan at saville[3] and went from there to Cadiz[+] and by water to this place. By this arrangement we will see every thing proposed and save about one half of the rail-road travel in Spain. There is no place in the world where travel is so uncomfortable as in Spain. We have fared much better than the public generally however, having had special cars provided for us all through the country. With the exception of a trip from Malaga to Grenada and back the balance of our travels in Spain will be by steamer along the east, or Mediterranean, coast, stopping during the day time at the different Ports. Spain gives some evidences of recent improvement, but there is great room for more. There seems to be no satisfaction with existing affairs and I would not be surprised to hear of a revolution breaking out at any time. A republic is inevitable at no distant day. I think now we will return to the states about next May. As we have seen every thing there is to be seen, without going through the east to San Francisco, I am becoming very homesick.

Your Ma has a little doll for Julia. It cost the $1000 bill you sent her and a frank & a half of money that these deluded people here insist upon having, besides.

We have met quite a number of people in Spain as well as in Russia who remember you very well.

Your Ma sends much love to you, Ida and little Julia in all of which I join. I rather think we will go back to Paris for the winter though we may not.

Yours Affectionately
U. S. GRANT

LT. COL. F. D. GRANT

ALS, USG 3.

1. On Nov. 12 and 14, 1878, John Russell Young wrote in his diary. "Left Cadiz at 8, and reached Gibraltar at 4.—Dined in the evening with Lord Napier. . . ." ". . . In evening to dinner at the American Consul—Ld Napier [t]here.—Afterwards a party of about 150, . . ." DLC-John Russell Young. Robert C. Napier, an accomplished engineer who spent most of his acclaimed British army career in India, became governor of Gibraltar in Sept., 1876. See *New York Herald*, Feb. 8, 1879; *Julia Grant*, pp. 258–59; H. D. Napier, *Field-Marshal Lord Napier of Magdala* (London, 1927).

2. Nov. 17. USG left Gibraltar on Nov. 18.

3. On Nov. 6, Young, Seville, had written in his diary. ". . . Remained up late and conversed with the Gen. about the war, and especially the movements that led to the

surrender of Lee.—" DLC-John Russell Young. See *ibid.*, Nov. 7–8, 1878; *Young*, I, 553–63; *Julia Grant*, pp. 257–58. USG had visited Cordova before his arrival in Seville. See Young diary, Nov. 3–5, 1878, DLC-John Russell Young; *Young*, I, 548–53.

4. On Nov. 9, USG, who felt ill, left Seville for Cadiz. See Young diary, Nov. 9, 1878, DLC-John Russell Young. On Nov. 10, Young, Cadiz, wrote in his diary. ". . . In the evening went around with the General, and came home late. Talked with the General an hour about Vicksburg." *Ibid.* See *ibid.*, Nov. 11, 1878; *Young*, I, 563–75.

On Nov. 15, Friday, Benjamin G. Haynes, vice consul, Cadiz, wrote to Young. ". . . I presume you are aware that Genl. Grant informed me that he would go on Sunday first in our Boat to Malaga and that we had agreed to keep back the hour for starting untill 8 a. m. The 2 Sheep and the Ram I will have the pleasure in Sending for General Grant by 1st Boat to New York Trusting you will continue to have in Comy with General and Mrs General Grant a pleasant Tour. . . ." ALS, DLC-John Russell Young.

To Richard W. Thompson

Gibralter, Nov. 14th /78

Hon. R. W. Thompson,
Sec. of the Navy,
Dear Sir:

On my arrival here two days ago I found your very considerate and highly appreciated letter of the 23d of ~~August~~ October, extending to me the use of the U. S. Steam Ship Richmond for my journey eastward should I be contemplating a trip in that direction. The time being so short between this and the departure of the Richmond from America I would cable you my determination not to go east,—certainly not this winter—only that I previously communicated the fact to Adm.l Ammen who I presume has informed the Department before this. It is a splendid opportunity however and I feel much tempted to accept. If I should change my mind I will cable you at the earlyest moment after having done so.

With many thanks for your courticy, I am,

With great respect
your obt. svt.
U. S. Grant

ALS, InFtwL. On Oct. 23, 1878, Secretary of the Navy Richard W. Thompson wrote to USG. "The U. S. Steamer Richmond, designed as the Flag ship of the Asiatic Naval Station, will probably leave the United States about the 10th of December, en route for

Singapore, and may be expected to reach Point de Galle in the Island of Ceylon by the middle of January next. If it is your purpose to visit British India, China, and Japan, it is probable that this vessel, being a flag ship, will afford you more facilities and conveniences of travel than you will be likely to obtain by any other method of conveyance. And if you consider it desirable to join her at any point en route to her station, upon notification of that fact the department will immediately issue the necessary instructions to carry out your wishes. As the North East monsoon may be expected to blow with great force in the China Sea, it is probable that the Richmond may visit Bankok, at the head of the Gulf of Siam, and Batavia in the Island of Java, and proceed from thence by way of the straits of Macassa to Manilla, in the Island of Luzon, and to Hong Kong. This route will undoubtedly furnish to you many opportunities of interesting observation and research. And if you shall conclude to avail yourself of the advantages of travel offered by the Richmond, the department feels assured that, apart from the personal gratification to yourself of observing the tastes, customs, and wants of the inhabitants of the countries visited, your intercourse with them would lead to more extended and intimate commercial relations between them and the United States. It is beleived that your presence on board a Man-ofwar, in the ports to be visited by the Richmond, will so arrest public attention as to bring prominently into view, not merely the character and extent of our commerce, but the nature and value of our institutions. You will be good enough to inform the department, at your earliest convenience, as to your wishes, in order that the necessary preliminaries may be arranged. If you decide to accompany the Richmond, orders will be issued to Captain Benham, who will command her, and to Rear Admiral Patterson, commanding the Asiatic Station, of similar import to the instructions to Commanders in Chief of Naval Stations in reference to yourself, and of which you have been heretofore advised—" LS, USG 3. See letter to Daniel Ammen, Dec. 6, 1878; letter to Richard W. Thompson, Dec. 25, 1878.

To Daniel Ammen

GIBRALTAR, Nov. 15th, 1878.

MY DEAR ADMIRAL,—

On my arrival here, three days ago, I found your letter of the 21st of October, and the very kind letter of the Secretary of the Navy tendering to me the use of the Richmond for an Eastern tour. I wrote to the Secretary at once, and said that I should have cabled, only that I had previously sent a message to you saying that I had determined on not going home by way of China and Japan, at least for this winter, and that no doubt you had communicated the message. I received your previous letter of the 15th of October, also. It seems a long journey to go from here to San Francisco by water for so little as there is to see along the coast. If I was alone, or with a party of gentlemen that could penetrate the interior of countries passed through, I should not hesitate.

We came here making our first stop, in Spain, at Victoria. The young king, hearing that I was on my way to Madrid, invited me to stop there where he was inspecting and reviewing some twenty-six thousand troops. I stopped two days.[1] The Spanish troops make a splendid appearance. The next stop was at Madrid, for a week.[2] Madrid is improving rapidly, and has evidently improved much in the last few years. It is now a beautiful city, with horse-cars running to every part. I saw but little evidence of improvement, however, elsewhere than in Madrid. It is hard to foretell the future of Spain. The people are good enough if, as you say, they could see any return for their labor. But, as it is, there seems to be no integrity among the ruling class. Those who do work receive but the barest subsistence. If a man raises a pig he cannot kill and eat it without paying an equivalent to five dollars of our money. The revenue-officers are so abundant that there is no chance of escaping any tax except by bribery, which is resorted to, to the extent of depriving the government of a very large percentage of its revenues. There is the greatest discontent, and the least thing would start a revolution. I have no idea that the existing state of affairs can last long. It will not be long before the experiment of a republic will be tried again, and probably with more success than the last time.[3]

From Madrid we went to Lisbon, being in the cars two nights and a day. The country passed through is highly *uninteresting*. There is no place of interest to stop to break the journey, and, if there was, one would have to take up his travel at the same hour of the day, or night, he left off. It is two nights and a day between Madrid and Lisbon, whether you take thirty-six hours to make the journey, or a whole year.

Coming here, we made stops at Cordova, Seville, and Cadiz. All of them are places of interest. On Monday[4] we will have a run, by an English man-of-war, for Malaga,[5] will visit Granada,[6] and return to the sea-coast and go by steamer to Barcelona.[7] From the latter place we will in all probability make our way to Paris, and remain quiet until about six weeks before the time to sail for home.

I want to spend about a month with Nellie before going back, and want to make a run through Ireland.

Mrs. Grant sends her love to Mrs. Ammen and the children, and her very kindest regards to yourself.

Very truly yours,

U. S. GRANT.

ADMIRAL D. AMMEN, *U. S. Navy.*

Daniel Ammen, *The Old Navy and the New* (Philadelphia, 1891), pp. 544–45. Daniel Ammen later commented. "On the receipt of this letter I wrote the general immediately that I hoped he would reconsider his determination to come home without having gone around the world. I said he would find Japan particularly interesting, and his visit to China and Japan would have an excellent result, in placing our people and our government in excellent relations with them; therefore it seemed to me very desirable that he should go around the world. I happened to meet General Sherman within a few days, and mentioned the above to him. He said he had received a similar letter from General Grant, and had written him almost in the same terms. Later on, when the Richmond did not sail for two months after the time named to General Grant, I wrote him that he should not wait for her, as the season in British India would not wait for him. Let the Richmond catch up with him if she could,—which she did at Hong-Kong or Shanghai." *Ibid.*, p. 545. See letters to Gen. William T. Sherman, Sept. 21, Dec. 8, 1878.

On Monday, Nov. 18, 1878, USG wrote to Lucius Fairchild, consul gen., Paris. "I am sorry to decline your invitation to dinner of[n] friday, but as Mrs. Grant will not be able to go I will remain with her." ALS, Paul Findley, Jacksonville, Ill.

1. USG had arrived at Vitoria on Oct. 15, inspected troops with King Alfonso XII of Spain on the next day, and departed for Madrid on Oct. 17. See John Russell Young diary, Oct. 15–17, 1878, DLC-John Russell Young.

2. See letter to Adam Badeau, Oct. 27, 1878.

3. The first Spanish republic ended in 1874. See *PUSG*, 25, 212–13.

4. Nov. 18, 1878. On Nov. 16 and 17, Young wrote in his diary. ". . . In the afternoon [w]ent out and saw Lord Napier [&] Gen. Grant review 4000 troops. . . ." "Arose early and went to church with the General. Heard a good sermon, the subject being the propriety of virtue. Then at noon we all went out to Mr Sprague's country seat. . . ." DLC-John Russell Young. Horatio J. Sprague, who succeeded his father as consul, Gibraltar, continued a prosperous merchant business. See *New York Herald*, Feb. 8, 1879; *New York Times*, July 19, 1901.

On Nov. 15, Robert C. Napier, governor of Gibraltar, had written to USG. "L homme propose, Dieu dispose! I am very sorry that the weather will not admit your free use and ride coming off to day—It looks settled for rain, but may perhaps clear up later in the day; if so I shall hold my self at your disposal for a ride should you feel inclined for one" ALS, USG 3. On [*Nov. 18*], Mary Cecilia Napier wrote to USG. "We shall be happy to send the carraige for you at whatever hour you intend starting— a verbal message to the Bearer will be quite sufficient—I should like to send up our 3 children with the governess in the carraige & they will wait outside till you go to the carraige just to shake hands with you as I should like you to see them—but don't let them put you out in any way—as at the last moment there is always a good deal to do. They will be quite happy in the carraige & walk back. Lord Napier intends going to wish you good-bye & will ride down either to your house or the New Mole when we learn the hour of starting . . . You will find it cold at Granada but very beautiful no doubt Should you again pass Gibraltar on your way to India or elsewhere we hope you will ~~join~~come & stay with us—& shall look forward to a visit from yo[u]" ALS, DLC-John Russell Young. See H. D. Napier, ed., *Letters of Field-Marshal Lord Napier of Magdala* (London, 1936), p. 53; letter to Adam Badeau, Dec. 19, 1878.

5. On Nov. 19, Sprague wrote to asst. secretary of state describing USG's visit and reporting that USG and Julia Dent Grant departed "for Malaga yesterday morning by H. M. gunboat 'Express,' which was placed at their disposal by the Senior naval officer on this Station, after having done me the honor of being my guests during their short stay here—" ALS, DNA, RG 59, Consular Despatches, Gibraltar. See Young diary, Nov. 18, 1878, DLC-John Russell Young.

USG's unfavorable opinion of John F. Quarles, consul, Malaga, prompted James Russell Lowell, U.S. minister, Madrid, to continue an investigation of this official. See Lowell to William M. Evarts, Dec. 11, 1878, May 27, 1879, DNA, RG 59, Diplomatic Despatches, Spain; *PUSG*, 24, 314.

6. For USG's stay in Granada, see Young diary, Nov. 19–22, 1878, DLC-John Russell Young; *Julia Grant*, pp. 259–60.

On Nov. 23, Young, Malaga, wrote in his diary. "Arose early this morning, and had breakfast with the Gen. Wrote to Mr. Lowell about thanking the Spanish government in the Gen.'s. name, . . . Gen. Grant & party left at 7.30 on the steamship for the coast, on the Mediateranean.—Am sorry to leave the General with whom I have been much this year and whom I esteem as a high-minded & peace-minded man—. . ." DLC-John Russell Young.

7. On Nov. 25, 29, and 30, Jacques Hartog, USG's courier, wrote to Young reporting USG's visits to Cartagena and Barcelona and plans to go to Toulouse and Pau, France. ALS, *ibid.*

To Daniel Ammen

Pau, France, December 6th, 1878.

My dear Admiral,—

On my arrival here, last night, I found a very large mail, and in it two letters from you. This is my first mail since leaving Gibraltar, from where I wrote you.[1] At that time I had fully determined not to go by India, China, and Japan, and so wrote the Secretary of the Navy, saying, however, that if I determined otherwise before the departure of the Richmond from America, I would cable him. This morning I sent him a despatch that I would accept his offer of a passage on that steamer.[2] I could not say much in a despatch, but I hope we will be able to join the steamer on the north side of the

Mediterranean, somewhere between Marseilles and Palermo. This will extend my trip and make my arrival in America some months later than I had expected, probably extending the time into the late fall. Of course going by San Francisco I shall want to spend at least a month going over old ground with which I was familiar a quarter of a century ago. That quarter of a century does not seem half so long as the one which preceded it, and passed, since you and I first received instruction under John D. White, and a *long beech switch*, cut generally by the boys for their own chastisement.[3]

Mrs. Grant wants me to say now that she regrets your retirement, because you might accompany us, and she has every confidence in you on your native element. I believe you are a first-class farmer besides.

I have not yet received your paper on the "Inter-Oceanic Canal,"[4] but will read it with great interest when it reaches me.

I have preserved with great care a letter you wrote me as much as nine months ago, giving the route and places to visit on naval vessels, after leaving the Red Sea, until since leaving Gibraltar. But I destroyed it a few days ago. I would be very glad to get a repetition of it now.

I am very sorry, with Mrs. Grant, that you cannot be the commander of our proposed trip, and that Mrs. Ammen is not to be with us. Mrs. Grant sends here love to Mrs. Ammen, Mrs. Atocha,[5] and the children. Regards to Mrs. A., Mrs. Atocha, and yourself.

Very truly yours,
U. S. GRANT.

ADMIRAL D. AMMEN.

Daniel Ammen, *The Old Navy and the New* (Philadelphia, 1891), pp. 545–46.

1. See previous letter.
2. On Dec. 6, 1878, USG, Pau, France, telegraphed to Secretary of the Navy Richard W. Thompson. "Accept passage on Richmond for Self and family" Telegram received, InFtwL. See letter to Richard Thompson, Nov. 14, 1878.
3. See Daniel Ammen, "Recollections and Letters of Grant," *North American Review*, CXLI, cccxlvii (Oct., 1885), 361–62.
4. On Nov. 12, Ammen read a paper entitled "Inter-Oceanic Ship Canal Across the American Isthmus" before the American Geographical Society in New York City.

See *New York Times*, Nov. 13, 1878; *Bulletin of the American Geographical Society*, No. 3 (1878), 142–62.

    5. Presumably Ammen's mother-in-law. See *PUSG*, 24, 428–29.

To Edward F. Beale

———

Pau, France,
Dec. 6th /78

MY DEAR GENERAL:

Your letter of the 29th of Oct. reached me,—or rather I found it—at Gibraltar about three weeks ago. It made me more homesick than I was to be back again and to be with you in some of your visits to the farm. I shall be sorry if Bob Akres[1] does not turn out a trotter. But my means will not allow me to indulge much in fancy stock.

We have nearly determined to go by the way of India, and to go by the U. S. Steamer Richmond which leaves for the Mediterranean on the 10th, four days from now. I have cabled to the Sec. of the Navy to-day accepting his invitation to take passage on her.[2] It would be delightful to have you along, as you propose but Mrs Grant would not give up the trip for the world.[3] In fact she has been urging me to go that way ever since I first announced my determination to return by the Atlantic.

We have seen the Capitols and most of the principle towns, and the people, of every Country in Europe. I have not yet seen any to be jealous of. The fact is we are the most progressive freest and richest people on earth, but do'nt know it or appreciate it. Foreigners see this much plainer than we do. While all other nations are ~~still~~ exercised how to raise more taxes out of an over burdened people to pay the interest on debts already contracted, and to support large Armies and Navies to protect themselves, we are reducing taxation and paying off our debt.

The results of the Nov. elections, in the North, are very encouraging.[4] I am glad the elections of Conkling & Cameron[5] are insured.

Mrs. Grant sends her love to Mrs. Beale and Miss Emily. Mrs. Grant says to tell Miss Emily that she has heard away out here of the swell team she and Buck attended the Wise-Hopkins weddin[6] with. My kindest regards to the ladies also.

Yours Truly

U. S. GRANT

ALS, DLC-Decatur House Papers.

1. See *PUSG*, 26, 180–81, 192; *ibid.*, 28, 299–300.
2. See previous letter.
3. Edward F. Beale had proposed "that Mrs. Grant might stay with Mrs. Beale in some pleasant climate during the journey around the world." Stephen Bonsal, ed., "General Grant's Letters to General Beale," *Scribner's Magazine*, L, 4 (Oct., 1911), 475.
4. Republicans carried most northern states, and Democrats nearly swept the southern states. For Republican assessments, see Charles Richard Williams, ed., *Diary and Letters of Rutherford Birchard Hayes* (Columbus, 1922–26), III, 508–10, and Harry James Brown and Frederick D. Williams, eds., *The Diary of James A. Garfield* (East Lansing, Mich., 1967–81), IV, 143–44.
5. U.S. Senator James D. Cameron of Pa.
6. Charlotte Everett Wise and Archibald Hopkins, both with distinguished ancestries, married in Washington, D. C., on Nov. 14. See *Washington Post*, Nov. 15, 1878, June 19, 1926, Sept. 7, 1935.

To Charles H. Rogers

———

Pau, France,

Dec. 6th /78

MY DEAR MR. ROGERS,

Your very kind letter of the 30th of Oct. reached me at Gibraltar just as I was leaving that place. I hardly know how to express my appreciation of your kind offer, and the sincere and friendly ~~offer~~ manner of the offering. I am equally undesided as to whether I should accept or decline. In either event I shall appreciate all the same your generosity and sincere friendship in making it. I remember the conversation referred to in your letter but had not thought of it in recent years. You are right in supposing that

I have not saved much, and could not, in the official positions I have held. They confered great honors on me and mine but they entailed heavy expenses also. In fact but for the generosity of New York & Philadelphia friends,[1] directly after the war, I should not have been able to make any european tour whatever. My expenses for the last twelve years have about equaled my pay and private income. We have about made up our mind to go home by India. In that event we will leave Paris for Nice—where we will take a Naval Vessel for Bombay—about the 20th of Jan.y. If you prefer my acceptance you might send me a letter of credit to Paris. My address there is always Drexel, Harjes & Co. No 31 Boulivard Haussmann.

Mrs. Grant & I have often spoken of you and Mrs. Rogers since our travels began, and often I have said that I must write to you. But in the matter of writing—and I fear in everything like work—I am a little indolent and procrastinating.

We have now been away from the United States more than a year & a half, traveling almost continuously, and have visited every Capitol and nearly every important town in Europe. Besides this we have assende[d] the Nile—in Africa—as far as the 1st rapids, have been to Jerusalem and other places in the Holy Land, or Palestine, Syria, and in Asia Minor. I have seen nothing yet to diminish my respect and love for our own country, people, institutions, climate soil or any thing else about us. The fact is we are the only first class power that is not compelled to grind the laborer to the last degree to pay the interest on debts already contracted and to support large Armies & Navies for their daily security. We should be a very happy people and are very rich by comparison but do not know it or appreciate it. This fact is much more recognized abroad than at home. When we return—probably about next Oct.—there will be nothing els but South America to see and as both Mrs. Grant & I are getting a along in years it is not likely that we will visit that country. We will probable get a quiet little place in Washington, retain our Galena home, and spend the Summers at Long Branch. I am getting so home sick that I would go back at once only that this is the last opportunity I expect to have to see the old world and desire to see as much of it as possible while the opportunity lasts.

With kindest regards of Mrs. Grant & myself to Mrs. Rogers, Miss Lilly[2] & yourself.

> I am, with great respect,
>
> U. S. Grant

P. S. Buck wrote us some time ago that you had great hopes of John's[3] recovery. I hope that he is still improving and that he may be fully restored to health. Remember us affectionately to him.

> U. S. G.

ALS, DLC-USG. USG addressed the envelope. "Chas H. Rogers No 173 Madison Avenue New York City U. S. America" AD, *ibid.* See letter to Charles H. Rogers, Jan. 14, 1879.

    1. See *PUSG*, 13, 234–35; *ibid.*, 15, 388–89; *ibid.*, 16, 74–75.

    2. Sarah Howell Post, nicknamed Lily, was a niece of Charles H. and Mary Rogers. Lily Post later married Henry N. Corwith, relative of her uncle's former business associates in Galena. See *New York Tribune*, Nov. 20, 1885.

    3. John Rogers, an unmarried son, born in 1838.

Addressee Unknown

> Pau, France
> Dec. 8th /78

Dear Sir:

Your letter of the 8th of Oct. only reached me about three weeks ago, at Gibraltar. It is impossible for me to state positively what took place, officially, some years ago. But I recollect well that the Craig claim was up before me very frequently both through the Interior Dept. and through Counsel. I recollect that there was great opposition to his getting a patent for a[ny land whatever . . . his purchase called for 123,000 acres . . . Col. Craig did not insist on the whole amount but wanted 97,000 by some ruling I now mis-remember . . .] by the Sec. of the Interior that Col. Craig had a valid title to a patent for 73,000 and was sustained in this view by . . . [I write this entirely from] memory of events that took place through several years of my public life and may not be as accurate as I could make myself if back in Washington where I could refer to all the action taken in that case.

Very Truly Yours
U. S. GRANT

ALS (partial facsimile), Alexander Autographs, Inc., April 20, 1999, no. 860; Superior Stamp & Coin, Nov. 16, 1996, no. 151. Possibly written to Robert H. Bradford, attorney for Thomas Leitensdorfer, party to a tangled Colo. land dispute with William Craig over the Las Animas grant. Craig, USMA 1853, resigned from the army in 1864 to manage his property interests. On Oct. 7, 1878, he filed a response to a legal bill meant to void a patent he had received from USG on March 2, 1877. See *HED*, 45-2-1, part 5, I, 275; *United States Reports: Cases Adjudged in the Supreme Court at October Term, 1887*, Volume 123 (New York, 1888), pp. 189–214; Morris F. Taylor, "Capt. William Craig and the Vigil and St. Vrain Grant 1855–1870," *Colorado Magazine*, XLV, 4 (Fall, 1968), 301–21, and "The Leitensdorfer Claim in the Vigil and St. Vrain Grant," *Journal of the West*, XIX, 3 (July, 1980), 92–99; Richard W. Bradfute, "The Las Animas Land Grant, 1843–1900," *Colorado Magazine*, XLVII, 1 (Winter, 1970), 26–43. See also *PUSG*, 26, 78–83.

On Sept. 11, 1876, Maj. Gen. John M. Schofield, superintendent, USMA, had written to USG, Long Branch. "I beg your pardon for troubling you with a matter of business while you are trying to get the rest you so much need. But I will be brief as possible J L. Rathbone, G. W. Schofield (my brother) and I, are interested in a tract of land in Colorado, purchased about *seven years* ago, from William Craig, under the St Vrain grant, as I believe. We have been waiting all this time for a confirmation of our title. Having been on the Pacific Coast during the six years I have I not been able to give the subject any personal attention. I am now informed that an award was made by the Register and Receiver and a decision rendered by the Attorney General that such award was final; that patents were about to be issued, when our attorney objected on the ground of injustice to us. We still believer the ground of his objection was correct, but we are anxious to have the matter settled and get it off our hands. Therefore I am authorized to say for J. L. Rathbone, and G. W. Schofield as well as for myself that we desire the matter to be settled without further delay, and respectfully request you to order the case closed and of in accordance with the Attorney General decision" Copy, DLC-John M. Schofield. See John M. Schofield, *Forty-Six Years in the Army* (New York, 1897), p. 426.

To Edward F. Noyes

Pau, France,
Dec. 8th /78

MY DEAR GENERAL:

You were kind enough to ask me, on my departure from Paris,[1] to let you know the day and train on which I might be expected to

return. My plans are well enough settled to speak with definite-
ness not only as to the time of my arrival in Paris, but with some
certainty as to my future movements. While at Gibraltar I received
a very kind letter from the Sec. of the Navy tendering me the use
of the Steamer Richmond—which leaves the states on Dec. 10th to
join the Asiatic Squadron, by way of the Mediterranean, Suez Canal &c.—to take me to India, China &c. I wrote thanking him saying that I had abandoned the idea of returning that way but that if I
should change my mind before the sailing of the Richmond I would
Cable him.[2] On my arrival here I concluded to go home by the
East, and so dispatched. We will therefore be in Paris but a short
time. On Wednesday, the 11th I shall leave here direct for Paris,
via Bordeau arriving in Paris at 5 25 am on the 12th. The hour is
so unseasonably early that I beg you will not attempt to meet me
at the station. I may conclude to rest over night in Bordeau and go
on the next morning. In that case I will arrive at the Orleans R. R.
Station five in the evening, and will telegraph you.

   Mrs Grant desires to be specially remembered to Mrs Noyes
and yourself.

                              Very Truly Yours
                              U. S. Grant

Gen. E. F. Noyes,
Min. Plen. Paris, France.

ALS, DLC-USG, IB.
   On Nov. 2[1], 1878, Robert R. Hitt, secretary of legation, Paris, wrote to USG.
"We were greatly [*pleas*]ed on yesterday to receive from you and Mrs. Grant your letter
from Gibraltar. [I] went down to the Continental [*Hotel*] in the afternoon and [*made*]
inquiry and looked at [—] rooms. You can have [—] [pa]rlor and two bed rooms [on
th]e first floor, looking south [—] Tuiliries Gardens, very well [and n]ewly furnished,
with meals served in your rooms, or with another room adjoining for dining room, at
100 francs per day, maid's room & board, and 'service' included—in fact everything. I
said to the proprietor that it was quite possible that you would be here the great part
of the winter. The rooms are large and all the appointments seem worthy. The price is
far below the regular rate, and I suppose it is made so partly because of their anxiety to
have you at the hotel, & partly because the hotels are just now at ebb-tide. The reflux
of the Exposition wave leaves them empty. I will take pleasure in making inquiries at
other hotels if you will authorise me to do so. I have received notice, only yesterday, of
the arrival of the cigars. You are now in the bright and interesting part of Spain—the
South—and I am sure you are having an agreeable tour. General Noyes requests me to
send you and Mrs. Grant cordial regards. If Mrs. Hitt knew I were writing she would

send messages of welcome to Mrs Grant & yourself returning to Paris, in which I join." ALS (press), DLC-Robert R. Hitt.

1. USG had left Paris on Oct. 12.
2. See letter to Daniel Ammen, Dec. 6, 1878.

To Gen. William T. Sherman

————

Pau, France,
Dec. 8th 1878.

My Dear General,

On my arrival here three days ago I found a very large mail, and in it your very kind one written just after your return from the Army meeting at Indianapolis.[1] A number of these letters—like yours— insisted that I ought to go back by the way of India, China & Japan. While at Gibraltar I received a very kind letter from the Sec. of the Navy tendering me the use of the Steamer Richmond—which leaves America on the 10th of Dec. to take her station in the East, via the Mediterranean &c.—to take me as far as she goes. I wrote the Sec. thanking him, but said that I had abandoned the idea of going home that way. However, I added, if I should change my mind before the sailing of the Richmond I would Cable him. On the 6th I sent him a dispatch accepting his offer of a passage.[2] So now, if nothing intervenes to prevent, I shall go back that way. Going by Cal. I shall want to remain there, and on the Pacific Coast, five or six weeks. It is impossible to say just when I will reach there, but the probabilities are that it will be in time to attend the next meeting of the society of the Army of the Tenn. in, say, October or Nov. On my arrival in San Francisco I should learn of the date of the meeting, and will make my arrangements to be in Chicago on that date, if possible

Mrs. Grant is not only delighted with this change of plan but she has urged it ever since it was first partially abandoned. She says for me to saus you for even suggesting the idea of her going back by the Atlantic.

We have had a delightful trip through Spain, Portugal and at Gibraltar. Met many persons who speak with pride at having met you.[3]

With kindest regards of Mrs. Grant & myself to Mrs. Sher[man] the children & yourself, I am Very Truly y[ours]

U. S. GRANT

GN. W. T. SHERMAN.

ALS, DLC-William T. Sherman. On Dec. 30, 1878, Gen. William T. Sherman wrote to Lt. Gen. Philip H. Sheridan concerning his reply to USG. ". . . I wrote him fully to the effect that the U. S. Frigate Richmond which he expected would leave NewYork on Dec 12, had not yet started, that this was a large Comfortable Ship, though slow— that instead of reaching Nice, by January 12, it could not possibly be there before the middle of February &c &c. I advised him to start on his own time, viz January 12 via Brindisi—to go to Alexandria, Suez—Aden, and Bombay, leaving word for the Richmond to follow to Point de Galle Island of Ceylon—that from Bombay he could put in the whole month of February & part of March—seeing the Interior of India—and be ready for the Richmond when she got there, which cannot be till in March. He can then use this Ship till he passes Canton which should be before the heat of June &c. I think this plan much better than to wait the Slow Movemt of the Richmond at Paris. I shall look out for him at San Francisco, in Sept or Oct, and as he proposes to go up to Oregon, & to pass five or six weeks on the Pacific this will give ample time to Call our Society Meeting at Chicago. . . ." ALS, DLC-Philip H. Sheridan. See Sherman to Sheridan, Jan. 10, 1879, *ibid.*; letters to Gen. William T. Sherman, Jan. 12, May 29, 1879.

1. The Society of the Army of the Tennessee met at Indianapolis, Oct. 30–31, 1878. See *PUSG*, 28, 478–79.
2. See letter to Daniel Ammen, Dec. 6, 1878.
3. Sherman traveled through Europe during 1871 and 1872.

To John Russell Young

Pau, France,
Dec. 8th /78

MY DEAR COMMODORE;

I am just in receipt of your note of 6th from Madrid.[1] On Wednesday, the 11th we start for ~~p~~Paris and will be there the next day, either at 5 a. m. or about the same hour the next day, depending on whether we break the trip by stopping over at Bordeau for the night or not.

On my arrival here I found a tremendious Mail and have spent two days, day-before-yesday and to-day, in writing up, and have three or four more to write yet. After our arrival at Pau we determined to make the trip eastward through India, China & Japan.

As, in my letter to the Sec. of the Navy, while deciding not to go home that way, I reserved, in my letter of thanks for his kind offer of a passage on the Richmond, the privilege of changing my intention, and to notify him if I did so, before the departure of the Richmond from America. She was to sail on the 10th of December. I telegraphed him on the 6th, from here, that I accepted his offer.[2] Unless therefore there is some slip we will go that way. I give you the earlyest notice possible so that you may prepare to go. I shall be delighted to have you go as Mrs. Grant is also.[3]

Present both of us kindly to Mrs. Young and Mrs. Brigh[t],[4] and give our love to Miss Young.[5]

Yours Truly
U. S. GRANT

COM. J. R. YOUNG.

P. S. If Mr. Bennett is in Paris please present my kindest regards. To Mr. Ryan[6] also.

U. S. G.

ALS, DLC-John Russell Young. On Dec. 9, 10, and 11, 1878, John Russell Young wrote in his diary. "Paris—. . . Called on Mr Bennett and received orders to go to Pau. Had long talk and walk with Mr. B. and left for Pau in the evening train . . ." "Reached Pau at two. Found the General well and walked [a]n hour with him. Dined [w]ith Mr. Doglass and later talked an hour [w]ith the General" "Walked an hour with the Gen, in the rain. Saw him off to Paris . . ." DLC-John Russell Young.

On Dec. 9, William P. Douglas, wealthy N. Y. sportsman, had held a dinner for USG at the Hotel de France, Pau, and asked the gathering "to drink to the health and prosperity of 'Unconditional Surrender' Grant." USG "said in response that it was grateful to him to meet so many American faces, to be among friends and to be the recipient of so distinguished a compliment as had been paid him by his countryman, Mr. Douglas. It was well known that he had no gift for speaking. Speeches might perhaps be made as battles had sometimes been won, by persistence and energy. He, however, would not venture the experiment, but would justify as far as he could the epithet of Mr. Douglas and make an unconditional surrender." *New York Herald*, Dec. 31, 1878. For Douglas, see *New York Times*, June 4, 12, 1919, Sept. 14, 1920, Feb. 8, 1921. USG also participated in a fox hunt at Pau and was honored at a dinner on Dec. 8. See *New York Herald*, Jan. 5, 1879; Pierre Tucoo-Chala, *Pau: Ville Anglaise* (Pau, France, 1979), pp. 180–81.

 1. Young had written to USG from Madrid on Nov. 29 and Dec. 1 and left Madrid for Paris on Dec. 4. See Young diary, DLC-John Russell Young.
 2. See letter to Daniel Ammen, Dec. 6, 1878.
 3. Young accepted this invitation to accompany the Grants on their trip to India. See Young diary, Dec. 16, 18, 1878, DLC-John Russell Young.
 4. Johanna F. Bright, widowed sister of Young's wife.

5. Young's infant daughter. See *PUSG*, 28, 374.

6. Probably John J. Ryan, *New York Herald* agent in Paris, who stood as godfather for Young's daughter with USG serving as a witness. See Young diary, May 28, 1878, DLC-John Russell Young.

To Michael John Cramer

———

Pau, France,
Dec. 10th /78

My Dear Mr. Cramer,

Since leaving Copenhagen Mrs. Grant & I have visited every Capitol in Europe not previously visited by us. I can say with great earnestness that no part of our journyings gave us more pleasure than that through the Scandinavian Countries, and no people have impressed me more favorably. If I were going to remain over another year I should go back to Norway at least, and far enough North to see the Midnight sun. But we expect to leave Paris about the middle of Jan.y to return to the states, but by the w[a]y of India, China & Japan. The Sec. of the Navy has been kind enough to invite us to go on a Man of War which leaves the States to day for the China squadron, via the Mediterranean and Suez. I first declined but since Cabled my acceptance.[1] This will probably bring us around home about next Oct. or Nov.

I am sorry to say that I do not get favorable news from Orvil. He does not seem to improve.[2] Buck has obtained for the two boys positions by which they earn $1,800 00 pr. annum.[3] This, with very little help, will probably enable them to get along.

Julia joins me in love to Mary and the children and in kindest regards to yourself.

I hope you did not forward the Sta[. .]s presented by the Consul.[4]—Julia says to tell Mary that she got a very rich fur cloak in Paris and hopes she got one also. Is there any thing we can do for you in Paris?

Very Truly Yours
U. S. Grant

ALS, deCoppet Collection, NjP.

    1. See letter to Richard W. Thompson, Nov. 14, 1878.
    2. Orvil L. Grant was under medical care for insanity. See *PUSG*, 27, 67–70.
    3. In 1880, Orvil Grant's two eldest sons, Harry L., born in 1858, and Ulysses S., born in 1861, worked as government clerks in New York City while living in the family home at Elizabeth, N. J. See letter to Horace Porter, [*1881–82*].
    4. Probably Henry B. Ryder, consul, Copenhagen, where Ryder's friend, Michael John Cramer, served as chargé d'affaires. For letters concerning Ryder, including one from Cramer to Hamilton Fish, Nov. 28, 1870, see DNA, RG 59, Letters of Application and Recommendation.

To Frederick Dent Grant

Paris, France.
Dec. 12th /78

DEAR FRED.

    You have seen by the papers that I am going to make the trip home via India, China & Japan. The Sec. of the Navy has been kind enough to offer me passage by the Steamer Richmond which left the states on the 10th, two days ago, for the Mediterranean.[1] We will probably get aboard of her somewhere from the 20th to the 25th of Jan.y, probably at Naples. Your Ma and I are both anxious to have you accompany us. It will be a splendid trip for you and I am sure Gen. Sheridan, and the War Dept. will be willing to give you a leave of absence for the purpose. We would like to have Ida also but she could not safely or pleasantly take the babe with her. Of course, I do not intend that the trip shall cost you a cent. The extra cost to me will be but little more than keeping a Courier which I have done heretofore but do not intend to do in the future.[2] If you come—and Ida must not let you fail to avail yourself of so fine an opportunity—you should start at once and join me here.—If you come telegraph Gen. E. F. Beale, Washington to get my trunk now at ~~your~~ his house house open and send my uniform coat, pants, chapeau &c.—all my uniform except the sword—to meet you at New York. These articles are in the bottom of the trunk. Bring them with you. If you cannot come ask Gen. Beale to send them to care of Drexel Harjes, & Co: by express.

With much love from your Ma & I to you, Ida and little Julia.
Yours Affectionately
U. S. GRANT

LT. COL. F. D. GRANT U. S. A.

ALS, Austin B. McLogan, Flint, Mich. On Dec. 18, 1878, John Russell Young, Paris, wrote in his diary that USG "sent a cable to his son F. D. to come and go to India." DLC-John Russell Young. On Dec. 19, Lt. Gen. Philip H. Sheridan, Chicago, telegraphed to Gen. William T. Sherman, Washington, D. C., concerning permission for Frederick Dent Grant to join USG in Europe for the trip to India, China, and Japan. ADfS (telegram sent), DLC-Philip H. Sheridan; copy, DNA, RG 94, ACP, 3744 1889. Additional telegrams between Sherman and Sheridan on this subject are *ibid.* On Dec. 20, Sherman wrote for AG Edward D. Townsend to Sheridan. "Your two despatches of yesterday have been laid before the Hon Secretary of War who authorises and instructs me to convey to you this his Answer—Inasmuch as Ex President U. S. Grant now in Europe, has requested the presence of his Son Lieut Colonel F. D. Grant, now serving on your Staff to accompany him on his travels, you are authorised to permit him to go, Still retaining him on your Staff, with the Same pay and allowances he would receive if remaining with you on duty at your HeadQuarters, and with the understanding that he may be Summoned back to his Post, at any time the public Service requires his presence, at his own Cost—The service not being strictly official, the Secretary of War does not feel warranted in ordering Lieut Col Grant in Such a way as to Entitle him to the usual travelling allowance, but he desires to do all he can to give pleasure to his Father General U. S. Grant—" ADf, *ibid.* Also on Dec. 20, Sherman wrote to Frederick Dent Grant, Chicago. "On the supposition that you will not start for Europe for a few days, under the authority sent you by telegraph and mail to-day, I want to congratulate you on thus being able to complete a journey around the world of which your trip with me is so good a foundation. I have written your father also your brother that we want your father to time his return to California and Chicago so that the Army of the Tennessee may meet him at the latter place on arrival. I feel sure that this will be agreeable to him and to all parties, and the nearer it comes to Christmas of 1879, the better for all. I hope he will not hurry too much, though I know he and your mother are anxious to get back home. . . . When you reach California I also want you to communicate to me, at the earliest date you can, the exact or approximate time when you will get back to Chicago, because I must call the meeting of the Society of the Army of the Tennessee for that date. Please make a note of this for it may be important. Give my best love to your father and mother and say that though anxious to see them back that we all want them to make this eastern trip and will welcome them back with increased force as coming by way of California. Wishing you also every pleasure, . . ." Copies (2), DLC-William T. Sherman. On Dec. 23, Sheridan wrote to Frederick Grant requesting observations "by letter one a month or oftener if practicable." ADf, DLC-Philip H. Sheridan. On Dec. 25, Wednesday, Frederick Grant, Philadelphia, wrote to Sherman. "I received your very kind letter & will do all I can to carry it out. I write to thank you for your kindness to me & wish you would also thank the Secty of War. I would write & thank him my self but do not know him personally and therefore do not like to write him a personal letter. I will write to you every once in a while so as to let you know all about our trip. I do not know when I will sail but think it will be saturday. Be so kind as to give my regards to Mrs Sherman & the children" ALS, DLC-William T. Sherman. See *New York Herald*, Dec. 28, 1878.

1. See letters to Richard W. Thompson, Nov. 14, Dec. 25, 1878.

2. USG's decision distressed his former courier Jacques Hartog. See Hartog to Young, Dec. 29, 1878, DLC-John Russell Young.

To Anthony J. Drexel

————

Paris, France,
Dec. 13th /78

MY DEAR MR. DREXEL;

We just arrived here yesterday morning from our tour through Spain. A most delightful trip it was, but with some discomforts of travel. We had however every comfort that could be given, and every attention. Spain is generally a very poor country, with re-sources destroyed, but a better people than I expected to find. My impression is that the spanish people would be industrious if they could find a reward for their labour, and that the Nation might become—again—prosperous. I wish you had been with me.

On my arrival at Pau I determined to change my mind and to return home by India, China & Japan. The Sec. of the Navy was kind enough to send me an invitation to accept passage by the Rich-mond, which was to leave the states on the 10th of of Dec. via the Mediterranean, for the Asiatic Squadron, which letter I received at Gibraltar. I acknowledged the receipt of the letter, with thanks for the courticy, but said that I had determined to return by the Atlan-tic.[1] But I added, that if I should change my mind before the sailing of the Richmond, I would cable him. On the 6th I did so.[2] I wish you could go along. It would be the best Medicine you could receive. The Sec. of the Navy would be glad to offer you a passage so far as Govt. Steamers carry us. When I sent my dispatch to the Sec. of the Navy Mrs. Grant said she wished she could take May Drexel[3] with her. It is probably too late for anything of that kind now; but if it is possible, and you wish it, ask the Sec. of the Navy if there would be any objection, and cable to me so that I may communicate with the Commander of the Steamer[4] on his arrival in the Mediterranean. But if you come we can fix a place for you either with me or in a hammock. Mr. Childs is such a sailor—having been in the Navy in early life—that I would not ask him to witness my contortion[s] in a heavy sea. He would not enjoy it for a six months voyage.[5]

I have written to Fred. to get a leave of absence to accompany me.[6] Whether he can do so I do not know. I hope he will be able to. It will be very valuable to him and a great pleasure to me.

Give our love to Mr. & Mrs. Childs, to Mr & Mrs. Borie and Mr. & Mrs. Paul,[7] and say to Mr. Borie[8] and Mr. Childs that I shall write to them before I sail,—and while away.

I hope you will write to me often if you do not conclude to join "the ship" and take a good rest.

Mrs. Grant's and my love and regards to all your family.

Very Truly yours
U. S. GRANT

ALS, Drexel University, Philadelphia, Pa. Anthony J. Drexel did not join USG.

On Dec. 7 and 9, 1878, George W. Childs, Philadelphia, wrote to U.S. Representative Alfred C. Harmer of Pa. "I return the papers with many thanks. I have good reason to believe that General Grant would like to have two gentlemen to accompany him on his trip and, one has been with him most of the time he has been abroad, and the other is a friend who has resided many years in India and is well posted as to that country and can be of great service to Genl. Grant. These gentlemen would not expect to be any cost to the Government but will be prepared to pay all their expenses. Thanking you for your part in the matters . . ." "The Secretary of the Navy has done himself, the Administration, and the country credit in honoring General Grant as he has done in tendering him the facilities of a U. S. Vessel. The Secretarys letter was admirable. I wrote you in regard to two friends accompanying General Grant, who are necessary to his comfort both of whom will expect to pay all their own expenses so as to be at no cost to the Government. Could you see the Sec. and let me know his decission so I can telegraph General Grant. I enclose our editorial to day. The Secretary's action in the matter has been telegraphed to Europe and appears in the leading papers there to day." ALS, InFtwL. Childs advocated John Russell Young and possibly Thomas W. Evans, an American dentist who had gained renown in Paris, or John Fayrer, a British surgeon noted for his service in India. Neither Evans nor Fayrer accompanied USG on his eastern trip. See letter to Richard W. Thompson, Dec. 25, 1878; *PUSG*, 12, 207; *New York Times*, Dec. 22, 1878, Nov. 16, 1897; *Washington Post*, Dec. 24, 1878. For Harmer's role in assisting USG's travel, see *Philadelphia Press*, Dec. 7, 1878.

In an undated memorandum, presumably for USG, Fayrer gave recommendations for travel in India. ". . . Take plenty of warm clothing for it is very cold in the Northwest Provinces—Do not over take too many things a few light flannel suits a light Tweed—an Alpaca coat or two—for the hot weather. It is always hot in the day time in the plains— Live in the ordinary way moderately and regularly. avoid exposure to direct sun's rays if possible. Drink claret, or light wine or weak brandy & water Attend immediately to any ailment however simple. Check diarrhea at once. Let the Doctor. They are to be found

at all stations decide whether further treatment is required—Dont remain in India after March.—" ADS, USG 3. At his dinner for journalists on June 29, 1877, Young had
seated Fayrer next to USG. Diagram (undated), DLC-John Russell Young. See *PUSG*,
28, 232–33; Fayrer, *Recollections of My Life* (Edinburgh, 1900), p. 424.

    1. See letter to Richard W. Thompson, Nov. 14, 1878.
    2. See letter to Daniel Ammen, Dec. 6, 1878.
    3. Drexel's daughter, Mae E., born in 1857.
    4. Capt. Andrew E. K. Benham.
    5. Childs spent an unhappy fifteen months of his boyhood in the navy. Childs,
Recollections (Philadelphia, 1890), p. 10.
    6. See previous letter.
    7. Drexel's son-in-law and daughter. See *PUSG*, 28, 317–18.
    8. On Monday, Dec. 23, 1878, USG wrote to Young. "Mr. Borie sails on thursday
to join us to accompany us to San Francisco. We can have Boston. Bring the material
from london with you. He will no doubt be provided, but it is better to be provided."
AL (initialed), DLC-John Russell Young.

To Adam Badeau

———

Dec. 19th /78

MY DEAR GENERAL:

I have your letter of the 17th, with Shermans to you inclosed. I
also received one from you at Pau, and one before the present one
here in Paris. I should have written to you earlyer but I found so
many letters to answer that I deferred.[1]

It is impossible yet for me to say when we will get off for our
trip around the world. The steamer on which we are to sail left the
states on the 10th of this month. If she crosses the Atlantic under
sail it will be about the last of Jan.y befor she will be ready for us. If
she steams over it may be as early as the 12th. Mrs. Grant & I want
to see Nellie before we go and have written asking her to come
here. She answers fearing that she may not be able to come, but has
written Mr. Sartoris, who is in Ireland, for his opinion. If she does
not come we will likely take a run over to London for a few days. I
will let you know by telegraph if we go. I shall be very glad, if we
do not go there, to see you here.

I am very glad to see Shermans letter to you. It only shows him
in the light I always regarded him; a warm friend as I shurely ~~was~~
am of his.

I do not see what the publication of your book, at any particular time, can have to do with the formation of publication opinion as to political objects. It has been a long time in preparation and the public has known all about it. If the work should be withheld the public might say that there was an object in that. I would go on as fast as possible and when the work is ready publish it: let the public say what they please.

Our trip through Spain, like all others, was very delightful. We received marked attention from the officials every where, and no place more marked than while we were at Gibraltar. Lord & Lady Napier, with the officers of the garrison, seemed not to be able to do too much for us.[2]

Hoping to see you either in London or Paris before our departure, I am, as always,

Yours Very Truly

U. S. GRANT

GEN. A. BADEAU,

CONSUL GEN. OF THE U. S.

LONDON ENG.

ALS, Munson-Williams-Proctor Institute, Utica, N. Y. See following letter; letter to Adam Badeau, Dec. 28, 1878.

1. On Dec. 10 and 19, 1878, Adam Badeau, consul gen., London, wrote to Orville E. Babcock. ". . . The telegraphic despatches in yesterday's London Times say that Genl Grant has accepted the Govt offer of a vessel to take him to India, China and Japan. I have not heard from him of this decision, but he is expected shortly at Paris. I write him today to say how glad I am of his decision; I shall go to see him before he starts— unless he comes to England. The question now will arise whether it will be better to publish my Military History before his return to America. I suppose his new tour will occupy a year, and I hope to have all done long before that. In any event I propose to begin the Civil Volumes at once. I can do most of A. Johnson's Administration from memory and documents that I have here: but for the Genls own administration it will be necessary for me to be in America some months. I suppose I can get a leave at the right time. But I think it wise to say nothing of this now. Let the Military work stand alone; and if it gets credit, that credit will help the civil one. I am very busy with my maps now. I wish I could consult you about them. I have not yet had your opinion about the March to the Sea chapter. . . ." ". . . I do not yet get any word from the General. He has not been so long without writing to me since he left America" AL (initialed), ICN.

2. On Jan. 19, 1879, Robert C. Napier, governor of Gibraltar, wrote to USG. "I have been anxious to write to you to thank you, on Lady Napier's behalf and my own, for your kind remembrance of us on Christmas day and for the pleasant tokens of it in the Photographs which arrived safely We think the likeness and the Execution very good and shall value them very highly as mementos of your & Mrs Grants visit here

which we hope you may be tempted to repeat. We have watched the reports of your progress in the papers and now hear that you will Embark at Marseilles where I will direct my letter. I am glad you have decided to visit India You will Enjoy your visit and, if well advised as to Times and Seasons, you will accomplish the journey with *benefit* to your health. If you should happen to meet with the letters of Victor Jacquemont, who travelled some forty eight years ago, you will be able to judge of the progress made since then. I hope you may find it convenient to go as far as Jullalabad or at least to the Khybur. Lady Napier desires to join me in the kindest regards to Mrs Grant and your self. With the best wishes for your journey . . ." ALS, USG 3. See letter to Frederick Dent Grant, Nov. 14, 1878; letter to Daniel Ammen, Nov. 15, 1878; *The Times* (London), Dec. 19, 1930.

To Adam Badeau

Dec. 24th /78

DEAR GEN.

I have just this moment rec'd yours of the 21st. I hasten to answer so that you may respond to such enquiries as you are receiving the best you can. Having visited Europe very thoroughly, except Ireland; I did think of running over there for a hasty trip before my departure for the east. It is extremely problematical whether I can go. I must stay here until I know all about the time to expect the Richmond in the Mediterranean; where I am to board her; how much she is to await my orders, &c. The mail which brings news to the 10th of Dec.—the day the Richmond was to sail from America—brings me no news on the subject. It is certain that I cannot go to Ireland—that is, leave here for there—before the 2d of Jan.y. Nellie & Mrs. Sartoris come here this week to remain with us until our departure for the east.[1] ~~You had~~ We will not go to London therefore unless I should go to Ireland. You had better come over here therefore, and, if you get this in time, why not come with Young this week?

Mr. Borie sails on thursday the 26th, by the Steamer Ohio from Phila. He will accompany me on the whole trip, much to both Mrs. Grant's and my delight.

Before your letter suggesting a letter of condolence to the Prince of Wales for the death of Princess Allice,[2] and requesting a word about you in a letter of thanks you supposed I would write to the President for his tender of a ship to take me east, I had written such a letter—as the latter—but to the Sec. of the Navy from whom the tender came, with allusion to the President.[3] On the whole I thought it out of place—in the estimation of the American critizen—to write to the Queen or for her.

We will be glad to see you over here at such time as you can best come before my departure. By the second of Jan.y I will know positively whether I can go to Ireland.

With kindest regards of Mrs. Grant & myself,

Yours Very Truly

U. S. Grant

ALS, Munson-Williams-Proctor Institute, Utica, N. Y. See *Badeau*, p. 511; letter to Adam Badeau, Dec. 28, 1878.

1. See *Julia Grant*, p. 261.
2. Younger sister of the Prince of Wales, Princess Alice, Grand Duchess of Hesse-Darmstadt, died on Dec. 14, 1878. See *The Times* (London), Dec. 16, 1878.
3. See letter to Richard W. Thompson, Nov. 14, 1878.

To Elihu B. Washburne

Paris, France.
Dec. 24th /78

My Dear Mr. Washburne:

Your very welcome letter of Nov. the 24th was awaiting me here on my return to Paris some ten days since. I was very glad to hear from you again, but sorry to hear the cause of the detention of your family East this winter. I hope your daughter is improving, and that she will soon be restored to entire health.[1]

You have seen by the papers that I have determined to go home by India, China & Japan? This will not probably delay my return, but it will land me in San Francisco about the time I expected to reach Phila—say the last of June. If we get to San Francisco as early as that—or nearly so—I shall want to remain on the Pacific coast six weeks or two months. I spent two years there, in early life, and always felt the greatest desire to make it my future home. Nothing ever fell over me like a wet blanket so much as my promotion to the Lt. Generalcy. As Junior Maj. Gen. in the regular Army, I thought my chances good for being placed in command of the Pacific Div. when the war closed. As Lt. Gn. all hope of that kind vanished. You wrote me that you had been all over the Pacific Coast before, and how much interested you were in that country.[2]

I anticipate great pleasure fro[m] the trip before me. The fact is I take much more interest in seeing countries but seldom visited by foreigners to seeing those where one comes but little in contact with others than those foreign to the soil visited. I shall endeavor to profit by the journey even if I should write nothing. So far I have abstained from giving my views about the institutions and peoples of the countries I have already visited. The fact is however that I have seen nothing to make me regret that I am an American. Our country: its resources; energy, inginuity and intelligence of the people, &c. is more appreciated abroad than at home. If our politicians and people could see us as others see us, and see how much better off all producing classes are with us than in the most favored nation of europe, they would have much less to complain of, and more to be thankful for.

I am much pleased with the result of the Nov. elections. It seems to me to put the republican party right for /80. Providence seems to direct that something should be done just in time to save the party of progress and national unity & equality. The Potter investigating committee[3] and the financial question did it the last time.

My mails for two months from this time should be sent to U. S. Consul Bombay.[4] I shall always be pleased to hear from you.

Mrs. Grant joins me in kindest remembrances to you and all your family.

> Very Truly Yours
> U. S. GRANT

ALS, IHi.

1. Elihu B. Washburne's two daughters, Susan Adèle and Marie Lisa, lived with their parents. Both later married.

2. Earlier in 1878, Washburne had traveled to the Pacific coast for health reasons.

3. U.S. Representative Clarkson N. Potter of N. Y. had led an extended investigation of the 1876 presidential election. See *HMD*, 45-3-31; Frank P. Vazzano, "The Louisiana Question Resurrected: The Potter Commission and the Election of 1876," *Louisiana History*, XVI, 1 (Winter, 1975), 39–57.

4. Benjamin F. Farnham.

To Richard W. Thompson

Paris, France,
Dec. 25th 1878.

HON. RICHARD THOMPSON,
SEC. OF THE NAVY:
MY DEAR MR. SEC.

I am just this day in receipt of your letter of the 10th of this month, enclosing also copies of yours of the 9th to Capt. Benham, Commanding Corvette Richmond and Adm.l Le Roy; Comd.g U. S. Naval Force, European stations. I hasten to reniew my thanks for the courticy thus extended, and to say that my accepting it will neither result in cost to the Department nor delay or prejudice to the public service. Should my desires lead me to visit parts of the east where Naval Vessels would not properly go, I shall either forego the pleasure, or take the ordinary means of travel provided for visiting those parts.

I shall put myself in communication with Adm.l Le Roy at once, and arrange to be on board the Richmond, at Ville-franche, sur mer, on the earlyest day she would sail if I were not to accompany her.

Please present my compliments to the President and your associates in the Cabinet, wish them all, for me, a merry Christmas, a happy New Year & many returns.

Very respectfully
your obt. svt.
U. S. GRANT

ALS, NjP. On Dec. 10, 1878, Secretary of the Navy Richard W. Thompson wrote to USG. "UNOFFICIAL . . . Since the receipt of your letter of the 14th ultimo, from Gibralter, expressing some doubt in reference to your trip to the East, I have received your cable telegram informing me that you had concluded to accept my invitation to take passage on the Richmond. I am glad you have done so, for if you had failed to avail yourself of so favorable an opportunity you might have regretted it hereafter. I have to day written Rear Admiral Le Roy, commanding the Mediterranean Squadron, requesting him, upon the receipt of my letter, to put himself in communication with you, so that all the necessary preliminaries for your voyage may be made before the Richmond reaches Europe. I have also written Capt Benham, who commands the Richmond, instructing him when he reaches Gibralter, to notify Admiral Le Roy, in order that there may be ample time for you to make such arrangements as you may desire. I have given no directions as to the port from which it will be best for you to embark, but have suggested Ville-franche as being probably the most convenient for you. I enclose copies of both these letters in order that you may be fully informed of their contents. And if after you confer with the Admiral you shall prefer some other than the port of Ville-franche, and will indicate it to him, he will make the arrangement to suit you. It is suggested to me by Geo W Childs Esq. of Phila, that it will be agreeable to you to have two friends accompany you, one of whom has already been your travelling companion and the other familiar with China and the East. Of course there can be no objection to this and I have also written to Rear Admiral Le Roy as well as to Capt Benham leaving this matter entirely at your discretion. Copies of these letters I also send you. I hope you will have a pleasant voyage and can see no reason why you may not, as the Richmond is in excellent condition and a good sailer. I almost envy you your visit to the Orientals and should like to enjoy it myself—but of course shall never do so. It is hardly probable that there will be a government vessel coming from China or Japan to San Francisco about the time of your return home, but if there is and I shall at that time occupy my present position of Secretary I will endeavor to provide for your passage across the Pacific, as I suppose it is not your design to return by way of Europe." ALS, USG 3. A letter of Dec. 9 from Thompson to Capt. Andrew E. K. Benham is *ibid.* See letter to Anthony J. Drexel, Dec. 13, 1878; Thompson to George W. Childs, Dec. 10, 1878, DLC–John Russell Young.

On Dec. 9, a correspondent had reported from Washington, D. C., that repairs would delay the U.S.S. *Richmond.* "General Grant has been informed of the change of time and will regulate his movements accordingly, and designate where he will join the ship." *Philadelphia Press,* Dec. 10, 1878. See letter to Gen. William T. Sherman, Jan. 12, 1879.

To Adam Badeau

Paris, France,
Dec. 28th /78

DEAR GENERAL:

I have again concluded to visit Ireland before my departure for the East. General Noyes[1] & I will leave here on the 2d of Jan.y. without servants, and only hand bags, for a flying visit through the principle cities. We expect to be in Dublin the next morning after we leave, only passing from one station to the other in London. We will not stop more than one day at any place in Ireland, and must be back here by saturday, the 11th of January. You might make your arrangements to join us in London on our return and come to Paris with us.

I have no information yet of the sailing of the Richmond, and can form no idea of the time of my departure. I cannot leave Paris however until after the 15th. Mr. Borie, who goes with me, will want a little rest here, and if Fred goes he cannot arrive in Paris before the 15th.

Very Truly Yours

U. S. Grant

Gn. A. Badeau. U. S. A.

P. S. Since sealing this a cablegram informs me that Fred. sails on the Britannia on Saturday, ~~next~~ to-day; Mr. Borie not until next week.[2]

U. S. G.

ALS, Munson-Williams-Proctor Institute, Utica, N. Y. See letter to Adam Badeau, Dec. 24, 1878.

On Dec. 30, 1878, Adam Badeau, consul gen., London, wrote to Orville E. Babcock. ". . . Gen Grant will be in London on the 2d of Jany, and go straight to Ireland, with 'Mr Noyes, no servants and only hand bags.' He means to pay a flying visit to the principal cities. It will be a bad time—mid-winter and *every body* in mourning for the Princess Alice. Besides (this of course is to *you* only) the consul at Dublin writes me that the Fenians are very hostile to him, because he refused to receive their deputation while he was President, There must be a demonstration the Consu[l] says, and there may be trouble. The Genl evidently wants to go with Noyes only, for he has invited me to join him *on his return*, and pay him a visit in Paris. Mrs Grant does not go.—You know of course that Fred and Mr. Borie are to go to India etc; also Russell Young. The Genl writes that he and Mrs Grant are delighted to have Mr. Borie accompany them. I hope it will do the dear old fellow good. Gen Grant has no truer friend. . . ." AL (initialed), ICN. See Note, [*Oct. 17, 1876*].

1. On Dec. 25, USG had written to Edward F. Noyes, U.S. minister, Paris. "Please send the Oysters & apples to the hotel—Liverpool—by any public carman and I will leave directions at the door to receive them in case of my absence from the house. Only send a few of the apples." ALS, DLC-USG, IB.

2. On Jan. 1, 1879, a correspondent reported from Philadelphia on Adolph E. Borie's opposition to the movement to nominate USG for a third term. *Cincinnati Enquirer*, Jan. 2, 1879.

To John Russell Young

Paris, France
Dec. 29th /78

MY DEAR MR. YOUNG:

I have your letter enclosing one from old Gen. Patterson.[1] You say Sec. Thompson letter to you leaves the whole matter of your accompanying me to me: Of course I not only want you to go but shall be very much disappointed if you do not go.

Fred. sailed yesterday, on the Brittania, to join our party. Mr. Borie did not get off on thursday[2] but is to sail this week.

Governor Noyes & I leave here thursday morning for Dublin direct. We will not be in London any longer than to pass from one station to the other. We take with us neither servant nor trunk; simply valises. Do you propose going with us? If so meet us at the station of the "Wild Irishman"[3] at 8 O'clock thursday evening, or at Charing Cross station a little after six.[4]

Yours Truly
U. S. GRANT

P. S. I did not invite Mr. Welsh to accompany us because I know he had been very sick. But if his health is sufficiently restored to permit him to go along I would be delighted to have him.[5]

U. S. G.

ALS, DLC-John Russell Young. See John Russell Young diary, Dec. 25, 27, 1878, DLC-John Russell Young.

1. Robert Patterson. See *PUSG*, 23, 255.
2. Dec. 26, 1878.
3. A train on the London & North Western Railway.
4. On Thursday, Jan. 2, 1879, Young wrote in his diary that he "went to Charing Cross to see Gen Grant & Mr Noyes who are coming over to go to Ireland.—Gen. comes in late and we all drive to Euston square & go to Dublin—We sit up & talk & play cards until we come to Holyhead, and embark on the vessel." DLC-John Russell Young.
5. Nominated as minister to Great Britain on Oct. 30, 1877, John Welsh did not accompany USG to Ireland. See *Calendar*, Jan. 19, 1877.

Speech

[*Dublin, Jan. 3, 1879*]

My Lord Mayor and fellow-citizens—I feel that I can address you as fellow-citizens, because I have been a voter here now, I think, about seven hours. There is no telling who I may come into competition with hereafter as a candidate for office. It may be with the Lord Mayor; it may be with my friend here to the right, who represents you in Parliament—at least I saw him there last year. It strikes me you did not know rightly what you were doing when you made me a freeman of your city—that you did not know the trouble you were about getting into—for I am a troublesome candidate, and may trouble some of you here. Now, you may be asking me many questions. Now, I rather like Ireland, and I wish you to know that I should like to have a high representative place here amongst you. You may put it that I am here rather bidding for votes. I have done it before to much larger crowds of Irishmen than here present, and have been successful. But I know we have a great deal of eloquence here, and people that can spread out what I say. I have talked to a much larger crowd than this smaller one—to a larger one than Mr Butt ever did. Gentlemen, I ask your patronage, if ever I come back here to settle, to make me Lord Mayor or Member of Parliament. I am modest. I don't know whether you think me a modest man, but I am. I don't want both places at once, but after I go out of one I may want the other. However, I will say a word or two a little more serious. We have heard some words spoken about our country—my country before I was naturalised in another. We have a very great country, a prosperous country, and room for a great many people. We have been suffering for some time a very great depre[s]sion, and the world has felt it. There is no question about the fact that when you have 45 millions of such consumers as we have and make them feel poverty, then the civilized world feels it. You have had here great prosperity from our great extravagance and our great misfortunes. We had a war which involved every man almost who could bear arms, and my friend who spoke so eloquently to you left a leg in it.¹ You did not observe, perhaps, that he has got a wooden one in place of it. I try to represent him in my humble way. When that great conflict was going on we were spending one thousand millions dollars a year more than we were producing, and Europe got every dollar of that—and it made for you a false property, which was a real property then to you. You were getting our bonds and our promises to pay—you were cashing them yourselves. That made very great prosperity, and made producers beyond the real wants of the world at peace. We got through that great conflict finally, and with an inflated currency which was far below the specie which you used here, it made our people still extravagant. Our speculations were going on, and we continued to spend four or five hundred, or three or four, hundred million dollars a year more than we were producing. We paid it back to you for your labour and manufactures, and it made you apparently prosperous, and really prosperous, while we were getting really poor. But being honest, however, we were bound to pay a solid, honest payment. We came down to the necessity of selling more than we bought. We have battled that day; we have turned the corner; we have had our depression—yours is just coming on—I hope it is nearly over. Our prosperity is commencing, and as we become prosperous you will too—because we become increased consumers of your products as well as our own. I think it is safe to say the United States, with a few years more of such prosperity as we have had for the last year or two, will consume as much more as she did. The increased consumption it would be hard to put into millions, but we have several men who put it into million[s]. One of them was the president of the United States in his Message to Congress. He speaks to that fact—that the prosperity of our country means the prosperity of the balance of the civilised world. Beaconsfield, who is a far-seeing man—he sees as far into the future as any man that I know of—he too saw the same thing—that American prosperity meant European prosperity. I don't speak of English or Irish prosperity, but I speak of European prosperity. Now gentlemen this is the longest speech I ever made. I have nothing more serious to say, but only to explain how I happen to make a speech of this length. I know it is because I have become an Irish citizen. I never kissed the blarney stone, and I don't think I ever shall, but I think it is because I have been looking at my friend Mr Butt. His countenance was so jolly and he said so many good things that I felt that if I ever had the opportunity I would say some good thing too. I think you won't give credit to my occupying too much time. Now gentlemen I am going to ask you to fill your glasses to the full and drink the toast I am about to propose—the health of the Lord Mayor who has been the cause of a great deal of my misery. I give you the health and long life all the Lord Mayor, and may he be as successful as through the carri[ag]e of his office as he has been on the present occasion.

The Irish Times (Dublin), Jan. 4, 1879; variant text, *Freeman's Journal* (Dublin), Jan. 4, 1879. USG spoke during an evening banquet at the Mansion House. Lord Mayor John Barrington of Dublin concluded his toast for USG by reading a telegram from F. M. Mullally, Islington, England. "I wish at the last moment to communicate to your lordship a noble act of General Grant towards a poor Irish and orphans—Mrs Carroll and children—whose husband was killed in the American War. . . ." *The Irish Times* (Dublin), Jan. 4, 1879.

On Jan. 3, 1879, USG, Adam Badeau, consul gen., London, Edward F. Noyes, minister to France, and John Russell Young arrived in Dublin during the morning and rapidly toured the Royal Irish Academy, Bank of Ireland, and Trinity College. At a city hall ceremony, Lord Mayor Barrington introduced USG. ". . . He fought the battle, he raised the sword, for the purpose of freeing his fellow-man. I recollect, fourteen years ago, when the people of this country received with a thrill of horror the announcement that President Lincoln had been assassinated. Ireland mourned for his loss when she heard the news that the great disciple of freedom had been struck down. A truly great General took his place and carried out the work that had been begun, and through the assistance of his generals, particularly Sherman and the illustrious Phil Sheridan, he might say that his was a real victory, and crowned with success—that the shackles of the negro and slavery disappeared from America, every part of which is now free. . . ." *Ibid.* USG responded. "My Lord Mayor, Gentlemen of the Town Council of Dublin, and ladies and gentlemen, I feel very proud to be made a citizen of the great city which you represent, and to be a fellow-citizen with those whom I see around me to-day. Since my arrival on this side of the Atlantic I have had the pleasure of being made a citizen of quite a number of towns and cities. None have given me more pleasure than being made a citizen of the principal city of Ireland. I am by birth a citizen of a country where there are more Irishmen, either native born or the descendants of Irishmen, than you have in all Ireland. I have had the honour and pleasure, therefore, of representing more Irishmen and their descendants when in office than the Queen of England does. Not being possessed of the eloquence of your worthy Lord Mayor, I shall say no more than simply to thank you again." *Ibid.* A certificate documented USG's freedom of the city. DS (dated Jan. 3), Smithsonian Institution. In the afternoon, the party lunched at Viceregal Lodge with the Lord Lt. of Ireland, John Winston Spencer Churchill, Duke of

Marlborough. See Young diary, DLC-John Russell Young; *Young*, I, 576–79. See also John Augustus O'Shea, *Roundabout Recollections* (London, 1892), II, 11–26.

Also on Jan. 3, the Cork Corporation debated a letter "informing the Mayor that General Grant, the ex-President of the United States, was about to pay a visit to Cork within a week." One official denounced USG, saying that he had "insulted the Irish people in America. He got up a 'No-Popery' cry there." Another official agreed: "I can't see anything in the career of General Grant, or ex-President Grant, that calls for the sympathy of the Irish nation. I have had interviews with many persons who spent years in America, and I learned from them that he never thought of the Irish race as he thought of others, and that he actually went out of his way to insult their religion." *The Irish Times* (Dublin), Jan. 4, 1879. An editorial characterized the Cork proceedings as "undignified and altogether out of place." *Ibid.* On Jan. 10, a correspondent in Washington, D. C., reported Gen. William T. Sherman's defense of USG. "I do not recall a single instance in which prejudice upon religious matters ever had the slightest influence in the discharge of his official duties. Many of his intimate personal friends are Catholics, and during his residence in St. Louis his circle of acquaintances was almost altogether among families of the Catholic faith. He nominated Henry T. Blow for the Brazilian mission, a gentleman well known as a member of the Catholic Church, and one of his old acquaintances in St. Louis. I do not recall just now any other name, but it is 'bosh' to talk about General Grant insulting any one on account of his religious convictions. The Des Moines speech was prompted by a desire to defend the freedom of our public schools from sectarian influence, and, as I remember the conversation which led him to write that speech, it was because of the ceaseless clamor for set religious exercises in the public schools; not from Catholics, but from Protestant denominations. His son Fred married a Catholic lady and his aunt, Mrs. Fred Dent, is a Catholic, so that I know there is no prejudice in the General's mind, such, at least, as he is accused of harboring against a class of people many of whom are his particular friends. . . ." *New York Herald*, Jan. 11, 1879. On Nov. 4, USG spoke to a Chicago reporter on the Cork affair. "I was in Dublin at the time, and had no intention of visiting Cork. . . . Their grievance, I believe, was that I was an enemy of the Catholics. Whatever I may have thought, I cannot remember that I had ever said anything in criticism of the Catholic or any other church, and Catholics cannot consider me their enemy unless they are enemies to the sentiments I expressed at Des Moines. If any Methodist friends should ever undertake to divert public funds to the support of sectarian schools, they and I would be at outs." *Chicago Inter-Ocean*, Nov. 6, 1879. See *PUSG*, 26, 342–45; *New York Herald*, Jan. 7, 9–10, 15, 27, 1879; *New York Times*, Jan. 12, 1879; *Washington Evening Star*, Jan. 27, 1879.

On May 10, John Beveridge, town clerk, Dublin, had written to Nathaniel R. Harris, Philadelphia. ". . . I have the honor to inform you, that the address expressive of Sympathy in the welcome of General Grant was duly laid before the Municipal Council, and recorded, and has been deposited in the Monument Room of the City Hall, and I am to add that its receipt would have been acknowledged at once, but that your address was omitted from your letter of the 18th January." Copy, USG 3. On Nov. 30, Harris wrote to USG. "The Citizens of Philadelphia, formerly Citizens of the City of Dublin Ireland, in token of their appreciation, of yourself being made a Citizen of the ancient City of Dublin Sent an address to the Corporation of that City, through the Honorable Benjamin H. Burrows United States Consul, which was duly delivered, to the Right Honorable (Sir John Barrington) the Lord Mayor, and cortiously received the consideration of the Corporation and his Honor. I am instructed by the committe, to forward to you, a copy of the acknowledgement of said address, and of its disposition, by a 'Special Meeting' (for Said purpose) of the Corporation of the City of Dublin. The Right Honorable the Lord Mayor, presiding. I am also instructed to inclose a Slip, cut from one of the Dublin papers, which gives a Statement of the facts as they occured. We rejoice at the safe arrival of yourself and companions to your native Land, and when you arrive in the City of 'Brotherly Love,' none of our fellow Citizens of this commonwealth, will be more willing to pay their respects to the Honored Citizen of two Hemispheres, and the first Citizen of this Republic. Without any intention of intruding upon your patience, I most respectfully ask you to receive the cordial greetings, of my companions, and signers of the above address, . . ." ALS, *ibid.* The enclosed undated newspaper clipping contains the communication from Harris *et al.*, dated Jan. 18, commending Dublin officials for honoring USG. *Ibid.*

On Jan. 6, at the Londonderry train station, laborers had pressed near USG "and inquired why he did not receive O'Connor Power when he went out with an address from the Fenian prisoners to America." *Londonderry Journal*, Jan. 8, 1879. See *PUSG*, 27, 336–37. On the same day, USG received an address conveying freedom of the city. DS (2 signatures, dated Jan. 3), Smithsonian Institution. USG thanked officials. ". . . My being here at the present time is a little bit accidental. My mind was only recently made up to come here now. But having visited every capital in Europe, and almost every important country except Ireland, and never having put my foot on your soil, I expected to make that my final visit on my way back to America. But recently I changed my mind, and concluded to go home by the East, through China and Japan, and return by way of San Francisco to my own home. But I could not think of having seen so much of the Old World, and pass by your little island without putting my foot on the soil. My time is so limited now that I have but a few days to spare. I must leave, on my way back to Paris and the Mediterranean, on Wednesday next, the day after tomorrow. Hence my short stay amongst you." *Londonderry Journal*, Jan. 8, 1879. Later, USG told a banquet ". . . that there is that kindly feeling existing between my countrymen and yours which has been spoken of here to-night. You have numerous relations with us, and we all of us have relations on this side of the water, although some of us would, unluckily enough, have to go back five or six generations to find them. But we are related, and the majority of our kindred come from this side of the water. We have them, of course, from other parts of Europe as well. We have a vast country, a productive country, a good climate, and a home for all who find themselves limited on this side of the water. We will make you all welcome when you come there to see us—and more than that, we will make you all citizens, but not so rapidly as you have made me a citizen here to-day. But, after a little probation, we will make you all citizens, and give you an equal voice with ourselves in saying who shall make the laws, and what laws should be made. With industry and frugality there is a home for many more millions there yet. We hope to see more of the people of Derry and Ireland there after a while, when you become more crowded and want more room. We hope you will go there and establish your shirt factories—and linen factories, and all your other factories. Just go there and build up your factories, where you will have sufficient room, and good markets, and you won't have a word to say about tariff. I think that this is the intrusion of the evening, my talking so long. I did not intend to say a word but to thank you, which I now do most heartily." *Ibid.* See *Freeman's Journal* (Dublin), Jan. 7, 1879; John Russell Young diary, Jan. 6–8, 1879, DLC-John Russell Young; *Young*, I, 579–84.

On Jan. 7, Joseph Cuthbert, chairman, Coleraine Town Commissioners, telegraphed to USG, Londonderry. "The town Commissioners request you will receive a short address from them at Railway Station when passing through to day" Telegram received (at 8:53 A.M.), DLC-USG, IB. At Coleraine, USG replied to an address. "Mr. Chairman, and members of the Coleraine Town Commissioners, it is with the greatest possible pleasure that I visit your ancient town, and received the very flattering address. I regret that my time is so very limited that I cannot reply as I would like; but representing, as I do, some forty-five millions of Irishmen, or descendants of Irishmen, I can't help expressing, however briefly, the pleasure I feel at seeing representatives of the ancient town of Coleraine." *Londonderry Journal*, Jan. 8, 1879.

Later, USG spoke in Belfast. "Mr Mayor and Gentlemen, I hardly know how to respond to the toast, and to the kind words which have just been delivered. I thank you very much for the compliments you have paid to my country. I admit they are only what is due to that country, and, while responding, I repeat the words of the Mayor, that it would only be an enemy of the two countries who would raise a hand to cause a difference between my country and yours. We have, if not one interest, a like interests. Our civilization and language are the same, and we (that is, the great English speaking nations of England and America) are two nations peculiarly adapted for impressing our customs upon other nations, and inducing them to become the consumers of our produce, and to labour to make the most of whatever their own soil or climate can produce." *The Irish Times* (Dublin), Jan. 8, 1879. See *Freeman's Journal* (Dublin), Jan. 8, 1879.

Also on Jan. 7, "Messrs Wm Barbour & Sons Hilden Flaxspinning Mills Lisbourn and Flaxspinning Mills Patterson New York" invited USG to tour their works near Belfast. N, DLC-USG, IB. On Jan. 8, USG visited several Belfast businesses. Irish insurgent John Rea demonstrated at the train station upon USG's departure. See *The Irish Times* (Dublin) and *Freeman's Journal* (Dublin), Jan. 9, 1879; D. B. Dunne to Young, Jan. 14, 1879, DLC-John Russell Young.

1. Edward F. Noyes, minister to France, had praised the Irish and USG in an earlier toast. *Irish Times* (Dublin), Jan. 4, 1879.

To John Barrington

———

January 4th, 1879.

My DEAR LORD MAYOR,—The artist, Mr Hartshorn, who drew the portrait of me which was hung in the banquet hall last evening has presented it to me to be presented again to such person as I may choose. As I am now an Irish citizen in good standing, I do not wish to carry it away with me. May I ask you to accept it?—Very truly yours,

U. S. GRANT.

To Sir John Barrington.

The Irish Times (Dublin), Jan. 6, 1879. On Jan. 4, 1879, Lord Mayor John Barrington of Dublin wrote to USG. "I accept with pleasure the portrait of your own good self which

you have so kindly presented me. The artist (Mr Hartshorn) has produced a most striking likeness, and I shall keep it as a pleasing souvenir of your becoming a Freeman of the
ancient and loyal city of Dublin." *Ibid.* A correspondent described the life-size likeness
of USG as "an admirable brazen portrait." *Freeman's Journal* (Dublin), Jan. 4, 1879. Born
in 1842 in N. H., Newton T. Hartshorn served in the Engineer Corps during the Civil
War before beginning a career as an artist. See *PUSG*, 23, 132; Hartshorn to James A.
Garfield, Oct. 1, 1880, DLC-James A. Garfield; Elizabeth Newell Berglund, "Newton
Timothy Hartshorn: Portrait Painter," M. A. Thesis, University of Maine, 1950.

On Feb. 14, 1879, President Rutherford B. Hayes wrote to George W. Childs,
Philadelphia. "Private . . . I am anxious to get for this house a portrait of Gen Grant,
and if it is not practicable to consult his, or his family's wishes, I prefer to procure a
portrait now without waiting for Gen G's return. There is a portrait here by Ulke
three fourths size, that is well thought of. But in this matter I would like your judgement. Do you know of any Satisfactory portrait, which could be copied?" ALS, Gilder
Lehrman Collection, NHi. See *PUSG*, 27, 95.

To John A. Kasson

Paris, Jan. 12th /79

HON. J. A. KASSON,
U. S. MIN. &c.
MY DEAR MR. KASSON,

On my return from a short visit to Ireland, a day or two since, I
found your very welcome letter of the 4th of this month. I hope you
may be in America on my return and that we may meet.—The Naval Vessel, on which we were to take passage was to have sailed for
the Mediterranean on the 10th of Dec. On the 10th of Jan.y she had
not yet started. I have determined therefore to go with[*out*] her and
to do up India at least before availing myself of th[e] kind invitation of the Sec. of the Navy to use a Govt. vessel We will probably
leave here the last of this week.[1]

As you say the Nov. elections—in the North at least—are very
satisfactory.[2] Resumption too has been a great success[3] The only
thing I fear in regard to the latter matter is the possible effect of
the rapid conversion of the five twenties of /67. Most of the bonds
held abroad are those of /67. The new bonds are taken at home.
Now that resumption is an actual fact the new bonds can be paid
for in currency. The foreign owner of called bonds must be paid in

gold coin or its equivalent. So long as the balance of trade is in our favor we can afford to call an amount of foreign held bonds equal to this balance. But any thing beyond that must be paid for in gold coin to be transported. Should the Amt. be large the Sec. might be compelled to sell bonds, at a higher rate of interest, to enable him to keep coin enough to enable him to hold fast to resumption. But it is a most desirable thing to have every form of indebtedness of the Country held at home. We will be the richest nation on earth when this is consumated.

Mrs. Grant desires to be specially remembered to you.

Very Truly yours

U. S. Grant

ALS, IaHA. John A. Kasson, minister to Austria-Hungary, visited the U.S. during the summer. While in New York City, he explained USG's strengths as a presidential candidate in 1880. See *New York Tribune*, July 12, 1879.

On Jan. 9, 1879, a secretary for John Shaw, gen. manager, South Eastern Railway, wrote to USG. "Mr John Shaw presents his complements to General Grant, and begs to state that he has had much pleasure in giving instructions for a Saloon Carriage to be attached to the Tidal train which leaves Charing Cross Station at 8.50 am. tomorrow (Friday) and a Deck Cabin will be reserved by the Boat from Folkestone to Boulogne. He has also telegraphed for a coupé to be provided on the Northern of France line from Boulogne to Paris, and trusts that the arrangements he has made will add to General Grant's comfort." N, DLC-USG, IB. On the same evening, John Welsh, U.S. minister, London, entertained USG. *Londonderry Journal*, Jan. 10, 1879.

1. See following letter.
2. See letter to Edward F. Beale, Dec. 6, 1878.
3. In accordance with legislation enacted in 1875, the U.S. had returned its currency to a specie basis on Jan. 1, 1879. See *PUSG*, 26, 35–39; message to Congress, Feb. 3, 1877.

To Gen. William T. Sherman

Paris, Jan. 12th /79

My Dear General,

On my return from Ireland night before last I found your letter of the 22d of Dec. past. I had learned in London, with great disappointment, of the delay of the Richmond, and determined to do the

very thing you advise; take a regular steamer and make my visit
to India before joining a Govt. steamer.[1] During the day I will find
out the date, and places of departure, of steamers from Mediterranean ports and start by the earlyest after the 16th. On that day
I have accepted an invitation to dine with the Marshall President
of the Republic. As the dinner is given to me I cannot well withdraw my acceptance so as to start at an earlyer day.[2] It does seem
to me the Navy was never up to time, except in war, and then only
with some of the Commanders.—Fred reached here on thursday.[3]
Mr. Borie is expected daily though I have no positive information
of his having left America.[4]

I have just received a letter from Dr. McMillan, Consul Gn.
at Rome, complaining of secret and underhanded efforts that are
being made to undermine him. You know the Dr. better than I do.
But I saw him constantly for three weeks last Spring both in his
office, at his house and at dinners, receptions &c. My judgement
is that he is a most capable & faithful officer.[5] If you feel disposed
you may say as much for me to the Sec. of State, or pPresident or
both.

I see by the papers that $30.000.000 of the five twenties of
/67 have been called in. This is an addition to an equal amount
that has been subscribed for since Jan. 1st. It is a grand thing to
get the public debt of the country—and all our securities of every
description—owned at home. But may we not be going too fast? A
large part of the bonds of /67 are held abroad. The new bonds are
being subscribed for by our own citizens. Now that we are back to
specie payments the new bonds can be paid for with currency. The
foreign holder of the redeemed bond must be paid in Gold coin or
its equivolent. So long as there is a balance of trade in our favor we
can stand this process to the extent of the balance. But beyond that
gold must go out of the country and either endanger permanent
resumption or enforce the sale of bonds bearing a higher rate of interest, to be sold abroad to buy gold with to maintain resumption.
It looks to me as though it would be well to make "haste slowly."
I have no doubt but the Sec. of the Treas. has considered all these
things and may be right. I hope most sincerely he is,[6] for as I said

in the beginning, it is a most desirable thing that all the countries indebtedness should be owned at home.

With kindest regards of Mrs. Grant, Fred, & myself,

yours Truly

U. S. GRANT

GEN. W. T. SHERMAN

ALS, DLC-William T. Sherman. See letter to Gen. William T. Sherman, Dec. 8, 1878.

1. On [*Jan.*] 11, 1879, USG, Paris, wrote to John Russell Young. "I have now determined not to wait for the Richmond, but to sail from Marseilles, by the French line of steamers on thursday, the 23d of Jan.y. and meet the Richmond at Calcutta or beyond. Possibly out there the Adm.l may assign some other vessel to our use." ALS (misdated Dec.), DLC-John Russell Young.

2. French president Maurice de MacMahon's dinner guests also included Chinese and South American diplomats. See *New York Times*, Jan. 17, 1879.

3. Jan. 9. See letter to Frederick Dent Grant, Dec. 12, 1878.

4. See letter to Adolph E. Borie, Jan. 13, 1879.

5. On Jan. 22, Gen. William T. Sherman wrote to Secretary of State William M. Evarts. "If parties are Engaged in Slandering Dr McMillan—U. S. Consul General, Rome, it is only fair play that he Should be heard. Please read the Enclosed letter just received." ALS, DNA, RG 59, Applications and Recommendations, Hayes-Arthur. The enclosure is a letter dated Jan. 3 from Charles McMillan, consul gen., Rome, to Sherman denying charges of drunkenness pressed by J. Schuyler Crosby, consul, Florence, "who since his insolent and personally and officially discourteous treatment of me on the occasion of General Grant's visit to Florence last April, has left no means untried to injure me here and at home—" ALS, *ibid.* See *PUSG*, 28, 379–80; McMillan to Sherman, April 25, 1879, DLC-William T. Sherman.

6. Secretary of the Treasury John Sherman was Gen. Sherman's younger brother. See following letter; *John Sherman's Recollections of Forty Years . . .* (Chicago, 1895), II, 686–725.

To Adolph E. Borie

———

Paris, Jan.y 13th /79

MY DEAR MR. BORIE:

I have only just heard of your actual sailing from America, and hasten to write welcoming you just as I expect you to reach Liverpool. I am very much disappointed in the delay of the Richmond—she only left N. Y. on the 11th—and have determined to go on to Bombay, and do up India, before she arrives there. We will leave here on saturday [1] for Marseilles, stopping over sunday

at Lyons, and await the departure of the steamer—on the following thursday—at Marseilles. I hope you will feel strong enough to
come over and go with us to Marseilles. We could wait just as well
as not until monday if you desire it. If you will telegraph me when
you will be here I will secure rooms for you at this hotel—Hotel
Liverpool—.

I have been feeling very anxious since your first delay lest you
might not come at all. We will have a jolly time on the trip with
our little game of Boston. Fred. Mr Young & Dr Keiting[2] gives us
a full table, with one to spare.

After we get to India I have no doubt but we will find Naval
vessels to take us where we want to go without waiting for the
Richmond.

Mrs. Grant joins me in anxiety to meet you, and have you again
as a traveling companion.

Very Truly yours
U. S. Grant

ALS, PHi. USG addressed the envelope. "Hon. A. E. Borie Care J. S. Morgan & Co. 22
Old Broad St. London England" AD, *ibid.*

1. Jan. 18, 1879.
2. John M. Keating, born in 1852, earned a medical degree from the University
of Pennsylvania in 1873 and practiced in Philadelphia. He served as Adolph E. Borie's
physician and wrote *With General Grant in the East* (Philadelphia, 1879).

To George W. Childs

———

Paris, France,
Jan.y 14th /79

My Dear Mr. Childs:

I have your letter of the 30th of Dec. and by the same mail
quite a number of others from the states. I had begun to fear that I
was not to have Mr. Borie with me after all. From London I learn
however that he was expected last night.[1]

I have been wofully disappointed at the delay of the Richmond. If we were to remain for her we would loose the India part

of our trip entirely. I have determined therefore to take a regular passenger steamer for Bombay, do up India first, and then take the Richmond, or such steamer as Adm.l Patter[son][2] may designate, to visit Chinese & Japanese ports in. It has been my expectation to reach San Francisco about the 1st of July next. But the delays have been such that we may not get there before Oct. Fred may be compelled to leave earlyer and take a packet for home in advance of the party. I feel that the rest, freedom from business cares & change of climate will be of great benefit to Mr Borie. I wish Drexel was along for the same reason, and for his company.

I had a delightful run through the North of Ireland. There is no indication of distress & poverty in that section. A more hearty, independent, self reliant people are not to be found. Their factories seem to be all running and while profits may not be as large as formerly they are sufficient to support the population & keep them contented.

Mrs. Grant sends her love to Mrs. Childs, Mrs. Drexel and Mrs. Borie. I join mine also. I will try and drop you, Mr Drexel or Mrs. Borie a line from time to time, and shall always be glad to hear from either of you.

Yours Truly

U. S. GRANT

ALS, DLC-USG. See letter to Anthony J. Drexel, Dec. 13, 1878.

1. See previous letter.
2. Rear Admiral Thomas H. Patterson commanded the Asiatic Squadron.

To Charles H. Rogers

Paris, France
Jan.y 14th /79

MY DEAR MR. ROGERS;

I am very much obliged for your letter of the 31st of Dec. just received. I have been exceedingly disappointed by the delay in the

departure of the U. S. Steamer Richmond which was to take my
party. We have concluded not to await her arrival but to leave Marseilles next week—thursday¹—for Bombay direct, and to do up
India before the arrival of the Richmond. Fred. is now with me
to accompany us around the world, and we expect Mr. Borie in
a day or two. I wish you,—and Mrs. Rogers to keep Mrs. Grant
company,—could be along. It is a great comfort to have my dear
old friend, Mr. Borie, with me. I hope the trip, and absence from
business cares, will do him much good. From what I understand he
sadly needs rest and recupuration. I would have taken Ulysses, Jr.
with me in stead of taking Fred. but I thought it improper to break
in upon the time of a young man just as he is trying to establish
himself in business. The whole would have to be done over again
on his return.²

I will drop you a line occasionally while on my travels, and will
always be glad to hear from you. My address will not be changed
so far as letters from the United States are concerned.

Mrs. Grant sends much love to Mrs. Rogers & Miss Lillie
and her kindest regards to you. Please remember me also to the
ladies.

With greatest esteem
your obt. svt.
U. S. Grant

ALS, DLC-USG. See letter to Charles H. Rogers, Dec. 6, 1878.

1. Jan. 23, 1879.
2. Ulysses S. Grant, Jr., worked as a lawyer in New York City. See *PUSG*,
28, 236.

To Edward F. Beale

Paris, Jan. 17th /79

Dear General.

I am in receipt of your letter of the 4th of Jan. Mr. Borie
has not put in an appearanc[e] yet though the papers notice his

arrival in Liverpool two or three days ago. We start in the morning for Marseilles, to take the French steamer for Alexandria, thence by rail to Suez; thence the ΘP. & O. line[1] to Bombey. But as the steamer does not leave Marseilles until the 23d Mr. Borie will have abundance of time to join us. Starting at this time we will be able to do up India while the season is pleasant, and in time to take the Richmond on her arrival at Calcutta. It is impossible for me to fix a time now when I will reach California. If I can not get to Japan early in May I will probably remain in China until the cool weather in the fall—say the 1st of Oct. In this case I would not reach San Francisco until some time in Dec. But I shall certainly be in the states before the end of the year, barring accidents.

You have seen by the the papers that I have just made a run through Ireland? I was only in the northern part. I was much pleased with the people. There are no more thrifty, self reliant & contented people in europe to-day than the people of north Ireland. I saw no idle factories and no indication of poverty. Business may not be so brisk or so remunerative as it was during, & directly after, our war, but it is on a solid basis.

I anticipate much pleasure from the trip before me; but, as I believe I have said to you in a previous letter, I get very homesick some times. I long for a quiet home.

Give Mrs. Grants love to Mrs. Beale & Miss Emily and my kindest regards. Tell Ammen that I may not write to him before we get to Bombey, but I am always pleased to hear from him. My address will continue to be same as before, or to the care of the U. S. Consul either at Bombey[2] or Calcutta.[3] Write to me often.

Very Truly yours

U. S. GRANT

GN. E. F. BEALE.

ALS, DLC-Decatur House Papers.

1. See Boyd Cable, *A Hundred Year History of the P. & O.: Peninsular and Oriental Steam Navigation Company 1837–1937* (London, 1937).
2. Benjamin F. Farnham.
3. Allyne C. Litchfield, consul gen.

To Adolph E. Borie

———

Paris, Jan.y 17th /79

My Dear Mr. Borie

I wrote you to the care of J. S. Morgan &co. London, that on account of the delay of the Richmond I had determined to take passage from Marseilles directly for Bombay so as to finish my visit to India before the weather gets to warm. The French steamer[1] to Alexandria I understan[d] is very fine and the accomodations better than on most of the Atlantic steamers. At the office they inform me that there are but few or no passengers besides our party for the next steamer so that we can get as many staterooms as we please. On the P & O Steamer[2] from Suez to Bombey they have assigned me three staterooms, and if I could have felt assured of you and Dr. Keiting being along, and taken the tickets, I could have had another. But there will be no difficulty about your getting the stateroom when you get your ticket. The office of the company is on Av. Opera, just opposite Spendide Hotel. Mr. Young, who goes with us, will see you and attend to this or any other matter for you. Mrs. Grant & I start in the morning for Lyons, where we will stay a couple of days, and then go on to Marseilles. Mr. Young will not leave Paris until tuesday evening.[3] I am sorry you are not here to go with us. But I presume you will want to rest in Paris until Monday or tuesday. Either day will give you the opportunity of breaking the journey at Lyons. I think we have the promise of a most delightful trip before us. I am most anxious to see you but Mrs. Grant has got very tired of Paris and wants to spend a day or two at each Lyons & Marseilles.

Very Truly yours,

U. S. Grant

ALS, PHi. See letter to Adolph E. Borie, Jan. 13, 1879.

1. For the *Labourdonnais*, see *Young*, I, 585–86, and *Julia Grant*, pp. 262–63.
2. *Venetia*.
3. On Tuesday, Jan. 21, 1879, 8:00 p.m., John Russell Young took the train from Paris for Marseilles with Adolph E. Borie and Adam Badeau, consul gen., London. Young diary, DLC-John Russell Young.

To Lt. Gen. Philip H. Sheridan

———

Paris, Jan. 17th /79

MY DEAR GENERAL:

To-morrow we leave here for Marseilles[1] to take the French steamer for Alexandria, Egypt, thence by rail, through Egypt, to Suez, where we get the Peninsular & Oriental Steamer— English—for Bombey. This will give us time to see India pretty thoroughly before the season becomes too warm, and before the Richmond, on which we expected to take passage, arrives. I have not heard from Mr. Borie yet though the papers announce his arrival in Liverpool two or three days ago. Fred. has been with us a week. I am under many obligations to you for allowing him to come and for what you say about him.[2] The trip will be of inestimable value to him if he remains in the service and of great value if he does not. If Congress keeps legislating against the Army[3] I hope he will find something else to do, and, in the language of the Hon. Bardwell Sloate become a P. I. G.—perfectly independent Gentleman.[4]

Tell Ingalls that I received his letter and would be glad to do what he asks, or anything to help him. But, if I understand the status of present Army legislation, the President can retire any Officer who is entitled to, or who may be subject to retirement under any past act of Congress; but he cannot fill any vacancy, no matter how created, above the rank of Captain. The retirement of the Qr. Mr. Gn. therefore would not benefit him. Am I not right in this? Ingalls, above every officer in the staff, deserves promotion. I regard his administration of the Q. M. D. during the war as far the ablest administration of any we had. I have always believed that it was unfortun[ate] for him that he was not in the line. I believed at the time that h[e] would have made the best commander for the Army of the Potomac that could have been selected from that army; and I mean no disparagement to the very able officers there.[5]

I shall always be glad to hear from you. Mrs. Grant sends her love to Mrs. Sheridan & the children, and I join in kindest regards to them & you.

Very Truly yours
U. S. Grant

Gn. P. H. Sheridan, U. S. A.

ALS, DLC-Philip H. Sheridan.

1. The Grants postponed their departure from Paris. See letter to Elizabeth M. Borie, Jan. 20, 1879.

2. See letter to Frederick Dent Grant, Dec. 12, 1878.

3. A joint congressional committee on army reorganization had recently proposed reducing the number of officers and trimming expenses. See *SRC*, 45-3-555; John F. Marszalek, *Sherman: A Soldier's Passion for Order* (New York, 1993), pp. 433–36.

Probably in late 1878 or early 1879, USG wrote to Orville E. Babcock concerning military legislation. "I'm sorry for you poor army fellows who are stirred up every year. *The army never seems to have any peace except in war.*" *New York Graphic*, Jan. 24, 1879.

4. In Benjamin E. Woolf's *The Mighty Dollar* that opened in New York City on Sept. 6, 1875, Bardwell Slote, a fictional congressman, used humorous acronyms. See Barrett H. Clark, ed., *Favorite American Plays of the Nineteenth Century* (Princeton, 1943), pp. xxiv–xxvi.

5. See *PUSG*, 28, 194, 427.

To Elizabeth M. Borie

Paris, France
Jan.y 20th 1879.

My Dear Mrs. Borie;

Mr Borie arrived here last night. To-day he is out calling, and says,—and Dr Keating says also—that he improved much by the sea voyage. To-morrow we start for Marseilles where we take passage on the 23d for Alexandria,[1] thence to Suez, then by the English line of steamers to Bombay. We will be five or six weeks in India after which we will be aboard of a Naval vessel all the time, except for short visits ashore, until we leave Japan for San-francisco. We will take the best of care of Mr. Borie and try to take him home to you much improved in health. I have told him that Dr. Keating was to be absolute master of the hours when Boston was to cease. Mrs. Grant was much pleased to receive your letter and says she will help to take care of Mr. Borie. She wants you also to consider this as a reply to your very kind letter to her.

Remember us to all the Bories, Mr. Drexel & family & Mr & Mrs. Childs. I will drop you a line occasionally to let you know how Mr. Borie is, and how he is behaving himself. We all anticipate much pleasure from our trip through the east, and much greater from our return to our old home and friends.

Very Truly Yours

U. S. Grant

ALS, PHi.

On Jan. 18, 1879, Vice Admiral Alexis Pothuau, Minister of the Marine and the Colonies, Paris, wrote to Edward F. Noyes, U.S. minister, Paris, that he had notified colonial governors and naval personnel to assist USG on his travels. Translation, USG 3.

1. See John Russell Young diary, Jan. 23, 1879, DLC-John Russell Young; *New York Herald*, Jan. 24, 1879.

Travel Diary

[*Jan. 23–July 26, 1879*]

No. 1

Left the wharf at Marseilles 1 5 p. m. thursday, Jan.y 23d 1879. by French Steamer La Bourdonnay Breese stiff from the S. E. At 10 35 the 24th passed Ajaccio, Corsica the birth place of Napoleon. Wind still strong from the S. E. At 4 p. m the 25 come to anchor in the Bay of Naples.[1] Lit at 7 p. m. same day

At 10 30 the 26 passed Strammboul and the straits of Messina by one. weather pleasant wind light. After passing the straits the wind became fresh again from the south East. Four cabin passengers—English—left the steamer at Naples & eight, all Americans, came aboard.

27th At sea, head wind but smooth sea. Ship made but about nine notts an hour the last twenty-four hours.

28th smooth sea but head wind. Passed Candia in full view for a number of hours

29th, noon. Best run of any twenty-four hours since leaving Marseilles. Distance to Alexandria however so great that it will be impossible to reach there to-day.

30th Anchored out side the harbor of Alexandria last night at 8 p. m. Entered at early dawn this a. m. Left for Ishmalea & Suez at 8 30 and arrived at the latter place at 6 30. Weather charming, fields green and flourishing. Party much pleased with the picturesque dress & manners of the people. Arrived at Suez 6 30

31st Delayed by steamer on which we are to take passage being blockaded by the sinking of another steamer in the canal. Mr Borie & I have just completed an inspection of the old city of Suez riding through on the diminutive donkeys of the country. Left Suez at 8 p. m.

Feb. 1st Passed Mt Sinia at 9 a. m. Air balmy and delightful.

Feb.y 2d Weather still delightful, sea smooth & passengers contented. Heat increasing however & light clothing coming into requisition. Met but one steamer—an English transport—during the day.

Feb.y 3d Weather delightful, sea smooth, vessel making from eleven to twelve knots.

Feb.y 4th About same as yesterday, heat increasing slightly as we approach Aden.

Feb.y 5th Wind strong & sea high. Coast of Arabia in full view Will not reach Aden much before midnight.

Feb.y 6th Arrived at Aden 2 a. m. left at 8.[2] From daylight to the hour of departure the native boys swam about the steamer ready to dive for sixpen. All the land seems to be of volcanic origin & entirely barren. The natives are of a low order of savages; hair died—or colored from some process—red, curled into small corkscrew tufts. It is fortunate that enlightened nations take possession of such people and make them, and their soil, produce something for the advancement of civilization of the human race.—We found while anchored off Aden that we had quite a number of Amiture Artists aboard. In walking the deck I noticed no less than five ladies taking sketches of the volcanic projection, the fortifications, neat frame building in view, and the general perspective. Some gentlemen were also engaged in the same pleasant task; one of them—I think a Judge of one of the Courts in India—used colors & seems to have quite a talent as an artist. About Aden, and the entire to the Red sea, is regarded as the hottest part of the world. But fortunately we found the weather delightful probably a circumstan[ce] not occurring many days in the year to persons accustomed to other, & cooler, climates. The troops stationed at Aden—always a native Indian regiment—are only required to serve one year. During that period they serve by detail for one month on the small barren island of   .[3] Sentence to the closest confinment given to criminals in our country could not be worse punishment, except the latter implies disgrace The former—successfully gone through without health impaired—is a pleasant reminicence through life Fairwell Aden.

Feb.y 7th Nothing to note only making a fair passage through the Indian Ocean with a refreshing breeze which has made the temperature delightful throughout the whole passage from Suez. This part of the voyage is usually looked upon with dread by the traveler often people succumbing to the intense heat. Run since noon yesterday to noon to-day 223 miles. Four of the lady passengers and one of the gentlemen Amature Artists, amused themselves by sketching me. to-day.

Feb.y 8th Still balmy & beautiful weather.

Feb.y 9th Nothing to note except continuance of favorable weather. Sunday & Service by a minister of the English church who is a passeng[er] aboard.[4] Over nine hundred miles from Bombay.

Feb. 10th Still beautiful mild & pleasant weather; sea smooth & passengers all contented. But few found below deck except for meals—at which all attend—from the hour of rising in the morning to the hour of retiring at night—with most passengers 10½ at night

Feb.y 11th No incident of the last twenty-four hours to record. Another day of delightful temperature & smooth sea. Passengers getting better acquainted and resorting to little games to pass away the evenings.

Feb.y 12th The same run of good weather & delightful temperature. The steamer is expected to arrive early to-morrow at Bombay. Passengers jubilant at the prospect of closing so long a sea voyage. Myself & party anticipate ninety days, at least, on shipboard before reaching our own shores.

Feb.y 13th Thursday 8 a. m just going into the first landing at Bombay. Passengers all on deck in improved garb from that worn during the passage. Many expecting to meet friends from whom they have been long separated. The voyage has been most delightful and the passengers most agreeable. Generally they are connected with the government service—Civil or Military—of India, or are the families of such. Though three weeks at sea—with the exce[p]tion of a day crossing Egypt—I almost regret that the voyage is so near at an [end] Before anchoring the ship was visited by representatives of the govt. the Steam company, foreign consuls & friends & relatives of the passengers; some of them long separated. Among the visitors to the ship were the ~~Aid de Camp~~ private Sec. to the Gov. General of Bombay—Sir Richard Temple[5]—and the American Consul.[6] The Gov. Gn was—is—on the frontier attending, in person, to the forwarding of supplies to the troops engaged in Afganistan[7] But learning of my expected arrival he directed that the Goverment House should be put at the disposal of myself & party, and that the chief official in the absence of the Gov and his remaining staff, should do all in their power to make our stay both pleasant and profitable. We have now been here twenty four hours. The whole party can bear testimony to the fact that the entertainment has been princely and the official household fully competant to dispense hospitalities Yesterday we rode through the old native city of Bombay. I have seen nothing in my Eastern travels to compare it to. Discription could not convey an accurate idea of either the city or the people. Every Nationality of the East is represented here. In passing through the city and seeing the people & the houses one must be impressed with the idea that it is impossible for all the former to get within the latter at one & the same time. Bombay differs from all the other Eastern cities I have yet seen in this regard; I have seen no beggars here yet. In the other one scarsely meets persons of the poorer classses—they nearly all are of this class—who is not ready to beg and to receive all that is offered. During the day there were quite a number of callers also, a number being ladies. I forgot to state that among the visitors to the steamer was the American Colony with two exceptions—it was stated that they were unavoidably detained—numbering seven gentlemen in all, enough however to show that wherever trade & trafic goes the universal Yankee may be found, Bombay is well gridironed with the Yankee Horse rail-road. It is conducted by an American and the stock all owned—I am told in New York City.[8] It seems to be fully patronized and, I understand, has been a paying consern from the start. Afternoon visited Elphantine Island some eight miles up the bay from the city Wharf. The island is celebraded for its cave and is the one attraction to all tourists who visit Bombay. The cave is artificial and is the work of a very Ancient people. I was disappointed in the extent of the Cave—or lack of extent. Descriptions have been so often drawn of this curiosity that I will not attempt it. In fact to do so I should have to resort to the guide book as most travelers have no doubt done.

Feb.y 15th Visited by invitation an old family of Parsees long engaged in mercantile pursuits & shipbuilding.[9] It is not common for the females to make their appearance. On this occasion however they departed from the rule and brought in all their families. Three generations were living under one roof. This too include[d] the families and descend[ants] of four or five of the brothers of the first generations but one of whom is now living. Their ancestors occupied probably the same premises for generations before The women and children were fancifully dressed, and all, except the oldest of the females, speak english well. The men, old & young, speak it without an accent. The reception was most cordial, Before each member of the party was presented with a boquet, a wreath of flowers over the neck and a Lotus leaf as token of respect and good wishes for our future success and happine[ss.] They also gave each some little token to keep as a reminder of our visit to Bombay and to a Parsee house. Visited also the Bombay Club house, an imposing modern building. From the latter drove through the dense, old part of the City to the Bycullus Club house and race course. Took lunch in the Club and then witnessed from the balcony two races. Running close between the leading horses but not remarkable for speed.[10] In the evenigh had a dinner party of forty-eight persons invited to meet my party. The guests included most of the American Colony, the Judiciary of Bombay and a few Military and Naval officers. Party broke up early and there was but little speaking, the abomination of such gatherings. I do not mean the little speaking is an abomination but that there should be any.

Feb.y 16th Sunday and the day before the departure of the mails. All have been busy in preparing their letters for friends at home. Lunched at 2 p. m. with Sir & Lady Westlopp[11] About twelve guests at the table; mostly the Judiciary of the Presidency of Bombay. The afternoon & evening spent quietly at home.

Feb.y 17th Visited a Parsee school for the education of Native young ladies in the English language. Shool numbered some sixty scholars. Progress seemed to be good. From the school visited Adm.l Corbett[12] on board the Ur Euryalus. Then the English Academy. In the evening had a dinner at the Government House, forty-eight at table.

Feb.y 18th Took another run through the city, visited a great diamond merchant, saw jewels of immense value kept as is common— universal—in this country, in the private residence of the owner, and without any indication of anything being kept on sale. At half past five left for Jubalapur. Pleasant run through the night thanks to the English Managers of the Indian railways.[13] Arrived at Jubilapur at half past ten the evening of the nineteenth. Was met at the train by the General in command of the district and many people. Rested for the night at a very good hotel and this morning—the 20th visited the Marble quarry. Distance from Jubulepur to the quarry about twelve miles. The first ten was made in carriages, the last two on elephants, our first experience in this mode of conveyanc[e.] Was much pleased with the intelligence of these animals. At the quarry & on the road returning had quite a heavy fall of rain with thunder & lightning a most unusual occurrence at this season of the year. Jubulpur is a city of about 60,000 people, unimportant except for its garrison & considerable trade over the road. At 10 30 left for Alahabad where we arrived at 8 a. m. to-day—the 221dst. Alahabad is situated at the junction of the Ganges and Norbudda Jumma, the latter former navigable to Calcutta. This Allahabad is only important as a city held as sacred by the Hindoos who make pilgrimages to it in great great swarms— at times by the 100 000, to bathe in the Ganges. Left Alahabad the on the evening of the 22d[14] and arrived at Agra this a m. the 23d. In the evening drove to the Targe. [*Taj Mahal*]   The splendor of this monument surpa[ss]es all the discriptons given of it. On the 24th went to Jaypore, the capitol of an independent principality, governed by a native Prince, or Maharajah.[15] The city is well built and presents a very peculiar style of Architecture to the European or American traveler. The ruler shews some signs of progress having introduced gass & water. The palace, which we visited, covers one seventh of the whole City—a city of 150.000. people—It is occupied by the ten wives of the Maharajah and their 3000 femal[e] servants. The Prince fitted the party out most sumptuously with carriages, elephants & palanquins to visit the ancient capitol,— Ulwur[16]—some seven miles distant. We visited this Capitol on the 25th   On the way out saw numerous monkey, three wild boars, several aligaters & quantities of wild peafouls. The city presents nothing remarkable, except the old palace of the Prince. At this palace a goat is sacrificed every day in the year, except some of the great feast days, when from twenty to fifty goats & buffalo are sacrificed. We arrive[d] just in time to witness this ceremony. In consists in incantations ove[r] the beast to be sacrificed and the sword which is to do the deed. This performance over the goat is held by two men, one at the head the other at the tail when a man with a sword takes of the head, clean, with a single blow.

Even when to buffalo is offered up his head must be taken of clean with a single blow. Otherwise the sacrifice is a failure. On the 26th returned to Burdpore, visited the Palace of the Rajah,[17] & took lunch, drove through the city & out about seven miles to Futtapur Secria. This is a very wonderful Palace built for the occupation of the Rajah. But has never been occupied, or if so but for

a very short time. On the 27th returned to Agra. In the evening
visited the Fort & drove through the city. The Fort, so called, is
the ancient palace of the Moguls when they ruled this country.
This, the 28th of Feb.y winds up our visit to Agra which has been
a most pleasant one, thanks to the English officials. In the evening
dined at the "Club House" about seventy-five guests being seated
at the table.[18] All were employees, civil or military of the Indian
Government, or members of the families of such employees except
my party and one other, an independent Prince—Prin[ce]   of   [19]
The evening was a very pleasant one & closed with an entertainment,—partly theatrical & partly ledgerdemain—by natives. I saw
nothing wonderful in tricks and, of course, could not understan[d.]
At Agra as at every place I have yet visited in India,—except Jubulpore,—I have not been permitted to go to a public house for entertainment. At Bombay myself and party were all entertained at the
Government House, most sumptuously though the Govr. Gen.—Sir
Richard Temple was necessaryly absent, at the front opening a new
route of supplies for the Army in Afghanestan. At Jubulpur there
was no one situated to accomodate us, but everything was done to
make our visit agreeable. At Alahabad we were sumptuously entertained by the Lt. Gov. Sir George Couper;[20] At Agra, on arrival
by Mr. Lawrence,[21] the second Civil officer of the place; at Jaypore
at the residence of the Resident Englishman—Mr. Bainoun [Bey-
non][22] though he too was absent, returning towards Agra we were
guests over night at the deserted palace of some former Maharajah
of Burdpore: At Agra, on returning, we were entertained by Mr.
Webster,[23] the senior in service to Mr. Lawrence, who had returned
during our absence. The 30 1st of March come to this place Dehli
arriving about 3 p m having left Agra at 6.45 a. m. In the afternoon drove through the city, visited "The Fort" (Jumma Musjid)
several public gardens, the leading Hindoo Temple &c. "The Fort"
is much the same as that at Agra. It is a magnificent old marble palace, the former residence of Moguls, surrounded by high red sand
stone walls. The 2d visited Minar, a pillar 238 ft. high, a number
of tombs, deserted villages and ruins of ancient Dehli. The Delhi is
well worth a visit and should require four days, dilligently put in, to

see to any advantage. The season is late and I cannot give the time.
The 3d was principally spent in viewing the positions taken by the
Europeans in their long siege of Delhi, after the mutiny of 1857
broke out.[24] It was fully explained by an intelligent officer—Col.
Harris—who was present at the siege, and badly wounded. In the
after noon, visited the city, the Library & Institute and made some
purchases from a native Jeweler. The 4th ~~was spent principally in
going about the outer & inner~~   We left Delhi at 11 35 for Lucknow, where we arrived this a m—the 5th at six oclock after a long
& dusty ride. There is one peculiarity about India at this season of
the year   All parts are alike. The whole looks like one arrid, dusty
fruitless plain with a sprinkling of small trees over the whole &
little patches of green here & there. These latter are the wheat
fields, and other products of the soil which have to be watered from
the numerous deep wells which are sunk at short distances apart all
over the country. The method of drawing the water is of the rudest
discription. The bucket used is a leather basket. A roped is passed
over a roller about 8 feet above the center of the well and attached
to the handle of the bucket. A native lets the bucket down the well
when an other hitches a yoke of cattle to the other end of the rope
and drives off until the bucket comes to the surface. The water is
then poured into a narrow ditch made on the top of a ridge raised
some foot or more above the land to be irrigated, and extending all
around it. Men are in the fields to draw the water from the ditch—
done by making a break in the ditch with their hands—and regu-
lating the amount of water to let on to each little ~~pat~~ patch. When
one has received enough the break is patched with a dab of mud &
the water is allowed to flow on to another. The process continues
throughout the dry season. I am informed that each patch of wheat
requires ~~six~~ three waterings by this slow process. Other crops have
far greater   It is a matter of mystery—to the American traveler
particularly—how a country less in area than that part of the U.
States east of the Mississippi river, with vast portions of this to-
tally barren & uncultivated, can feed 230,000,000 of people. But it
does, & has large exports, beside. Spent the 5th & 6th in Lucknow
visiting all points of interest and left the morning of the 7th for Be-

naris in the evening—10 O'clock—at night. This—the 8th—have
visited the city and taken a litt[le] steamboat ride on the Ganges
getting a view of the city from the river. Benaris is regarded by
the Hindoo as a sacred city and is believed by them to have existed
from the begining of time. It is well and solidly built, many of the
houses going up three or four stories high. The streets are very
narrow and many of them do not admit even a pack animal. The
sight of the natives worshiping—which seems to be their principle
occupation—is a curious one There can be no doubt about their
sincerity. It is a grave question whether they should be disturbed in
their faith. It teaches no cruelty to beast or man, and sets up a good
system of morals for the guidence of its followers.

Left Benares at 11 30 a m on the 9th & reached Calcutta at
5 30 a. m. the 10th after the warmest and dustyest ride we have
yet had in India. Calcutta is a disappointing city. The native part
is principally built of Bamboo, many of the houses being nothing
more than sheds supported by a few posts. The English part of the
city is well & substantially built and beautifully laid out. Calcutta
does not present many objects of special interest to the traveler.
The drives however are beautiful and the public gardens & parks
are very attractive. On the 11th we had a picnic party some sixteen miles up the river, at the country Gov.t House. The Picnic was
held under ~~the~~ a celebrated Banyon tree This tree has extended,
and sent down branches to take root, until now a thousand persons
could take shelter under it. Have visited the zuological garden.

After six days pleasantly but fatiguingly spent in Calcutta,
sightseeing, visiting places of note, with late dinner parties evry
night, we left for Rangoon, Buhrma Sunday²⁵ at 4 a. m. ~~and~~ which
place we are just now, the 19th arriving at. The voyage has been
without incident but to warm to remain below deck day or night.
At night all the passengers—fortunat[e]ly there are but four, first
class, beside my party—have their beds move[d] on deck where we
sleep. During the day we loll, read and play Boston to while away
the day. Fortunately we received a mail, with the latest home papers, just as we left Calcutta. Fortunately also there has been breeze
enough to make it very tolerable on deck. But I would advise trav-

elers to India to start in time to leave the country a month earlyer than we are doing. If however they should be going West, through Russia, they might be a month later. It is always pleasant in the Himalaya and the trip is carrying the traveler North all the time. At 11 a. m. of the 19th we reach the wharf at Rangoon Burma. Mr. Chas Aichison, Chief Commissioner[26] and a number of Civil, Mil. & Naval officers were ready to meet us with carriages to conduct us to Govt. House, occupied by the Chief Commissioner where all my party are to stay as guest while we remain here. This is the hospitality that has been extended throughout India and all other British possession. In the evening took a drive about the suburbs of the City—European part—and through a few of the principle streets of the native part. To day—the 20th—rose at 6 a. m. and visited   one of the most noted—probably second—Pagodas in the World.[27] From a short distance it gives the idea of a highly gilded spire resting on a dome built on the ground, with no building un- der it; & not remarkable for hight or other proportions. When vis- ited on foot we found that we had to assend numerous flights of steps, between smaller pagodas to the hight of ft. before reaching the paved plateau on which the dome rests. Its proportions

No 2

After the Pagoda visited the Bazaars.[28] The traveler through In- dia is much impressed on coming to Burma with the difference be- tween the natives of the two. The contrast is all in favor of the Burmese. In India they are divided into Casts. Those of one Cast must stick to it, and their descendants to all time unless per chance they may fall from it and loose all Casts. Females have no rights and must not remain single. The may be betrothed at any time from conception to the age of puberty. By the latter time they are disgraced if not married. Generally however their parents betroth them before they are five years of age, and when the two parties reach puberty they are sent to live together. Often when the male is much the oldest the female is sent at the age of seven to nine to live with the man to whom she was betrothed and who possibly she had never seen. Many become widows before they are five years of age and can never after marry. Through widowhood—life—they are a disgraced & despised life.—This may have originated in the fact that a plurality of wives is authorized by their religion, and as this might give rise to jealousies & revenges, and often to poisning of the husband of plural wives, or even of the husband of a single wife some times, it might have been thought a wise protecting measure for the stronger sex. No woman except of the very lowest Caste is allowed to be seen by men other than their own family.

With the Burmese marriage is a matter of choise between the contracting parties. The man must ask and the girl give consent before the contract can be entered into. They have no Caste and all can compete to better their condition. Females are not shut up but visit and receive visits. They act as salesmen and do business as frely as in Europe. The Burmese are not bigoted and do not object to the intermarriage of their race or religion with people of any other race or religion. The Burmese appears to be of the Mongolian race the other the pure Indian.

But the first great difference that strikes the traveler is the greater prosperity of the Burmese, and their much better personal appearance. They like to dress—in gay colors—and all do wear clothing. The Indian covers but little of his person and cares but little about what portion is covered. Burma is also the most prosperous portion of British eastern possessions. Nothing could more clearly demonstrate the fact than that labor here commands about three to four times the Amt. it does in India, and servants receive twice as much. The latter all come from Madrass or other parts of India. The Burmese scarsely ever accepts menial service. The exports from Burma exceed the imports as three to two. This proportion can be largely increased with an increase of imports. They send out yearly many thousand of tons of rice, 7 to 800.000 tons Vast amounts of valuable woods, dyestuffs, hides and many other articles.

Rangoon is a city of about 100,000 inhabitants now but is growing rapidly in population and commercial importance. Its first rail-road reaching the interior has been completed but one year, and has paid two per-cent over expenses on cost. Anothr road is in contemplation, and is partially constructed.[29] With these roads and the navigable river, Rangoon, navigable for some eight hundred miles to the interior I predict that Rangoon will outstrip either Calcutta or Bombay, in wealth, in ten years and in population in twenty-five

Left Rangoon Saturday March 22d Arrived at Maulmein at 3 p. m the 23d after a most pleasant run. Maulmein is a very ancient city, about the oldest in Burmah. It is situated on the Salween river about thirty miles from its mouth. The country about, and to the very edge of the city, is hilly, the highest peakes almost entitled to be called mountains. They are covered with tropical trees of various sorts giving a much more picturesque appearance to the country than is generally seen along the coast of British India. There is but little back country to support Maulmein hence it is declining in Commercial importance as Rangoon goes up. The principle export is timber   Both at Rangoon and at this place I have visited the saw mills to see the elephants at work. The intelligence shewn by these beasts looks like reas[on] rather than instinct. Their strength too is wonderful. I have seen them place one foot against the end of a log sixteen to twenty feet long and fifteen inches square in the cross section and walk across the yard pushing the log before them, and without taking the foot off or placing it on the ground. When the log is much larger they place their tusks against the log with their trunk between the tusk and the log. When the log is moved to its place for stacking the elephant will place his tusks under it, a little distance from the end, and with his trunk hold it on the tusk, raise it up until he can deposit the end on top the pile where it is to be stacked—often twelve feet high—and then from the end on the ground push it to its place. After the center of gravity has passed the edge of the pile the log will tip and become higher than the back of the animal. He then turns ~~up~~ his trunk up into the air, places the underside against the end of the log and pushes it to his place. The elephants employed here were all capture[d] and it is often asserted that they will not breed after being domesticated. But that theory is exploded as millers here have found to their regret. There are a number of young elephants here from three weeks to two years old, conceiv[ed] & born in captivity. When the female bears young the proprietors must loose the use of the animal entirey for six months, and partially much longer. The young is not fit for any work for nine years, and not for full work for twenty. The enormous amount it takes to feed the elephant makes capturing, and training, the mature animal much more economical than raising them. Some that I have seen at work are supposed to be as high as seventy years old, and seem to be as good as ever.

To-day—the 25th—leave Maulmein for Penang, Melacca & Singapore. Arrived in harbor at Penang at 5 30 p m the 28th All the shipping in port except one or two French vessels were decked with flags and all saluted the tug as we went on shore. The Lt. Governor Mr Irving[30] was in waiting on the wharf with a guard of honor to receive us, thousands of natives were also present to greet the American party. The Governor had carriages ready to conduct the party to Govt. House, situate[d] on the top of the mountain— 2670 ft. above the city below. The island of Penang is beautiful to behold being mostly composed of mountain peaks from 1000 to 2700 ft. above the sea. Here rain falls every month in the year which, with the tropical climate, keeps vegitation green and beautiful the year round, strongly in contrast with India in the dry season. The mountains are covered with tropical trees, in great variety to the very summit. The valleys and more level places are cultivated, the coconut being the principle production. The nutmeg was formerly the leading product of the island, but some years ago the most of the trees were killed by an insect—a borer—that destroyed the roots. There is yet some nutmegs raised also cinamon & coffee The island is about 36 miles in circumference and contains a population of about 100,000 souls; Maylayans, Chinese Hindoos and traders from all parts of the world. It is difficult to see how such a population can find a support on such an area and where so small a proportion is susseptible of cultivation. But when we reflect how little the native of all the East requires for his support the problem is half solved. They require neith clothing or fuel to protect them against the season, and modesty does not dictate the necessity of more than covering for the loins; with children under ten years not even this. For food a family of eight are quite content with five or six pounds of rice a day—costing about two cents pr pound—or its equivalent in banas coconuts or almost any fruit, ~~or~~ vegitable or grain that grows. There is "richness" in the sugar cane for the native. This grows in great luxurience on the main land only a mile off. This p m we start for Melacca & Singapore expecting to reach the latter place on the morning of the 30th of March.

In coming to the Govt. House one is struck with the contrast in temperature. It was a great comfort to be able to sleep in bed again, under cover in a room with closed doors after having been compelle[d] for so many nights to make beds on the upper deck of the vessel to exist atall. 31 of March arrive[d] at Malacca at sunrise. Remained until three in the afternoon. Visited the city taking a short ride into the country. The town has about 25,000 inhabitants, mostly Chinese with a few Malayans, a few Hindu and scattering others of different East India indians. The houses are generally two stories high, blue fronts to the street and are scrupulously clean Industry seems to be the order of the day among the inhabitants, peopl[e] of one trade generally living in the same quarter. One would judge that there were more barbers than of any other one calling. The suburbs is one mass of coconut groves, which are said to produce about one dollar per tree pr. annum. Considering that the coco does not require more than ten square feet,—or that near five hundred—can be produced to the acre even this woud seem to make the raising of them very profitable. To-morrow morning we expect to be in singapore. From there we will feel as if we were on the "homestretch."

Arrived at Singapore Apl. 1st at 6 a m The entrance to the harbor presents a beautiful & picturesque appearance. The harbor is formed by numerous islands which separate the Indian Ocean from the Chinese sea at this point. These islands are high & broke[n,] covered from the waters edge to the summit of the hills, with the richest virdure & tropical trees & schrubery. Singapore is a much smaller city than I supposed the whole island on which it stands not containg over 100 000 people. The business of a large nature is conducted principly by European[s.] But the Chinese & some ~~May~~-alayans & some other natives of the east form no inconsiderable competitors. The mechanics and small traders are almost exclusively Chinese. There is not that objection here to Chinese immigration that exists in Australia & the United States, but the reason is that the european cannot, nor would not if he could, settle here to do the drudgery of cultivating the soil, the mechanical work or serve in menial capacities. All who come wish to direct, and are willing to take labor where they can get it the best for their money The same reasons exist here however which makes the Chinese so objectionable a class in both Australia & the U. S. If there is any one thing in the religion of the Chinese that they adhere to under all circumstances, and is adhered to by all classes, it is their veneration of their dead ancestors. Their graves must be watched and have certain rights performed by their descendents to the end of time, on pain of the souls of the departed becoming wanderers & vagrants over the world. This prevents the emmigration of families. The wives & children are left at home to attend these observances. The men emigrate alone. Here they marry again and rear families without objection of the govt or of the natives among whom they marry. No european nation would tolerate this admixture.

My self and party are at the Govt House, the guests of Colonel Anson, Act. Governor Straits Settlement.[31] We find here the same hospitality that has been extended throughout our travels in the East.

Apl. 8th to-morrow leave for Bangkok Siam. During our stay at Singapore have dined with the Maharajah of Jayhore and visited him at the Capitol of his country. Jahore is a small independent province taking in the southern end of the Malay peninsula, extending north nearly to Melacca. The present pPrince speaks english well and is a very progressive man. He entertains as well, and with as much ease and grace of manners as any of his more civilized European fellow Princes. He is doing much for his country & people, and if not involved in debt by unscrupulous and bad advisors will, in a very few years, be a very rich & independ[ant ruler].[32] The Chinese do most of the work of clearing & tilling the soil running saw mills, building house boats &c. and all the mechanicle work. They are much encouraged in settling in his territory as

in fact in almost all parts of the East. They—the Chinese—leave
their families behind and scarsely ever return to them. But here
they marry native women with as much impunity as if they were
not already married. In fact where they have the means of supporting them no hostility exists against their marrying as many as
they please. On Friday the 5th—we lunched with Mr Whampoa, a
wealthy Chinese.[33] He is a most advanced man for his race speaking, reading and writing the English fluently. His house is large &
richly furnished in Oriental style. The enclosed grounds about the
house embraces about 25 acres, most beautifully & ornimentally
cultivated as only the Chinese & Japanese know how to cultivate.
Within the grounds may be found every tree, schrub, flower & fruit
produced in the tropics. Many scrubs & plants are trained in the
shape of men, women, fish animals, birds, ships houses &c. Fish are
cultivated in artificial ponds. There is also an aviary and zological
collection within his grounds. He preserves however the religion &
dress of his countrymen.

At 10 a m—one hour less than three days from Singapore Apl.
12th—arrived off the bar of Bangkok. Passage smooth and the living good on board the little but neat & fast running steamer Kongsee. No insident on the passage to note. A few minuets later run
on the bar where we remained until seven at night. The extreme
darkness of the evening, owing to clouds and rain, made navigation so extremely difficult that we soon found ourselves aground
again. Daylight this a. m.—the 13th disclosed the fact that we
were far out of the channel where she will have to remain for extreme high tide. At 11 were taken off by the King of Siam's yacht—
Rising Sun—and expect to reach Bangkok at 1.30. The rain has
been pouring all day except for a few minuets at a time intermit-
tently. We hope for a cessation long enough to debark in comfort.
In assending Chowphya river to Bangkok the traveler is struck
with the luxurient growth of the various Palms—the Beetle, the
Coconut, the ~~Chowphya~~ Atapa &c; the swampy appearance of the
country the native houses &c. Generally the houses stand on posts
high enough to raise them above high tide, but many of them float
but a few inches above the water and rise & fall with the tide. In the

latter houses the bamboo is used as a raft to build upon and to give
the proper flotation. To secure them from being carried away by
the current they are secured by a pair of long polls, or piles, driven
into the bottom of the river and extending up some feet above extreme high tide. The building[s] are made of the lightest material,
the walls and roofs being made of the Atapa leaf, the rafters &
frame work of Bamboo or other light wood. The natives require no
clothing to protect them from the weather* and but very little to
satisfy their modesty. For the balance they can secure to make life
pleasant to them—food—they have to go but a few feet from their
doors to secure an abundance   The Banana, Coconut & Beetle nut
are abundant throughout the year and the river supplies fish by
simply raising their nets once a day.

   *Modesty makes but little demand in this way.

   At 3 p m arrived at the landing where the party were received
by a guard of honor—50 men—and members of the royal family.
Carriages were in waiting to conduct us to the Palace occupied by
the Kings brother, a lad of 19 years of age,[34] where we are to be
entertained during our stay. At the Palace the Ministe[r] was in
waiting to receive us, also a guard of 200 men. On entering the
Palace a salute of 21 guns was fired. Fourteenth were conducted in
boats to call upon the Minister of state, the ex Regent & the Chief
Prince of Siam—the eldest brother of the King—each in their Palaces.[35] Bangkok resembles Venice very much in the facility of getting from one place to another by boat. But there is no resemblence
in the people or building. Here it is constantly the floating house,
or the Bamboo, built upon high poles. The people with but little
clothing and only the lowest class of females socially, being seen.
The ease and grace and high degree of civilization of the ruling
class among a people who have made so little advance in civilization strikes one with amazement. The whole of Bangkok looks like
an immense jungle, so luxurient is the growth of trees & fruits, &
vines, covering every foot of ground not occupied by buildings In
the evening dined at the Palace set apart for my party. The service cooking & attendence was much the same as would be seen
in the best European or American houses. On the 15th made fur-

ther calls upon the chief dignitaries of the Govt. Among them the
King. The latter is a young man, 25 years of age, quite impressive
in appearance and intelligent; speaks english farely well and understands perfectly. He is evidently a progressest but is restrained by
the older men in counsil.[36] The country is capable of great developement, probably not producing now to more than one fifteenth
of its capacity. But the country is out of debt and the people apparently happy. There is no beggars or deformed people to be seen,
and no indication of poverty or distress. The trade & Mechanical
pursuits seem to be wholly, or nearly so in the hands of the Chinese & a few European firms doing business here. In the evening
dined with the Minister of Foreign affairs.[37] The table was fine &
the service superb. After dinner examined the curios in the house.
The collection was very rich, much of it pure gold & ivory richly
carved. The 16th was spent in receiving calls, visiting   .[38] The
dinner with the Minister of Foreign Affairs was on the 14th. The
15th dined with the Ex-Regent. Also the evening of the 15th held
a reception which was attended by all the male members of the
ruling families of Bangkok, and by the Europeans residing here,
of both sexes. During the reception had native music, the members
of the band being females, mostly young. After the reception had
a theatrical performance. The actors were all young girls They
were very richly dressed, well formed & graceful. They would have
been good looking but for the horrid practice here of blackening
their teeth. When one of them opens their mouths it presents the
appearance of a black hole in the face. On the 16th dined with the
King in the evening and visited the Queen[39] during [th]e day and
also the [H]arum, both special [m]arks of favor rarely bestowed
upon strangers. There seemed to be several hundred females in the
harum, ranging from little children up to old gray headed women.
Their life must be desolate. They are cut out from all outside view,
and never see a male, except the King himself, only on occasions
like the present. At dinner, and after, the King was very much interested in making enquiries about my own country.[40]

   17th we are now assending the river in the private Yacht of
the King. Expect to visit the old capital of Siam,[41] destroyed over

one hundred years ago by the Burmese and return as far as the country Palace of the King, where we will stay over night. 18th. returned by the same conveyance we assended the river upon Spent an uncomfortable night at the "Old Capitol." The city shows by the standing steeples of old ₱Pagodas, or Temples, that it was a very populous place. Now probably not a thousand inhabitants remain. There is still however a vast population in the vicinity, along the the streams and bayous, in new abodes of the ordinary, native character, and such as can be put up without expence. It is in the midst of a very productive region and which is more cultivated from the fact that the river affords a cheap—or rather easy—for every thing is cheap in this country—to a market. On the way down stopped for Tiffin at the American Consulat[e.] Met there most of the foreign population occupying official position in Bangkok. In the afternoon decended to the mouth of the river where we were transferred to the steamer Bangkok. ~~in a gale with rain falling. The water was rough and the transit was made with difficulty. Our approach~~ The Steamer was obliged to lay until 2 a m, on the 19th, to take advantage of the tide to get over the bar. The passage back to Singapore was a very pleasant one, without incident, except that we caught a few fish from lines put out from the stern of the steamer baited with white clothes. The fish in the Gulf of Siam seam to be very abundent. The wonder is that with the teaming population of this section of the world, all fish eaters—or of any thing they can get—more are not caught. We arrive at Singapore about five in the afternoon of the 22d. Were very much disappointed, and disgusted, that the Richmond, which we had expected so long, had not yet arrived. Found that she had reached Pt. de Gall on the morning of the 13th of April, and from a dispatch from the Commander that she was still there on the 18th. I determined therefore not to take her even if I should be compelled to wait a week—or any other length of time—after her arrival to get other mode of conveyance. Fortunately we found that the French steamer, Iriwad[y] was in port, bound for Hongkong; delayed for the arrival of the steamer from Java. We determined to take this steamer, which was to sail at seven the next morning. Made our transfer—about four miles—in the morning through a most violent tropical rain storm.[42] At 8 30 we were off, and now, 2 p m. Apl. 25th are approaching Saigon, Cochin China. The steamer will lay over one day giving an opportunity of comparing an Easter French Colony with the English so many of which we have visited. Spent the night of the 25th and the day following at the Govt House, a most spacious Palace the finest I think we have yet seen in the East. The Governor General, a Rear Adm.l in the French Navy, we found a most hospitable and pleasant gentleman[43] During the 26th visited all the places of interest in the new—or Europea[n]—town and also the old city some four miles further up the river The people of Saigon—the natives—seem to be prosperous & happy. They would not probably change their condition if they could. But here like every place in the East the Chinese are the leading people. They monopolize all the small trades, do all the mechanical work, are the house servants & market gardners, stevodores & often the largest merchants. The women never seem to leave their own country except for immorral purposes. The evening of the 26th there was a large dinner party at the Govt House after which a reception at which all the Europeans residing, and present in Saigon attended. The boat intending to sail ~~on the~~ at 4 O'clock a m on the 27th we went aboard after the reception. The night was the most suffocating we have experienced in the tropics. Since starting however the weather has been delightful.

Arrived at Hong Kong at 3 p m. the 30th of Apl. Found preparations for our reception, people assembled on shore the Governor of the colony who took us to the Govt House. An American vessel was in port—the Ashuelot Capt. Perkins[44] in command—who immediately came aboard to welcome us and to take us aboard of his vessel before going ashore. On reaching the vessel a salute of 21 guns was fired. Half an hour later, on leaving, a similar salute was fired from the American vessel. No salute was fired from the English side, said to be in obedience to orders received from the Colonial Govt. A Japanise Man of War, in port gave a salute however.—She was sent in anticipation of my arrival in Hong Kong to extend an invitation to that country—But the Governor ~~was pre~~ of Hong Kong—Pope Hennessey—was present to receive us and

to conduc[t] us to Govt. House. From the 30th of Apl. to the 5th
of May we staid there an received the greatest hospitality from a
really hospitable man During the interval ever[y] place has been
visit[ed] and I must give my judgement that Hong Kong is the most
beautiful place I have yet seen in the East. This colony is on an island reaching 1700 ft. above the Sea. The city is well built—mostly
of Granite—and the harbor is a magnificent one both in scenery
and security. To-day—the 5th—we are assending the river to Canton. The Chinese extended the most cordia[l] invitation to their
country not only on learning my intention of visiting their country
while in Paris, but since my arrival in Hong Kong. On our way up
we have been board twice by Chinese Gun Boats to do honor to
the occasion, but the last intimates British interferece—on the part
of an officious Consul I suppose—to their making the demonstration they had intended. We will see. Tide, and delays in receiving
persons who come aboard by way of compliment, made it late for
our arrival in Canton—about 9 O'clock. We found that much of the
population had been assembled for hours to see so many yankees.
On the 6th called on the Vice Roy [45] which gave an excellent opportunity of seeing the city. The distance is over three miles from the
european quarter and through the dense part of the city. I would
estimate the number of people lined along the street to see the
visitors at not less than 100 000 me[n.] The city is certainly very
remarkable. The streets are paved with flat granite stone and are
only from five to eight ft. wide. The houses are of brick—a beautiful brown colored brick—and what might be considered from two
to three storey high. But the houses generally present no front. The
seem to be merely walls separating lots, roofed over, and the interior fixed up according to the taste and occupation of the owner.
The fronts are generally—I might say universally—occupie[d] as
as stores or work shops. The backs seems to be arrange[d] in land-
ings at different stages, reached more by ladders than by stairs,—
for the occupation of the family. The population is very dense and
must far exce[ed] 1,000,000 of peopl[e.] The Chinese seem to be
a most industrious and frugal people. It is from here a majority
of the emigrants to the United States go. It might be said that

Malay, Burma and the Straits Settlements are populated from here. I am satisfied that the Chinese are badly treated at home by europeans as well as when they emigrate I blame them for submitting to such dictation. I should not blame them if they were to drive out all europeans—Americans include[d]—and make new treaties in which they would claim equal rights. Treatie[s] at present are like [the arrangement entered] into between the white man & the indian who had shot a Crow & a turkey. The white man proposed that he would take the turkey & the indian the crow, or the indian might take the crow & the white man would take the turkey. No show was given the indian to get the turkey. The 7th dined with the Vice Roy. It was a regular Chinese entertainment except that knives and forks were supplied in addition to the chop sticks. The 8th was spent in viewing this remarkable city both on foot & by boat. We entered some of the noted flower boats also. They are fitted up very fancifully and at night when lit up must look very gorgeous. In the day time no indications of the character given to the inmates of these boats are distinguishable.[46] On the 9th left Canton and desended the river amidst the booming of canon from Chinese gunboats & forts all along the way to the Ancient Portuguese town of Macao.[47] This was the first settlement on Chinese soil held and governed by a foreign power. Macao is beautifully situated on a high promontory almost surrounded by water The view to the sea is cut off by numerous islands of conciderable elevation. It was a most flourishing city until the Coolie trade was put a stop to by more civilized and more humane nations. Now it is in a languishing condition and derives a large part, possibly the largest part of revenue, from license[d] gambling. It is to be hoped that the Chinese will retake this place.

No 3

Spent the night of the 9th of May at Macao Hotel, visited one of the licensed gambling houses and the following morning took a short run through the private garden of a wealthy Portuguese citizen. The garden is on a high hill overlooking the city and commands a fine view of the surrounding country.[48] At 9 a m left Macao on our return to Hong Kong where we had an engagement for a dinner party at the Government Ho[use] and a garden party in the evening. The garden party did not come of however owing to the threatening condition of the weather.[49] On Monday, the 12th, bid good buy to Hong Kong and took passage on the U. S. S. Ashualot for Singapor[e.][50] At 8 a m the 13th arrived in port, at Swatow where we spent the day. Took a walk through the city—the dirtyest I ever saw or ever imagined—and at two took tiffin with the U. S. Vice Consul. The quarter of the European residents is on an island opposite to the city and has all the appearance of a refined european settlement. In fact at every place I have visited in the East there is a quarter set apart for European residents and all present the appearance of cleanlyness & luxury, strongly in contrast with the native towns. In the evening set sail for Amoy where we arrived about 11 O'clock May 14th. Had tiffin with the American Vice Consul where we met all—or substantially so—the foreign citizens of the place. The foreigners here have—like those of Swatow—an island opposite the city set apart for their residences. The city, if possible, is more filthy than Swatow. Left Amoy about 7 in the evening for Shanghai not intending to stop further on the way. May 17th 11 a m just running into the mouth of the Wusung river some twelve miles below Shanghai. The weather has been delightful all the way from Hong Kong, the last two nights being cool enough to sleep comfortably in the cabins, the first time since leaving Calcutta, in fact since leaving Suez in Jan.y last.

May 23d Five p. m. Just leaving the mouth of the Woosung river. Expected to meet the Richmond which left Hong Kong on the 18th. She is not in sight. Spent six days in Shanghai, the principle commercial city of China. The reception by foreigners of all nationalities, was the mos[t] cordial & most enthusiastic we have witnessed since leaving England. Almost every hour, an[d] every day, was taken up with entertainments in honor of our country.[51] Shanghai contains a population of from six to eight hundred thousand people. The impression given of the Chin[ese] is that they are an industrious frugal people and while slow to adopt new ways are nevertheless progressive. They seem to possess the schrewdnes[s] to realize that their safety consists in holding back in modern civilication & progress until they can educate their own people to take the management in building roads, constr[uct]ing machinery &c. and until it can be done with their own capital. They realize the danger of placing themselves at the mercy of foreign bond holders. My impression is that the day is not very far distant when they will make the most rapid strides towards modern civilization, and become dangerou[s] rivals to all powers interested in the trade of the East. They are patient enduring and of long suffering in their weakness. But once feeling themselves strong they are likely to become cruel overbearing and vindictive. They cannot be much blamed if this prediction comes true. At present their rights are scarsely respected in any open port where foreigners are admitted. I am not prepared to justify the treatment the Chinese have recei[ved] at the hands of the foreigner.

After a most pleasant run of three & a half days from Shanghai we arrive[d] at the bar of the Peiho sixty miles below the City of Tientsin. The first indications that anything we know as a sea, with high waves to toss a vessel, in the eastern waters were encountered on this trip. From the Mediterranean to Shanghi hardly a wave was encountered. We found that the Viceroy had sent two gun boats outside the bar to meet us, with an officer of rank to welcom[e] us to his territory. We are now—May 27th 4 p m just approaching the City. of The Peiho, while deep, is narrow and very crooked, making it difficult of navigation for a vessels of any length to navigate. With the Ashuelot,—less than 260 feet in length—we have been obliged to have a tug tow us, or rather go in advance with a line out, to pull us around sharp curves in the river. The country is a delta, very low and flat the whole distance, teaming with population and covered with little mounds, the final resting place of the dead.

May 31st left Tientsin by house boat for Peking. The visit to Tientsin was one of great interest though the city itself possesses no attractions The present ruler of the province—the most populous in China—Vice Roy Lee—is probably the most intelligent and most advanced ruler—if not man—in China.[52] On the present occasion, having American guests, he departed widtely from Chinese

customs, and from any thing he had done heretofore in receiving
them. Two gun boats with a Mandarin of his personal staff, was
sent outside the bar two days before our arrival to escort us in. The
Viceroy met us in person just before arrival at the landing having
come from his palace in a tug for the purpose. He also gave an
entertainment—dinner—at his palace to which the Consular Corps
of the port were invited to meet my party. This I believe is not an
unusual thing, but the Viceroy accepted, & attended, a dinner given
by the Consular corps to me and has invited Mrs. Grant to meet
Madam Lee on our return from Peking.

June 1st We have been polking along since yesterday at the rate
of about two miles per hour. This is as fast as boats can be pulled
against the current of one & a half to two miles per hour. We have
a company of eight boats with a smal skiff along side which makes
visiting from boat to boat easy. It looks now very much as if we
would be three days on the river.

Arrived at Tunjo the end of navigation, and twelve miles from
Peking, June the 3d at daylight. Met arrangement—that is horses
and litters for the party and wheelbarrows for the bagge—made
by Prince Kung, the practical head of the Chinese Govt. So far the
official authorities of China have shown every politeness and attention in their power. Reached Peking after more than five hours in a
chair or palanquin. The road is over a dead level, the distance about
twelve miles, and is one of the numerous works of far past dinasties
which markes the degeneracy of the Chinese Govt. & people. The
bed of the road is raised from three to eight feet above the natural
level for a width of probably forty feet. The whole is paved with
artificial stone of large size which, though artificial, have stood the
ware of cart wheels and wheelbarrows which carry great burdens,
for centuries. But it is worn into a wretc[h]ed condition for want of
repairs. There has probably not been a repair made on any road in
the empire for several generations. But all the bridges I have seen
are substantial yet and work could not be improved on by the modern engineer. The trip at this season of the year is a trying one. It
is close to the end of the dry season when every thing is as dry as
a hot sun can make it and every breeze carries with it a cloud of

dust. Even the journey by boat on the river is dusty. The morning of the 4th arose early and ascended the great wall and walked from one of the entrances through it to another. The work is faced on either side with brick & filled in with earth the whole of the top being paved with large artificial ston[e.] The thickness of the wall is about fifty feet & the hight nearly the same. The whole length around the city—the length of wall—is said to be twenty-five miles. But there is another wall connecting with the south side of this & enclosing the Chinese city of nearly equal extent, the south wall of the capitol however forming the north wall of the latter. It is hard to see any practical use these walls can serve in the present age unless they should be converte[d] into drives which they would be admiral for by simply making good road beds and the construction of ramps for assending up. Their hight would be no objection because each side has a thick wall some four feet above the roadway terreted, through their whole length. In the afternoon called—by appointment—on Prince Kung, the practical head of the govt. Found him very affible and apparently very strongly inclined to cultivate the most friendly relations with the U. S.[53] The following morning—the 5th[54]—get up early and visited the Temple of Heaven. This has been so often described that I will not attemp[t] it. Suffice it to say that, but for the nave of the thing, it is not worth the trouble of a visit. It had been my intention to make an excursion to the Summer Palace, twelve miles distant, and to the great wall forty five miles distan[t.] But as what I had seen in the way of sights had proven such a great disappointment, and as the weather was so intensely hot—the thermometer ranging at 101° 104° 97° & 95° degrees on the days set apart for these journeys—I concluded to give them up. I did not feel like encountering this heat & a ride of 114 miles in a mule litter for the pleasure to be derived. On the 9th Prince Kung returned my call and spent an hour in most earnest conversation.[55] He was most anxious that I should act the part of pacificator between his country & Japan. I believe he feels so anxiously about the matter that he would agree if Japan would that my decission should govern both nations in regard to their territorial difficulties. I promised to look into the matter and to converse

with our minister to Japan—and with the Japanese authorities if
the opportunity occurred—when I get there.[56] China is in a very
weak condition and her enlightened men—of whom Prince Kung
is one—begin to see it and to realize the importance for a new
civilization.

To day—the 10th of June—said good buy to Peking and took
our departure. Five hours more brought us to the Peiho which we
are now descending in small boats with accomodations of but for
two each. As there are five of my party, & fourteen Naval officers
from the Ashuelot & Richmond, beside a boat for kooking and one
for eating in, it makes quite a fleet, twelve boats in all. The wind is
against. But this great relief from the intense head which we have
endured for the past week.

June 15th at 2 30 a m left Tientsin on the Ashuelot for the
mouth of the river & steamer Richmond. The Viceroy accompanied
on a Chinese gunboat. Reached the Richmond by 12 m. Received
salutes from the forts at the mouth of the river & from the gunboat. The sea was very smooth & the transfer easily effected. The
Viceroy spent over an hour on the Richmond and inspected it very
thoroughly. He was received with a salute of 19 guns & the yards
manned. He seemed highly pleased with his reception and with all
he saw.[57] About four we will start for the great wall at its eastern
extremity.

16th At about 12 m. anchored off the sea end of the great
Chines[e] wall at less than a mile distance from shore. The sea was
very smooth and consequently an easy landing was effected on a
serf beach where no artificial means have been resorted to make a
landing place. The wall at this place is fallen much into decay. Instead of being built of stone as generally supposed it is faced with
brick and filled in with earth between the walls. Probably in the
mountains, and where rock prevails near the work, it may be constructed of that material. An hour on shore satisfied the curiosity of
all and after painting the name of our vessel—the Richmond—and
the date of our visit on the walls,[58] we took our departure for Chefoo, the only Sanitarium—I believe—in China. Reached Chefoo the
following morning. Extensive preparation had been made for our

reception and entertainment for the fiew hours it was understood
we would remain ~~Expecting to~~ It being understood that we would
depart the day of arrival the Deputy Commissioner of Customs,
Mr. Simpson—an Englishman [59]—and the Tartar of the place combined in a dinner at the house of the former at 8 in the evening, to
be followed by a reception & ball in the evening. The Vice Consul
of the United States—an Englishman also—met us at the dropping of our anchor in harbor & invited us to his house—about the
best in the foreign settlement, and far better than any in the native city—to tiffin & to spend the afternoon until time for the later
entertainments of the day. We spent a pleasant afternoon seeing at
the Consulate about all the foreign element of the place. In the evening they were present again at Mr Simpson's keeping up the dance
until midnight—when we left—how long after I do not know. At 4
the next morning—or in the morning—we set sail for Nagasaki,
Japan, where we arrived this noon, the 21st of June. The Ashuelot
started out with us but encountering a heavy storm on the 18th
while we were still hugging the Chinese coast, and being more a
still water vessel than a sea going one, she put back for the cover of
islands which were not far off. We hope to see her this evening or in
the morning, and will feel restless until she does come up.

At Nagasaki we found every preparation for our reception. The
Govt. had prepared and put at our disposal a house; had sent a man
of war; a committee composed of a Native Prince—dethroned of
his territorial inheritance & powers since the marvilous changes of
the last twenty-five years in this most interesting country, but still
holding high rank [60]—Mr Yoshada, the present Minister to the
United States, and others of rank, beside interpreters, servants &c.
Salutes were fired, troops formed on the Bund, and the population,
big & little, lined the sidewaw from the landing to the house where
we are quartered.

June 26th at half past four p m. left Nagasaki for the inland sea;
the Richmond bearing my party and Judge Bingham, U. S. Minister to Japan, & Mr. Yosheda, the Minister to the U. S.—temporarily on leave visiting his own country—in addition. The Ashuelot
also accompanies and a Japanese man of war [61] sent from the Capi-

tol with a committee to accompany us through Japan. Nagasaki we found a most beautiful city located on the slope of Green hills at the head of a narrow bay some nine miles in from the Yellow Sea. We were entertained at a govt. house occupied as a female seminary and furnished for the occassion with furniture and servants brought from Tokio. All classes of officials from the Govr of the province down and all citizens joined in doing us honor and in efforts to make our stay pleasant. Six days were agreeably spent in Nagasaki and a longer time would have been but for the fact that Cholera broke out at various points in the province which kept us from making ex̶k̶cursions to the interior which we had intended. The morning of the 27th found us entering the straits connecting the Yellow & Inland seas. Nothing can be more picturesque than the scenery of the straits; narrow, deep, filled with islands large & small, all high out of water and green to their summit. Villages dot the whole picture. The waters are filled with small fishing vessels, and junks engaged in transporting the products of the country to a market. Cholera prevailing at all points i̶n̶ along the inland sea where there is population prevented our landing at different points as we had expected. At Kobe we had anticipated a week with excursions to the interior.⁶² As it was to loose nothing of the beauty of scen[e]ry throughout this se[a] we anchored at night and traveled by day only contenting ourselves with remaining on shipboard. On the 1st of July arrive[d] at   a small fishing villege, surrounded by eight or ten other villeges of the same character, at the head of   bay. We went ashore and through two of the villeges but saw nothing to interest except the general neatness of the simple homes of the people, the perfection of the cultivation of their patches of ground, and the great & simple curiosity of the people, of all ages and both sexes, to see so many foreigners. This not being a port open to trade cannot be visited by foreigners except by permission of central authority hence it is probable that our party was the first white people ever seen by the majority of these people. All day our steamer was surrounded by native boats filled with men, women and children exhibiting a quiet curiosity. This place is but six miles distant from   the Capitol of the province.⁶³ The

Govr had learned in some way of our coming and sent three of his staff to welcome us, and later in the day came himself, to extend an invitation to his Capitol. To-day—the 2d of July—we go. Visited   the 2d. The distance from the landing is six miles, through a beautiful fertile and highly cultivated valley. The road is lined with a succession of villeges every house having out the Japanese flag. Jap[an] has a most [thoroug]h school system and on this occassion the scholars with their teachers were lined along the road to make their bow of welcome as we passed. There were litterally miles of them. At   we were first entertained at an old temple in the edge of the city surrounded by magnificent grounds where nature and art have competed to see which could do most to beautify. Nature got the best of it, but art has no reason to be ashamed. Here we witnessed day fire works. This consists in firing in to the air a shell which explodes about the time of its greatest elevation throwing out light cotton material mad[e] into [many] devices such as flags birds representations of men animals [&c The ma]terial being [light] floats with the [breeze] for some time before coming to the ground. From the temple we were taken to a large academy where we were beautifully entertained at tiffin—~~by~~ in Japanese style—by the Governor. Returning to the steamer we set sail, at once, for Yokohama which place we reached at about 11 O'clock the 3d of July. The scene was a grand one, the vessels of all nations being decked with flags all over, the stars & stripes being conspicuous in all, and a number of them firing salutes. The English were conspicuous for their lack of courtisy. But this is understood to be in consequence of orders from the home govt and to annow exceeding the officials in these waters. No blame to them. By 2 p. m. we were installed in our quarters in Tokio. The palace[64] is spacious, beautifully decorated, and built for summer purposes. The grounds about it are spacious, extending to the bay on one side and is in a high state of ornamental cultivation. Old trees, beautifu[l] lawns, artificial lakes of several acres in extent, gravel walks dwarfed trees in pots, summer houses on the banks of the lakes, &c, make up the picture. On the 4th my party, with quite a delegation of our naval officers, were presented to the Emperor & Empress.[65] I believe this is the first occasion when the Empress has ever given a formal reception to foreigners. But Japan is striving to become both liberal and enlightened. She deserves success for her efforts are honest and in the interest of the whole people. In the evening we were entertained in a public park of the city by the American residents of Tokio. The usual 4th of July speeches were delivered toast drank, music and fireworks.[66] On the 5 Mrs. Grant & myself, with party were received by the Emperor & Empress with no more ceremony than is observed at the smaller and less ostentati[ous] courts of Europe. Both the Emperor & Empress came forward and shook hands with Mrs. Grant & myself. Each delivered little speaches of welcome to us which were read in english. Our stay continued in Tokio until the 17th of July when we left temporarily for this mountain resort, Nikko Every day and almost every hour of the stay was taken up in entertainments which although they became very fatiguing, were very instructive as to the rapid progress made by the Japanese Govt. & people. Generally our engagements required us to start out at about nine in the morning and provided something to take up almos[t] every hour until 12 at night. In this way I visit[ed] & inspected the Military school; the Naval Academy; the school of science; the Normal school for girls; the Govt. Bazarre containing almost every thing of Chinese production; witnessed the review of their troops—on this occasion the Emperor ~~was in the earr~~ and I in his carriage—the target practice of their soldiers, &c. All these were morning occasions. Each was followed by a breakfast—called tiffin all through the east—about as elaborate as a set dinner at home. One of these breakfasts was with the Emperor. The Empress was not at this breakfast not having sufficiently broken through ancient customs of seclusiveness yet for this. But she was replaced at table by several Princesses of royal blood who now visit and receive visits. Every was a dinner party except Sundays and two evening given up to re-receptions by the citizens—native—of Tokio and Yokohama. These were gorgious affairs consisting of brilliant alluminations of the two cities, extensive fireworks, theatrical and musical performances, banquet &c. We also visited an annual ceremony still observed in Tokio of opening the river, with fire works ~~and~~ &c.[67] On this occasion all the population of Tokio that could be was out. The river was filled for a long distance up and down, brilliantly illuminated and each boat filled to its utmost capacity with people. Every available place on shore was also filled. The fireworks which followed were in the best Japanese style. All this time the days were intensely hot, and the evenings to in the brilliantly lighted, and pack[ed] halls, where the entertainments took place. I felt much relieved to get away for the country although it involved three days ride in the hot sun, two in carriages & one in Jenrikshais. The road from Tokio to Nikko— about 85 miles in length—was built about 350 years ago by

It is a perfect avenue the entire distans. Excep[t] places after reaching the foot hills the road is a high embankment and ~~with~~ the grade is perfect. Although wheeled vehicles did not exist in the country when the road was built the projector made it wide enough for a good carriage road with a row of trees on each side. These trees were set close together and consist entirely of the yellow pine & Japanese Cedar. These trees have attained great size now as well as antiquity The cedars are specially beautiful. They have grown to great hight as well as diameter, an[d] are generally very straight. Having been so closely planted it is not an uncommon thing to find four, and even six, of these trees grown together so as to form but a single stump for a few feet above the ground. The whole country is beautifully cultivated. Arrived at Nikko July the 19th and were comfortably installed in the house of the Priest of the Temple of Manguanji, on a hill overlooking the villege of Hachi-shi, below & ~~Nikko~~ Jumachi above. The temple is one of the most noted in Japan and the most sacred.[68] ~~At~~ Above it some hundreds of feet is the tomb of Iyeyasu the first Shogun of the Tokugawa family,[69] and the builder of the road above described. He also planted trees about the temple covering many acres on the mountain sides which have survived, and now make a magnificent park. The scenery through this section of Japan is much like that of the White Mountains in our own Country. The streams are very beautiful and constant waterfalls & rapids are encountered. On the 21st we visited the falls of Kirifuri.[70] The distance from Nikko is only three miles, but the road is so difficult to travel that it took nearly three hours of very hard travel to reach there. On the 25th visited Lake Sachino[71]-

Midzumi[72] six or seven miles from Nikko & 2400 feet above it, and a smaller lake beyond and some 800 feet high[er.] These lakes are in the midst of mountains of great beauty. The former is about seven miles in length, the latter about one. The outlet of the second to the first is through a deep canion with numerous waterfalls & rapids present much such scenery as some parts of Clear creek Canion in Colorado. Uno-Wooni—Hot springs—on the smaller lake are much visited by natives for

July 25th

Lachi-no-Midzuma & Uno-Wooni—Hot Springs—the baths which are supposed to possess fine medical qualities. The lame and the halt flock there by the thousands. On the 26th we returned making two very fatiguing days travel but, very enjoyable ones.

AD, George Washington University, Washington, D. C. For USG's own allusion to his travel diary, see letter to Elihu B. Washburne, April 4, 1879. Major sources for USG's trip through Asia are John Russell Young diary, Jan.-Sept., 1879, DLC-John Russell Young; *Young; Julia Grant;* John M. Keating, *With General Grant in the East* (Philadelphia, 1879).

1. On Jan. 16, 1879, B. Odell Duncan, consul, Naples, wrote to USG, Paris. "I have just received your note of the 13th Inst. & regret to learn that we shall see so little of you in Naples. . . ." ALS, DLC-John Russell Young. See Duncan to John Russell Young, Jan. 12, 1879, *ibid.*

On Feb. 17, 1869, James L. Orr, Anderson, S. C., had written to USG recommending Duncan. ". . . He was graduated at Furman University and went afterwards to one of the German Universityies. He speaks French & German fluently. . . . He was a member of the Constitutional convention in this state under the reconstruction acts of Congress and took a leading part in framing that Constitution He is a consistent and influential republican—was a delegate to the Chicago Convention and warmly supported by his speeches & pen the election of Gen Grant. . . ." ALS, DNA, RG 59, Letters of Application and Recommendation. Related papers are *ibid.* On Dec. 6, USG nominated Duncan as consul, Naples. See Augustus C. Rogers, ed., *Our Representatives Abroad: . . .* (New York, 1874), pp. 269–73.

2. On Feb. 6, 1879, John Russell Young, "On the Red Sea," wrote to Thomas Nast. "A letter of yours long unanswered has been lying among my papers,—a bundle I always carry with me,—called my portfolio of Good Intentions. I should have answered it before, but since seeing you in Paris, I have been in Spain, and Portugal, in Ireland and France,—and now I am on the Red Sea, under full steam to Bombay. General Grant was so earnest and kind in his wish to have me with him, that here I am, on my way around the world.—We have had a perfect trip thus far,—all of which, you will, I hope, find in the *Herald.* The General, Mr Borie, and I spend most of our time looking out on the waves, and *scheming for a third term*!!!! You never knew such a schemer as the Gen. He sits up for hours and hours, late and schemes.—Don't tell Mr. Harper about this it will distress him. . . . I left General Grant on deck talking to

his wife. He was scheming for a third term. I told him I was coming down stairs to write to some people, to whom I was shamelessly in debt,—you among them. The General sent you his kindest wishes, and his regards to J W. H.—& Mrs. Grant sent you her love.—Please do not tell Mrs. N. of *this* message.—We think of returning home in October." ALS, CSmH. For Joseph W. Harper of Harper & Brothers, see *New York Times*, July 22, 1896.

3. Perim, a five-square-mile island situated 100 miles west of Aden.

4. On Feb. 9, Young wrote in his diary. "Rose early, and went to church—The service read by Mr. Stokes & was very interesting—. . . Had a long talk with Gen Grant & the tiger colonel about Vicksburg campaign. Gen. said intercepting despatch from Joe. Johnston led to his awaiting battle at Champion *Hill.*" DLC-John Russell Young. See *PUSG*, 8, 213–14.

5. Representing Richard Temple, governor of Bombay, both Charles Gonne, chief secretary, and Capt. John S. Frith, aide-de-camp, greeted USG. See letter to Anthony J. Drexel, Feb. 16, 1879; Frith to Young, Feb. 28, 1879, DLC-John Russell Young.

6. Benjamin F. Farnham.

7. The Second Afghan War began in Nov., 1878.

8. For the Bombay Tramway, see *The Gazetteer of Bombay City and Island* (Bombay, 1909), I, 358–60.

9. USG visited the Wadia family. See *The Times of India* (Bombay), Feb. 17, 1879; Ruttonjee Ardeshir Wadia, *The Bombay Dockyard and the Wadia Master Builders* (Bombay, 1955).

10. See *The Times of India* (Bombay), Feb. 17, 1879; Samuel T. Sheppard, *The Byculla Club 1833–1916: A History* (Bombay, 1916).

11. Born and educated in Ireland, Michael R. Westropp went to India (1854) and was knighted upon being named chief justice of Bombay (1870). See *The Times* (London), Jan. 20, 1890.

12. Rear Admiral John Corbett commanded British naval forces in the East Indies. See *ibid.*, Dec. 12, 1893.

13. USG traveled over the Great Indian Peninsula Railway. See *Gazetteer of Bombay*, I, 342–50.

14. On Feb. 22, 1879, Lt. Gen. John A. Ewart, British army commander, Allahabad, wrote to USG. "A Telegram has just arrived asking the date of your probable arrival at *Calcutta*. If you would kindly let me know, a reply by telegram shall be sent at once. I am sending instructions to the officers Comdg at Cawnpore and Benares to give you every assistance; perhaps you could also kindly inform me on what dates you expect to reach these Stations. If I can be of any further service to you before you leave Allahabad I shall be only too glad." ALS, DLC-USG, IB.

15. Ram Singh.

16. See Thomas Holbein Hendley, *Ulwar and its Art Treasures* (London, 1888).

17. Seswaut Singh.

18. See Speech, [*Feb. 28, 1879*].

19. Identified as the "young Maharajah of Dholepore." *The Statesman and Friend of India* (Calcutta), March 4, 1879.

20. George Couper entered the Bengal civil service (1846) and rose to lt. governor of the North West Provinces (1877).

21. See Alexander J. Lawrence to Young, March 4, 1879, DLC-John Russell Young.

22. For William H. Beynon, see *The Times* (London), Oct. 15, 1903.

23. Possibly Henry B. Webster, British magistrate and collector, North West Provinces.

24. Sepoys (natives in the British army) mutinied in 1857, triggering widespread revolt against colonial rule in India. The British recaptured Delhi after a siege lasting over three months.

25. March 16, 1879.

26. Among the first to enter the Indian civil service through competitive examination (1855), Charles U. Aitchison held several responsible posts before his transfer to Burma (1878).

27. See Elizabeth Moore *et al.*, *Shwedagon: Golden Pagoda of Myanmar* (London, 1999).

28. On March 23, 1879, a correspondent reported from Rangoon on USG's visit. *The Statesman and Friend of India* (Calcutta), March 29, 1879.

29. The first Burmese railroad, opened in 1877, connected Rangoon with Prome. A second railroad from Rangoon was not completed until 1884.

30. Starting in 1879, Charles John Irving served as resident councillor, Malacca. He probably greeted USG at Penang in the absence of the local resident councillor, Col. Archibald Anson, then serving as act. governor, Straits Settlements.

31. See letter to Archibald Anson, April 22, 1879.

32. Adolphus G. Studer, consul, Singapore, offered a less flattering assessment. See letter to George W. Childs, April 5, 1879.

33. Hoh Ah Kay Whampoa prospered as a merchant, performed consular services for various countries, and earned a reputation for gracious hospitality. See *The Times* (London), May 22, 1880.

34. Prince Kaphia died shortly after USG's visit. See Adolphus G. Studer to John Russell Young, May 18, 1879, DLC-John Russell Young.

35. For Siamese officials, see David K. Wyatt, *The Politics of Reform in Thailand: Education in the Reign of King Chulalongkorn* (New Haven, 1969).

Young reported a conversation between Si Suriyawong (former regent) and USG. "The Regent, after some meditation, spoke of the great pleasure it had given him to meet General Grant in Siam. . . . The General thanked the Regent, and was glad to know that his country was so much esteemed in the East. There was a pause and a cup of the enticing tea and some remarks on the weather. The General expressed a desire to know whether the unusual rain would affect the crops throughout the country. The Regent said there was no such apprehension, and there was another pause, while the velvet coated cigarettes and cigars passed into general circulation. The General spoke of the value to Siam and to all countries in the East of the widest commercial intercourse with nations of the outer world, and that from all he could learn of the Siamese and the character of their resources any extension of relations with other nations would be a gain to them. . . . Then the Regent responded:—'Siam,' he said, 'was a peculiar country. It was away from sympathy and communion with the greater nations. It was not in one of the great highways of commerce. Its people were not warlike nor aggressive. It had no desire to share in the strifes and wars of other nations. It existed by the friendship of the great Powers. . . . What he valued in the relations of Siam with America was the unvarying sense of justice on the part of America, and as the hopes of Siam rested wholly on the good will of foreign Powers she was especially drawn to America.'" *New York Herald*, June 9, 1879.

36. King Chulalongkorn of Siam assumed the throne in 1868 and ruled through a regent until Nov., 1873. See *New York Times*, Oct. 24, 1910; Wyatt, *Politics of Reform*

in Thailand; David M. Engel, *Law and Kingship in Thailand During the Reign of King Chulalongkorn* (Ann Arbor, 1975).

37. Phanuwong Mahakosathibodi, brother of Si Suriyawong. See Wyatt, *Politics of Reform in Thailand*, pp. 46, 85.

38. USG continues the entry for April 16, 1879, below.

39. Probably Queen Saovabha Phongsri, born in 1864, the first of Chulalongkorn's many wives.

40. See Speech, [*April 16, 1879*].

41. Ayuthia.

42. USG's party left behind their Indian servants. On April 24, 1879, Studer gave USG's servant forty-one dollars to cover expenses from Singapore to Bombay. DS, DLC-USG, IB. See also Studer to Young, April 26, 1879, DLC-John Russell Young.

43. Rear Admiral Louis Lafont governed a restless native population. See G. Vapereau, *Dictionnaire Universel Des Contemporains . . . Supplément a la Sixième Édition* (Paris, 1895), pp. 901–2; James A. Bising, "The Admirals' Government: A History of the Naval Colony that was French Cochinchina, 1862–1879," Ph.D. Dissertation, New York University, 1972.

44. A U.S. Naval Academy graduate, George H. Perkins participated in operations against New Orleans and Mobile during the Civil War and took command of the U.S.S. *Ashuelot* in 1877. For his remarks on USG, see Susan G. Perkins, ed., *Letters of Capt. Geo. Hamilton Perkins, U. S. N.* (1886; reprinted, Freeport, N. Y., 1970), pp. 190–202. See also Carroll Storrs Alden, *George Hamilton Perkins Commodore, U. S. N.* . . . (Boston, 1914).

45. See letter to Liu K'un-i, May 16, 1879.

46. For USG's visit to Canton, see letter to Elihu B. Washburne, May 4, 1879.

47. See *The Celestial Empire* (Shanghai), May 20, 1879.

48. See C. A. Montalto de Jesus, *Historic Macao* (2nd ed., 1926; reprinted, Hong Kong, 1984), pp. 283–93.

49. See letter to William H. Forbes *et al.*, May 10, 1879.

50. Actually Shanghai.

51. See letter to Edward F. Beale, May 23, 1879.

52. For Viceroy Li Hung-chang of Chihli, see Speech, [*May 30, 1879*].

53. See conversation with Prince Kung, [*June 5, 1879*].

54. Actually June 6.

55. USG misdated this entry. See conversation with Prince Kung, [*June 8, 1879*].

56. See letter to Prince Kung and Iwakura Tomomi, Aug. 13, 1879.

57. See Speech, [*June 13, 1879*].

58. See *New York Herald*, Aug. 18, 1879.

59. Born in London, Charles Lenox Simpson entered the customs service in China (1861) and was promoted to commissioner (1877).

60. Date Kunitada, not to be confused with Date Munenari, another prominent Japanese official. See *The Japan Biographical Encyclopedia . . .* (Tokyo, [1958]), p. 120.

61. The *Kongô*, a new ironclad in the Japanese fleet.

62. See letter to Julius Stahel, May 18, 1879.

63. USG landed along the western coast of Suruga Bay at Shimizu, close to Shizuoka, capital of the prefecture. On July 1, 1879, Young wrote in his diary. ". . . About two we came to anchor in [—] Bay with Fusiyama in sight. The bay as beautiful as Naples. . . ." DLC-John Russell Young.

64. Enryōkan.

65. See first Speech, [*July 4, 1879*].

66. See second Speech, [*July 4, 1879*].

67. USG was the guest of Prince Hachisuka for the traditional opening of the river on July 12. For USG's activities, July 5–16, see Speech, [*July 3, 1879*]; letter to Ellen Grant Sartoris, July 15, 1879.

68. See Robert Charles Hope, *The Temples and Shrines of Nikkō, Japan* (Yokohama, 1896), pp. 18–19.

69. See A. L. Sadler, *The Maker of Modern Japan: The Life of Tokugawa Ieyasu* (London, 1937).

70. Translated as "falling mist cascade." Hope, *Temples and Shrines*, p. 94.

71. More commonly known as Lake Chuzenji.

72. Mizuumi is Japanese for a lake or pond. See E. M. Satow, *A Guide Book to Nikkô* (Yokohama, 1875), pp. 31–36.

To Anthony J. Drexel

Bombay, Calcutta,
Feb.y 16th /79

My Dear Mr. Drexel:

We arrived at this place the morning of the 13th[1] after the most delightful sea voyage I ever had from Suez on. The sky was clear, the air balmy & the sea smooth. I think even Mr. Childs would have enjoyed it. We had also a most agreeable set of passengers. Mr. Borie seems to be doing well and is begining to have a good deal of fun in him. I hope to return him to the many friends he left behind a well if no a young man.—We are staying here at the Government House guests of the Governor of this Presidency,[2] and receiving the most bountiful hospitality. All the Governors of India, and the Viceroy[3] have extended the hospitality of their official residences to myself and party on our arrival within their domains. But Young will give full descriptions of all this in the Herald. I refer you to the Columns of that paper for full information of "The Innocents Abroad"[4]—On the 18th we start for the interior & round to Calcutta. There we hope to take the Richmond and to be able to controll our movements somewhat until we reach Japan, say about the first of June. I doubt whether we will be able to visit Madras. The Duke of Buckingham[5] has given us a special invitation, but it is back this way from Calcutta.

Give Mrs. Grants love to the ladies of your family, to Mrs. Childs & Mrs. Borie, and my kindest regards. We think of you all very often and wish you could see us in our light summer clothes keeping in the shade to keep cool.

Very Truly yours
U. S. GRANT

A. J. DREXEL, ESQ.

ALS, Haverford College, Haverford, Pa. For USG in Bombay, see *Young*, I, 606–22; John M. Keating, *With General Grant in the East* (Philadelphia, 1879), pp. 39–52; *Julia Grant*, pp. 265–67.

On Feb. 11, 1879, the Bombay Rifle Vols. invited USG to attend its annual ball on Feb. 14. N, DLC-USG, IB. Also on Feb. 11, the Bombay Club enrolled USG as an honorary member. ANS, *ibid.*

1. See *The Times of India* (Bombay), Feb. 13–14, 1879; *Bombay Gazette*, Feb. 14, 1879.

On Jan. 17, Henry S. King & Co., London, had written to USG, Paris. "Your approaching visit to the East affords us reasonable excuse for troubling you with the offer of the services of our Branch Houses at Bombay, and Calcutta, for any business which you may require to be transacted during your stay in India. . . ." L, DLC-John Russell Young. On Feb. 13, Thomas W. Cuff, branch agent of Henry S. King & Co., Bombay, wrote to USG. "We beg to tender our Services for the clearance of your baggage from today's mail steamer, as well as for the execution of any commissions during your visit to Bombay. A gentleman of our Firm would have been on board to render any assistance that might have been required, but unfortunately was unable to reach the Steamer before your departure." LS, *ibid.* See *The Times* (London), Nov. 15, 1933.

2. Active in Indian colonial government since 1847, Richard Temple took over as governor of Bombay in 1877. On Feb. 14, 1879, Temple telegraphed to USG "offering him the heartiest welcome to the Bombay Presidency, and assuring him that, although the Governor himself was detained by duty in Sind, everyone in Bombay, including both Government servants and the general community, would do their utmost to make the General's stay pleasant to him and to show him and his party everything that was worth seeing in Bombay or the interior. General Grant, in reply, telegraphed that he had been extremely gratified by the cordial welcome given to him on landing at Bombay, which was everything he could have desired. He and his friends, he added, were now settled in very comfortable quarters, thanks to His Excellency's kindness and the great attention of the officers of the household. General Grant concluded his message with an expression of great regret that he should not have the opportunity of making Sir Richard Temple's personal acquaintance during his short stay in Bombay." *Bombay Gazette*, Feb. 15, 1879.

On Feb. 15, USG attended a state dinner at the Government House. Replying to a toast, he "said how much he regretted being unable to make the personal acquaintance of Sir Richard Temple, to whom he was indebted for a most hospitable reception at Bombay. . . ." *Ibid.*, Feb. 17, 1879. See Temple, *The Story of My Life* (London, 1896), II, 24–25, 173–74, 213–14.

3. Edward Robert Bulwer-Lytton, poet and career diplomat, accepted appointment as viceroy of India in 1876. He telegraphed to USG "a message of wel-

come, of considerable length." *The Statesman and Friend of India* (Calcutta), Feb. 22, 1879.

On Feb. 27 and March 3, 1879, Allyne C. Litchfield, consul gen., Calcutta, wrote to John Russell Young. "Yesterday morning I received a note from Col. Colley—Lord Lyttons private Secty of which the following is a copy—DEAR GENL—Would you mind telegraphing to Generl Grant or his Secty to ascertain how long he proposes to remain here? It might not seem civil for a *host* to ask such a question, but we want to know with a view to laying out a programme of entertainment for his stay'—To which I replied that I would wire with pleasure but I feared Genl Grant would find it difficult to reply difinetely since the 'Richmond' which was to take him from Calcutta had not been heard from as I was aware—. . ." "Your favor of the 27th at hand—I regret to say that up to the present time I can give you no news concerning the 'Richmond'—I have telegraphed to Point de Galle and shall know to-morrow if she has passed there. Whatever information I receive I will despatch to General Grant at once—You say in your letter 'I think we will be there on the 10th perhaps the 11th' Lord Lytton has issued invitations for the evening of the 10TH & I hope nothing will prevent the arrival of General Grant & party on that day—. . ." ALS, DLC-John Russell Young. On March 4 and "Monday Morning," probably March 10, Litchfield again wrote to Young. "I this morning received a telegram from the Master Attendant at Point de Galle as follows: 'Have no information of Richmond'. . . I have arranged to have a telegram from Galle when the Richmond arrives there & will telegraph to General Grant promptly" "I hastily note a few thoughts that will doubtless help to answer queries that may arise in General Grants mind. *Richmond*: Not yet passed Aden—I have arranged to have a telegram when she does pass—. . . *Letters*: I presume the inclosed and many others the Gen will receive may be begging letters for various institutions (or individuals even) written under the impression that as General Grant conquered a continent he must be very wealthy, and according to a custom which, I daresay he has already found, prevails in the East—If he will give you authority to open such as have nothing on the outside to indicate that they are of any consequence it will save him much trouble—" ALS, *ibid.*

4. An allusion to Mark Twain, *The Innocents Abroad* (1869). For Young's columns on USG's voyage to India and travels through that country, see *New York Herald*, March 10, 24, April 11–12, 14, 22–23, May 2, 24, 26–28, 30, 1879.

5. Richard Grenville, Duke of Buckingham and Chandos, appointed governor of Madras in 1875.

To Edward F. Noyes

Bombay, India,
Feb.y 16th /79

MY DEAR GENERAL,

We arrived at this place on the 13th after a most agreeable trip. On the Mediterranean it was a little cold and, at times, quite rough. But from Suez on it was as smooth as a mill pond, the sky clear and the temperature just right to keep the passengers on deck in light summer clothing. From Suez to Bombay, thirteen days run, there is but one stop—at Aden, in Arabia. Our stop there was at night so I did not go ashore. From the appearance of the savages who swam around the boat to dive for six pences I should judge them to be about the lowest order of people in Asia. Immediately on arrival here I was waited on by an Aid to the Govr with an invitation from that official for myself and party to occupy the government house during our stay. We are doing so, and it is one round of gaiety. The reception has been quite as cordial as what you witnessed in Ireland. The hospitalities of the officials, and Citizens is Princely. On the 18th we start for the interior. Everywhere the leading officials have telegraphed their invitations for my party to be their guests. I must admit the great hospitality of the English people wherever I have met them. Mrs. Grants & my kindest regards to Mr[s]. Noyes, Mr. & Mrs. Hitt.

Yours Truly
U. S. GRANT

ALS, Cincinnati Historical Society, Cincinnati, Ohio. See previous letter.

To Adam Badeau

Bombay, India
Feby 17th /79

MY DEAR BADEAU:

We reached this place on the 13th after a most pleasant voyage. From Suez to Bombay the temperature was just right to keep all the passengers on deck from the hour of rising in the morning to the hour of retirement in the evening. The sky was clear and the sea so smooth that you might almost play billiards on deck. The reception here has been most cordial from the officials, foreign residents, Parsee merchants and the better to do Hindoo natives. Myself and party were invited to occupy the Government House, where we are now staying, and where we have received princely hospitalities. Young has described the whole thing very fully in his article for the paper. I hope you will see it.

To-day we start for the interior[1] where we expect to see more characteristic phases of Indian life & habits. Bombay has much in common with European cities. It is a manufacturing and commercial city. The old—native—portion of the city however is different from anything I have yet seen either in Egypt or Turkey. Like in New York City one may find people from every know part of the world.

The party are all well and join me in kindest regards to you. Please present my complements to Mr & Miss Welsh[2] and Mr. Hopping.[3]

yours Truly
U. S. GRANT

ALS, Munson-Williams-Proctor Institute, Utica, N. Y. See letter to Anthony J. Drexel, Feb. 16, 1879.

1. USG left Bombay on Feb. 18, 1879.
2. John Welsh, minister to Great Britain, had eleven children from two marriages.
3. William J. Hoppin, Harvard Law School graduate (1835) and member of the Union League Club in New York City, served as first secretary of legation, London. See *New York Times*, June 20, 1872; *New York Tribune*, Sept. 4, 1895.

To Edwards Pierrepont

Bombay, India,
Feb.y 17th /79

My Dear Judge:

Just before leaving Paris I received your very kind letter which I did not find time to answer. Since that we—myself & party—have had a very pleasant run from Marseilles to this place. We have now been here four days and have pretty well seen the city. I am staying at the Government House, guest of the Governor of this province. The hospitality of the officials, foreign residents & natives is boundless. Something takes place both day & evening for our entertainment.—To-morrow we start for the interior.[1] There we expect to see something more characteristically Indian. Bombay is a commercial and manufacturing city, and has much in common with an European town. But every type of Asiatic is found here and every variety of dress from no clothes to the well clad. Mrs. Grant joins me in kind regards to Mrs. Pierrepont and yourself.

yours Truly

U. S. GRANT

P. S. We have no later news from America than we brought with us from ~~America~~. Paris. We hope for a mail however in a day or two, and with it letters and papers of a week later date than any we now have. I hope Congress is doing nothing to disturb specie resumption which seemed to commence with so little disturbance.

U. S. G.

ALS, OHi. After resigning as minister to Great Britain in late 1877, Edwards Pierrepont practiced law in New York City. On Oct. 31, 1878, Pierrepont praised specie resumption at a Republican gathering. See *New York Tribune*, Nov. 1, 1878.

On Feb. 17, 1879, USG replied to a toast at a state dinner supervised by James Gibbs, Bombay judge. *The Times of India* (Bombay), Feb. 18, 1879.

1. On Feb. 18, John Russell Young wrote in his diary. "... At six we left Bombay with guard of honor and all display. I saw Olcott for an hour who was full of his Theosophy and new form of religion." DLC-John Russell Young. USG also met Henry S. Olcott, former agricultural editor of the *New York Tribune* and New York City attorney, who had gone to India to promote his unorthodox beliefs. See *Bombay Gazette* and *The Times of India* (Bombay), Feb. 19, 1879; *Young*, I, 622–23.

Speech

[Agra, India, Feb. 28, 1879]

I cannot undertake to reply to all that has been just now so eloquently said. I therefore confine my remarks to the subject of pacification. When the war was concluded a great difficulty met us. About a million of armed men had to be disbanded and sent back to be absorbed in civil pursuits. Feelings of excitement had to be assuaged, not only in our own population, but on both sides of the Atlantic. That all this was accomplished so soon was greatly to the credit of the nature of the Anglo-Saxon people, not only in America, but in the mother-country. In thanking you for the manner in which you have drunk our healths, I must add that we shall not forget the kindness with which we have been received wherever we have been; and I hope the good feelings of which it is an evidence will be extended by constant visits of Americans to Britain and of the British to America.

The Pioneer (Allahabad), March 3, 1879. USG spoke following a dinner at the Agra Club after being introduced by Henry G. Keene, British official and a prolific writer, who praised USG as "the unconquered, the pacificator of his country, the worthy successor of George Washington." *Ibid.* See *The Statesman and Friend of India* (Calcutta), March 4, 1879; Keene, *A Servant of "John Company": Being the Recollections of an Indian Official* (London, 1897), pp. 281–82, and *Here and There: Memories Indian and Other* (London, 1906), pp. 84–85; *The Times* (London), March 29, 1915.

On Feb. 23, 1879, John W. Tyler, prison superintendent and honorary secretary, Agra Club, wrote to USG's private secretary, presumably John Russell Young. "I am desired by the Committee to inform you, that they have Elected General Grant & his Staff Honorary Members of this Club, during His Excellency's visit to Agra." LS, DLC-USG, IB.

On Feb. 28, W. A. McIntosh, special correspondent, *Indian Daily News*, Agra, wrote to USG. "I arrived here last night, from Allahabad, on my way to Jeypore and other Rajputana States to report 'famine' matters in those States for the 'Indian Daily News' of Calcutta, and as I should like to telegraph your movements, after you leave this, to the newspaper in question I shall feel very much obliged if you will kindly let me know what places you visit on your way down to Calcutta—I presume you go down to Calcutta from here. I shall in all probability be at the 'Club' dinner tonight but as I am anxious to wire a faithful report, of your 'reply' to the toast of your health, may I beg you will kindly favor me with a M. S. S. of what you intend to say. I shall feel extremely thankful if you will do me this favor and I promise you that I shall make no use of the M. S. S. until after the dinner. Trusting you will excuse the liberty I have taken . . ." ALS, *ibid.*

To John Russell Young

[*Delhi, India*]
March 4th /79

DEAR YOUNG.

Just in from a ride through the city with Mrs. Grant, and found your note. Met many merchants who accosted us on the streets, and more beggars. Purchased from the former—at their own prices—and contributed to the latter. Will not be able to purchase your watches even at rates at which Parsee Brokers would take them in our own country. But we will try to get through to Calcutta, even if we have to leave a hostage. I should fear to leave Mr Borie

because he would contract such obligations that we could never re-
deem them. I suggest we should sacrifice Dr. Kaiting. By providing
for four meals a day for him—with a lunch between each meal—he
would be content. At Calcutta we can make all arrangements for
the immediate future.

[Yours truly,

U. S. GRANT.]

AL, DLC-John Russell Young; John Russell Young, *Men and Memories* (New York,
1901), II, 269. After arriving in Delhi on March 1, 1879, USG left for Lucknow on
March 4. See John Russell Young diary, March 1–4, 1879, DLC-John Russell Young;
Young, II, 53–64; John M. Keating, *With General Grant in the East* (Philadelphia, 1879),
pp. 74–79.

On Feb. 27, G. Gordon Young, "Officiating Commissioner," Delhi, had written
to USG. "I hope you will allow me the pleasures of receiving you & Mrs Grant at my
house here during your stay—and of showing you such sights as are to be seen in the
City and neighborhood. I shall do myself the pleasure of meeting you at the Station
when you arrive, which if I am rightly informed, will be on Sunday the 2d March. You
will perhaps intimate to me by telegraph any change of plan, that we may be prepared
for your reception." ALS, DLC-USG, IB.

To Charles H. Rogers

Calcutta, India,
11th March, 1879.

MY DEAR MR. ROGERS.

My party arrived at this place at 5 30 a. m. all well, and having
done India very well. We landed first at Bombay and after six days
started for the interior, and North west provinces of the country.
Our stops were at Jubulpore, Allahabad, Agra, Jaypore, Burdpore,
Fettipore [S]egra, Delhi, Lucknow, Benares, and lastly here.[1] I have
now a very good idea of India, its people and the effect of English
rule. I shall not bother you with these views however, but will only
say that while progress in the direction of civilizing the natives has
been very slow I believe that if the English were to withdraw the
whole population would return to barbarism at one bound. The
people are inferior to our North American Indian. The English who
are sent here to direct government are, so far as I have seen them,

a very superior set of men. Indeed I believe they all have to pass a rigid examination to enter even the lowest place in the India service.[2] The kindness of all the officials, Civil & Military, to me and my party has been most marked. No where are we allowed to stop at public houses, but are taken in by the highest official of the place.

Mrs. Grant sends her love to Mrs. Rogers and Miss Lilly, and kindest regards to you & John in all of which I join.

Very Truly Yours
U. S. GRANT

ALS, DLC-USG. On March 10, 1879, John Russell Young wrote in his diary. "Arrived in Calcutta at five, & were met by the Viceroy's aide. Drove to the Government House, and had quarters. Lord Lytton met us at lunchen.—In the evening a drive and a grand dinner, in which Lord L. made a charming speech on the General" DLC-John Russell Young. After celebrating U.S. and British relations and toasting the U.S. presidency, Edward Robert Bulwer-Lytton, viceroy of India, commended his guest. ". . . General Ulysses Grant, like his classic namesake, has seen men and cities in almost every part of the world, enlarging the genius of the statesman and the soldier by the experience of the traveller. Let us hope that when he returns to that Great Empire of the West, which he has once rescued and twice ruled, he will at least take with him a kindly recollection of his brief sojourn in this Empire of the East, where his visit will long be remembered with gratification by many sincere friends and well-wishers." *The Statesman and Friend of India* (Calcutta), March 13, 1879. See *Young*, II, 135–37; John M. Keating, *With General Grant in the East* (Philadelphia, 1879), pp. 94–97.

On March 11, 12, and 13 (Thursday), Young wrote in his diary. ". . . In the evening we have another state dinner, and remain up late,—with the Gen. & Vicery playing cards." ". . . In the afternoon we go to the house of Sir Ashley Eden the Lt. Gov. of Bengal.—A dinner party and a reception & many natives. Have a long talk with Lord Lytton the Viceroy, on American & Indian affairs." ". . . Lunchen with the Consul General. I come home hot & tired. A Garden Party, & a resolution to sail for Rangoon on Monday morning. This prevents our going to Ceylon & Madras—Am sorry." DLC-John Russell Young. See *The Statesman and Friend of India* (Calcutta), March 11, 1879; *Young*, II, 137–49; Keating, *With General Grant*, pp. 97–98.

1. At Jabalpur, USG's party rode elephants for the first time, and at Agra, visited the Taj Mahal. At Jaipur, they witnessed Hindu religious ceremonies and were entertained by the local maharajah. To reach Fathipur-Sikri, USG's party rode camels. See Young diary, Feb. 19–28, 1879, DLC-John Russell Young; *Young*, I, 623–27, II, 3–50, 122–34; Keating, *With General Grant*, pp. 53–74; *Julia Grant*, pp. 267–72; H. G. Keene, *A Handbook for Visitors to Agra and its Neighbourhood* (4th edition, Calcutta, 1878), pp. 42–69, and *A Handbook for Visitors to Lucknow, Allahabad, and Cawnpore* (Calcutta, 1880), pp. 1–19.

On Feb. 26, Sydney Hartwell, United Service Club, Lucknow, wrote to USG's private secretary, Agra. "It is believed that General Grant will pay this Station a visit early next month and the Residents of Lucknow propose doing themselves the honor of inviting General & Mrs Grant & party to a Ball at the Chuttee Munzil Club on the 7th March. I now write to ask whether this proposal will be acceptable to General

Grant, also whether the date fixed (7th March) will be convenient, and if not whether you will kindly fix some other day" ALS, DLC-USG, IB. For USG's party in Lucknow and Benares, see Young diary, March 5–8, 1879, DLC-John Russell Young; *Young*, II, 65–71, 98–121; Keating, *With General Grant*, pp. 80–92; *Julia Grant*, pp. 272–74.

2. The British began competitive examinations for Indian Civil Service positions in 1855. Earlier candidates received special collegiate training. See Naresh Chandra Roy, *The Civil Service in India* (2nd edition, Calcutta, 1960), pp. 60–86.

To Adam Badeau

Calcutta, March 15th /79

DEAR BADEAU,

We have now done India from Bombay to Delhi and back to this place. We leave here to-morrow morning for Singapore, by a regular steamer, the Richmond not having put in an appearance yet.[1] Our visit to India has been a most delightful one. The English people have exceeded themselves in hospitalities. No where but at one place have we been permitted to stop at a hotel, and there—Jubulpore—it was because no official had the spare room for our accommodation. The rail-road officials have been equally attentive giving us all through India two special cars, provided with every convenience, including bath rooms, for our party of six.

I have a letter from a cousin of mine who says that she has been informed that a brother of her Grand father, by the name of Mordecay Levy died in London some fifty years ago leaving a large fortune to her grandfather, and that the will was recorded, as she says, in parliment. Will you do me the favor to have some one examine whether they can find any such record.[2]

Mrs. Grant and all my party desire to be specially remembered to you. I will continue to drop you a line occasionally, but you must not expect much to interest you

Very Truly

U. S. GRANT

ALS, Munson-Williams-Proctor Institute, Utica, N. Y. On March 15, 1879, USG purchased quinine pills and quinine powder from R. Scott Thomson & Co., Pharmaceutical Chemists, Calcutta. Receipt, DLC-USG, IB. On the same day, USG mingled with sailors at "the Seaman's Coffee Rooms in Lall Bazar." *The Statesman and Friend of India* (Calcutta), March 18, 1879. Also on March 15, John Russell Young wrote in his diary. ". . .

Did a lot of work for the General—In the evening went to dine with Sir Richard Garth the chief justice, and ~~in the~~ at 11 drove with the Gen. on board the str. Simla to embark for Burmah." DLC-John Russell Young. Viceroy Edward Robert Bulwer-Lytton of India, who had left Calcutta on March 14, later alleged that USG was drunk and licentious at Chief Justice Richard Garth's dinner. See Mary Lutyens, *The Lyttons in India:* . . . (London, 1979), pp. 149–50; William S. McFeely, *Grant: A Biography* (New York, 1981), pp. 472–73; Geoffrey Perret, *Ulysses S. Grant: Soldier & President* (New York, 1997), p. 455.

On March 14, USG met Garth at the Bengal High Court and participated in graduation ceremonies at Calcutta University. USG later attended a party given by the influential Tagore family and praised the traditional entertainment. USG's invitation, dated March 11, is in USG 3. See *The Statesman and Friend of India* (Calcutta), March 17, 1879; *Native Opinion* (Bombay), March 23, 1879; *China Mail* (Hong Kong), April 5, 1879; John M. Keating, *With General Grant in the East* (Philadelphia, 1879), pp. 98–102; Alexander J. Arbuthnot, *Memories of Rugby and India* (London, 1910), pp. 232–34.

1. On March 2, Capt. Andrew E. K. Benham, U.S.S. *Richmond*, Naples, had written to "Sir," possibly Benjamin F. Stevens, U.S. dispatch agent, London. "In reply to your telegram, I beg to say that the ship will leave this point, as soon as some repairs, that are now in progress, are completed, probably by the middle of this week and certainly by the latter part, when I shall make all possible despatch to India. The ship will, I think, reach point de Galle, Ceylon, by the 20th of April, should the General wish to join her at Bombay, that point can be reached earlier, I should like to hear from Genl Grant, at either Suez or Aden, that I may know his wishes, and be governed accordingly. The private Stores mentioned in the Telegram were received at Ville Franche and are now on board . . . P. S. Should I fail to meet Genl G. at Pt de Galle or to hear from him I shall proceed to Singapore and await him there," Copy, DLC-John Russell Young.

On March 12, Col. G. Pomeroy Colley, secretary, viceroy of India, wrote to USG. "I enclose the reply just received from Captain Willoughby, our transport agent at Suez, regardig the Richmond—" ANS, DLC-USG, IB.

2. On April 17, 1870, Mordecai Marshall, Brookfield, Mo., had written to USG. "I understand that you are somewhat acquainted with the estate of Mordecia Levi of London to Judas Levi of the U. S. Being one of the heirs of that Estate I am anxious to learn all I can in regard to the matter and if not intruding to much upon your valuable time would like you to inform me what you have learned in regard to the Estate There are I understand four hundred and fourty thousand pounds sterling belonging to the estate now on deposit in the bank of England and has been there for the last fourty seven years I understand you have raised an heir to the estate is my reason for addressing you in regard to the matter" ALS, DNA, RG 59, Miscellaneous Letters.

To Michael John Cramer

Rangoon, Burma
March 20th /79

MY DEAR MR. CRAMER,

We have now been very well through India and are this far on our way to the further East. The weather has been pleasant until within the last few days. But now it is becoming very warm and as we have yet to go through the straits of Melacca, near the equator, before turning north we must expect some discomfort.—I have been very much pleased with English rule & English hospitality in India. With that rule—250.000.000. of uncivilized people are living at ~~peopl~~ peace with each other and are not only drawing their subsistence from the soil but are exporting a large excess over imports from it. It would be a sad day for the people of India and for the commerce of the world if the English should withdraw.—We hope to be in Hongkong by the middle of April, and further North in China as soon thereafter as possible. When a good climate is reached we will regulate our further movements by the reports of weather on seas to be traversed, and climate of places to be visited. At present however we expect to reach San Francisco about the first half of July. Although homesick to be settled down I dread getting back. The clamor of the partisan and, so called, independent press will be such as to make life there unpleasant for a time.

Mrs. Grant joins me in love to you, Mary and the children.

I have to-day written a letter to Mr. Corbin.[1]

Very Truly yours
U. S. GRANT.

P. S. Julia asks me to add, to tell Mary that the English speak in the highest terms of the work being done all through this country by the Missionaries, especially in an educational way. They say they are doing much good.

ALS, Gilder Lehrman Collection, NHi.

1. In June, 1879, George A. Townsend ("Gath") spoke to one "of the household and a connection of the President," possibly Abel R. Corbin, concerning USG and his father. "The General was the only one of the children with any generosity about money. Having been sent to West Point, brought up with the cadets and open and candid in the army, he terrified the old man by not worshipping money. The old man would take a drink but never pay for it. Grant was as likely to pay for it and never drink it. . . . He was dumbfounded that Grant would play poker or occasionally faro. You know how a man of Grant's temperament would bet; the first wager he made would be with all he had for all on the cloth. 'All the downs' was his favorite bet. He did the same in war. Consequently, when his opportunity came he didn't aim to be a major or lieutenant-colonel, as his father might have wished, to save some salary. He felt the spirit of the game and played for big victories and high promotions. In short, if he had been the kind of man his father wanted he probably never would have amounted to much." Asked whether USG drank,

the informant said. "Occasionally he does. Give Grant something to do and he gets all the mental excitement he wants out of that duty and task. He has such fidelity and honesty that he was never known in any event or expectation to be off guard. But he has a very active brain and in holiday times takes his syrup. I never heard of a military man of genius or activity who hadn't his convivial side. . . . Nobody knows how to fight Grant, he's so perfectly simple and square. They will insist that he has gone abroad on a scheme and is being worked up by parties here. Until they understand that he's destitute of all cunning and arrangement they never can beat him. I would no more think of doubting the truth of anything he told me than of flying. . . . It was informally proposed that he become the President of a railroad consolidated upon the Erie. But the arrangement would take time and Grant would not wait. He is very particular about lending his name to any speculative matter where shares of stock are to be sold. He had numerous offers to be the President of compounded mining interests in California and the West, but he felt that all mining was uncertain, and he might lay himself open to the imputation of dishonesty, and even without cause. . . ." *New York Graphic*, June 11, 1879.

To Daniel Ammen

SINGAPORE, April 2d, 1879.

DEAR AMMEN,—

Since my letter of yesterday I have been thinking if I have been in any way remiss in not informing the Secretary of the Navy of my determination to proceed in advance of the Richmond. In thinking the matter over, I have come to the conclusion that if there has been any neglect to complain of I am the one to complain. The Secretary was kind enough to voluntarily offer me a passage on the Richmond, which his letter [1] said would leave the States for the Mediterranean on the 10th of December. I accepted, and was quietly waiting in Paris until I should hear of her passing Gibraltar before starting. I remained there until home papers of a later date than the 10th of December reached me, and, seeing no notice of her departure, I got Mr. Harjes to cable to Drexel to find out whether she had yet started. By this means I found that she would not leave until the 10th of January. If there is punctilio in the matter, why was I not informed? I also telegraphed to Admiral Pattison,[2] who replied that he had not a word from the Richmond. I wrote to Le Roy three times, the third letter because so long a time had elapsed without a reply to my second that I feared he had not received it.

An answer came, however, from a hotel in Nice, written evidently by his secretary and sent through Stevens in London,[3] stating that he had been relieved, and that Captain Davis[4] was in charge and would no doubt forward my desires in any way he could, if I would write to him,—or words to that effect.

> Very truly yours,
> U. S. GRANT.

Daniel Ammen, *The Old Navy and the New* (Philadelphia, 1891), p. 546. On April 1 and 2, 1879, John Russell Young wrote in his diary. "We arrived this morning very early at Singapore. Were received by all the people. Came to the house of the Colonial Secy Cecil C. Smith, . . ." ". . . In the evening a state dinner at the Gov. House, all the great folks in town being there. . . ." DLC-John Russell Young. See *North-China Daily News* (Shanghai), April 18, 1879; Cecil C. Smith to Young, April 26, 1879, DLC-John Russell Young.

1. See letter to Richard W. Thompson, Nov. 14, 1878.
2. Rear Admiral Thomas H. Patterson.
3. Benjamin F. Stevens, U.S. dispatch agent, London.
4. Capt. John Lee Davis served in the European Squadron.

To Elizabeth M. Borie

> Singapore
> Straits Settlements
> Apl. 3d 1879.

MY DEAR MRS. BORIE:

Mr. Borie and Dr. Keating write to you very regularly, and keep you fully posted of all we see and do, but I thought you might not object to a line from me to confirm what they say: that we have actually been through India, and seen a great deal of it: through Burma[1] and the Straits Settlements[2] and seen a great deal in them beside very clever and hospitable people. We have been most hospitably treated every place we have yet been where British rule prevails. Mr. Borie enjoys it very much, though I think he would be rather glad to avoid the swallow tail and white cravat at dinner occasionally. Every night since we reached Bombay has been either a dinner party—often a reception following—or we have been traveling. I think Mr. Borie is much improved since we started.

He looks so and has got well enough to quarrel with the Dr. who tries to restrain him in his diet occasionally.—It looks now as if we would reach Japan by the middle of May if we do not go to Peking, and by the first of June if we do. I want to spend about a month in Japan and hope to hold Mr. Borie until I leave. But he seems anxious to hurry on home. If we are all together on our arrival in San Francisco—and I trust we will be—I hope we will meet you, Mr. Childs, Mr. Drexel and other Phila friends in San Francisco prepared for long excursions in that most interesting country. Mrs Grant joins me in much love to you and all our Phila friends.

Very Truly Yours
U. S. Grant

ALS, PHi. An envelope stamped as received in Philadelphia, May 17, 10:00 P.M., is *ibid.*

1. See John Russell Young diary, March 19–25, 1879, DLC-John Russell Young; *New York Herald*, May 1, 1879; *Young*, II, 170–87; John M. Keating, *With General Grant in the East* (Philadelphia, 1879), pp. 108–20; *Julia Grant*, pp. 277–80.

2. See Young diary, March 28–29, 1879, DLC-John Russell Young; *Young*, II, 187–94; Keating, *With General Grant*, pp. 121–28.

On March 29, Walter Scott, chairman, Penang Chamber of Commerce, welcomed USG. ". . . Should you by God's Providence again assume the reins of Government, we feel convinced that the interests of America will not suffer in your hands, and that the Bond of friendship now existing between your nation and ours will be cemented if possible more strongly than ever. We hope that the remainder of your tour will prove as successful as it has hitherto been, And we sincerely trust that your life may long be spared to your family and Country." DS, Smithsonian Institution. USG replied "that he was extremely obliged to the gentlemen of the Chamber of Commerce of Penang, for their address, and for the reception that had been accorded to him. This however was only in keeping with the cordiality and hospitality he had received from every part of the British empire he had visited since his landing in Liverpool nearly two years ago. His reception in England was continued with unabated, he might say with increasing kindness, in the colonies of Great Britain and throughout the vast Indian empire which he had just visited. This was very grateful to him, not alone because of the kind and f[la]ttering words with which these receptions were always accompanied, and to which he was far from being insensible, but because it showed a good feeling towards his own country. In that sense, more than any other, the kindness he had received in England, and in English colonies was grateful because he believed that the welfare of the Anglo Saxon race,—he might say of the world depended more than upon any other cause upon the harmony and good feeling of this one people—one people in race and civilization, although two nations. He did not think it was any disrespect to the other great civilized powers of Europe,—he certainly did not so intend—when he said that the civilization which finds its home in England is better calculated than any other to bring the greatest good to mankind. Wherever he saw a new growth of this civilization, as in Penang, he felt that it would be in the end, a great blessing to the people of all classes. An allusion had been made to his own efforts when he was in office, to bring about a settlement of the questions at issue between England and America at the close of the war. That policy he wished to say, was simply carrying out a conviction which he had entertained long before he held any office, that the first thing to be considered in our relations with other nations was a good understanding with England. With this conviction, he felt it his first duty to urge with all his ability the settlement of the questions arising out of the war, and the removal of all festering sores between the two countries. He regarded the existence of such questions as a scandal. He had no reason to feel dissatisfied with the results of those efforts, and his experience since he came abroad only confirmed him in that belief. The two nations were now as one nation in the development of their civilization, and he wished every effort of the English success because the advancement of the common civilization of the two countries meant the happiness, the prosperity and the peace of the world." *Straits Times Overland Journal* (Singapore), April 5, 1879.

Also on March 29, Chinese merchants and residents welcomed USG, noting "that it is the first time that a visit has been paid to Penang by so distinguished a representative of the United States of America. We therefore avail ourselves of this occasion to bring to your Excellency's notice that formerly no restrictions were placed on emigration from China, but, latterly, restrictions have been imposed, and we solicit your Excellency's powerful influence on our behalf to advocate the removal of these restrictions and thus restore the intercourse between the two nations to its former footing. Should your Excellency be instrumental in reopening the ports of America to free emigration from China, your Excellency's name will ever be held in grateful remembrance." *Ibid.* USG replied that "it afforded him a special pleasure to receive the address which had just been read. He was about to visit China,—having received a warm invitation to do so, and he was very anxious to see with his own eyes the institutions and people of that country. To be met with a welcome from Chinamen in this Colony, therefore, was gratifying. There was one point in the address, in reference to the passage by Congress of a Bill restricting the emigration of Chinamen to the United States. He knew nothing of such a Bill, except what he had read in the telegraphic despatches in the last English newspapers. He knew nothing of the details of the Bill. He had been absent from the United States for some time, and was imperfectly informed of the public sentiment which had supported the Bill. In all questions like this, there were demagogues who would pander to prejudices against race or nationality, and favor any measure of oppression that might advance their interests. A good deal of the feeling against people of other races in the United States,—was demagoguery, and did not represent the better feeling of the country. In this question of Chinese emigration there was something to be said in favor of those who advocated a measure limiting emigration of the Chinese to America. In his earlier years, when a young officer in the army, the General said he spent some time in California, and saw then something of the beginning of Chinese emigration to the United States, and of the objections to that emigration on the part of good people. That was the beginning of this whole agitation. He remembered very well the objections. It was not to the Chinamen coming to the United States,—but to their coming in a condition of slavery. He hoped when he visited China to look into this question more closely, to see for himself the practical operations of the Chinese emigration to the United States, as it was a question on which he felt the deepest interest, affecting as it did the welfare of the two nations. But the gentlemen who presented this address could well understand the objections on the part of the American people to receiving emigrants who come, not as citizens, but as slaves. It was in order to free one race from slavery, to put an end to a condition of things that was degrading to both races,—black and white,—that we fought a long war, losing a great number of lives, with an enormous waste of treasure. This was a terrible sacrifice,—he questioned if any nation ever made a greater one. It was to suppress slavery. Having made these sacrifices to free the negro, it would not be expected that the Americans would consent to the revival of another victim of slavery in which the Chinaman and not the negro was the form. As he understood this question of Chinese emigration, the Chinese did not come as the people of other nations, of their own free will, to enjoy the benefits and the protection of the American Government, to have the fruits of their labor, and accept the responsibilities as well as the benefits of residence in America,—but as dependants, slaves of companies, who brought them as merchandize, held them in practical bondage, and enjoyed the fruits of their labor. As a consequence the Chinaman in America was not a member of our society, on the same footing with other races, entitled to all the benefits of our laws, with chances for improvement and prosperity, but the slave of a company. He felt sure that the gentlemen who had signed this petition, and who represented the flourishing Chinese community in Penang, would agree with him, that emigration to the United States, under those circumstances was not an advantage to us, and was a wrong to the people who were sent as emigrants. This in brief, said the General, was the objection to Chinese emigration on the part of Americans who had none but the kindest feelings towards the Chinese people and nation, and who would extend to them if they chose to make their home with us, the same welcome they extended to all the rest of the world. He mentioned these views, not as bearing on the Bill to which allusion had been made in the address, beceuse of the Bill he knew nothing, but as giving in a general way the feelings of the American people to the Chinese. He was only a citizen of the United States, without authority, in the councils or the government of the country, and consequently the authors of the address have overrated his influence in the settlement of the question. But it was one, which, as an American citizen, interested him greatly, and he looked with pleasure to his visit to China as enabling him to look into it, and make up his mind. He never doubted, and no one could doubt, that in the end, no matter what agitation might for the time being affect at home, the American people would treat the Chinese with kindness and justice, and not deny to the free and deserving people of that country what they offer to all the world. He begged again to thank the members of the Chinese community for their address, the reception of which had given him an especial pleasure." *Ibid.* For an editorial endorsing USG's remarks, see *China Mail* (Hong Kong), April 16, 1879.

To Elihu B. Washburne

———

Singapore,
Straits Settlement
Apl. 4th 1879.

MY DEAR MR. WASHBURNE:

Since my last letter to you I have seen much of the world new to me, and but little visited by our countrymen. The reality is different from my anticipations as to climate, characteristics of the natives, the Governments that have been forced upon them &c. &c. My idea had been rather that English rule in this part of the globe [w]as purely selfish, all for the benefit of "Old England" and pampered sons sent here to execute laws enacted at home, and nothing for the benefit of the governed. I will not say that I was all wrong, but I do say that Englishmen are wise enough to know that the more prosperous they can make the subject the greater consumer he will become, and the greater will be the commerce and trade between the home government and the colony, and greater the contentment of the governed. This quarter is governed on this theory, and, as far as my opportunities have given me the power to judge, by a most discrete, able and well chosen set of officials. My opinion is that if the English should withdraw from I[n]dia, and the East, they would scarsely get off the so[il] before the work of rapine and murder and wars between native chifs would begin. The retrograde to absolute barbarism would be more rapid than towards civilization is possible, it would be almost instantanious. As Mr. Young, who is traveling with me, gives accurate and detailed accounts of every place we visit, and all we see, nothing of this sort is necessary from me. I keep somewhat careful notes however—have since leaving Paris for the east—but doubt whether I shall ever use them further than for my own reference

The weather is getting very warm in this section and we must expect a good deal more of it before we get to a cool climate. In a few days we start for Bankok, Siam, and return here—within a degree of the equator—to take steamer for Hong-Kong. I shall then visit Chinese ports as far North as Shanghai—and possibly go to Peking—before visiting Japan. It looks now as if we would reach San Francisco as early as August. I am both home sick and dread going home. I have no home but must establish one after I get back; I do not know where.—Mrs Grant joins me in love to Mrs. Washburne and the children as well as to your. ~~self~~.

Yours Truly

U. S. GRANT

ALS, IHi.

To George W. Childs

————

Singapore
Straits Settlement
Apl. 5th 1879.

My Dear Mr. Childs,

It looks now as if my party would reach San Francisco some time in July. But when we leave Japan our departure will be telegraphed to the States so that it will be easy to calculate within a day when we will arrive. I shall hope to meet you, Mr. Drexel, Mrs. Borie and as many friends as will join you, there, prepared to make excursions to all points of interest on the Pacific coast, and to stop on our return at Virginia City, Salt Lake and in Colorado long enough to visit several places I know you would enjoy seeing. It will be a more interesting journey to you than a trip to the continent and will be free from the sea voyage.

We leave here on the 7th or 8th for Bangkok, Siam, and a few days thereafter for Hong-Kong & Canton. We will then coast up China,—stopping at all points of interest,—as far as Shanghai. If the inconveniences of travel are not too great we will go to Peking. The weather is getting very warm in this lattitude, but we are all as well as we can be. Mr. Borie is much improved and will claim the title, when he returns home, of the "Great Continental, African & Asiatic Explorer" in addition to the title of the "Great American Traveler.—Give all our love to all our Phila friends.—Take Gen. Patterson with you to San Francisco.

Yours Truly
U. S. Grant

ALS, ICarbS.

On May 14, 1879, Adolphus G. Studer, consul, Singapore, wrote to Frederick W. Seward, asst. secretary of state, that USG's party arrived "from Rangoon, all in good health, on the 1t ultimo, remained until 9th ultimo, when they, upon an autograph letter of invitation from the King of Siam, which I handed to the General here by request of Mr Sickles, our Consul at Bangkok, left for Bangkok, ~~left for Bangkok~~, returning hither on the evening of 22d ultimo and finding the U. S. S. 'Richmond' was not here to receive them they sailed early on the following morning on the French Messagerie Steamer 'Irawaddy,' touching at Saigon, for Hongkong. The Administrator, or acting

Governor of this Colony (Sir William Robinson, the actual Governor, went to England on leave about four months ago) Colonel Anson (Lieut Governor at Penang for several years), told me, before General Grants arrival that he would receive him with great honors, a salute and guard of honor, on arrival, and extend to him and party the hospitalities of Government House; but, I have been informed, two days before the General's arrival, that he received instructions from the Secretary of State for the Colonies not to receive the General with official honors, but to show him the honor and courtesy due a distinguished foreigner. I am told that the administrator was greatly grieved over this prevention to receive the General in the manner above shown, as originally intended. He did, however, extend to him the hospitalities of government House in a most liberal and courteous manner, as far as I have been able to observe, . . . I managed to find a quiet moment, within which I could inform the General, that he would not receive an official reception and only such as would be due to a 'distinguished foreigner' etc. but his equanimity did not seem in the least disturbed. . . . On the following day, April 3d H. H. the Maharajah of Johore, who, I had noticed, took great pains from the very beginning, to show great friendliness to the General and party (the sincerity of which I doubt greatly) gave a large banquet at his large mansion, a little distance from the city, in honor of the General and party, . . . It was a very quiet, spiritless sumptuous dinner—no more, no less!—The same 'ubiquitous magnitude,' the 'Maharajah' (a title received from the British, not from the Malays, who know him only, and very justly too, as 'Tumongong of Johore.' Tumongong, in Malay, means 'Chief of Police') subsequently invited the General and party and a few others, among which the Administrator and family to a Pic-Nic party or Excursion to his residence at Johore-Baru, on the mainland, which I did not attend. Among those showing hospitality to General Grant not one deserved more to be honored that the Hon. H. A. K. Whampoa, a Chinaman, member of the Colonial legislature, Consul for China and Vice Consul for Russia. . . . On landing, when all the different officers, Officials and Consuls were introduced to him, he shook hands with none, but broke through all the reserve when Mr Whampoa was introduced, by shaking hands warmly with him and saying: 'Mr Whampoa I am glad to meet you, I have heard of you before and how kindly you have always treated my countrymen.' That was a distinction for which the good old gentleman could hardly find an expression of gratitude and pride, as he himself assured me. He invited the General and party, the administrator and family and a few friends to luncheon on Friday, April 4th, and a very pleasant and happy entertainment it was. After luncheon he showed his guests his fine collection, and conducted them through his incomparable grounds, making here and there interesting explanations. It will be a great matter of pride and satisfaction for the rest of my days that General Grant and party also honored myself and daughter by accepting our invitation to luncheon on Saturday April 5th, at this Consulate, . . ." LS, DNA, RG 59, Consular Despatches, Singapore. See *China Mail* (Hong Kong), April 16, 1879; Studer to John Russell Young, May 23, 1879, DLC-John Russell Young; *Young*, II, 195–209; Keating, *With General Grant*, pp. 128–36.

A Hong Kong newspaper reported on "a letter from General Grant to the U. S. Consul (Colonel Moseby), in which he states that, while it is impossible for him to say when he will reach Hongkong, his plans are briefly these. He was to leave the Straits Settlements on the 6th or 7th for Bangkok, Siam; he spends several days there, and leaves for Saigon about the 18th. He takes the first steamer offering there for Hongkong, whether mail or no, and will advise the authorities here by telegraph when he leaves Saigon. It was the General's expectation to make the trip in the U. S. naval vessel

Richmond, but she was a month late in leaving the States, and has travelled very slowly. He has heard of her passing Aden, and hopes to see her in Hongkong when, or soon after, he arrives." *China Mail* (Hong Kong), April 15, 1879. See *ibid.*, April 24, 1879.

On May 10, a correspondent reported from Washington, D. C. ". . . In a private letter received from Gen. Grant, dated at Singapore, he says that he hardly expects to reach the United States before September; that he has found the wonders of the far East even more interesting than the attractions of Europe; that they represent a civilization so different from that of the Western Nations that he has only regretted that he could not delay his journey, which, however, the seasons would not permit. The whole party are enjoying excellent health, and are looking forward to their return home almost with impatience." *St. Louis Globe-Democrat*, May 11, 1879.

Speech

[*Bangkok, April 16, 1879*]

Your Majesty; Ladies and Gentlemen:—I am very much obliged to Your Majesty for the kind and complimentary manner in which you have welcomed me to Siam.—I am glad that it has been my good fortune to visit this country, to thank Your Majesty in person for your letters inviting me to Siam and to see with my own eyes your country and your people.—I feel that it would have been—misfortune if the programme of my journey had not included Siam.

I have now been absent from home nearly two years, and during that time I have seen every capital and nearly every city in Europe, as well as the principal cities in India. Burmah and the Malay Peninsular.—I have seen nothing that has interested me more than Siam, and every hour of my visit here has been agreeable and instructive.

For the welcome I have received from Your Majesty, the princes and members of the Siamese Government and the people generally I am very grateful. I accept it, not as personal to myself alone, but as a mark of the friendship felt for my country by Your Majesty and the people of Siam. I am glad to see that feeling, because I believed that the best interests of the two countries can be benefitted by nothing so much as the establishment of the most cordial relations between the two countries.

On my return to America I shall do what I can to coment those relations. I hope that in America we shall see more of the Siamese.—that we shall have embassies and diplomatic relations, that our commerce and manufactures will increase with Siam, and that your young men will visit our country and go to our colleges as they now go to colleges in Germany and England. I can assure them all—kind reception, and I feel that the visit will be interesting and advantagous. I again thank your Majesty for the splendid hospitality which has been shown to myself and my party, and I trust that your reign will be happy and prosperous and that Siam will continue to advance in all the act of civilization.

Copy, DLC-USG, IB. King Chulalongkorn of Siam welcomed USG. "Your Royal Highnesses Ladies and Gentlemen now assembled. I beg you to hear the expression of the pleasure which I have felt in receiving as my guest a President of the United States of America. Siam has for many years past derived great advantages from America whose citizens have introduced to my kingdom many arts and sciences, much medical knowledge and many valuable books to the great advantage of the country. Even before our countries were joined in treaty alliance, citizens of America came here and benefitted us—since then our relations have greatly improved and to the great advantage of Siam, and recently the improvement has been still more marked. Therefore it is natural that we should be exceedingly gratified by the visit paid to us by a President of the United States. His Excellency General Grant has a grand fame that has reached even to Siam that has been known here for several years we are well aware that as a true soldier he first won glory as a leader in war and thereafter accepting the office of President earned the admiration of all men as being a statesman of the highest rank. It is a great gratification to all of us to meet one thus eminent both in the government of war and of peace, we see him and are charmed by his gracious manner and feel sure that his visit will inaugurate friendly relations with the United States of a still closer nature than before and of the most enduring character. Therefore I ask you all to join me in drinking the health of His Excellency General Grant and wishing him every blessing." Translation, *ibid.* USG proposed a toast. "I hope you will allow me to ask you to drink the health of His Majesty the King of Siam. I am honoured by the opportunity of proposing his health in his own capital and his own palace, and saying how much I have been impressed with his enlightenal rule.—I hope you will unite with me in drinking the health of his Majesty and the prosperity of the people of Siam." Copy, *ibid.* On April 16, 1879, John Russell Young wrote in his diary. "We remained around home all morning & had portraits taken in Siamese costumes—Very Amusing—. . ." DLC-John Russell Young.

On Feb. 4, Chulalongkorn had written to USG. "Having heard from my Minister for Foreign Affair on the authority of the United States Consul that you are expected at Singapore on your way to Bangkok, I beg to express the pleasure I shall have in making your acquaintance. Possibly you may arrive in Bangkok during my absence at my country residence Bang Pa In in which case a steamer will be placed at your disposal to bring you to me. On arrival I beg you to communicate with His Excellency my Minister for Foreign Affairs who will arrange for your reception and entertainment." LS, DLC-USG, IB. On March 18, David B. Sickels, consul, Bangkok, wrote to USG from Singapore. "I have the honor to hand you herewith a letter written by His Majesty, the King of Siam, inviting you to visit Bangkok and become his guest. I have arranged with Mess Katz Brothers, the agents of the steamer *Kongsee*, for the conveyance of yourself and family and the members of your suite to Paknam (the mouth of the Menam river) where the King's steam yacht will await your arrival. I have to inform you that the Ambassador's House has been prepared for your accommodation and that every thing will be done by my self and the American residents at Bangkok to contribute to your enjoyment. It is my intention to return to Siam to-morrow for the purpose of completing the arrangements for your reception there." ALS, *ibid.* In an undated note, Frederick Dent Grant wrote to Young. "will you be kind enough to send the letter of invitation from the King of Siam to father up here. father wants to see it" ANS, DLC-John Russell Young.

On April 11, Chulalongkorn wrote to USG. "I have very great pleasure in welcoming you to Siam. It is, I am informed, your pleasure that your reception shall be a private one, but you must permit me to shew, so far as I can, the high esteem in which I hold the most eminent citizen of that great nation which has been so friendly to Siam, and so kind and just in all its intercourse with the nations of the far East. That you may be near me during your stay, I have commanded my brother His Royal Highness The Celestial Prince Bhanurangsi Swangwongse to prepare rooms for you and your party in the Saranrom Palace, close to my Palace and I most cordially invite you, Mrs. Grant and your party at once to take up your residence there, and my brother will represent me as your host" LS, DLC-USG, IB. See Young diary, April 12–13, 1879, DLC-John Russell Young; *New York Herald*, June 9, 1879.

On April 14, Robert O. Fuller wrote to USG, Bangkok. "Probably you were surprised at seeing me at the palace yesterday. I wish to explain, how it came about. When I landed the two gentlemen that came on board for you invited me to get into a carriage. I declined saying 'I did not belong to Gen. Grant's party.' One of them said 'I better go if I did not stay, as it would be worth seeing.' Hoping this explanation will be satisfactory to you, and wishing you and Mrs. Grant a pleasant and prosperous journey." ALS, DLC-USG, IB. Fuller was on a world tour of Baptist missions. See *New York Times*, March 10, 1903.

On April 14 and 15, USG and Chulalongkorn exchanged visits. Young diary, DLC-John Russell Young. The two discussed U.S.-Siamese relations during their second meeting. Young reported USG saying "that the policy of the United States was a policy of non-intervention in everything that concerned the internal affairs of other nations. It had become almost a traditional policy, and experience confirmed its wisdom. The country needed all the energies of its own people for its development, and its only interest in the East was to do what it could to benefit the people, especially in opening markets for American manufactures. The General, in his travels through India and Burmah, had been much gratified with the commendations bestowed upon American products; and, although the market was as yet a small one, he felt certain that our trade with the East would become a great one. There was the field at least, and our people had the opportunity. Nothing would please him more than to see Siam sharing in this trade. Beyond this there was no desire on the part of the American government to seek an influence in the East." Chulalongkorn lamented Siam's small population. "General Grant thought this difficulty might be me[t] by the introduction of skilled labor, such, for instance, as mining experts from Nevada and California, who could prospect and locate mines and labor-saving machinery in which the Americans especially excelled."

Chulalongkorn questioned USG "about the Chinese in America. The General said that there had been a large emigration of Chinese to the United States; that they brought with them many of the best qualities of laborers, but there was an objection in the minds of many good people at home to their arriving, as they did, in a condition of practical slavery." Asked if the Chinese came with their wives and children, USG "said that this was one of the difficulties—one that most offended the moral sense of people at home, the absence of domestic ties. This, and the condition of servitude in which they came, were the only objections that had any standing against the Chinese. As laborers they were good, and there were many fine points in their favor, many reasons why their labor was a benefit to a country with so much to develop as the United States." Asked whether Chinese immigrants paid taxes, "General Grant answered that in America there could be no tax upon labor, and that there could be no distinction between the labor of Chinamen and the labor of another race. What the State laws in States like California provided he was not aware, but his impression, as far even as California is concerned, was that the Chinaman paid nothing to the government in the way of taxation. A few large merchants in San Francisco paid taxes on their property. This, however, would not be regarded as a special hardship, if there were no slavery and the laborers came with their families. . . . The General said that it would be well for Siam to have embassies or diplomatic relations with other nations, and he asked why it would not be a good thing for Siam to send an embassy to the United States." Told that cost constrained the Siamese government, USG said "he felt sure that the government would receive any embassy His Majesty chose to send with the utmost cordiality. . . . The General asked whether it was not possible for the King to visit the United States and see the country. Such a visit would have a good effect, and he himself would be delighted to have the opportunity of entertaining his Majesty in the United States and returning some of the hospitalities he was now enjoying. . . . General Grant then referred to education in the United States and to the fact that the Siamese government had sent some of the young men to Germany and England for education. He suggested to His Majesty that it would be well to send some of these young men to American colleges. Other nations had done so, ruling families in Europe as well, notably the Chinese and Japanese. We had splendid schools in the United States, and the young men would return home with a better idea of the American people and the country. The King might depend upon those young men having the best reception; not merely a good education and careful training, but every personal courtesy. . . ." *New York Herald*, June 22, 1879.

On April 16, Joseph W. Torrey, vice consul, Bangkok, wrote to Young. "The Consul desires me to inform you that the Foreign Consuls propose calling on Gen. Grant. this p. m. between the hours of 4.30 and 5.30. as arranged yesterday" ALS, DLC-John Russell Young. On April 18, John H. Chandler, interpreter, Bangkok, wrote to Young denigrating U.S. consuls as "played out politicians and adventurers." ALS, *ibid.* For Torrey's eventful career, see *New York Times*, July 5, 1885.

On April 17, Chulalongkorn wrote to USG. "I am sorry that my Private Secretary Phyā Bhāskarawongse could not accompany you this morning as it was necessary for him to attend the family ceremony of pouring water on his brother the Ex-Regent. I performed that ceremony this afternoon and now have commanded him to rejoin you. Mr. Alabaster if his health permits will also place his service at your desposition tomorrow morning" LS, DLC-USG, IB. On April 18, USG, Paknam, telegraphed to Chulalongkorn. "On my departure from your territory allow me to renew my thanks for your many acts of courtesy during my brief visit to Siam. I shall ever remember it with

pleasure and entertain the hope that I may be able some day to return it, in part by receiving and entertaining in my own country some of those near and dear to you." Copy,
ibid. See letter to King Chulalongkorn, May 16, 1879; Young diary, April 17–18, 1879,
DLC-John Russell Young; *Young,* II, 218–60; John M. Keating, *With General Grant in
the East* (Philadelphia, 1879), pp. 137–57; *Julia Grant,* pp. 281–83.

On Monday, April 14, 11:00 A.M., Sickels had written to "My Dear Sir," presumably Young. "I sent Mr Torrey this morning to inform the General that the Steamer
'*Thales*' would leave here for Hong Kong on Friday or Saturday. I write now to state
that I have since learned that she may not depart until Sunday. I have engaged passage
for the party, subject, of course, to the General's approval. She is a fine vessel and the
apartments are equal to those of the *Kongsee.* I have arranged for a ball at the Consulate on Friday night. . . . *P. S.* I have opened this letter to add that I have just received
unofficial informati[on] that the Siamese governmen[t] intends to send Genl Grant &
his party on the Str. *Bangkok* to Saigon." ALS, DLC-John Russell Young.

To Archibald Anson

———

           Steamer *Bangkok.* Singapore, April 22nd, 1879.
Col Anson, Administrator Straits Settlements.
MY DEAR COLONEL,

    I have just returned this p. m. to Singapore from a very pleas-
ant visit to Bangkok, expecting to find the U. S. steamer *Richmond*
here to take myself and party away. She not being here however,
and not likely to arrive before the end of the month, I have determined to take the French steamer, now in port, and which leaves
at seven o'clock in the morning. This will prevent me calling in
person to pay my respects to you and Mrs Anson, and thanking
you again for your kind hospitalities while we were guests at your
house. On the part of Mrs Grant and myself, and all those with me,
we renew our invitation to yourself and family to make our houses
your home if you should ever visit the United States.

                        Very Truly Yours
                        U. S. GRANT.

Archibald Edward Harbord Anson, *About Others and Myself 1745 to 1920* (London,
1920), pp. 363–64. Archibald Anson, veteran British army officer and colonial administrator, served as act. governor, Straits Settlements. Anticipating USG's return to the
presidency, Anson questioned Julia Dent Grant on her plans for the White House. She
answered, then added with reference to her husband, "If he heard me he would knock
my head off." *Ibid.,* p. 362. See *The Times* (London), Feb. 27, 1925.

To Ellen Grant Sartoris

Apl. 30th /79

DEAR DAUGHTER:

We are now approaching Hong-Kong, China, from where I understand a mail leaves to-morrow noon. As we are to be the guests of the Governor General,[1] and there may be a dinner party, receptions &c. I may not have the opportunity of writing to you after landing and before the departure of the Mail. Your Ma is in deep anxiety of hearing from you on our arrival at Hong-Kong, and hopes to find a dispatch saying that you are well.—I have been writing to you very regularly, but do not recollect whether I said any thing about our visit to Siam? We went there, spent six days most pleasantly, and returned to Singapore where we confidantly expected the Richmond. But learning that she was at Ceylon and would not reach Singapore for a week I determined to leave by the first steamer going my way. Fortunately one was in port, bound for Hong-Kong, and to sail at seven the next morning. We took it—a very fine steamer of the Messajerie line—and are now here not expecting ever to see the vessel which was fitted out for us until we get to Yokohama, Japan, and then it will be too late to use her.[2] From Yokohama we will go to San Francisco by the regular Mail Steamer. Our stay at Hong-Kong will probabl[y] be over a week. Before leaving there we will visit Canton, one of the most charistic of the Chinese Cityies, and some nine hours up the river from Hong-Kong. From the latter place we will go direct to Shanghai, thence to Peking, bringing us to Yokohama, probably, about the middle of June. Spending three or four ~~months~~ weeks there we will sail direct for San Francisco.—Your Ma, Fred, & I send much love to you Algie & the babe.[3]

Yours Affectionately

U. S. GRANT

ALS, ICHi. For USG's arrival at Hong Kong, see John Russell Young diary, April 30, 1879, DLC-John Russell Young; *China Mail* (Hong Kong), April 30, 1879; *Young*, II, 309–10; John M. Keating, *With General Grant in the East* (Philadelphia, 1879), pp. 164–67.

1. John Pope-Hennessy, appointed governor of Hong Kong in Nov., 1876. See *The Times* (London), Oct. 8, 1891.

2. On April 23, 1879, John Russell Young, Singapore, wrote in his diary. "Mailed my letters home, and went on board the Irawaddy for Hong Kong.—General has a despatch from *Richmond* that it will be in Singapore on the 28th and is very angry at apparent trifling with him We play at Boston until four in the afternoon and are all tired out." DLC-John Russell Young. See Adolphus G. Studer to Young, May 2, 1879, *ibid.*; *Young*, II, 262–63; Keating, *With General Grant*, pp. 158–61.

In April, USG drafted a telegram to Rear Admiral Thomas H. Patterson, Yokohama. "Will be HonKong with Richmond thirtyeth." ADf (undated telegram sent), DLC-John Russell Young. On the same sheet, USG wrote to Young. "Will the Commodore please put this on a form and forward it. We will be in Hong-Kong before the 30th but will not get away before that time. The object is to give Adml Patterson as much time as possible to join us if he wishes to go along as I suspect he does." AN, *ibid.* On May 4, USG, Hong Kong, wrote to Patterson. "Capt. Perkins was kind enough to place the *Ashuelot* at my disposal and to say that he had instructions from you to do so. To-morrow I avail myself of your kindness and . . . go to Canton. I think I shall also take her to run up to Shanghai. . . ." Kenneth W. Rendell, Inc.

3. On April 7, Ellen Grant Sartoris gave birth to her third child, Vivien May.

To Elihu B. Washburne

Government House,
Hongkong. May 4th /79

MY DEAR MR. WASHBURNE,

I am just in receipt of your letter of the 4th of Feb.y, from SanaAntonio. I was in San Antonio in Dec. 1845 when it was but little else than a Mexican Town, and isolated from all settlements. From Corpus Christy to San Antonio there was not a family except a few Mexicans scattere[d] along the San Antonio river for some miles below the town. From there to Austin there was not a habitation except at New Bransfelt, which which had been colonized, I think, that year.

We are now on the home stretch, letters going much quicker to America by the East than by the West. Up to this time myself and party have had the same hearty welcome and kind hospitalities as we experienced throughout India. It promises to be the same thing throughout China & Japan. At this place I have received official notification from both governments of their desire to make my stay among them as pleasant as possible.[1] This is really the most beautiful place I have yet seen in the East.[2] The City is admirably built & the scenery is most picturesque. The harbor is made by the irregular high land on the main shore and innumerable islands coming up out of the sea and rising to a height of from 500 to 1700 ft. above. We go to-morrow to Canton,[3] thence to Shanghai[4] & Peking. On the way we will make short stops at several Chinese Sea Ports. I expect to reach Yokohama about the last of June, and San Francisco late in August. I expect to remain on the Pacific for some weeks and then to go to Galena to remain until the weather gets cold. Where we will spend the winter I have not determined. We may go to Florida & Havana—With kindest regards of Mrs Grant, Fred, & myself to you and all your family,

I am, very Truly yours,

U. S. GRANT

ALS, IHi. On June 14, 1879, Elihu B. Washburne wrote to USG. "I write this at a venture and send to Yokohamo, but am very doubtful whether it will reach you. I therefore send [p]ress copy to San Francisco. I received yours, d[a]ted Hongkong on the 4th ulto. a few days ago. I was very much gratified to know that you would go to Galena on your return. That determination will be well received by all your friends. Gov. Rice of Massachusetts, one of your best friends, breakfasted with me the very morning I got your letter and he expressed the utmost satisfaction in learning what you proposed to do. I returned from Galena this morning. I saw to it that your friends will have everything in perfect order to receive you. I found all inside the house in as good order as could be expected. Mr. Felt will see that everything is made ready and comfortable. It would perhaps be well for Mrs. Grant to have some few things sent out by Buck, such as the crockery, cutlery table linens etc. etc. and perhaps some pictures for the parlor. I think there is a full supply of bedding. There will be plenty of time to have this done after your arrival at San Francisco. I assure you that you will find the place delightful, and have no doubt you will enjoy some weeks of rest there very much. To be sure most of your old friends have gone, but you will see all the people you want to, and others besides. I hope you will be good enough to keep me posted as to your movements after you reach California as I must arrange many matters so as to be at Galena before and at the time of your arrival. I suppose Fred will arrive here in advance of you and he can tell me a good deal. Mrs. W. and the childr[en] were quite well at last accounts. Kindest regards to Mrs. G. and Fred. . . ." ALS (press), DLC-John Russell Young. See *Galena Gazette*, June 12, 1879.

1. On April 9, Durham W. Stevens, secretary of legation, Tokyo, had written to Secretary of State William M. Evarts. "I take pleasure in informing you that the Japanese Government have expressed the desire to make General Grant their guest during his anticipated visit to Japan. At the request of Mr Terashima I telegraphed this to General Grant at Calcutta, and I understand that instructions have been given to the

Japanese Consul at Hong Kong to formally tender to the General on his arrival at that place the invitation of the Japanese Government to accept their hospitality during his sojourn in Japan. . . ." LS, DNA, RG 59, Diplomatic Despatches, Japan.

2. At a dinner on May 3, Governor John Pope-Hennessy of Hong Kong introduced USG, who replied. "I am very grateful to you for your kind address, to which I would be happy to respond, but there is so much personal and flattering to myself that I find it impossible. It is only a continuance of the kindness that I have received not only in England, but in India, and in the British colonies; wherever, in fact, I have met Englishmen, I have met nothing but courtesy, hospitality, and good-will to myself and my country. As you have said, I am about to leave the British and pass into the Chinese Empire. I have met no gentlemen so kind as the gentlemen of England. For this reception, more especially for the reception in Hongkong, I am grateful, as I know my friends and countrymen at home are grateful for the kindness that I have been honoured with during the last two years. I do not know that I can say anything better, nor anything which is nearer to my heart, now that I am leaving the British Empire, than to ask you all to unite in this sentiment: 'The perpetual friendship and alliance of the two great English-speaking nations of the world—England and America.'" *Hongkong Government Gazette,* May 14, 1879. See *China Mail* (Hong Kong), May 5, 1879.

3. In April, Charles P. Lincoln, consul, Canton, had "received a letter from General Grant, in which the General accepts the Viceroy's invitation to visit the provincial capital." *North-China Herald* (Shanghai), April 29, 1879.

On May 6, Young wrote in his diary on USG's three-mile trip to visit Viceroy Liu K'un-i of Canton. ". . . I regard this Canton procession, as among the most extraordinary scenes in my life.—Estimated that two hundred thousand people on the way to meet & see the General." DLC-John Russell Young. On the next day, the viceroy returned USG's visit and later provided "a long and curious dinner." *Ibid.,* May 7, 1879.

Also on May 6, Gideon Nye *et al.,* "American residents of Canton," presented an address, dated May 5, to USG expressing "the hope that your personal observation among the people of Canton,—where the Chinese can be best studied understandingly in their own homes,—will enable you to correct the misconceptions among our Countrymen of the Pacific States which tend to impair the compact of friendly comity to which our Government constrained the reluctant Rulers of China in 1844 and again in 1858. Trusting that you can afford time for such study; and offering our individual personal aid to that end, . . ." DS (14 signatures), DLC-USG, IB; Df (printed), DNA, RG 59, Applications and Recommendations, Hayes-Arthur. In response, USG "expressed his gratification at the unanimity of his countrymen in approval of his public services, and alluded to his and Mrs Grant's happiness in meeting in their travels communities of Americans, especially when, as here, they found them in friendship with each other; that he had visited many peoples and received many hospitalities, but always felt that the attentions he received were not for himself personally, but in honor of the Great Nation from which he and all who heard him came: and in his travels nothing pleased him more than to meet his own Countrymen. That in communities of Americans like that in Paris, for instance, the attractions to continued residence were largely in their own circle as a distinct colony, and that this home-like association reconciled many to absence from home: But that for mere travellers like himself, seeking pleasure, they should go home as soon as they could; and that was what he was now doing. That the pleasure they had in meeting the American community here was all the greater because of the distance from home." *China Mail* (Hong Kong), May 10, 1879. See also *ibid.,* May 6–8, 1879.

At a banquet on May 8, Lincoln toasted USG by stating "his deliberate judgment, that the good of the United States will be promoted in the highest degree by the resumption of office by the ex-President; who, in the maturity of his strength and judgment, and enriched by the experience gained in travel, possesses an assemblage of qualities of incomparable value to the Nation." Replying, USG "adroitly evaded the eulogium of his host, after acknowledging its warmth and the reception accorded it by those present, by recalling that in the various countries of Europe which were represented on this occasion by their respective Consuls and citizens, he had received the utmost courtesy and kindness from both Rulers and people and was therefore doubly gratified now, in that the present reminded him of his European experience of pleasurable intercourse, whose associations thus followed him around the world towards his home; where they would remain in cherished remembrance." *Ibid.,* May 10, 1879.

On May 16, Lincoln wrote to Charles Payson, 3rd asst. secretary of state. ". . . I am pleased to say that notwithstanding the advice of the British Consul to His Excellency the Viceroy, that General Grant was not entitled, more than any private Citizen—to any recognition or reception at the hands of the Native Authorities, they received him with courtesies never before extended to any Foreigner—. . ." ALS, DNA, RG 59, Consular Despatches, Canton. Related clippings are *ibid.* See letter to Liu K'un-i, May 16, 1879; *New York Herald,* June 27, 1879; *Young,* II, 311–44; John M. Keating, *With General Grant in the East* (Philadelphia, 1879), pp. 170–94.

4. On April 7, Shanghai residents had held a public meeting to prepare for USG's visit. See *North-China Daily News* (Shanghai), April 8, 1879.

To William H. Forbes et al.

———

Hong Kong, 10th May /79

Messrs Forbes, ~~Hopkins~~ [Hoppins] and Keswick: Committee
Gentlemen:

I am just this moment—4 30 p. m.—put in possession of your note of this date informing me that the Committee of arrangements for the Garden party to be given this evening have appointed you a special committee to notify me that on account of the threatning bad weather they propose to postpone the party until Monday evening—the 12th—and ask me to accept for that evening. I am sorry to say that my arrangements for leaving here on Monday morning are such that I do not feel justified in making any delay beyond that date. Answers have been sent to enquiries as to the date of my arrival at Shanghai, and at two or three other points we expect to touch by the way. I regret not meeting, in a social way, the Citizens of Hong Kong who have been kind enough to give me this invitation and hope I may meet each and all, if not together, separately, at a later day in some part of the world.

> I am, with great respect,
> your obt. svt.
> U. S. GRANT

ALS (bracketed word in another hand), ICU. For William H. Forbes and William Keswick, see *New York Tribune*, July 11, 1897; *The Times* (London), March 11, 1912.

On May 4, 1879, Forbes and his wife invited USG and Julia Dent Grant to "dinner on Friday evening next the 9th instant at eight o clock." D, DLC-USG, IB.

Speech

[*Hong Kong, May 12, 1879*]

Mr. NG CHOY and Gentlemen, I thank you for this valuable address. It will be kept by me as a pleasing memento of the Chinese community of Hongkong. In other Colonies during my recent travels I have also met countrymen of yours, and I have found the rulers of those Colonies recognising your good qualities of frugality, industry, and enterprise. Such qualities go far to account for the prosperous condition in which I see you all here. I am now leaving Hongkong to visit your country,[1] and I am sure I shall see much that will be very interesting to me. For this handsome address[2] I must again thank you most sincerely, and I shall never forget the kindness shown to me by the people here. I wish that prosperity may continue to be enjoyed by you.

Hongkong Government Gazette, May 14, 1879. Chinese residents of Hong Kong composed an address, dated May, 1879, to welcome USG. ". . . We have been delighted to find that, in international questions you have shown a spirit of impartiality and fairness, treating Americans and Foreigners alike: and the Chinese who have been trading in the United States have sung, and continue to sing, praises of the many good actions done by you while in office. . . ." Translation (95 names), DLC-USG, IB. For Chinese lawyer Ng Choy, or Wu T'ing-Fang, see Howard L. Boorman, ed., *Biographical Dictionary of Republican China* (New York, 1967–79), III, 453–56.

On May 1, USG had visited John S. Mosby, consul, Hong Kong. "Whilst there he received a deputation from the Chinese community, consisting of Messrs. Ng Choy, Lee Tuk Cheong, and Lee Sing, who waited upon him to invite him to attend a Chinese dinner, and asking him to fix a time to suit his convenience. The General replied that he was much obliged to them for their kindness in wishing to provide for his entertainment, but that at present he was unable to fix any definite period, though he would most certainly accept the invitation. . . ." Visiting Mosby again on May 2, USG "said that on his arrival here he was very much surprised to see so many American ships in port, and he had not seen so many vessels flying the stars and stripes together since he had left England." *North-China Daily News* (Shanghai), May 8, 1879. See *China Mail* (Hong Kong), May 1–2, 1879; Charles Wells Russell, ed., *The Memoirs of Colonel John S. Mosby* (Boston, 1917), pp. 396–98.

1. For USG's departure from Hong Kong, see *China Mail* (Hong Kong), May 12, 1879.

On May 6, Isaac F. Shepard, consul, Hankow, had written to USG. "I have the honor to invite you to visit Hankow while you are in China, and to tender you all the attention in my power. . . ." ALS, DLC-USG, IB. USG did not visit Hankow.

2. "The address, which was sixteen feet long by four feet wide, and extremely handsome, was embroidered in gold on a strip of crimson satin about ten feet long, with a rich deep border exquisitely embroidered. The characters are written in Chinese. On the top of the scroll is written the address, on the right side is General GRANT's name in Chinese, and on the opposite side are the signatures. . . ." *Hongkong Government Gazette*, May 14, 1879.

To King Chulalongkorn

UNITED STATES STEAMER ASHUELOT,

NEAR SHANGHAI, May 16, 1879.

TO HIS MAJESTY THE KING OF SIAM:—

DEAR SIR—Just before leaving Hong Kong for Shanghai I received your very welcome letter of the 20th of April,[1] and avail myself of the first opportunity of replying. I can assure you that nothing more could have been done by Your Majesty and all those about you to make the visit of myself and party pleasant and agreeable. Every one of us will retain the most pleasant recollections of our visit to Siam and of the cordial reception we received from yourself and all with whom we were thrown in contact.

I shall always be glad to hear from you and to hear of the prosperity and progress of the beautiful country over which you rule with so much justice and thought for the ruled.

My party are all well and join me in expression of highest regards for yourself and Cabinet and wishes for long life, health and
happiness to all of you and peace and prosperity to Siam. Your
friend.

U. S. GRANT.

New York Herald, June 30, 1879. On Oct. 8, 1879, King Chulalongkorn of Siam wrote to
USG. "I have received Your Excellency's two letters date 16th May and 22nd August
and am very pleased to hear that you still look back with satisfaction to your visit to
Siam and keep in friendly remembrance myself, my country, and those who assist me
in governing and taking care of the prosperity of my people. I also have most pleasant
recollections of your visit I regard it as most fortunate and advantageous to my country, and myself that so eminent a man should have come here and himself seen the condition of things in Siam, and enabled me to have his intimate friendship. I thank you
for the expression of your conviction of what is certainly true, that Asiatics have much
to complain of in the treatment they received from other nationalities, and I trust that
your opinion will led all foreigners to reflect and see the truth that hitherto in their
dealings with Asia they have mostly shown very little consideration of the difficulties
and troubles they have brought on Asiatics. I am very glad to be able to inform you that
the diplomatic troubles which was vexing us at the time of your visit is now at an end.
His Excellency Phya Bhaskarawongse my private secretary was sent to England as my
Envoy and was well received by H. B. M. Government which gave careful consideration to his representations, acknowledged the right of Siam as an independent Kingdom to deal with its own people according to its own laws, and has replaced Mr. Knox
by another Political Agent. Phya Bhaskarawongse is now on his return journey. I know
that you who saw and knew our trouble will be very glad to hear that we are now clear
of all difficulty. On September 4th My Royal Consort gave birth to a second Prince,
and both she and her son remained strong and well for three weeks when the child died
almost suddenly, and the mother sorrowing fell ill, but I trust her illness will not prove
serious. I am glad to hear that Mr. Borie and Dr. Keating have reach home well but I
am sorry that you should have lost the companionship of Mr. Borie whose genial society must have much enlivened your travels. Short as was my acquaintance with him,
I often think of him. Please assure Mrs. Grant and the gentlemen who travelled with
you of my high regard, and remembrance, and hope that their return to America may
be happy and prosperous. I trust that Your Excellency's own life may continue to be
blessed with all honour and happiness, and I beg you to continue a regular correspondence with me." LS, Mrs. Paul E. Ruestow, Jacksonville, Fla. See Adolphus G. Studer
to John Russell Young, June 9, 1879, DLC-John Russell Young.

On May 26 and Oct. 8, David B. Sickels, consul, Bangkok, had written to Young.
"*Personal*. . . . I enclose herewith an autograph letter recently received from His Majesty
and a translation of the same, relative to the death of Prince Kaphia, of which sad event
I informed you in a previous letter. Permit me to say in this connection that it would be
highly gratifying to the King if Genl Grant would write a letter of condolence to him.
This young Prince was very attentive during the General's visit and it is stated that his
exposure and exertions hastened his death. . . . I am having some Siamese publications
on *Gunnery* translated for Genl Grant." "*Personal* . . . The letter addressed to the King
by General Grant and which was forwarded to me sometime ago, was personally presented to His Majesty during a private audience at the palace. The King permitted me

to read the letter and desired me to communicate the fact of its receipt by him together with the assurance that its friendly tone and generous sentiments afforded him great pleasure. The General's letter of condolence, which you intimated it was his intention to write, before his departure from Japan, has not, as yet, reached me. . . . Please say to Mrs Grant that I am gathering the seeds and some other little curios for her and will send them as she directed me to do. . . ." ALS, *ibid.* See Sickels to Young, May 18, Nov. 15, 22, 1879, *ibid.*

1. On April 20, Chulalongkorn had written to USG. "I received your kind telegram on leaving Siam and was very pleased to hear that you were satisfied with your reception. Your reception was not all I could have wished for I had not sufficient notice to enable me to prepare much that I desired to prepare, but the good nature of your Excellency and Mrs. Grant has made you excuse the deficiencies. You will now pass on to wealthier cities, and more powerful nations, but I depend on your not forgetting Siam, and from time to time I shall write to you and hope to receive a few words in return. I shall certainly never forget the pleasure your visit has given me and shall highly prize the friendship thus inaugurated with Your Excellency and Mrs. Grant. I send my kind regard to Mr. Borie wishing him long life, health and happiness, and with the same wish to yourself and Mrs. Grant and your family . . ." LS, USG 3. On April 25, Sickels wrote to Young. "*Personal* . . . I herewith enclose a letter received from His Majesty's private Secretary with instruction to forward it to Genl Grant. I am informed that it is His Majesty's reply to the General's telegram. An answer was received by wire at Paknam and delivered to Mr Alabaster, but it came too late—just after the 'Bangkok' left. . . . Please say to Mrs Grant that I will carefully select the Lotos and other seeds she desired and send them in a small tin case to her son in New York   I send by the Steamer 'Dale,' a bottle of 'Lotos Perfume' for Col Grant, which will be hande[d] to Col Moseby for delivery to him   With many pleasant remembrance[s] of the General and party, . . ." ALS, DLC-John Russell Young. See Speech, [*April 16, 1879*].

To King Kalakaua

UNITED STATES STEAMER ASHUELOT,
NEAR SHANGHAI, May 16, 1879.

His Majesty King KALAKAUA:—

DEAR SIR—On the eve of my departure from Hong Kong for Shanghai, China, I was put in possession of your very polite invitation of the 18th of February for me to visit your kingdom, and to be the guest of Your Majesty. I can assure you that it would afford me the greatest pleasure to accept your invitation if I could do so. I have always felt the greatest desire to visit the Hawaiian islands, and cannot say positively yet that I may not be able to do so. But it will be impossible for me to give a positive answer until I get to Japan and learn of the running of the vessels between Yokohama and Honolulu, and between the latter place and San Francisco.

I shall visit Pekin before going to Japan, and remain in the latter country a month or six weeks. As soon as it is determined whether I am to have the pleasure of visiting your most interesting country or not, I will inform you, hoping that I may be able to go. Your friend,

U. S. GRANT.

New York Herald, June 30, 1879. On Feb. 18, 1879, King Kalakaua, Honolulu, wrote to USG. "The public newspapers give me the information that you are at present on your passage to the East and are intending to return to the United States across the Pacific Ocean. When I was in the United States during your Presidency, you manifested such interest in the prosperity of my Kingdom that I am proud to think it will not be uninteresting to you to observe the progress we have made and the general state of the Country. I need not remind you that other travellers have found the natural features of the Islands, and more especially their volcanic phenomena interesting, and I entertain a hope that if you accept the invitation which I now tender to you to visit us as a guest of myself and this nation on your return to your native country, such a visit will be a pleasant remembrance to you. For myself it will afford me a great gratification to receive and entertain you, and my people will be proud to do everything in their power to make your visit agreeable." ALS, USG 3. On Feb. 17, James M. Comly, U.S. minister, Honolulu, had written to Secretary of State William M. Evarts transmitting King Kalakaua's autograph letter and a copy (dated Feb. 16). ". . . His Majesty requests me to ask that the Department telegraph to San Francisco, to be forwarded to me here, information as to when General Grant may be expected to reach here." LS, DNA, RG 59, Diplomatic Despatches, Hawaii. On March 10, Frederick W. Seward, act. secretary of state, wrote to Comly that King Kalakaua's letter "has been forwarded to General Grant through the United States Legation at Tokei, Japan." Copy, *ibid.*, Diplomatic Instructions, Hawaii.

On March 3, John Russell Young, Delhi, wrote to Comly. "General Grant received your letter dated 24 Decr. today. He requests me to thank you for your invitation to make his home with you. He thinks he will be in Honolulu sometime in June, as he hopes to be home in July, but cannot say definitely. Of course you will know his movements after leaving China and Japan. They include a visit to the Sandwich Islands which he is anxious to see. We hope to be in Calcutta in a week, and to be in Ceylon the latter part of the month.—" ALS, OHi.

On Sept. 24, Comly, San Francisco, wrote to USG. "If it is possible, will you be kind enough to wedge me in somewhere for a five or ten minutes talk about the Sandwich Islands? We are all much disappointed that we are to miss seeing you at the Islands, and I would like to take back some pleasant message to the King. If you can see me late this evening, after the crowd is over, I will wait your direction, and will be extremely gratified." ALS, *ibid.* USG endorsed this letter. "I will be glad to see Gen. Comly after my return from the 'Camp Fire' this evening, say about 11 o'clock." AES (undated), *ibid.* USG attended this veterans' event on Sept. 27. On Oct. 25, 1880,

Comly, Honolulu, wrote to a State Dept. official that he and USG discussed the importance of advantageous U.S. relations with China and Japan. ALS, DNA, RG 59, Diplomatic Despatches, Hawaii.

To Liu K'un-i

UNITED STATES STEAMER ASHUELOT,
NEAR SHANGHAI, China, May 16, 1879.
HIS EXCELLENCY THE VICEROY OF KWANGTUNG AND KWANGHAI:—

DEAR SIR—Before leaving Hong Kong for more extended visits
through the Celestial Empire, I was placed in possession of your
very welcome letter giving expression to the best wishes of Your
Excellency and of all the high officials in Canton for myself and
mine. Since then it has been my good fortune to visit Swatow and
Amoy, both, I understand, under Your Excellency's government,
and have received at each the same distinguished reception accorded at Canton. Myself and party will carry with us from China
the most pleasant recollections of our visit to the country over
which you preside and of the hospitalities received at your hands.

Mrs. Grant desires to thank you especially for the beautiful
specimens of Chinese work which you presented to her. With the
best wishes of myself and party for your health, long life and prosperity, and in hopes that we may meet again, I am your friend,

U. S. GRANT.

New York Herald, June 30, 1879. In early May, 1879, Viceroy Liu K'un-i of Canton wrote
to USG. "It has been a high honor and a source of the deepest satisfaction to myself,
the High Provincial Authorities and the gentry and people of Canton that Your Excellency whom we have so long desired to see, has thus been so good as to come among
us. Upon learning from you of your early departure while I dared not interfere to delay
you I had hoped, in company with my associates to present my most humble respects
at the moment of your setting out, and I refrained from doing so only in obedience to
your command I have ventured to send a few trifles to your honored wife which I hope
she will be so kind as to accept. I trust that you & she will have a prosperous journey
throughout all your way, and that you may both be granted many years and abundant
good. Should I ever [b]e honored by my Sovereign with a mission abroad it will be
my most devout prayer and earnest desire that I may meet you again I Respectfully
wishing you the fulness of peace" L (undated translation), DLC-USG, IB. For Liu
K'un-i, see Arthur W. Hummel, ed., *Eminent Chinese of the Ch'ing Period (1644–1912)*
(Washington, 1943–44), I, 523–24.

To Julius Stahel

Shanghai, China
May 18th 1879.

My Dear General:

I have your letter of the 23d of Apl. enclosing the kind invitation of Mr. Walsh for myself & party to occupy his & his firms houses during our stay at Hiogo, and also at Yokohama. I find here a telegram of the 14th of May saying that the Governor of the province requests us to occupy at Hiogo the house specially prepared for myself & party, by order of his Imperial Majesty. Of course this latter will be accepted, and an acknowledgement of the invitation will be made as soon as the letter extending the invitation is received.[1]

Please say to Mr. Walsh that I feel under the same obligations to him & Mrs. Walsh[2] for their kind kind invitation that I would if it was accepted.

Very Truly Yours
U. S. Grant

Gen. J. Stahel U. S. Consul.

ALS, NjP. Julius Stahel, consul, Yokohama (1866–69), served as consul, Osaka and Hiogo, after USG's presidency. See *PUSG*, 11, 131; DNA, RG 59, Letters of Application and Recommendation. On April 23, 1879, Stahel, Hiogo, wrote to USG. "It gives us much pleasure to know that we shall soon have the honor of welcoming you to our little settlement, and I enclose herewith an invitation from Mr. Th. Walsh in which I most heartily join.—Pray be assured that we shall use our best efforts to make your, Mrs Grant's and your guest's stay here as pleasant a one, as is within our power. I also enclose a communication from the American Missionaries residing at Hiogo, Osaka and Kioto—Trusting that your arrangements will permit you to honor us by making our house your home during your stay at Hiogo—. . ." ALS, DLC-John Russell Young. On the same day, Thomas Walsh, Kobe, wrote to USG, Shanghai. "My friend General Stahel informs me that you and your party may shortly arrive in Japan, and I therefore address you to say that I shall be very happy to place my firm's house here at your disposal during your stay—General Stahel, who has apartments and his Consulate in our house, joins me in this invitation and writes to you accordingly—If you will do us the honour to accept it kindly mention the probable date of your arrival so that arrangements may be made for your comfort—I beg at the same time to say that it would give Mrs Walsh and me much pleasure to receive you and Mrs Grant in our house, at Yokohama, where we intend returning shortly—Should you prefer the peaceful liberty of a private dwelling to the ceremonious civilities which are in store for you, we shall feel honoured to have you as our guests, and to do whatever we can to render your visit enjoyable to you—" ALS, DLC-USG, IB. Jerome D. Davis, former lt. col., 52nd Ill., and four others "representing nearly fifty American missionaries" also had written to USG. "In common with all Americans residing in Japan, the American Missionaries laboring in the cities of Kobe, Osaka, and Kioto welcome you to the shores of their adopted country. . . . Again, not only did the success of the Armies under your command make Americans living abroad proud to own their nationality, it also put our Country in position to join with other Christian and civilized nations in extending the hand of Sympathy and help, to those nations and peoples less favorably situated.—Not to speak of advantages given in the way of commerce, it may be safely said that America has taken the lead of all other nations in advancing the educational interests of Japan—But the *Preserved Union* has enabled us especially to give to other nations that institution more than all else characteristic of the American people, more closely than all else inwoven with the very life of our nation, the religion of our fathers,—the Religion of Jesus Christ; and so you will not be surprised to find that the number of Christian missionaries from America laboring in Japan is more than double the aggregate from all other lands—Proud as we are, that for months and years we were allowed to follow the Star-spangled banner through Evil and good report, we are far gladder and prouder to follow the Banner of the Cross on to its sure victory. Such are a few of the many reasons which prompt us to give you a special welcome to Japan. We therefore ask that, if your other arrangements allow it, you will honor us and the other American residents of the community, with a quiet social interview at the *Girl's School* of the *American Board, Kobe* or at such other place, and at such time as may suit your convenience—" LS (undated), *ibid.* See *PUSG*, 21, 311–17; *New York Tribune*, Sept. 4, 1901; J. Merle Davis, *Davis: Soldier, Missionary* (Boston, 1916).

1. For this invitation, dated Hiogo, May 16, see DLC-USG, IB.
In late June, USG telegraphed to Stahel indicating his inability to stay at Kobe. *Japan Herald* (Yokohama), July 1, 1879. On June 30, John Russell Young, U.S.S. *Richmond*, wrote in his diary. "This afternoon we come to anchor in the bay of Hiogo,—or Kobe. The cholera interferes with landing. The Consul Mr Stahel comes off and we have a pleasant chat. The Gen. gives a dinner party to *Richmond* people, and we all remain up late conversing—The town is in illumination, and makes a most beautiful effect. . . ." DLC-John Russell Young. See *Japan Herald* (Yokohama), July 10, 1879; *Young*, II, 509–12. Quarantined from Toyko in early July, Stahel sought assistance from USG, "who, however, replied that he was bound to obey the regulations issued to guard against the spread of the epidemic." *Japan Herald* (Yokohama), July 7, 1879.
2. Walsh's wife, Katharine, was the youngest daughter of John A. Dix, former governor of N. Y.

To Edward F. Beale

UNITED STATES CONSULATE GENERAL.
SHANGHAI. May 23d 1879,

MY DEAR GENERAL:

A mail is just in and brings your letter of the 13th of March. Yours of the 3d reached me at Hong Kong. The dialogue which you give that took place between you and a Northern democratic Congressman is discouraging enough. But I have strong faith in the people when real danger comes. The experience of the rebellion is not going to be thrown away. Should there be a second rebellion during the life of people engaged in the last it would be dealt with most summarily, and would be so thoroughly put down as to keep it down for ever. You would not witness again the instigators of rebellion dictating laws for the govt. of the loyal.

I have now been in this greatest commercial city of China six days. My reception has been the most cordial and most demonstrative I have witnessed since leaving England. But Young's letters to the Herald will give full description. We leave in an hour for Tientsin & Peking.¹ After going to the great wall we will go to Japan where I shall stay five or six weeks. I should like to go back by Honoluluʸu but doubt whether I will be able to do so.²

Mrs. Grant joins me in much love to you and all your family.

Very Truly your friend

U. S. GRANT

GN. E. F. BEALE.

ALS, DLC-Decatur House Papers.
On May 17, 1879, R. W. Little welcomed USG on behalf of "the Foreign Community of Shanghai." ". . . Devoted as we are to trade, we have little to shew that is of interest to the ordinary traveller. But as the head for two periods of a great cosmopolitan, commercial State, we trust that you will find something to interest you in this small commercial Republic, itself as cosmopolitan as the great country from which you come. . . ." USG replied. "Gentlemen of the Committee,—I am very much obliged to you for the very hearty welcome which you have extended to me, and I must say I have been taken a little by surprise—an agreeable surprise. I have now been a short time in the country of which Shanghai forms so important a part in a commercial way, and I have seen much to interest me, much to instruct me, and much I wish I had known ten or twelve years ago. I hope to carry back to my country a report of all I have seen in this part of the world that will be of interest, and possibly something new to the people at Home. I thank you again for the hearty welcome which you have have given me." *North-China Daily News* (Shanghai), May 19, 1879. See also *The Celestial Empire* (Shanghai), May 20, 1879.
Also on May 17, H. H. Winn, Shanghai Bowling Club, wrote to David H. Bailey, consul gen., Shanghai, inviting USG to visit the club. ALS, DLC-USG, IB.
On May 18, John Russell Young, Shanghai, wrote in his diary. ". . . In the evening a dinner and a long talk of the war, and war events until late Gen. said if he had known the ground as well after the battle of Mission Ridge as before he would have destroyed the army of Bragg. Thinks Thomas should have done so,—certainly" DLC-John Russell Young.
On May 19, Shanghai fire brigades paraded by torchlight to honor USG. An accidental explosion marred the event. See *North-China Daily News* (Shanghai), May 20–21, 1879; *The Celestial Empire* (Shanghai), May 20, 1879.

On May 21, USG attended a ball at the Shanghai Club. In response to a toast, USG said "that he was really much interested in one matter that was spoken about, and for which he had been given some credit. He referred to the *Alabama* affair, in regard to which he had felt that all differences between the two countries should be settled in an amicable matter, and that they should go along peaceably and pleasantly together. He gave great attention to the affair, endeavouring to bring about a peaceable settlement so that they might live as good friends and brothers." Concerning his visit to Shanghai, "he was happy to meet so many Europeans—so many English, French, Germans and members of all nationalities—people who represented the high civilisation and the whole civilised world, and he hoped that the same brotherhood which existed between the two English speaking nations would exist between other countries." *The Celestial Empire* (Shanghai), May 27, 1879.

On May 22, W. Saunders photographed USG. *North-China Daily News*, May 30, 1879. On May 27, Saunders billed USG $21 for twenty-four cabinet portraits. D, DLC-USG, IB.

Also on May 22, USG breakfasted with George French, chief justice of the supreme court for China and Japan at Shanghai, and later attended a garden party at the residence of Francis B. Forbes, agent, Russell & Co. *North-China Daily News* (Shanghai), May 23, 1879. See French to Young, May 17, 1879, and Forbes to Young, June 17, 1879, DLC-John Russell Young.

On June 2, Bailey wrote to Charles Payson, 3rd asst. secretary of state that USG's "reception here, by the entire community, Foreign and Native, marks an era in the history of Shanghai, as being the grandest ovation ever given to any person since the establishment of Foreign Relations with China. I may mention that as the escort filed through the Consular Compound in review by the General, the refrain of 'John Brown's Body' was involuntarily taken up, making a striking and touching incident of the reception in this 'Far off Land.'" LS, DNA, RG 59, Consular Despatches, Shanghai. Related clippings are *ibid.* On March 9, 1869, U.S. Representative John A. Smith of Ohio had written to USG. "Hon David H. Baily of Wilmington, Ohio is an applicant for Consul General to the Port of Shanghai, in China—. . . He has made the peculiar civilization of China an object of close investigation and thought, and has special fitness for that service in behalf of his goverment—. . ." ALS, *ibid.*, Letters of Application and Recommendation. On July 19, 1870, Jesse Root Grant, Cincinnati, wrote to USG. "I learn that you sent in the name of D H Bailey, the Elector of the 6th Ohio District, as Consul at Hong Kong, and that the Senate did not have time to act on his nomination. The Senate having failed to confirm Col Golding there is a vacancy. Now I write this letter to urge you to appoint Mr Bailey to the vacancy. Mr B is in every way fitted to fill the place, and certainly he is entitled to some recognition at your hands. For some time past Mr B has been connected with the Editorial Staff of the Cincinnati Chronicle, and has ably and faithfully supported your administration through the columns of that paper: He has also in several instances defended you in the paper from personal attacks made by malicious enemies in other papers. Mr Baileys endorsements are of the highest character and his appointment would give satisfaction to many of your personal as well as political friends. I earnestly reccommend that you appoint him." LS, *ibid.* Related papers are *ibid.* On Dec. 6, USG nominated Bailey as consul, Hong Kong. In 1879, after his appointment as consul gen., Shanghai, Bailey was charged with corruption while at Hong Kong. See *HED*, 46-2-20.

1. See Young diary, May 23, 1879, DLC-John Russell Young; *North-China Daily News* (Shanghai), May 24, 1879.

2. See letter to King Kalakaua, May 16, 1879.

To Gen. William T. Sherman

Tientsin, China,
29th May 1879.

MY DEAR GENERAL:

I am now getting so far on my way round the world that it is time to give you an opportunity of fixing the date for the meeting of the ~~Army~~ Society of the Army of the Tenn. I go from here to Peking, and on my return will go directly to Nagesaca; stop there a few days and one or two days at each of two other cities before going to Yokohama, reaching the latter place about the last of June. I will want from four to six weeks in Japan after reaching Yokohama, so that if I should go directly to San Francisco I will reach there the last of August or first of Sept. But when I get to Yokohama I may find Adm.l Patterson inclined to run up to the Amoor river in which case I would go with him. This would entail a further delay. Then too I have not been on the Pacific coast for a quarter of a century and naturally feel desirous of visiting all the places I have seen before, and which it is probable I will never have another opportunity of visiting. I would suggest therefore that you fix the date of the Army meeting now for some time about the middle of October and if I can be there I will; if not will send you a letter setting forth my regrets and reasons for my absence.

I have been much interested in my eastern trip, but have seen no place, except the upper Nile, that I would care to visit the second time. The fact is I have found no place abroad, no country, equal to our own as a permanent home.

Mrs. Grant joins me in kindest regards to yourself, Mrs. Sherman & the children

Yours Truly
U. S. GRANT

GEN. W. T. SHERMAN
COMD.G ARMY OF THE U. S.

ALS, DLC-William T. Sherman. On July 17, 1879, Gen. William T. Sherman wrote to USG, via San Francisco. "I was glad to receive your letter of May 29th from Tien Tsin,

China, and to learn your purpose to come home, to reach San Francisco in Early September, and Chicago in middle October. I have notified the officers of the Society Army of the Tennessee, but at the same time intimated my purpose not to publish a call for the annual meeting until you have actually reached San Francisco—Three or four weeks, which you propose to pass in California and Oregon, will be ample time for us. The telegraph now announces, that by reason of a declared purpose of some of your friends to go out to San Francisco to meet you, having a political purpose, you have changed your mind, will visit Australia and so manoeuvre as *not* to reach the United States until after the Convention has actually met and named the next Republican candidate for President. I hope this is not true, but that you will consult your own convenience and come home when you have completed one of the grandest and most complete tours of the world ever made by any man. You remember I was earnest for you to make this trip so as to reach California en route for Chicago, about October of this year, and I am now of the same mind & conviction, and will be much disappointed if you vary your plan because of the indiscreet purpose of irresponsible men, acting from selfish motives, and not from the impulse of a pure friendship & respect. I am sure your real friends will prevent the intrusion upon you of any except the people of San Francisco & California, who are perfectly able & perfectly willing to make your welcome back as warm & enthusiastic as you can wish or hope for. Afterwards, the people of Oregon, Nevada, Utah, Wyoming, Nebraska &c. can each in turn receive you at their doors, and do what hospitality and cordiality require, but that no set of men should intrude on you outside their 'bailiwick.' This is what I understand is your wish, and if made known in advance, would be respected, and you would be free to settle down at such place as you please, uncommitted till forced to act. I therefore hope you will come home as soon as you feel so disposed and not change your purpose, because some indiscreet friends have talked of coming to San Francisco to meet you. It seems to be my fate to be placed in delicate relations with my friends & comrades. At this moment a fierce political contest is about to be inaugurated in Ohio, between the two great parties, of which my Brother John and my Brother in Law, Tom Ewing are the leaders. The second places on the tickets being filled by two of my personal favorites among the younger Brigadiers of the army—viz: Hickenlooper & Rice. Already have I been solicited to make public expressions in favor of one or the other of these parties, but decline emphatically. As soldiers I stand ready to endorse *both*, as politicians, they must blow their own trumpets. And now it looks as though in 1880 I would be forced into a similar relation between U. S. Grant and John Sherman. I know what you will say, but don't know what false impressions may be made by mischievous gossips. I will endeavor now to make my feelings plain to you, hoping this letter may catch you when about to embark on the ocean with plenty of leisure to read long letters. Had the Democratic party held out as they began at the outset of the extra session— General U. S. Grant would have been the inevitable candidate for President in 1880, and would have been elected, because the people were alarmed at the declarations of purpose of the southern leaders—Blackburn, Beck, Tucker &c. &c. These in effect threatened to force the President to get along without money to support the army and the Judiciary, unless he consented to ignore the laws made in pursuance of the new amendments to the Constitution. Indeed I myself heard Blackburne & Tucker assert on the floor of the House that the Democratic party had an inherited right to govern this country; that they meant to do it, and to obliterate from the Statute Book ever[y] law made since 1861. This alarmed the country very much, and all minds turned naturally to you. But the Democrats soon perceived their mistake; receeded from their position, and after three months angry debate, made all the necessary appropriations except for the US. marshals—

nominally claiming that the Democratic party would sustain the Executive in every thing Except the use of Deputy marshals to be employed to influence the elections of members of Congress. The general impression of danger to the country from the Democratic party has now died away and the two parties are manoeuvering to elect their own Congress and their own President, with far less apprehension of actual danger than was naturally felt last summer. John Sherman has gained large fame in managing the Treasury, and has his circle of Satellites. He wrote a personal letter to some friend in New York, in which he used an expression:—'If selected by the Convention as Presidential candidate in 1880, I would advocate honest money; the union of all men who fought in the Civil War' &c &c. This letter was given to the public, which has jumped to the conclusion that thereby he has indicated a wish & purpose to be such a candidate. If that be his wish & purpose he conceals it from me, but I know him to be ambitious and confident of his power and nerve, he would doubtless accept a nomination and of course it would be unnatural for me to oppose or qualify his purpose. He once asked me if you would be content to have your name placed on the Retired list as General—like General Scott; and Secretary of War McCrary asked me if I thought you would accept the mission to England if Mr. Welsh insisted on his own recall, intimating the propriety of such an offer to you, because Nellie resided in England. So I infer your existence is the subject of discussion among the powers that be. All I have ever answered was that such offer should be made you, when the emergency arises, and when your answer would be followed by speedy fulfilment. I doubted however if you would answer a supposititious question. Some of your real friends have expressed to me a doubt if you can be nominated & elected by reason of the general objection to the Third Term, unless there was actual danger apprehended, but this danger, it is contended, has already passed away, and the Republican party has many able & ambitious competitors for the office, who are unwilling to admit that there is but one man however eminent, able to fill the place—such as Blaine, Conkling, John Sherman Logan & other comparatively young men. All your friends contend that you have not and will not, by word or deed, indicate a wish to be the nominee unless the country call again for you with a uninimity which is overwhelming but they further contend that in every event the country must provide for you some honorable employment, to consume your time, and to provide for the necessary wants of your family and dependants. Thus stands the case today, and I hope you will come home quietly at your own time—see your friends & let Time solve this question for you, as it has many others in the past. Many changes are occuring daily among our old Comrades showing that our age is approaching the limit of activity and usefulness. New men are arising equal to the duties of the day & hour; and our country generally seems to be on the eve of a new epoch of prosperity if not of speculation. Your eye will take in evidence of this fact at every step of your progress after you reach our shores at San Francisco. No matter what the papers say, you will find all the machinery of Government working as smoothly & harmoniously in America as at any former period of our history. My folks are now at the sea shore—Atlantic City, N. J. My best love to Mrs. Grant & Fred." Copies (2), *ibid.* A recent column had identified "a private letter received from General Grant" as the source for reporting USG's intention to extend his time abroad. "He expects that his Australian tour and possibly a voyage along the west coast of South America, the isthmus and Mexico will consume the period between the present and the early part of June next, by which time he expects that the excitement incident to a Presidential nomination will be over. He, however, is much gratified at the tone of the leading republican and independent journals of the country in condemning, as they have, the machinations of these people, as he thinks a political movement inspired and operated by such influences could only bring the party into discredit and throw it on the defensive; that it was important for the party to purge itself of such material rather than to encourage it. The General has not forgotten the kind offices of his real friends, and the step which he has now taken has been as much out of deference to them as a matter of personal relief to himself. He feels that by this course he can make that discrimination between those who have been worthy of his confidence and those who have betrayed him for their own selfish purposes." *New York Herald*, July 10, 1879. See also *ibid.*, May 31, Oct. 6, 1879; *Chicago Inter-Ocean*, Aug. 1, 1879. In late April, Sherman had exchanged views with Hamilton Fish on USG's return to San Francisco. See Sherman to Fish, April 28, 1879, DLC-Hamilton Fish; Fish to Sherman, April 29, 1879, Sherman to Fish, April 30, 1879, DLC-William T. Sherman; *New York Times*, April 22, 24, 1879; *New York Herald*, April 22, 26, 1879. In July, Frederick Dent Grant, Tokyo, wrote to Sherman on travel to San Francisco, Chinese affairs, and dishonest consuls. ALS, DLC-William T. Sherman.

On May 16, Adam Badeau, consul gen., London, had written to Sherman. "... My last letter from Genl Grant was written when he was leaving India. It seems uncertain when he will reach the Pacific coast. The longer he stays away the better I shall like it. No matter what his future is to be—he will be better off out of America for a whole year yet. It will be impossible to persuade those who hate him and the cause he represents that he is not their most formidable enemy, and as soon as he lands in America the attacks will begin. Why should he not escape them for another year? I confess I look upon his return to politics with no feeling of exultation. Now he is *above* them. If his own happiness only were consulted, he would remain there. ..." ALS, *ibid.* See also Badeau to Sherman, June 7, 1879, *ibid.*

Speech

[*Tientsin, May 30, 1879*]

Your Excellency and Gentlemen,—I am very much obliged to you for the welcome I have received in Tientsin, which is only a repetition of the kindness that has been shown to me by the representatives of all nations since I came within the coasts of China. I am grateful to the Viceroy for the especial consideration which I have received at his hands. His history as a soldier and a statesman of the Chinese Empire has been known to me—as it is known to all at Home who have followed Chinese affairs for a quarter of a century, and I am glad to meet one who has rendered such great services to his country. My visit to China has been full of interest. I have learned a great deal of the civilization, the manners, the achievements and the industry of China that I had never known before. My visit to China has increased my estimate of the civilization and the character of the Chinese people, and I shall leave the country with increased feelings of friendship towards them, and a desire that they may be brought into relations of the closest commercial alliance and intercourse with the other nations. I trust that the Viceroy will sometime find it in his power to visit my country, when I shall be proud to return as far as I can the hospitality he has shown me. Again returning to you all—to the Viceroy whose guests we are, and to you who represent here the nations of Europe—my thanks for your courtesy, I ask you to join with me in a toast to the prosperity of China and the health of the Viceroy.

North-China Daily News (Shanghai), June 10, 1879. Through a translator, Viceroy Li Hung-chang of Chihli had toasted USG. After the banquet, "the whole party assembled in a group, and were photographed, the General and the Viceroy sitting in the centre, with the foreign guests standing on the General's side and the Chinese on the Viceroy's side." *Ibid.* Li, who advocated the modernization of China, greatly admired USG. See *ibid.*, June 2, 1879; John Russell Young, *Men and Memories* (New York, 1901), II, 303–25; Arthur W. Hummel, ed., *Eminent Chinese of the Ch'ing Period (1644–1912)* (Washington, 1943–44), I, 464–71.

On May 29, 1879, USG and Li attended a dinner arranged by the French consul and enjoyed "a lengthy conversation and quiet smoke." *North-China Daily News* (Shanghai), June 10, 1879. See also *North-China Herald* (Shanghai), June 10, 1879.

Speech

[*Peking, June 5, 1879*]

GENTLEMEN—I am much obliged to you for your welcome and for the compliments you pay me. I am glad to meet you and to see in the capital of this vast and ancient Empire an institution of learning based upon English principles, and in which you can learn the English language. I have been struck with nothing so much in my tour around the world as with the fact that the progress of civilization—of our modern civilization—is marked by the progress of the English tongue. I rejoice in that fact, and I rejoice in your efforts to attain a knowledge of English speech and all that such a knowledge must convey. You have my warmest wishes for your success in this and in all your undertakings, and my renewed thanks for the honor you have shown me.

New York Herald, Aug. 13, 1879. USG replied to an address, dated June 5, 1879, from tutors and students at Tung-wen College, Peking. "We have long heard your name, but never dreamed that we would have an opportunity to look on your face. . . . It is our sincere hope that another term of Presidency may come to you, not only that your own nation may be benefitted, but that our countrymen resident in America may also enjoy the blessings of your protection." *North-China Daily News* (Shanghai), June 17, 1879. USG then toured the college with its president, Presbyterian missionary William A. P. Martin. See Martin, *A Cycle of Cathay* . . . (New York, 1896), pp. 324–25.

On June 3, Martin, representing U.S. citizens in Peking, had read an address to USG. "Twenty years ago, the American flag for the first time entered the gates of this ancient Capital. For the greater part of that time your countrymen have been residing here under its protecting folds; and it is with feelings of no ordinary type that we gather ourselves beneath its shadow this day to welcome your arrival; because, to you, Sir, under God, it is due that its azure field has not been rent in fragments and its golden stars scattered to the winds of heaven. . . . Hoping that your influence may contribute to the adjustment of difficulties which threaten to reach so disastrously our American interests in China; and that thereby you will add another to the many laurels that crown your brow, we hail your visit as both opportune and auspicious; and again, with one heart, we bid you welcome to the Capital of China." *North-China Daily News* (Shanghai), June 13, 1879. USG replied that "he was always glad to meet his fellow countrymen, and the kind words in which he had been welcomed added to the pleasure which such a meeting afforded in Pekin. The Americans were a wonderful people, he said, smiling, for you found them everywhere, even here in this distant and inaccessible capital. He was especially pleased with the allusion in the address to the fact that in America a career was possible to the humblest station in life. His own career was one of the best examples of the possibilities open to any man and every man at home. That feature in America he was proud to recognize, for it was one of the golden principles in our government. The General again thanked the delegation for their kindness, wished them all prosperity in their labors in China and a happy return to their homes, where he hoped some day to meet them." *New York Herald*, Aug. 12, 1879. See *North-China Daily News* (Shanghai), June 5, 1879; *Young*, II, 379–402; *Julia Grant*, pp. 287–89.

Conversation with Prince Kung

[*Peking, June 5, 1879*]

General GRANT—I have long desired to visit China, but have been too busy to do so before. I have been received at every point of the trip with the greatest kindness, and I want to thank your Imperial Highness for the manner in which the Chinese authorities have welcomed me.

Prince KUNG—When we heard of your coming we were glad. We have long known and watched your course, and we have always been friends with America. America has never sought to oppress

China, and we value very much the friendship of your country and people. The Viceroy at Tientsin wrote of your visit to him.

General GRANT—I had a very pleasant visit to the Viceroy. He was anxious for me to visit Pekin and see you. I do not wish to leave Pekin without saying how much America values the prosperity of China. As I said to the Viceroy, that prosperity will be greatly aided by the development of the country.

Prince KUNG—I suppose your railways and roads have been a long time building?

General GRANT—I am old enough—almost old enough—to remember when the first railway was built in the United States, and now we have 80,000 miles. I do not know how many miles there are under construction, but, notwithstanding the arrest of our industries by the war and the recent depression of trade, we have continued to build railways.

Prince KUNG—Are your railways owned by the State?

General GRANT—It is not our policy to build roads by the State. The State guaranteed the building of the great road across the continent; but this work is the result of private energy and private capital. To it we owe a great part of our material prosperity. It is difficult to say where we would be now in the rank of nations but for our railway system.

Prince KUNG—China is not insensible to what has been done by other nations.

General GRANT—The value of railroads is to disseminate a nation's wealth and enable her to concentrate and use her strength. We have a country as large as China—I am not sure about the figures excluding Alaska, but I think practically as large. We can cross it in seven days by special trains, or in an emergency in much less time. We can throw the strength of the nation upon any required point in a short time. That makes us as strong in one place as another. It leaves us no vulnerable points. We cannot be sieged, broken up and destroyed in detail, as has happened to other large nations. That, however, is not the greatest advantage. The wealth and industry of the country are utilized. A man's industry in interior States becomes valuable because it can reach a market. Otherwise his industry would be confined necessarily to his means of subsistence. He would not enjoy the benefits enjoyed by his more favored fellow citizens on the ocean or on the large rivers in communication with the markets of the world. This adds to the revenue of the country.

Prince KUNG—If the world considers how much China has advanced in a few years it wi[l]l not be impatient. I believe our relative progress has been greater than that of most nations. There has been no retrocession, and of course we have to consider many things that are not familiar to those who do not know China.

General GRANT—I think that progress in China should come from inside, from her own people. I am clear on that point. If her own people cannot do it it will never be done. You do not want the foreigner to come in and put you in debt by lending you money and then taking your country. That is not the progress that benefits mankind, and we desire no progress either for ourselves or for China that is not a benefit to mankind. For that reason I know of nothing better than to send your young men to our schools. We have as good schools as there are in the world, where young men can learn every branch of science and art. These schools will enable your young men to compare the youngest civilization in the world with the oldest, and I can assure them of the kindest treatment, not only from our teachers but from the people.

Prince KUNG—We have now some students in your American colleges.[1]

General GRANT—Yes, I believe there are some at the college where one of my sons studied, Harvard.

Prince KUNG—We propose to send others to your schools and European schools, so long as the results are satisfactory. What they learn there they will apply at home.

General GRANT—I understand China has vast mineral resources. The Viceroy at Tientsin told me of large coal fields as yet undeveloped. If this is so the wealth of such a deposit is incalculable and would be so especially in the East. America and England have received enormous advantages from coal and iron. I would not dare to say how much Pennsylvania, one of our States, has earned from her coal and iron. And the material greatness of England, which, after all, underlies her moral greatness, comes from her coal and iron. But your coal will be of no use unless you can bring it to a market, and that will require railroads.

New York Herald, Aug. 13, 1879. Interjections by other Chinese officials omitted. Prince Kung, or I-hsin, directed the Chinese foreign office, or Tsungli Yamen. John Russell Young compressed the discussion into dialogue. "What I have written may seem a short conversation. But it was really a long conversation. In the first place it was a deliberate, slow conversation. There was a reserve upon the part of the Chinese. They were curious and polite.... The part of the conversation which impressed Prince Kung most was the suggestion that real progress in China, to be permanent, must come from the inside—from the people themselves." *Ibid.* See *North-China Daily News* (Shanghai), June 17, 1879; *Young*, II, 404–9; Arthur W. Hummel, ed., *Eminent Chinese of the Ch'ing Period (1644–1912)* (Washington, 1943–44), I, 380–84.

1. Since 1872, Yung Wing, or Jung Hung, who graduated from Yale in 1854, had administered the education of Chinese students in the U.S. See Wing, *My Life in China and America* (New York, 1909); letter to Samuel L. Clemens, Dec. 24, 1880.

To Daniel Ammen

PEKING, CHINA, June 6th, 1879.

MY DEAR ADMIRAL,—

I have now been in Peking three days, and have seen all there is of interest to see in this forsaken city. Since our arrival we have received an American mail, and with it your two letters of the 6th and 17th of April. I am delighted that you consented to be our representative at the Congress to discuss the question of the Inter-Oceanic Canal,[1] because I do not believe there is another American who understands the relative advantages of the one feasible route over all others, nor who can state the advantages and obstacles in the way of other routes as clearly as you can. If any of the officers who made surveys of any of the proposed routes for the canal had been sent, they would have been mere representatives of the particular route they had surveyed. It might have done to have sent all of them, as witnesses to testify to their work, but under one who had examined the whole field impartially.

I have found China and the Chinese much as you have often described it and them. It is not a country nor a people calculated to invite the traveller to make a second visit. But they are a people of wonderful shrewdness and industry, and are rapidly monopolizing the trade, as carriers, merchants, mechanics, market-gardeners, and servants, from Bombay eastward. Then, too, their leading men seem to have a thorough appreciation of the necessity for internal improvement, such as railroads, etc., but have a horror of introducing them with foreign capital and under foreign control. Their idea seems to be rather to educate a sufficient number of their own young men abroad to fit them as engineers, machinists, soldiers, sailors, etc., and then to make their improvements with their own men and means. My belief is that in less time from now than the half-century since you and I first went to J. D. White's school in Georgetown elapses, Europe will be complaining of the too rapid advance of China.

Mrs. Grant joins me in love to you, Mrs. Ammen, and the children, and also to Mrs. Atocha.

Very truly yours,
U. S. GRANT.

ADMIRAL D. AMMEN, *U. S. Navy.*

Daniel Ammen, *The Old Navy and the New* (Philadelphia, 1891), pp. 546–47.

1. This congress convened in Paris on May 15, 1879. Elected a vice president, Daniel Ammen abstained from the vote approving a canal across Panama. See *ibid.*, pp. 475–76; letters to Daniel Ammen, July 16, Aug. 7, 1879; Ammen, *The American Inter-Oceanic Ship Canal Question* (Philadelphia, 1880).

To Adolph E. Borie

Peking, China,
June 6th /79

MY DEAR MR. BORIE,

We have now been in this Capitol three days and have seen all there is to see, and that precious little to interest. You have lost nothing, except the society of the party, by not coming. Tientsin is a more populous city than Shanghai and more repulsively filthy. The passage from there to within twelve miles of this city is made in what are called House Boats, and they can be made very comfortable. Judge Denny, our Consul at Tientsin,[1] fitted ours up for us from furniture from his own residence. The kitchen was in a separate boat drawn along side. Fred. & the Commodore had a separate boat, three of the young officers from the Ashuelot another, a Mandarin, sent by the Vice roy, another, the vice consul of Tientsin[2] and an American—Mr. Hill[3]—another; and then two Gunboats sent by the Vice roy. The motive power for all this fleet was men—trackers—who pulled the boats the whole distance. We made the distance—170 miles by river—in two & a half days. The country past through is the most unattractive imaginable. It is a dead level all the way, and but little above low water. The population—a teaming one—reside in villages along the banks with the ground raised some few feet above the natural level to protect them from the annual overflows. It is safe to say that where you find Chinese homes—in their own country—you may put down the population at 150.000 to the square mile. I do not know that this would include women and children. But few of the former are seen, but from the number of the latter—generally seen naked up to ten years of age—it is inferable that the former must be somewhere about. I do'nt see how the fact is explainable otherwise.

The Commodore promises me that he will write you a letter also. I leave him for the discriptive part of our journey. Mrs. Grant sends her love to Mrs. Borie, and all our Phila friends, as I do. Remember us specially to your brother,[4] Mr. Drexel, Mr. Childs & Gen. Patterson.

Very Truly Yours
U. S. GRANT

P. S. Give my special regards to Dr. Keating and tell him to kiss the little girl for me. U. S. G.

ALS, PHi. On May 21, 1879, Adolph E. Borie and John M. Keating left Shanghai for Philadelphia. See John Russell Young diary, May 20–21, 1879, DLC-John Russell Young; *North-China Daily News* (Shanghai), May 22, 1879; Keating, *With General Grant in the East* (Philadelphia, 1879), pp. 214–27.

1. On March 10, 1873, U.S. Senator John H. Mitchell of Ore. wrote to Secretary of State Hamilton Fish recommending Owen N. Denny, Portland lawyer and police

court judge, as consul, Amoy, China. ALS, DNA, RG 59, Letters of Application and Recommendation. On Feb. 13, 1875, USG nominated Denny as collector of Internal Revenue, Ore. In 1877, Denny accepted appointment as consul, Tientsin. See letter to James A. Garfield, Feb. 18, 1881; Robert R. Swartout, Jr., *Mandarins, Gunboats, and Power Politics: Owen Nickerson Denny and the International Rivalries in Korea* (Honolulu, 1980), pp. 1–16.

2. William N. Pethick. Probably in early June, 1879, Denny wrote to John Russell Young. "If Mr Pethick *can* go to Peking with the General he would have an *honest* interpreter at the yamen & Perhaps if the Genl would request him he might go—. . ." ANS (undated), DLC-John Russell Young. See letter to Chester A. Arthur, Dec. 5, 1881.

3. Born in Maine, Charles E. Hill went to China in 1859 and worked as a commercial agent. See *HMD*, 45-2-31, 3–5, 63–97.

4. Borie was the eldest of twelve children in his family.

To Edward F. Beale

UNITED STATES CONSULATE GENERAL,
~~SHANGHAI.~~ Peking, China
June 7th /79

MY DEAR GENERAL:

I have now been to the limit of my travels in China. From here we take the back track to Tientsin, and thence to Japan as rapidly as a U. S. Vessel of War—seven knots an hour—can carry us. I must say that neither the country nor the people attract the traveler to pay them a second visit. But I have visited the country under the most favorable circumstances to see and study the people, institutions &c. and have drawn rather a favorable view of their future from all I have seen. In the first place they are enduring, patient to the last degree, industrious, and have brought living down to a minimum. By their shrewdness and economy they have monopolised nearly all the carrying trade—coastwise—of the east, they are driving out all other merchants; through India, Malay, Siam, and the islands from the shores of Africa to Japan, they are the mechanics, market gardeners, Stevedors, small traders, servants and every thing els that goes to mark material progress. They are not a military power and could not defend themselves against even a small European power. But they have the material for a strong

independent nation and may, before many years roll around, assert
their power. Their leading men thoroughly appreciate their weakness, but understand at the same time the history of Turkey, Egypt
and other powers that have made rapid strides towards the new
civilization on borrowed capital, ~~capital~~, and with foreign management and controll. Their idea seems to be to gradually educate a
sufficient number of their own people to fill all places in the developement of rail-roads, manufactories, telegraphs, and every thing
new to them, but common—if not old—with us. Then, with their
own men, and capital, to commence a serious advancement. I would
not be surprised to hear within the next twenty years, if I should
live so long, more complaint of Chinese absorption of the trade and
commerse of the world than we ~~do~~ hear now of their backward position. But before this change begins to show itself there will be a
change of dinasty. The present form of government gives no state
power whatever. It may take off the heads of weak offenders, or of a
few obnoxious persons, but is as weak against outside powers as we
would be if "States Rights," as interpreted by Southern democrats,
prevailed. There are too many powers within the government to
prevent the whole from exercising ~~their~~ its full strength against a
common enemy.

Mrs. Grant's & my love to you & all your family.

Very Truly Yours

U. S. Grant

Gen. E. F. Beale

ALS, DLC-Decatur House Papers. USG assessed China similarly to John Russell
Young. See *Young*, II, 441–43.

Conversation with Prince Kung

[*Peking, June 8, 1879*]

Prince Kung—I am delighted to see you again, and hope you
have enjoyed your visit to Pekin. It is a pity that you have had such
warm weather, for in this season Pekin is always trying.

General GRANT—I have found it warmer than in the tropics, where we expected, of course, much warmer weather than in this high latitude. I presume, however, that you leave Pekin when the warm season sets in and go to the sea shore or the hills.

Prince KUNG—No. I remain here all the year round. The business of the Empire requires constant attention, and can only be attended to at the capital. We manage, however, to transact all of our important business early in the morning. The hours before dawn are our important hours. I rise at two o'clock in the morning. At the same time we have business that often carries us late into the afternoon.

General GRANT—I want to thank you and the Yamen for the handsome presents you sent to Mrs. Grant. It was a delicate and unexpected attention, and Mrs. Grant desires me to express her thanks.

Prince KUNG—We did not wish you to leave China without one or two souvenirs of the country representing those branches of industry and art in which our people have won distinction. Our regret is that your stay is so brief that we could not send Mrs. Grant something worthy of her acceptance and worthy to be given to one held in such high honor by China as yourself. I hope you will also prolong your stay.

General GRANT—I would be happy to remain longer in China; but the weather is so oppressive that I have been compelled to abandon many of the excursions I proposed to myself when coming to Pekin, and I have made engagements with the Japanese government to be in Japan at a certain time. I hear that arrangements have been made in Japan consequent upon my coming, and I do not wish to cause the authorities any inconvenience.

Prince KUNG—How long do you propose remaining in Japan?

General GRANT—That will depend upon what is to be seen; but I hardly think more than a month.

Prince KUNG—You have been in China a month, I think.

General GRANT—More than a month already; and by the time I leave it will be a good deal more than a month.

Prince KUNG—I suppose you will stay some time in Tientsin?

General GRANT—Two or three days. I have made engagements for two days, and have promised the Viceroy[1] to meet him on my return. That engagement also compels me to leave Pekin.

Prince KUNG—I am sorry you leave so soon for other reasons. We are very anxious to have you with us because China has never been honored before with the presence of so illustrious a guest, and, apart from the personal desire of all connected with the government to do honor to one so well known in China, we wish to show our kind feelings to the people of America in honoring one who has been the head of America. China has always been treated well by your country, and never more so than under your administration. We can never forget the services rendered to us by Mr. Burlingame.[2]

General GRANT—The policy of America in dealing with foreign Powers is one of justice. We believe that fair play, consideration for the rights of others and respect for international law will always command the respect of nations and lead to peace. I know of no other consideration that enters into our foreign relations. There is no temptation to the United States to adventures outside of our own country. Even in the countries contiguous to our own we have no foreign policy except so far as it secures our own protection from foreign interference.

Prince KUNG—There is one question about which I am anxious to confer with you. The Viceroy of Tientsin writes us that he has mentioned it to you. And if we could secure your good offices, or your advice, it would be a great benefit, not only to us, but to all nations, and especially in the East. I refer to the questions now pending between China and Japan.

General GRANT—In reference to the trouble in the Loochoo islands.

Prince KUNG—Yes; about the sovereignty of Loochoo and the attempt of the Japanese to extinguish a kingdom which has always been friendly and whose sovereign has always paid us tribute, not only the present sovereign, but his ancestors for centuries.

General GRANT—The Viceroy spoke to me on the subject and has promised to renew the subject on my return to Tientsin.

Beyond the casual references of the Viceroy in the course of conversations on the occasion of interviews that were confined mainly to ceremonies I am entirely ignorant of the questions.

Prince Kung—We all feel a great delicacy in referring to this or any other matter of business on the occasion of your visit to Pekin—a visit that we know to be one of pleasure and that should not be troubled by business. I should not have ventured upon such a liberty if I had not been informed by the Viceroy of the kind manner in which you received his allusions to the matter and your known devotion to peace and justice. I feel that I should apologize even for the reference I have made, which I would not have ventured upon but for the report of the Viceroy and our conviction that one who has had so high a place in determining the affairs of the world can have no higher interest than furthering peace and justice.

General Grant—I told the Viceroy that anything I could do in the interest of peace was my duty and my pleasure. I can conceive of no higher office for any man. But I am not in office. I am merely a private citizen, journeying about like others, with no share in the government and no power. The government has given me a ship of war whenever I can use it without interfering with its duties, but that is all.

Prince Kung—I quite understand that, and this led to the expression of my regret at entering upon the subject. But we all know how vast your influence must be, not only upon your people at home, but upon all nations who know what you have done, and who know that whatever question you considered would be considered with patience and wisdom and a desire for justice and peace. You are going to Japan as the guest of the people and the Emperor, and will have opportunities of presenting our views to the Emperor of Japan and of showing him that we have no policy but justice.

General Grant—Yes, I am going to Japan as the guest of the Emperor and nation.

Prince Kung—That affords us the opportunity that we cannot overlook. The Viceroy writes us that he has prepared a statement of the whole case, drawn from the records of our Empire, and he will put you in possession of all the facts from our point of view.

General GRANT—The King of the Loochoo Islands has, I believe, paid tribute to China as well as Japan?

Prince KUNG—For generations. I do not know how long with Japan, but for generations Loochoo has recognized the sovereignty of China. Not alone during the present, but in the time of the Ming Emperors, the dynasty that preceded our own, this recognition was unchallenged, and Loochoo became as well known as an independent Power in the East owing allegiance only to our Emperor as any other part of our dominions.

General GRANT—Has Japan made her claim upon Loochoo a subject of negotiation with China? Has she ever presented your government with her view of her claim to the islands?

Prince KUNG—Japan has a Minister in Pekin.[3] He came here some time since amid circumstances of ostentation, and great importance was attached to his coming. There was a great deal said about it at the time, and it was said that the interchange of Ministers would be of much importance to both nations. We sent a Minister to Japan, an able and prudent man,[4] who is there now. This showed our desire to reciprocate. We supposed, of course, that when the Japanese Minister came there would be a complete explanation and understanding in Loochoo. We welcomed his coming in this spirit and in the interest of peace. When he came to the Yamen, and we brought up Loochoo, he knew nothing about the subject, nothing about the wishes or the attitude of his government. We naturally inquired, what brought him here as Minister? of what use was a Minister if he could not transact business of such vital consequence to both nations and to the peace of the world. He said he had certain matters connected with the trade of the two countries to discuss—something of that kind. It seemed almost trifling with us to say so. When we presented our case he said that anything we would write or say he would transmit to his government—no more. He was only a post office. When our Minister in Japan presented the subject to the authorities he had no better satisfaction, and was so dissatisfied that he wrote to us asking permission to request his passports and withdraw. But we told him to wait and be patient and do nothing to lead to war, or that might be construed as seeking war on our part.

General GRANT—Any course short of national humiliation or national destruction is better than war. War in itself is so great a calamity that it should only be invoked when there is no way of saving a nation from a greater. War, especially in the East, and between two countries like Japan and China, would be a misfortune— a great misfortune.

Prince KUNG—A great misfortune to the outside and neutral Powers as we[l]l. War in the East would be a heavy blow to the trade upon which other nations so much depend. That is one reason why China asks your good offices and hopes for those of your government and of your Minister to Japan. We have been told of the kind disposition of Mr. Bingham toward us. Our Minister has told us of that; and one reason why we kept our Minister in Japan under circumstances which would have justified another Power in withdrawing him was because we knew of Mr. Bingham's sentiments and were awaiting his return. It is because such a war as Japan seems disposed to force on China would be peculiar[l]y distressing to foreign Powers that we have asked them to interfere.

General GRANT—How far have the Japanese gone in Loochoo?

Prince KUNG—The King of the islands has been taken to Japan and deposed. The sovereignty has been extinguished. A Japanese official has been set up. We have made a study of international law as written by your English and American authors, whose text books are in Chinese. If there is any force in the principles of international law as recognized by your nations the extinction of the Loochoo sovereignty is a wrong, and one that other nations should consider.

General GRANT—It would seem to be a high handed proceeding to arrest a ruler and take him out of the country, unless there is war or some grave provocation.

Prince KUNG—If there was provocation, if Japan had suffered any wrong in Loochoo that justified extreme action, why does not her Ambassador at our Court or their own ministers at home in dealing with our embassy give us an explanation? China is a peaceful nation. Her policy has been peace. No nation will make more sacrifices for peace, but forbearance cannot be used to our injury, to the humiliation of the Emperor and a violation of our rights. On this subject we feel strongly, and when the Viceroy wrote the Emperor from Tientsin that he had spoken to you on the subject, and that you might be induced to use your good offices with Japan, and with your offices your great name and authority, we rejoiced in what may be a means of escaping from a responsibility which no nation would deplore more than myself.

General GRANT—As I said before, my position here and my position at home are not such as to give any assurance that my good offices would be of any value. Here I am a traveller, seeing sights, and looking at new manners and customs. At home I am simply a private citizen, with no voice in the councils of the government and no right to speak for the government.

Prince KUNG—We have a proverb in Chinese that "No business is business"—in other words, that real affairs, great affairs are more frequently transacted informally, when persons meet, as we are meeting now, over a table of entertainment for social and friendly conversation, than in solemn business sessions at the Yamen. I value the opportunities of this conversation, even in a business sense, more than I could any conversation with ambassadors.

General GRANT—I am much complimented by the confidence you express, and in that expressed by the Viceroy. It would afford me the greatest pleasure—I know of no pleasure that could be greater—to be the means, by any counsel or effort of mine, in preserving peace, and especially between two nations in which I feel so deep an interest as I do in China and Japan. I know nothing about this Loochoo business except what I have heard from the Viceroy and yourself, and an occasional scrap in the newspapers, to which I paid little attention, as I had no interest in it. I know nothing of the merits of the case. I am going to Japan, and I shall take pleasure in informing myself on the subject in conversing with the Japanese authorities. I have no idea what their argument is. They, of course, have an argument. I do not suppose that the rulers are inspired by a desire to wantonly injure China. I will acquaint myself with the Chinese side of the case, as Your Imperial Highness and the Viceroy have presented it, and promise to present it. I will do what I can to learn the Japanese side. Then, if I can in conversation with the Japanese authorities do anything that will be a service to the cause of peace, you may depend upon my good offices. But as I have said, I have no knowledge on the subject and no idea what opinion I may entertain when I have studied it.

Prince KUNG—We are profoundly grateful for this promise. China is quite content to rest her case with your decision, given, as we know it will be, after care and with wisdom and justice. If the Japanese government will meet us in this spirit all will be well. I shall send orders to our Minister in Japan to wait upon you as soon as you reach Japan and to speak with you on the subject. Your willingness to do this will be a new claim to the respect in which you are held in China, and be a continuance of that friendship shown to us by the United States, and especially by Mr. Burlingame, whose death we all deplored and whose name is venerated in China.[5]

General GRANT—An arbitration between nations may not satisfy either party at the time. But it satisfies the conscience of the world, and must commend itself more and more as a means of adjusting disputes.

Prince KUNG—The policy of China is one of reliance upon justice. We are willing to have any settlement that is honorable and that will be considered by other nations as honorable to us. We desire no advantage over Japan. But, at the same time, we are resolved to submit to no wrong from Japan. On that point there is but one opinion in our government. It is the opinion of the Viceroy, one of the great officers of the Empire, and, like yourself, not only a great soldier, but an advocate always of a peaceful policy, of concession, compromise and conciliation. It is my own opinion, and I have always, as one largely concerned in the affairs of the Empire and knowing what war entails, been in favor of peace. It is the opinion of the Yamen. I do not know of any dissentient among those who serve the throne. Our opinion is that we cannot, under any circumstances, submit to the claims of Japan. We cannot consent to the extinction of a sovereignty, of an independence that has existed for so long a time under our protection. If Japan insists upon her present position there must be war.

General GRANT—What action on the part of Japan would satisfy China?

Prince KUNG—We would be satisfied with the situation as it was.

General GRANT—That is to say, Loochoo paying tribute to Japan and China.

Prince KUNG—We do not concern ourselves with what tribute the King of Loochoo pays to Japan or any other Power. We never have done so, and although there is every reason why an Empire should not allow other nations to exact tribute from its vassals we are content with things as they have been not only under the dynasty of my own ancestors and family, but under the dynasty of the Mings. We desire Japan to restore the King she has captured and taken away, to withdraw her troops from Loochoo and abandon her claims to exclusive sovereignty over the island. This is our position. Other questions are open to negotiation and debate. This is not open, because it is a question of the integrity of the Empire. And the justice of our position will be felt by any one who studies the case and compares the violence and aggression of Japan with the patience and moderation of China.

General GRANT—I shall certainly see the Viceroy on my return to Tientsin and converse with him, and read the documents I understand he is preparing. I shall also when I meet the Japanese authorities do what I can to learn their case. If I can be of any service in adjusting the question and securing peace I shall be rejoiced, and it will be no less a cause of rejoicing if in doing so I can be of any service to China or be enabled to show my appreciation of the great honor she has shown to me during my visit and of the unvarying friendship she has shown our country.

New York Herald, Aug. 15, 1879. John Russell Young described his account. "I have written down this conversation at length, so far as I can remember it, and have tried to give you some idea of the accessories, because of the historical value of the scene. . . . The Prince spoke during this interview with great animation. . . . When he spoke of China's resolve to defend her sovereignty he showed emotion, something extraordinary in an Oriental, . . ." *Ibid.* On June 8, 1879, Young wrote in his diary. "At two to day Prince Kung & the members of the Yamen came to the Legation and had an interview with General Grant. The Prince remained an hour, and talked all the time about LooChoo. . . ." DLC-John Russell Young. See conversation with Prince Kung, [*June 5,*

1879]; *Young*, II, 409–14; Edwin Pak-wah Leung, "The Quasi-War in East Asia: Japan's Expedition to Taiwan and the Ryūkyū Controversy," *Modern Asian Studies*, 17, 2 (April, 1983), 257–81, and "Li Hung-chang and the Liu-ch'iu (Ryūkyū) Controversy, 1871–1881," in *Li Hung-chang and China's Early Modernization*, ed. Samuel C. Chu and Kwang-Ching Liu (Armonk, N. Y., 1994), pp. 162–75.

1. Li Hung-chang.
2. Anson Burlingame, U.S. minister to China (1861–67), then served as a Chinese envoy until his death in 1870. See David L. Anderson, *Imperialism and Idealism: American Diplomats in China, 1861–1898* (Bloomington, Ind., 1985), pp. 36–45.
3. Soejima Taneomi.
4. Ho Ju-chang.
5. Young interjected: "An allusion was made to the convention between Great Britain and America on the Alabama question—the arbitration and the settlement of a matter that might have embroiled the two countries. This was explained to His Imperial Highness as a precedent that it would be well to follow now. The Prince was thoroughly familiar with the Alabama negotiations." *New York Herald*, Aug. 15, 1879.

Conversations with Li Hung-chang

[*Tientsin, June 12–14, 1879*] [1]

There will be no Executive who will not do all he can to protect the people, Chinese or Europeans. The opposition to the Chinese at home comes from various causes. There is a class of thriftless, discontented adventurers, agitators and communists, who do not work themselves and go about sowing discontent among honest workingmen. This class is always ready for trouble, and of course as soon as there is trouble the criminal class asserts itself. This class always has a grievance over which to fight and disturb society. Sometimes it is a religious outbreak like what was seen thirty years ago or thereabout when there was an uprising against Catholics, or more recently in New York, when there was a fatal street fight arising out of the attack of Protestants by Catholics.[2] During the war the grievance was the negro, and there was an outbreak in New York that required us to withdraw troops from the field in presence of the enemy to put it down. Two years ago it was a war upon railways, in which millions were destroyed. Your Excellency can understand that in all large nations the turbulent class can give trouble. What they want is trouble. The pretext is nothing. Then we have demagogues in politics—men who know better, but who always seek advancement by pandering to this class. I attribute the worst features of the Chinese agitation—the threats of violence, the outbreaks in sections of California—to this class, the agitators and communists, men who believe that nothing is right that is orderly and legal, and the criminal classes. Your Excellency may rest assured that the great mass of the American people will never consent to any injustice toward China or any class.

I am ready to admit that the Chinese have been of great service to our country. I do not know what the Pacific coast would be without them. They came to our aid at the time when their aid was invaluable. In the competition between their labor and ours, of course if we cannot hold our own we confess our weakness and go to the wall. If the Chinaman surpasses us in industry, thrift and ingenuity, no law can arrest the consequences of that superiority. I have never been alarmed about that, however. The trouble about your countrymen coming to America is that they come under circumstances which make them slaves. They do not come of their own free will. They do not come to stay, bringing their wives and children. Their labor is not their own, but the property of capitalists. On that point our best people feel very strongly, because we consider nothing so carefully as the elements that go toward building up the nation. Its future depends on that. We had slavery some years since, and we only freed ourselves from slavery at the cost of a dreadful war, in which hundreds of thousands of lives were lost and thousands of millions of dollars spent. Having made those sacrifices to suppress slavery in one form, we do not feel like encouraging it in another, in the insidious form of cooley emigration. That is a wrong to your government and our own, and to the people especially.

If you can stop the slavery feature then emigration from China is like emigration from other countries. Then, as there is a complaint on the Pacific coast of Chinamen coming too rapidly, coming so as to glut the labor market, emigration might be stopped for a period—for three or five years. I infer from what you say that, with the indisposition of the government to have Chinamen leave home, there would be no objection to such a measure.[3]

That would enable us to see how much foundation there is in the belief that our labor market in California is overstocked. I have no ideas of my own on the subject. I have not been in California since I was there as a young man. I rather suspect that many generations must pass before so great an empire as California would have too much labor. At the same time the complaint comes from good people, and should be considered. If you stop emigration for five years before the five years are over we shall know all about the question. It may be that the complaint is well founded; but it is just as possible that before the five years are over there will be a clamor for the removal of the restriction by the men who foster the present agitation against the Chinese.

You have many young Chinamen in our schools. What reports do they send home? [4]

Yes, I remember. I was anxious to have this done. The proposal was defeated, mainly, if I remember, through the influence of Mr. Casserly, then Senator from California.[5] I wish you would send some of your boys to West Point. It is one of the best schools in the world.

But if there is any trouble about entering the schools why not do like the Siamese government? We have on board one of our men-of-war in the China waters two Siamese noblemen, one a brother of the King, who entered as seamen. They are now serving before the mast. That was the way seamanship was learned in the past, and although it was, of course, not as good as the school, it was a great deal. Why would not the Chinese do the same thing with their young men—with youths of intelligence and good family? [6]

General Upton is a distinguished and able officer.[7] When Mr. Burlingame was alive he asked me to name an officer to enter your service and organize the army. I selected Upton. But Mr. Burlingame died and the matter fell through. General Upton has a high rank in our regular army, especially for a young man, and I have no idea that he would care to leave. But there is no nation in the world where there are so many competent military men as in America. The war was an educator, and so large a proportion of the population, North and South, were in the army that at the close there was scarcely any department of business or industry where you could not find men competent to hold high commands.

Of the South as well as the North.[8] The soldiers in the Southern army have shown themselves by all odds the best part of the Southern population. Our armies were not mercenaries—not on either side. Mercenary armies give trouble. No people are more peaceable in civil life than those who have seen war. They know what war is.

Your Excellency is very kind, but there could be no wish more distasteful to me than what you express.[9] I have held the office President as long as it has ever been held by any man. There are others who have risen to great distinction at home and who have earned the honor who are worthy, and to them it belongs, not to me. I have no claims to the office. It is a place distasteful to me, a place of hardship and responsibilities. When I was a younger man these hardships were severe and never agreeable. They would be worse now.

No man who knows what the Presidency imposes would care to see a friend in the office. I have had my share of it—have had all the honors that can be or should be given to any citizen, and there are many able and distinguished men who have earned the office. To one of them it should be given.

I would much rather time my arrival so as to avoid it.[10] But most of these paragraphs are exaggerations and others are written in an unfriendly spirit. It is possible some personal friends may come to meet me from the East—a half dozen perhaps—who will take the occasion to run over to California. I have a good many friends on the Pacific coast, whom I will be glad to see. But my time of return is unknown and indefinite, and the stories that have crept into the Chinese papers about monster excursions are exaggerations.

New York Herald, Aug. 16, 1879. "The Viceroy spoke of the stories which came to China of the oppressions of the Chinese by evil disposed persons in California, and said that China was compelled to trust entirely to the justice of other nations in the treatment of her people. General Grant said that he had no doubt that the stories of ill treatment were exaggerated; that neither in California nor in any settled section of the Union would violence be allowed as a rule to any class. The fact that Chinamen come to

America in a constantly increasing stream showed that they were not deterred by violence. The cases that did occur were sporadic, and deplored and punished. The Viceroy said that in China the safety and protection of all people was a matter of imperial concern; that foreign nations held the imperial government responsible. General Grant answered by explaining the relations of the States to the general government, showing the existence of three powers in the State—legislative, judicial and executive—and that while the Executive was a part of the government he was not altogether so. The Viceroy said that he was familiar with the general features of the government, but it was difficult for foreigners to divest themselves of the idea that the protection of the people and the prevention of unjust laws was the mission of the Chief of the State. General Grant answered that the Executive of the United States, no matter what party succeeded, would look at the Chinese question from the highest point of view, and not as the Governor of a State like California. . . . The Viceroy said that his government never lost its confidence in the justice of the United States. If there was a grievance—a real grievance—in America on account of the emigration of Chinamen to that country, his government was prepared to do what it could to remove it. General Grant answered that the Chinese question at home was not free from embarrassments—serious embarrassments. . . . The Viceroy said that it was a mistake to suppose that the emigration of the Chinese to America or to any other part of the world was the desire of the government. If the government had its way it would keep all the Chinamen at home. General Grant said that this was natural. The Viceroy continued that he was willing to consider any proposition to relieve the Americans from the burden of Chinese emigration. General Grant answered that no doubt the American Minister, Mr. Seward, came back instructed on the subject. He did not know, however. Mr. Seward was the proper person to consider the question. He was not in China in a diplomatic capacity, and did not know the feelings of the administration, and he would not like to say or do anything to interfere with the Minister or the administration. The Viceroy said he quite understood that. He himself was conversing unofficially. 'I know,' he continued, 'that a hint or a suggestion from you would have weight in China, and my object is to have your advice as to the best way to satisfy the American people.' General Grant said, 'You can put a stop to the slavery system.' The Viceroy answered that the government would do so if possible. But many things were hard to do, like, for instance, the suppression of the opium traffic, which was the desire of every statesman in China. . . . The Viceroy said that he was glad he had the expression of the General's views as to what would be satisfactory to the United States. They would have great influence with his government, and he would communicate them to Prince Kung. At the same time he hoped that the General would use his influence to secure protection to the Chinese now in America. The government was distressed when it heard of the attacks on Chinamen. General Grant said that it was not alone his duty to do that, but the duty of all citizens. But the Chinese could have no better protector than the present administration. Mr. Hayes will do all a President can do. . . ." Li Hung-chang asked what became of vol. officers after the Civil War ended. "General Grant said that officers as well as men went back to civil affairs. He meets men who had held important commands under him constantly, and in all departments of business. He told a story of meeting a blacksmith on one occasion, his arms bared and standing over his anvil, who had been a colonel under him during the war. The Viceroy was amused with this incident. He said China had not been so fortunate in dealing with her armies. There was always friction and irritation. If men had been officers they wanted to remain so. He asked about the policy of the government in dealing with the sick and wounded. General Grant explained our pension system. The Viceroy asked the General how far America had progressed in the development of the torpedo service. He attached a great deal of importance to the torpedo as a defence for a long coast. He had given some attention to the subject, because the defence of the coasts was under his charge. The General said that he only knew in a general way that great attention was paid to the torpedo system at home. He had always when President encouraged its development. He could not say he had any especial information on the subject. It might be assumed, however, from the character of the men at the head of the army and navy, and, indeed, from the character of army and navy officers generally, that whatever was known in torpedo service in any part of the world was known in America. The Viceroy asked whether the General was familiar with the Lay torpedo. General Grant said that the Lay torpedo had within it the elements of a startling and great invention; but it was undeveloped. In time the principle would succeed. Our people have had a way of working and working at an idea, once that they found it, until they developed it. While the Lay torpedo was crude now he believed in its ultimate success. The Viceroy said he had seen the Lay torpedo and witnessed some interesting experiments. But it appeared to him to be a crude machine. He asked whether the defences of the American coasts were committed to the army or navy." USG responded. "To both branches of the service. The actual defences of harbors like New York in the engineering are under the engineers. But in the navy we have a special torpedo school." Li Hung-chang "said that he had given much attention to torpedo defences, and watched with interest all the developments of the science in other nations. He looked to America's important discoveries, and hoped some time to see China avail herself of the services of competent Americans. General Grant said that in this as in other matters of the greatest importance to the welfare of China much advantage would be gained by the advice and aid of Americans, and of skilled men from other nations. Since he came to China he had learned a great many things about China in the way of the resources of the country that interested him. There seemed to be no end of the resources of China, and it was a mistake in the authorities not to avail themselves of modern knowledge. The Viceroy said that he had given much thought to the development of the country. He had opportunities of seeing the advantages of outside aid not enjoyed by others who had not been so much in relations with foreigners. There was an apprehension of foreign ideas and foreign aid which he did not share. This came also from the conservatism of the people, and the fact that the government had to consider the peculiar conditions of the Empire, the vast population and the existence of traditions and customs that had grown for centuries. General Grant said that he had no confidence in any development or progress that did not come from the people themselves. No other would be sound. But in the matter of famines, of which he had heard so many distressing stories since he came to China, it would be a blessing to the people to have railway communications. In America there could be no famine such as had recently been seen in China, unless, as was hardly possible in so vast a territory, the famine became general. If the crops failed in one State supplies could be brought from others at a little extra expense in money and time. We could send wheat, for instance, from one end of the country to another in a few days. The same in case of invasion. The resources of the country in men and arms could be massed in a short time at any menaced point. That gave a nation a great advantage. So in mineral resources. The coal and iron of America, upon which so much of the wealth of the nation depends; the gold and silver of the Pacific, which had played so great a part in the welfare of the world, would be valueless without railways. This led to a long conversation, in which the Viceroy went over many of the points embraced in his talk with Prince Kung.

The Viceroy said he was anxious to see China introduce railways and telegraphs. Already he had a telegraph of his own from the forts at the mouth of the river to Tientsin. He would be glad also to have small steamers on the Peiho River. He was sorry his opinions on this were not shared by some of his colleagues. But in time he hoped wiser opinions would prevail. The Viceroy then referred to the questions at issue between China and Japan, as to the occupation of the Loochoo Islands by the latter Power. Turning to a secretary he produced several maps and books—some in Chinese and some in English. The maps were of China and Japan on a large scale. The books were copies of the treaties between the Chinese Empire and other governments, in English and Chinese. The Viceroy began the conversation by saying that he had received a letter from Prince Kung, asking him to lay before the General the Chinese side of the Loochoo discussion. Prince Kung had also written him of General Grant's willingness to look into the question and give his good offices to China. General Grant said that he had said to his Imperial Highness that he was only a private citizen at home, with no authority to enter into negotiations or to speak for the government. Mr. Seward and Mr. Bingham, who were Ministers to the respective governments of China and Japan, had only returned from home, and they may have instructions from the administration. At the same time, if any advice or aid he could give could serve the cause of peace, he would be glad. He had a horror of war, and there could be no greater calamity, both to Japan and China, than war. He believed where there was an honest difference of opinion between two countries wisdom and patience could always adjust it. The Viceroy said he knew that the General was not a diplomatist nor an official. But for this purpose he might say that neither was he an official. When he heard that the General was coming to China his heart was glad, for he felt that he could talk to him about Loochoo. If the General chose to speak on the subject he would speak with an authority greater than that of any diplomatist. There were men to whose words nations would listen, and the General was one of those men. His own government was willing to put its case unreservedly in his hands, and as he was going to see the Mikado a word from him to that sovereign might serve the cause of peace and justice. The General said if he could ever speak words with such a result he would not hesitate to speak them. As to the Loochoo question, he knew nothing beyond what he had heard from Prince Kung. He might add that since seeing Prince Kung he had conversed with Mr. Seward and others and had heard their opinions. But he felt that he knew only the Chinese case, or at least a hurried statement of the case, and he had no idea what his view might be when he conversed with the Japanese. The Viceroy opened a volume in Chinese containing the treaties and read from an early treaty made when Mr. Cushing was Minister, in which the United States held herself ready to offer her good services between China and other Powers in the event of any question arising. He asked whether the General did not think that the difference with Japan about Loochoo did not come within the limits of the treaty. General Grant read over the clause and said he thought it did. The Viceroy then read from the Burlingame Treaty assurances of the same character. He read from a treaty between China and Japan engagements on the part of the two countries not to invade the territory of the others. He pointed out the existence of a treaty between the United States and the Loochoo Islands, showing that the American government dealt with the Loochoo King as an independent Power. He then called the attention of the General to the international law on the subject and held that the course of Japan was one that called for the intervention of outside Powers. Otherwise there was no use of that international law which foreign nations were always quoting to China. General Grant said the argument seemed to be sound, but it belonged to diplomacy. From the fact that the Viceroy quoted a treaty in which the United States acknowledged the Loochoo Islands as an independent Power he supposed that China in dealing with Japan was also willing to regard them as an independent Power. The Viceroy said as an independent Power, certainly. But to be entirely accurate Loochoo should be described as a semi-dependent Power. China had never exercised sovereignty over the islands, and did not press that claim. But China was as much concerned in the maintenance of the independence of a Power holding toward her coasts the relations of Loochoo as in the integrity of her inland territory. As a matter of fact, because of the great powers allowed by China always to her provinces and dependencies the emperors had never exercised the rights of sovereignty over Loochoo. As a matter of law and right, however, the right was never alienated, and the sovereigns of Loochoo always respected it by paying tribute to China until Japan came in and forbade the tribute. General Grant asked if the sovereigns did not also pay tribute to Japan." Li Hung-chang replied. "In this way. Before the revolution in Japan, and the consolidation of the power of the princes into the imperial power, the feudal lords had great authority. They did as they pleased. Perhaps none of these lords were more powerful than the Satsuma princes. These princes occupied the islands of Japan nearest to Loochoo. To protect themselves from the raids and exactions of the Satsuma princes the Loochoo people paid tribute only to the princes, never to Japan. Well, when the revolution came, and the powers of the princes were absorbed, the Emperor claimed that the payment of tribute to the princes was recognition of the sovereignty of Japan. That is the only claim that the Japanese have ever made." USG interjected. "And in the meantime tribute has been paid to China." Li Hung-chang replied. "In the meantime and for centuries before. . . . The Loochoo kings always received more from the Emperor than they gave. For centuries this has gone on. . . . They always valued the relation with China and we gave them special trade facilities. . . . They prefer the Chinese connection, infinitely prefer the mild and friendly relations that have subsisted for so many centuries to the destruction of their government." USG asked. "Is the Sovereign a native?" Li Hung-chang replied. "He is a native. . . . The people of Loochoo are not Chinamen, but we have an important part of the population. It came in this way. During the Ming dynasty the emperors came to know of the islands, and thought it would be well to civilize them. Thirty or forty Chinese families, with different surnames—good families— were selected and sent to Loochoo to civilize the islands. Their descendants are in Loochoo now. Consequently we have a special claim over them." USG then "asked what was the progress of the negotiations between China and Japan on the subject. The Viceroy answered that there were no negotiations. The Japanese sent troops to the islands and forbade the payment of any more tribute to China. They then commanded the King to abandon his government and repair to Japan. The King was ill and said he could not go to Japan. He was told that unless he was better in a certain time, eighty days I think, he would be taken. He was so taken. Representations were made to Pekin. We addressed remonstrances to the Japanese. No response was made. Our Minister was treated in a manner that none but a people as patient as ours and as averse to difficulties with other nations would tolerate. Then we addressed the Japanese Minister in Pekin. He had no instructions, no advice, no information. Japan has treated the whole question as an accomplished fact, as something done, an incident about which we had nothing to say. A Governor was appointed. Loochoo was made an integral part of the Japanese Empire, and unless something is done to restore things to their former position the world would see the extinction of a nation with which other nations had made treaties for no fault of its own, and not as an act of war. If that could be done of what value is international law? General Grant thought it was unfortunate that there should have been no negotiations, so that some thread could be found which could be taken up and pursued to a harmonious and honorable result." Li Hung-chang continued. "We have strained every effort to open negotiations. Apart from the feeling of wounded honor in the Chinese mind at the sudden extinction of a nation that has been friendly and tributary there are other reasons. If you look at the map you will find that the Loochoo Islands block the coast of China, that they spread between our shores and the Pacific Ocean, and virtually command all the channels of our commerce. Such a command in the hands of a Power like Japan is a menace to our commerce. At any time it may be interrupted. Then the Loochoo Islands come close to Formosa. We have already had trouble about Formosa. The possession of Loochoo brings Japan within a step of Formosa, which is but a step from our coasts. These are considerations that, of course, concern China more than the other Powers; but when you add them to our unquestioned rights under treaty law and international law they will explain our own feeling, and especially what you heard from Prince Kung in Pekin." USG "asked if, in the absence of negotiations, the Viceroy was in possession of any unofficial information as to the views of the Japanese government? The Viceroy said from all he could learn the Mikado was not in favor of any policy like that shown in the occupation of Loochoo. But there was a party—among them men like the Princes of Satsuma—who were urging the Japanese to annexation. His own belief was that if the foreign Powers were to strengthen the Mikado in resisting the wishes of this party its influence would die out, and the Loochoo Islands be restored. General Grant wished to know if the Viceroy had had any expression from the foreign Powers. The Viceroy said he believed that Mr. Bingham, the American Minister, was friendly to the views of China. He supposed so, at least, from the anxiety in Pekin to have Mr. Bingham return to Japan. Of the wishes of the other Powers he had no information beyond rumor. General Grant felt certain that Mr. Bingham would consider the matter. He (Mr. Bingham) had just returned from home, and no doubt had been in conference with Mr. Evarts. He would see Mr. Bingham as soon as he reached Japan, and learn all the facts. He did not know what he could do, or how far he would go until he saw Mr. Bingham. The Viceroy asked if the General found on reaching Japan that Mr. Bingham had given no attention to the subject, or had formed opinions hostile to negotiation, he would then pursue the matter. The General said the Viceroy was supposing a condition of things that could not exist. Mr. Bingham was an able man, one who had had large experience in affairs at home—a conspicuous lawyer, especially fitted in every way to enter into the consideration of a question resting, as this appeared to rest, on treaty and international law. The Viceroy still pressed the point, and asked whether the indifference of the Minister, which he only spoke of as a possible thing, would prevent the General's giving these good offices requested by Prince Kung. General Grant said, of course, if he found that so important a question had been overlooked by the Minister, and if it was in a position where he as a private gentleman could aid the cause of peace, he would do all he could. But he had every confidence in Mr. Bingham. The Viceroy said this confidence was shared by the Chinese. But Prince Kung and himself laid especial stress upon the name and influence of the General. The Loochoo question could not be considered as within the range of diplomatic action. The Japanese had not allowed it a diplomatic standing. Consequently there was no chance of reaching a solution by the ordinary methods of diplomacy. How can you talk to ministers and governments about matters which they will not discuss? But when a man like General Grant comes to China and Japan he comes with an authority which gives him power to make peace. In the interest of peace China asks the

General to interest himself. China cannot consent to the position Japan has taken. On that point there is no indecision in the councils of the government. The Viceroy had no fear of Japan or of the consequences of any conflict which Japan would force upon China. General Grant said his hope and belief were that the difficulty would end peacefully and honorably. He appreciated the compliment paid him by the Chinese government. The Viceroy and Prince Kung overrated his power, but not his wish, to preserve peace, and especially to prevent such a deplorable thing as a war between China and Japan. When he reached Japan he would confer with Mr. Bingham and see how the matter stood. He would study the Japanese case as carefully as he proposed studying the Chinese case. He would, if possible, confer with the Japanese authorities. What his opinion would be when he heard both sides he could not anticipate. If the question took such a shape that, with advantage to the cause of peace and without interfering with the wishes of his own government, he could advise or aid in a solution, he would be happy, and as he remarked to Prince Kung this happiness would not be diminished if in doing so his action did not disappoint the Chinese government. An allusion was made to the proposed constitution now pending in California. General Grant said he had no information from California that enabled him to have an opinion of his own as to its success. People who knew the country best informed him that it would be defeated. The best people in California hoped for its defeat. There were other questions besides the Chinese which the new constitution covered which excited deep feeling at home. But California has had peculiar experiences. There are the best and the worst people in California. The best men had to struggle before in the days of the Vigilance Committee. They may have to do it again if the bad influences gain the supremacy. But in the long run, whatever the fate of the new constitution, the best people will assert themselves in California. . . ." *Ibid.* See Ari Hoogenboom, *Rutherford B. Hayes: Warrior & President* (Lawrence, Kan., 1995), pp. 387–91; Charles I. Bevans, ed., *Treaties and Other International Agreements of the United States of America 1776–1949* (Washington, 1968–76), 6, 659–660, 680–84; 9, 692–93.

1. John Russell Young combined several conversations into a single account. See Young diary, June 12, 14, 1879, DLC-John Russell Young; Owen N. Denny to Young, June 3, 1879, *ibid.*; *North-China Daily News* (Shanghai), June 25, 1879; *Young*, II, 415–17.

2. See Michael A. Gordon, *The Orange Riots: Irish Political Violence in New York City, 1870 and 1871* (Ithaca, 1993).

3. "The Viceroy said that if such a measure would be an advantage to America the government would consider it, and, in his opinion, consent. He himself would have no hesitancy in supporting it." *New York Herald*, Aug. 16, 1879.

4. "The Viceroy answered that the reports were most satisfactory. They were treated with kindness, and he wished to send more. He was anxious to send some to West Point. The government had tried to do this before, but the Americans, to his surprise and grief, would not consent. . . . The Viceroy asked whether there was any idea that another application to the American government would be favorably entertained. General Grant said he did not know; he had been away from home so long that he did not know the public temper." *Ibid.* See Yung Wing, *My Life in China and America* (New York, 1909), pp. 207–9.

5. On Feb. 26 and 29, 1872, U.S. Senator Eugene Casserly of Calif. had opposed a bill to admit Japanese pupils to USMA. See *CG*, 42-2, 1209, 1283–84; *HED*, 42-1-17.

6. "The Viceroy said he would be delighted. If General Grant would use his good offices and would secure the admission of young men on men-of-war he would send them. General Grant answered that he would see Admiral Patterson when he reached Yokohama and communicate with the Viceroy." *New York Herald*, Aug. 16, 1879.

7. "The Viceroy said he was anxious to have the advice and aid of the Americans so far as possible. There were several things which could be learned from Americans, and in that event he would like General Grant to select competent persons. There was General Upton, who had been in China. He wanted him to take a post." *Ibid.* Emory Upton then held the rank of lt. col., 4th Art. See Upton, *The Armies of Asia and Europe: . . .* (New York, 1878), pp. 13–32, 385–97; Peter S. Michie, *The Life and Letters of Emory Upton, . . .* (New York, 1885), pp. 284–98, 318–26. On March 15, 1881, Upton died at San Francisco. On March 16, USG, New York City, told a reporter, "I am at a total loss to understand what could have induced such a man as Gen. Upton to commit suicide. He never was of a morbid nature; his temperament was, to all appearances, ever of the sunniest. He had no bad habits, nor could there exist any just reason for his feeling dissatisfied with himself or his achievements. As a soldier his career was remarkably brilliant; particularly gallant was his conduct at Spottsylvania, where, for his bravery and what it accomplished, he was accorded, upon my recommendation, a Brevet Brigadier-Generalship. As a military student and author, Gen. Upton unquestionably ranked far above the average; he has long been rated as excellent authority in this country in many military matters. He gave us the first really American system of tactics, a want our Army had long felt. Those tactics were suggested to him in our campaign from the Rapidan to the James. Our old systems of tactics were translations from the French, and altogether not adapted to territory such as that in which the greater part of the rebellion was fought. In a wooded country with narrow roads we might as well have had no tactics at all, so far as the old system served us. Indeed, it was not infrequently the case that we were obliged to entirely abandon the system and depend upon plain common sense. Gen. Upton overcame the seemingly insurmountable difficulty, and his system of tactics adopted by the War Department made intelligent operations possible on any kind of ground." *New York Times*, March 17, 1881. ". . . Gen. Grant said that while Gen. Upton was stationed at West Point by his orders in 1870–75, as commandant of the Cadets, he was rated by some as severe, but he was always thoroughly just." *Ibid.* See *ibid.*, April 5, 1885; *PUSG*, 10, 434.

8. "The Viceroy asked General Grant whether at the close of the war any difficulty was experienced in sending the soldiers back to civil life. General Grant replied that, on the contrary, the men who had been in the army reverted to their old homes and occupations and became the best portions of society. He did not think it a reflection upon those who did not go into the war to say that no classes were more loyal, industrious and peaceful than those who had been in the war. The Viceroy asked if this was true of the South as well as the North." *New York Herald*, Aug. 16, 1879.

9. "The Viceroy said with a smile that he had received much pleasure from the kind words spoken by the General about China, and he hoped they would not be forgotten when the General became President again. Of course the General would become President again, and the Viceroy hoped this would be, and that when President the General would remember him and write to him." *Ibid.*

10. "The Viceroy said he had read in some Chinese papers translations from the American papers about the great reception that was awaiting the General in California, and supposed he would time his arrival so as to meet it." *Ibid.*

Speech

[*Tientsin, June 13, 1879*]

Your Excellency, Ladies and Gentlemen,—I am much obliged for the honour you do me, and especially for the complimentary terms in which the Viceroy proposes my health. I have enjoyed exceedingly my visit to China. It has been full of interest, and the recollections of the trip will remain with me all my life. There is no part of those recollections that I shall dwell upon with more pleasure than my meeting with the Viceroy, of whose fame I had heard before I came to China, and whom I was glad to meet. I can never forget his kindness, and now that I am leaving China, I hope that I may express the wish that I may not altogether be forgotten by him. To you all, ladies and gentlemen, I return my thanks for the hospitality shown to my party and myself in Tientsin. In conclusion, I ask you to unite with me in drinking the health of the Viceroy and prosperity to the Empire of China.

North-China Daily News (Shanghai), June 20, 1879. USG replied to the sentiments of Viceroy Li Hung-chang of Chihli at a dinner given by Gustav Detring, customs official. *Ibid.* See John Russell Young diary, June 13, 1879, DLC-John Russell Young; *New York Herald*, Aug. 17, 1879; *Young*, II, 417–18.

On June 13, 1879, 10:00 A.M., USG received a Chinese deputation seeking money for famine relief from a U.S. indemnity fund. "The General replied to the address by saying that he had always been in favour of returning the money to China, and that during his administration, the Government had frequently brought the matter before Congress, asking favourable action thereupon; but for various reasons, chiefly because of the pressure of other business, or that there was no one to take an active interest in the question on behalf of China, it had been put off from year to year. He was sure the money would be returned to China, and promised to do what he could to have the matter acted upon after his return to the United States. The General asked several questions of the members of the Committee, and, among other things, they stated that the distress was yet very great in Shansi, and in the Northern provinces, where famine had prevailed for three years past, they estimated that more than 13,000,000 of people have died as victims. The General expressed his deep sympathy, and after some further conversation the Committee withdrew." Newspaper extract filed with David H. Bailey to Charles Payson, July 15, 1879, DNA, RG 59, Consular Despatches, Shanghai. See *HED*, 41-2-69; *SRC*, 41-2-230, 48-2-934; *SMD*, 42-3-49; *HRC*, 45-3-113.

During the early evening of the same day, USG talked with Li, who "asked the General if he had ever been wounded in battle. The General replied that he had not, though he had often had his horse killed under him, his sword and parts of his uniform shot away and his clothes torn by bullets. The General then gave interesting reminiscences of some of his battles and answered many questions regarding them put by the Viceroy. He concluded by saying that perhaps the most remarkable feature of the war was seen in the way that the whole Union Army, numbering at the close of the war over 1,000,000 of men, was quietly disbanded, the soldiers returning to their various callings as private citizens, leaving a regular standing army of 50,000 men, which has since been reduced to 25,000. . . ." Newspaper extract filed with David H. Bailey to Charles Payson, July 15, 1879, DNA, RG 59, Consular Despatches, Shanghai.

On June 14, 3:00 P.M., Li sent gifts to USG, Frederick Dent Grant, and John Russell Young. "Accompanying the presents were some fine coloured photographs for each of the General's party. These photographs included a large sized picture of the General and Viceroy sitting together (taken in the Viceroy's yamên when the General made his first visit there)—. . ." *Ibid.*

On June 15, USG and party transferred from the U.S.S. *Ashuelot* to the U.S.S. *Richmond* for their voyage to Japan. Li's farewell remarks were translated. "I greatly regret having to part with you, and wish you could have stayed longer here that we might have become still better friends. But I will always entertain the warmest regard for you and remember all that you have said to me. You are now leaving the last port in China where you can meet a high provincial officer. It is therefore a duty, as well as a great pleasure for me, to come with you to say farewell at the farthest limit of my jurisdiction. I regret that you have not been entertained better in my country. It would have been different had our Emperor been of mature years. But I hope that you will think charitably of the little that has been done, and consider it a slight token of true admiration and respect. I wish you and your whole party a pleasant voyage and safe return to the United States, with an abundance of present and future happiness." *Ibid.* USG replied. "I feel very grateful for all the kindness and courtesy you have shown to me and my party. I part from you with feelings of the highest respect and admiration for your character and talents. You must always think of me as your friend. I thank you heartily for coming so far and regret the inconvenience I have put you to. I hope to be able to welcome you some day in my own country, but wherever you may be I wish you long life, prosperity, and increasing honours. Good bye, and let us always think of each other as good friends." *Ibid.*

On June 17, Jan H. Ferguson, Dutch consul gen., Chefoo, China, wrote to USG. "In May 1868 I have had the honour to be introduced to your Excellency, in Washington, by General Rickets,—when on a trip to the United States,—being then Governor of the Netherland Island of Aruba (West India) with leave of absence to visit America. I am sorry I was not at the Capital when your Excellency arrived there, being obliged, for my health, to be a resident of this more healthy seaport, where your Excellency arrived to-day on your 'tour du monde'. I will be very happy to call on your Excellency with the Secretary of the Legation—. . ." LS, DLC-USG, IB. On June 28, a customs official, Chefoo, wrote to USG, Yokohama. "In conformity to your desire I have the honour to hand you enclosed the Chinese Address presented to you by the Superintendent of Customs at Chefoo and its translation in English.—" ALS, *ibid.* An incomplete enclosure is *ibid.*

To Adam Badeau

Nagasaka, Japan,
June 22d /79

MY DEAR GENERAL:

The two enclosed chapters were received at Tientsin China just on the eve of my departure from there, so I brought them here to mail. The last chapter I think is one of the best in the book. It shows Early in an unpleasant light and shows the Southern character— for lying—as it should be shown.[1] I have no corrections to suggest in either chapter.

My visit through China was a pleasant one thoug[h] the country presents no attractions to invite the visitor to make the second trip. From Canton to Peking my receptions by the Civil & Military authorities was the most cordial ever extended to any foreigner no matte[r] what his rank. The fact is Chinese like Americans be[tter,] or rather perhaps hate them less, than any other foreigne[rs.] The reason is palpable. We are the only power that recognize[s] their right to controll their own internal affairs. My impression is that China is on the eve of a great revolution that will land her among the nations of progress. They have the elements of great wealth and great power too and not more than a generation will pass before she will make these elements felt.

I received your letter suggesting that I should write to Mr. Welsh on my departure from the last British Colony, in time to have written from Hong Kong. But I did not do so because I did not feel like making acknowledgement to the Govt. for any exhibition of respect on their part while I do gratefully acknowledge the most marked hospitality & kindness from all British officials in the east. I do not care to write the reasons for distinguishing between the people official & unofficial—of England and the Govt. But I will tell you some day.[2]

We arrived at this place yesterday & found the most extensive arrang[e]ments for our reception. The Japanese have made my party their guests during our stay in the country, and have a house he[re,] at Kobe & Tokio, fitted up for our accomodation.

Mrs. Grant Fred & Young—dubbed the Commodore—join me in kin[dest] regards to you. It looks now as if we would leave for home about the 10th of August. But I may change my mind and go back to visit Australia, and some other places left out, and go back by [the] Sandwich Islands.[3] In this case we wi[ll] not reach San Francisco before M[ar]ch.

Yours Truly

U S GRANT

GN. A. BADEAU.

ALS, Munson-Williams-Proctor Institute, Utica, N. Y.

On June 9, 1879, John A. Bingham, U.S. minister, Tokyo, wrote to USG, Nagasaki. "I have the honor to enclose herewith three letters addressed to you and two addressed to Mr Young who, I understand is with you. I beg leave to acquaint you that in accordance with the request contained in your letter to Mr Stevens of date the 18th ultimo, I have officially conveyed to His Excellency Mr Terashima His Majesty's Minister for Foreign Affairs, the information that you accept with pleasure the invitation of His Imperial Majesty's government to be during your stay in Japan the guest of the Empire. Prince Katè [*Date*] and Mr Yoshida the Japanese Envoy to the United States will leave Tokio on the 11th inst. for Nagasaki for the purpose of receiving you officially upon your arrival at that port. These gentlemen have kindly requested me to accompany them which I would do but for the belief that it is not probable that you will reach Nagasaki before the 23d of June at which time I have advised them it is my purpose to join them. Be assured that your visit to Japan will give great pleasure to the Emperor, his Ministers and his people, and that they will cordially and gratefully receive you as the friend of their country and also as the representative of the only Western Power that has by Solemn Treaty declared a willingness to assure to Japan her essential right, (so long, and still withheld from her) to regulate her foreign and domestic commerce, by laws of her own enactment. Permit me to add that I too, will be glad to receive and welcome you and your's to Japan. I beg leave to present my compliments to Mrs Grant. With sincere wishes for your health and prosperity, . . ." ALS, DLC-John Russell Young. On May 30, Bingham had written to Terajima Munenori, Japanese minister of foreign affairs. "I beg leave to acquaint Y. E. that Mr Stevens is this morning in receipt of a letter dated May 18 from General U. S. Grant, late President of the United States, in which the exPresident requests the acknowledgment to be made on his behalf to H. I. J. M's Government of the obligations of himself and party 'for the more than cordial invitation that they should be the guests of H. I. M's. Govt. during their stay in Japan.' I have the honor and pleasure further to say that the General accepts the invitation thus given in these words, 'I accept the same as a very high honor which I shall ever remember.' This Legation will in due time be advised by the General on what day he will sail direct from Tientsin for Japan, of which I will promptly inform you. He leaves Tientsin this day for Peking. What stay the General will make in China is not yet determined." Copy (filed with Bingham to William M. Evarts, June 7, 1879), DNA, RG 59, Diplomatic Despatches, Japan.

On June 18, Thomas B. Van Buren, consul gen., Kanagawa, wrote to USG. "This will be handed you by my friend Mr Tileston, one of a large number of *attenuated*

Americans here, who has lived in the Country a long time and who is, in all respects a very charming gentleman—I am extremely disappointed that my duties are so pressing as to prevent my going to meet you, but I beg to tender my congratulations upon the success so far attending your journey and to bid you in my own behalf and that of the Foreign residents of this community a most cordial welcome to Japan. Hoping to see you soon, and that you will adopt Mr Borie's suggestion to remain *at least* two months in Japan, I am with Kindest regards to Mrs Grant . . ." ALS, DLC-USG, IB.

On June 21, Edward G. Furber, Pacific Mail Steamship Co., and twelve others, Nagasaki, welcomed USG. "You have been so fêted in other lands during your two years' tour, that now, as you cross the threshold of this ancient Empire, which in twenty-five years has attempted to revolutionize the traditions of twenty-five centuries, we, representing the Foreign Community of Nagasaki, are sensible that any welcome we can offer you will appear but a poor one, compared with the receptions you have met with from the larger and more wealthy ports in China. . . ." *North-China Herald* (Shanghai), July 1, 1879. USG replied. "Gentlemen—It is very gratifying to me to have this welcome from the foreign residents of Nagasaki on the occasion of my landing in Japan. It has long been my wish to visit Japan, a nation which has always interested me and for whose efforts to advance in all the benefits of our civilization the American people have had so much sympathy. I hope that all foreign nations will continue to give Japan sympathy and encouragement. I hope also that she will long enjoy peace and especially be at peace with her neighbors. This will be a blessing to her as well as to the rest of the world. I thank you very much for your kind words of welcome, which show not alone your good feeling to me, but what I value more—your good feeling to my country." *New York Herald*, Aug. 22, 1879. On Aug. 23, Van Buren wrote to USG from Yokohama. "A few of the Foreign residents of Nagasaki who received you, when there, with a short address of Welcome, have had the latter printed upon silk within a wreath of flowers Exquisitely Embroidered, and have asked me to present the same to you in their names. I have therefore Very great pleasure in handing it to you herewith . . ." ALS, USG 3.

On June 22, USG had written a memorandum. "At the request of Governor Utsumi Tadakatsu Mrs. Grant and I each planted a tree in the Nagasaki park I hope that both trees may prosper, grow large, live long, and in their growth, prosperity and long life be emblematic of the future of Japan." ANS (facsimile), MoSHi. Also on June 22, Governor Utsumi Tadakatsu of Nagasaki invited Julia Dent Grant to dinner the next day. D, DLC-USG, IB.

On June 23, Utsumi addressed USG. "After a two year's tour through many lands, Nagasaki has been honored by a visit from the Ex-president of the United States, General Grant. Nagasaki is situated on the western shore of this Empire, and how fortunate it is, that I can greet and welcome you (on my official Capacity as Governor of Nagasaki) as you land for the first time on Japanese soil. Many years ago, Honored Sir, I learned to appreciate your great Services, and during a visit to the United States, I was filled with an ardent desire to learn more of your illustrious deeds, then you were the President of the United States. How could I then anticipate this occasion, the first Kenrei (governor) to receive you—Words cannot express my feelings. Nagasaki is so far from the seat of Government, that I fear you cannot have matters arranged to your satisfaction. It is my earnest wish, that you and Mrs Grant may safely travel through Japan and enjoy the visit." Translation, *ibid.* USG replied. "Your Excellency, ladies and gentlemen: You have here this evening several Americans who have the talent of speech and who could make an eloquent response to your address. I have no such gift, and I never lamented its absence more than now, when there is so much that I want to say about your country, your people and your progress. I have not been an inattentive observer of that progress, and in America we have been favored with accounts of it from my distinguished friend whom you all know as the friend of Japan, and whom it was my privilege to send as minister. I mean Judge Bingham. The spirit which has actuated the mission of Judge Bingham—the spirit of sympathy, support and conciliation—not only expressed my own sentiments but those of America. America has much to gain in the east. No nation has greater interests at stake. But America has nothing to gain except what comes from the cheerful acquiescence of the eastern people, and insures them as much benefit as it does us. I should be ashamed of my country if its relations with other nations, and especially with these ancient and most interesting empires in the east, were based upon any other idea. We have rejoiced in your progress. We have watched you step by step. We have followed the unfolding of your old civilization and its absorbing the new. You have had our profound sympathy in that work,—our sympathy in the troubles which came with it, and our friendship. I hope that our friendship may continue,—that it may long continue. As I have said, America has great interests in the east. She is your next neighbor. She is more affected by the eastern populations than any other power. She can never be insensible to what is doing here. Whatever her influence may be, I am proud to believe that it has always been exerted in behalf of justice and kindness. No nation needs from the outside powers justice and kindness more than Japan; for the work that has made such marvelous progress in the past few years is a work in which we are deeply concerned, and in the success of which we see a new era in civilization. This we should encourage. I do not know that I can say anything more than this in response to the kind toast of the governor. Judge Bingham can speak with more eloquence, and, as minister, with authority. But I could not allow the occasion to pass without saying how deeply I sympathized with Japan in her efforts to advance, and how much these efforts are appreciated in America. In that spirit, I ask you to unite with me in a sentiment:—'The prosperity and the independence of Japan.'" *Tokio Times*, July 12, 1879. See *New York Herald*, Aug. 22, 1879.

Also on June 23, Nagasaki citizens invited USG and Julia Grant to dinner the next day "at Fukusaiji, Chikugamachi, at 3 o'clock in the afternoon." D, DLC-USG, IB. Two local merchants presented an address, dated June 24. "General U. S. Grant—In the name of the citizens of Nagasaki we offer you a sincere welcome to this small town. We feel greatly honored by your visit to Nagasaki, and still more so by your becoming our guest this evening. Any outward signs of respect and hospitality we offer you are but a fraction of our kindly feelings toward you, . . ." *New York Herald*, Aug. 25, 1879. USG replied. "Gentlemen—I am highly honored by your address and also by this sumptuous entertainment. I have enjoyed exceedingly my visit to Japan, and appreciate more than I can say the kindness that has been shown me by all persons. But I have enjoyed nothing more than this, because it comes from the citizens of Nagasaki and is entirely unofficial. That I take as an especial compliment, coming, as it does, from the people and not the government. For while I am deeply gratified for all that your government is doing to render my trip here agreeable and instructive I have a peculiar pleasure in meeting those who are not in authority, who are the citizens of a country. I shall take away from Nagasaki the most grateful remembrances of your hospitality and the most pleasant recollections of the beauty of the place. Again, accept my sincere thanks for your kindness." *Ibid.* See *Julia Grant*, p. 293.

On July 1, Viceroy Li Hung-chang of Chihli, Tienstin, wrote to John Russell Young. "Since bidding you farewell at Taku I have not ceased to think of you, and I have now to thank you for your letter of 23d ulto. from Nagasaki, which tells me of your safe journey. The remarks made by General Grant to those who received him when he first landed in Japan, regarding the importance of preserving friendly relations with other countries, and especially of avoiding the interruption of long existing peaceful intercourse with neighboring Governments, are regarded with pleasure as an evidence of the General's philanthropy and comprehensive grasp of the whole situation, and show that he has not forgotten the appeal made to him by my Government and myself. For this I cannot sufficiently express my gratitude. In the letters I have received from Mr. Ho, our Chinese Minister in Japan, he has mentioned the friendly regard and the just sentiments towards China entertained by His Excellency the American Minister, Mr. Bingham; and now that Mr. Bingham has been in Consultation with General Grant regarding the Loo choo question, and his views are in accord, no doubt means may be adopted to meet the present exigency; so that a rupture of friendly relations between China and Japan may be averted. I am deeply moved by feelings of thankfulness, and would express my hope that General Grant and Mr. Bingham will be enabled to realize my poor desires; and for what they do I now offer my earnest thanks in advance. I would feel much obliged, also, by your writing me fully upon the course of affairs, and I now avail of this opportunity to wish you every prosperity." Translation, DLC-John Russell Young.

On Aug. 25 and Dec. 15, Utsumi wrote to USG. "I have the honor to respectfully offer you my congratulation upon the good health, which you have enjoyed, since you left Nagasaki, and during your excursions to the different localities. During your stay at this port, I expressed to you my desire, that I might go to the capital and again have the pleasure of seeing you there. But, greatly to my regret, I have been suffering from a disease of the stomach and still being under medical treatment I cannot gratify this desire. The tree, which you planted in the public garden of this port, has met with a good success and is growing more and more luxuriant. The monument for the same is now being prepared and it is my desire to be able to erect it shortly and to maintain it forever together with the tree. I would beg to express my sincere prayer that you will take a good care of yourself during the heat of the season" "It gives me the greatest pleasure to congratulate your excellency on the excellent health you have enjoyed, and I am very glad to learn of your safe arrival at Washington, after your long journey around the world. Accept my profound thanks for the Photograph you have so kindly favoured me with, It is an admirable likeness, and I wished to thank you before, but have been waiting for a favourable opportunity. It gives me the greatest pleasure to inform you that the Banyan tree planted by Mrs Grant and yourself, is growing fast and is in a most flourishing condition. The monument is erected near the middle of the group of trees, with the inscription engraved, after your autograph, and especial care will be taken that the monument may endure for myriads of years. I beg to enclose herewith, a lithographic copy of the inscription on the monument." L, USG 3.

1. See Adam Badeau, *Military History of Ulysses S. Grant,* . . . (New York, 1881–82), III, 81–114, especially pp. 112–14.
2. See *Badeau,* pp. 310–11.
3. See letter to King Kalakaua, May 16, 1879.

Speech

[*Tokyo, July 3, 1879*]

GENTLEMEN—I am very much obliged for this kind reception, and especially for your address. It affords me great pleasure to visit Tokio. I have been some days in Japan, having seen several points of interest in the interior and on the inland sea.[1] I have been gratified to witness the prosperity and advancement of which I had heard so much, and in which my countrymen have taken so deep an interest. I am pleased to hear your kind expressions toward the United States. We have no sentiment there that is not friendly to Japan, that does not wish her prosperity and independence, and a continuance on her part of her noble policy. The knowledge that your country is prosperous and advancing is most gratifying to the people of the United States. It is my sincere wish that this friendship may never be broken. For this kind welcome to the capital of Japan I am again very much obliged.

New York Herald, Aug. 31, 1879. USG replied to an address, dated July 3, 1879, from the Tokyo Reception Committee. "On behalf of the people of Tokio we beg to congratulate you on your safe arrival. How you crushed a rebellion, and afterwards ruled a nation in peace and righteousness, is known over the whole world, and there is not a man in Japan, who does not admire your high character and illustrious career. Although the Great Pacific Ocean stretches for thousands of miles between your country and ours, your people are our next neighbors in the East, and as it was chiefly through your initiative that we entered upon those relations and that commerce with foreigners, which have now attained such a flourishing condition, our countrymen have always cherished a good feeling for your people, and look upon them more than on any other foreign nation as their true friends. Moreover, it was during the happy times of your Presidency, that the two countries became more closely acquainted and connected, and almost every improvement that has been made in our country may be traced to the example and lessons received from yours. For years past, not only our Minister, but any one of our countrymen, who went to your country, was received with hospitality and courtesy. It is therefore impossible that our countrymen should now forbear from giving expression to their gratification and gratitude. Your visit to our shores is one of these rare events, that happen once in a thousand years. The citizens of Tokio consider it a great honor that they have been afforded the opportunity of receiving you as their guest, and they cherish the hope that this event will still more cement the friendship between the two nations in the future. We now offer you a hearty and respectful welcome." *Japan Herald* (Yokohama), July 4, 1879. See also *ibid.*, July 3, 1879; *Tokio Times*, July 5, 1879.

On July 4, John A. Bingham, U.S. minister, Tokyo, wrote to USG. "I am just in receipt of a letter dated the 2d instant from Shibusawa Yeichi and Fukuchi Kenichiro, a committee appointed to make suitable arrangements for your reception 'in the name of the people of this city.' I enclose a translation of the Committee's letter, and will be pleased to receive and communicate a letter from you indicating your purpose to accept the proposed courtesy at such time as may be agreeable after today. You may remember that Mr Kusumoto, the Governor of the capital, yesterday at the Palace made mention of this desire of the people to tender a reception, and that upon my calling your attention to the matter you indicated a willingness to accept their courtesies after today, of which I at the time advised the Governor." LS, DLC-USG, IB. The enclosure is *ibid.* For Shibusawa Eiichi and Fukuchi Gen'ichirō, see Richard T. Chang, "General Grant's 1879 Visit to Japan," *Monumenta Nipponica*, XXIV, 4 (1969), 373–78, 385–91; James L. Huffman, *Politics of the Meiji Press: The Life of Fukuchi Gen'ichirō* (Honolulu, 1980).

On July 6, Shibusawa and Fukuchi wrote to USG. "We are instructed, on behalf of the Tokio Citizens Committee of Reception, to inform you that the Citizens of Tokio desire to offer you a Public Reception at the Hall of the Kobu Dai Gakko, Tokio, on Tuesday evening July 8th 1879, at half past nine o'clock. We therefore respectfully request the honor of your presence at the time and place above stated, together with all the members of your family and Suite. If agreeable to yourself, the Chairmen of the Committee will wait upon you at 9 o'clock on the evening of the 8th instant, and escort you to the place of the Reception." LS, DLC-USG, IB. On July 8, John Russell Young wrote in his diary. ". . . In the evening we all went to the fête in honor of Gen Grant by the people of Tokio. This was a most beautiful scene. Lanterns by the hundred thousand. Remained until eleven when a slight rain came on, and we all came home drenched. In all respects memorable." DLC-John Russell Young. See *Japan Herald* (Yokohama), July 9, 1879; Charlotte T. Marshall and John Z. Bowers, eds., *Letters From Meiji Japan: Correspondence of a German Surgeon's Wife 1878–1881* (New York, 1980), p. 75.

On July 12, Shibusawa and Fukuchi invited USG and party to "the Shintomiza Theatre at 8.30 P. M on wednesday the 16th inst to witness some Japanese performances especially arranged for the entertainment." DS, DLC-USG, IB. On July 16, USG attended a play, intended to celebrate his own achievements, depicting the suppression of a revolt in eleventh-century Japan. See *Japan Herald* (Yokohama), July 17, 1879; *Tokio Times,* July 19, 26, 1879; Donald Keene, *Emperor of Japan: Meiji and His World, 1852–1912* (New York, 2002), p. 318. On Sept. 2, Shibusawa and Fukuchi wrote to USG. "We have the honor to inform your Excellency that we have immediately forwarded to Morita Kanya, the Proprieter of the Shintomiza theatre, a curtain presented to him through us by your Excellency together with a translation of your letter addressed to us. He has been deeply pleased with the same and has forwarded to us a letter returning his warmest thanks, which we beg leave to herewith enclose to your Excellency. . . ." Translation, USG 3. The enclosure is a letter of the same day from Morita Kanya to USG. "I have the honor to offer, in behalf of myself and all at my theatre, the highest appreciation for the honor you conferred upon us by being present at the theatric entertainment held for you by the Reception Committee of the Citizens of Tokio, and also by your presenting me a beautiful curtain which we will always regard as the boundless honor of my theatre and which we will forever keep for the remembrance of your visit to the City of Tokio. . . . P. S. I would pray your Excellency to accept this trifling offering of a set of the old Japanese Saddle in token of my highest regard to your Excellency." Translation, *ibid.*

1. After leaving Nagasaki on June 26, USG's ship anchored off Hiogo (June 30) and Shizuoka (July 1). See letter to Julius Stahel, May 18, 1879; *Young,* II, 514–19; *Julia Grant,* pp. 295–96.

Speech

[*Tokyo, July 4, 1879*]

Your Majesty: I am very gratified for the welcome you accord me here to-day, and for the great kindness with which I have been received, ever since I came to Japan, by your government and your people. I recognize, in this, friendliness toward my country. I can assure you that this feeling is reciprocated by the United States; that our people, without regard to party, take the deepest interest in all that concerns Japan, and have the warmest wishes for her welfare. I am happy to be able to express that sentiment. America is your next neighbor, and will always give Japan sympathy and support in her efforts to advance. I again thank your Majesty for your hospitality and wish you a long and happy reign, and for Japan prosperity and independence.

Tokio Times, July 12, 1879. USG replied to a translated address of Emperor Meiji. "Your name has been known to us for a long time, and we are highly gratified to see you. While holding the high office of president of the United States you extended to our countrymen special kindness and courtesy; and when our ambassador Iwakura visited the United States he received the kindest civilities from you. The kindness thus shown by you has always been remembered by us. In your travels around the world you have reached this country, and people of all classes feel gratified and happy to receive you. I trust that during your sojourn in our country you may find much to enjoy. It gives us sincere pleasure to receive you; and we are especially gratified that we have been able to do so on the anniversary of American independence. We congratulate you, therefore, on this occasion." *Ibid.* On July 4, 1879, John A. Bingham, U.S. minister, Tokyo, wrote to USG. "I have the honor to acquaint you that I am in receipt of an official communication from His Excellency Mr Terashima, His Imperial Japanese Majesty's Minister for Foreign Affairs, in which the Minister is pleased to say that His Majesty will receive you together with Mrs Grant, Colonel Grant and your Secretary, Mr Young, at 2 o'clock P. M. this day. I will join you at the Palace of Enriokuan at 1 P. M. to accompany you and your family to the audience." LS, DLC-USG, IB. See *PUSG*, 23, 35–40, 192–94, 202–3; *Young*, II, 523–31; *Julia Grant*, p. 297.

On Friday, probably July 4, Durham W. Stevens, secretary of legation, Tokyo, wrote to John Russell Young seeking an appointment "for General Grant to see Mr Soyeshima [*Soejima*]? Mr S was formerly Minister for Foreign Affairs and is now attached to the Court in the capacity of 'Reader' to the Emperor, a private, confidential and very important office. . . ." ALS, DLC-John Russell Young.

On July 15, Bingham wrote to Secretary of State William M. Evarts. "I have the honor to inform you that General U. S. Grant and suite arrived at Nagasaki, Japan, on the 20th ultimo, and that on the 21st ultimo I met him at that port, . . . The General arrived in Yokohama on the 3d of July, and was saluted by the war vessels of Russia Japan, France and the United States, the German man-of-war displaying the Imperial Ensign in honor of the General. The English men-of-war in port made no recognition of the General, owing to the order issued by Her Britannic Majesty's Colonial Secretary Sir Michael Hicks-Beach to the effect that Her Majesty's war vessels should not salute General Grant as he was but a private gentleman. After the salute the General was received at the Japanese Admiralty landing by His Majesty's Ministers of State, and conducted at once to Tokei, where he was met by the Governor and received an address of welcome from the citizens of Tokei, after which he was conducted by Japanese officials, under a guard of honor to the Palace of Enriokuan which had been assigned to him by the Emperor. The Palace assigned to the Ex President with all its surroundings is the finest in the Empire. On the 4th of July Their Majesties the Emperor and Empress gave audience to General and Mrs. Grant and received the distinguished visitor with marked consideration, in the presence of the Princes of the Empire, the Prime Ministers, Admiral Patterson and several Naval officers and the officers of this Legation. . . ." LS, DNA, RG 59, Diplomatic Despatches, Japan. *Foreign Relations, 1879,* pp. 643–44.

Speech

[*Tokyo, July 4, 1879*]

LADIES AND GENTLEMEN—I am unable to answer the eloquent speech of Judge Bingham, as it is in so many senses personal to myself. I can only thank him for his too flattering allusions to me personally and the duty devolving on me during the late war. We had a great war. We had a trial that summoned forth the energies and patriotism of all our people—in the army alone over a million. In awarding credit for the success that crowned those efforts there is not one in that million, not one among the living or the dead, who did not do his share as I did mine, and who does not deserve as much credit. It fell to my lot to command the armies There were many others who could have commanded the armies better. But I did my best, and we all did our best, and in the fact that it was a struggle on the part of the people for the Union, for the country, for a country for themselves and their children, we have the best assurances of peace and the best reason for gratification over the result. We are strong and free because the people made us so. I trust we may long continue so. I think we have no issues, no questions that need give us embarrassment. I look forward to peace, to generations of peace, and with peace prosperity. I never felt more confident of the future of our country. It is a great country—a great blessing to us—and we cannot be too proud of it, too zealous for its honor, too anxious to develop its resources, and make it not only a home for our children, but for the worthy people of other lands. I am glad to meet you here, and I trust that your labors will be prosperous, and that you will return home in health and happiness. I trust we may all meet again at home and be able to celebrate our Fourth of July as pleasantly as we do to-night.

New York Herald, Aug. 31, 1879. USG replied to a speech by John A. Bingham, U.S. minister, Tokyo. "General Grant:—On behalf of the citizens of the United States of America here assembled, I beg leave to bid you a hearty welcome to Japan. Here, as elsewhere, your countrymen hold you in the highest regard. In common with all Americans, we are not unmindful that in the supreme moment of our nation's trial, when our heavens were filled with darkness and the habitations of our people were filled with dead, you stood with our defenders in the forefront of the conflict, and with them achieved, amid the fires of battle, the victory which brought deliverance to our imperiled country. . . . I venture to say that this recognition of your services will not be limited to the present age and the present generation of men, but will continue from age to age through all the future. . . ." *Tokio Times*, July 26, 1879; ADf, Milton Ronsheim, Cadiz, Ohio. See *Japan Herald* (Yokohama), July 5, 1879.

On July 11, 1879, Samuel R. Brown, Yokohama, wrote to USG. "Will you excuse the liberty I take in addressing this note to you? I have been a missionary of the Reformed Church in America at this place sin[*ce*] the [1]st of Nov. 1859, and am now in my seventieth year, an invalid making preparation to go home to my native land; with my wife and daughter by the 'China,' which is to sail on or about the 27th inst. Tomorrow my wife and daughter propose to pay their respects to you at Tokio, with other missionaries & their wives. . . . I am delighted to observe the cordial reception given you by the Mikado, & the rulers and the people of this most interesting country." ALS, DLC-USG, IB. See William Elliot Griffis, *A Maker of the New Orient: Samuel Robbins Brown, Pioneer Educator in China, America, and Japan. . . .* (New York, 1902).

To Ellen Grant Sartoris

Tokio, Japan.
July 15th /79

DEAR NELLIE:

It has been longer since I wrote you last than between any two of my letters since leaving Paris. But we are now in a country where the regular mail goes but once a month. We arrived in Japan—at Nagasaki—about the 20th of June. Since that time we have been the guests of the Nation and have received every possible attention by all classes of people from the Emperor down. Japan is a most interesting ~~people~~ country and so are the people. The country is mountainous, with fine streams, fertile but narrow valleys and a teaming population. The hills are green to the very summit, and many cultivated, by terracing the sides, to quite a high elevation. All in all Japan & the Japanese are worth all the trouble, time and expense of visiting. I might give you some account of our reception here and in this country but Mr Young will give so full an account that I will trust to your reading that.

AL, ICHi. Julia Dent Grant concluded this letter. "your Papa has been called off to see some callers, I see your Pap has been telling you how charming & delightful the people & country are & What a kind & Princely man[ner] They are treating us—We are now occupying a beautiful Japanies Palace The growns are magnificent groves & Lakes & Lawns with lovely flowers The decorations of the house are simply lovely. I do nothing (whilst I am alone) but wander around & admire the lovely things—Fred & I are geting some very pretty things to take home Fred got several handsome double gowns yesterday for Ida & Mrs Sheridan. I will also get some for myself & you I know you would like to have one by this time I am so sorry that I cannot send my little *Violets* little dresses—untill I get home & if she is already out of long dresses I will send her the short ones as I can give to Ida the long dresses. (no doubt but she will need them soon) We are having Balls dinners, receptions Lunchons Thearitials & Mesicals, The most magnificent Fireworks all the time This is The Capitol & all the Legations are located here & The Japanies court is very magnificent, *We* have three ships of war here & the officers are all nice & do enjoy all the festivitys with us Kiss the dear little chicks for me The babys name is just the thing Violet (So Buckee tells me) Thank Algee for his letter to me, & remember me to him . . ." ALS, *ibid.* Ellen Grant Sartoris had named her new baby Vivien May.

On July 5, 1879, Inoue Kaoru, minister of public works, and his wife, invited USG and Julia Grant for dinner on July 6. D, DLC-USG, IB. Inoue had directed the renovation of Enryōkan, USG's residence while in Toyko. See *Young,* II, 534–39.

Also on July 5, Walsh, Hall & Co., Yokohama, wrote to John Russell Young, Tokyo. "We beg to acknowledge receipt of Messrs Drexel Harjes & Co's Letter of Credit No 1305 in favor of General U. S. Grant, upon which the General wishes to draw 5000 Francs. We much regret to say however that today being Saturday and a Bank Holiday, we are obliged to wait until Monday before sending the money. In the meantime we enclose a Draft (in Triplicate) on Messrs Drexel Harjes & Co. for the above amount, which we will thank you to have signed by the General and return to us. We will also forward the sum of $100. as requested by Messrs Russell & Co. Shanghai, and we will pay $180. to Mr. Mr. Thornton Paymaster U. S. N." L, DLC-John Russell Young.

On the same day, Tokudaiji Sanetsune, minister of the imperial household, wrote twice to USG. "I have the honor to inform you that on the 7th inst. a Military

Parade has been ordered in your honor at 9 o clock A. M. at the Hibiya Parade ground and to request you to be present on the occasion with Colonel Grant and your Secretary." "I have the honor to inform you that I am ordered by His Majesty the Emperor to request the pleasure of your company at breakfast to be given in your honor on the 7th instant at 12 o clock, at the Shiba Palace, and I am also ordered to convey to you His Majesty's desire that you will be pleased to accompany Mrs Grant and Colonel Grant." Translations, DLC-USG, IB. A guest list for the breakfast is *ibid.* See John Russell Young diary, July 7, 1879, DLC-John Russell Young; *Young*, II, 533–34; Donald Keene, *Emperor of Japan: Meiji and His World, 1852–1912* (New York, 2002), pp. 312–13.

On July 6, Iwakura Tomomi wrote to USG. "I have the honor to request that you will give me the pleasure of your company at luncheon on the 8th instant at 1 oclock P. M." L (in Japanese), DLC-USG, IB; translation, *ibid.* A related letter (in Japanese), dated July 5, is *ibid.* Also on July 6, Japanese officials escorted USG to a rifle-match. See *Japan Herald* (Yokohama), July 7, 1879.

In early July, "The Governor of Kanagawa on behalf of a committee of the citizens of Yokohama" invited USG and Julia Grant to a "party at the Town Hall on Wednesday Evening, the 9th July, at nine o'clock—" D (undated), DLC-John Russell Young. An itinerary for USG's train travel to Yokohama for this event is in DLC-USG, IB. See Young diary, July 9, 1879, DLC-John Russell Young; *Japan Herald* (Yokohama), July 10, 1879; *Japan Weekly Mail* (Yokohama), July 12, 1879. Also in early July, "representatives of the merchants of Yokohama" had welcomed USG. "That such an illustrious Visitor should honour us with his presence is a source of great pleasure to us, and in greeting Your Excellency to-day we would pray you to believe that no outward expression of welcome can adequately express our joy at your safe arrival and our hope that your sojourn among us may be a prolonged one—" D (undated), DLC-USG, IB.

On July 10, Prince Hachisuka invited USG and Julia Grant to attend an evening party on July 12. D, DLC-John Russell Young. See Young diary, July 12, 1879, *ibid.*; *Japan Herald* (Yokohama), July 14, 1879; Toku Baelz, ed., *Awakening Japan: The Diary of a German Doctor: Erwin Baelz* (1932; reprinted, Bloomington, Ind., 1974), pp. 46–47.

On July 11, Tanaka Fujimaro, vice minister of education, wrote to USG. "I have the honour to present to Your Excellency the copies of the annual reports of the Department of Education, the calendars and regulations of the schools under the control of the Department and also some other books selected from among the publications of this Department as mentioned in the list herewith enclosed. I shall feel very happy if Your Excellency will kindly accept them." LS, DLC-USG, IB. On July 10, Young had written in his diary. "This morning we drove to the normal school and were taken through by Minister Tanaka. The whole affair most interesting especially the children. Then we had tiffin, and back to the palace.—In evening we drove to the commencement of the University of Tokio and had a reception with displays illuminations and all kind of festivities. Nothing could be more interesting and worthy of note." DLC-John Russell Young. See also F. V. Dickins and S. Lane-Poole, *The Life of Sir Harry Parkes . . .* (London, 1894), II, 278–81; E. G. Holtham, *Eight Years in Japan 1873–1881 . . .* (London, 1883), pp. 254–58; Clara A. N. Whitney, *Clara's Diary: An American Girl in Meiji Japan*, ed. M. William Steele and Tamiko Ichimata (Tokyo, 1979), pp. 251–53, 255–61, 264–71.

To Daniel Ammen

Tokio, Japan, July 16th, 1879.

My dear Admiral,—

I have received several letters from you since I wrote last, the last one from Paris. I had previously read in the New York *Herald* the result of the Paris Conference on the Inter-Oceanic question, and of your triumph over deeply-seated prejudices. In my judgment it was very fortunate that you were selected to go, and consented.[1]

We have now been nearly a month in this interesting country and among these amiable people. The changes, however, have been very great since you were here last, and there is much that you would not recognize.[2] They have now a very perfect school system which enables all classes, male and female, to get a fair education. They have a Military and Naval Academy, both on a better basis than ours were for many years after their establishment.[3] They have colleges for the higher branches, both for those going into the public service and those who wish to obtain the highest education attainable, for their own gratification. The gentlemen connected with the government in any way, and many merchants and other people, dress in European style, and not unfrequently the ladies do also. The Japanese are altogether the superior people of the East. I think I see, however, dawning a new era for China. They have been learning two things from the experience of other Eastern countries; first, they must not mortgage themselves to European powers by borrowing their money; the second, the necessity of advancement with their own means and the employment of as few foreigners as possible as instructors. Their advance will therefore be slow until their own people are instructed sufficiently to become teachers. I see by the latest home papers that the Sultan of Turkey has carried out his design and sent me two Arab horses; I wish you would say to Beale, after giving him the respects of myself and Mrs. Grant, that I hope he will take care of them until I return.[4] If he chooses to send one to any one having a brood farm, he is at liberty to do so.

With kindest regards of Mrs. Grant, Fred, and myself to Mrs.
Ammen and the children,

I am yours truly,

U. S. GRANT.

ADMIRAL D. AMMEN.

Daniel Ammen, *The Old Navy and the New* (Philadelphia, 1891), pp. 547–48.
    On July 16, 1879, USG received receipts for eighteen letters and five letters. ADS,
DLC-USG, IB.

    1. See letter to Daniel Ammen, June 6, 1879.
    2. Daniel Ammen visited Japan in 1846 and 1868. See Ammen, pp. 137–42,
443–54.
    3. On July 16, 1879, USG planned to visit the Japanese naval academy, Kaigun
Heigakkō, established in 1869, to witness gun practice and training ship maneuvers.
Japan Herald (Yokohama), July 15, 1879. For USG's earlier tour of the military acad-
emy, Rikugun Shikan Gakkō, established in 1874, see *Japan Weekly Mail* (Yokohama),
July 26, 1879.
    4. Later in 1879, three men conspired to steal these horses. See *Washington Post*,
Dec. 26, 1879; letter to Edward F. Beale, March 6, 1878.

To Adam Badeau

———

Tokio Japan
July 16th /79

MY DEAR GENERAL:

Your letter inclosing the chapter on Hatchers Run reached me
last night. I have read it carefully and see nothing to correct unless
it might be to let Warren off a little lighter. But in that respect do
as you please for I think you are entirely correct.[1]

We have now been in Japan for nearly a month. The country
is most beautiful and the people charming. There is nothing they
are prouder of than their institutions of learning, from their common schools up the highest college, including their Military & Naval schools. There is no country where the arrangements are more
complete for giving every child, male and female, a fair common
school education than in Japan. Their higher institutions compare
favorably with those of the oldest countries of the highest civilization. The better class of males wear the european costume and

many of the ladies are begining to adopt it also. From China to Japan the change is very great both in the people and country. But I though[t] I saw jerms of progress in China. The country has great resources and a wonderfully industrious, ingenious & frugal people. The end of this century will probably see China looming up.

To-morrow we go to the interior for a week or two.[2] After that I shall visit some other points of interest in the country and set sail for home on the 27th of August.[3] I dread going home but must do so.

Remember Mrs. Grant and I to Mr. Welsh and his family with him, and be assured of our kind regards for yourself. Young & Fred join me in this.

Very Truly yours

U. S. Grant

Gen. A. Badeau.

ALS, Munson-Williams-Proctor Institute, Utica, N. Y.

1. Adam Badeau discussed Maj. Gen. Gouverneur K. Warren at Hatcher's Run, Oct. 27–28, 1864. See Badeau, *Military History of Ulysses S. Grant,* . . . (New York, 1881–82), III, 114–28. See also *PUSG*, 12, 360–61; David M. Jordan, *"Happiness Is Not My Companion": The Life of General G. K. Warren* (Bloomington, Ind., 2001), pp. 198–99.

2. For the journey to Nikkō, see John Russell Young diary, July 17–19, 1879, DLC-John Russell Young; *Young*, II, 552–54; *Julia Grant*, pp. 300–301.

3. On May 3, Russell & Co., agents, Pacific Mail Steamship Co., Hong Kong, had written to Frederick Dent Grant. "We have received instructions by wire from the President of the Pacific Mail Steamship Company, to furnish General Grant and party with a free passage hence, or from Yokohama to San Francisco. Will you kindly advise us or the General Agent at Yokohama, about the date General Grant proposes leaving for the United States, so that the necessary arrangements can be made for his accommodation. Our probable departures from Yokohama are S. S. 'City of Tokio' June 1st S. S. 'City of Peking' July 1st" L (tabular material expanded), DLC-USG, IB. On May 28, an agent for the Occidental & Oriental Steamship Co., Yokohama, wrote to USG, Shanghai. "I am instructed by the President and Board of Directors of this Company to extend to yourself, Mrs. Grant, and the gentlemen accompanying you, the hospitalities of the Co. between this port and San Francisco, together with the hope that you will avail of them. Our Steamers leave Yokohama for San Francisco about the 10th of each month, & if you will, at your leisure and convenience, kindly signify your proposed date of departure from Yokohama, every thing will be done to make your voyage across the Pacific a pleasant one. Should our sailing dates not be in accord with your proposed movements, we can easily alter the same, and we trust you will not hesitate to make your wishes known in this direction, in order that we may have the pleasure of conforming to them." LS, DLC-John Russell Young. See John Haskell Kemble, "The Big Four at Sea: The History of the Occidental and Oriental Steamship Company," *The Huntington Library Quarterly*, III, 3 (April, 1940), 339–57.

To Adolph E. Borie

———

Tokio Japan,
July 16th /79

MY DEAR MR. BORIE:

We have now been in Japan nearly a month. The country is beautiful—as you saw—and the people most kindly. Our first landing in the country was at Nagasaki, where we remained a week. From there we came through the inland sea—which you did not see—to Yokohama, traveling only by day. There is nothing pictured in novels half so beautiful as the inland sea. We anchored at nights but unfortunately the Cholera was—and is now—very virulent around the entire coast of the inland sea so that we could not land.

Our reception and entertainment has been different from any thing you saw while with us. Siam came the nearest. I will not describe because Youngs letter, by this mail, will give full description.[1] This much I will say however: since we have been in the country we have been on the continual go, day & night. I have visited their schools, colleges, Naval and Military Academies and feel sure they compare well with ours at home. In fact the authorities seem prouder of their institutions of learning than of any thing else. But I will not bore you further on this subject. Our officers of the Ashuelot, who you know intimately, are here and we have been the means of giving them opportunities of seeing what they may not have had the opportunity otherwise of seeing. We found the officers of the Richmond quite as agreeable, and much more numerous. The ship too is commodious and a good sea goer. No cleverer a man sails a ship than Capt. Benham.[2] It is certain they did all they could to reach us, and it was a great disappointment to them that they did not succeed at least as early as Singapore. I would write to Drexel and Childs by this mail but it closes to-night. I have already this a. m. visited the Naval Academy; at 12 30 go to tiffin to visit the last institution I I have not yet seen;[3] after which two temples. In the evening we go to a theatrical—Japanese—performance specially got up for us.[4] We go to the interior to-morrow, to the mountains, for some days. On the 27th of August we sail for San Francisco. It is my intention to remain on the Pacific coast for a number of weeks, long enough to visit my old stoping grounds not only in the state but in Oregon and Washington territory.

Remember me to all my old friends in Phila and give Mrs. Grant's Fred's and my love to Mrs. Borie. For yourself the same.

Ever Truly yours
U. S. Grant

ALS, PHi. On Sept. 1, 1879, Adolph E. Borie, Philadelphia, wrote to USG, San Francisco. "I still owe you a reply to your's of 16 July from Tokio, as if sent you previously, it would have reached Japan after your departure thence Since my last in answer to yrs of 6th June from Pekin, we have read all the very interesting letters of our good 'Commodore' in the 'Herald' describing your visits to & from Pekin &cer, & to and at Nagasaki and Tokio &cer and I now drop him a line to express the great satisfaction we *all* (ladies particularly) have experienced from the able descriptions. Let me here, correct an item in yrs of 16th July. I did see, with great pleasure the full beauties of the 'Inland sea' from Nagasaki to 'Kobé', & only missed seeing Tokio only having 1 day in 'Yokohama' which turned into a very busy one and all taken up in a pretty full collection of bronzes silks, porcelains, fans &cer, (I hope Mrs. Grant found plenty left.) How shocked we all were for nearly two days by the unpardonable cable of 16 June about 'Nelly,' I need not tell you, and we trust most warmly it never reached you. I have remained since my last out here nearly every day, trying to regain my strength, as against the heats in town, and altho these have been rather moderate, I have but partially succeeded and still await the permanently cooler weather now approaching, before abandoning good hopes Business has continued to improve in all but Coal, the managers of which article have shown great imbecillity, and permitted it to reach prices which are terribly low, but so low that I cannot but believe that they must bring about very soon, a better agreement &cer. Coal stocks have fallen very heavily, Reading from 20 to 16½, but we [— — — — —] many of us have to sell. 'Iron' has kept up very nicely, in spite of a good steel coming up from England, and this is of great importance to Reding, and most of my Iron Co stocks have risen from 30 [—] of the value up to 100 at which they are *selable*. So, I keep up my spirits and trust to 'Gould', (now back from London and very well and in good spirits, particularly about the confidence evinced by our Stock & bond holders in Great Britain) to bring Reading out all right I notice all said about you in regard to the Panama Canal: if that is offered to you *in the proper shape*, I should be delighted to see you accept; but not unless in that shape *beyond a doubt*, and then, only in case a proper person can be found to take your place, at Washington, to save the Country from the 'infamous conspiracy now threatning' it between the Democrats and ex Rebels. Drexel & Childs are well and send love. Genl Patterson, also, nears to 88 Mrs B. & all our folks send their love also to you & Mrs G. in which I fervently join." ALS, DLC-USG, IB. See Borie to John Russell Young, Sept. 1, 1879, DLC-John Russell Young.

On July 8, John M. Keating, Philadelphia, had written to John Russell Young. ". . . What an awful time I had with reporters when I got back. I managed to dodge all but one chap, by flying to the country, but poor old Mr Borie was corner[e]d & in his innocence put his foot into it & the papers have been giving it to him ever since—He has been quite feeble since his return, the sudden cessation of all excitement now that he is settled down has brought on a very depressing reaction. . . ." ALS, *ibid.* On June 16, Borie had answered a San Francisco reporter's question on another presidential nomination for USG. "I hope he will refuse to accept the infernal office. I call it infernal because I consider it the most trying and difficult position in the world. In fact, so anxious have I been for him to decline that it was for the sole purpose of endeavoring to dissuade him from making a sacrifice of himself that I left Philadelphia and joined him when I did. . . . I didn't have an opportunity to talk directly to him on the subject. In fact, I never got any further than hints, insinuations and suggestions. . . ." *San Francisco Chronicle*, June 17, 1879. For additional Borie remarks, see *New York Herald*, June 26, 29, 1879.

   1. For Young's account of USG's reception at Tokyo, see *ibid.*, Aug. 31, 1879.
   2. Andrew E. K. Benham joined the navy as a midshipman (1847) and rose through the ranks to capt. (1878). See *Washington Post*, Aug. 12, 1905.
   3. On July 14, Kuroda Kiyotaka, minister of colonization, Tokyo, wrote to USG. "I have the honor to inform you that it is my desire to show you the productions of Hakkaido collected at the branch office of Colonization Department and to offer you Tiffin prepared of Hakkaido products on the 16th instant at half past twelve o clock. You will therefore be pleased to accompany Mrs Grant and Colonel Grant." Translation, DLC-USG, IB. On July 15, Kuroda invited Young to join USG. Translation, DLC-John Russell Young.
   On Aug. 30, Kuroda again wrote to USG. "It would give us much pleasure to have you visit Hokkaido and show you some progress we made there in industry, mining & agriculture, of which Gen. Horace Capron, while engaged in our services, took an active part. We feel very sorry that time does not allow you to make a trip there, but desire to show you some things of Hokkaido and present you two rolls of Japanese silks (Kohaku-ori & Kaiki) & 3 doz. of Handkerchiefs, which were all manufactured in Hokkaido with materials produced there and hope you would accept them as a specimen of Hokkaido manufacture" LS, USG 3. See *PUSG*, 22, 37–38, 45–46; David F. Anthony, "The Administration of Hokkaido under Kuroda Kiyotaka, 1870–1882: An Early Example of Japanese-American Cooperation," Ph.D. Dissertation, Yale University, 1951; John A. Harrison, *Japan's Northern Frontier:* . . . (Gainesville, 1953), pp. 59–120.
   4. See Speech, [*July 3, 1879*].

Addressee Unknown

———

Tokio, Japan, July 16th [*1879*]

. . . We expect to sail on the *City of Tokio*, which is to leave here for San Francisco on the 27th of August. . . . We have now been in Japan nearly a month, the guests of the nation, and have received the most unbounded hospitalities. Our first stop in the country was at Nagasaki, where we remained a week. It was a continuous ovation while we remained. From Nagasaki, we came up through the inland sea to Yokohama, anchoring at night, so as to lose no part of the scenery. It is grand beyond description, and strongly in contrast with what we had left in China. In Japan, the country is mountainous, and green and fresh to the very summit of the highest hills. In China—so far as the foreigner usually sees it—it is a flat, desert-looking dust or mud plain—depending upon whether it is the dry or rainy season—without anything to rel[i]eve the eye. The scenery up through the inland sea is very grand, and we got as good a view of it as is possible from the deck of a steamer, but we did not land anywhere. The cholera had broken out a few days before our arrival, all along the borders of the sea, and was carrying off the people by hundreds. . . . What I said at Penang about the Chinese question was without previous thought or preparation. I had no idea what the address to me was to be until it was read in the presence of an assembly. The response had to be spontaneous, and now I see nothing in particular to alter or take back.[1] The fact is, the Chinese question is not going to agitate the country long. The Chinese Government are very anxious to keep all their people at home, and, if not interfered with, they will stop emigration. . . .

Very truly yours,

U. S. GRANT.

Alta California, Aug. 3, 1879. The San Francisco newspaper printed portions of a USG letter "to a personal friend in our city." *Ibid.*

1. See letter to Elizabeth M. Borie, April 3, 1879.

To Elihu B. Washburne

Nikko, Japan.

July 23d /79

MY DEAR WASHBURNE:

Some weeks since I received your letter written after you had received mine from Bombay. You had not received one from me written after your suggestion had been received to go to Galena on my return home: I answered that letter saying that I should go there,[1] and presume you rec'd it after yours was written. Lest you may not have rec'd it however I repeat that it has been my intention to go to Galena on my return.

Since my last to you I have visited the principle sea coast cities in China and Peking in the interior, and have now been nearly a month in this most interesting country, and among these interesting people. China stands where she did when her ports were first open to foreign trade. I think I see dawning however the begining of a change. When it does come China will rapidly become a powerful and and rich nation. Her territory is vast and is full of resources, agricultural & mineral. Iron, coal, copper, silver & gold, beside nearly every other metel abounds as they does with us. The population is industrious, frugal, intelligent and and quick to learn. They are natural artisans and tradesmen. From Bombay to Hongkong they monopolize all the trades—mechanical—the market gardening; trucking, stevodoring; small shopkeeping, &c. and are rapidly driving out the larger merchants. They cannot do so well however in their own country. They must have the protection of a better and more honest government to succeed. Neither the country, cities or people present attractions to invite the traveler to make a second visit. Japan is different. The country is beautiful beyond description. Every street and every house is as clean as they can be made. Good water prevails every where and it is freely used. The progress that has been made in the last dozen years is almost inconceivable. Free schools abound all over the land giving facilities for every child, male & female, to get a fair education. Attendance is almost compulsory between certain ages. In the cities they have Academies, Colleges and Normal schools both to prepare males and females. It has been my privilege to visit at Tokeo (Yeddo) their Military & Naval Academies, their school of science; their College; their Normal school for young ladies; a very large school for children, taught by female teachers prepared at the Normal school, and other places of learning. The two former compare very well with our own Military & Naval Academies in course taught, discipline, drill and progress of the students. A student to enter the school of science must be a good english scholar, and, after entering, all his text books and resitations are in english. The course is six years, the last two in application of what they learned in the first four. A portion of each year—taking the place of vacation with us—is also spent in the workshops making parts of machinery, models of engines, of looms, machinery for spinning and weaving, &c. &c. Many of their teachers are natives though the studies are in english. It will be but a few years before they will be able to dispense with foreign instruction entirely.

We leave for home by the City of Tokeo which will sail from Yokohama about the 27th of August. I shall be glad to be settled down at home.

With kindest regards of Mrs. Grant and myself to you, Mrs. Washburne and the children, I am,

Very Truly Yours

U. S. GRANT

I forgot to mention that students to enter the college must study english five years first making a nine year course. Here too they have one or two native professors.

ALS, IHi. On Sept. 13, 1879, Elihu B. Washburne, Chicago, wrote to USG. "When I got back from the East a week ago, I found yours of the 23d July from Nikko. I wrote you fully about what I had done at Galena about your house and sent duplicates to San Francisco. I presume you will get either one or the other. All will be ready for Mrs. Grant and yourself when you shall arrive. As I wrote, it would be well for Mrs. G. to have Buck send some cutlery and crockery as they are the only things wanting. I have not been at Galena since I ordered the repairs made, but learn from a friend that the place now looks very well. I wish you would drop me a line, or send special word by Fred, how long you will remain on the Pacific Coast and about what time we may expect you at Galena. Mrs. W. has not yet returned from the East, but remains a short time to put our youngest daughter at school in Boston. I dont wonder that you have a longing to get home and settled down. Galena will be a good place for rest. It may be thought too quiet, but you will have a great many people to see you. I hope you will get to G. in season to vote at the local election early in November. I am still annoyed by the bronchitis and fear I may have to seek a milder clime than Chicago during the severe winter months. Kind regards to Mrs. G. . . ." ALS, DLC-John Russell Young.

On July 22, Tashiro Arajiro and three others had written to USG. "Since the distinguished name and magnanimity of your Excellency have been known to us who are living in the Eastern Hemisphere, we were desiring to have once the honor of access to your Excellency. It was beyond our expectation that your Excellency should come to this country and confer a great favor upon us by visiting Nikko. We consider your Excellency's visit as the highest honor that we have ever received. Now we the members of the local assembly of this Ken & the deputies of those who desire to receive your Excellency with hearty welcome express our congratilations for your Excellency's safe arrival here, and beg to present to your Excellency some specimens of hemps caltivated in this part of the country. We take this opportunity of expressing our sincere desire that your Excellency will enjoy long life & continue in happiness & prosperity, and also our warm thanks for the sincerity & kindness of your Excellency's country." Translation, DLC-USG, IB. USG remained at Nikkō until July 28. See John Russell

Young diary, July 20–21, 28, 1879, DLC-John Russell Young; *Young*, II, 562–64; Robert Charles Hope, *The Temples and Shrines of Nikkō, Japan* (Yokohama, 1896).

Also on July 22, Kimura Uzo wrote to USG. "... Ashikaga, in the county of Ashikaga, where we inhabit, and places in its vicinity, are noted in Japan for the woven goods which amount in value to more than three millions and five thousand yens every year. But we are not satisfied with this and in connection with those of the same view, have formed a society at Ashikaga, called the 'Kogiokai (Industrial Society) for the purpose of increasing a Knowledge and of encouraging the growth & manufacture of woven goods. Now I have the honor of offering Your Excellency through the hands of the local authorities, one volume containing specimens of the woven goods manufactured by that society & of requesting you to look it through, ..." Translation, DLC-USG, IB. USG visited Ashikaga on his way to Nikkō.

On July 30, Shirane Tasuke, governor of Saitama-ken, wrote twice to USG. "During my nine year's service in the local government, I have never been honored by the visit of a foreign distinguished guest, although I have already twice received His Majesty the Emperor. When your Excellency was lately passing through the district under my jurisdiction, it was my great regret that I was not able to have the honor of receiving your Excellency, on account of the visit of the Empress Dowager to the Warm Springs at Ikawo. Now, I avail myself of this opportunity of your return from Nikko to confer on me such great honor as personally appearing before your presence on behalf of a million of inhabits under the jurisdiction of the Saitama Ken. This honor is so great that it can never be obtained for many centuries. Again I avail myself of this occasion to express my earnest desire that in future, also, friendly relations between Japan and the United States will be continually strengthened, and also that your Excellency and your family will continue in happiness and prosperity." "Being intrusted with the office of governor of this province, it is my desire to promote the good administration of the government and place the people under happy and prosperous conditions of life, but owing to a want of Knowledge and experience, I am not able to accomplish a thousandth part of what I expect to do ... It is true that Japan and the United States are separated far from each other, and the mode of administration differs, yet if your Excellency will be kind enough to give me some instructions on the general principles which may be taken as a future guide, not only I, but the whole people under my jurisdiction will feel highly gratified and much indebted for your Excellency's kindness." Translations, *ibid.*

1. See letter to Elihu B. Washburne, May 4, 1879.

To Adam Badeau

Tokio, Japan
August 1st /79

MY DEAR GENERAL:

Your letter enclosing the within chapter reached me in the interior of Japan—at Nikko—just the evening before I started on my return here.[1] The chapter is so personal to myself that I can say nothing about it. But I have corrected two or three little errors of fact.[2] My visit to Japan has been the most pleasant of all my travels. The country is beautifully cultivated, the scenery is grand, and the people, from the highest to the lowest, the most kindly & the most cleanly in the world. My reception and entertainment has been the most extravigant I have ever known, or even read, of.[3] But as Young will probably give a full description of which you will read not long after receiving this, I will not attempt it. You speak of only receiving two letters from me since my departure from Marseilles! Probably since your last letter you have received two or three others. At all events I have returned all your chapters, with letters accompanying, and hope you have received them. I assure you that I am always glad to hear from you even if I do not answer as promptly as I might.

On the 27th of this month we sail for San Francisco. At the end of the first year abroad I was quite home sick but determined to remain to see every country in europe at least. Now at the end of twenty six months I dread going back and would not if there was a line of steamers between here and Australia. But I shall go to my quiet little home in Galena and remain there until the cold drives me away. Then I will probably go south—possibly to Havanna & Mexico—to remain until April.

Mrs. Grant, Fred & Young desire to be specially remembered to you.

Yours Truly
U. S. GRANT

GN. A. BADEAU

ALS, Munson-Williams-Proctor Institute, Utica, N. Y. See *Badeau*, p. 517.
    On Aug. 1, 1879, USG spoke. "Gentlemen and foreign residents of Yokohama, I am proud of the opportunity to be with you, and to be your guest this evening. In my journey round the world I have not enjoyed my visit to any country more than I have to this. And without saying more I wish to propose a toast. It is 'The foreigners residing in, and the Government and people of this country.' May they all live together in harmony, and may Japan increase in prosperity, power, and influence." *Japan Herald* (Yokohama), Aug. 2, 1879. On July 10, Thomas B. Van Buren, consul gen., Kanagawa, had invited USG to a garden party on behalf of "the Foreign Community of Yokohama—a community composed of all nationalities and gathered from almost every clime. . . ." *Ibid.*, July 11, 1879. USG replied "that he would be most happy to accept the hospitality of the Foreign Community of Yokohama, but it was impossible for him at present to fix a date. He would leave here on the 16th on a trip to Nikko, and expected to be absent about 10 days, and allowing even 12 days, he would return on the 28th. Any date therefore in the first week of August would be convenient to him. After that he expected to

make a trip up north to Hakodate, and he would leave Japan on the 27th August. It was therefore agreed that the Garden Party should take place at the time suggested." *Ibid.*

1. July 27.

2. For this description of USG's life at City Point, Va., see Adam Badeau, *Military History of Ulysses S. Grant,* . . . (New York, 1881–82), III, 135–49.

3. On Aug. 4, John A. Bingham, U.S. minister, Tokyo, wrote to USG. "At noon to-day I received through the Post Office an Enclosure printed in Japanese without a name attached though the name Murayama Kiyoshi as was endorsed on the enevelope. I shall bring the matter to the attention of the Government which as you will see by the enclosed translation made by Mr Thompson Interpreter to this Legation knows that mischief is intended & murder, if the writer is not demented in sending to me such a statement. You notice his envelope bears date yesterday the 3d. inst—& he concludes his printed enclo-sure with the words 'this out-break is near at hand, & cannot be averted. Hence notice is given before hand.' I hope to call & see you this evening or in the morning" ALS, DLC-USG, IB. The enclosed translation also is dated Aug. 4: "Recently many foreign visitors have come to Japan, as Reid, the Prince of Germany, Hennessy, & Grant. In entertaining them there has been boundless extravagance, and needless expenses have been incurred, the like of which have never been ~~witnessed~~ seen in our country in ancient or modern times. Does any one say ~~this~~at this was the will of His Majesty the Emperor? Such ~~is~~was not all the case. Does any one say the people loved to have it so? Such was not the case at all. The responsibility of this wrong lies with certain corrupt Officials, who to secure their own ends flatter the foreign visitors, and that too while difficully is pending be-tween this country and China, respecting the Settlement of the Riu Kiu matter, a matter in which China is ready ~~to~~ to appeal to the sword. Surely the Safety and reputation of the country is at stake. The offense of those who have committed such extravagance to the dishonor & injury of their country and people is one that neither Heaven ~~and earth~~ nor earth cannot forgive. Hence Soldiers of the Sei-gi-to-ron, (Right discussion party) have agreed to ~~exceut~~ kill, for the countrys benefit, Okuma Shigenobu & Ito Hirobumi, the ~~crimin~~ guilty ringleaders, and then they wish to assassinate Grant and Hennessy. Fur-ther: Shibusawa Sakarichi [*Eiichi*] & Fukuchi Genichiro & the like ~~are all~~ fellows are all vile as dirt & not fit to be mentioned Still as they countenance the corrupt officials and help them to gain their private ends & thereby poison Society, it only remains for them to be butchered along with the others. This outbreak is near accomplishment & cannot be averted Hence notice is given beforehand." D, *ibid.* On Aug. 16, Bingham wrote to Secretary of State William M. Evarts reporting the threat and the inconclusive Japa-nese investigation. LS, DNA, RG 59, Diplomatic Despatches, Japan.

To Daniel Ammen

———

Tokeo, Japan
Aug. 7th 1879.

MY DEAR ADMIRAL,

Your letter of the 2d of July reached me a few days since. After two days reflection on your suggestion of the part I should take—

or consent to take if offered—in the matter of the Inter-Oceanic Canal, via Nicaragua I telegraph[ed] to the Sec. of the Navy, Washington: "Tell Ammen approve. Grant." I hope you received the dispatch?[1] On the 27th, two weeks after this leaves Yokohama we sail for San Francisco. I do not feel half as anxious to get home as I did eighteen months ago. There is no country that I have visited however this side of Europe, except Japan, where I would care to stay longer than to see the points of greatest interest. But Japan is a most interesting country and the people are quite as much so. The changes that have taken place here are more like a dream than a reality. They have a public school system extending over the entire empire affording facilities for a common school education to every child, male & female They have a Military & a Naval Academy that compare well with ours in course taught, discipline and attainments of the students They have colleges at severa[l] places in the empire on the same basis of instruction as our best institutions. They have a school of science which I do not believe can be beat in any country. Already the great majority of their professors—even in teaching European languages—are natives, most of them educated in the very institutions where they are now teaching. But I hope to meet you soon and then I will say more on this subject than I care to write in the limit of a letter.

Mrs. Grant sends her love to Mrs. Ammen and the children. Please remember me kindly also.

Yours Truly

U. S. GRANT

ADM.L D. AMMEN

ALS, DLC-John Tyler Morgan. On Sept. 12 and 13, 1879, Daniel Ammen, "'Ammendale' near Beltsville, Md," wrote to USG, San Francisco. "I have to apologize for not acknowledging the receipt of the several letters from you to my address as above—I have received also your note of August 7th from Tokio stating that you would leave for home in a fortnight. On the receipt of your telegram of August 7th I informed the President of its contents and sent its import to prominent gentlemen in Nicaragua for the purpose of preventing any untoward action on the part of that Government in granting a concession for a canal to speculators to hawk about the World, or to persons who might wish to hold it merely to embarrass or prevent the construction of the canal. There seemed to be no reason or advantage in having the public precipitately informed of your willingness to aid in the construction of the work.—In the N. Y. World of the 22nd of August I read an editorial urging you as the fittest person for the Presidency of the Nicaragua Canal.—It seemed to me proper then, to write a letter to that paper which was published on the 26th a copy of which I enclose.—This called forth a general and very favorable expression of opinion of the press, with one or two exceptions wherein I was considered as officious and noisy and not knowing fully what I was talking about. As you are aware on my return from Paris I endeavored to have our Government call a Commission without delay, as stated in the terms of my Report, copies of which I send you, but although the idea was approved by the press of all parties it has not been carried out.—Whilst I feel satisfied that the President is entirely favorable to the project it would be purely *supposititious* were I to express an opinion why this commission had not been called.—It seemed to me of great moment that it should be done without delay to prevent losses abroad if not at home by investments in the Panama project of ignorant people.—Happily however, and the result of attempts to raise the money has proven the assertion, the decision of the Congress had no force inasmuch as almost all of the able Engineers regarded it as Mr Menocal and I did.—Such a Commission seemed to me necessary too, in order to enlighten the public both at home and abroad in relation to the comparative merits of the Panama and Nicaragua routes through a full discussion of the surveys made by the order of our Government, by able Engineers. To complete the work fully it seemed to me advisable that this Commission should name from its members such as were willing to visit the two routes and that our Government should provide the necessary means and ask an appropriation for a moderate compensation to them.—The object of this visit would be to ascertain the relative facilities of execution through the existence or absence of material for construction and other conditions affecting the execution of the work.—Also, after a careful examination of the note books if it was thought necessary, to verify any part of the surveys that they regarded with doubt. In a conversation with Mr Cyrus W. Field touching the non-action of our Government he thought it of much importance that Sir John Hawkshaw of England, and a Civil Engineer designated by the Society of Civil Engineers of Paris, and another selected by our Society of Civil Engineers should make a personal visit to both Panama and Nicaragua to perform the functions of the Commission proposed by me.—Five days ago I wrote to Sir John Hawkshaw as to this and sent the letter through Mr Field. It is proper to inform you if I have not done so before that Mr Field was in England just on the adjournment of the Congress at Paris, and saw Sir John Hawkshaw with whom he had several conversations, the result of which indicated apparent agreement between those two gentlemen and myself touching the merits of the Canal question and the desirability of forwarding the execution of the work. A week ago I was in New York and had a general conversation with Mr Field touching the adoption of some plan of procedure but arrived at nothing further than that I should write to Sir John Hawkshaw in relation to the question which I did, as before stated.—Mr Field seemed to think it advisable to have your views regarding the organization of a Company, the terms of a concession and such other matters as seem of moment to you. Some two or three weeks after my return from Paris I had a visit from Mr F. Morris who has a farm in an adjoining county where he resides a part of the year at least on account of the health of his wife.—He is a New Yorker, a gentleman of good manners and address and was the President of the old Nicaragua Transit Company.—He wished to be informed of the proceedings of the Congress, and particularly what I thought of them. A month later he wrote me asking whether I would be disposed to forward to you his ideas and a plan for forming an Inter-Oceanic Canal company of which he proposed you should be the President.—I replied that I would do so and stated that you would arrive about the middle of September.—A week ago when I was in New York he asked that I would call and see him.—He then showed me a concession which he purposed asking of the Nicaraguan Government which from a cursory reading I thought to be a fair one.—He stated that with your consent obtained it was his purpose to ask it in your name his own and mine in behalf of some or a certain number of men of influence and wealth whose names were known to me.—I replied that I would forward to you what he proposed; that so far as I was concerned I did not *wish* to be upon it or to have any active participation in the work.—He insisted that my name would be of service in obtaining a concession in Nicaragua and I informed him that I would consider his proposal.—He has been to Nicaragua within the past two or three years one or more times for the purpose of obtaining a concession. I have advices indirectly from President Zavala of Nicaragua and persons of prominence that they will grant any concession that seems necessary to you to any company of which you will be the President.—Of course I construe this to mean that they do not doubt that your ideas would accord with their own as to the proper terms of the concession. Whilst undue haste seems unnecessary, it is plain that any great delay would appear to manifest on the part of our countrymen an indifference and would naturally lead to a less earnest and enthusiastic consideration of the subject by the Nicaraguans. The prominent position Mr Field occupies at home and abroad and his connection with and in the management of great public works would in my belief fit him specially for the organization of an initiatory company in relation to which he will doubtless inform you ere long if he thinks of endeavoring to develop the project. Many thanks for the admirable photograph of yourself and the Viceroy which arrived to-day.—Please present Mrs Ammens and the childrens love to Mrs Grant and my kind congratulations and remembrances." "Yesterday when I wrote you on reaching Washington I found that I had not brought with me the copy of the letter I wrote published in the New York World of the 26th August, which I now enclose.—I brought in by mistake Mr Field's arraignment of Mr Tilden which strikes me as convincing in matter and especially able in manner.—I sent that to you. When Mr Field was made aware of the receipt of your telegram he was much gratified and expressed the opinion to me that you were especially able to carry the work to a successful execution when I was in New York a few days ago. I forgot to mention in my letter of yesterday that the import of my letter to Sir John Hawkshaw was to the effect that our Government had not yet acted on my suggestion of forming a Commission to examine into and report upon the Interoceanic Canal question and with a view in the end to send suitable delegates of their number to personally inspect the Nicaragua and Panama routes to ascertain the relative facilities of executing the constructions and the presence or lack of material which would so materially affect the cost of construction. Under the actual conditions I suggested the great advantage that would probably result from Sir John making a personal visit to Nicaragua and Panama accompanied by an Engineer selected by the Society of Civil Engineers in Paris, and one selected by the Society of Civil Engineers of the United States for the purposes above named. To-day I have written to Mr Field that it seemed to me advisable that he should inform you with the least possible delay what he thought should be the terms of a concession by Nicaragua and his ideas as to the formation of an initiatory company; that surrounded and occupied as you would be perhaps it would be quite impossible for you to outline these points whilst you might be able to consider or amend them if presented. Should it not be considered advisable by you to adopt or to accept what Mr Field or Mr Morris may propose, it may be worth while for you to consider whether I could not visit Nicaragua to ask a concession in

your name singly which would have been carefully considered by you in advance.—
This would leave you entirely a free agent in establishing a Directory of the Company
and would without doubt in the end secure funds for the construction of the work."
ALS, DLC-USG, IB.

On Aug. 25, Ammen had written *"To the Editor of The World."* "I had the pleasure
of reading an editorial in THE WORLD of the 22d inst. in relation to the construction
of the Nicaraguan interoceanic ship-canal, with your suggestion in regard to the fitness and advantage of General Grant's being offered the presidency of the company.
Since the early part of 1866 General Grant has taken a special interest in bringing
about the necessary surveys and satisfying himself as to the results obtained and as to
the sufficiency of our information in relation to all of the routes supposed to be practicable. He has a full and minute knowledge of the advantages and difficulties attending
the construction of the canal considered as a commercial question wherever it may be
located. It was assumed by the congress in Paris that nothing but a canal at the level
of the sea would satisfy the demands of the world's commerce, and as well that the
cost of execution of the work was hardly a question to be considered. It is plain to see,
however, that the vessels making use of the canal and their cargoes must pay for this
disregard of a commercial principle. . . . In general, all that I have said, as far as relates
to the Paris Congress and the contruction of a ship-canal, has been presented to General Grant, and also the difficulty now existing growing out of the action of the Paris
Congress in considering the question otherwise than as an economic one, and he has
been requested to aid and participate in the construction of a ship-canal via Nicaragua,
and asked to say whether, if invited by a board of directors of a responsible interoceanic
ship company having a proper concession, he would serve as president of the company.
I feel warranted in the assertion that for the purpose of promoting this great object,
so advantageous to our commerce and that of all nations, General Grant will consent
to these requests. On the 7th of the present month a telegram was received from him
to that effect. The Nicaraguan people and their Government have been duly informed
of this. As Americans generally can now see that the difficulties of the situation will
be met by the ability and services of General Grant, so the Nicaraguans will see that a
concession may now be safely given to proper persons, who in due time will be named,
with every assurance of a speedy execution of the work, and they will doubtless grant
the most favorable concession possible. Had the congress in Paris considered the question commercially, as indicated in my address, and had not the supposed value of a
concession granted by the Government of Colombia dazzled those having control, so
that physical conditions were lost sight of, the exigency would not have arisen which
will make it advantageous in the highest degree to our commerce and that of other
nations that General Grant should devote himself to these great interests instead of
enjoying the repose which would otherwise no doubt be far more acceptable to him."
New York World, Aug. 26, 1879. Ferdinand de Lesseps, who led a competing effort to
build a canal, reportedly proposed USG as honorary president of that co. See *New York
Herald*, July 6–8, 19, 1879.

On Aug. 26, a correspondent in Washington, D. C., interviewed Ammen, who said
that "General Grant has been in constant correspondence with a prominent officer of
the Engineer corps of the United States army since his visit to Europe, and in all the
letters received from him he never alluded to the subject of politics or the Presidency,
but the tenor of every letter indicated an absorbing interest in the Interoceanic Canal.
He declared that it must be an American project and carried out by American engineers. He said that during his stay in London and Berlin he had frequent interviews

with capitalists, and they all expressed their doubts of De Lesseps and regarded him as visionary and impracticable, but declared that if it were an American scheme in the hands of American engineers any amount of capital could be got to carry out the project." *Ibid.*, Aug. 27, 1879. An editorial supporting USG's involvement in the canal initiative is *ibid.* See *ibid.*, Aug. 28, Sept. 1, 6, 8, 1879; letter to Daniel Ammen, Sept. 28, 1879.

1. Ammen later recollected: "On my return from Paris I wrote an earnest letter to General Grant, then in Japan, stating that it seemed to me of the utmost importance to our national interests and welfare that we should construct the canal, and expressing the hope that he would send me a telegram without delay announcing his willingness to place himself at the head of a movement to construct it. A telegram of assent was received by me, and in due time two letters from him written before he left Japan, expressing more fully his intentions in relation to forwarding, as far as he could, the construction of the Nicaragua Canal." Ammen, *The Old Navy and the New* (Philadelphia, 1891), pp. 476–77. See letter to Daniel Ammen, June 6, 1879; *New York Times*, Sept. 10, 1879.

Conversation with Emperor Meiji

[Hama Rikiu (Shore Palace), Japan
Aug. 10, 1879]

His Majesty:—Tell general Grant that it was my intention to meet him sooner, but being prevented from so doing by the presence of public business, this is the first opportunity I take;[1] and I am very glad to meet him here today and find him so well.

General Grant:—Please say to His Majesty that it is now nearly two months since I arrived in this country; and being so cordially received by His Majesty's government and people, and treated with such great kindness and courtesies wherever I've been, the time has rolled away more quickly than I imagined; and now I shall leave on Tuesday next[2] for the Hot Springs at Hakoné and come back about 19th or 20th inst.; and I shall, with my party, take the Steamer "City of Tokio" for San Francisco on the 27th inst.; I wish I could stay somewhat longer, but to my regret I must take that Steamer.

His Majesty:—Tell genl. Grant that I wish he could stay with us longer. But if he must leave by that Steamer it cannot be helped. Now that he has seen some of our country, I will be very glad

to hear whatever general Grant wishes to make known in the
way of suggestions or talk generally upon affairs in Japan.

General Grant:—I am very glad to be received by His Majesty in
this manner. Of course no one can know as to what is the best
national policy to be pursued in a foreign country so well as
the people themselves. But such as I have in view to say to His
Majesty I shall be happy to say now.

Since my arrival at Nagasaki I have watched with interest
and much care the agricultural aspects of the country and the
progress of the people generally; and have learned to know the
people and status of this Empire much more than before. Although I have for a long time been greatly interested in Japan
and its progress, my interests and sympathies, if anything, have
increased since. And I can say this: None, except His Majesty's
own subjects, can feel more warmly interested for Japan's welfare than I do. In this regard, however, I am a fair representative only of the most of the American people.

This side of Singapore I have found but few newspapers or
periodicals that are capable or willing to reason things upon
common footing between the Asiatics, and European and
American. "The Tokio Times" and "The Japan Mail" are the
only papers I have seen that treat eastern nations as if they too
had rights that ought to be respected.[3] All the western officials,
except very few, are the same. Whatever is their interest they
advocate it without regard to the right of China or Japan.

Sometimes my blood boils to see this unfairness and
selfishness.

His Majesty:—I appreciate your good wishes.

General Grant:—In all civilized countries there are generally political parties; their existence is very useful for checking each
other from misrule; but parties trying to destroy the existing
government are, of course, very mischievous. I dare say there
are also parties here. There may also be leading men who
might be called in our country demagogues. They must find
some pretext against government to secure followers. If I mistake not, the theme now so popularly advocated by the press

and some of the people of this country seems to be that of Elective Assembly.[4]

I do not know whether the proper time for it has come or not. But such assemblies are very good for all countries in due time. All the European nations including even Russia have Elective Assemblies for legislative purposes. No government, monarchical or republican, is as strong as the government that rests on the people, and enables those in authority to know what the people wish and what is best for them. An assembly will have to be established in this country sooner or later, and therefore the government ought to hold out to the people this idea, and educate them to the fact that in due time such assembly shall be established for them. The people shall know that it is coming and they should be educating themselves for the responsibility. But you must always remember that privileges like this, can never be recalled. When you give suffrage and representation you give them forever. Consequently in establishing such assembly too great caution can not be taken. It is exceedingly dangerous to launch out too suddenly. You do not want to see anarchy as the result of any premature creation of an assembly. Nor should too much be expected from an assembly. The surest way would be the slowest, approaching the result step by step, carefully educating the people as you go on. It seems to me that the first step should be an advisory assembly, a counsel of the leading men in Japan, with power to debate but not to legislate. This power would give the members confidence and knowledge, and teach them the nature of the responsibility they had assumed. Above all, the best assurance for suffrage and representation, is in the education of the people, and Japan has done in that wonderfully.

His Majesty:—This is a very interesting view on the whole.

General Grant:—Another subject that occurs to me is the question of foreign indebtedness. There is nothing a nation should avoid as much as owing money abroad. Any individual, who borrows money from others to such extent that he can not repay at his will, is altogether helpless and becomes enslaved to the principal. Indeed none can feel more humiliated than he! Being so in the case of any individual it is far more so in the case of any nation. Look at Egypt, Spain or Turkey; how helpless they are! National resources are all hypothecated to such an extent as they have now nothing that they may call absolutely their own. In Egypt the Kedief is forced to abdicate! See in Spain the extravagant rate of internal taxes of all sorts as the necessary result of superfluous foreign loans. There the corruption among revenue officials of all grades are fast ruining the nation, a nation of great capacity and resources.

I am glad to learn that the foreign loan of Japan is not so large; at any time it might be paid off if holders of her bonds would receive the money before they are due. The sooner it is paid back the better it will be for Japan. Japan, if possible, ought never to borrow any more from foreign nation.

You are doubtless aware that some nations are very desirous to loan money to weaker nations whereby they might establish their supremacy and exercise undue influence over them. They lend money to gain political power. They are ever seeking the opportunity to loan. They would be glad, therefore, to see Japan and China which are the only nations in Asia that are even partially free from foreign rule or dictation, at war with each other so that they might loan them on their own terms and dictate to them the internal policy which they should pursue.

It may not be improper in this connection to say that, while I was in China I had several interviews with Li-Hung-Chang and Prince Kung.[5] They spoke to me at length regarding the Loo Chu question; and requested me to speak to the members of the Japanese Government in favor of its proper and moderate settlement. I promised them I would do my best, though I declined to act as their agent in the matter. I then told them I would first speak to the U. S. Minister Mr. Bingham which I did, and many times too.[6] I also had a talk on the subject with Mr. Ito and Genl. Saigo while at Nikko.[7] And I have of late informed myself more fully on the subject than before. As is the case in all controversies— there are two sides,—and what I have learned in Japan, is far different from what I was told in China. I am not, of course, in a position to know definitely the merits of the case. On that I would not feel myself justified in expressing an opinion. I can see how impossible it is for Japan to recede from her position. I can see how her case has features that cannot be answered.—A nation having gone as far as Japan, and having acted as she believed in her unquestioned sovereignty, must consider what is due to her people. But while all that should be recognized and conceded, there is an aspect to the Loo Chu affair, which seen from the Chinese point of view is worthy of attention. That is the only point that I would care to mention. China feels that she has not received from Japan the consideration due to her as a sovereign power,—as a friendly nation,—and as a nation which had for a long time enjoyed a certain relation to Loo Chu. She feels this more keenly now, because she feels that the case of Formosa was a humiliation.[8] Suffering from that remembrance, she looks upon Japan's action as wanting in respect and friendship, and as indicating a disposition upon the part of Japan to again occupy Formosa and in doing so bar the channel between China and the Pacific Ocean. The result of this is that the Chinese statesmen feel a sense of wrong and irritation towards Japan. Now without, as I was saying, entering into the discussion, nor denying to Japan every right claimed by the government, it seems to me that this feeling in the minds of Chinese statesmen should be well-considered by Japan, and that Japan in a spirit of magnanimity and justice should make concessions to China. The importance of peace between China and Japan is so great that each country should make concessions to the other. I have heard it suggested, but I have no authority to speak on the subject, that a boundary line running between the islands so as to give China a wide channel to the Pacific would be accepted. I have no idea how true it is.[9] I mention it to show that while in the minds of Chinese statesmen there is a feeling of anger, they are open to accommodation.

His Majesty:—As regarding Loo Chu, Ito etc. are authorized to talk with you and will do so shortly.

General Grant:—I would say one word more on this question. In
your discussions with China on Loo Chu, and on all matters at
issue, do not invite or permit so far as you can avoid it, the intervention of a foreign power. European powers have no interests in Asia, so far I can judge from their diplomacy, that do not
involve the humiliation and subjugation of the Asiatic people.
Their diplomacy is always selfish, and a quarrel between China
and Japan would be regarded by them as a quarrel that might
ensue to their own advantage. China and Japan—approaching
this question in a spirit of friendship and concession, as ancient
allies and of the same race, can adjust it in a manner honorable to both, and lay the foundations of a lasting peace. I may
add that nothing would give me more pleasure than to be able
to carry back to my own country to which I am about to sail,
the knowledge that peace between China and Japan had been
assured.

His Majesty:—Expressed his hope for the most peaceful and harmonious relations with China.

General Grant:—I have now seen some part of Japan; I see that
the people are all intelligent, industrious, and painstaking; and
their various industries are in flourishing state. I fear, however,
they are as yet rather heavily taxed and their surplus fund is
generally small; and though I see marked indication of their
steadily growing richer yet so long as the present tariff convention shall remain in force their growth must be necessarily
very slow. Five per centum on all imports whatsoever is exceedingly small. And export duty is the worst possible thing
for any country to have. It is against all sound reason alike
economic principle; it acts directly against the interests of the
country which imposes it. The amount levied upon exports is
clear loss to the producers themselves; and not only so, but it
discourages industries of the country. Hence it ought, by all
means, to be abolished as soon as possible. Foreign Government should agree to the proposed revision of treaty. At least
25 per cent on some articles of imports must be levied so as to

act as protection of national industries as well as to serve revenue purposes. The sooner this is done the faster and greater will be the development of the National resources. Hence the vast importance of the revision of treaties.

I think I have one thing more I would like now to say: I have seen many schools, academies and colleges here. Their system seems to be as good as any of the United States or of European Countries. Their professors and tutors are mostly of Native Scholars; and they are, I've no doubt, as efficient as desirable. But in all educational institutions there is certain danger which ought to be avoided. Where young teachers, though they may be very able as teacher, are alone intrusted with the work of instruction chiefly from the text books, the steady advancement of educational standard is impeded; because their knowledge is more or less limited and the necessary amount of experience wanted. Educational institutions must either make progress or retrograde. Whenever they come to a stationary point they begin at once to retrograde. In order to check this we find it necessary in America, to have one or two old professors of long experience to oversee the younger and working teachers or in other words to superintend such institution. These old professors are generally in intercollegiate communication with similar institutions of all countries, exchanging views and adopting each other what is good and improved. This system will also be found necessary in Japan. While I look forward to the time when Japan will have her own people in all engagements she should not be hasty in terminating her *enjoyments* with foreigners who are worthy. In the United States we never hesitate to employ foreigners if they are useful to keep them. The men who made your Engineering school which has no superior in the world, are men who should be kept as long as you can keep them.[10]

I think this is about all I wished to say to-day. Please thank His Majesty for his kindness to give so much of his valuable time to listen to me.

His Majesty:—I have listened with much interests to all that Genl.
Grant has kindly said, and I will give deliberate consideration
upon those subjects. Thanks to him.

Guranto shōgun to no go-taiwa hikki (Tokyo, 1937), pp. [13–26]. Printed text and facsimile of one draft page. See John Russell Young diary, Aug. 10–11, 1879, DLC-John Russell Young; *Young*, II, 540–47; Donald Keene, *Emperor of Japan: Meiji and His World,
1852–1912* (New York, 2002), pp. 314–17.

On Aug. 4, 1879, an unidentified person wrote to John Russell Young that the private secretary of Itō Hirobumi, minister for the interior, sought a conference "in regard
to the subject of your talk with me the other evening viz: Gen. Grant's receiving The
Mikado on board the Flagship. What time will it be fconvenient to you to meet us? We
can come to see you at any time you may name.—I think the matter can be arranged,
as you wish, only I recommend the *utmost secrecy*." ALS, DLC-John Russell Young.

1. On July 7, USG had reviewed Japanese troops with Emperor Meiji, who later
in the day "expressed a desire to have a private and friendly conference with the General, which it was arranged should take place after the General's return from Nikko."
New York Herald, Aug. 31, 1879. See Keene, pp. 312–13.

2. Aug. 12. USG returned to Tokyo from Hakone on Aug. 19. See Young diary,
Aug. 19, 1879, DLC-John Russell Young; *Julia Grant*, pp. 303–4.

3. See James L. Huffman, *A Yankee in Meiji Japan: The Crusading Journalist Edward H. House* (Lanham, Md., 2003), pp. 117–51; Grace Fox, *Britain and Japan 1858–
1883* (Oxford, 1969), pp. 429–33.

4. On Aug. 3, Young had written in his diary. "Iwakura called to day—and there
was a long talk with General Grant, the old Premier remaining all the morning. The
theme that interested him was the proposal to found a Japanese national assembly."
DLC-John Russell Young.

5. See conversations with Prince Kung, [*June 5, 1879*], [*June 8, 1879*]; conversations with Li Hung-chang, [*June 12–14, 1879*].

6. On Aug. 6, Young wrote in his diary. "Mr. Bingham came over and we had a
long talk.—Mr B. takes the side of China on the LooChoo question. . . ." DLC-John
Russell Young.

7. On July 22, USG had heard the Japanese case from Itō, Saigō Tsugumichi,
minister for war, and Yoshida Kiyonari, envoy to the U.S. In reply, USG "said in substance that he had been anxious for a conference with the Japanese authorities in fulfilment of a promise he had made to Prince Kung and Viceroy Li-Hung Chang. When in
China these officials had spoken with great feeling, Prince Kung especially, upon the
Japanese action in Loochoo, and had asked him to use his good offices for peace. The
General had told Prince Kung that he was a private citizen and not an official, and that
he was travelling for pleasure and not on business, and that he felt sure the whole question would be safe in the hands of Mr. Bingham, so far as America was concerned. He
had spoken fully with Mr. Bingham, who was a lawyer, a just and able man, and this
opinion was confirmed. But the Chinese authorities were so urgent that he could not
decline without declining a duty that might devolve upon any man, the duty of preserving the peace. He knew nothing about Loochoo except what had been published
in the papers. But since he gave the promise to the Chinese he had obtained all the
information he could. He had heard the Chinese case and studied it. He had heard with
great interest the case of Japan, not only what was now presented to him formally by

the government, but from other sources. As to the merits of the case, the right or the wrong, he had no opinion to express. There were many points in both cases which were historical and could only be determined by research. His main interest—he might say his entire interest—in the subject arose from his kind feelings toward both Japan and China, countries in whose prosperity Americans and the world, but America especially, was deeply interested. Japan had done wonders in the past few years. She was in point of war materials, army and navy, stronger than China. Against Japan China, he might say, was defenceless, and it was impossible for China to injure Japan. Consequently Japan could look at the whole question from a high and magnanimous point of view. At the same time China was a country of wonderful resources, and, although he had seen nothing there to equal the progress that delighted him in Japan, there had been great progress. It was beginning, and no one could foresee what might come from it in twenty or thirty years. Japan should be in a position where she could assist China, and not allow this grievance to grow up and fester and be the source of alienation and irritation now and of trouble in the future. Mr. Yoshida said that there was no higher consideration in the minds of Japanese statesmen than friendly relations with China. China was their near neighbor. Their commerce had continued for centuries. There were points of identity in their civilization, religion, language, laws and customs, which made the friendship of China very dear to Japan. General Grant said that what China felt now was that Japan desired to humiliate them. The Formosan expedition had been attended with circumstances that looked like a humiliation. They regarded the occupation of Loochoo as an advance to Formosa. They looked upon these islands as controlling the channels of their trade with the Pacific, and that whoever held them would be able to check this trade at any time. This was an argument presented by the Viceroy at Tientsin, a distinguished and an able man. It had not been alluded to in the argument of the Embassy, but no doubt it had more weight with such a man as Li-Hung Chang than any other. It was an argument that would be apt to strike a statesman who was looking out for the welfare of his own country. If Japan holds Loochoo she dominates all the channels of the Chinese trade. This was a most important matter to China. This point evidently had not occurred to the Japanese Ministers, and it was explained with some minuteness. Colonel Grant illustrated his father's argument by tracing with a pencil the lines of the Loochoo Islands and their contiguity to the China coast, and the control they would exercise over the trade. General Grant continued by saying that there were other reasons why Japan should, if possible, have a complete and amicable understanding with China. The only Powers who would derive any benefit from a war would be foreign Powers. They knew that the policy of some of the European Powers was to reduce Japan and China into the dependence which had been forced upon other nations. He had seen indications of this policy during his travels in the East which made his blood boil. He saw it in Siam and China and Japan. In Siam the King was unable, as he had told the General, to protect his people from opium. In China opium had been forced upon the people. That was as great a crime against civilization as slavery. In Japan, only the other day, he saw the Germans deliberately violate a Japanese quarantine by sending down a German gunboat and taking a German merchantman out of quarantine. No European power would dare to do such a thing in the United States. But it illustrates European policy in the East. If war should ensue between China and Japan European Powers would end it in their own way and to their own advantage, and to the disadvantage of the two nations. Your weakness and your quarrels are their opportunity. Such a question as Loochoo offers a tempting opportunity for the interference of unfriendly diplomacy. Minister Ito said that these were all grave considerations, but

Japan, standing on her immemorial rights, had simply carried out an act of sovereign power over her own dominions. General Grant answered that he could not see how Japan, having gone so far, could recede. But there might be a way to meet the susceptibilities of China and at the same time not infringe any of the rights of Japan." Young added. "The conversation here took a range that I do not feel at liberty to embrace, as propositions and suggestions were made which it would be premature to disclose, and which, in fact, would have no value until they were considered and adopted by the Cabinets of Japan and China. I have only given you the threads of General Grant's conversation, which covered a great many points and went over the whole field of politics in Asia. The Japanese Ministers showed the most conciliatory spirit. General Saigo did not speak English, but Mr. Ito and Mr. Yoshida both conversed fluently in that tongue. The Formosan expedition, which General Saigo commanded, came up, and was discussed for some time. Various points in the Japanese statement were commented upon and explained, and from a formal conference upon grave questions of State the meeting ran into a most interesting and suggestive conversation. . . . When the talk ran out and the rain ceased Minister Ito said that what had been communicated by General Grant would be submitted to the Cabinet and be considered very carefully. He had no idea what the Cabinet would say. He would probably have occasion to speak with him again on the subject. But on behalf of the government of Japan he desired to express their thanks and their gratitude to General Grant for having presented this question, and for his efforts to continue between Japan and China relations of peace, based upon the honor and independence of both nations. Japan had no desire but peace, and no feeling toward China but a desire to preserve the friendship which had existed so long. The Ministers dined with General Grant in the evening." *New York Herald*, Sept. 1, 1879. See *Young*, II, 558–62.

8. In 1874, Japan landed troops on Formosa to avenge the killing of a shipwrecked Ryukyu fishing crew and withdrew only after China paid an indemnity. On July 18, John A. Bingham, U.S. minister, Tokyo, wrote to USG. "I today send to Mr Fish a dispatch No 98. with many enclosures in relation to the Formosan Expedition &c. Among other Enclosures in this dispatch is No 7—being the reply of Prince Kung the prime Minister of China to the note of our Chargé d'Affaires at Peking Mr Williams— informing the Prince of my action here in protesting against the employment of the S. S. 'New York' an American vessel in the armed Expedition to Formosa in violation of our Treaty obligations & of our laws & also of the sovereignty of China. It gives me pleasure as I doubt not it will give you pleasure to know that my conduct is heartily approved by the Government of China as it was also by this government. The Prince says to Mr Williams in this communication speaking of me & my action, 'his conduct shows clearly that the U. S. is ready to maintain its peaceful relations with China and this effort of the American Minister in Japan to up-hold treaty obligations is very honorable to him and we are deeply sensible of it and shall feelingly remember it.' Although I have now a response from China thanking me for my action I regret that I have no response yet from the Department to my dispatches No 76 & 78 sent forward as Early as the 25 of Apl. last. This I have no doubt is owing to some delay in the Mail. The dispatch now sent by me No 98—with Enclosures together with my other dispatches therein referred to by numbers shew the real nature as I believe of this Formosan expedition & as the question now stands as therein stated upon official proclamations &c. fully & literally verifies all the views expressed by me in my former dispatches I may say to you privately that the German Minister took the same action that I did and that his government promptly approved by telegram. That is he it gave orders to his Con-

suls not to permit any German Ship or German subject to engage in the Expedition by leaving port in aid of it or in company with it. It looks as if China though slow to strike may declare formal war against Japan—as her official declaration has been made that the act of Japan is no less than a hostile invasion of the domain of the Chinese Empire resulting in a conflict of arms there with Chinese subjects under Chinese jurisdiction. It is greatly to be deplored if these two great powers of the East so rapidly advancing in civilization should plunge into a national conflict. I have no doubts that Japan was forced into this wild & foolish adventure by the clamor of the clans lately engaged in insurrection—and I am justified in saying that the Government ordered the expedition not to leave Nagasakai until further orders & the consent of China was should be obtained, to the end that the savages of Formosa might be subdued—and that in violation & defiance of this order the Expedition sailed I hope I may find approval of my action in dispatches by next mail I congratulate you upon your final success on the currency question as well as upon your firm action in the first instance now so fully understood & approved by the country. I regretted to find in the Japan Herald of the 16th inst—one of the defamatory articles copied from the Washington 'Capital' abusive of you. The paper is one of several English Journals published in Yokohama that are constantly seeking occasion to abuse America, her institutions and her Representatives at home & abroad. It pains me that any portion of the American Press should live by malicious defamation. I am sure our Country & its defenders and officials deserve better treatment—I see by a recent article that some people are of opinion that the Herald's efforts on the third term whether so intended or not have resulted in confirming the people in the belief that they may of right elect & re-elect to the office of President whoever suits them best as many terms as they think best without being called to account for it." ADf, Milton Ronsheim, Cadiz, Ohio. See *PUSG*, 24, 463–64; Sophia Su-fei Yen, *Taiwan in China's Foreign Relations 1836–1874* (Hamden, Conn., 1965), pp. 156–295.

9. On July 16, 1879, Divie B. McCartee, Tokyo, wrote to Young. "Referring to my note to you of the 12th inst., upon conversing with those who have had better opportunities than I to ascertain the views, with reference to the Liu Kiu question, held by the Viceroy Li Hungchang, and others of the high Chinese officials; I would like to modify what I said, although I took care to state that I had no (*sufficient*) authority for saying it,—about the willingness of the Chinese Government to give up *Liu Kiu proper* to Japan;—and suggest that the islands and the strait lying *south* of the *26th parallel* of North latitude, should be given to China; on account of their connection with or proximity to Formosa;—While the islands and seas to the *north* of the *29th parallel* of north latitude should belong to Japan, (and *might* be called *Okinawa ken*,) as being in close proximity to or connection with Satsuma—and that the islands & seas *between* the *26th* and *29th* parallels of north latitude constitute a *neutral* ground, the (King of Liu Kiu being reinstated in his sovereignty over so much of his former dominions) under the joint protection of China and Japa[n] (it would I suppose be impossible to add—*and of the U. S. A.*) each of the protecting powers to have a *Resident* or *Consul* or Commissioner, with a staff limited to __ persons to look after the interests of their respective countries—" ALS, DLC-John Russell Young. See Robert E. Speer, ed., *A Missionary Pioneer in the Far East: A Memorial of Divie Bethune McCartee* (New York, 1922), pp. 163–67.

10. The Imperial College of Engineering, or Kōbu Daigakkō, chartered in 1871. See Fox, pp. 464–66; W. H. Brock, "The Japanese Connexion: Engineering in Tokyo, London, and Glasgow at the End of the Nineteenth Century," *British Journal for the History of Science*, XIV, part 3, no. 48 (Nov., 1981), 227–43.

To Edward F. Beale

———

Tokio, Japan
Aug. 10th 1879.

MY DEAR GENERAL:

The time is now near at hand for my departure for the states.
On the 27th of this month we sail on the steamer City of Tokio. It
is my intention to remain several weeks on the Pacific and visit Oregon & Washington territory. On the way home I shall stop over a
few days at Virginia City, a few days at Salt Lake, and from Chienne
I shall go south to Denver, where—or at Colorado Springs—I shall
leave Mrs. Grant while I run out to Leadville. Returning from the
latter place we will go directly to Galena, the only place where I
have a residence. I shall not go east probably before the Holidays.
I will then accept yours & Mrs. Beales proffered hospitalities for
a few days, while there. I shall not want to remain in Washington
long while Congress is in session.[1]

I have now been six or seven weeks in Japan. The country and
people are exceedingly interesting. The progress that has been
made in this country in a few years is more like a romance than
a reality. They have school facilities for every child in the empire
male & female, equal to the Northern states of the Union. Their
Naval & Military Academies, their Colleges and their school of science are equal to the best of ours in the course taught and mode
of instruction. In all these higher educational institutions the text
books are in English hence the students must learn the english. Already the mass of their professors are natives, many of them having
been educated in the schools where they now teach. Remember us
all to Mrs. Beale and all your family.

Very Truly yours
U. S. GRANT

GN. E. F. BEALE

ALS, DLC-Decatur House Papers.

In early Aug., Arisugawa Taruhito, Japanese army gen., wrote to USG. "It is my
desire to entertain you at a soiree to be held at Shiba Palace on the 7th instant at nine

oclock P. M. and I would request that you and Mrs Grant will be pleased to be present." L (in Japanese), DLC-USG, IB; translation (undated), *ibid.*

On Aug. 8, John A. Bingham, U.S. minister, Tokyo, wrote to John Russell Young. "I pray you to convey to General & Mrs Grant the thanks of my family & myself for their kind invitation to dinner this Evening—and our acceptance of the same except Mrs Bingham who I regret to say by reason of indisposition has not been able for some days to go out & is not able now to do so." ALS, DLC-John Russell Young. On the same day, John Pope-Hennessy, governor of Hong Kong, Tokyo, wrote to Young. "We shall be delighted to dine with the General & Mrs Grant tonight at ½ p 7. It is my birthday, & I shall think of it as a birthday dinner." ALS, *ibid.*

1. The congressional session started on Dec. 1.

To Ellen Grant Sartoris

Tokio, Japan,
August 10th /79

DEAR DAUGHTER;

We are now nearly through our visit to this interesting country, and ready to start home. We sail on the 27th of this month for San Francisco. We expect to meet Buck & Ida there, and possibly Jesse. Our visit here has been very delightful. The country is beautiful abounding in green mountains, beautiful & highly cultivated vallies, clear mountain streams & picturesque waterfalls. The people are docile & intelligent as well as industrious and frugal. Education is now becoming universal both among the Mails & females. The country is advancing beyond all precedent. How the Goverment & the people retain their temper and kind treatment to the foreigner under the insults heaped upon them and overbearing and bullying policy of the foreigner and their diplomatic representatives I cannot understand.[1] The course of the average Minister, Consul & merchant in this country & China towards the native is much like the course of the former slave owner towards the freedman wh[en] the latter attempts to think for himself in matters of choice of candidates. The present policy towards these two countries cannot continue much longer without a terrible calamity and one that will fall heavy upon life and property. I hope there will be a speedy change. We should change the most of our representatives in these two countries. Not our Minister here however.

Your ma will send from here, by express, a double gown— silk—which she has got for you. It should arrive soon after this. We will stop a few weeks on the Pacific Coast and visit Oregon & Washington Territory. On the way east we will stop a few days at Virginia City, Nevada, a few days at Salt Lake, and go from Chienne to Denver where I will leave your Ma & Ida while I and the boys go to Leadville, the new Eldorado. When we leave there we will go directly to our home in Galena. What we will do for the winter is not yet determined. But if your Ma is willing we will go to Havanna & Mexico. Your Ma & Fred. join me in love to you Algie & the children. Remember us also to Mr. & Mrs. Sartoris.[2]

Yours Affectionately

U. S. GRANT

ALS, ICHi.

1. On Jan. 7, 1876, George B. Williams, Japanese commissioner to Europe, London, wrote to John A. Bingham, U.S. minister, Tokyo. *"Confidential . . .* At Washington I met many of your friends and had many enquiries regarding you. As I indicated to you before leaving Japan I had quite a long talk with the president regarding the Japanese Tariff and explained to him the difficulty under which Japan labored. The president listened attentively and at the conclusion said he was not aware that the customs duties of Japan were determined by Treaty and that he did not see the justice or necessity of so determining them; that possibly some reason existed when the Treaty was made but that the times had changed and he thought Japan should be left untrammelled in this matter; and he concluded by saying that if Japan wished a change for me to tell Yoshida to present some proposition from the Japanese government, or to advise his government to take some action that could be acted upon by the United States. Of course your name was mentioned frequently but I did not feel at liberty to say much regarding the opinions I know you to hold, as I did not deem myself, under the circumstances, the proper channel of communication. The president told me to talk to Mr Fish, which I did, Mr F. was non-committal beyond saying he could do nothing until Japan presented a proposition, when he was prepared to act promptly. . . ." ALS, Milton Ronsheim, Cadiz, Ohio. See *PUSG*, 23, 37; *New York Times*, Nov. 2, 1871, Dec. 10, 1875.

2. See letter to Ellen Grant Sartoris, Sept. 28, 1879.

To Prince Kung and Iwakura Tomomi

––––––

Tokio, Japan.

August 13, 1879.

Since my arrival in Japan I have been favored with several interviews with the cabinet of His Majesty The Emperor, on the subject
which His Highness Prince Kung and His Excellency the Viceroy
Li Hung Chang have so much at heart, to wit an honorable and satisfactory settlement of the Loo Choo question; a settlement which
will be alike honorable to both nations. While the statement of facts
relating to this question as stated by the Japanese side differ in many
material points from the statements made to me both in Peking and
Tientsin yet I feel that what I have heard will justify me in saying
that the Japanese are most anxious to preserve the most amicable
relations with China, and to this end would magnanimously make
sacrifices of what she believes to be her just rights if China would
meet her in the same spirit. But in the heated controversy which has
already taken place between the two governments on the LooChoo
question there have been one or more communications on the part
of China so threatening in tone, or if not threatening so offensive,
that I do not believe that the Japanese would consent to treat with
any commission from the other side, until China consented to withdraw such despatch or despatches. This being done I believe Japan
would gladly appoint a commission or commissioners from among
her able citizens, to meet a like commission or commissioners, appointed in like manner, by China from among her own representative citizens.[1] They would not only meet to confer, but would meet
determined to bring about permanent good feeling among the two
peoples if China would meet them halfway in concessions.

No foreign power should be brought into such a convention, nor
should any foreigner, except it might be as interpreter and with the
consent of both parties. It might be that such a convention would
fail to agree entirely, or fail upon some minor points, in which contingency the two nations might agree upon an arbitrator whose

decision on the disputed points, after hearing both sides, should be binding. In such case, while it is entirely the business of the two nations, I would earnestly Suggest that no representative of a foreign government abroad should be selected.

In the vast East,—embracing more than two-thirds of the human population of the world,—there are but two nations even partially free from the domination and dictation of some one or other of the European powers with intelligence and strength enough to maintain their independence.—Japan and China are the two nations. The people of both are brave, intelligent, frugal and industrious.—With a little more advancement in modern civilization, mechanics, engineering, &c., they could throw off the offensive treaties which now cripple and humiliate them, and could enter into competition for the world's commerce.—Much more employment for the people would result from the change and vastly more effective would it be.—They would become much larger consumers as well as producers, and then the civilized world would be vastly benefited by the change, but none so much as China and Japan.

Japan is rapidly reaching a condition of independence, and if it had now to be done over such treaties as exist could not be forced upon her. What Japan has done, and is now doing, China has the power,—and I trust the inclination,—to do. I can readily concieve that there are many foreigners, particularly among those interested in trade, who do not look beyond the present, and who would like to have the present condition remain, only grasping more from the East, and leaving the natives of the soil merely "hewers of wood and drawers of water," for their benefit. I have so much sympathy for the good of their children if not for them, that I hope the two countries will disappoint them.—

I leave Japan in two weeks from now, for my American home. If I could hear there, that amicable and most friendly relations had been established between China and Japan I should feel delighted.— If anything I may have said or done should have any effect in producing so desirable a result I shall feel that my visit has not been in vain, though made without thought of taking any part in the affairs of the two countries.

With many thanks for the great courtesy shown me by all Chinese officials during my visit to the country, and with the assurances of my highest consideration,

I am very truly & respectfully
Your Obedient Servant
U. S. GRANT.

Copies, DLC-USG, IB (in John Russell Young's hand); USG 3. On Oct. 9, 1882, John Russell Young, U.S. minister, Peking, wrote to Secretary of State Frederick T. Frelinghuysen recounting a conversation with Viceroy Li Hung-chang of Chihli on the strained relations between Japan and China. "*Confidential.* . . . Three years ago, when General Grant was here; Prince Kung and himself had asked General Grant to use his good offices with the Emperor of Japan, and try and undo the enormity of the Loo Choo annexation. General Grant saw the Japanese Emperor and wrote a letter to Prince Kung proposing a settlement. China was willing to accept the terms, but Japan refused. The question was still open and he hoped I would be able to take it up and help China to her own. I replied that I was familiar with all that had taken place in China and Japan on the occasion of General Grant's visit and knew of this letter. . . . It has never to my knowledge before been printed or even made a matter of record in the Department. At the time it was written it was held as a confidential communication at the request of Mr. Iwakura. Time has removed that reserve, and I give it now, because it is necessary as throwing light upon the views of the Viceroy, and the sentiments of the two Governments. I may add a word as to the history of this letter with which I am familiar. When Ex President Grant was in Peking H. I. H. Prince Kung asked him to use his good offices with the Japanese Cabinet to have a settlement of the Loo Choo Islands claim. The Ex President answered that he was a private citizen without warrant to speak for his Government, and not even in a position to give effective advice. The Prince answered that advice thus given was sometimes the most effective. The Ex President said that if occasion served while he was in Japan, and he could give any counsel in the interest of peace he would do so. Sometime after the arrival of the Ex President in Japan; Mr. Iwakura said he understood that Prince Kung had spoken about Loo Choo. Mr. Iwakura said that, if General Grant wished it, certain members of the Cabinet would confer with him and tell the Japanese side of the case. The result was that Mr. Ito, Secretary of the Interior, General Saigo, Secretary of War, and Mr. Yoshida, Japanese Minister at Washington, came to General Grant and spent several hours with him. General Grant, at the request of the Japanese Prime Minister, drafted a joint letter to both Governments. This letter, which I enclose, was submitted to the Emperor of Japan and approved before it was sent to Prince Kung. I regard the document as of the greatest importance. It had the effect at the time, as I have been told by many Japanese, of preventing what threatened to be a serious disagreement, and perhaps war. It is much to be regretted that the advice given by the Ex President was not followed to a complete settlement. . . ." LS, DNA, RG 59, Diplomatic Despatches, China. The enclosure, a misdated copy of USG's letter to Prince Kung and Iwakura Tomomi, is *ibid.* See following letter; letter to John Russell Young, May 18, 1883; *Foreign Relations, 1881*, pp. 243–44; Frederick T. Frelinghuysen to Young, March 16, 1883, DNA, RG 59, Diplomatic Instructions, China.

On July 11, 1879, Ho Ju-chang, Chinese envoy, had written to USG. "I am in the receipt of Communications from the Prince and Ministers of Our Office of Foreign

Affairs, and His Excellency Li, Northern Superintendant of Foreign Trade; stating, that, 'In the matter of the abolition of the government of Liu Kiu, and its erection into a *ken*, by Japan;—At a recent interview with the Honorable Ex-President of the United States of America, the whole facts were comprehensively laid before him; and the Honorable Ex-President has done us the great favor to promise to exert his good offices, to bring about an amicable arrangement, in accordance with the provisions of the treaty; [with the United States of America, in 1858;] and also to promise that, upon his arrival in Japan, he will personally confer with the Honorable United States Envoy Bingham, and will thoroughly deliberate the matter with him, and take satisfactory measures; so that the peace and unity of Asia may be preserved inviolate; not only to the sincere appreciation of China, but to the boundless gratitude of Liu Kiu. He is therefore Commanded, upon obtaining an interview [with the Honorable Ex-President], and after having first expressed his acknowledgements,—to lay before him a translated comprehensive statement of the whole case.' The undersigned accordingly comes specially to present his acknowledgements; and he also begs to submit for Your Condescending inspection, a translated, detailed account of this case from beginning to end." L (in Chinese), USG 3; translation (brackets in original), *ibid.* See John A. Bingham to William M. Evarts, Sept. 18, 1879, DNA, RG 59, Diplomatic Despatches, Japan; Evarts to Bingham, Oct. 25, 1879, *ibid.*, Diplomatic Instructions, Japan.

On Aug. 23, Owen N. Denny, consul, Tientsin, wrote to USG. "Your welcome favor of August 6th, together with one in my care to His Excellency the Viceroy, came by the last mail. We were all glad to hear of your continued enjoyment and safe return to Tokio. Yesterday I gave your letter to the Viceroy, who manifested very great pleasure in its reception as well as eagerness to know its contents. He sat at the table and with his own pen wrote the Chinese as it was translated to him by Pethic. He will send a copy of it to the Prince and the answer will be sent to me, which I will take great pleasure in forwarding to you. Your letter put the Viceroy in splendid humor, and he said: 'Now I have hopes that a settlement may be had of the serious matter which will at least "save the face" of China; that whatever settlement is arrived at will be due entirely to the friendly effort of General Grant, who will ever be held in grateful remembrance by the Chinese Government.' I have just finished quite a lengthy dispatch to the Department of State in regard to the material progress of China, in which I refer to your cordial reception by the Chinese Government. Their unlimited confidence in you is shown in their asking you to come forward in behalf of the United States and settle the question of Chinese emigration to our country, and by the good results already beginning to flow from your visit here, as well as those which are sure to follow. Please say to Mrs. Grant that Lady Li (wife of the Viceroy) a few weeks ago was taken dangerously ill, and came so near dying that all the native physicians gave her up and said she must die. It was then the Viceroy, as a last and vain hope, was induced to try foreign physicians, and Dr. Irwin and Dr. McKenzie as well as Miss Howard, M. D., of Peking, were called to attend the case, and in their hands she soon recovered. The news of the success of the foreign doctors spread rapidly in all directions, and it will be the means, coming as it does from the Viceroy, of breaking down an infinite amount of prejudice among the official classes against progress and foreign skill. . . . I doubt if the Viceroy even could have been induced before your visit to have thought of such a thing. The prejudices of these people must be broken down and forgotten before foreign ideas can prevail here, and that which will break it down in one direction tends to remove it entirely. It is only the first of many more which are sure to follow from your visit here." *Sacramento Record-Union*, Nov. 1, 1879. See Denny to Frederick W. Seward, Aug. 12, 1879, DNA, RG 59, Consular Despatches, Tientsin.

Also on Aug. 23, Li, Tientsin, wrote to USG. "When Your Excellency visited China I had the pleasure of making your acquaintance and enjoying your conversation, and I cannot find words to express the regard I formed for you. Though your entertainment here was very meagre I constantly keep your visit in memory. I have just received your letter dated Aug. 1st from Tokio, and thank you very much for it. Several letters received from Mr. Young had informed me of your efforts in the Loo Choo question, and of your earnest representations to the Japanese Ministers in the interests of peace—urging them not to be influenced by the bad councils of those who wish to bring about a war. In this I perceive your Excellency's generous remembrance of your promises here, and your admirable desire to advocate the best interests of both countries. I at once had your letter, and that of Mr. Young, translated and sent to the Tsung-li Yamen for perusal by Prince Kung who joins in my thanks to you. In this question Japan has really practiced great imposition. Proofs can be shown that Loo Choo has for over five hundred years been tributary to China—as all Foreign Countries well know. Japan now with no provocation suppresses Loo Choo without first so much as consulting with China, and then invents many falsehoods, disputes with the Tsung-li Yamen regardless of truth and justice and will not acknowledge any wrong Committed. But all this having, I believe, been already explained, Your Excellency no doubt clearly sees where the wrong lies. Your Excellency's remark that both Countries should make mutual concessions in the interests of peace, is most wise and just. Yet Japan was first in fault and has not shown a yielding disposition towards China. In the Formosa affair several years ago China made concessions so great that her officers and people have never yet become resigned to them. If on this present occasion China yields again, it is to be feared that the honor and integrity of the nation will be compromised. As I do not know how Your Excellency has discussed this question with the Japanese Ministers so as to preserve the dignity of both countries, I will anxiously await the favor of your further instructions. Your Excellency after attending to this business will soon be returning to the United States, but perhaps will first arrange for H. E. Mr. Bingham, the American Minister, and H. E. Ho, the Chinese Minister, to carry on the negotiations so as to bring about an amicable settlement:—this is my most fervent wish. My Government is unanimously in favor of undertaking such measures as will establish China as a great Power, and thus will realize the kind wishes to that effect expressed by Your Excellency and by Mr. Young. I have now to wish Your Excellency a prosperous voyage home and a hearty public welcome when you reach there; and I hope that you may succeed to the next Presidency, in which event the friendly relations between our two Countries will become firmer than ever. In future when in need of friendly counsel I will take the liberty of writing to you specially as occasion requires. Mr. Consul Denny is an officer of the highest integrity and has always been held in great regard by me. I trust that you may be able to do something for his advancement after your return to the United States. I avail of this occasion to most respectfully wish for you every happiness. . . . I beg to present my compliments, likewise to Col. Grant and Mr. Young. P. S. Referring to our conversation at Tientsin regarding Chinese emigration, and your expressed hope that a satisfactory adjustment of the Chinese labor question in California would be made, I beg to say that I communicated your valuable views to the Prince and Ministers of the Tsung-li Yamen, with a request that they would deliberate upon some convenient settlement. But Mr. Seward, the U. S. Minister, subsequently entered into a discussion with the Yamen upon a proposition he made for China to prohibit the emigration to California of prostitutes, criminals, diseased persons and persons under contract for labor. The Prince and Ministers, considering the advice that they had pre-

viously received from you, and remembering the terms of friendship so long existing
between the two countries, met Mr. Seward in a friendly spirit and as an especial mark
of favor consented to his proposition, leaving regulations to be arranged afterwards. I
presume that Mr. Seward has already informed you of this." Translation, USG 3. On
restricting Chinese emigration, see conversations with Li Hung-chang, [*June 12–14,
1879*]; David L. Anderson, *Imperialism and Idealism: American Diplomats in China, 1861–
1898* (Bloomington, Ind., 1985), pp. 105–12.

On Sept. 3 and 9, Harry S. Parkes, British minister, Tokyo, confidentially wrote
to Thomas F. Wade, British minister to China. "I have the honour to acknowledge
the receipt of your Confidential Despatch of the 13th Ultimo relative to the difference
which has arisen between China and Japan on the Loochoo question. . . . I do not think
that Japan would consent to any mediation on the part of foreign powers in the matter.
I do not know what General Grant has been able to accomplish. He told me that he had
written to Prince Kung informing him of all he had observed in Japan, but with his
usual regard for silence, said nothing that led me to believe that he had succeeded in
bringing about a better understanding. . . ." "In continuation of my despatch of the 3rd
inst: I may mention that I have now learned on good authority that General Grant advised the Japanese Government to endeavour to keep on good terms with China, as his
own observation had convinced him that in a few years that power might prove a formidable enemy. Also that he advised them not to seek or admit the mediation of foreign
powers in their present difference with China respecting Loochoo, as the mediating
powers would only be too likely to have ends of their own to serve. . . ." Copies, British
Foreign Office, Japan, Part I, Correspondence, 1856–1905, Section II, FO 46/89–404,
1868–1890.

On Sept. 19, Yoshida Kiyonari, envoy to the U.S., Tokyo, wrote to USG. "Since
your departure sixteen days have just rolled away: & it looks to me as though a month
had gone. I hope that you are, if not already on your beloved soil, very near now to
San Francisco, & that you had a pleasant voyage. We had very unpleasant & stormy
weather recently: & although it was of a local nature we could not but feel somewhat
concerned about your party: we trust the storm did not reach you. There is no news of
any importance to report to you except one: we received some ten days since a communication from the chinese Govt in reply to our last ultimatum. It is of a calm & moderate tone. Gov. Ito promised me a copy of its English translation as soon as it is made.
I am not yet in receipt of it; or I would send it to you by this mail. By the next mail
I hope to forward it to you. The main points in it are briefly as follows: The chinese
Govt expresses deep regrets that an *independent* Kingdom (though tributary to both
countries—Japan & china) should so suddenly be absorbed by Japan. It does not, however, put advance any grievance regarding the fact that it loses a tributary. It expresses
a desire that the friendly relations between china & Japan should not be disturbed by
such a comparatively small matter as the Liu Kiuan question; that the past should not
be chased, [or followed up] but the future ought to be admonished; finally that there
may be some one who, knowing the principle of the international intercourse, may well
adjust the troubled question &c. &c. &c. On the whole it does not seem to me that the
Chinese Govt intends to insists upon any fixed proposition whatever of the adjustment
of the question Regarding to the Eight Hundred & Ten Yens you left with us to be
distributed among the Employes I have this day addressed to you an official note. We
distributed among them 510 Yens as was deemed by all ample & enough; & have taken
the liberty to in sending in *your name* to the Gov. of Tokio Mr Kusumoto the remaining 300 Yens to be added on your behalf to the fund contributed to the relieve of the

sufferers from the epidemic cholera; & I hope this will meet your hearty approval as it was unanimously agreed upon by us all as being the best & most approp[ri]ate disposal of the balance. Treaty revision business is progressing but very slowly: I hope you will do all in your power to help us in the matter in such a way as you may deem best. I have mailed to your address a few copies of Yokohama paper. My wife joins me in heartily wishing you & Mrs Grant ever good health & happiness. . . . P. S. I am sorry to say that we have not as yet found the originater of that nefarious note, though we have arrested 4 or 5 men employed in the printing thereof. we shall find the *one* sooner or later. Gov. Hennessey issued order that the Japanese Trade Dols should be circulated in Hong-Kong on the equal footing with Mex. Dols. Our Govt. has also issued proclamation to the same effect." ALS (brackets in original), USG 3. For USG's threatened assassina-tion, see letter to Adam Badeau, Aug. 1, 1879.

On Sept. 20, Prince Kung, Peking, wrote to USG. "In June last I had the honor of paying my respects to you here, but as your stay was very short I was deprived of a much-desired fuller acquaintance. On the 23d ulto I received your letter regarding the Loo Choo question, and I beg to thank you heartily for the pains you have taken and sense of justice you have displayed in dealing with it. You state that Japan does not wish to disturb friendly relations with China: I am highly pleased to hear this; and since Japan is thus returning to what is reasonable, it is right that the advice in your letter should be followed and that China and Japan should deliberate upon some plan whereby relations of perpetual friendship may be preserved between the two coun-tries. This end once accomplished, will be due to your efforts which will have secured benefits to both China and Japan. Your remarks as to what China should do for herself in the future meet my full approval and prove that you are indeed a genuine friend of this country, for such advice could not be given by one who is indifferent. Having now heard of your prosperous voyage to Japan, I wish you good fortune in continuing the journey to your native land, where I hope you may again be at the head of the Govern-ment, and thus fulfill the hopes of all here and abroad and strengthen the bonds of friendship between our two countries. In returning these my thanks, I avail of the oc-casion to wish you increasing happiness." Translation, USG 3.

On Sept. 24, Li wrote to USG. "On the 23d August I sent you through Mr. Consul Denny a letter which was no doubt duly rec'd by you. Yesterday Consul Denny handed me your letter dated Aug 23d addressed to Prince Kung, which I forwarded to him after perusal, and I now hand you his reply. I also received your separate letter to me dated Aug. 20th regarding Loo Choo; and I am inexpressibly grateful for your care and your exertions in this matter. Y. E. mentions that the Japanese Government is of-fended at a despatch sent by Mr. Ho, the Chinese Minister, and hence will not discuss public business with him. The Tsung-li Yamen has, in accordance with your advice, sent a despatch to the Japanese Foreign Office, proposing that special Ambassadors be appointed by the two countries to discuss a settlement. If, therefore, Japan gives heed to your advice and sends an officer to China to make proper arrangements, it may be hoped that an early settlement may be effected; and so by removing a source of discontent to the Chinese people further misunderstandings may be avoided, and your action will thus result in good to both countries. The despatch sent by Mr. Ho is really a trifling matter. Loo Choo having been suppressed, for Japan now to withdraw from her position in a way that China may not lose dignity, is certainly difficult; and fearing lest the officers appointed by both countries should be unable to come to terms, I beg that Y. E. will write as occasion requires to counsel friendly measures. I hear that Y. E. starts for home Sept. 2d I wish you a quick and pleasant voyage. You have now been traveling more than a̶two years and should enjoy a period of rest and quietness after your exertions. May you, at some future day, again resume the guidance of the Government, and thus bring benefits to our respective countries. Regarding the favors I have asked I hope that I may enjoy the privilege of hearing from you when opportunity offers; and I now avail of this opportunity to wish you increasing happiness" Translation, *ibid*. On the same day, Li wrote to Young. "I have now to acknowledge the receipt of your four letters of the following dates—July 5th, 15th, 25th and Aug. 24th, and assure you that I highly appreciate all that you have said and done. That General Grant succeeded in inducing the Mikado and his Ministers to listen and give heed to his views regarding the Loo Choo affair is very gratifying: were it not for his great reputation for fairness the Japanese would hardly have been persuaded, and had it not been for your untiring and ceaseless efforts this change of feeling among the Japanese could not have occurred. For these efforts of the General and yourself in behalf of the best interests of the two countries, I have not words to sufficiently express my thanks. In conformity with General Grant's advice the Prince and Ministers of the Tsung-li Yamen have sent a despatch to the Japanese Foreign Office proposing that both countries appoint special Ambassadors to meet and settle the question. If Japan sends such an officer to China for this purpose, it may be hoped that an early settlement will be made and thus remove cause for unfriendliness—which is my earnest desire. Your remark that China's wish to first discuss this LooChoo question with Japan is a proof of China's regard for Treaty obligations and unwillingness to think lightly of going to war,—is most correct and just. Loo Choo was reduced by Japan to a dependent district without consulting with China; and when China several times introduced the question for discussion, Japan acted in a most unreasonable manner. And now that China, acting on General Grant's advice, has sent a despatch asking that officials be appointed to consult upon the question, another proof is given of China's great respect for Treaty stipulations and desire to maintain friendship. As the Mikado himself saw and approved of General Grant's letter to Prince Kung and myself and directed his ministers to act in accordance therewith, I hardly think there will be subsequent change of policy. But if an Ambassador is not promptly sent to China on this business, not only with this be treating China with contempt but it will show that the promises made to General Grant were from the lip and not from the heart, and as such a breach of good faith. China from first to last has acted with courtesy and can justify herself before the world. As to Mr. Ho's despatch that gave offence to the Japanese Govt it is, as you say, a trifling matter,—a mere error of language, and can rightly have no bearing on the settlement of the Loo Choo matter. Japan seems to be putting forward excuses to avoid a discussion with China, using this device to cloak the act committed. If anything in the despatch had given offence there would have been no difficulty for the Japanese Minister in Peking to have brought the matter before the Tsung-li Yamen. Why then should they have hastened to suppress Loo Choo as they did and then attempt to justify themselves by that despatch. General Grant and yourself are too intelligent to be deceived by this pretext. If an Ambassador is appointed to discuss this question, then the withdrawing of the despatch can be easily arranged. Though I have given the subject careful reflection yet I cannot think of a satisfactory plan whereby this Loo Choo question can be arranged with credit to both countries and so as to secure permanent friendly relations. If Japan should deny her fault and attempt to put China in the wrong, then China, being really without fault, would have to consider other ways for a just settlement. Although General Grant and yourself will soon return home, I trust that you will both keep these matters in mind and continue to favor us with your help. In your letters you urge that China should adopt measures to become a powerful country. This advice can come only from a heart that cherishes genuine friendship and I have been deeply moved by what you have said. From time to time I will consult with the Prince and Ministers of my Govt with a view to carry out measures that will realize what you have recommended. In two of your letters you have spoken of the advantage of entering into a Treaty for offensive and defensive alliance between the United States and China, which would secure lasting peace for China and immunity from wrongs imposed by other countries. This suggestion is somewhat similar to the terms of Art. 1 of the Treaty of 1858, but is more plain and positive. China will be extremely desirous that the plan may be supported by Gen. Grant, and I hope that you will carry out your intention to bring the matter forward at Washington. If Gen. Grant should again be President the plan would be certain of success. I shall therefore rely upon you to keep it in mind and do what you can as opportunity offers. I wish you a pleasant voyage from Japan and a safe return to your native land. I entertain such feelings of respect for the General and yourself, because of the sincerity you have shown, that I wish to enter into a compact of firm and lasting friendship with you both. And although in future we will find it difficult to meet, yet I hope that we may as friends keep up a pleasant correspondence as a relief to our thoughts of each other when far away. I take this opportunity to wish you increasing happiness." Translation, DLC-John Russell Young. See *Foreign Relations, 1880*, pp. 194–201.

On Oct. 11, Yoshida, Yokohama, wrote to USG. "I hope you & your party arrived at home long ago & are enjoying all good health as ever. Since my last writing there is no news regarding to the Loochoo question. Mr. Terashima has been appointed as minister of Education the Foreign Office being filled by Mr. Enouye. The Revision business is not much progressing but I hope will be soon attended to in earnest. The Prince Hennerich is now here & he is intending to visit Hokoné soon. He is not going around in official style but in incognito. Italian Prince is soon to arrive from the Northern waters. There have been about 8 or 10 person's arest in Osaka &c. &c. they are supposed or rumoured as having counterfieted a large amount of currency. It is however difficult to believe when we find so very few counterfiet Cy of very apparent order. The supposed chief in the crime is a man of considerable influence in Osaka by the name of Fügita. He is of Chashin clan. & to some extent friend of some leading members of the Govt. Hence there has been some political commotions here. but I believe this is not going to disturb the harmony of the Govt. In fact I do not believe that Fügita & others have had any thing to do with the counterfiet money Sir Harry Parkes is going home via America per S. S. 'City of Peking' which leave here by 12 n. today He goes, he says, on a/c of Lady Parke's illness, but it is doubted whether he is ever coming back here again My wife joins me in wishing you & mrs Grant good health and happiness. . . . P. S. Please donot forget to send seeds to different Governors as they are all waiting for them." ALS, USG 3. On Oct. 31, Yoshida, Tokyo, wrote to USG. "At the instance of Messrs Ito and Enouye I have the honour to enclose herewith for your confidential information two copies of the translation into English of the recent correspondence between Japan & China relating to the Liu Kiu question. You will observe that the chinese Government have only in part accepted your confidential advice, & apparently ignoring what you mentioned as the necessary preliminary step or condition (that is to say: first 'to withdraw such despatch or despatches so threatening in tone or offensive &c &c.') they simply request to be informed in what manner the high commissioners suggested should be appointed for the desired end. Our government have written a reply (enclosure No. 8.) from the perusal of which you will be pleased to observe that the controversy once so threatening is assuming a more pacific aspect. I presume that the Chinese Government have already addressed you on the subject, in which event will you be good enough to let us have a copy at an early date? Again thanking you for very cordially for your good offices & good will towards Japan . . . P. S. I have forwarded the papers mentioned herein in our regular mail bag to the Japanese Consulate in San Francisco, Cal. whence they will be forwarded to you at once. Six more papers are also enclosed for your ready reference though you may have read most of them. An extract from your own note to Prince Kung &c. is herewith also enclosed for reference. Pray excuse me for this manner of writing for the want of time as the mail is just closing On the 25th inst I received your kind letter from San Francisco which gave me *great pleasure.* I am trying to communicate in person to His Majesty your kind & courteous words which, I have no doubt, I shall soon succeed. I have communicated your kind wishes to every one I met since, & will do so to as many more as I may meet hereafter. With the warmest regards & best wishes to you & mrs Grant, & Col. & mr Young" ALS, *ibid.* A printed document, "Riu Kiu. Reply of H. I. J. M's Minister of Foreign Affairs to the Chinese Despatch of 20th September 1879," dated Oct. 22, 1879, left China to act first on USG's suggestion for the appointment of commissioners to negotiate a resolution. *Ibid.* See Bingham to Evarts, Dec. 11, 1879, DNA, RG 59, Diplomatic Despatches, Japan; Evarts to Bingham, Jan. 10, 1880, *ibid.,* Diplomatic Instructions, Japan.

On [*Oct. 23*], while on a visit to Sacramento, USG had discussed the dispute. "The nature of the difficulty has been known in this country as the Formosa trouble, though it related chiefly to a series of islands north of that island. The people inhabiting the islands were wreckers and pirates and murdered all the unfortunate sailors who by shipwreck were cast upon their shores. China claimed jurisdiction of the islands until some Japanese seamen were murdered there, when Japan called the Government of China to account for the conduct of the people, whereupon China had in a measure repudiated its responsibility in the matter. These islands had for many years been under the jurisdiction of Japan, and while under that jurisdiction the people had been well governed. Japan recalled this jurisdiction, but the question was still unsettled, as China had never acknowledged officially the rights claimed by the Japanese Government." The reporter continued. "While General Grant did not accept, in a formal and official way, the office of mediator, or the conferring of plenipotentiary powers, he did consent to give his personal advice and to hear both sides of the case from the two nations. During his visit to Japan he did represent the case and make the necessary inquiries at the court of that Empire; and since his return to San Francisco has forwarded to the courts of both countries, to their several Ministers of State, his opinion or award in the matter." *Sacramento Record-Union,* Nov. 1, 1879.

On Dec. 30, John Hay, asst. secretary of state, wrote to Young, London. "*Unofficial.* . . . I have just received your letter of the 16th December, and am very glad to have your suggestions in regard to those Eastern matters. I am sorry that I was not able to see you here and talk with you more fully in regard to them, but I am glad that you saw the Secretary and the President. General Grant was in the Department yesterday and made several suggestions exactly in the line of your letter, and approved, as you did, in the heartiest way, the change the Department has made at Shanghai." ALS, DLC-John Russell Young. Denny had replaced David H. Bailey as consul gen., Shanghai. Young visited officials at the capital on Nov. 21. John Russell Young diary, *ibid.* On Dec. 12, Young had written to the editor, *The Times* (London), reporting USG's extensive conversations with Chinese and Japanese officials and diplomatic communications signaling the likely peaceful resolution of the Ryukyu dispute. *The Times* (London), Dec. 17, 1879. See *ibid.,* Dec. 12, 1879.

On Jan. 23, 1880, Yoshida wrote to USG. "Your favour of Dec. 5th of the last year was received, through the U. S. Legation, & I read it with great pleasure. The Liu Kiu question, I have pleasure to report, is progressing as well as any one might have expected. On our side the principle, you were good enough to advocate while in Japan, has been stuck to so far. China seems, however, to be rather disinclined to withdraw those 'offensive correspondence' as you, per letter, advised Prince Kung & Li to do. We are now trying to find out what would satisfy the chinese Government for the amicable settlement of the said question. The chinese translation (per chinese official translator) of your letter addressed to Prince Kung, does not, I fear, clearly convey the same meaning as the original. Hence a slow action on their part, I venture to presume! You will do an additional goodness if you would once more write a private letter to *Kung* & *Li* urging to *act out, without unnecessary delay,* the good & confidential advice you offered them. Of course, it should clearly be understood that so far as the *Liu Kiu Island* PROPER, which is the origin of the present controversy, is concerned no question should be raised by China; neither should China construe the phrase: 'to this end [Japan] would magnanimously make sacrifices of what she believes to be her just rights' as meaning that even Liu Kiu I. itself might be included in such sacrifices. We shall leave Japan on or about 14th of next month for the U. S. but knowing that you would be either in Cuba or Mexico when we shall arrive in washington, I write these brief lines to save time. My wife joins me very cordially in presenting you & mrs Grant the warmest personal regards and compliments of the season. . . . 1. P. S. I enclose herewith a copy of your letter to Pce Kung for your reference. 2d P. S. I need hardly add to assure you that, regarding certain sacrifices which may be made to china in case china should withdraw those 'offensive despatches', our governt. abides by the same decision come to, at the interview with you at Enriokwan before you drew up your note to Prince Kung." ALS (brackets in original), USG 3.

On March 31, an American living in Japan wrote to USG. "Since your departure from this country—it seems hardly possible that it was more than six months ago—I have many times been tempted to send you a brief recital of leading events, with such general and personal intelligence as might perhaps be agreeable to you. I will endeavor to set before you a swift review of what has passed during the last half-year Japan and China are free from all danger of a rupture. It can hardly be news to you that the final correspondence on the Rin Kin (Loo Choo) question was colored with your counsel throughout, and that the first completely pacific proposal was in the form of inquiry from Japan, 'If China would consider the affair in the spirit of General Grant's suggestions?' A cordial response having been given, there was little further difficulty. . . . The government is stronger than ever, as the recent consolidation proves, and means to devote its strength to domestic improvements. If it were a bad government, selfishly disposed; if it had not given repeated manifestations of devotion to the country, and shown in practical ways its determination to bring the people forward, I should feel some anxiety at its unchecked power. . . . They encourage local suffrage assemblies in every part of the country, in order that experience in the working of representative bodies may be diffused; and they are planting schools with absolutely lavish hands. But they are sternly resolved, from the Emperor to the last appointed Sangi, to sanction no premature agitation for parliamentary institutions. In maintaining this ground, I may tell you, they consider themselves greatly fortified by the recollection of your conversation with the Emperor, on that lovely but tropical August afternoon, when I found you, at Hamagoten, in stately and oppressive black—a necessary condition of an imperial conference, no doubt. And I can add, parenthetically, that owing to the wide range of your discussions with various members of the ministry, there is hardly a topic that comes up for debate upon which your views are not brought forward. You are an unseen attendant at every council board; an invisible but an influential participator in every cabinet meeting." *Chicago Inter-Ocean*, April 28, 1880. See conversation with Emperor Meiji, [*Aug. 10, 1879*].

On June 26, Yoshida, Washington, D. C., wrote to USG. "I now have the pleasure to present you & mrs. Grant my hearty thanks for the kind reception you gave us the other day. We enjoyed the visit very much indeed. We arrived safely in Washington Tuesday evening the 22d. I have already & *in full* reported to my Government the result of my interview with you regarding to Liu Kiu question submitting at the same time copies of your letter & those of Prince Kung & Li Hung Chang which latter were addressed to you last year. In regard to the letters of Prince Kung & Li, I urged my government never to use in any correspondence or negotiations with the Chinese Government as they were obtained from you only on these conditions, and I am quite confident that they will never be used by my Government. I have no doubt that your letter to me will fully be appreciated by my government & made such use of as may be deemed proper & most effective for bringing about the peaceful settlement of the pending dispute. I now return herewith to you with many thanks the three original letters (Chinese version) addressed to you by Prince Kung & Li, respectively. Thanking you again for your friendly feeling & good wishes towards Japan & with very high personal regards & esteem for you and mrs Grant, . . . P. S. Accept also our united thanks for ~~the~~ your kind accord to name our second son after you—My wife was exceedingly delighted when I told her the boy's big name." ALS, USG 3. On June 19, USG had given a dinner party at Galena in Yoshida's honor. See *Galena Gazette*, June 21, 1880. On Nov. 16, Yoshida wrote to USG, New York City. "*Strictly Confidential.* . . . I have great pleasure to inform you, privately, that I am in receipt of a telegraphic communication from home, announcing a good result of the long pending negotiation between Japan and China, growing out of the Loo-Choo question. It seems that the Chinese Government has at last come to the agreement, as proposed by Japan, and, at the time when the above mentioned despatch was sent, a protocol or convention was about to be signed by the Representatives of the two Governments. The peaceful settlement of the controversy, I have no doubt, is greatly due to your good offices, for both countries, and I take this occasion, in behalf of the Japanese Government, to render to you grateful thanks, for your ever friendly advice and assistance in the matter. As soon as I have received fuller advices from home I will at length communicate with you." LS, USG 3.

On Feb. 14, 1881, Li wrote to USG. "You will probably have learned before this letter can reach your hand that China and Japan have as yet not come to an understanding respecting the fate of the Liu-Kiu Islands. An agreement recently entered into by the Japanese Minister and the Tsung-li-Yamen could not be ratified because our Emperor's advisers—and I among them—thought it incompatible with the dignity of China to share in the spoliation of a tributary prince against whom she had no grievance whatsoever. Indeed, China, after protesting against the annexation of Liu Kiu by Japan, could not without losing all self-respect and the esteem of the rest of the world suddenly turn round and participate in an act which at the outset she condemned as arbitrary. The final issue in this matter now entirely depends on the attitude of Japan. I, for my part, hope that the discussion will cease and not become a cause of further trouble just after our protracted dispute with Russia has been settled amicably.—I am informed that Mr Angell intends to ~~retire~~ retire shortly from the position he so ably holds at our capital. If this be so, I should indeed regret it, because Mr Angell has during his short stay already gained for himself much esteem and confidence. As to the nomination of Mr Angell's successor I would ask you to recommend, if possible, to the attention of the President elect Consul General Denny who by his antecedents and experience is above all others most likely to foster the already existing intimacy between our respective countries and to benefit both.—As you know Mr Denny and no doubt also appreciate his many qualifications I feel confident that your influence on his behalf will not be wanting at the proper time and in the right quarter. Hoping that you and your family continue to enjoy good health and wishing you all happiness . . ." LS, *ibid.* See letter to Chester A. Arthur, Dec. 5, 1881.

On March 31, Iwakura Tomomi, Tokyo, wrote to USG. "Allow me to take the liberty of writing to you a few lines and thanking you for the very kind inquiries you constantly make after me through our Minister Yoshida who reports to us from time to time what is going on in Your Country. Though years have passed since you left our shores yet the pleasant time I spent with you while you were in this country is still fresh in my memory, but you will please excuse my long silence attributing it to my ignorance of the art of writing English. I am however very happy to learn from Mr. Yoshida that you always enjoy good health and prosperity and that you are ever ready as in the past to help us in whatever involves the interest of this Empire. We feel much indebted to you for this friendly disposition and I have little doubt that the efforts which an influential man like yourself may make for us will hardly fail in bringing about good results, and any assistance you may give us will be always highly appreciated by us. You have no doubt heard from Mr. Yoshida all the particulars of what passed between this government and that of China concerning the Loo Choo question. In accordance with your advice we endeavoured to come to a peaceful solution of this affair for the interest and welfare of the two countries and with this end in view we did our best to show to the Chinese good will and friendly feelings. It is to be much regretted that they would not accept them but it is not our fault and cannot be helped. A memorandum of the conversation which took place between the Tsungli-Yamen and our commissioner before the latter's departure from Peking has been sent to Mr. Yoshida from whom I hope you will hear all the details. You will be pleased to learn that our Emperor enjoys good health and that the country is in perfect peace. He often speaks about you. I hope that the United States will enjoy the same tranquility under the new President as it did under his predecessor and that the day will not be very far distant when we shall see you raised to this honorable position again. The Hawaiian king recently arrived in Japan on his way to China India and Europe and we did our best to please him. I shall be always happy to render you any services here and hope you will not hesitate in charging me with them. My colleagues join me in sending their kindest regards to Mrs Grant and Yourself" Translation, USG 3.

On June 27, 1882, Iwakura wrote to USG. "I have duly received your kind letter through Mr. Young, and it gave me much pleasure. I cannot but thank you for the unceasing interests you take in our welfare. I am much pleased with Mr. Young's appointment, and congratulate your country for securing the services of such an able man. With reference to Riu Kiu question, I have together with Mr. Inouye &c. explained to Mr. Young its later development and the state in which it now stands. Mr. Young will no doubt fully communicate with you on the subject. In spite of your good offices (requested especially by China) towards the satisfactory settlement of the pending controversy, and despite our proposed concessions which were based upon your wise suggestions, the sister Empire has, I regret to say, decidedly taken backward steps rendering further progress toward its settlement almost impossible. I trust however that the day may not be far distant when the dream of imaginary suzerainty over RiuKiu will pass away and the recognition of the stern necessity of Asiatic concert will take its place. I wish to emphasize the fact that on our part we have already done all we could to settle the question, and whatever steps to be taken in future must necessarily be initiated by China. I forward this letter through Mr. Young, and if you will accept the contents of the box which accompany this letter for Mrs. Grant as a triflying mark of my respect to her I shall feel very happy indeed. Wishing you good health, happiness and prosperity . . ." LS, Nellie C. Rothwell, La Jolla, Calif. See Young to Frelinghuysen, March 22, 1883, DNA, RG 59, Diplomatic Despatches, China; John Davis to Young, May 26, 1883, *ibid.*, Diplomatic Instructions, China; Payson J. Treat, *Diplomatic Relations between the United States and Japan 1853–1895* (1932; reprinted, Gloucester, Mass., 1963), II, 141–44; George H. Kerr, *Okinawa: The History of an Island People* (Rutland, Vt., 1958), pp. 376–92; Edwin Pak-wah Leung, "General Ulysses S. Grant and the Sino-Japanese Dispute over the Ryūkyū (Liu-ch'iu) Islands," *Proceedings of the First International Symposium on Asian Studies*, II (1979), 421–49.

1. Negotiations between Chinese and Japanese commissioners broke off without agreement in early 1881. See *Foreign Relations, 1881*, pp. 229–32.

To John Russell Young

——————

Miyanoshita, Japan,
May [*Aug.*] 13th /79

MY DEAR COMMODORE.

We arrived here at 11 am. to-day, all well. Our quarters are very fine for a public house; the best I have seen in Japan, in a public house. After looking around for a half hour I set about writing the letter to ~~Japanese~~ China which you remember I promised I would write. I send it to you for you to deliver, first, because I want to know that it goes safe, and second, because I would like you to read it.—I would like you to deliver it in person and say that if it does not suit please destroy it. If it answers the purpose ask that the letter should be retained until I return to Tokeo. I have not spent an hour in the preparation of the letter and may think of some improvement.

The scenery here, and on the way, is grander than the Nikko scenery.

Please give the bearer a receipt for this.

Yours &c.

U. S. GRANT

P. S. You may notice that I have not addressed my letter to any one. I have avoided this because I do not know but the letter should go to Prince Kung. At the same time I want the Viceroy to see it. If then he thinks it should go to Prince Kung he can put it in the envelope I address and forward it.

U. S. G.

ALS, DLC-John Russell Young. Miyanoshita is in the hot spring district around Ha-kone. On Aug. 12, 13, 15, and 18, 1879, John Russell Young wrote in his diary. "Came down to Yokohama this afternoon. The Gen and party went to Hakune. Resolved that I would not go but try and push ahead my matters with my book. . . ." ". . . Letter from the General ~~and~~ enclosing one to Prince Kung about LooChoo. Wrote the General an answer." ". . . Telegraphed Governor Ito who came down and saw me at Grand Hotel. Read him the letter of the General, . . ." "Dine with the Chinese ambassador. Ito came down and returned the Generals letter and said the Emperor approved it. . . ." *Ibid.* See *ibid.*, Aug. 23, 1879; previous letter.

To Adam Badeau

Tokio, Japan
Aug. 25th /79

MY DEAR GENERAL:

My visit to this interesting country—and abroad—is now drawing to a close. On the 2d of Sept.[1] we sail for San Francisco. Our reception and entertainment in Japan has exceeded anything preceeding it. Youngs account will not be very full until his book comes out because two firms have already pirated his work and advertise cheap additions compiled from his letters to the Herald. Since learning the fact he has written but little for the paper intended for the book.[2]

This is a most beautiful country, and a most interesting people. The progress they have made in their changed civilization within twelve years is almost incredible.[3] They have now Military & Naval Academies, Colleges, Academies, Engineering schools, schools of Science and free schools for male & female as thoroughly organized, and on as high a basis of instruction, as any country in the world. Travel in the interior is as safe for an unarmed, unprotected foreigner as it is in the New England states. Much safer from extorsion. This is marvelous when the treatment these people—and all eastern peoples—receive at the hands of the average foreigner residing among them. I have never been so struck with the heartlessness of Nations as well as individuals as since coming to the east. But a day of retribution is sure to come. These people are becoming strong and China is sure to do so also. When they do a different policy will have to prevale from that enforced now.

I send to-day addressed to your care a small box containing some small presents to Nellie which I wish you would be kind enough to pay all charges upon and forward to her, with the bill for the Amount you may have to pay. The box is marked: Mrs. Nellie Grant Sartoris; Care General A. Badeau; U. S. Consul General London, England.

Mrs. Grant, Fred, & Young join me in kindest regards to you.

Very Truly yours

U. S. GRANT

GN. A. BADEAU

ALS, Munson-Williams-Proctor Institute, Utica, N. Y.

On Aug. 19, 1879, Terajima Muneori, Japanese foreign minister, and his wife, invited USG and Julia Dent Grant "to dinner on Friday, the 22nd Inst. at half past 7 o'clock P. M." D, DLC-USG, IB.

On Aug. 20, John Russell Young wrote in his diary. "There was a visit to the Military school and afterwards we all drove with Saigo to see the races. A large crowd the Emperor coming also. After the race we went home and several of the *Richmond* gentlemen remained to dinner" DLC-John Russell Young.

On Aug. 21, Thursday, Oscar G. Sawyer, "Flagship Richmond," wrote to Young, Tokyo. "The Admiral will send the Steam launch to the English Hatoba on Saturday, to await Gen'l Grant and party; also an Officer to meet him at the Station. It is presumed that you will come down on the 6,30 P. M. train. Will the Japanese furnish a carriage for the General at Yokohama?" ALS, *ibid.*

On Aug. 22, Governor Watanabe Noboru of Osaka wrote to Yoshida Kiyonari and Date Kunitada. "It is my great regret that the prevalence of epidemic decease has prevented General Grant, Ex-President of the United States from visiting Osaka, although the preparations have been made to receive him; I wish now to present to Mrs Grant the herein aftermentioned articles, which were manufactured in this city, and which I intended to offer on their visit to osaka. . . . One Flower vase with several kinds of artificial flowers, and its Stand." Translation, USG 3. See Rokuro Takano *et al., Studies of Cholera in Japan* (Geneva, 1926), pp. 89, 96.

On Aug. 25, Young wrote in his diary. "To-day there was a festival at Uyeno gardens which was very beautiful. We went out in the afternoon, and saw the Emperor. Came home at ten, the whole town a glow of light. . . ." DLC-John Russell Young. See

"Programme of the Fête Champétre at Uyeno Park," USG 3; *Foreign Relations, 1879,*
pp. 682–85; *Young,* II, 572–75.

1. Actually Sept. 3.
2. Popular accounts were James D. McCabe, *A Tour Around the World By General
Grant.* . . . (Cincinnati, 1879), and L. T. Remlap [Loomis T. Palmer], ed., *General U. S.
Grant's Tour Around the World,* . . . (Chicago, 1879). For other early derivative books, see
J. T. Headley, *The Travels of General Grant.* . . . (Philadelphia, 1879), and *The Life and
Travels of General Grant.* . . . (Philadelphia, 1879); *General Grant Abroad.* . . . (Chicago,
1879); J. B. McClure, ed., *Stories, Sketches and Speeches of General Grant* . . . (Chicago,
1879); *General Grant's Tour Around the World* . . . (Chicago, 1879); J. F. Packard, *Grant's
Tour Around the World* . . . (Philadelphia, 1880).
3. The establishment of a new government in early 1868 marked the success of a
Japanese revolutionary movement intent on modernization.

Speech

[*Tokyo, Aug. 30, 1879*]

I come to take my leave of your Majesty and to thank you, the
officials of your Government and the people of Japan for the great
hospitality and kindness I have received at the hands of all during my most pleasant visit to this country.[1] I have now been two
months in Tokio and the surrounding neighborhood and two previous weeks in the more southerly parts of the country. It affords
me great satisfaction to say that during all this stay and all my
visiting, I have not witnessed one discourtesy towards myself nor a
single unpleasant sight. Everywhere there seems to be the greatest
contentment among the people and while no signs of great individual wealth exist, no absolute poverty is visible. This is in striking and pleasing contrast with almost every other country I have
visited.

I leave Japan greatly impressed with the possibilities and probabilities of her future. She has a fertile soil not yet one half subdued
to man's use,[2] great undeveloped mineral resources, numerous and
fine harbors, an extensive sea coast abounding in fish of almost end-
less variety, and above all an industrious, ingenious, contented and
frugal population. With all these nothing is wanted to insure great
progress except wise direction by the Government, peace at home

and abroad, and non-interference in the internal and domestic affairs of the country by the outside nations. It is the sincere desire
of your guest to see Japan realize all the strength and greatness
she is capable of, to see her as independent of foreign rule or dictation as any western nation now is, and to see affairs so directed by
her as to command the respect of the civilized world.[3] In saying
this I believe I reflect the sentiments of the great majority of my
countrymen. I now take my leave without expectation of ever again
having the opportunity of visiting Japan, but with assurances that
pleasant recollections of my present visit will not vanish while my
life lasts. That your Majesty may long reign over a prosperous and
contented people and enjoy every blessing is my sincere prayer.

Copy, USG 3. Emperor Meiji's response to USG's speech was translated into English.
"Your visit has given us so much satisfaction and pleasure, that we can only lament
that the time for your departure has come. We regret also that the heat of the season, and the presence of the epidemic, have prevented several of your proposed visits
to different places. In the meantime, however, we have greatly enjoyed the pleasure
of frequent interviews with you; and the cordial expressions which you have just addressed to us, in taking your leave, have given us great additional satisfaction. America and Japan being near neighbours, separated by an ocean only, will become more
and more closely connected with each other as time goes on. It is gratifying to feel
assured that your visit to our Empire, which enabled us to form very pleasant personal acquaintance with each other, will facilitate and strengthen the friendly relations that have heretofore happily existed between the two countries. And now, we
cordially wish you a safe and pleasant voyage home,—and that you will on your return
home find your nation in peace and prosperity, and that you and your family may enjoy long life and happiness." *Japan Herald* (Yokohama), Sept. 1, 1879. See *Young*, II,
600–604.

On Sept. 2, 1879, John A. Bingham, U.S. minister, Tokyo, wrote to Secretary of
State William M. Evarts. "General Grant being about to quit Japan for the United
States it pleased His Majesty the Emperor to give a farewell audience to the General
and Mrs. Grant and their suite on Saturday the 30th ultimo at the Imperial Palace. I
too had the honor to be present. . . . A final reception will be given this evening in honor
of General Grant at the Palace Enryoquan in which the Emperor has entertained his
distinguished guest during his sojourn in this city. . . ." LS, DNA, RG 59, Diplomatic
Despatches, Japan. *Foreign Relations, 1879*, pp. 685–87. On Sept. 3, USG left Japan on
the *City of Tokio*. See *ibid.*, p. 694; *Young*, II, 609–13; *Julia Grant*, pp. 305–6.

In Oct., John Russell Young reviewed his travels with USG. "I met General Grant
when he landed in Queenstown in May, 1877, and accompanied him to Liverpool. I saw
a good deal of him while in England, although not specially interested in his movements, having other duties for the *Herald*. I went with him to France when he first visited that country, but that was through the accident of my happening to have business
in Paris at the time of his visit. I really first accompanied General Grant when he left
Nice on the American man-of-war Vandalia. This was the first part of the tour 'round

the world. We visited the Mediterranean ports, the Holy Land, Egypt and Malta and had a very pleasant stay at Naples. . . . Our visit to the Holy Land was exceedingly interesting because of its associations, although we were unfortunate in our journey so far as the weather was concerned. There is no harbor on the Syrian *cost*, and the landing at Joppa is always perilous, but we fortunately found a pleasant day for that purpose. But from the time of landing until we left there was rain and snow—the heaviest snow-storm that had been known in Jerusalem for twelve years. . . . I remember, as we rode across the plains of Sharon, General Grant saying (and he has a keen eye for such matters) that that plain alone, properly cultivated, would supply the Mediterranean nations with wheat and corn. . . . We saw a great deal of the King of Greece, a bright, interesting young gentleman, who came on board the Vandalia and spent an afternoon with General Grant. They talked a great deal about the relations of Greece and Turkey, and the King was anxious, I observed, to have General Grant's advice as to the best attitude for Greece to take. . . . I saw a great deal of the General on his return to Paris. He seemed to enjoy Paris, not at first, but in time. It was interesting to me to observe the change of his mind in reference to France. He went to France with the old-fashioned American feeling about the French: that they were an inferior race, giddy, given to pleasure, suffering, perhaps, from the paramount influence of the Catholic Church, and that the Republican leaders were communists. This is the opinion of the average American, as a general thing. But France grew upon General Grant bit by bit. When he came to see the leaders of French politics, M. Gambetta especially, he found them, so far from being visionary enthusiasts, conservative men, patriotic and of great ability. Gambetta, in fact, he came to look upon as one of the foremost statesmen in Europe. The industrial condition of the French people, their thrift, their untiring patience under the burdens of a heavy debt, their communal governments, all impressed the General very much, and I know he left France profoundly convinced with the fact that nothing but a republic ever would live in France and that that people were destined to a great future. . . . The General arrived in Berlin in the evening, and the next morning, instead of making calls (which, in fact, was something that never occurred to him), we strolled out around Berlin, got on top of the street cars, where you ride for half fare, and rode around and around the city among the workmen. This was one of General Grant's favorite methods of amusing himself abroad. I know that he used to go down to Versailles from Paris in a third-class train so as to see the workingmen. On our return from this trip through Berlin on the top of the street cars we found General Grant's table covered with cards, and among them four cards from Bismarck—he had either called or sent four times to see the General. The General remarked: 'I do not want Bismarck running after me; he has a great deal of business to do, while I am simply a wanderer;' and he sent a message to Bismarck at once, saying that he would call upon him at any hour that he would name. Bismarck named the next afternoon at 4 o'clock. At General Grant's request I accompanied him. I wrote an account of this interview, which was published at the time. . . . When Bismarck returned Gen. Grant's call he came in full General's uniform and remained half an hour, talking mostly with Mrs. Grant, in a charming, light, domestic conversation, about his wife, his children and his home, running off into playful things. I saw him again at the dinner he gave General Grant. When the dinner was at an end a long conversation was had between them, Bismarck smoking a huge pipe, with the great hound crouching between his knees. General Grant saw Bismarck on many occasions after this, when I was not present, and they became quite cronies. . . . I have heard General Grant say he regarded Bismarck, Gambetta and Beaconsfield as the three greatest men he had met in Europe. . . .

Mr. Moran, our Minister in Portugal, was quite ill while we were there. General Grant used to go around, sit and talk with him by the hour about his (Moran's) experiences in London during the war. After Portugal we visited Gibraltar, and after visiting there we met Lord Napier. . . . Lord Napier and General Grant became very friendly, spent a great deal of time riding around the fortifications and on the beach together. General Grant said that Lord Napier was the best informed man he had ever met, outside of America, on the events of the American war; he seemed to know of it in detail, of the different movements, tactics and strategy. While at Gibraltar the General reviewed the British garrison, and was struck with the discipline of the British army. . . . Our trip through India was hurried on account of the season being late. India should be visited in December or January. We did not arrive until the middle of February. The Viceroy, Lord Lytton (Owen Meredith), telegraphed General Grant that he would wait for him in Calcutta, and this hurried General Grant's movements, as he did not wish to keep the Viceroy from going to the hills, where he spent his summer. . . . General Grant is a severe traveler, one of extraordinary endurance. Always prompt and anxious to get on, he saw things very rapidly, and never was more satisfied than when he could travel all night and see sights all day. He seemed to enjoy sea life more than anything else. On his way home from China [*Japan*] he read a great deal, being especially interested in Hugo's Les Miserables, especially in the account of the Battle of Waterloo, which, he, said was one of the best accounts he had ever read. I remember his saying that he agreed with Hugo in one thing about the battle, that it seemed the time had come for Napoleon to fall; that the battle was a perfect one so far as any military genius could devise it, and there could be no criticism made upon Napoleon's manner of planning it and fighting it. He had a great detestation of the character of Napoleon, whom he regarded as one of the most selfish men in history. 'I think if Napoleon,' General Grant said on one occasion, 'had been a thoroughly unselfish man, a patriot, and one who cared about his country, not about the advancement of his family and his personal power, he would have been without comparison, the greatest man in history; but, as it turned out, he was one of the worst. I never had any sympathy with him nor respect for his achievements, although, of course, I cannot but wonder at his marvelous genius.' I remember that when we were on the French ship going to Hong Kong, one of the young ladies asked Gen. Grant to write in a book called 'Questions and Answers,' a sort of a young ladies' album much in vogue. One of the questions was, 'Which two characters in history do you dislike most?' He wrote, 'Napoleon and Robespierre.'" *Philadelphia Times*, Oct. 20, 1879.

1. For a list of presents given to USG and Julia Dent Grant in Japan, see DLC-USG. On Dec. 18, Frederick Dent Grant, Chicago, wrote to Bingham. "I express to you today One Diamond ring from Father to Prince Date . . . will you be kind enough to have these things turned over to the persons named they are sent by father for the Gentlemen that were near us during our stay in Japan—Father intends sending some other things as soon as he can collect them . . ." ALS, Milton Ronsheim, Cadiz, Ohio.

2. Young recalled a conversation toward the end of USG's visit. "The General pointed out to his Japanese friends the large area of fertile land awaiting cultivation, and how much might be added to the wealth and revenues of the country if the people were induced to develop the whole territory. This led to a discussion of the land tax, so heavy a burden to the people, and which the government is compelled to impose for revenue. If, instead of taxes on land the authorities could levy a tariff for revenue—such a tariff as we see in Germany and France—then the tax on land could be abated." *Young*, II, 582.

3. Some Japanese believed that aggressive efforts to revise treaties would provoke a hostile response, especially from Great Britain. USG advised: "If there is one thing more certain than another, it is that England is in no humor to make war upon Japan for a tariff. I do not believe that under any circumstances Lord Beaconsfield would consent to such an enterprise. He has had two wars, neither of which have commended themselves to the English people. An Englishman does not value the glory that comes from Afghan and Zulu campaigns. To add to these a demonstration against Japan, because she had resolved to submit no longer to a condition bordering on slavery, would arouse against Lord Beaconsfield a feeling at home that would cost him his government. Just now is the best time. Lord Beaconsfield must soon go to the people. His Parliament is coming to an end, and even if he had adventurous spirits in his cabinet or in the diplomatic service disposed to push Japan, he would be compelled to control them. Japan has a great many friends in England who are even now making her cause their own, and who would support her when she was right. More than all, there is a widespread desire for justice and fair play in England, to which the Eastern nations, and especially Japan, need never appeal in vain. Japan has peculiar claims upon the sympathy and respect of mankind, and if she would assert her sovereign rights she would find that her cause met the approval of mankind." *Ibid.*, p. 583.

To Adam Badeau

———

Tokio, Japan.
Aug. 30th /79

MY DEAR GENERAL:

You will see from the date above that we did not get away from here on the 27th as I wrote you we would. The steamer on which we are to sail postponed her departure until the 3d of Sept. otherwise I should not have received your letter of the 9th of July. I do not know how it can be that you have not received letters from me. I have written to you oftener than to anyone else [ex]cept my children and possibly Ammen. I have received, since leaving you at Marseilles, three or four batches of your book, and returned all of them. I hope you have received them all back.

Mrs. Robeson is no friend of mine to tell you of my intend book in competion with yours when she knew yours was not yet in print and might be changed to suit the altered circumstances. On lookin[g] at your letter again I see that Mrs. R. did not tell you that, but you got your information from an obscure paper published in the Western part of Kansas. Well, I thought by letting the information out so far from London you would not find it out before your work was completed and then it would do you no good nor me any harm. But as you are posted now I give you my written pledge that the work described in the Wichita Eagle[1] shall not appear in time to do you any harm.—I do not feel bad over the information Mrs. Robeson gave you. I am not a candidate for any office nor would ~~not~~ I hold one that required any maneuvering or sacrifice to obtain.

We are all well. Mrs. Grant, Fred & Young join me in kindest regards to you.

Yours Truly
U. S. GRANT

GN. A. BADEAU, U. S. CONSUL GENERAL.

ALS, Munson-Williams-Proctor Institute, Utica, N. Y. See *Badeau*, p. 519.

On Aug. 26, 1879, USG and Julia Dent Grant attended a reception given by Thomas B. Van Buren, consul gen., Kanagawa. In response to Van Buren's toast, USG said. "Ladies and Gentlemen,—I thank you most sincerely on behalf of Mrs. Grant and myself for this hospitable reception, and for your kind wishes; and I cordially join in your expressed desire that we may have a peaceful and prosperous voyage, and find our friends at home in health and prosperity." *Japan Herald* (Yokohama), Aug. 27, 1879. See *Young*, II, 600. On Aug. 20, Van Buren, Yokohama, had telegraphed twice to USG, Tokyo. "My invitation all out what can I do" "Will postpone what date will suit you best answer" Telegrams received (11:10 A.M. and 11:30 A.M.), DLC-USG, IB.

On Aug. 27, USG wrote to John A. Bingham, U.S. minister, Tokyo. "As I understand the tide will be low, and running out, at the time we must start for Prince Datés to-morrow afternoon, and to avoid detention of either your party or mine I think it will be better if you will come over here to start soon after 4 O'Clock, p. m. I am told the boat will not be able to get in at that time at your house so that it will be as easy to come here as to go to Hamagaten and will ~~delay~~ be more pleasant." ALS, Milton Ronsheim, Cadiz, Ohio. See *Young*, II, 596–99.

On Aug. 29, Harada Jirō, president, 74th National Bank of Yokohama, and his manager, wrote to USG. "We have long since been attracted by your Excellency's illustrious name to have great respect toward you and our joy was boundless when you arrived in Japan in the seventh month of this year and we had the honor of having several interviews with you. It is our great regret that after your two months stay in this country, it has happened to us to part with you and we would therefore pray your Excellency to accept this trifling offering as shown on the annexed list as a souvenir of our sincere feelings towards you. . . . One Tablet, with thereon embroidered Cock and hen on silk. One round Tablet, with thereon lacquered picture of a young cowherd on an ox." Translation, USG 3.

On Aug. 30, Saturday, F. E. Foster, Yokohama, telegraphed to John Russell Young, Tokyo. "please present my compliments to General & Mrs Grant & say that Mrs Foster & myself will have great pleasure in dining with them on Monday evening the steamer will not leave before Wednesday morning at ten oclock about Honolulu I will try to

give a difinite reply tomorrow I shall extend gen grants invitation to Captain Maury—"
Telegram received, DLC-John Russell Young.

On Sept. 1, Miyashima Seiichiro wrote to USG. "I have long cherished a high
respect for you but to-day for the first time it is my happiness to be favored with a personal interview, a happiness which I had never dared to hope for. I beg to congratulate
you upon your continued good health notwithstanding the sultry weather. When your
honored contrys envoy Perry came to Yedo, I was but sixteen years of age, and was
too young to understand the questions of the day, but heard the discussions that were
going on through the empire as to the propriety of entering into treaties of peace and
friendship with foreigners. Perry said that, Commercial intercourse conducted upon
the principles of justice would benefit the empire beyond the possibility of a doubt. As
for example to borrow an illustration from every day affaires. It need no argument to
prove that, glass windows will keep out wind and rain much better than paper ones,
and the benefits that would arise from the introduction of steamboats and electric telegraphs would also be very great. Why not make the experiment of commercial intercourse for five or six years, and then if it should prove hurtful instead of beneficial at
the expiration of that time, alter the arrangements accordingly. Since that time twenty
seven years have gone by like a dream and the present commercial intercourse between
Japan and all the nations of the world, certainly owes its origin to the favor of your
honored country. During the period referred to we have passed through many troubles
and experienced many vicissitudes and have gradually attained our present state of
prosperity. Your excellency who have just in this time come to Japan may imagine to
yourself the circumstances of that time. Since the revolution (on 1868) our sovereign
and people have diligently labored to correct what was wrong, and to draw from every
foreign country the means to remedy our own deficiencies. But imports from abroad
are greatly in excess of the exports of native products, and this cannot fail to produce
embarrassment and difficulties, which are truly to be defprecated. The time having arrived for the revision of the treaties, it appears I understand that, before all the treaty
powers, your country has consented to it in the favorable terms to our country. We
know from this that, Commodore Perry did not deceive us, and that persons of sincerity and humanity abound in your honored country. May our country forever continue
in relations of peace and intimate friendship. I keep the picture of your great and good
friend Mr. Lincoln hanging in my room, and cherish the memory of his many solid vir-
tues, but now having the exceeding good fortune to see you in person, I beg to present
these lines for your acceptance." L (in Japanese), USG 3; translation, *ibid.*

1. "GRANT CRAMMING FOR A BOOK. It is perfectly wonderful to think of
the amount of studying Grant is doing and with what zeal he is improving his mind
all this time. A friend of mine who was with him frequently in Paris, said that while
there, notwithstanding he was the object of almost constant adulation, every meal a
banquet, with every night a reception by some high dignitary in his honor, he yet found
time to make a long and deep study of the communism of 1871 and the revolution of
1789. Every day he would gather some of the learned French statesmen and historians
and talk for two or three on a specific part of this topic, and would then dismiss them
to read and make notes of his investigations on the subject. At times he would go to
the prisons and talk with some of the famous communistic leaders still incarcerated,
or, again, he would have some of the officers who captured the barricades come to him
and give him their testimony on communism with a gun or petroleum can in its hand.
In Spain, England, and everywhere, it was always the same with Grant—he was quiet,
philosophical and contemplative, and modest under all circumstances, and though na-

tions were waiting to do him honor, he always preferred the reserve and unostentatious society of his family, travelling friends and a few learned men of the country which he was visiting, to the pomp and display of royal honors. I predict that when Gen. Grant again rests on his native land, not only will he be the greatest living military chieftain, but he will be the greatest traveller and best-posted man on foreign affairs that has ever lived. He will be a man of the great world in the grandest sense of the term. The gentleman who told me of his Parisian habits says Grant expects to write a journal of his travels and memoir of his life when he returns, and that he will probably remain in private life to do it." *Wichita Eagle,* June 12, 1879.

To Owen N. Denny

———

Tokio, Japan.
Sept. 1st 1879.

My Dear Judge;

This will present to you W. G. Markham, a gentleman who has been largely & intelligently—as his letters will show—engaged in stock breeding and raising, of latter years particularly in sheep breeding & raising. Mr. Markham has recently brought to Japan two hundred head of very fine sheep which I have seen myself. He goes to China hoping to be able to introduce there some to improve their present stock. He can tell you what has been the effect here of crossing the fine American sheep with the Chinese which are at present the most numerous here. If you will aid Mr. Markham to an interview either with His Excellency, Li Hung Chang,[1] or other authority that will give him the opportunity of representing his desires I will be much obliged.

Please present Mrs. Grant's and my kindest regards to Mrs. Denny & Miss Denny, and also to the Viceroy.

Very Truly Yours
U. S. Grant

Judge O. N. Denny
U. S. Consul,

ALS (facsimile), eBay, July 12, 2005. William G. Markham began breeding registered cattle and sheep in upstate N. Y. (1860) and served as an official in national and state associations devoted to wool and sheep interests. See Markham to James A. Garfield, Nov. 26, 1877, DLC-James A. Garfield; *New York Times,* May 17, 1922.

1. Markham "visited China and the pastoral plains of Mongolia and in an interview with his excellency the viceroy Li Hung Chang so impressed him with the value of American sheep that a subsequent shipment was made to China." Undated newspaper clipping (filed with Markham to Elijah W. Halford, June 18, 1891), DLC-Benjamin Harrison.

Speech

[*San Francisco, Sept. 20, 1879*]

Mr. Mayor: I accept with great pleasure the cordial invitation of the citizens of San Francisco to be their guest during my stay in the city. I once lived here, and it gives me great gratification, after quarter of a century's absence, to come back and witness the wonderful change which has taken place in that period. I know it has been marvelous, because I have read and heard so much of it; but I have no doubt that when I see it for myself, I shall find that what I have read has given me but a faint idea of your wealth and prosperity. Let me ask you to express to the citizens of San Francisco my sincere thanks for their hospitality.

San Francisco Chronicle, Sept. 21, 1879. USG spoke on arrival in San Francisco, after a welcoming address by Mayor Andrew J. Bryant. Earlier, USG spoke to a reporter on board the *City of Tokio* in San Francisco Bay, "remarking that if any other evidence of the near approach of American civilization were needed, it was the presence of the interviewer, a species of the human family he had not met with abroad." "I cannot say I am not glad to get here, though the latter part of my tour has been extremely pleasant. A year and a half ago I was thoroughly homesick, but the variation of scene and the kindness which I have met with have almost done away with that feeling. I have enjoyed it very much and particularly the latter part of it. There was so much that was entirely new to me in China and Japan that it was very interesting. As an incident I can mention the pyrotechnic displays in China, which were most remarkable and exceeded anything I ever saw. They made figures of every conceivable kind in the shape of lanterns—men, beasts and birds and combinations of the three, which were hoisted in the air and disposed about the trees and streets to produce a marvelous effect. The trip up the inland sea in Japan was very pleasant. In fact, the most beautiful scenery I ever saw was on that trip. . . ." Asked about his presidential prospects, USG replied. "Well, I don't aspire. . . . My time is all my own and there is nothing to hurry me. I can simply say that traveling as I am I shall stay as long as it is agreeable. I want to visit Yosemite, and I propose to go to Oregon, and just how long I shall remain I can't tell. I should like to see Benicia again, for that and the Columbia were my old 'stamping-grounds.'" The reporter pointed out Alcatraz in the distance. USG said, "I recognize it. I have been here before. It was twenty-seven years ago when I arrived here and twenty-five years ago when I left, but after coming into the bay after a Panama voyage you recollect it pretty distinctly." When the reporter asked, "I presume, General, you have had a good opportunity to study the Chinese question abroad?" USG replied, "No; I have not. You will recollect that I left here before it attained any prominence or political importance whatever, and I have had no opportunity of examining it in its California bearings. My views on it were expressed, as far as I could form them, in my speech at Penang, which was delivered hastily and without warning. Mr. Young tells me that your papers published it. I said then that the importation of a race of slaves to this coast, if such were their condition, was a great evil; but if they came as citizens of other countries did, I saw no objection. But as I said before, the Chinese question is a new one to me. . . . I heard enough to know that [*Chinese officials*] are opposed to Chinese emigration to this country, except for commercial purposes, and that they are ready to co-operate with the United States in ameliorating the evil. I received it from the highest dignitaries of the empire. I have been away from home so long, however, that it is a dead question at present to me, but I hope to know something about it before long." Asked where he would go after leaving Calif., USG said. "To Galena. I am going home for a little rest. I have not had any private life for eighteen years, and I expect the change will be pleasant." The reporter said that newspapers "estimate your fortune variously from $75,000 to $500,000." USG responded. "Well the first figure is much nearer the truth, although I trust it is largely over that. Perhaps if I were to sacrifice it under the hammer it would not bring more, but I have enough to live on. I have a brick house and a fine place in Galena, but in the present condition of commercial affairs, instead of renting it profitably it is necessary to pay somebody to take care of it. The Lesseps Canal Presidency, which you mention as a rumor, I don't know anything about." At this point, "one of the bands on the accompanying schooners struck up a pot-pourri from the *Pinafore* and Senator Cole called attention to the fact." USG remarked, "I have heard a great deal of this *Pinafore* and would like to hear it. I never happened to be in a place, however, where it was being played." *Ibid.* On Sept. 27, 1879, USG attended a California Theatre production of Gilbert and Sullivan's *HMS Pinafore*.

Later on Sept. 20, at the Palace Hotel, USG told well-wishers "that he was glad to return to San Francisco after an absence of twenty-five years and to receive so warm and generous a welcome from its citizens. He hoped now that he was here to remain long enough to see and be seen by all his friends, but for the present he must say, Good night." *Ibid.*

On April 2, 1879, Alexander D. Sharon, San Francisco, had written to USG. "Learning that you intend soon to visit our Coast I take great pleasure in tendering to yourself and family, the freedom of The Palace Hotel during your Stay in San Francisco Your acceptance of its hospitalities will give me great satisfaction" ALS, DLC-USG, IB. See Oscar Lewis and Carroll D. Hall, *Bonanza Inn: America's First Luxury Hotel* (New York, 1939), pp. 82–89.

In July, William Roy, former lt. col., 1st Ind. Art., and more than seven hundred others, New Orleans, addressed USG. "With unfeigned pleasure we beg to tender you our greeting on your return to your native land, and most heartily congratulate you on the distinguished honors conferred upon you while abroad. . . . You must be aware of the trying ordeal through which the country has passed (politically) during the years of your absence, and the odium which some would attach to the great Republican Party of which you were once its honored head and of which we form some humble part. We would challenge her accusers and again honor you. In doing so, however, we would be as frank and fair in the criticism of our own faults as we would be of those of others. Republicans in the HIGHEST, NOBLEST and BROADEST sense, our heartfelt aim and desire is simply, Good Government over a UNITED, HAPPY and CONTENTED People. Actuated by a motive SO SIMPLE, SO PURE, WHO throughout the length and breadth of our entire land can EXCEPT? WHO ASK MORE? All this, under your leadership, sustained as you will be by an OVERWHELMING MAJORITY of your fellow countrymen, we believe, WE KNOW awaits us, under the blessing of an over-ruling Providence. Thus briefly. we tender you an earnest, honest greeting, and with the greeting, echo back from the South the welcome sound which greets our own ears, as it comes from the North, from the East. and from the West. Assuring you of the honest beat of thousands of hearts, all over this Southern land, in response to what we here express, and their longing desire for the early dawn of brighter, happier days, we bid you WELCOME, and hail you to the OVATION which awaits you." DS (printed), ICarbS.

On Sept. 8, the San Francisco Board of Supervisors passed a resolution welcoming USG. DS, Smithsonian Institution. On Sept. 17, Wednesday, Martin C. Briggs and two others, San Jose, resolved: ". . . By the California Annual Conference of the M. E. Church now in session and representing a large and respectable body of Citizens of the state, that we respectfully request the authorities and Committees of arrangement of San Francisco so to order the public demonstration in honor of our Eminent fellow Citizen, that it shall not take place on the Sabbath day." DS, DLC-USG, IB; *San Francisco Chronicle*, Sept. 19, 1879. A nearly identical notice in the same newspaper, purporting to request a similar observance of the Jewish sabbath, was exposed as a hoax. See *Alta California*, Sept. 20, 1879.

On Sept. 13, Hamilton Fish, Garrison, N. Y., had written to USG, San Francisco. "You will be overwhelmed with the welcome of grateful Millions, on your Arrival. I will not occupy your time further than to add the welcome of one who has followed you in your travels, with the most affectionate interest. My wife, who has been *very seriously* ill, but is better, sends love to Mrs Grant. Present to her my most sincere regards. We long to see you again—when shall that be? Be assured of the ever sincere regard & affection . . ." ALS, DLC-USG, IB. On Sept. 17, George W. Childs, Philadelphia, telegraphed to USG. "Welcome you are not more rejoiced to be home than we are to have you. Your philadelphia friends in Still Stronger Friendship & affection have followed with close interest your Journey around the World. They have enjoyed to the fullest the unexampled welcomes and honors by People & Governments that everywhere greeted the American Citizen whose service to his country has added so largely to the lustre of her fame. They can wish for you nothing higher after the honors you have received and the broad & priceless experience you have gained than continued health & happiness to you and yours" Telegram received, *ibid.* On Sept. 21, Lt. Gen. Philip H. Sheridan, Chicago, telegraphed to USG. "Please accept my congratulations for your safe return. Mrs Sheridan sends her love to Mrs Grant, in which I join" Copy, DLC-Philip H. Sheridan. Also on Sept. 21, Governor John C. Frémont of Arizona Territory and Col. Orlando B. Willcox, Prescott, telegraphed to USG. "On the part of the people and military in Arizona we welcome you home" Telegram received (at 6:16 P.M.), DLC-USG, IB. On the same day, U.S. Senator James D. Cameron of Pa., Harrisburg, telegraphed to USG. "Congratulations upon your safe return and love from us all to Mrs Grant and yourself" Telegram received (at 9:20 P.M.), *ibid.* On Sept. 22, Governor William E. Smith of Wis., John P. Newman, New York City, and Anthony J. Drexel, Philadelphia, Pa., all sent similar messages to USG. Telegrams received (at 11:55 A.M., 1:20 P.M., and 3:20 P.M.), *ibid.* Also on Sept. 22, Frank Jaynes, San Francisco, wrote to USG. "On behalf of the Western Union Telegraph Co. I have the honor to extend to you the freedom of its telegraph lines during your stay upon the Pacific Coast; and I take great pleasure in handing you herewith a book of franks for the most convenient use of the same." LS, DLC-

John Russell Young. On Sept. 23, George C. Bates, Leadville, Colo., wrote to USG. "Congratulating you on your safe return from your triumphant trip around the world; I deeply regret that I could not have received you there, in that same old Room at the corner of Montgomery & Merchant street where a quarter of a century ago, I gave you the California HUG on the arrival of your old 4th Regiment whith its cholrea stricken ranks.—Genl you have seen the wonders of the old world, but you never saw *Leadville*— a baby town, of less that *two* years with a population of 30.000; with over 200 drinking houses 150 gaming houses, 6 churches 3 daily papers 2 miles nearer hHeaven than you have ever been before, and which turns out at least $75.000 silver dollars every day the 8th wonder of the world Genl Come and see it.—and you & your good wife will find me; not as in Detroit years ago, in a handsome Brick on Fort Street; but in a *Log Cabin* leased at 50 dollars per month, where my new wife and my self will give you and your Lady a regular Pioneer Welcome—When you have seen the wonders of these Mountains and these Gulches and this Infant city you will be more amazed than ever, at the future greatness and glory of our beloved country whos every nook & corner whos Mountains & Valleys have been Illuminated by your achievements and gallantry—I salute you as of olden times in Detroit and Sanfrancisco" ALS, *ibid.* See *PUSG*, 22, 208; letter to Jesse Root Grant, Jr., July 30, 1880. Also on Sept. 23, President Rutherford B. Hayes, Gen. William T. Sherman, and Sheridan, Quincy, Ill., telegraphed to USG. "The ladies and gentlemen just from Chicago all unite in heartest greetings to Mrs Grant and yourself" Telegram received (at 10:15 P.M.), DLC-John Russell Young. On Sept. 24, Sheridan, Chicago, telegraphed to USG. "Your telegram of this date received. Mrs. Grant and Julia are especially well, and anxiously awaiting Fred's return. We are all well here and send our warm regards" Copy, DLC-Philip H. Sheridan. Also on Sept. 24, John Calvin Brewster, San Buenaventura, Calif., wrote to USG. "Doubtless you are the recipient of many weighty communications from distinguished statesmen and politicians but as I am neither I beg pardon for this encroachment upon your valuable time My object in addressing you is to ask, and if you please obtain your photograph I mail to your address a photo print (my own make) of the old mission buildings of this place, erected 102 years ago . . ." ALS, DLC-John Russell Young. See William A. Bullough, "History Through a Lens: The Photographs of John Calvin Brewster, 1874–1909," *Ventura County Historical Society Quarterly*, 41, 1 (Fall, 1995), 5–29.

On Sept. 22, John Russell Young had spoken to a reporter about USG's political intentions. ". . . If he is nominated by an enthusiastic convention, then he will decide what is the best thing to be done. He never plans ahead. He is not a schemer. The talk which I have heard since our return, to the effect that Grant and the party managers were arranging all this thing is simply disgusting. Let me tell you that during his absence abroad Grant did all of his own correspondence, and let me say that he is a very poor correspondent. He has written a few letters to Commodore Ammen (who is one of his old school-day friends), a letter to Mr. Borie, a letter or two to Mr. Childs, a few letters of courtesy, and a few letters on private business. Take the entire correspondence of the General during the past two years and a half, and I believe the number of letters written by him will not exceed two dozen. I know what I am saying when I assert that none of the letters received from Gen. Grant's personal friends hinted at the probabilities of the future, and I am positive that he did not allude to politics himself. Let me illustrate the alarming character of Grant's correspondence: He has a friend named Borie. They are old chums. Borie has been in the habit of writing letters to the General. His letters are always acceptable. The General has answered a few of them. In this way an American newspaper reporter finds out that a deep-laid scheme is on foot to capture the country for Grant, and Borie is at the bottom of it. The newspapers teem with rumors of the supposed contents of Grant's letters to Borie. Now the truth of the matter is that nearly all the letters that have passed between Mr. Borie and Gen. Grant have been, on the one side, letters of information regarding the progress of Edison's wonderful inventions, and, on the other, inquiries regarding them. The General is a great admirer of, and an enthusiastic believer in, Edison. He would not be surprised at anything Edison might do. If he were to invent an automatic lamp-post that would collar a drunken man on the street and take him home and put him to bed the General would not be surprised. It is my honest opinion that Grant has no more idea of what he may do in the future than you have. If you were to ask him he couldn't tell you. He acts only when the moment for action comes. He never blows a fog-horn." *Chicago Tribune*, Sept. 23, 1879.

On Oct. 25, Joseph Tuttle, San Francisco, wrote to USG. "I beg leave to hand you herewith, a Photograph picture of Benicia Depōt, which I beg you to accept as an offering of love from an Old Soldier who knew you in early days. At this Depōt you turned in your public property, and I received it from you on your arrival in California. This is the only picture in existence of the Depot as it appeared at the time of your arrival, and I trust it may bring to mind many pleasant remembrances." ALS, USG 3. On Aug. 30, 1866, Tuttle, Fort Yuma, Calif., had written to USG seeking a commission as lt., 14th Inf. ALS, DNA, RG 94, ACP, 3817 1871. No appointment followed. See *PUSG*, 1, 256.

During his visit, USG received honorary memberships in the Association of the Territorial Pioneers of California, dated Sept. 16; the Mercantile Library Association and St. Andrews Society, Sept. 22; and the Caledonian Club, Oct. 3. DS, Smithsonian Institution. USG also received invitations from the Society of California Pioneers and the Sonoma and Marin District Agricultural Society, dated Sept. 22, and the California Theatre, Oct. 6. DLC-USG, IB.

Speech

[*San Francisco, Sept. 24, 1879*]

I am very glad to meet the representatives of the Chinese community and receive their address. I have, as you say, just returned from a visit to your country. It was a most interesting visit, one that I shall always remember, especially because of the kindness and hospitality shown me by the people and the authorities of China. For that I am grateful, and glad of the opportunity of expressing that gratitude so soon after my arrival at home. I hope that the remark you make about China breaking down the seclusion in which she has been shrouded for ages will prove true, in all senses, and that China will continue to draw near to her the sympathy and the trade of the civilized world. The future of China will largely depend upon her policy in this respect. A liberal policy will enlarge your commerce and confer great advantages upon the outside world. I hope, as an American, that America will have a large share in this. Again I thank you.

San Francisco Chronicle, Sept. 25, 1879. USG spoke during a reception at the home of Maj. Gen. Irvin McDowell, at Black Point. Frederick A. Bee, Chinese consul, welcomed USG on behalf of a delegation of Chinese diplomats and merchants. *Ibid.*; copy, DLC-USG, IB. The delegation also presented USG with a scroll. *San Francisco Chronicle*, Sept. 25, 1879; DLC-USG, IB. Bee also addressed Julia Dent Grant. "Mrs. Grant: The Chinese merchants of this city desire to present you with this beautiful testimonial of their high regard for you. Inasmuch as it required foreign fleets and armies to break down Chinese exclusiveness and open commercial relations, they recognize that you, in your recent visit to the capital of the Chinese Empire, broke down that Chinese domestic exclusiveness which had existed for centuries. In commemoration of that event they desire to give you this casket as a memorial thereof." *San Francisco Chronicle*, Sept. 25, 1879. Bee presented Julia Grant with a "satin-lined ivory casket . . . embellished with delicate and elaborate carvings in the highest style of Chinese art." *Ibid.*

Also on Sept. 24, 1879, USG visited the produce exchange and received a delegation of former citizens of Galena.

On Sept. 21, Isaiah W. Lees had presented USG with a written invitation (dated Sept. 20) to attend a Sept. 23 ball to benefit the Widows' and Orphans' Aid Association of the San Francisco Police Dept. USG "accepted the invitation on behalf of himself and suite, and said that a policeman's life was similar in many respects to that of the soldier, and as nothing was ever done to provide for the widows and orphans of the brave dead who laid down their lives defending their country, he heartily indorsed every measure having for its aim the alleviation of the weak and helpless." *Ibid.*, Sept. 22, 1879.

On Sept. 22, during a visit to Cliff House, USG received a telephone call from Governor-elect George C. Perkins of Calif. "The General was immediately informed and betrayed much interest. He stated that he had never seen the telephone, excepting so far as the crude predecessors of it in use in the English mines and the small telephonic prototypes of Japan were concerned. As soon therefore as the last yielding spoonful of ice cream had been overwhelmed by the cafe noir finale, he was conducted to the telephone, and for some minutes interestedly examined the silver-glistening bells and the mysterious box. Intrepidly clutching the two ear-pieces attached to cords, he waited and the following impressive dialogue ensued: . . . Dropping the handles he said: 'It's wonderful. I heard every word he said of the latter portion. I suppose that in a year or two the world will wonder how it ever did without it.'" *Ibid.*, Sept. 23, 1879.

Also on Sept. 22, a reporter asked Julia Grant when the trip abroad had been planned. "Oh, long, long ago. We were always planning it. When we were young people we talked of it, and always meant to go some day. During the war the General used to say: 'When the war is over we will go to Europe, anyhow.' But when the war was over he was elected President, and that prevented us from carrying out our plan. Then we said that when his term expired we would go; but he was elected a second time, and we had to put it off again. It seemed as if we should never be able to go." Julia Grant also spoke of plans to visit Washington, D. C., where she "has so many friends that she feels almost more at home there than in Illinois." "Every large city that I looked upon abroad I have mentally compared with our capital, and the verdict has always been the same: 'No, you are not so beautiful as Washington.'" *Ibid.*

On Sept. 25, John P. Jackson, *San Francisco Evening Post*, toasted USG during a banquet at the Palace Hotel, given by members of the San Francisco press in honor of John Russell Young. USG responded. "I thank you, gentlemen, and the public of

San Francisco, for the kind manner in which I have been received, and for the hospitality shown me. I shall feel highly gratified if as hearty a welcome awaits me on my return to my home in the East. The good opinion of my countrymen is dearer to me than that of the whole world besides." *Ibid.*, Sept. 26, 1879. On Oct. 7, Jackson wrote to USG. "The 'Soscol Orchards' in Napa County raise the finest fruit in this state—The owners Simpson Thompson (father, aged 80 yrs) and Son James M. Thompson, are old Pennsylvanians and early Californians—They are anxious that you should enjoy some of their fruit and hence send you a box of apples representing the two extremes of our country—The dark-red are *Hoovers*; origin Georgia—The light red are *Northern Spy*, origin New-York—and are considered the most delicious of all dessert apples—I have said to Mr. Thompson that I would see these apples delivered to Gen'l and Mrs. Grant, which herewith I beg to do." ALS, DLC-John Russell Young.

On Sept. 26, Mayor Lawrence Archer welcomed USG to San Jose. USG replied. "I am glad to see you all and to thank you for your kind reception. You speak of my reception by the sovereigns and princes of the world. I am prouder of all this kindness from the sovereigns—the people of my country. Ladies and gentlemen, I thank you." *San Francisco Chronicle*, Sept. 27, 1879. A similar brief speech is *ibid.* At a banquet, USG responded to a toast. "Gentlemen of Santa Clara county: It is with extreme diffidence that I rise to thank you for the very hearty reception I have received at the hands of the people of your county. I cannot express all that I feel and it is hardly necessary that I should do so. I have a friend here who has never been wanting to do me a kindness, and I know he will do better than I can. I call on Colonel Jackson." Jackson responded. ". . . I wish to draw a lesson that was pointed to-day by the tanners of Santa Clara. It is the pride of our nation that the humblest man in it may aspire to the highest office. . . ." *Ibid.*

Speech

[*San Francisco, Sept. 27, 1879*]

Comrades, it will be impossible for me to make any large percentage of you hear me, even if it is possible to respond properly, as I will try to do, to the toast you have just drank so heartily. I will say to you, however, that it does my heart good to meet so many with whom I served during the trials through which our country passed but a few years ago. It affords me special pleasure, mingled with gratification, to meet at this reception those opposed to us in that conflict. We have a country now which they as well as ourselves may be proud of. It is their country as well as our country. All that we ask of anybody here is to be a good American citizen, and he may then enjoy all the rights and privileges any of us expect to enjoy who fought under the old flag. I repeat again that it is highly gratifying for me to be here with you under these auspices.

San Francisco Chronicle, Sept. 28, 1879. Stuart M. Taylor, former capt. and asst. AG, toasted USG before veterans at a "campfire" held at the Mechanics' Institute Pavilion. "We honor one who has done more than any other to secure the perpetuity of this great nation. Our Confederate brothers have joined to do honor to their magnanimous victor. These men, once our foes, are now our brothers, striving to do what they can to add a new glory to our common country. Taking by the hand our comrade, I bid him welcome, aye, thrice welcome. Comrades, fill your glasses and drain bumpers to our honored guest." *Ibid.* See *Alta California*, Sept. 24, 1879.

On Sept. 23, USG spoke to a committee representing former C.S.A. soldiers and sailors. ". . . If you had traveled around the world as I have for the past two or three years you would appreciate, like me, the value of our common country more completely than any man can who stays at home. . . . It affords me very great satisfaction and pleasure to receive these gentlemen who were long ago opposed to us, and I hope that if this country ever sees another war we shall all be together under one flag, fighting a common enemy." *San Francisco Chronicle*, Sept. 24, 1879.

On Sept. 25, USG addressed veterans at Badger's Park, Oakland. "Soldiers and sailors of two armies who fought years ago, I am very proud of the welcome which has been given me to-day. I am particularly pleased and happy to think that the gentlemen who were once opposed to each other are now gathered together in common unison and friendship. I hope the day will never come when it will be necessary for you to take up arms again. I have an abiding faith that we will remain together in future harmony. So far as we are concerned, our mutual welfare will be our mutual trust. I have no doubt that if ever we are called upon to war again, we or our children, without regard to services rendered a few years since, will be found side by side fighting against a common enemy. I am perfectly satisfied, from my recent travels and a comparison of our country with all the foreign Powers, that there is none of them who desires to come into contact with us. They will submit to just and fair arbitration rather than fight. And when a grand people ask for nothing but what is just and fair from other nations, I think we have a promise of a long period of peace and prosperity such as was never known to the civilized world before." *Ibid.*, Sept. 26, 1879. Mayor Washburn R. Andrus presented USG with the freedom of Oakland. DS, Smithsonian Institution. On Sept. 28, Etta King, Oakland, wrote to USG. "You will see by this we live in Oakland. I feel as though I would like to have a shake of your Paw for old acquantance sake we have lived here two years, could you spare time to come and see us if so drop me a line, when I would like you and family to come and take lunch with us, if wont have time tell me when you will have time to see us in San or Oakland. The best wishes of Mr & Mrs Etta S. Chesnut . . . We live out side of city so we have no number or Po Box." ALS, DLC-USG, IB.

To Daniel Ammen

SAN FRANCISCO, CAL., Sept. 28th, 1879.

MY DEAR AMMEN,—

We arrived here on the 20th, after a most pleasant and smooth sail of nineteen days from Yokohama. On my arrival I found a letter from you, and have received one since. But the kindness of the people here has prevented me from writing a single letter to any one until to-day. This is Sunday, and I have gone to another room, and consequently am "out."

I have had no time to read the Eastern papers since my arrival, and there are many that I have not seen; hence I do not know the present prospects of the Inter-Oceanic Canal. I approve, however, what you have done in the matter, and if the people of the United States will take hold of the Nicaragua route in earnest—the only practicable route, comparatively—I will give all the aid in my power.

I start for the Yosemite on Tuesday,[1] and after my return go to Oregon, so that I shall not start East before about the 27th of November. Even then I do not expect to go east of Chicago before the holidays; but if I could do any good for the canal enterprise by doing so, I would go earlier.

The papers have told you of my reception here. It has been exceedingly friendly, and apparently by the whole people. I appreciate it, of course, very highly, but it makes hard work.

Give Mrs. Grant's love to Mrs. Ammen and the children, and remember me most kindly. If you see Beale, tell him that I shall write to him in a few days.[2]

Very truly yours,

U. S. GRANT.

Daniel Ammen, *The Old Navy and the New* (Philadelphia, 1891), p. 548. See *PUSG*, 28, 448–51; *New York Herald*, Sept. 30, 1879.

On Sept. 22, 1879, a San Francisco reporter interviewed Frederick Dent Grant, who, "upon the interoceanic ship canal project being broached, stated that as yet his father had received no *popositions* to take the presidency of the Nicaragua Company, and even if he did, it was not probable that he would accept them. . . . As for Captain Eads' marine railway the Colonel thought that was entirely impracticable. His father, he said, had a fine opinion of Captain Eads and his ability as an engineer, but did not think the marine railway would be a success. The General did not pretend to be an engineer, but as an army officer he knew something about engineering, and formed his opinion from what he knew of the Panama route and the obstacles that lay in the way of a ship canal or railway. For ten miles out of Aspinwall there was no foundation on which to build a railway that could carry ships. The ground was a soft deposit, which permitted the roadbed to sink, and as bedrock was some three hundred feet beneath the surface it would be a gigantic work to sink enough granite on which to construct a solid track. . . . In relation to his father's trip to Oregon, it having been stated that the General would not make it, Colonel Fred said that he would, but the date was not yet settled. The

General had a desire to visit the localities where he served before his present greatness had been thrust upon him. Mrs. Grant wished to forego the Oregon trip, being desirous to return home, but the General, he thought, would overcome her objections. The General had accepted an invitation to dine with Senator Sharon at Belmont on the 9th, after his return from Yosemite." *Ibid.*, Oct. 1, 1879. On Oct. 8, USG and 2,000 guests attended a dinner in his honor at Belmont, the estate of U.S. Senator William Sharon of Nev. See *San Francisco Chronicle* and *Alta California*, Oct. 9, 1879.

1. Sept. 30.

2. On Oct. 7, a correspondent reported from Washington, D. C. "In a private letter to a friend in this city, received to-day, Gen. Grant says that he thinks it likely he may not reach Chicago before the latter part of November, and does not expect to be in Washington until about the Christmas holidays, unless something in connection with the interoceanic question should call him sooner. The letter is mainly devoted to the canal question, and shows that the General is in earnest in his determination to do everything within his power to further this great work. . . ." *St. Louis Globe-Democrat*, Oct. 8, 1879.

On Oct. 25, another correspondent reported from Washington, D. C. "General Beale, who has taken up his abode in his handsome mansion here for the winter, told me the other day that he had a letter from General Grant and that the latter had accepted an invitation to spend the Christmas holidays with him (Beale) in this city. Grant will, therefore, not arrive here in time to participate in the ceremonies of unveiling the grand equestrian statue of General Thomas by the Army of the Cumberland on the 20th of November. I hear from a very high source that General Grant's two years of idleness have given him a craving for an active, severe and confining business life, where sagacity, good judgment and hard work will be rewarded by a fortune. Grant is a poor man, having spent almost his entire fortune in traveling, and for this reason, as well as his longing for occupation, he is anxious to go into business. . . . Should Grant, junior, however, marry Miss Flood, there will be no occasion for the old man to go into business to retrieve his fortunes. Jennie Flood, in all human probability, will be the richest heiress in America. Her brother and herself are the only children of the great bonanza king, who once told me that he was worth at least fifty millions of dollars. The brother, a young man of about twenty, has always been in feeble health." *Philadelphia Times*, Oct. 26, 1879.

To John A. Bingham

San Francisco, Cal.
Sept. 28th /79

MY DEAR JUDGE.

After a very pleasant but slow passage we arrived here on the 20th of this month. The papers that go out by this mail will tell you of the more than enthusiastic reception given me by the people of California. This is the first time, day or night, since our arrival that I have been able to put pen to paper to write a letter. This is sunday and I have left my own quarters to get the time now.

On tuesday we start for the Yosemite, and on our return will go to Oregon. About the 25th of Oct. we start for Galena where I expect to get some rest.—Since my arrival here I have had occasion to speak much of my travels—in private conversation with limited company—and all seem to be much interested in what I say about Japan. The fact is the people here are so absorbed with their anti-Chinese discussions that they hardly know anything about Japan except that there is such a country that one has to pass to reach the territory of their aversion. I think this will be changed now and that a more friendly intercourse will spring up between Japan and the United States. I should say more intimate, for they are friendly now. I will probably drop a line to Mr. Yosheda[1] to-day. If I do will enclose it in this and ask you to be kind enough to have it delivered.

Please present Mrs. Grant's & my kindest regards to Mrs. Bingham, and all the members of your family.[2]

Very Truly Yours
U. S. GRANT

JUDGE JNO A. BINGHAM U. S. MINISTER, JAPAN

ALS, Milton Ronsheim, Cadiz, Ohio.

1. Born in 1845, Yoshida Kiyonari studied in England and entered Japan's foreign service, where he served as minister to the U.S. For his role as liaison between the Japanese government and USG during efforts to resolve the Ryukyu dispute with China, see conversation with Emperor Meiji, Aug. 10, 1879; letter to Prince Kung and Iwakura Tomomi, Aug. 13, 1879.

On Sept. 21, 1876, Yoshida, Washington, D. C., wrote to John A. Bingham, U.S. minister, Tokyo. *"Personal . . .* The other day I went to the White House & saw Mr President; he then intimated to me that he is intending to make a tour of World soon after the next March—& that he desire to go to Japan where he would likely stay a few weeks to travel in the Country. I trust this will be realized for I know that our people—to say nothing of His Majesty & his Cabinet &c—will be exceeding glad & happy to welcome him. . . ." ALS, Milton Ronsheim, Cadiz, Ohio.

2. Bingham's daughter, Marie, married James R. Wasson in 1876. On Jan. 23, 1877, Eli T. Sheppard, consul, Tientsin, Washington, D. C., wrote to Bingham. "Since writing you a day or two ago, I have seen the President and had a long talk with him. He was exceedingly glad to hear that you are in good health, and asked me how you were pleased with the appointment he had given Col. Wasson. He told me he regarded Wasson as one of the most promising young men in the country; and then he gave me a long account of his early life and of his success at the Military Academy. I will when I see Wasson, if I do see him—tell him how kindly the President has spoken of him. The President also told me he intended to start for Japan & China & India sometime in June, in company with his family—You will no doubt have him for your guest in due time; During our Conversation he spoke of Peshine Smith; He did not before know that Smith was out of

the Japanese service. He said he hoped the Japanese Governmt would fill the place with some American. Just on the impulse of the moment, I told him the Japanese had offered it to me. I had before told him I was going to resign as Consul at Tientsin on account of my ill health. He said he was very glad I was going to get the place—and asked me if I had told Mr Fish. I told him I had not spoken of it to any one and had not thought of doing so. He said Mr. Fish would be glad to know of it, and said I would better just mention it, and when I again saw Mr Fish I did so—. . ." ALS, *ibid.* See *PUSG*, 21, 474–75; *ibid.*, 22, 37–38; *ibid.*, 27, 303, 309–14; Erving E. Beauregard, *Bingham of the Hills: Politician and Diplomat Extraordinary* (New York, 1989), pp. 14, 156–57, 160, 187–89.

To Adolph E. Borie

San Francisco, Cal.
Sept. 28th /79

My Dear Mr. Borie:

I have now been in San Francisco eight days and this is the first opportunity I have had of putting my hand to paper to write a letter. You know we had a highly interesting visit to Japan. I became very much interested in both the people and the country. I hope to see the relations of our country and Japan become much more intimate & close in the future. But as I hope to see you before a great while, and have a number of letters to write now, I will wait to talk over these matters.

The papers will inform you of the overwhelming reception the Californians have given. This place is just as Phila was at the close of the war. I cannot venture in the streets except in a carriage for the mob of goodnatured and enthusiastic friends, old and young.

On the 30th we start for the Yosemite to visit that world renowned scenery. On our return we go to Oregon, and about the 27th of Oct. we will start east. I shall make several stops on the way, one at Virginia City, Omaha & Desmoines, possibly others, making about a weeks detention in all. I must be in Chicago on the 12th of Nov. for the soldiers meeting. I do not think I shall go further east before about the holidays. If I do however I have promised Mayor Stokely to inform him, in time, when I will be in Phila[1] I wish you and Mrs. Borie were with us. The weather is delightful and the trips would do you good.

Give Mrs. Grant's & my love to Mrs. Borie and all our Phila friends.

Very Truly Yours
U. S. GRANT

ALS, PHi.

1. On Sept. 22, 1879, Mayor William S. Stokley of Philadelphia telegraphed to USG, San Francisco. "When you departed from Philadelphia I bade you God speed upon your journey, and now desire to congratulate you on your safe return to your native land, and to assure you that our citizens anxiously await your arrival here to extend a hearty welcome." *Philadelphia Public Ledger,* Sept. 24, 1879. On Sept. 23, USG telegraphed to Stokley. "Thanks for your kind despatch and for the good wishes you express in the name of Philadelphia. I cannot now name a time for visiting Philadelphia, but will let you know." *Ibid.,* Sept. 25, 1879. On Nov. 14, George W. Childs, Chicago, telegraphed to Stokley. "General Grant requests me to inform you that he has made his arrangements so as to be in Philadelphia on December 16th." *Ibid.,* Nov. 15, 1879.

To George W. Childs

———

[*San Francisco, Sept. 28, 1879*]

Thanks to my numerous California friends, about the 27th of October we will start for Galena, making probably a week's detention by the way. It is not probable that we will go further East than Chicago before the holidays, but if we do I have promised to notify Mayor Stokeley in time. . . . You have seen the kind reception I have had here. It seems the people cannot do too much. It is very kind of them, and I appreciate it very highly.

New York Herald, Oct. 8, 1879.

To Abel R. Corbin

———

San Francisco, Cal.
Sept. 28th /79

MY DEAR MR. CORBIN:

We arrived here a week ago yesterday. This is the first day, or night, my kind friends have given me an opportunity of putting pen to paper to write a letter. This is Sunday and I have gone into another room than my own too get the opportunity now. I received your last letter a few days ago and take the first—as you see—too respond.

You see the magnificent [ovation of] the people of California [have g]iven me! It is a little [hard on] me, but very clever [in them], and I appreciate it [highly.] On tuesday we [start for the] Yosemite and [*on* our re]turn go to Oregon[. About] the 27th of Oct. [we start] for Galena and [will be deta]ined probably abo[ut a week,] in the aggregat[e, at different] points on th[e way.] I do not thi[nk we will] be going east of [Chicago before the] holidays, but [when I do go] one of the fir[st] places will be to Jersey [City to] see Mother and all [of you.] My whole trip has been one of great interest, and I am glad that it has not been marred by anything that has taken place on landing on our own shores. I shall always retain pleasant recollections of the cordial treatment I have received everywhere, but will appreciate none more highly than my reception by our own people.

Give Julia's & my love to Mother & Jennie and accept the same for yourself.

Very Truly Yours
U. S. GRANT

ALS (partial facsimile), Profiles in History, Catalog 35, Winter 2003, no. 30.

To Horace Porter

San Francisco, Cal.
Sept. 28th /79

MY DEAR GENERAL.

I received your very kind letter, tendering the use of a Pullman Car, a few days ago. I am very much obliged, but it will not be necessary to send one this side of Omaha. The officers of the Central Pacific have been kind enough to offer to send me over their road, and the Union, in a special, and to give me the officers car for my own use. I shall start east probably on the 26th or 27th of Oct. and delay over at different points on the road, ~~for~~ about a week in the aggregate. It is not my intention now of going east of Chicago before the holidays. When I do go it is not likely that I shall return to Galena before next spring.

You have seen the kind of reception the Californian's have given me? It is eight days now since our arrival and this is the first day, or night I have had an opportunity of putting pen to paper to write a letter. This is Sunday and I have gone into Youngs room without giving notice of my where-a-bouts or I should not be able to write now. I appreciate fully the great kindness of the people and shall always remember it. Present my kindest regards to Pullman and to all my New York friends. When I see you I will have much more to say than I can write in a letter.

Very Truly yours
U. S. GRANT

GN. HORACE PORTER,

ALS, Horace Porter Mende, Zurich, Switzerland.

On Sept. 1, 1879, Lt. Gen. Philip H. Sheridan, Chicago, wrote to USG. "The enclosed letter from the Burlington & Quincy R. R. was sent to me with the request, that I would have it presented to you on your arrival in San Francisco—I think the object the officers of the Road had in making me the medium of transmitting this communication, was to assure you that the only motive they had in offering you the courtesies of the road was personal regard & friendship. I take this occasion to offer to you & Mrs Grant the warm congratulations of Mrs Sheridan & myself on your safe return, & our continued love and attatchmt." ALS, DLC-USG, IB. On Sept. 27, William H. Stennett, Chicago and Northwestern Railway Co., Chicago, telegraphed to Maj. Gen. Irvin McDowell, San Francisco, tendering USG the use of a special train from Omaha to Chicago or Galena. Telegram received (at 11:55 A.M.), *ibid.* On Oct. 22, William J. Mauriac, Illinois Central Railroad Co., Chicago, wrote to Elihu B. Washburne, Chicago. "In order to gratify the citizens, living along the line of our Road, who wish to be at Galena when Genl. Grant arrives, we will have to run special Excursion trains. To meet the public requirements of such an occasion and to avoid complication in Train matters, it is desirable that we should know the day and, if possible, the hour at which the General and his party will be likely to arrive. In Mr. Ackerman's absence at New York, I take the liberty of asking information from you on these points." ALS, DLC-Elihu B. Washburne. On Oct. 29, USG, Humboldt, Nev., telegraphed to Governor John S. Phelps of Mo. "Thanks for your Cordial Invitation regret that I cannot accept I go directly to Galena via Omaha Burlington & Quincy" Telegram received (at 9:00 A.M.), CtY.

To Ellen Grant Sartoris

San Francisco, Cal.

Sept. 28th 1879.

MY DEAR DAUGHTER:

We arrived here one week ago yesterday after a smooth passage of nineteen days from Yokohama. We are all very well. The reception of the people of California, and their attentions, have been so warm and so constant that I have not had time to touch my pen to paper to write a letter until to-day. Just before leaving Japan we received a dispatch from Buck saying that "rumor Nellies death untrue." We had heard nothing of the rumor, but surmized at once that your Mother-in-law was dead.[1] We heard nothing more until our arrival here when we found our surmize confirmed. We condole with Mr. Sartoris, Algie and the family.

On tuesday—this is sunday—we start for the Yosemite; on our return from there go to Oregon, and will start east about the 27th of Oct. For the present we do not go further east than Galena. It will probably be a little dull there, but from all we hear through letters and the press we will have but little quiet for the present except while we stay in Galena. You will no doubt see from home papers how splendidly we have been received here. Buck come out to meet us and will remain with us until we get to Galena. Fred. started home last tuesday and is no doubt now in Chicago. Jesse is so absorbed in his studies and business that he could not come out. All send love and kisses to you and the children and love to Algie.

Yours Affectionately

U. S. GRANT

ALS, ICHi.

1. Adelaide Kemble Sartoris, mother of Algernon Sartoris, died Aug. 4, 1879. A press error confused Adelaide Sartoris with Ellen Grant Sartoris. See *New York Herald*, Aug. 16, 19, 1879. On Sept. 22, Julia Dent Grant recalled: "We were in Tokio. A telegram reached us saying simply that a false report of her death had been circulated. I had just received a long letter from her three days before—such a bright, cheerful letter—telling how she had just come back from London and was going to a ball the next week; what a pretty new bonnet she had, and a lot of bright, happy home-talk.

She mentioned also that they felt very much troubled about the health of her husband's mother, Mrs. Sartoris, but I could not remember that when we received the telegram. The very suggestion of such a thing seemed so terrible. I just turned to my husband and said, 'Oh, Ulysses!' He said, 'Don't trouble about it; you know there are three or four Mrs. Sartoris. Probably some one of them has died, and the report sprang from that.'" *San Francisco Chronicle*, Sept. 23, 1879.

On Aug. 16, Isaac H. Sturgeon, St. Louis, had written to USG. "How shall I write you and what shall I say that may at all comfort and console you and Mrs Grant for the loss of your dear child. I with my wife and children came down to breakfast this morning together and as usual Mrs Sturgeon gives us coffee from the head of the table and then reads to us the papers—and I was shocked when with a sad look to me she said Nellie Grant is dead—I could not help saying My God is it so? are you not mistaken? Does the paper say so? When she sadly replied it is so telegraphed from London—. . ." ALS, DLC-John Russell Young.

On Aug. 22, Friday, Gen. William T. Sherman wrote to Lt. Gen. Philip H. Sheridan. ". . . What a Cruel Mistake that was about Nellie Grant—I hope the Genl & Mrs Grant will hear the Exact truth before they Start from Japan about next Monday we will all meet in Chicago about Novr 1.—" ALS, DLC-Philip H. Sheridan.

Speech

——

[*San Francisco, Sept. 29, 1879*]

To see so many children of the public schools present on any occasion is a most gratifying sight, but to see them here in honor of myself is doubly so to me. From what I see to-day I know that your city must be provided with schools sufficient to diffuse knowledge through all branches of society, and it is only through these that you can insure the permanency and perpetuity of our institutions. They are in greater danger from the neglect of schools than from any outside source, but with wise government they are certain to be maintained. I thank you again for the reception given me here, and I shall long remember it.

San Francisco Chronicle, Sept. 30, 1879. Amos C. Hiester, president, San Francisco Board of Education, greeted USG before an estimated 12,000 children in the pavilion at Woodward's Gardens. "Your loyalty to the public-school system of the United States has impelled the school children of San Francisco to extend this special greeting. The children, their parents and the Board of Education recognize in you a true and fearless friend of popular education, and are proud to look you in the face and take you by the hand. Allow me, sir, to present you to the children and teachers connected with the public schools of San Francisco. These happy faces will tell their own story." A reporter noted: "Several minutes elapsed before the recipient of these honors could control his emotions sufficiently to speak, . . ." *Ibid.*

On Sept. 22, 1879, Hiester and Azro L. Mann, superintendent, wrote to USG. "You have always expressed a deep interest in the public schools of this country, and on several occasions you have expressed that interest in weighty and well-remembered words. We have public schools in this westernmost city of the republic of which we are justly proud. As you may not ever visit us again, the Board of Education invites you to name a day when you can spare an hour or two for the purpose of visiting a few of our prominent public schools. Carriages will be provided for yourself and as many of your family and friends as may wish to join you." *Ibid.*, Sept. 23, 1879.

Speech

————

[*Stockton, Calif., Sept. 30, 1879*]

Gentlemen of Stockton: I am very much pleased to be back in your city once more, not having beheld it since twenty-five years ago. I am sincerely obliged to you for the hearty reception I have met with at your hands to-day, and will state that it is pleasant to have the first roof that ever sheltered me in Stockton cover so much kindness to me. I passed through your city several times when I was on this coast before, but never stopped as long as I have to-day. My reception has been so pleasant that I hope I may come back here at some future time. The only untoward event of to-day was the news which I gained from a gentleman whom I met, that he had known me at Knight's Ferry in 1849. I did not come west of the Rockies till 1852, so I am sorry to think that some one must have been personating me there. I was in Knight's Ferry at three different times after that, in 1852 and 1854. However, I am very glad to meet you all to-day, and if any one hereafter says that he met me in Stockton in 1879, I shall have the pleasure of not being able to deny it.

San Francisco Chronicle, Oct. 1, 1879. USG spoke during a banquet at the Yosemite House. On Oct. 1, 1879, a correspondent reported from San Francisco. "General Grant's speech at Stockton yesterday is the theme of general interest here to-day. Ever since his name has been associated with politics the democratic press has assailed him furiously, to the annoyance of republicans, on his alleged life at Knight's Ferry and Stockton in 1849, and through constant repetition was believed by many. The speech was evidently the result of a quiet waiting of years for an opportunity, and yesterday the General found it, to the great gratification of his friends. . . ." *New York Herald*, Oct. 2, 1879. See *PUSG*, 1, 258–59.

From Stockton, USG and party traveled by train to Madera, Calif., where they embarked on a six-day stagecoach tour of the Yosemite Valley. On Oct. 1, at Mariposa, "General Grant was asked if he had ever been in Yosemite. He said he had not; in 1854, before the valley was known, except to a few pioneers, he came to Tuolumne in the employ of the Government. At the village and in riding about the region he spent fourteen days. He had at that time never heard of Yosemite." *San Francisco Chronicle,* Oct. 3, 1879. On Oct. 4, during lunch at Nevada Fall, USG talked of "the early days of California, when men talked rough, wore their pantaloons in their boots, and carried about with them an arsenal of bowie-knives and pistols. Money, he said, had little value, and personal labor was overhigh. . . ." *Ibid.,* Oct. 6, 1879. On Oct. 5, USG and party visited the giant sequoias. *Ibid.,* Oct. 7, 1879. On Oct. 6, on his return from Yosemite, USG spoke at Merced, "saying that he had had many foreign receptions while traveling, but none of which he felt half so proud of as this. The honor was entirely unexpected; the more so, as when he left the State the place where Merced now stands was uninhabited." *Ibid.*

On Oct. 8, Walter de Sanno, Lathrop, Calif., wrote to USG. "*Private* . . . I had the honor of being the engineer of your Special train from Merced to Oakland Wharf on the night of Oct 6 and morning of 7th Will you honor me with your Autograph? as a souvenir of the event." ALS, DLC-USG, IB.

Speech

[*San Francisco, Oct. 9, 1879*]

Mr. President, Gentlemen of the Board of Trade and Chamber of Commerce of San Francisco: I hardly know how to express my gratitude for the cordial and kind reception that you have extended me, and indeed, for that I have received from all citizens of the State wherever I have been. There is no question that the prosperity of the State, as well as of the nation depends on such as you. It is domestic and foreign trade that gives the means of support to the great laboring classes in our midst. It is to just such as you we must look for the proper development and encouragement of trade. Any one who has been abroad as I have, especially in the Orient, can see the depth of degradation to which labor is brought when not directed by able heads. They will see people who live on what would elsewhere be considered meager support for the meanest pauper. Here, while of course we have ample provision for the sick or disabled, we have not a healthy person in all America, willing to help himself, who is not better off than he would be in countries

where I have seen some of the most abject and pitiable labor conditions. Gentlemen, you have much to congratulate yourselves upon,
and you have such a country that you need be jealous of no other.

San Francisco Chronicle, Oct. 10, 1879. "The General's somewhat lengthy speech was
received with considerable satisfaction and applause, as many of the gentlemen present
considered it to be an expression upon the Chinese question." *Ibid.* USG responded to
an address by Governor-elect George C. Perkins, president, San Francisco Chamber
of Commerce. The address, signed by Perkins and three others, is in the Smithsonian
Institution.

Speech

[*Astoria, Ore., Oct. 13, 1879*]

Mr Mayor and Gentlemen of the Council of Astoria: I thank you
and the citizens of Astoria for this kind reception. Twenty seven
years ago I first visited your state, and I have ever felt a strong desire again to behold this important section of our common country.
This will make the ninth time I shall have passed up and down this
beautiful and grand river. Every point of interest between Astoria
and the Dalles returns to my memory. I never had the pleasure of
stepping ashore at this particular place before, but it seems to me
that when I last passed by here the hills forming the background
of this thriving town, were much higher than they are now. This,
I presume, is a mark and sign of the improvement and growth of
your promising city, which I am rejoiced to see presents a striking
contrast to the Astoria of twenty-seven years ago Gentlemen the
geographical position of this city over which you preside, together
with evidences of enterprise, thrift and industry, which caught my
eye as we entered your h[a]rbor, is a sure indication that ere long
one of the most important commercial cities of the Pacific coast,
will be your city of Astoria. That this may soon be accomplished
and the prosperity of your town be uninterrupted, you have gentlemen my most hearty wish. I regret that my stay will be so short, as
I would be pleased to visit every portion of the North Pacific coast.
It seems like returning home again. Thanking you for your kind

and cordial welcome, I assure you it will ever be cherished in my memory.

Oregonian, Oct. 14, 1879. USG responded to a welcome address by Mayor Wilder W. Parker of Astoria, Ore. Copy, USG 3. On Sept. 29, 1879, Parker telegraphed to USG, San Francisco. "I am authorized by the citizens and City Council to invite you with your family and companions to visit this City on your entrance to Oregon our people will give you a cordial reception and conveyance to Portland be furnished you and suite—Please answer as early as convenient" Telegram received (at 10:55 A.M.), DLC-USG, IB. On the same day, Parker telegraphed to George L. Woods, former Ore. governor, San Francisco. "See Gen Grant and urge him accept invitation to visit Astoria third city in size and importance in Oregon and oblige me" Telegram received (at 11:00 A.M.), *ibid.*

On Aug. 8, Brig. Gen. Oliver O. Howard, Vancouver Barracks, Washington Territory, had written to USG. "I have just learned that you will probably visit my Department in September next. I have quite sizable quarters at Vancouver and with Mrs Howard's most cordial concurrence send you a hearty invitation to make my house your home during your stay—I mean of course you & yours. As you wish peace & quiet, this I think you can find with us. Give our kindest regards to Mrs Grant & any of the family who may be with you. I have been, now, five years in command of the Dept. of the columbia." ALS, *ibid.* On Sept. 20, Governor Elisha P. Ferry of Washington Territory telegraphed to USG, San Francisco. "A Cordial invitation is extended to you to visit this territory" Telegram received, *ibid.* On Oct. 10, territorial legislators passed a resolution welcoming USG. DS, USG 3. At about this time, Mayor Orange Jacobs of Seattle and seven others wrote to USG. "Recognizing your distinguished services as a civilian and soldier, and hoping that you may visit Puget Sound, the mediterranean of America, the Mayor and Common Council of the City of Seattle on behalf of themselves and the good people of the city whom they represent, would cordially and urgently request, a visit to our youthful City and an acceptance of Pioneer hospitality" DS, *ibid.*

On Oct. 13, Mayor Louis Sohns greeted USG on arrival at Vancouver. "*General:*— The humble individual who has the honor of addressing and welcoming you now in the behalf of the people of our town, had also the pleasure of landing with you and the old gallant 4th Infantry, 27 years ago at this very spot. . . ." *Vancouver Independent*, Oct. 16, 1879. Later, Ferry welcomed USG. ". . . Should you visit the eastern portion of the Territory, you would obtain personal knowledge of a large acreage of agricultural land, capable of producing one hundred million bushels of wheat annually, and from twenty-five to fifty bushels per acre. At the present time you would find several thousand tons of wheat awaiting export on account of inadequacy of transportation. You would be also confirmed in the opinion which I think you entertain that it is the duty of the government to remove obstructions to navigation existing in that noble river, a portion of which you traversed to-day, to enable those who inhabit the head waters to obtain an unobstructed outlet to the sea. Should you visit Western Washington, and particular[l]y Puget Sound, you would discover the great commercial and manufacturing facilities of that locality. . . ." *Ibid.* USG replied. "*Governor and members of the Legislature:* I regret exceedingly that I shall not be able to remain long enough to visit any other portion of the Territory. I had expected to spend several weeks on the Pacific coast, but the reunion of the Army of Tennessee, Which I commanded during 'the late unpleasantness,' was postponed for my return, and I have promised to meet them.

They did not fix the day until I promised to be with them early in November. That, with other appointments, compels me to leave not later than the 17th. You can easily see the impossibility of accepting your invitation. Your statement of the producing capacity of the Territory surprises and gratifies me. I lived a year on the spot on which I now stand, but never visited that portion of which you speak. I always supposed that while a part was productive, a greater share was too unproductive, except of fish and timber, to justify enough population to make a state, unless there should be some mineral development. From your statement I have no doubt of your soon becoming a state, and we can't have too many in this latitude." *Ibid.* On Oct. 14, USG addressed a crowd of 500 on the city square. "Citizens of Washington Territory: I can hardly express my gratification at the reception I have received at your hands. I can assure you that it affords me great pleasure to come back to the spot where I spent much of my time many years ago and note the vast improvements that have taken place during my absence. I am very sorry that my stay will be necessarily short in your Territory, but previous engagements will prevent me from visiting many points of interest in your thriving country. I thank you for the hearty receptions which have met me on all sides, and assure you that none have afforded me greater pleasure." *San Francisco Chronicle*, Oct. 15, 1879.

On Sept. 22, K. Van Oterendorp, Oregon Steam Ship Co., San Francisco, had written to USG. "The Oregon Steamship Company have the honor to tender to your Excellence and party the freedom of their ships from San Francisco to Portland, Oregon and return. Should your Excellence wish to avail yourself of this offer please notify me in time, so that I may be able to reserve proper accommodations. Enclosed herewith please find list of sailing-days." ALS, DLC-USG, IB. On Sept. 23, Woods, San Francisco, telegraphed to Mayor David P. Thompson of Portland. "Have conferred with Grant. He goes to Oregon certainly; time undetermined. Can I serve you? Command me" *Oregonian*, Sept. 24, 1879. On Sept. 24, Thompson telegraphed to USG, San Francisco. "In behalf of the general committee and the citizens of Portland, I am authorized to extend to you and party an invitation to visit our city and other such places in Oregon as your may desire. Should you accept our invitation, please indicate what time would suit your convenience." *Ibid.*, Sept. 25, 1879. On the same day, USG telegraphed to Thompson. "Hope to be in Portland on 14th, but will telegraph you day of departure." *Ibid.* On Oct. 14, USG and party left Vancouver aboard the *St. Paul*, which briefly ran aground. "Mrs. Grant, like most other ladies, is afraid of storms, and frequently on their journeyings has given utterance to fears of going to the bottom of the sea. Yesterday, when the *St. Paul* ran on the sand, Gen. Grant, addressing his wife familiarly, said: 'Julia, you ought to be satisfied now, we've gone to the bottom at last.'" *Ibid.*, Oct. 15, 1879. On the same day, USG spoke to Union and C.S.A. veterans at a Grand Army of the Republic reception in Portland. "*Comrades*—It is gratifying to me to meet my old comrades again; and it is particularly gratifying now in the time of perfect peace, to take by the hand those who fought against us. This is a great country and they have a right to participate in its benefits. I wish for them all the benefits that have accrued, provided they remain good and true citizens. Again let me say that I am pleased to be here, and meet so many of you." *Ibid.* On Oct. 15, after a trip up the Columbia River to the Upper and Lower Cascades, USG toured Portland public schools. At Harrison School, Principal Irving W. Pratt introduced USG to assembled students and joked "that the children evidently considered him a second Alexander, and looked for a man about sixteen feet high." USG replied "that as to the reference to his height the children would certainly be disappointed. He said it was a real pleasure to him to see so many happy faces. He had learned with much satisfaction that Portland had such facilities for public instruction that all her children were amply provided for. Also, that he had been informed that, for discipline, thoroughness and general culture, the Portland public schools do not yield the palm to any city in the west; and from what he had observed, he himself thought the claim to these excellencies well founded." *Ibid.*, Oct. 16, 1879. Later, William Strong, former territorial judge, introduced USG to a crowd of 4,000 at the Mechanics' Pavilion. USG responded. *"Judge Strong, Ladies and Gentlemen of Portland, of Oregon of the Northwest;* I am proud of the reception now tendered me, and those which have been tendered me at your hands. It is a pleasure to be back again near the place I enjoyed so much 26 or 27 years ago. I am glad to note evidences of your prosperity, and I take it as only a beginning of the great improvement in the near future. When I first came here Oregon and Washington were one territory, small in population, but large in area. Now you have one prosperous state and a territory which I hope soon to see become a state. You have the soil and climate to support a population sufficient for many states. In your remarks you have alluded to the struggles of the past I am glad that they are at an end. It never was a pleasure to me that they had a beginning. The result has left us a nation to be proud of, strong at home and respected abroad. Our reputation has extended beyond the civilized nations; it has penetrated even to the less civilized parts of the earth In my travels I have noticed that foreign nations appear to respect us more than we respect ourselves. I have noticed the grandeur at which we have been estimated by other powers, and their judgment should give us a higher estimate of our greatness. They recognize that poverty, as they understand it, is not known with us, and the man of the comparative affluence with them is sometimes no better clad or fed than our pauper. Nowhere are there better elements of success than on the Pacific coast. Here those who fought on opposite sides during the war are now peacefully associated together in a country of which they all have the same right to be proud. I thank the people again, through you, Judge Strong, for this reception." *Ibid.*

On Sept. 15, Mitchell Wilkins, president, Ore. Board of State Fair Directors, Mayor George W. Gray of Salem, and two others had written to USG. "As one of America's most worthy and honored soldiers and civilians, we, who speak for a large portion of the people of this State, hereby earnestly solicit you to visit our State Fair and Capital City, the hospitalities of which we now tender you. If you could be here about the 3d or 4th day of October, it would contribute greatly to the pleasure of many thousands of our citizens who will then be present to welcome you to your old home, 'where rolls the Oregon', as well as to greet you on your return from foreign Lands and distant Courts, their honored and distinguished guest." LS (4 signatures), DLC-USG, IB. Governor William W. Thayer of Ore. and Rockey P. Earhart, Ore. secretary of state, favorably endorsed this letter. ES, *ibid.* On Sept. 27, Earhart and three others telegraphed to Woods. "Thousands of our people will attend State Fair to see General Grant, the only opportunity they may ever have to see him. The disappointment will be general and very great if he does not come, urge upon him the acceptance of invitation heretofore sent answer" Telegram received, *ibid.* On Oct. 1, Woods, San Francisco, wrote to Earhart and Gray. "I laid your telegram before General Grant and urged that he comply with your wishes, explaining to him the large presence at the State Fair, etc. He fully appreciated the reasons given, and wanted to go, but was embarrassed by previous engagements to go to Yosemite. It is his purpose to visit all points in your State possible during the short time allotted him, so as to meet the people. His stay at each point will necessarily be brief. It is now understood that we leave here for Oregon on October 9th." *Portland Standard*, Oct. 8, 1879. On Oct. 16, USG spoke in Salem. "*Gentlemen*—I thank you most heartily for the cordiality manifested in this your reception of myself and party. This is the first opportunity I have ever had of visiting this portion of the Willamette valley, and I have enjoyed it heartily. Again accept my thanks for the honor shown me." *Oregonian*, Oct. 17, 1879.

On Sept. 12, John H. Mitchell, Washington, D. C., had written to USG. "It is with extreme regret I am detained here on business connected with my profession—(my family being in Europe) thus preventing me from joining *personaly* with your many friends in Oregon and California in extending cordial welcome to you on your return in America. Permit me to say, however, that I, in common with the people of the Pacific Coast, feel a just pride in the manner in which you have been received and honored by all the nations and peoples of the Old World. . . ." ALS, DLC-John Russell Young.

To Henry M. Cist

———

Palace Hotel.
San Francisco, Oct. 21st *1879.*

H. M. Cist,
Cor. Sec. Society Army of the Cumberland,
Dear Sir:

On my return from Oregon this a. m. I find your invitation for me to be present at the meeting of the Society of the Army of the Cumberland on the 19th & 20th of November. I would like specially to be present at your next meeting to testify my profound respect & esteem for the worthy, patriotic and brave old soldier, Gen. Geo. H. Thomas, whos monument is to be unveiled on that occasion, but fear I shall not be able to do so. But I do not pronounce yet positively that I will not be there. I have telegraphed to Gen. Sherman to-day on the same subject saying that I would be able to decide when I meet him in Chicago one week before your meeting.

Be assured if I am not there my desire to be will be as great as that of any one.

Very Truly yours
U. S. Grant

ALS, Lincoln College, Lincoln, Ill. On Oct. 18, 1879, Gen. William T. Sherman telegraphed and wrote to USG, San Francisco. "Equestrian Statue of General Thomas will be unveiled here in Washington November 19th–20th, just one week after our Chicago Meeting. The Army of the Cumberland earnestly desire your presence, and for reasons which I will explain by letter are very anxious for you to be present. Is it possible? I make this at suggestion of many of your personal friends, that you may not make other appointments to conflict. A conditional answer would satisfy present purposes, and a perfect answer after receipt of my letter of this date." Copies, DLC-William T. Sherman (2); DNA, RG 94, Letters Sent; *ibid.*, RG 107, Telegrams Collected (Bound). "Extensive preparations are made here to unveil Thomas' Equestrian Statue, said to be unusually good, at the intersection of 14th, and Mass. Avenue Nov. 19th–20th. I suppose you know well that certain mischief makers have tried to array you, and also me, against Thomas, because of the Battle of Nashville and subsequently the promotion of Sheridan as Lieut. Genl. I think I knew Thomas personally as well as any man living—We were classmates, members of the same section for four years, of the same Regiment, 3rd. Artillery, for 10 years, and correspondents to the day of his death. He always confided to me his inmost secrets, so that I claim to be a staunch admirer of his Great Qualities, and charitable to his defects—I also believe that you had occasion to know him thoroughly, and that you too bore him in the most exalted respect, whilst you had to guard the Great Public interests against what seemed slowness and deliberation when vehement and prompt action was called for—Now as I say such fellows as Boynton, pure mischief makers, wish to create the impression that you and I were envious, jealous of his great fame, and his deserved popularity. If you could attend this last tribute to his noble memory, it would disarm this class of men. Of course I will be on hand, and it may be that you also will, and this will prove what is true, that in action you measured him according to your better knowledge, but at the same time loved, respected and encouraged the man & Patriot. Of course my feelings are even stronger, and I am sometimes mortified to find such men as Hooker and Boynton, for whom Thomas had no love or respect in life, now become his worshipers and the traducers of his oldest and best Friends." Copies (2), DLC-William T. Sherman. On Oct. 21, USG telegraphed to Sherman. "Will see you in Chicago about going to unveiling of Thomas monument Have accepted invitations in Chicago until after time of unveiling these might be deferred but want to avoid going east until I decide where to spend the winter" Telegram received (at 5:35 P.M.), *ibid.* See Sherman to Adam Badeau, Nov. 4, 1879, copies (2), *ibid.*

On Nov. 5, Henry M. Cist, Cincinnati, wrote to Sherman. ". . . I understand and appreciate your feeling in regard to the attendance of General Grant at the unveiling of the Gen'l Thomas statue, and I think every right minded member of our society would do the same. I see by the morning dispatches from Indianapolis that General Grant has decided to go to Washington and to be there on the 20th and that the Indianapolis meeting is postponed until after our meeting, so I presume it is all settled. I am very glad that [*it is*] all arranged and I think that this is the best arrangement of the matter. There are very many members of our society and others outside of all army connection in civil life here some of our very best citizens who think that it would have been a great mistake not to have had General Grant at Washington at our meeting and that it would have appeared ungracious in the General not to have gone. . . ." ALS, *ibid.*

Grenville M. Dodge recorded an Oct. 27, 1882, conversation with USG. ". . . I asked the General if he had read Van Thorn's life of Thomas, and suggested that it was a great wrong to Thomas to have such a life written; that he would go down to History as a disappointed, disgruntled and complaining officer, which was just the contrary of my views of him. The General said he had not read it, but had read some criticisms on it. He had had a talk with Badeau and explained some matters to him. He said that Badeau brought in the Evening Post, which had an article in that must have been written by him, (Badeau) as it expressed his (Grant's) views. The General said he had nothing but kindly feelings for Thomas; said that he was slow, and never desired an independent command. That when he was ~~put to the~~ placed in command of the Army and Department of the Cumberland, he expressed a regret at relieving his own commander. That before the battle of Chattanooga, he gave Thomas a week's notice of his plans, and wanted him to be ready when Sherman was ready, to strike; told him he must be sure and be ready at the moment, so as to surprise the enemy. He again told him the night before he (Grant) was ready. Thomas then came to his headquarters, and told him he could not get ready. When the General asked him how soon he could be ready, he replied: 'In another day.' So he delayed the attack another day. That he is ~~made no~~ plans of the battle; ~~that it was~~ were in orders simply, and those were never changed, except as to time. and the Battle more nearly followed the Plans and orders then any other in the war ~~He~~ His orders intended to draw from Bragg's centre to fronts of Sherman and Hooker and Thomas to attack the enemy's center. That after watching Sherman's fight and Hooker's progress for some time he saw a division of troops too far away to be used, and ordered Thomas to bring them to the center. That he waited an hour, and saw they did not move, when Gen'l Jo Reynolds, an old classmate, and chief of staff of Thomas, came up and he (Grant) spoke rather roughly to him, asking him why those troops had not come up, and Reynolds said he knew of no orders, and Grant then told him he had ordered them up some time ago, and now ordered Reynolds to see that they came up to the front, which they soon did Grant said that after the progress of the battle on the flanks convinced him that it was time to attack in the center, and he had given Thomas the order to attack, he was looking to see the effect of this attack, and waited nearly an hour, when, becoming impatient, he turned around, and to his surprise saw Thomas talking to T. J. Wood in the rear; he (Grant) was angry and called Wood up and said: 'I ordered your attack an hour ago. Why has it not been made?' Wood replied: 'I have been ready for more than an hour, and can attack in five minutes after receiving the order.' Grant then said: 'I order you to attack.' and in about five minutes he saw Wood's forces going forward. As soon as they rose the hill, he (Grant) followed; and after reaching the ridge he went on to join Hooker, while Thomas returned to Chattanooga and went to bed. Gen'l. Grant said Thomas did not give an order that day. Grant rode forward, and it was midnight when he returned to Chattanooga. He then went to Thomas's headquarters, and told him to hold Gordon Granger, who had been ordered to move to Knoxville to relieve that place, stating that he had come from the front, and did not know but Bragg might make a stand. A steamboat loaded with provisions was ready to go up the river. He told Thomas to hold Granger ready to move at any moment. Gen'l. Grant took two hours sleep, then rode ~~twenty-five miles~~ Twenty miles to the front, where Hooker was fighting Bragg's rear guard; reached there early in the morning and saw that Bragg was trying to get away, and had no idea of stopping; and before he dismounted, he sent an Aid back with orders to Thomas to have Granger move on to Knoxville immediately. He stayed with Hooker and attended to having provisions, &c., brought forward; he then came around by Georgetown next day where Sherman was. and stayed that night. Sherman's army was without transportation, clothing or shoes. Gen'l. Grant said to me that he had a feeling of instinct that Granger had not moved on, that he might need Sherman. He explained the situation to Sherman and told him to remain where he was until he heard from him (Grant) and he (Grant) returned to Chattanooga, the next day and found Gordon Granger at his headquarters. He had not moved. Then he became alarmed and ordered Sherman forward, telling him he must reach Knoxville within six days, and told him to take Granger along. Sherman started from where he was without returning to the camps and was illy prepared for the march his army leaving without water overcoats or blankets. Grant said that Thomas was a good soldier but was slow, deliberate, and did not appreciate the value of time in combined movements. He, (Grant) wished that on the fall of Hood he would take a position as far east of Knoxville as possible, and accumulate provisions that were transportable, so that in the combined movement towards Richmond, he could move a force from that point; his intention being to concentrate all he could and infringe on Lee's army. He said that when he ordered Thomas to move he was informed that Thomas had no mules. He sent out orders to buy at any price, but Thomas did not get them together so he could move. That the war closed and the contractor who had bought the mules under Thomas's orders claimed to have paid some six or eight thousand dollars more than his contract price allowed and from this order of Thomas grew the Kentucky claims, that finally reached the Court of Claims, and on which judgment was rendered for $108,000,—and Bristow received ten per cent for collecting it. Gen'l Grant said that Thomas expressed himself as gratified when he gave Gen'l Sherman the military Division of Mississppi; that all he wanted was his army and department; and that he preferred to serve under a superior. Grant said Thomas should not feel sore, and he did not believe he did. He contrasted his actions with Sherman's, who was in his Thomass class, and ranked him in class and in the army. He said that Thomas commanded a brigade under Sherman in Kentucky—Sherman being Department Commander; that Sherman was relieved and sent to command a camp at St. Louis; that he never murmured. Was sent to him (Grant) at Paduca. That Sherman ranked him (Grant) but did not say a word or murmur, but took hold and did all he could to aid the cause along, and no one heard a lisp from him here. Grant said he was never aware that Thomas was dissatisfied with his assignment to California; that he (Thomas) could have had any command that he desired that a General had not requested or been assigned to. I told the General that Thomas enroute to California, stopped at Council Bluffs and visited me; that we then talked over matters; that he said he had not seen me since the Battle of Nashville, and he thanked me fervently, as he had done before in letters, for stripping my department and sending him all the troops in it. That he spoke in the highest terms and kindliest manner of Sherman and Grant, and said that he preferred a command East, but knew that it was for the best that he was going to California. Mrs. Thomas was with him, and we spent the day reviewing old battles, especially the move to the rear of Dalton, and that I thought him a very happy, contented man. I know he talked and seemingly felt that all and more had been done for him than he deserved,—while I felt that too much could not be done for him. I said to General Grant that my criticism on Thomas's campaign in Tennessee was, that he should have concentrated all his forces in the Department immediately, and fought Hood at Pulaski or Columbia. I know the ground well, and thought that country offered a great opportunity to face him, and I said: 'General, if any of us had been there, neither you or Sherman would ever have been so lenient to us, if we had not done it.' The General made no answer and made no criticism, except that: 'Thomas was a fine soldier, but slow, and preferred to serve under some one, rather than be responsible himself.' He was very emphatic in his description of the whole matter, so much so, that the attention of a great many people in the car was attracted to us, and I never heard the General give a more clear, decided description of his plan, orders, &c.," Typescript, IaHA. See Thomas B. Van Horne, *The Life of Major-General George H. Thomas* (New York, 1882), pp. 167–200.

Memorandum

Arrived in San Francisco—first time—in Sept.—possibly late in August—1852, via Panama, coming up the coast on the Steamer Golden Gate. Was stationed a few weeks at Benetia; then went to Fort Vancouver, now of Washington Territory. Remained there until Sept. 1853 when promotion to a full captaincy in the 4th U. S. Infantry carried me to Humboldt Bay, Cal. where I remained until the spring of 1854. Left San-Francisco in July 1854 via Nicaragua and only returned to the Pacific coast again on the 21st of Sept. 1879, coming from Japan, or by the East the entire way from our eastern seaboard. This day made a member of the Sacrimento Society of Cal. Pioneers, an honor which I highly prize.

U. S. GRANT

OCT. 23D 1879 ULYSSES SIMPSON GRANT

ADS, Sacramento Society of California Pioneers. On Oct. 23, 1879, during a reception at Pioneer Hall, N. Greene Curtis presented USG with a certificate of election as "an Honorary Member" of the Sacramento Society of California Pioneers. DS (two signatures, dated Oct. 22), Smithsonian Institution. USG responded. "Ladies and Gentlemen: I am very happy to become a member of this Society. I have already accepted an invitation to an honorary membership of the Society of Pioneers in San Francisco. I am glad to find that I am eligible to become a full member. This, as I understand you, is a full membership? . . . I thought you a kind of close corporation, and did not believe myself eligible to full membership because I was not so fortunate as to be here in 1849. However, I thought myself eligible for honorary membership on the ground that I had been here in the early days of California, and that I participated in the war which gave California to our country. We are all proud of California and we are all proud of Californians. We are proud of what you have done here and we are proud to have had our flag extended over this side of the continent. This acquisition to the country has not only made us felt and known on the east side of the mountains, but it has been heard of in the very far East where I have been traveling lately. I have been in no country where they have not known California and Californians. It gave me pleasure to find that wherever Californians had been they left an impression that they thought a great deal of their country. I have never seen a Californian yet who did not speak well of California. I thank you, gentlemen." After greeting members, "General Grant, in signing the roll of membership of the Pioneer Association, wrote out this record: . . ." *Sacramento Record-Union*, Oct. 24, 1879.

On Sept. 22, in San Francisco, "a delegation of fifty citizens of Sacramento, headed by Governor Irwin and N. Greene Curtis, waited upon General Grant at the Palace and gave him a formal invitation to visit the capital." USG replied. "I thank you for the kind manner in which you have welcomed me to the capital of the State. The feeling manner in which you have expressed the wishes of the people of Sacramento is very gratifying to me. Say to your people that I will visit them before I leave the coast, and will notify you of the time." *San Francisco Chronicle*, Sept. 23, 1879. On Sept. 25, USG telegraphed to Mayor Jabez Turner of Sacramento. "I will telegraph the time when I hope to reach your city, although I cannot now do so. I may not be able to come until after my return from Yosemite and Oregon." *Sacramento Bee*, Sept. 25, 1879. On Oct. 13, Marcus D. Boruck, San Francisco, telegraphed to USG, Portland, Ore. "People Sacramento very desirous Mrs Grant accompany You—Ladies there having arrangements to make Connection therewith would like to Know Soon as possible—" Telegram received (at 11:10 A.M.), California Historical Society, San Francisco, Calif. On Oct. 22, before leaving San Francisco, USG telegraphed to Elihu B. Washburne, Chicago. "I will leave here on the night of the 25th instant, stop two days at Virginia City, and about the same time in the aggregate at other places on the way to Galena. This will land me in Galena about the 6th or 7th of November. On the road I can give the time accurately." *San Francisco Chronicle*, Oct. 23, 1879. En route to Sacramento, USG spoke during a brief stop at Vallejo. "A quarter of a century ago I visited this place and shook hands with the inmates of every house here, but there were only five houses then." *Ibid.*, Oct. 23, 1879.

Also on Oct. 22, outside the state capitol, USG thanked "the citizens of Sacramento and of California for the welcome I have received at every place that I have been since my arrival on your coast." USG spoke of his reception abroad and concluded: "If we all—every one of us—could see other countries as I have seen them, we would all make better citizens, or at least the average of citizens would be better, and there would be less discontent with their own country." *Sacramento Record-Union*, Oct. 23, 1879.

On Oct. 23, USG toured Sacramento and discussed his travels in the Far East and other subjects. A reporter rendered his remarks both directly and in the third person. When officials touted local schools, USG replied. "Yes, your school buildings are very creditable, but they have very good schools in Portland—some really elegant buildings—and for the population of the city I should judge that in this respect Portland might challenge comparison with any city of its size. . . . [T]his is very good, in fact a very creditable building, but they have good school-houses in Portland, a good system of schools, and all the children of the city have an opportunity to acquire a good common school and high school education. When a city accomplishes that it may be said to be on a par with any other, for none of them can do more." *Ibid.*, Nov. 1, 1879. USG admired the horses drawing his carriage. "I have a pair of white elephants, in the shape of a couple of Arabian horses, presented to me by the Sultan. They have a pedigree extending back five hundred years. . . . The value of the Arabian stock is due to the indispensable use the horse is to his master. He has an intrinsic value which is not known and cannot be appreciated elsewhere. All his high qualities of endurance and speed have been bred up because those qualities possess a higher value to the breeder than elsewhere perhaps. Now, in China they have only an inferior breed of scrubs, because in that country human labor is the cheapest thing known. The greater part of the transportation is performed by men. They have a vehicle, the name of which when translated is 'man-pull-cart,' literally, or perhaps as we would say 'man-cart,' in which you ride with considerable ease. Journeys are made long distances with these. A man works in the shafts, pulling them with his hands, without harness of any kind, and much of the travel in the country is performed in that way." USG characterized China's military as "very inferior; that the tactics in use were those formerly according to regulation in the armies of England and America, but that the arms were cast-off and rejected weapons, of a very inferior quality, of the American and European nations. The Chinese do not possess the soldierly quality common to civilized peoples. He said that at a public reception given to him by the Viceroy at Tientsin a military display constituted one of its features, which gave him an opportunity of forming a judgment as to the quality and bearing of the soldiers. He did not believe the Chinese people to be in any sense a military people." USG also discussed Chinese agriculture, infrastructure, and social policies. He had been "shown a piece of land which had been under cultivation every year for five thousand years without deterioration of the fertility of the soil. This result is effected by returning to the soil everything taken from it. Fish constitutes a large proportion of the food of the people, and all the offal not consumed for human food is carefully applied to the soil, and fish is a great fertilizer. Even the roots of the wheat—wheat is grown to a very limited extent—are taken and rotted in a compost heap and returned to the soil. All the leaves and garbage are utilized in the same manner. Famines occur in the interior of China in which thousands die of starvation. This is due to the want of facilities of transportation. In the aggregate the country produces enough to support even the dense life of China, but in every season there are portions of the country where crops are total or partial failures, while in these same seasons crops are abundant and successful in other parts. Facilities for transportation would enable the more favored districts to supply the destitution in the localities of want, but no such facilities exist. . . . The architecture of the public buildings, of the palaces of the nobles and the official residences of the Emperor and public officers, is much like that of the western civilization—of course, nothing like the capitols of States or the grand public edifices of Europe, but in the same style of architecture, and unlike the style of architecture of houses devoted to other uses in the country. . . . The Government gives no encouragement to the accumulation of individual wealth. If a man is energetic and enterprising and begins to accumulate money, a process of squeezing is applied to him by an unequal system of taxation, such as has often been mooted in this country to destroy large land holdings and to tax large properties out of existence. The system is in very successful operation in China, and its results can be seen there. Men who are successful and are accumulating property hide their wealth and assume a poverty which is not real, and the system reduces everybody to a level, arrests civilization, operates to stagnate all progress and generally results in poverty, ignorance and squalor. Some of the Chinese deposit their money in foreign banks established in seaport towns, and a larger part of the toleration shown foreigners in these towns is due to the fact that wealth deposited there escapes the confiscating process of unequal taxation. In the city of Hongkong the European residents there and the upper class of Chinese treat the lower caste of Chinese very much as they are treated by the hoodlums of San Francisco. They are kicked and cuffed, and bear it with the same stoical indifference they manifest here. Their compensation is that the authority extended over the city by the British Government gives them protection for whatever property they may possess—a protection they would not have under their own Government. He remarked that at seaport towns silver was abundant, but that in the interior copper and brass coin was the only money known; that a coin was in use there of the equivalent value of one mill, or one thousand of them for a silver dollar. He spoke of the people of the northern part of China as an educated and civilized race, while those of the south, particularly of the lower caste, were a very ignorant, debased and servile race. From this latter class the immigration to America, Australia and the Pacific islands was chiefly drawn, and from the lowest order even of this lowest caste. They possess physical energy, industry and great economy. They subsist at home on much less than their fellow-countrymen require, even in San Francisco or California, and by reason of this they operate to drive out other species of labor. Even all down the Malay coast this same order of Chinese which has emigrated here is working its way in and disturbing the labor system of that country, successfully competing and supplanting the cheap labor there." USG turned next to Japan. After discussing his role in mediating the Ryukyu Islands dispute between China and Japan (see letter to Prince Kung and Iwakura Tomomi, Aug. 13, 1879), USG turned to Japan. "I witnessed a very fine military review in Japan, and I must say that I have never seen in any country a more thoroughly martial exh[i]bition. The Japanese make good soldiers. Their army is thoroughly drilled and disciplined, is well armed with arms of modern invention and precision, and in all respects is equal to those of European nations. The Japanese people are light in weight, but they are very muscular and possess iron constitutions. I was informed that for a single day's march a distance of 80 or 85 miles could be accomplished by a Japanese soldier, carrying the accouterments, which weigh about twenty-five pounds. Besides this, the rations furnished to the Japanese soldier for one week do not exceed in quantity that furnished to the American soldier for one day. You will readily perceive the advantage such an army would have in the marching incident to campaigning. A force of 10,000 of these Japanese troops, armed as they are and disciplined as they are, could march 3,000 miles through China as a hostile or invading force without meeting successful resistance. The Japanese are adopting the manners and habits of Western civilization rapidly. Not more than six years ago it would have been impossible for a stranger to penetrate to the interior of that country. Now, a man may pass through Japan with as much safety and comfort, so far as the opposition of the natives of that country is concerned, as in any country in Europe. Not more than five or six years ago the traveler would have been met with hostile demonstrations on every hand. This opposition would have proceeded from the two-sworded gentry of that country, the remnant of the old aristocratic class who live without work, and constituted the soldiery of Japan. The habits of the people, as to matters of diet, are changing. Mutton and beef are rapidly becoming articles of food. Some change is to be noted in the customs of dress, but the most rapid progress has been made in the science of government. Brief summaries of the histories of all the nations of the world have been translated and printed for general distribution. Books on international law, agriculture, science and the arts have been translated from the English, French and German into the Japanese, and are extensively read by the educated classes. The arts and sciences of western civilization are receiving marked attention, and are springing up rapidly throughout the country. They have navy yards which would compare favorably in point of machinery and other equipments with those of the European nations and with those of our country. Their people learn our mechanic arts readily, and are fast adopting our ideas of government. In the olden time the Mikado, or Emperor, was the spiritual head of his people. The government of the country was left largely to subordinate Governors, called Tycoons, or the heads of provinces. The Mikado was a sacred being, a veritable child of the sun, never to be looked upon by common mortals. Members of his Cabinet were permitted to come into his presence by lying upon their faces, but were not permitted to cast profane eyes upon his sacred person. In this royally superstitious seclusion Mikados of Japan have dwelt for many centuries, but a great change has taken place and is going on now. The Mikado, a young man about 30 years of age, now mingles freely with his people, and is indeed the Emperor of the country. Instead of the traditional seclusion in which his great ancestors lived he goes about the country freely, mingling everywhere with the people and seeming to have an ardent desire to understand their wants and to meet and to mingle with them. This change has taken place within the short period of the reign of this young man, and when we realize how strong a hold the superstitious awe of this great sacred personage had upon the minds of the people of Japan, there is something almost miraculous in the change which has taken place in this regard. . . . [T]he Japanese are really in earnest in abandoning the old and adopting the new systems both of government and of social and personal customs. The tendency of the Government is to extend power to the people, and with 35,000,000 of inhabitants a civilization is dawning upon the islands of Japan which within a single generation will make that Government a first-class power. Before the changes of which I have spoken had taken place in that country it was the universal custom of the sexes to bathe together in a perfectly nude condition. The streets of the cities of Japan are narrow, the climate is warm, owing both to latitude and thermal currents, while the absence of sprinkling and other municipal regulation to keep them clean makes the streets very dirty. The Japanese, therefore, bathe two or three times a day, and through their streets there is a frequent recurrence of these bathing houses. For the most part they are public institutions, maintained at public expense. Well, before the communication with foreigners, and even as late as five or six years ago, it was the custom for the entire population, without regard to sex or age, to mingle freely in these bathing places in a state of nudity. With the adoption of some of our ideas of civilization a sense of modesty seems to have taken complete possession of the people. They now have separate bathing places for men and for women, and the practice of indiscriminate bathing is as completely unknown as in this or any European country. This change involved a good deal of trouble and expense, for separate houses for women had to be built, or those in existence had to be effectually partitioned. The Japanese have had a civilization from time immemorial It possessed many elements and attributes of great value. In mathematics they are the equal if not the superior of other peoples. But their civilization, both in its religious and intellectual aspects, developed in them very largely a single faculty, to which I attribute the readiness with which they have adopted the new civilization. I mean the capacity of comparison and the willingness to adopt that which under comparison proves to be the best. Religious and civil and social traditions have never produced in them that rigid orthodoxy of spirit which would operate to make them hold on to old things simply because they are old. Their ability to compare and form a judgment from the materials obtained by such comparison is associated with that spirit of liberality enabling them to discard the old and adopt the new if the latter vindicates its title to be adjudged the best. . . . Most certainly, there is a party of conservatives, composed mainly of very old people, of the most ignorant class and of the class privileged under the old order of things, and who will lose their dominance by the present tendencies to adopt broader and more liberal principles of government. The two-sword fellows of the old time, whose social and civil rank enabled them to live without work, understand the significance of the present tendencies and see clearly that in the distribution of opportunities among all classes every man will be put to his metal. The privileges and immunities this class have enjoyed are very rapidly passing away. It would be but natural to suppose that they would not give up these good things without some resistance, but as a party or an element in the government they are growing smaller and weaker. Nothing can arrest the present tendency to adopt our civilization on the part of the Japanese Government. The national character and the national characteristics of mind are such as to readily assimilate civilized ideas and adopt civilized customs. The change that has been wrought is almost marvelous, but it must be remembered that the peculiar civilization which for centuries has existed in Japan have prepared that people in a remarkable way for the adoption of the new order of things. The people may be said to have been thoroughly ripened for the era of European civilization now dawning on that country. When we are better acquainted with the old civilization of Japan and its ideas the historian will find a ready solution for the changes now taking place. The new condition of things must have arisen naturally and legitimately out of the old." Reverting to China, USG "spoke in terms of the severest reprobation of the conduct of the English Government toward China in forcing opium upon that people. He said that the Chinese Government would stop the traffic in opium at once if the British Government would permit it; that it brought to their people misery, poverty and death, and yet the Government was powerless to arrest the evil. Great Britain had derived large revenues from the opium traffic, amounting to thousands of millions to the treasury of that country alone; and that no greater injustice was ever practiced by one people upon another, and particularly by a strong Government against a weaker one. The matter was under discussion in England, and the best men of that country heartily disapproved of the course of Her Majesty's Government." Turning to domestic matters, USG ignored a reference to his possible candidacy for a third term, but discussed the presidency of the Nicaragua Canal Company. "That is a Presidency I will accept. If they will raise the necessary subscriptions and desire me for President, I will see that the work is carried through promptly." USG affirmed that the canal was feasible. "I *know* it is." He then "took up the subject of ship canals in a spirited manner and dilated upon it in a manner that proved his thorough familiarity with the whole subject. He said that he had six complete plans for ship canals, and the one for the Nicaraugua Canal, with some trifling alterations, he was perfectly satisfied, was feasible. It was a work in which he had taken great interest, and one that he thought ought to be carried forward to success." Asked whether travel to the Orient fostered appreciation of life in the U.S., USG responded: "It will enhance our appreciation of the liberty and prosperity we enjoy to travel anywhere in the world. America is respected throughout the world, but it must not be presumed from that fact that she is necessarily loved. Our institutions are in a measure a rebuke to the aristocratic classes of the old civilizations." As to whether the U.S. was feared, USG said: "Not in a sense that her existence or power is a menace to the peace of other countries, or that a disposition of aggression on our part is a danger to any country But the United States Government is the most powerful on the earth. Our navy is not equal to the navy of a third class power, but there is no power possessed of a navy greater than we can build on very short notice. We have all the resources of power, the wealth, the materials of war, with the necessary mechanical capacity to make them effective. . . . We have, say, fifty millions of people that are physically the equal of other people. We have, of course, no standing army, but every man in that crowd under 40 years of age can become a good soldier in five minutes. And this would be as true of every other crowd in the country. Besides this there is the superior power which the faculty of command gives. Our capacity for command is greater than that of other people. I have no reference to the military capacity of Generals in command. I refer solely to the general aggregate capacity of command among the people. Our people from boyhood, we may say, have the control and direction of somebody else. There are more Americans who are employers of labor, or in positions where they direct other men, than any other people on the earth. Some have command of but one, some of five, others of fifty, and even in groups where one man commands there are foremen down below. This produces and develops among our people the faculty of accomplishing a desired result through others, and this capacity is of the highest value in an army. The command of an army in its aggregate sense resides in the entire rank; that is to say, in every man who holds any position above that of private, and the higher this capacity in the people from which the army is drawn the higher its manifestation in the operations of war. It is this faculty of command which gives discipline. Whoever knows best how to command knows best how to obey. Discipline is not the result of mere docility; it is the intelligent perception of the necessity of obedience." *Ibid.*

To Edward F. Beale

————

Palace Hotel.
San Francisco, Oct. 24th *1879.*

My Dear General.

If you read all the papers say you will see that I have had but very little solid rest since landing in San Francisco. I am just back from Sacrimento where I had a most delightful but active visit, having to shake hands with nearly the entire population, big & little. The people in Oregon too were equally cordial. The change that has taken place in the two states since I left here is marvelous, not to be realized by people who return from time to time as you have done.

To-morrow evening we start for Galena where we will make our home for some weeks. In December late we will probably go east and determine upon some place to spend the winter. We expect to make a short visit to Washington when we will accept yours and Mrs. Beales tendered hospitalities. But do'nt be having dinner parties and other entertainments to take up all the time. I want to get out to the farm to see the horses and colts.

Will you be kind enough to ship by express, on the receipt of this, to my address in Galena, the trunks & boxes we have at your house?

Mrs. Grant joins me in love and regards to you and family.

Very Truly Yours
U. S. Grant

Gn. Ed F. Beale

ALS, DLC–Decatur House Papers.

On Oct. 24, 1879, A. C. Bradford, act. president, California Pioneers, introduced USG during an afternoon reception at the Pioneers' Hall. USG replied. "Mr. President and California Pioneers: The pleasure of being associated with you, and as far as possible being made a member of your association, is an honor which I highly appreciate.

I had the good fortune to spend two very pleasant years on this coast, and formed an attachment for the country and people. I have never abandoned the hope of making my permanent home among you. When I left in 1854 it was with the hope of returning in a few years, as a private citizen, and spending here the rest of my life; but events transpired that prevented the consummation of my wish. Years rolled on, nearly seven, and I did not see my way clear to return. The war broke out, and as did a million others, I entered as a volunteer. It was my good fortune in the course of two years to be promoted to the rank of Major-General in the regular army, the highest grade then existing. I hoped that the war would soon be terminated, and that I, as the junior Major-General, would be left Hobson's choice, and be enabled to select this coast as my command. But in less than a year the Act of Congress creating the office of Lieutenant-General threw a wet blanket over my hopes, and instead of making my home in the extreme West, I was obliged to reside in the extreme East. I had been in Washington but once or twice, and did not fancy it as a place of residence, but as time rolled on I found it not so bad, and now I think the Capital a place to be proud of. Gentlemen, allow me to reassure you that this introduction into the fellowship of your Society gives me great pleasure and honor." *San Francisco Chronicle*, Oct. 25, 1879. After his speech, USG toured the building. "In the library he was shown the coat he wore at Vicksburg. He examined it closely, and remarked: 'Yes, I recognize those shoulder straps.' A table was also shown him, which he was reported to have made at Humboldt in 1853. He looked at it smilingly, and said: 'That's a fraud; I never could handle tools; I couldn't even make a sled that would stay together long enough to slide down hill once. However, I may have ordered a soldier to make it for me;' and then added, facetiously: 'Perhaps I made it in' '49.'" *Alta California*, Oct. 25, 1879. See Speech, [*Sept. 30, 1879*].

Also on Oct. 24, USG addressed "Comrades and Veterans of the Mexican War." "I receive this badge which you have presented me with sincere gratification. I have been much pleased at all the receptions tendered me since my arrival, to meet so many with whom I served nearly a third of a century ago, and to find them not such very old men after all. A third of a century ago we could hardly look at men as old as we are now without considering them pretty well along in life; but now we don't look upon ourselves as very old men, and in fact I find myself putting off for a few years the time when I shall become old. That war served the purpose of educating all of us to render efficient service to our country when she needed it; and no one regretted more than I did the sad occasion for such service. We were then fighting side by side under one flag for the ultimate acquisition of all this glorious territory. We all vied in love for this coast, and I am sure that we all would now render equal service for perpetuating it and maintaining it as an integral and perfect part of the whole great nation. Gentlemen, I thank you for your kindness." *San Francisco Chronicle*, Oct. 25, 1879.

On the same evening, USG spoke at a Pioneers banquet attended by U.S. Senator William Sharon of Nev. "California Pioneers: When your worthy President began and mentioned 'Ohioan' I didn't know whether he was addressing his remarks to me or the Senator from Nevada, who has commanded almost everything on the coast, who lives in California, votes in Nevada and carries the State in his pocket. I have already to-day thanked some of you at your hall and others at another society to which many of you belong—the Mexican War Veterans—and I again thank you for the distinguished honor which you have paid me." *Ibid.*, Oct. 25, 1879.

On Oct. 25, USG spoke at Mills' Seminary in Oakland. "Young Ladies and Friends: I feel a greater embarrassment in speaking to you on this occasion than I have felt when addressing those of stronger arms. I reciprocate the feeling expressed, and assure you that the recollection of this day will remain with me when the memory of many former occasions shall have passed from my mind." *Ibid.*, Oct. 26, 1879.

Also on Oct. 25, USG addressed a farewell banquet at the Palace Hotel. "Gentlemen of San Francisco: The boundless hospitality and cordiality with which I have been received since I have put my foot on the soil of California, has taken a deep root in my heart. It was more than I could have expected, and while it has entailed some little fatigue at times, I assure you that I have been only gratified by it. I had previously been in California and on the Pacific coast, but I had been away a quarter of a century and a little over from the time when I landed here the first time. I hope that another quarter of a century will not elapse before I shall be able to visit you again. Although I see no old men yet among the Pioneers, if I remained away another quarter of a century I might be compelled to confess that some of you had become old. I want to see you again in your prime and in your youth. Gentlemen, in taking my departure I want to thank you all for the farewell reception which you have given me this evening, and to express the hope that whether I may be fortunate enough to visit your State again or not, I shall meet you one and all elsewhere, and that if not in this life, that it will be in a better world." *Ibid.*

Speech

———

[*Virginia City, Nev., Oct. 28, 1879*]

Mr. President and Ladies and Gentlemen of the Society of Pacific Coast Pioneers: Your President has already expressed in his remarks in regard to the honors I have received in foreign countries what I feel, and the feeling of appreciation which moves me in my reception in my own country. No honors that I received abroad were such a real pleasure to me, nor were any so deeply felt, as are those bestowed upon me by my own people in their reception of me on my coming home. I do not mean by this to say one word in disparagement of my greeting abroad, for it seemed honest and hearty, and was given in token of the high appreciation of this country and the high position it now occupies in the eyes of foreign nations. It would have been very different a quarter of a century ago. Then we were hardly looked upon as being a nation; now they not only regard us as a nation, but also as one of the most powerful of all nations. We have much that European nations have not, and cannot have. We have not yet a population which crowds every habitable district, and threatens to exhaust the productions of the soil, as in the Old World is often the case. In those countries the question in many places is

not how to obtain the luxuries, but how to obtain the actual nec-
essaries of life. It is not so with us; we have an extensive domain,
a fertile soil, and immense and wonderful resources of every kind
to exhaust before our population shall become so dense as to make
the raising of sufficient food to support life a serious problem. Our
land is capable of supporting millions and hundreds of millions. In
this respect we have great promise for the future. Indeed our people
are regarded better abroad than they regard themselves, unless we
come down to individual opinions, when some of us think very well
of ourselves and are probably often not a little conceited. The newspapers and politicians, however, would seem to believe that there
are a good many bad people in the world and would have us believe
that we are always on the verge of ruin, but I think we shall be able
to worry along for a considerable time yet. Still I don't say but some
of us might be improved. If I was not an American I would not dare
say this—I would be in danger of being mobbed. But I am just as
good an American as I was when I went away. I thank you heartily
for the kind reception you have given me and the honor you have
done me in making me a member of your Society.

Virginia City Territorial Enterprise, Oct. 29, 1879. USG responded to an address by
Robert H. Taylor.
     On Sept. 19, 1879, Governor John H. Kinkead of Nev. wrote to USG. "I beg to
tender you for myself and the People of the State of Nevada the hospitalities of our
Commonwealth, coupled with the earnest hope that you will honor us with a visit prolonged to the utmost limit consistent with your plans and engagements, I can assure
you of a cordial and heartfelt welcome from every citizen of our rugged, Silver-lined
Domain" ALS, DLC-John Russell Young. On Oct. 27, Kinkead welcomed USG to Carson City. USG spoke on the steps of the capitol: "GOVERNOR AND LADIES AND GENTLE-
MEN: It gives me great pleasure to acknowledge your welcome. It has been my fortune
to be quite a traveler over the country, but this State I have never visited before. I am
especially pleased, therefore, to be with you even for a brief time, and to see the capital
of the State which has done so much to swell the prosperity of our growing country,
and I am glad also to be for a time in a State which has done so much to restore our
currency to a sound basis." *Chicago Inter-Ocean*, Oct. 28, 1879.
     On Oct. 7, Mayor J. S. Young of Virginia City had telegraphed to USG. "If possible
please inform me when you will visit us and how long you can remain with us" Telegram received, DLC-John Russell Young. On Oct. 22, Wednesday, Mayor Andrew J.
Bryant of San Francisco telegraphed to Young. "Grant will leave here on next Saturday at midnight on a special train. He will reach your city on Monday morning about
9 o'clock." *Virginia City Territorial Enterprise*, Oct. 23, 1879. On Oct. 27, USG spoke on
arrival at Virginia City. "*Fellow-Citizens:* I am glad to meet you here to-day, and I feel

under many obligations for the fine reception you have given me. It is impossible for me to make a speech on this occasion. I am not like your Senators, who are in the habit of making long speeches to you and catching your votes. I can't talk in that way." *Ibid.*, Oct. 28, 1879.

On Oct. 28, USG, Julia Dent Grant, and others visited the Consolidated Virginia mine, accompanied by two reporters. "The General thinks it would be a good plan to sentence convicts to work eight hours a day down here. 'Anyhow,' he says, red in the face from heat, and mopping his face with the sleeve of his blouse, 'this is the place to leave the newspaper men.' 'Would you not leave the politicians, too?' asks Governor Kinkead. 'Yes, but there ain't room for all that ought to be put here,' the General replies, without a smile, and maybe he meant it." *Chicago Inter-Ocean*, Oct. 29, 1879. See *Julia Grant*, p. 311.

On Oct. 29, USG spoke on his departure from Virginia City. *"Fellow-Citizens of Virginia:* I thank you for all your kindness to me. I should, if it were possible, greatly enjoy staying a good deal longer with you. I have found very many things to interest me here besides the warm hospitality of your people. Once more I thank you." *Virginia City Territorial Enterprise*, Oct. 30, 1879.

On the same day, USG spoke on arrival at Reno. "It affords me great pleasure to see this bright spot in Nevada. I did not expect to see such agricultural land. I know what Nevada has done and is doing to bring about the general prosperity of our country. I thank you, ladies and gentlemen, for the greeting you have given me." *Ibid.*

On Oct. 27, USG, Carson City, had telegraphed to Governor John W. Hoyt of Wyoming Territory. "Will reach Cheyenne by train leaving Sanfrancisco twenty eighth thank you for invitation to lay over but will not be able to do so longer than the train consents to stop" Telegram received (at 7:30 P.M.), Wy-Ar. On Nov. 1, Hoyt twice telegraphed to USG, Virginia City and Carson City. "Learning that you are about to resume your way across the continent, in the name of the people of Wyoming, who, in common with the people of all sections of our country, have watched your progress around the World with very great interest, I welcome your approach, and tender you a cordial invitation to this Territory and to its capital. Begging your acceptance, and that you will be kind enough to inform me of the probable date of your arrival on Wyoming soil, with the length of time we may hope to detain in Cheyenne, . . ." "Your despatch, in answer to mine, rec'd. It had been my purpose to meet you at the western boundary of Wyoming; but owing to the rapidity of your movements, illness, & the pressure of duties connected with the Legislature about to convene, that is impossible. You will be met at the railway here, with a few words of greeting; after which it is hoped that you will lunch at my house and thereafter receive as many of our people as the limit of time and your own convenience will allow." ALS (telegram sent), DNA, RG 48, Territorial Papers, Wyoming Territory.

Speech

[*Ogden, Utah Territory, Oct. 30, 1879*]

LADIES AND GENTLEMEN: I thank you for this welcome. I would like very much indeed to spend several days in your Territory and examine your industries, resources, and growth if my time would permit. I cannot even stop at my home in Galena, but I must hasten on my journey, for I have promised to be present at the unveiling of the monument of the brave but lamented General Thomas, which occurrence has been postponed to give me time to reach the capital of the nation. You will excuse me for not making a speech as I am suffering very severely, and have been for an hour or two from a sprain in my back, received while preparing to pass to another car, by a sudden lunge of the cars on a sharp curve in the road.

This is the first and only thing that has happened to me to mar my pleasure on my long continued journey, indeed the first thing of the kind that ever happened me, and I think it will be all right in a day or two. I again thank you for this very kind welcome, and wish you all well.

Salt Lake Tribune, Oct. 31, 1879. See letter to Alexander M. Kenaday, Nov. 11, 1879.

En route to Ogden, Utah Territory, USG spoke to a reporter about his frequent public speeches since returning to the U.S. "Well, I couldn't help it. When I was in Europe I had to speak, and, having done so, it seemed to me it would be very uncivil to refuse the folks at home. It is very embarrassing. I think I am improving, for my knees don't knock together like they did at first, but I don't like it, and I am sorry I yielded the first." Told that Eastern audiences would expect longer speeches, USG replied: "Well, I fear they will be disappointed. I am just going to say I am glad to see you, and that's all." USG then discussed public figures, including Samuel J. Tilden. "O, I guess he will be nominated, won't he? Hancock would be a stronger man, but poor Hancock would be assailed by the Catholics for hanging the sainted Mrs. Surratt, when he was really no more responsible for it than you were." USG called George H. Thomas a "brave, honest soldier" and spoke "of the embarrassment which the invitation to the unveiling of the Thomas statue, coming after engagements made in Chicago, had given him, and of his indecision as to whether he would not change all his plans about not going East now, and try to be in Washington on this occasion." USG also discussed meeting John S. Mosby, consul at Hong Kong. Asked whether Mosby's public charges of consular corruption were true, USG replied: "Yes, they are; and not only true there, but in some other places in the East. In fact, we have very few men there who ought to be allowed to remain, and very few in Europe who should be recalled." USG "then went on to show in detail how peculations in the Hong Kong Consulate were carried on, and how this corruption was responsible for much of the Chinese emigration, because the consuls were so greedy for the fees that they did not carefully administer the oath regarding voluntary emigration required by law. Of the Chinese bill, he said he should have vetoed it as Hayes did, because it was a pettifogging bill, and not the right way to correct what he believed to be a great evil." *Chicago Inter-Ocean*, Oct. 31, 1879.

On Oct. 29, 1879, William E. Chandler, Salt Lake City, wrote to USG. "Allow me to congratulate you upon your safe return; ~~here,~~ upon the cordial ~~reception you received~~ attentions rendered you everywhere abroad and upon the ~~sp~~ ~~universal~~

spontaneous demonstrations with which the American people will universally ~~greet~~
receive you at home. I am only prevented from expressing my ~~own~~ congratulations
in person, by the dangerous sickness of my oldest son here in this city." ADfS, New
Hampshire Historical Society, Concord, N. H.

Speech

————

[*Ogallala, Neb., Oct. 31, 1879*]

COMRADES: On the occasion referred to I had taken a few minutes' time before the meeting to prepare what I was going to say,
and read it from manuscript. On this occasion I have not prepared
anything to say, and may not be able to say anything even as well
as I said it on that occasion; but I will say this, gentlemen, that I
think this organization of the Grand Army of the Republic is calculated to render good service in the future. It isn't, as I understand
it,—and I am a member of the Grand Army,—a political organization, but it is sound on one point, and that is that this is a Nation;
that this is a Union of States; and that it is to be preserved as a
Union of States forever. No matter what our political faith may be,
whenever the integrity of this Union is assailed we are all on one
side in that conflict. When all sections of the country agree with us
in this, they are, if not eligible to membership, at least eligible to
our respect and good opinion. Now as to telling stories I have no
particular gift in that way. Sometimes conversing about the affairs
of the War, something that is said calls up an anecdote or a good
story, where something occurred of a ridiculous, pathetic, amusing,
or illustrative character. I might tell, if I could happen to think of
them, of some things that occurred that Mr. Lincoln told me at
times when he visited me in the field, and I will tell you one thing
that occurred just after the surrender of Lee at Appomattox. I have
often heard the same story attributed to Mr. Lincoln in different
ways; but this is the way it occurred with me. After the surrender
of Lee, I hurried back to Washington with all haste to stop the
enormous expenditure the Government was making at that time
in the way of purchases, enlistments, and drafting. While I was not

positive that there would be further hostilities or any further efforts made on the part of the Rebel armies, yet I though it was not unlikely there would be, and that it was better to take proper precautions. So I ordered the Army of the James back to Burke's Station, to remain while we could go over to Washington and do as I say, stop expenditures that were being made. As you all remember, the authorities in Richmond had taken flight, and they never stopped till they got to Danville. Finding we were not pressing them, they did not stop there, supposing I was at Burke's Station. Extra Billy Smith, as he was called, was Governor of Virginia at that time, and he sent a letter through by a flag of truce to me, which Gen. Meade received, and, without letting them know I was not there, telegraphed to me at Washington. The letter was to this effect, that he was Governor of the Commonwealth of Virginia, and, as such, he had temporarily removed the seat of Government from Richmond to Danville, and he was desirous of knowing from me whether he would be permitted to exercise the functions of his office in Danville unmolested, or, if not, if he and a few friends would be permitted to leave the country. I was in doubt about the best way to answer it, when I happened to meet Mr. Lincoln on the sidewalk and told him about it. He supposed I was asking him for instructions, and his answer was this: "I will tell you," he said; "it's like an Irishman I once heard of who was in the habit of drinking whisky; he had done so for a long time. At last he joined a temperance society, but the habit of drinking was strong upon him. He wanted to take something, and so, for a time, he took soda-water; but one day he put his glass around and said: 'Doctor, can't you put a drop of brandy in that unbeknownst to me?'" Mr. Lincoln couldn't have said any plainer than that Extra Billy Smith could have gone and taken as many of that sort of drinks as he pleased.[1]

Chicago Tribune, Nov. 1, 1879. USG spoke to veterans aboard his train. Charles F. Manderson, former col. and bvt. brig. gen., presided and "alluded at some length to the famous Grand Army reunion at Des Moines, and Grant's speech on that memorable occasion." *Ibid*. See *PUSG*, 26, 342–51.

Earlier on Oct. 31, 1879, USG and party stopped at Laramie and Cheyenne, Wyoming Territory, and at Sidney, Neb., where "One of the bumpkins, who must have been slightly muddled, sang out: 'General, I'm from Connecticut, and when you go back there, tell 'em you saw out West a s-- of a b---- from the old Nutmeg State.' Grant, with great dignity, simply replied: 'You should never swear. It has been a principle of mine never to swear at any time in my life.'" *Chicago Tribune,* Nov. 1, 1879.

1. See Speech, [*Feb. 13, 1882*]; *PUSG,* 14, 389; *Memoirs,* II, 532–33.

Speech

[*Schuyler, Neb., Nov. 1, 1879*]

SENATOR: I am very much obliged for the kind words which you have said on behalf of your people of this prairie town, and I only express the gratification that I have felt at all other points in your State through which we have passed, when I say that apparently you have all been out. I am glad to see this prairie State growing as it appears to be, the ground being dotted all over with farms and prosperous villages, and I hope that you may realize your expectation after the census of 1880, in having at least three Representatives in the Lower House of Congress.[1] I thank you, gentlemen, for your attendance and for your kindness to me.

Chicago Tribune, Nov. 2, 1879. Neb. Senator John T. Clarkson introduced USG, who had earlier told the crowd: "Gentlemen, your towns out here in Nebraska, since I was along here the first time, have got to be as thick as blackberries, so that there is hardly time to read a newspaper article between two stations here." *Ibid.*

Also on Nov. 1, 1879, USG spoke at Grand Island, Neb. "I am very glad to meet you here, and I am sorry I was sound asleep when we arrived, and knew nothing about being here till they got me up." *Ibid.* At Columbus, USG regretted that he could not stop "and take you all by the hand, but it is arranged that I shall be in Omaha at 2 o'clock this afternoon, and the train, in consequence of the great number of trains passing, has already made its arrangements. It would, therefore, be impossible for me to do so; but I hope you are well, and that I will meet all of you again, as I expect to pass over this road often, now that I am a sovereign, and can go where I please and as often as I please." *Ibid.* At Fremont, USG spoke again. "GENTLEMEN: I am very glad to see you, but your towns in Nebraska are too thick for me to talk at every place the train stops. They are springing up here so rapidly that I scarcely know the country in passing through, although I have been out here three times before. This is my fourth trip." *Ibid.*

At Omaha, USG spoke about his travels and observed that "to-day the credit of the United States in the European market is higher than that of any other country in the world. We are there more highly appreciated than we appreciate ourselves as a whole, and I can and will say that as individuals we do not think well enough of ourselves." *Ibid.* Later, USG addressed a Grand Army of the Republic banquet. "It is exceedingly doubtful, gentlemen, whether I shall ever travel with Gen. Manderson again. I am sure that it would hardly be of my own choice if I did, for he has been imposing speeches upon me ever since I came into this State, and we have not passed a single depot on all these prairies that he has not had assistance in bringing me out. And now, gentlemen, I will leave it to you what would be left for me to say by the time I got to New York or Philadelphia, or where I started from to go around the world, if I found such companions. I will leave it to a vote whether I ought to be expected to say anything more. If I am expected to, it is only to repeat my thanks to the citizens of Nebraska for the treatment I have received, leaving out the desire to hear something from me. Even your worthy Mayor has been trying to hold out inducements to me to come and settle in Omaha. If I should do so, from what I have seen around me since I came to your State, I am sure I should be a formidable rival of his the first time he wanted to be elected to an office. As a friend of the Mayor, and from a desire that he shall have no further competition, I propose, if I should come this way to settle, I should go farther." *Ibid.*

1. Nebraska's delegation increased from one to three representatives in the 48th Congress, elected in 1882.

To John Russell Young

———

Burlington, Iowa,
Nov. 3d 1879.

MY DEAR COMMODORE:

Your dispatch and letter announcing the unexpected death of your father [1] were received while I was in Oregon. I intended writing immediately on my return to San Francisco expressing my sympathy and condolence. But every moment of my time was taken up after my arrival there from the hour of rising to a late hour at night. The same kind attentions you witnessed in San Francisco were continued up to the hour of my departure, and were shewn along the entire route of travel up to this point. I dread going to Chicago and the east though I fully appreciate all the hospitalities shewn.

Since you left me I have received two letters from Yosheda [2] and one from Judge Denny. The latter I enclose with this. In one of Yosheda's letters he says that a very satisfactory letter had been received from the Chinese Government on the Loo Choo question which indicated that the matter was not likely to give them any further serious trouble. [3]

I am receiving dispatches every hour almost asking me to stop at different places between Chicago and the east, and urging me to be at the unveiling of Thomas' monument. I would like very much to express my respect and admiration for the grand old Hero by being present on the occasion of the unveiling of his statue but it would be very inconvenient for me to go. I am going east, but when I do go I want to fix upon a place for the winter and not make the trip twice. I do not want to reach Phila before from the 15th to the 20th of Dec. a month later than the unveiling.

Mrs. Grant & Fred. join me in kindest regards to Mrs. Young & yourself.

Yours Truly
U. S. GRANT

J. R. YOUNG, ESQ.

ALS, DLC-John Russell Young. On Oct. 17, 1879, a Philadelphia reporter interviewed John Russell Young, who said "General Grant did not wish to go out of his way to snub Kearney, as has been asserted, but when the 'Sand lot orator,' as you call him, visited him the first time, the General, not wishing to offend him, sent down word to 'excuse' him, as he was much engaged. Kearney, however, persisted in calling not twice, but three times, and at the fourth visit the General was so vexed at the persistence of the man that he sent word that he 'couldn't and wouldn't' see him. Then Kearney attacked him on the sand lots, to which General Grant remarked: 'I would see any working man or any man in California, but I won't see a ruffian.'" Questioned on a third term for USG, Young replied. "That was a thing that General Grant never talked about. It was never a subject of conversation. All this so-called third-term movement was unknown to us, because we had no consecutive news, only straggling items, since May last. The General rarely saw an American paper, being most of his time in the middle of China, Japan, etc. The only thing about home matters that interested him then was the Nicaragua canal scheme. Of this he heartily approved, and I myself sent, at his request, to Admiral Ammen, his dear friend, the 'I approve' cable. He meant by this, as he explained it to me, that he approved of the whole plan as projected by the Nicaragua canal men, not that he opposed the different schemes of friendly English, French or other projects, but this Nicaragua one was, in his opinion, the only practicable route. This he knew, or believed, from his own personal observation of the country, having traveled the different routes when he was a young officer. If Lesseps could build the canal by that route he hoped he would, but, says General Grant, 'he can't; nature is against him.' . . . Borie, Drexel, Childs, General Patterson, Admiral Ammen, General Sherman, Washburne, but more especially General Beale, General Sherman and Admiral Ammen were his American correspondents beyond members of his family. Indeed, he seemed to let go of all cognizance of American affairs from the time he reached India. Therefore, it is not at all surprising that neither he nor I should know absolutely nothing of this third-term business. . . ." *Philadelphia Times*, Oct. 18, 1879. See letter to Daniel Ammen, Aug. 7, 1879.

1. George R. Young died in Philadelphia on Oct. 9.
2. Yoshida Kiyonari.
3. See letter to Prince Kung and Iwakura Tomomi, Aug. 13, 1879.

Speech

[*Burlington, Iowa, Nov. 4, 1879*]

SCHOLARS OF BURLINGTON:—Looking over this vast assemblage of children and knowing the numbers occupying the halls and rooms below, I should think that illiteracy in Burlington would be a thing unknown; and, knowing that it is the same in every city in Iowa, I believe that the men of the coming generation will know their rights, and how to preserve them. Education is so universal that, as I have said on a previous occasion, when I had preparation to speak, should a warfare again occur in this country, it would be between ignorance and superstition on one side, and intelligence and liberty on the other.[1] In a contest of this kind, I know Iowa is on the right side, and, I am sure, will remain so.

Burlington Hawk-Eye, Nov. 5, 1879. USG spoke at the public high school.

On Nov. 3, 1879, USG spoke at Council Bluffs, Iowa. "GOVERNOR GEAR, THE GRAND ARMY OF THE REPUBLIC AND PEOPLE OF IOWA: I am very glad to meet you here, and accept your escort with great pleasure. I had on a former occasion an escort of the Grand Army of the Republic when it was absolutely necessary. I believe I might go through this State without an escort or with an escort without arms, and it would be perfectly safe. It is not necessary for me to say more than to thank you and the people of Iowa both for this escort and for their good will." *Council Bluffs Nonpareil*, Nov. 4, 1879. On the same day, en route from Council Bluffs to Burlington, Iowa, USG spoke at Creston. "MR. MAYOR AND FELLOW CITIZENS: It looks as though a great many people had settled in this part of the country since I was last here a few years ago. Where prairie grass and prairie chickens were principally to be found there now are sufficient people to stamp out the prairie chickens and in their stead raise millions of bushels of that grain which has sustained and supported American life, and which has made America prosperous. I can only add that I thank you sincerely for your expressions of good will, and that I am very glad to see you all, citizens and everybody else." *Ibid.* Also on Nov. 3, USG spoke on arrival at Burlington. "LADIES AND GENTLEMEN— The welcome which I have received since coming into Iowa is to me exceedingly gratifying. I have seen a population in crossing your state, on a single line of railroad, greater than that of the entire state a quarter of a century ago. This is remarkable, and shows a growth and enterprise in this grand state that is most gratifying. The impossibility of making you all hear will make me cut short my remarks, and as they often do down at Washington, I will ask permission to have my speech printed." *Burlington Hawk-Eye*, Nov. 4, 1879. See Charles Mason diary, Nov. 3, 4, 1879, DLC-Charles Mason.

1. See *PUSG*, 26, 343.

Speech

[Galena, Nov. 5, 1879]

Mr. Mayor and Ladies and Gentlemen of Galena: It is with extreme embarrassment that I stand here to-day to receive the welcome which you are according me. It is gratifying; but it is difficult for me to respond to what I have just heard and to what I see, properly. I can say that since I left here, more than eighteen years ago, it has always been a matter of pleasure to me to be able to return again to Galena. Now, after an absence of two and a half years from this city, having been in almost every country north of the equator, it is with special pleasure that I return here again to be greeted by the citizens of this city, Jo Daviess County, and the surrounding country. In my travels abroad, as has been alluded to by the speaker who has just sat down, I have received princely honors, but they have been honors due to my country, and due to you as citizens and sovereigns of our great country. It but requires a person to travel abroad, and to get an insight of life in all of the foreign countries, to appreciate how happy we ought to be with the country we have here. It makes better Americans of us all to see the struggling there is, particularly in the Far East, to gain what would be a starving support in our own country. It should be a gratification to us to feel that we are citizens of this country, where want is scarcely known, and where the question of subsistence is not one we think of now. Fellow-citizens, I renew to you my thanks for your presence and for the welcome which I have received at your hands.

Chicago Tribune, Nov. 6, 1879. USG responded to an address by Ill. Senator Robert H. McClellan.

On Nov. 3, 1879, USG told a reporter he had not spent much time in Galena. "I was there in 1861 eleven months, in 1865 a few months, and in 1868 a few weeks, and

I don't think I have been there for more than a day or two at a time since, and then I stopped with friends, although my house is always there furnished and ready for me, a family who lives in the back part taking care of it." USG said that "not over a half dozen whom I used to know" remained in Galena, which had changed "[f]rom the richest and most prosperous town of its size in the West to about the poorest. It used to be the shipping point for all the lead mines in that region; but a railroad was built near there—first from Chicago, then one from Southern Wisconsin, and they kept coming into that section, every time cutting off some of Galena's territory, until its population has been reduced from 12,000 to 6,000 inhabitance, and from a fast mining town changed to a slow town supported by a farming country." USG looked forward to the slower pace. "When I was in Japan I went up in the mountains and stayed ten days almost alone. It was a novel experience for me, but I enjoyed it. I shall not be able to do much more than call Galena my home after a while. It is a good place to live now, as on my income I can live there much cheaper than in a large city, and live better than most of my neighbors then. My income is not large enough for me to live as I would like, and I will have to find something to do after a while. I have two farms near St. Louis, and some real estate in Chicago, which if I could sell I would feel better off. My land in Chicago is thirty-one acres, just outside the western limits of Chicago. Eleven years ago I was offered $1,500 an acre for it, and now, after paying taxes on it all that time, I couldn't get $250 an acre for it. But I did better in some other investments, or I could never have traveled abroad as long as I have. I had stock in the Adams Express Company, which went up; and I bought right after the fire in Virginia City, Nev., Union and C. & C. stock, when it had gone down from $700 a share to $130, and made $50,000 or $60,000 there. . . . Galena is a good town, with good schools and churches. . . . My father and mother were both Methodists, and I have always preferred that church." Asked "whether he considered the chances for Republican success next year as good now as they were" in 1876, USG replied, "Well, if they ain't, we will be beaten, for those fellows in the South will see to it that the Republicans don't carry Louisiana, Mississippi, or any Southern State . . . We will have a solid South, but the chances in the North are very much better, I think, than then. We don't need to carry only two of the Northern States which we lost last year, or New York alone. . . . I have been reading to-day what the papers say of Chandler's death, and I see it amounts almost to a universal expression of sorrow. I will be curious to see what the Southern papers say. Some of them will be cautious, but papers like that one in Okolona (what is its name?) will say what they think. I am sorry people think down there as they do, but as long as they do I am glad there are papers like that one to tell us of it." *Chicago Inter-Ocean*, Nov. 4, 1879. USG referred to *The Southern States*, a weekly published in Okolona, Miss. See *PUSG*, 25, 265; *ibid.*, 27, 15–16; Endorsement, Nov. 9, 1879.

On Nov. 4, USG spoke at Monmouth, Ill. "GENTLEMEN: I am very glad to get back to Illinois again, and very glad to see you all, but I have a great deal of sympathy with these press-men who are along with us, and who take down every word I say. I am a man of economy. I believe in economy, and they telegraph every word, and I want to save them expenses." *Chicago Tribune*, Nov. 5, 1879. Later on Nov. 4, USG spoke at Galesburg. ". . . I have had the pleasure of seeing the people of Galesburg out on one other occasion. I passed through in 1868, when I thought all the people in the city were about this spot. I am very glad to see you all again to-night." *Ibid.* Asked to speak again by those who could not hear him, USG said: "MY FRIENDS: I have only been in Illinois one hour, and during that time I have already made two speeches, and feel talked out." Someone answered. "We didn't hear the one you made here, General." USG replied: "Well, some one will be pretty sure to print what I said. You can buy a copy of the morning paper and find it all." *Chicago Inter-Ocean*, Nov. 5, 1879. After speaking, "the General was about to return to the car, when some rebel miscreant in the crowd flung an egg, whch struck him on the side of the head. John B. Colton stepped forward and offered $100 reward for the detection and arrest of the ruffian. Of course General Grant was indignant, but no more so than the thousands of loyal citizens, who would probably have hung the scoundrel could they have laid their hands upon him." *Chicago Evening Journal*, Nov. 5, 1879. Police in Galesburg later arrested three boys, "each about 13 years of age." *Chicago Tribune*, Nov. 11, 1879.

On Nov. 5, USG spoke at Mendota. ". . . In getting back now, to my own home, I feel specially gratified to meet the citizens of my own State, and to be welcomed by them. I am sure I shouldn't want to stay long in Illinois if I didn't feel that I could have a good feeling and a reception of the people of this State. . . ." *Ibid.*, Nov. 6, 1879. A second speech is *ibid.* On the same day, en route to Galena, USG spoke briefly at Dixon. *Ibid.* At Forreston, USG answered calls for a speech. "You've got several men around here who are fond of talking. Call them out. This is a free country, her gift of gab is fully developed; here's Ryan for instance." *Ibid.* A reception committee escorting USG to Galena included brothers James M. and William Ryan. See letter to John Thompson, May 18, 1880.

Also on Nov. 5, John G. Walker, secretary, Chicago, Burlington, and Quincy Railroad, asked USG "if he did not think the election of another Republican President would put an end to a condition of affairs in the South, of which the North had reason to complain." USG replied: "Why, yes, I think so; and I thought Hayes was elected; but, despite all he has done to further the end, things have not improved there, and still it seems they must change the programme when they see themselves at a stand-still, while the North is developing and growing all the while. Now just see the contrast. The land here and in Iowa, where we passed day before yesterday, is worth from thirty to forty dollars an acre, while just across the line south, for land as good, and having the advantage of climate, five dollars is asked with no takers. . . . [E]migrants will not go there until they become down there less intolerant. I think Chandler put the thing in a forcible way when he said in his speech just before he died: 'The mission of the Republican party would not cease unless a Northern man could travel through the South and take his politics with him with just the same safety that a Southern Confederate could go to Chicago and run for Judge.' I don't know that I have his words, but his idea was the true one, and was expressed in the short, forcible way which Chandler always used." *Chicago Inter-Ocean*, Nov. 6, 1879. On the same day, discussing recent municipal elections in Chicago, a reporter referred to Adolph Moses, Democratic candidate for superior judge, as "the worst beaten man in the lot." USG remarked. "And he's the last man in the world to complain. He was a Rebel soldier and then a carpet-bagger, but he was allowed to make the canvass without anybody interrupting him; and his friends had the same privilege." *Chicago Tribune*, Nov. 6, 1879. See *ibid.*, Oct. 24, 1879; *PUSG*, 19, 26–27, 37–38.

On Nov. 6, a reporter asked USG about a report "that Gen. Sherman had said that he (Grant) would make an important statement to the Army of the Tennessee at their reunion in Chicago next week." USG replied. "I received a telegram from Sherman this morning, and he says that as far as he is concerned there's nothing in it, and that he never made any such assertion. So far as I am concerned, I know nothing of it. I have nothing of any importance whatever to communicate to the Army of the Tennessee or to anybody else." *Chicago Tribune*, Nov. 7, 1879.

On Nov. 11, USG spoke to a Cincinnati reporter at his Galena home. "I have been stopping here quietly a few days to rest a little from the fatigues of our trip from San Francisco. I always like to come here, because I can take my quiet and ease here better than any-where else. . . . My health has been very good, but I begin to feel that I'm growing stouter than I like. While I was traveling I did not grow heavy, but it seems as soon as I stop the flesh grows on me again." Asked about a rumored winter trip to Cuba, USG replied. "My plans are not fully made up, though it is possible that I may go to the West Indies and spend a part of the winter season there, returning through Mexico. It may all be changed, however. When I start East in December it is possible that I may get employment at something, and in that case my other plans might be changed." Concerning reports that he had been tendered the presidency of the Texas Pacific Railroad, USG said "the only information I had of it was that I saw in the papers. Nothing of the kind has been offered me." As to a possible presidential run, "That, too, is said without any authority from me. The fact is, I haven't been disturbing my mind about any thing since I went away, and any plans that are made for the future for me are without consultation with me." USG also discussed his daughter's rumored death, plans to visit Cincinnati, and lastly his imminent visit to Chicago. "My son lives there, and my engagements there are for every evening for the week, to be entertained by various societies. . . . I think Chicago a great city. It is one of the few cities where a stranger can go and not feel that he is alone. San Francisco, Chicago, and New York are the three great cities of America in that respect. They are metropolitan." *Cincinnati Enquirer*, Nov. 12, 1879.

On Sept. 15, William H. Powell, former brig. gen., Belleville, Ill., had written to USG. "Learning that you are at this date enroute for your Home, and feeling assured that you will not only be glad to meet the Thousands of your own Country men who are waiting to extend to you a hearty welcome back to your Native land, we doubt not but that you will be more than pleased to meet with the *veterans* of *your own State* in a re-union to be held as you will see the latter part of Oct. It is therefore with great pleasure, that we extend to you our urgent and Cordial Invitation to meet with us on the 23d day of Oct 1879—being but 14 miles from St Louis the occasion will furnish a very fine opportunity to your Thousands of old Friends and Comrades of Illinois and adjoining States to Welcome you Home to your Native land and to their Hearts. do not fail to come dear General if possibly within your power. please advise us of your purposes at as early a day as possible—" ALS, DLC-USG, IB.

To Rutherford B. Hayes

Galena, Ill.
Nov. 7th 1879.

HIS EXCELLENCY, R. B. HAYES,
PRESIDENT OF THE U. S.
DEAR SIR:

Your very kind invitation of the 27th of Oct. for myself and party to be your guests at the Executive Mansion during our stay at the Capital on the occasion of the meeting of the Society of the Army of the Cumberland, Nov. 19th & 20th, and as long thereafter as we may wish to remain thereafter, I found on my arrival here. Mrs. Grant joins me in thanks to you & Mrs. Hayes for the cordial invitation, which we would accept with pleasure, but it is not my intention to visit the Capital at that time. Later in the winter, when I leave this place for winter quarters, at some place not yet definitely fixed upon, I have promised General Beale to spend a few days with him in Washingington. I will take occasion then to call and pay my respects and to thank you and Mrs. Hayes in person.

> With best wishes
> sincerely
> U. S. GRANT

ALS, OFH. On Oct. 27, 1879, President Rutherford B. Hayes, Washington, D. C., wrote to USG, Galena. "Mrs. Hayes and myself will be glad to receive you and Mrs. Grant with any members of your family who may be with you, as our guests on the occasion of the unveiling of the statue in honor of General Thomas. It occurs on the 19th & 20th of next month, and long enough after the Chicago reunion to enable you to be present, if other engagements do not prevent. Preparations are making to give you a hearty reception here. Your welcome back will be a warm and friendly one. We shall be glad to have you remain with us as long as it may be convenient for you to do so." Charles Richard Williams, ed., *Diary and Letters of Rutherford Birchard Hayes* (Columbus, 1922–26), III, 575–76.

To Bela C. Kent

> Galena, Ill.
> Nov. 7th 1879.

DEAR SIR:

Your letter of the 4th of Nov. informing me of the resolution of [the] Council of New Al[bany] inviting me to visit your city, and to name the time when I can do so, is received. I expect to go east on my way to visit my mother in Jersey City, N. J. some time during the first half of Dec. I expect to go by Indianapolis, Louisville & Cincinnati making a short stop at each of those cities. This will take me through New Albany, and if [the] hour of arrival shou[ld] be such as to ma[ke] it possible I will be glad to stop for an hour or two.

Very Truly Yours

U. S. Grant

Hon. Bela C. Kent Mayor of New Albany

ALS, New Albany-Floyd County Public Library, New Albany, Ind.; *New Albany Ledger-Standard*, Nov. 11, 1879. See letter to Newland T. DePauw, Nov. 25, 1879; *New Albany Ledger and Tribune*, Oct. 25, 1940.

To Ellen Grant Sartoris

———

Galena, Ill.

Nov. 8th 1879.

My Dear Daughter,

We arrived in Galena on the 5th—three days ago—amidst great enthusiasm by all the citizens of the Citizensy and surrounding country. The whole trip from ~~Omah~~ San Francisco was an ovation. But your ma will probably send you papers giving an account of it. We will remain here until some time in Dec. and then go east and to some place for winter quarters, we think now of going to Havanna & Mexico.—The papers announce that you and Algie will sail for America in about two weeks. But as we have just received a letter from you and you say nothing about it I presume the rumor is without authority. But when we get to our Long Branch house next June we want you to come and to bring the babies prepared to make a long visit. I hope Mr. Sartoris, Sr. will come also. We can make him very comfortable and I am sure a trip among the many watering places of the east will do him good. Probably I might go with him on a trip to the great Mining regions of the Rocky Mountains. I think Buck has made a small investment for you in a mine in Leadville which promises now to give you five or six hundred per cent on the investment. He is now in Leadville looking after it. Jesse is in San Francisco full of business and much elated at the idea of doing something for himself. I believe he has made some $4.000 00 this year.

Fred, Ida & little Julia went out to Omaha to meet us, and returned with us to Galena. Julia is going to be very pretty, and she is very smart. At present however she is like the Dutchman's horse, "tallest when she lays down."

All send love and kisses to you, little Algie & the babe, and our kindest regards to Algie & your father-in-law.

yours Affectionately
U. S. GRANT

ALS, ICHi.

On Nov. 9, 1879, Julia Dent Grant "expressed deep regret at the ridiculously false report alleged to have been circulated by Olive Logan to the effect that, owing to incompatibility and other causes, her daughter, Nellie, and Mr. Sartoris did not live happily together." Julia Grant added "that the report that Mrs. Sartoris had set sail for America was not true, and that she had received no intimation of her intention to visit this country; that her daughter was at present spending the fall at the Sartoris residence in London, and that she would pass the winter months with her husband in Italy, as she has always done since their marriage." *Chicago Tribune*, Nov. 10, 1879.

Endorsement

A nation, as well as the state of Michigan mourns the loss of one of her most brave, patriotic & truest citizens. Senator Chandler was beloved by his associates and respected by those who disagreed with his political views. The more closely I become connected with him the more I appreciated his great merits

U. S. GRANT

GALENA ILL NOV. 9TH 1879.

AES (facsimile), *Zachariah Chandler: An Outline Sketch of His Life and Public Services* (Detroit, 1880), p. 393. Written "upon the reverse of a funeral order issued by the Detroit Commandery of Knights Templar." *Ibid.*, p. 394. U.S. Senator Zachariah Chandler of Mich. died on Nov. 1, 1879, while in Chicago on a speaking tour. On the same day, a correspondent reported USG's reaction to the news of Chandler's death. "It is the saddest piece of news I have heard yet. I have known him a long time, and he was a man for whom I had a personal regard. I look upon his services to the country as having been great in a political field, and I think his loss will be very severely felt, not only by his State but by the country at large. I was much shocked to hear of his death. I regarded him as a man of very great integrity, and bold and fearless in the enunciation of his views. I saw him the last I saw of any of my American friends at home. He went with me down the Delaware River as far as I was accompanied by any of my friends. I received a letter from him a short time ago, a personal letter, which reached me before I left San Francisco, and which I was going to answer to-morrow at Fort Omaha. I knew him slightly a good many years ago, and I have been intimate with him ever since 1864, when I went east to take command of the Army. He was a member of my Cabinet, Secretary of the Interior during my second term, and it was then that I was possibly more intimate with him than before and learned to know him better. His death is a loss to the whole country, and its suddenness adds greatly to the shock." *New York Times*, Nov. 2, 1879.

To Silas F. Miller et al.

GALENA, ILL., Nov. 9, 1879.—*Silas F. Miller,*[1] *Walter Evans*[2] *and Horace Scott,*[3] *Committee*—Dear Sirs: Your letter of the 3d of November is just now before me. I presume it was here on my arrival, but the mail awaiting me was so large that I am not yet thr[o]ugh with it. On my arrival in Galena I received a dispatch from the managers of the roads between Indianapolis and Louisville, and Louisville and Cincinnati, tendering me transportation for myself and party over their routes, which I accepted.[4] The escort which you tender I accept with pleasure, and any arrangement for transportation will be agreeable to me. I can not now fix the time for leaving Indianapolis, but it will be during the first half of December. Very truly yours,

U. S. GRANT.

Louisville Courier-Journal, Nov. 14, 1879. On Nov. 3, 1879, Silas F. Miller *et al.*, Louisville, wrote to USG, Galena. "Allow us to congratulate you on your safe arrival home after your long journey, the triumphal character of which we have watched with the liveliest gratification. We trust that your approaching visit to our city will be as pleasant as we have reason to expect it will be From the time you reach the city the reception will, of course, be entirely non-partisan in its character; but at a meeting of some of your personal and political friends here we were appointed a committee to provide an escort and transportation for yourself and friends from Indianapolis. We hope you will gratify us and all your political friends in the city by allowing them specially to show you this much courtesy and attention while you pass between the two cities. If this will be agreeable to you, please telegraph us to that effect when you receive this letter. With expressions of our highest and most distinguished consideration, . . ." *Ibid.* See *ibid.*, Nov. 19, 1879; *Louisville Commercial*, Nov. 14, 1879.

On Sept. 21, Eli H. Murray, Louisville, had telegraphed to Frederick Dent Grant, San Francisco. "I have sent an invitation to your Father the General He should by all means accept this invitation Please urge him in my name to Come It is the best judgment of all his friends in this section In any event this is the thing at this time" Telegram received, DLC-John Russell Young.

On Oct. 27, Mayor John G. Baxter of Louisville telegraphed to USG, Virginia City, Nev. ". . . Your visit to this place will be marked by a genuine Kentucky hospitality. . . ." *Louisville Courier-Journal,* Oct. 28, 1879. On Oct. 28, USG telegraphed to Baxter. "Your kind invitation to Louisville received. I do not know when I will be going east of Illinois, but when I visit Indianapolis I will extend my trip to Louisville." *Ibid.,* Oct. 29, 1879.

On Nov. 6, John W. Almy, Louisville, telegraphed to USG, Galena. "Allow me to extend to you the hospitalities of the Galt House during your visit to Louisville, and should be pleased to have you accept." *Louisville Commercial,* Nov. 8, 1879. On Nov. 7, USG telegraphed to Almy. "I accept your invitation for the Galt House. Will probably be in Louisville about December 10." *Ibid.* On Nov. 17, in Chicago, USG spoke to a Louisville reporter about his upcoming visit. "Mr. Almy, of the Galt, some time since invited me to accept his hospitalities, and I accepted them, but since then the committee having the matter in charge informed me that other arrangements were made, and I was compelled to telegraph the facts to Mr. Almy, thanking him for his kindness. I believe, however, the reception is to be held at his house." USG also acknowledged "kindly sentiments" addressed to him by Southerners. "They have been more grateful to me than I can express; you may tell the COURIER-JOURNAL, and through it the people of the South, that in whatever position I may in future be placed, that while always determined to support the National Union, I am for those and only those things which will allay all bitterness of the past—all sectional animosities—and those which will make us a united, great people, such as we are now really believed to be by the great nations of the old world." *Louisville Courier-Journal,* Nov. 18, 1879.

1. A Ky. delegate to the Republican National Convention at Chicago in June, 1880, Silas F. Miller joined the 306 stalwarts who supported USG.

2. A former capt., 25th Ky., Walter Evans was another of the 306 supporters at the Chicago convention. See Endorsement, Dec. 18, 1880.

3. Born in 1826 in Vt., Horace Scott rose from railroad switchman to gen. superintendent of the Jeffersonville, Madison, and Indianapolis Railroad.

4. On Nov. 1, 1879, James B. Wilder, president, Louisville, Cincinnati, and Lexington Railway, telegraphed to USG, Omaha. "In your visit to our city we beg to tender you the courtesies of our road, and shall be pleased to transport your car to and from Cincinnati or Central Kentucky, at such time as may suit your convenience." *Louisville Commercial,* Nov. 6, 1879. On Nov. 4, Frederick Grant, Fort Omaha, Neb., telegraphed to Wilder. "General Grant thanks you for your courtesies, and will be glad to accept them when he visits Louisville. At present he does not know when he will be there, but thinks early in December." *Ibid.*

To Emmons Clark

Galena, Ill.
Nov. 11th 1878[9]

COL. E. CLARK.
DEAR SIR:

I have your letter of the 7th of Nov. inviting me to visit the Seventh Regt Fair, to be held in New York City, between the 17th of Nov. & the 1st of Dec. It would afford me pleasure to accept this invitation, but I shall not be able to go east of this state until after the last mentioned date.

Please excuse the half sheet. I was not aware that it was not a full one until the first page was written.

Very Truly yours
U. S. GRANT

ALS, IHi. Emmons Clark enlisted in the 7th N. Y. Militia in 1857 and rose to col. in 1864. In 1866, Clark was appointed secretary, New York City Health Board. See *New York Times*, Aug. 10, 1905.

On Sept. 18, 1879, S. Oscar Ryder, New York City, telegraphed to USG, San Francisco. "The ninth Regiment national guard state newyork respectfully tender you their services as an escort on your arrival in newyork" Telegram received (at 3:40 P.M.), DLC-USG, IB.

On Nov. 22, USG, Galena, wrote to Francis B. Thurber accepting an invitation for "the Exposition of the 'International Dairy Fair Association,' to be held in New York City . . . I expect to be in New York City during the holding of your Fair . . ." Charles Hamilton Auction, Sept. 4, 1975, no. 192.

To Alexander M. Kenaday

————

GALENA, Ill., Nov. 11, 1879.

To ALEXANDER M. KENADAY, Secretary, &c., Washington, D. C.:—

DEAR SIR—Your letter of the 8th inst. conveying the invitation of the veterans of the Mexican war to join them in the procession at the unveiling of the statue in honor of the patriot—the pure, brave and noble General George H. Thomas—is just received. It would afford me much pleasure to accept this invitation if I could be present on that occasion, but I cannot. The distance is long and the time is earlier than I can well break up here for the winter. I want to avoid two trips to the East so close together. I had, also, previous to hearing of the proposed time of the meeting of the Society of the Army of the Cumberland, accepted invitations in this State covering the time of the society meeting. I would like to testify my heartfelt respect and admiration for the soldier who in life had no personal enemies, and whose memory will be forever revered in the history of his country. Very truly yours,

U. S. GRANT.

New York Herald, Nov. 16, 1879. In Oct., 1879, Alexander M. Kenaday, journalist, labor organizer, and founder of the National Association of Veterans of the Mexican War, launched *The Vedette*, a monthly advocating veterans' interests. See *New York Times*, March 26, 1897; letter to Henry M. Cist, Oct. 21, 1879.

Speech

[*Chicago, Nov. 12, 1879*]

COMRADES OF THE SOCIETY OF THE ARMY OF THE TENNESSEE: After an absence of several years from the gatherings of the Society of the Army of the Tennessee, it affords me heartfelt pleasure to again see you, my earliest comrades in arms in the great conflict for Nationality and the Union of all the States under one free and always-to-be-maintained Government.

In my long absence from the country I have had the most favorable opportunities for seeing and comparing in my own mind our institutions and those of all the European countries, and most of those of Asia, and comparing our resources and their development, and the capacity and energy of our people for upholding the Government and developing its resources, with most of the civilized peoples of the world everywhere, from England to Japan, and from Russia to Spain and Portugal. We are everywhere understood; our resources are highly appreciated, and the skill and energy and intelligence of the citizen recognized. My receptions have been your receptions. They have been everywhere a kind of an acknowledgment that the United States is a Nation, a strong, independent, and free Nation, composed of strong, brave, and intelligent people, capable of judging of their rights, and ready to maintain them at all hazards.

This is a non-partisan association, but composed of men who are united in the determination that no foe, domestic or foreign, shall interfere between us and the maintenance of our grand, free, and enlightened institutions and the unity of all the States. The area of our country, its fertility, and the energy and resources of our people, with the sparsity of population compared to area, postpone the day for generations to come when our descendants will have to consider the question how the soil is to support them and how the most can be produced for the support of human life, without reference to the taste or desire of the people, or when but a few can exercise the privilege of the plain luxury of selecting the articles of food they are to eat or the quality and quantity of clothing they are to wear, but will remain the abundant home of all who possess the energy and strength to make good use of them, and if we only remain true to ourselves.

Such a country is one to be proud of. I am proud of it,—proud that I am an American citizen. Every citizen, North and South, East and West, enjoys a common heritage, and should feel an honorable pride in it. I am glad these Society meetings keep up their interest so long after the events and scenes which they commemorate have passed away. They do not serve to keep up sectional feeling or bitterness toward our late foe, but they do keep up the feeling that we are a nation, and that it must be preserved one and indivisible. We feel the kindest for those who fought and fought bravely on the opposit side from us. They equally claim with ourselves the blessings of our great common country. We claim for them the right to travel all over this broad land, to locate where they please, and the right to settle and become citizens and enjoy their political and religious convictions free from molestation or ostracism, either on account of this, or their connection with the past. We ask nothing more for ourselves, and we rejoice to see them become powerful rivals in the development of our great resources in the acquisition of all that should be desirable in this life, and in patriotism and love of country.

Chicago Tribune, Nov. 13, 1879. *Report of the Proceedings of the Society of the Army of the Tennessee at the Thirteenth Annual Meeting Held at Chicago, . . .* (Cincinnati, 1885), pp. 349–50. USG spoke during a reception at Haverly's Theater, and prefaced his remarks with a brief question. "COMRADES OF THE ARMY OF THE TENNESSEE: Do not you think it would be much better now to let the program of the evening go on, and let us have this song, and then you shall hear from me in the time that is put down on the program?" *Chicago Tribune*, Nov. 13, 1879.

Earlier on Nov. 12, 1879, Mayor Carter Harrison of Chicago welcomed USG at the Palmer House. USG replied. "MR. MAYOR, GENTLEMEN OF THE COMMITTEE OF RECEPTION, GENTLEMEN OF CHICAGO AND OF ILLINOIS: I feel very much honored by the welcome which I am receiving at your hands to-day. I feel highly honored by the speech of welcome which has just been uttered by your worthy Mayor. It is something that is so personal to myself that it would hardly be in good taste for me to respond to the language of it, and it leaves nothing, therefore, for me to do than to repeat my thanks to this committee and to the citizens of your city for the hearty reception which they have given me. In regard to one allusion, to my receptions abroad, I will say that in every case I felt that it was a tribute to my own country. I will add, further, that our country stands differently abroad in the estimation of the Europeans and Eastern nations from what it did a quarter of a century ago. An American citizen is regarded in a different light from the American citizen of a quarter of a century ago. At that time it was believed that we had not a nation; that it was merely a confederation of States tied together by a rope of sand, that would give way upon the slightest friction. They have found out their grand mistake. They know that we have now a government, that we are a nation, and that we are a strong, intelligent, and brave people, capable of judging and knowing our rights, and determined on all occasions to maintain them against either domestic or foreign foes. And that is the explanation of the receptions which you have received through me while I was abroad. Gentlemen, I thank you." *Chicago Inter-Ocean,* Nov. 13, 1879.

On Oct. 6, 7, and 9, Lt. Gen. Philip H. Sheridan, Chicago, had telegraphed and written to USG, San Francisco, care of Maj. Gen. Irvin McDowell. "The Executive Committee of the Chicago Club through the Secretary Mr W. Scott Keith request me to notify you, that at their meeting on Saturday evening they unanimously tendered to you a reception on your visit to this city, in November A copy of its action will be forwarded to you by mail. I would like to be present at this reception, but cannot, unless it would be convenient for you to accept for evening of fourteenth or fifteenth of November, as I am obliged to go to Washington for unveiling of Thomas' Statue If either of those evenings are not convenient, the Club will be ready for any other evening you may designate." LS (press) and ADfS, DLC-Philip H. Sheridan; telegram received (at 6:30 P.M.), DLC-USG, IB. "It gives me great pleasure to be the medium of forwarding to you an invitation from the Chicago Club, concerning which I telegraphed you yesterday, a copy of which telegram is with the invitation herewith enclosed. Should you be pleased to accept this courtesy from the Club I can assure you, as a member of it, an agreeable reception, and a generous and hearty welcome." "After a consultation with Colonel Grant, the Chicago, and Calumet clubs have fixed the following days of November for the receptions accepted by you: Chicago Club, November fourteenth, Calumet Club November Seventeenth, eighteen Seventy nine" LS (press) and ADf, DLC-Philip H. Sheridan. A certificate welcoming USG to the Calumet Club is in the Smithsonian Institution.

On Oct. 29, Frederick Dent Grant, Chicago, wrote to Edwards Pierrepont. "Father & mother will arrive here Nov 12 at about 1 P. M." ALS, Keya Gallery, New York, N. Y. A newspaper reported: "Col. Fred Grant has received a telegram from his father, instructing him to make engagments up to the 18th." *Chicago Daily News,* Nov. 1, 1879.

On Nov. 11, Alfred F. Foll *et al.,* Lena, Ill., wrote to USG "regretting your inability to accept our invitation to pause a few moments amongst us while on your way to Chicago." DS (23 signatures), USG 3. See *Chicago Evening Journal,* Dec. 4, 1879.

Also on Nov. 11, Governor Henry M. Hoyt of Pa. telegraphed to Melville E. Stone, editor, *Chicago Daily News.* "The people of Penna note with pleasure the completion of the circuit around the globe by Gen Grant on his second round by their acclaims

They will arrest him here on a 'Lap' until in Eighteen Eighty one he shall inaugurate as the Chief Magistrate of a nation, the full purposes of a free people & in Eighteen Eighty five sixty millions of us will bid him God speed to the fulfilment of a perfect career" Telegram received (at 9:28 P.M.), USG 3. Eight other governors telegraphed congratulations to USG on his arrival in Chicago. *Ibid.* On the same day, James Longstreet, Gainesville, Ga., telegraphed to the *Daily News.* "I beg leave to congratulate you and the good people of Chicago upon the return of General Grant to your City— Attentions received during his tour around the world were just tributes to the great American soldier statesman and should be remembered with pride and all should express appreciation to the great man safely returned to his native land. We have many Excellent men who most naturally and properly aspire to the highest office of the people but it seems deeply set in their hearts to Enoble the nation by again honoring Grant." Telegram received (at 12:17 P.M.), *ibid.* Also on Nov. 11, U.S. Representative Alexander H. Stephens of Ga. telegraphed to [Stone] expressing "kind regards" toward USG. ". . . His generous, magnanimous and patriotic sentiments, expressed to the ex-Confederates at San Francisco, met a warm response from [t]he breast of millions in this country without regard to sections or those political differences of opinion which led to the late lamentable conflict in arms. That no such differences may ever arise again, should be the earnest desire of every patriot." *Chicago Daily News,* Nov. 12, 1879. On Nov. 12, Robert Toombs, Atlanta, telegraphed to Stone. "Your telegram rec'd. I decline to answer, except to say, Present my personal congratulations to Gen'l. Grant on his safe arrival to his country. hHe fought for his country honorably and won. I fought for mine & lost I am ready to try it over again Death to the Union" Facsimile, *ibid.,* Nov. 22, 1879. See *ibid.,* Nov. 18, 1879. On Nov. 13 and 14, "AN EX-REB" and "AN EX-CONFEDERATE," Chicago, wrote to the editor. "There are a great many ex-Confederate soldiers in Chicago who are desirous of paying their personal respects to Gen. Grant, but whom the different committees seem to have forgotten or ignored in their arrangements. I, as one of them, have a high regard for the man as a soldier, and also on account of his magnanimous treatment of Gen. Lee when he surrendered his sword under that historical tree at Appomattox. Unlike Gen. Toombs, the majority of us in Chicago are reconstructed, and, as I have said, are desirous of paying our respects to the returned hero." ". . . Not an ex-Confederate soldier in Chicago who done duty on the battle-field but honors Grant, and loathes and hates such sentiments as Toombs, the double-dyed traitor, utters. . . ." *Chicago Tribune,* Nov. 14, 15, 1879.

Speech

[*Chicago, Nov. 13, 1879*]

MR. PRESIDENT, AND GENTLEMEN OF THE SOCIETY OF THE ARMY OF THE TENNESSEE AND GUESTS: Notice was sent to me some days ago that I was to respond to a toast here, but I paid no attention to it at the time, and had no idea, until I got here, of the toast that I was to reply to. I had relied upon it that there would be half a dozen or more speakers before I would be called upon, and that during that time there would be a man out in the hall that I would want to see; or that I would execute a flank movement by which I would get out of it. Finding, however, a[f]ter my arrival here, that I was to be the first one called upon, and hardly feeling that it would be proper to look for that man so early in the evening, I made a substitute here myself, but the president of your society has not called upon that man. I know if he had called it as it reads upon his paper, you would have heard much more said about the position of our country among the nations of the earth than I can say [t]o you. I can feel what your mayor probably would have said if the president had ever called upon the name that he sees on his paper.[1]

But as I have to say a word, I shall rely now upon your signifying in a very few moments your disapprobation of what I am saying, so as to let me off.

The president has given notice that we are not to speak any longer than we can hold the audience.

Our nation, we have been in the habit ourselves of looking upon as being one of the first nations of the earth. For a long period back the "Yankee" had not only a respectable opinion of himself individually but of his country as a whole. It has been our own opinion that we had nothing to fear in a contest with another power. I am pleased to say that, from the observations that I have been able to make in the last two years and a half, we are beginning to be regarded a little by other powers as in our vanity we heretofore regarded ourselves. We do, among the nations of the earth to-day, not only in our own conceit, but with the acknowledgment of other nations, occupy the position of one of the first powers in all that goes to make up a great nationality.

We have the strength. We have the individual self-assertion and independence, and we have, to a greater degree than almost any other nation, the power of colonizing, of settling up new country, opening it, and developing it. We have also the very great advantage of being without neighbors to molest or make us afraid.

It is true, we have a northern frontier, and we have a southern frontier, but we get along with a very small army. We keep no standing army, but what little we do, as some one remarked the other day, "It is a standing army because it has no time to sit down." Mr. President, I find you are filling the chair with a good deal of ability.

I do not know anything that I can specially add to what I have said, except in the way of advice, and that is, let us be true to ourselves, avoid all bitterness and ill-feeling, either on the part of sections or parties toward each other. Avoid quarreling among ourselves, and we need have no fear for the future of maintaining the standing that we have taken among the nations so far as opposition from foreign nations goes.

Gentlemen, I am very much obliged to you.

Chicago Times, Nov. 14, 1879. *Report of the Proceedings of the Society of the Army of the Tennessee at the Thirteenth Annual Meeting Held at Chicago,. . .* (Cincinnati, 1885), pp. 418–19. Gen. William T. Sherman presided over a banquet at the Palmer House. USG responded to the first toast of the evening: "Our Country—Her Place Among Nations." See Albert Bigelow Paine, *Mark Twain: A Biography* (New York, 1912), II, 652–57.

Earlier on Nov. 13, 1879, USG spoke at a Union Veteran Club reception at McVicker's Theater. "COMRADES AND FRIENDS OF THE LATE WAR: I was entirely unaware of the object of my coming here this morning. I thought it was to see the place where you were to meet this evening or some other time. I was not aware that I was going to meet so many of my old comrades, but I assure you it affords me very great pleasure to meet you here, and to meet you everywhere. Veterans of the late War to me are companions, and in all my travels I have not been in hardly a country, in hardly a town, or hardly a place in the two and a half years that I have been away from my own country that I have not met some of your number. As we heard last night, wars, while not desirable, are not perhaps unattended with good. We believe sincerely that the War which we waged has been attended with solid good to our country. We believe that our victory redounded to the benefit of the vanquished as well as to ourselves. We believe that they would have been in a very much worse condition than they are now had their cause succeeded, and we certainly would have been infinitly worse off. But wars render another benef[i]t. People who grow up in a time of profound peace are very much accustomed to vegetate and live along in or near the place of their birth; but having been torn away from their homes, as all of you were, they get weaned from their homes, and at the close they seek the best place for the development of their energy and their talents, and in that way the veterans of our War are scattered over all of this broad land, and are now developing our Territories, building railroads, opening mines, opening farms, cultivating the soil over a vast territory which can be made, and is being made, available for the support of man. They have scattered, and are building homes in foreign lands, and opening in that way the commerce of our country; they are making our country felt, and known, and appreciated wherever a flag can float. Now, gentlemen, I have said a great deal more than I had any idea I should say when I came here. And, as Mark Twain very aptly remarked last night, I could make a very much better extemporaneous speech if I had a couple of hours to prepare it in." *Chicago Tribune*, Nov. 14, 1879.

On Nov. 15, USG received a delegation of Mexican War veterans at the home of Frederick Dent Grant. "A very small boy, adorned in a very loud brigade major's uniform—sword, bucklets, spurs, etc.—stepped up to the general, to whom he presented a basket of flowers. . . . [USG] patted the lad on the shoulder, and remarked: 'My military friend, I suppose you will be in the next war with Mexico, when they attempt to annex our country to theirs.'" *Chicago Times*, Nov. 16, 1879. Later, during a reception at the Grand Pacific Hotel, USG greeted a well-wisher. "I have met you before. I met you here in 1866 when I was 'swinging around the circle' with Andy Johnson. I remember it well,—when he nearly forgot what we came out here for,—when he made a political speech. . . . He almost forgot that we came to build a monument." Presented with a badge as president of the Union Veteran Club, USG replied: "I didn't know that I was President still of that organization. . . . I don't know but I ought to be impeached for neglect of duty." *Chicago Tribune*, Nov. 16, 1879.

1. USG had bet Mayor Carter Harrison of Chicago, who was not a scheduled speaker, that Sherman would call on him. ". . . Meanwhile the general had stealthily got possession of President Sherman's paper, and sure enough when the mayor referred to it he found that the general had erased his own name, and inserted that of Harrison. The bet was declared off, and the programme was carried out as Sherman had originally prepared it." *Chicago Times*, Nov. 15, 1879.

To Daniel Ammen

———

CHICAGO, ILLINOIS, Nov. 16th, 1879.

MY DEAR ADMIRAL,—

Your letter of the 12th is just received, and the despatch referred to I have only just seen, although it was probably promptly delivered at the house while I was out.

I do not expect to be east as far as Philadelphia before the 16th of December,—cannot well be, because I have promised to stop a day at Indianapolis, Louisville, Cincinnati, Columbus, and Pittsburg, by the way, and have set December 9th for being in Indianapolis. If Mr. Franco[1] desires to see me before I go East, and it is not too much trouble for him to do so, he might come West and meet me in Chicago. I will be back here as early as the 6th of December. I would be glad to meet him in Galena; but my accommodations there are small and the public accommodations are not attractive.

In regard to the Nicaragua Canal: It seems to me the concession should be made by a treaty between the United States and the Nicaraguan governments, and that there should be an act of incorporation by Congress. The former could be had without trouble or delay. The latter, I think, also might be obtained without trouble, and conditional subscriptions might be taken up without waiting for the concession.

The latter should amount to $100,000,000 before any work is commenced. My idea is that subscribers should receive bonds, interest payable semi-annually, as the money is called for, and on completion of the work should receive stock to the full amount of the bonds. But all this would be determined after the organization of the company.

It is not certain now that I will be in Washington this winter, but make my head-quarters in Philadelphia during my stay in the East.

Mrs. Grant joins me in kindest regards to Mrs. Ammen and the children.

Yours truly,

U. S. Grant.

Daniel Ammen, *The Old Navy and the New* (Philadelphia, 1891), pp. 548–49. On Nov. 13, 1879, a correspondent reported from Chicago. "General Grant received a telegram this morning from Washington of such an important nature as may require his personal attention in the East next week. The telegram is from a personal friend, informing him that he had received this morning from Paris a letter . . . to the effect that the writer of the letter is now on his way across the Atlantic with full assurances of subscriptions amounting to one-third of the capital necessary to construct the Nicaragua Canal, provided General U. S. Grant asks the necessary concession for the Nicaragua grant and becomes the president of the company." The reporter asked USG whether he would accept such a proposal. "I should not like to say I would accept it upon a rumor simply that the money could be raised. I should want to know first that ample subscriptions had been made and that certain concessions had been obtained from the Nicaraguan government." Asked if he favored the Nicaragua route, USG replied. "Yes; it is by far the best. The surveys made while I was President were at my instigation. In fact I instigated the plan indirectly. I tried to get an appropriation for the purpose of carrying out the work, and had I been in office a little longer I think I could have accomplished something." Concerning management of the project, USG said: "I think it should be neutral waters, and that Congress should pass an act assuming some sort of supervision over it, simply to have an eye to its protection, because it is on our continent." Asked whether his acceptance would help to raise money, USG answered: "I am not sure that the French capitalists would be influenced at all by that. At any rate I should want to know authoritatively just what will be done if I consent." USG said the proposal might affect his plans. "I should perhaps go to Cuba for the winter, but I would defer my visit if I could assist this project in any way. I have always felt a great interest in it, and, whether I am an officer in the company or not, shall always aid the accomplishment of the plan in any way I can." *New York Herald*, Nov. 14, 1879. On Nov. 20, Daniel Ammen told a reporter that he had communicated the French proposal to USG. "I have every reason to believe that General Grant will take control of this canal enterprise, provided such a company is organized and sufficient capital is subscribed to insure its success. General Grant will not connect himself with it as long as there is a possibility of its failure. Another of his conditions is that the Nicaraguan Government shall grant the right of way. . . . General Grant thinks we can build the canal for $80,000,000, but my own belief is that the capital stock of the company should not be less than $100,000,000, and then it would be necessary only to call for as much as was needed. The cost cannot be estimated very closely. If we can raise $20,000,000 in this country, the remainder can be procured in England and France without difficulty, provided General Grant will take hold." *Chicago Inter-Ocean*, Nov. 21, 1879. See letter to Edward F. Beale, Nov. 27, 1879.

1. "Señor Thomas de Franco, Minister to Italy from the Republic of Nicaragua, arrived in this city last week, and started yesterday for Washington. Señor de Franco comes directly from Paris, where he has been engaged in working up the Nicaraguan Canal project. It was rumored before he arrived that he was the bearer of pledges from French bankers to subscribe $30,000,000 to the project on condition that General Grant should become president of the company. . . . Señor de Franco said that the question of General Grant's connecting himself with the work will probably be decided when the General comes to Philadelphia on the 17th of December. . . ." *New York Tribune*, Nov. 25, 1879. On Nov. 25, in Washington, D. C., Thomas de Franco said he had "no doubt that Gen. Grant, who is deeply interested in the subject of a canal, would look with favor upon the office, if tendered by a company in which he could have confidence and pride. . . ." Aniceto G. Menocal (civil engineer, U.S. Navy) added that "Gen. Grant will accept the presidency of the Nicaraguan Canal Co. if the right kind of men take hold of it. I have a letter in my pocket from him, received yesterday, in which he says he will accept under such conditions." *Washington Post*, Nov. 25, 1879. On the same day, a correspondent reported from Washington, D. C. "Mr. Thomas De Franco had a long interview with Admiral Ammen to-day in regard to the Nicaragua Canal and the documentary evidence submitted more than confirms previous reports of the willingness of French capitalists to subscribe largely for the stock of the company. . . ." *New York Herald*, Nov. 26, 1879. On Dec. 3, in New York City, de Franco said that if USG accepted the canal co. presidency, "he would be bound to devote himself entirely to the enterprise and would not feel at liberty to engage in political movements. . . . I shall meet him in Philadelphia on the 18th, in company with other friends of the canal project." *New York Tribune*, Dec. 4, 1879. See letter to Elihu B. Washburne, Dec. 22, 1879.

On Feb. 28, 1880, a correspondent reported. "The arrival in Managua is announced of Don J. Tomas De Franco, who is proclaimed as the bearer of important propositions from Gen. Grant and Admiral Ammen, looking to the obtaining of a concession from the Government of Nicaragua. . . ." *New York Times*, March 9, 1880. On April 5, Cornelius A. Logan, U.S. minister, León, Nicaragua, wrote to Secretary of State William M. Evarts. ". . . I have learned that Thomas De Franco has again sailed for the United States, but whether with special powers from the Government or not, I am uninformed. The street report is, that he was summoned by telegram, with the information that his supposed Paris backers had gone over to Lesseps. My advice is, that care be exercised in treating with him, as his general business reputation in Central America, seems none of the best. . . ." LS, DNA, RG 59, Diplomatic Despatches, Central America.

To Edward F. Beale

———

Chicago, Ill.
Nov. 16th 1879.

MY DEAR GEN.

The trunks &c. sent from your house come duly to hand. I should have written before but, as you may have seen from the papers, I have been very busy since my return. I have been pulled nearly to pieces since my arrival here. But the welcome has been most hearty and gratifying. I will be in Phila on the 16th of Dec. and make that my Hd Qrs. until I go some place into winter Qrs. probably in Havana. I hope to see you there. It is doubtful whether I go to Washington at all. If I do go it will be but for a day or two to see you, and in that case Mrs. Grant and I will slip down quietly so that it will not be known until ~~I~~ we get there. But I will see you in Phila and we can talk the matter over. I will expect Ammen up there soon after my arrival and would be glad if you would go at the same time. He will want to talk the Nicaragua Canal project over and I would like you to be present.

Mrs. Grant joins me in best regards to Mrs. Beale and Miss Emily.

Yours Truly
U. S. GRANT

GN. ED F. BEALE.

ALS, DLC-Decatur House Papers.

To John A. Bingham

———

Chicago, Ill.
Nov. 16th 1879.

MY DEAR JUDGE.

Since my arrival at San Francisco my time has been taken up so, day & night, with social matters, in reading and disposing of large amounts of mail matter, &c. that I have had but little time to attending to any thing els. I did however find time to drop you and Mr. Yosheda a line before the departure of the first mail for Japan after my arrival. I fear those letters never reached you. I wrote and directed a large number of letters intending to put stamps on them when I was through. Being called out however before finishing them Mr. Young, or some one, sent them to the post office. I sent afterwards to have stamps put upon the letters but no one in the office seemed to know anything about them.

No doubt you have seen from the American papers the receptions I have rec'd from San Francisco to this place? It has been very flattering but very hard work. I shall always recollect my travels with great gratifications, and no part with more pleasure than my visit to Japan. The unequaled hospitality of the government and the people, the beauty of the country, the progress of her citizens in a new line of civilization, has been a constant source of conversation with me since my return. I can safely say that an interest in Japan and the Japanese has been awakened in this country that was never known before. It is safe to predict that the number of visitors from the U. S. to Japan will multiply very rapidly hence forward.

Please present my kindest regards and well wishes to his Majesty, Cabinet and those with whom I was brought in contact during my visit. Mrs. Grant & the Col. join me in kindest regards to you, Mrs Bingham and family.

Yours Truly
U. S. GRANT

ALS, Milton Ronsheim, Cadiz, Ohio.

To John Russell Young

———

Chicago, Ill.
Nov. 16th 1879.

MY DEAR COMMODORE.

This chapter is not just what I would like to make it if you were here to make the alterations. But I have not the time to make the changes I would like. I will be in Phila about the 16th of Dec. and if it is not then published if your brother will bring it to me I will go over it with him and make suggestions which will insure it from any just criticism.

I wrote you from Galena inclosing a letter from Denny. Did you get it? I thought the letter would interest you. It was addressed to you at the Herald Office.

I have been kept so busy here that I have not had time for even the necessary sleep. It will continue so until I get back to Galena. The turn out of people, decorations &c. were much the same as in San Francisco. The roads the day of my arrival brought in from the country 100.000 people.

I am sorry you go to Europe; but you know your own business best. I hope there will be such a turn in affairs as to bring you back into a perfectly independent position.

With the respects of Mrs. Grant, Fred & myself, I am

Very Truly Yours

U. S. Grant

J. R. Young, Esq.

ALS, DLC-John Russell Young.
On Nov. 19, 1879, John Russell Young, New York City, wrote to Julia Dent Grant. "I have been intending to write you ever since I came home.—But you have been overwhelmed with care and ceremony and I felt that not to trouble you would be a kindness. I am sorry,—that I could not go to Chicago. But since I came home, business matters arising out of my father's death, and the closing of my book have absorbed all my time. I found Mrs Young very well, and the baby pretty and thriving.—Mrs Young wants me to thank you for all the good care you took of me, and would write you herself.—Mrs Bright is very well, and talks of her Spanish trip as the dream of a lifetime. I have seen a good many people since I came home, and I have felt often like sitting down and writing you a wicked letter about all the humbugs I see. But it would do no good, although I do wish Pierrepoint would get a better preparation of dye for his whiskers.—My book is done, and should be out by Christmas. It will make two volumes, and I had to cut out 200 pages and leave out what I had written. I have cancelled and rewritten the pages in the early parts where some one in my absence made blunders, and I would like to have done more.—You see I have beaten Badeau.—who makes a great blunder not to hurry his work out. I send you a batch of odds and ends from the newspapers.—It may be that you have seen some of them before,—But if not, it will give you an idea of the drift of sentiment in the country for and against the General. I give you *both* sides, and it may interest you in your far Galena home.—Tomorrow I go to Wn and hope to see the face of the great and good R. B. Hayes.—Excuse my paper [bu]t I want some for the extracts;. . ." AL, WHi. The newspaper clippings, mostly undated, are *ibid.*

Speech

——

[*Chicago, Nov. 18, 1879*]

It is a pleasant sight to see what is so common in America, and, I am afraid, not so common in any other country—to see the destitute children provided for as they are in this country, where they not only are taken care of, but are taught and brought up as well as favored children with good parents. Where it is a matter of law simply to provide by taxation a home for the destitute, and they are looked to by officials appointed with a salary, it is true starvation is kept from overtaking them and that they are furnished homes. But their morals and their education are neglected, and their condition more resembles that of prisoners than of children being brought up to become suitable members of society. This institution, like others of its kind in the country, will serve to bring these little children up as useful members of society, and for that they will be ever grateful in their future lives to you and to the charitable people who support you without an enaction of law to compel support by taxation.

Chicago Tribune, Nov. 19, 1879. USG spoke at the Protestant Orphan Asylum. Earlier, USG received a delegation of four War of 1812 veterans at the home of Frederick Dent Grant. One of the veterans criticized conditions in the South. USG replied: "Oh, we'll get along all right down there when a new generation springs up and when we begin to have a little prosperity in the South." *Ibid.*

On Nov. 17, 1879, USG addressed students at Chicago's Exposition Building. "I am always glad to be received by the school children. Receptions of the same kind took place at San Francisco and elsewhere. It is the condition of our future success to secure general education. With education universal there need be no apprehension of danger to our country in the future. Without education I should despair of the future of the republic." *Chicago Inter-Ocean*, Nov. 18, 1879. USG and Julia Dent Grant returned to Galena on Nov. 19.

To Adam Badeau

——

Galena, Ill.
Nov. 21st 1879.

MY DEAR GENERAL.

I have just read the inclosed and see nothing to suggest in the way of change except there are three or four typographical errors which you will correct. I have no one with me now and have consequently mail enough to keep about six hours a day reading and answering such as must be answered. You must be satisfied therefore with a very unsatisfactory letter. There is one omission I would suggest in the notes to the first chapter here returned. I doubt the policy of giving Butler's intention to hang McClellan in a certain contingency.[1] He might deny it and your Authority for the statement—Rawlins—is dead.

The papers have probably kept you posted as to the manner of receptions I have had since my arrival in San Franc[isco.] They have been very flatter[ing.] I go East so as to reach Phila on the 16th of Dec. I will remain there until I go to take up winter quarters. My present intention is to go to Havana & the City of Mexico and return to Galena about the last of Apl. next year. In this case I will not meet you on your arrival.[2] But you can get your book out just as well without me. I think you can not get it out too soon after your return to America. It will be the most authentic book published on the war, and I think the most truthful history—except what you say about me—published this many a day.

Mrs. Grant joins me in kindest regards and well wishes for you.

Very Truly yours
U. S. Grant

Gn. A. Badeau,

ALS, Munson-Williams-Proctor Institute, Utica, N. Y. About this time, USG wrote to Badeau. "I neglected to inclose this in my last letter. I gave your summing up of Thomas' characteristics to the press thinking it appropriate as the Society of the Army of the Cumberland were about meeting in Washington to unveil the Equestrian Statue to his memory. All well" ALS, *ibid.* The Society of the Army of the Cumberland met Nov. 19–20, 1879.

1. "In 1864, at the time of the Presidential election when McClellan was a candidate against Lincoln, disturbances were apprehended in New York by the Government, and General Butler was send to that city to assist in maintaining the public peace. No disorder occurred, but General Rawlins told me shortly afterward that Butler had intended, in case of a riot, to send out to Orange where McClellan was living, and have him tried by a drum-head court-martial for inciting treason, and if found guilty, he meant to hang him at once. I have, as General Grant said, no authority for this statement but Rawlins's declaration that Butler had so assured him. Acting upon Grant's advice I did not give it a place in my history." *Badeau*, pp. 520–21.

2. See *ibid.*, p. 521.

To Virginia Grant Corbin

Galena, Ill.
Nov. 23d /79

DEAR SISTER:

The boxes you sent we found safely here on our return from Chicago four days ago. I should have written to you at once but my mails take up day and night, to a late hour, to read and answer.

We leave here for the East on the 3d of Dec. We will stop six days however in Chicago, and make stops at other places, so that we will not be in Phila until the sixteenth. The programme marked out will keep me three or four days in Phila before I can go anywhere. But as soon as I can I will run over—probably in the night train from Washington—and spend the day with you without it being known if possible. When we go to New York City, a few days later, Julia and I can both go over and spend the day and have you come and spend the day with us sometimes too. We expect to stay with Buck.

Bella leaves us when we go East. Julia wants to ask if she can get Anna, the girl you spoke of before we left, in her place. She would expect to pay her $15 00 pr. month. You will know what her work will be. We expect to go to Havana Cuba & Mexico for the winter so that she will have a fine opportunity to travel. Kitty Felt goes with us.

I hope this will find Mr Corbin much better than when you wrote.[1] I want to go over quiety to your house the first time so as not to be interrupted. If it is known that I am there people will be coming so that I will not get to talk to you and mother any.

Love to all of you. Julia asks if you will make enquiries about the girl and let her know what she says.

Truly &c
U. S. GRANT

MRS. JENNIE CORBIN.

ALS, Nellie C. Rothwell, La Jolla, Calif.

1. Abel R. Corbin died March 28, 1880. See *New York Times*, March 29, 1880.

To Newland T. DePauw

GALENA, ILL., Nov. 25th, 1879.

DEAR SIR—I fear I have not made myself entirely understood in regard to visiting New Albany. Before receiving your first letter or any letter from New Albany, I had accepted an invitation from Indianapolis, and one from Louisville. I am to be in the former city on the 9th, and the latter on the 10th of December. As I go to Cincinnati on the 11th, it will be impossible for me to stop at New Albany unless it is taken on the way between Indianapolis and Louisville. A committee of citizens of the latter city, appointed by the mayor, accompany me from Indianapolis. Any arrangement they may make for stopping at New Albany will be agreeable to me. I will be very glad if arrangements can be made to stop, even for a short time, at New Albany, but I fear it cannot be done.

Very truly yours,
U. S. GRANT.

New Albany Ledger-Standard, Nov. 28, 1879. Newland T. DePauw, son of New Albany, Ind., industrialist Washington C. DePauw, served as secretary of a committee appointed to welcome USG. See letter to Bela C. Kent, Nov. 7, 1879; *PUSG*, 25, 251–52.

To Eustace S. Morrow

GALENA, ILL., November 25, 1879.

E. S. Morrow, Esq, City Clerk:

DEAR SIR: Your letter of the 13th of November, enclosing a copy of the resolution passed by the Councils of Pittsburgh inviting me to visit your city, was duly received. I do not remember whether it has been formally acknowledged or not, but I believe it is understood that I had accepted. I take great pleasure now in saying that I expect to go from Columbus, Ohio, to Pittsburgh on Saturday, December 13th, and to remain there until the following Monday, leaving Pittsburgh in time to reach Harrisburg about dark of that day. Respectfully, &c.,

U. S. GRANT.

Pittsburgh Commercial Gazette, Nov. 28, 1879.

To Adolph E. Borie

———

Galena, Ill.
Nov. 26th /79

MY DEAR MR. BORIE

I was sorry you did not get out to Chicago with Drexel & Childs. They seemed to enjoy their trip and I know you would have done so also. They both invited Mrs. Grant & I to make their houses our home during our stay in Phila and I have yours & Mrs Borie's standing invitation. But I thought it would be better on this occasion to go to a public house.[1] I probably will be going out very much through the day & night, and when in the house receiving so many calls as to make it unpleasant for a private family. You had better finish up your travels now while you are young & go with us to Cuba & Mexico.

Mrs. Grant joins me in love to you and Mrs. Borie.

I received your letter a day or two ago and read nearly the whole of it the first trial almost like print. You must be getting much better.

yours Truly
U. S. GRANT

ALS, PHi.

On Dec. 15, 1879, Adolph E. Borie spoke about USG to a reporter at his Philadelphia home. "He's the most modest great man I ever met. Tennyson once spoke of the Duke of Wellington as being 'in his simplicity sublime.' Now, I never knew the Duke of Wellington, and I never happened to be acquainted with any one who did. I know General Grant, and that phrase of Tennyson's describes him exactly. Why, I've seen him blush like a school-boy, clear up to his ears, at the receptions tendered him in Europe. Adulation has no effect on him whatever. In that respect he is nothing less than a wonder. Day by day, as our acquaintance continues, new phases of his character are developed that challenge my respect and esteem, and I love him more and more." Borie also discussed USG's plans. "The General to-day has an income of about ten thousand a year. I happen to know this, because I've often talked the matter over with him. He would like to control some corporation, as I said in June on my return from traveling with him, and as was reported in the papers of Philadelphia at the time. Now he don't want any fifty thousand dollars a year salary, and the reports circulated to that effect are untrue. As a matter of necessity he has no need of work at all. What he wants is something to occupy his mind." Asked whether USG would accept a presidential nomination, Borie replied: "That's hard to tell. I don't imagine he could answer it himself. The way it looks now he will be forced—that's the word, forced—to accept it. For the General's sake I sincerely trust that matters will not take that turn, but there's no telling. If he is nominated he will be elected, and if he is elected it will be the General and not the people who will suffer by the bargain." *Philadelphia Press*, Dec. 16, 1879. Borie spoke to another reporter concerning USG. ". . . In regard to my appointment in the Cabinet, I wrote a letter at once declining the appointment. Mr. Stuart told me it was my duty to see the General, and he called with me. It was a surprise, and I found that the President had not told one of them any more than he told me. I told him I did not consider that I knew enough about the navy and naval affairs to fill the position. He said that was all nonsense; that I knew about ships and one thing and another. Still I persisted until he told me he would appoint Admiral Porter as my assistant. There was no Assistant Secretary of the Navy at that time. He asked me to take it for a little while and see if things went on comfortably, and if I still persisted in it and desired not to remain he would appoint somebody else. It was perfectly unexpected, going into that Cabinet. . . ." *Philadelphia Times*, Dec. 17, 1879. See *PUSG*, 19, 145–46, 200–202.

On Nov. 28, Hamilton Fish had written to George W. Childs, Philadelphia, accepting an invitation to meet USG in Philadelphia. ALS (press), DLC-Hamilton Fish.

1. On his visit to Philadelphia, USG stayed at the Continental Hotel. Proprietor J. E. Kingsley recounted meeting USG during the war. "He had Mrs. Grant with him and he walked in that side-door and up to the counter to register. I saw a man with his body bent forward and his toes and knees pointed toward each other, as if he stood on the balls of his feet or had lived in stirrups. His uniform contained the stars of a high officer, but was a very seedy uniform, worn and whitened like a farmer who had ploughed in his regimentals. . . . He went out to take a walk, and after a while I saw him come in, followed by a swarm of people, who filled up the lobby here. Said I: 'General, they have found you out.' 'Yes, Mr. Kingsley;' he answered, 'can't I go somewhere to eat a few oysters quietly?' I took him into the private office, convenient to the restaurant-car, and he sat down there and began to talk and lunch. I put several questions to him and found he was more of a man of information than he looked. I saw that there was mettle in him. He has ever since stopped with me in Philadelphia, except when he has gone to a private house." *Philadelphia Press*, Dec. 16, 1879.

To Alfred H. Love

GALENA, Ill., Nov. 26, 1879.—Alfred H. Love, President Universal Peace Union—Dear Sir: Your letter of the 18th of Nov., asking if I can give your Society an evening or an hour during my visit to Philadelphia, only reached me yesterday. It will afford me much pleasure to comply with your request. The time can be better arranged after my arrival in Philadelphia, and had better be fixed for the day time. It is probable the few evenings I expect to be in Philadelphia, before going to New York city, are already assigned.

With many thanks for the kind expressions in your letter, I am,

With great respect,

U. S. GRANT.

Philadelphia Public Ledger, Dec. 1, 1879. Born in 1830 to Philadelphia Quakers, Alfred H. Love refused to serve in the army or to hire a substitute during the Civil War. He founded the Universal Peace Union in 1866. On Nov. 18, 1879, Love, Philadelphia, wrote to USG, Chicago. "Many of your friends who are not connected with military companies, and who do not seek political positions, desire to testify their appreciation of your eminent services in behalf of peace. You will recollect our pleasant communications while you were in office, and we will never forget the encouragement you gave us in your first inaugural address, and then on frequent occasions for the Indian peace policy, the arbitrations with foreign Powers, the care of the Modoc children, and similar peaceful movements, and while abroad your excellent remarks at Birmingham, England, and in China and Japan. Can you give us an evening or an hour or two when you visit this city? Our reception would be comparatively a plain one and yet a very sincere one. When you come to this city next month you will see the same familiar military display. Already the Academy of Music is planned, so that every person admitted to the desirable seats must be in uniform. We have formed an opinion that you care less for this grand display than for the sincere friendship and welcome home again of your true friends. Not that the same feeling may not animate all, but if you can give your peace friends the opportunity to meet you and to refer to those noblest acts of your life, which have advanced the cause of Christian civilization, we shall be pleased to be informed at your earliest convenience. Lucretia Mott and some of the veterans in the cause of liberty and peace still remain with us, and Philadelphia seems a proper place for a meeting of those who love the highest purposes of our lives, and if less formal and less ostentatious, equally genuine and appreciative." *Philadelphia Press*, Dec. 2, 1879. See Speech, [*Dec. 26, 1879*]; *Voice of Peace*, VI, 11 (Feb., 1880); *PUSG*, 23, 159, 271; *ibid.*, 24, 202–3; *ibid.*, 25, 430–31.

To Horace Porter

———

Galena, Ill.
Nov. 26th /79

MY DEAR GENERAL,

I have been intending to write you a long letter when ever I could get time. But I get about sixty letters a day, most of them

requiring answers, and as many papers as almost any country journal; so I dispair of getting the time. I will have to put off what I
want to say until I meet you in New York or some place else. I will
be there about the 20th or 22d.

You have no doubt seen then I intend going to Cuba & Mexico for the Winter! My party will consist of Mrs. Grant and myself, Miss Felt[1] and a man from the Inter-Ocean[2] who will act
as my private sec. We hope to get off near the 1st of Jan.y /80. I
did intend to sail from New York direct to Havana; but I do not
know now but we will go by rail to Fla. and take a steamer across
from there. Gen. Butterfield[3] writes me that he is part owner of
a Steamer in the South that we can have for the trip from Fla. to
Cuba.

I have written to Badeau returning him the chapters he
last submitted. I suggested no change except the omition from
the notes of Butlers design to hang Gn McClellan if there had
been election riots at the time he—Butler—was sent from City
Point to New York City for temporary duty during the elections. Rawlins, Badeaus authority for the statement, is dead,
and if B should deny it it would place Badeau in an unpleasant
position.[4]

With kindest regards to Mrs. Porter & the boys,

yours Truly

U. S. GRANT

GN. HORACE PORTER

ALS, Horace Porter Mende, Zurich, Switzerland.

1. Katherine (Kitty) Felt, born about 1847, was the eldest daughter of Lucius S.
and Katherine Felt of Galena.

2. Born in 1852 in Wis., Byron Andrews graduated from Hobart College in 1875,
moved to Chicago, and entered journalism. In 1879, Andrews visited Mexico as secretary to an American industrial deputation.

3. In 1869, USG had appointed Col. Daniel Butterfield as asst. treasurer, New
York City. Ousted after the gold panic scandal, Butterfield resigned from the army in
1870 to resume a career in railroads, steamships, and real estate. See *PUSG*, 10, 60;
ibid., 16, 74–75; *ibid.*, 19, 258–59.

4. See letter to Adam Badeau, Nov. 21, 1879.

To Edward F. Beale

———

Galena, Ill.
Nov. 27th /79

MY DEAR GENERAL,

Your letter of the 24th is received. It is my intention to visit Cuba & Mexico this Winter. I shall go to Cuba first, and some time in Feb.y leave there for Vera Cruz & the City of Mexico. Now that the Mexican Minister has been kind enough to make the enquiry will you please inform him of my intentions, and thank him for his thinking to make the enquiry. Our party will consist of four persons beside two servants. I will have a sec. with me and Mrs. Grant take a lady friend from here, Miss Felt.

I wrote to Ammen at the same time I wrote to you, sending the letter to the Navy Dept. A letter just received from him would indicate that he had not rec'd it at the time of writing.— Will you tell Ammen that I think the "Act of Incorporation" he has drawn out is exactly the right thing. If he would submit it to Senator Edmunds he would advise him if any change was necessary, and whether the names of incorporators should be inserted before action by Congress could be taken. Also whether it would not do to name a few of the American Corporaters and leave the European names to be filled in after. The Concession might be agreed upon with Mr. Francho & have it submitted to the Nicaraguan Govt. All this arranged and $100.000.000, millions subscribed I think one pr. ct. of the subscription would be sufficient to call for at first. This sum would defray the expenses of the preliminary surveys before commencing work, and other expenses of organization.

Very Truly yours
U. S. GRANT

GN. E. F. BEALE

ALS, DLC-Decatur House Papers. See letters to Daniel Ammen, Nov. 16, Dec. 5, 1879; Gerald Thompson, *Edward F. Beale & The American West* (Albuquerque, 1983), pp. 215–19.

To Rutherford B. Hayes

———

Galena, Ill.
Nov. 30th 1879.

My Dear Mr. President,

Your kind letter of the 25th, inviting Mrs. Grant & myself to visit you, or be your guests, while we are in Washington, and saying that you see it announced we are to be there about the 16th or 18th, was duly received. It is now very doubtful whether I shall ~~now~~ be in Washington at all this Winter. If I am it will be but for a single day, and that after the 1st of Jan.y. I go to Cuba early in Jan.y and may go through by rail to Fla. In that case I should probably pass through Washington and stop over one day. But I had previously accepted an invitation to stay with Gen. Beale—who lives on La Fayette Square, near the Ex. Mansion—if I go. I hope therefore you will excuse me, particularly as you will be so crouded at that time; for keeping my former engagement.

I am very desirous of seeing you and the Sec. of state before leaving the country again, and hope I may have the opportunity of doing so.[1] With many thanks for your kind invitation,

Sincerely Yours
U. S. Grant

His Excellency R. B. Hayes
Pres. of the United States.

ALS, OFH.
On Nov. 16, 1879, John Russell Young, New York City, had written to John Hay. "I know of nothing that has rejoiced me more than your appointment as Ass't Sec'y State. I wish you all success in your office, and I have no doubt of that, because I know you will have ~~an~~ a brilliant and enviable career.—There is one department of our service abroad that will merit your attention,—the service in China and Japan and Siam. We have great interests in those countries and they are paralyzed by a degraded public service. General Grant said to me that one of the reasons why he was anxious to go to Wn was to talk with Mr Hayes & Mr Evarts on the subject. Mosby should be supported to the utmost. . . ." ALS, RPB. On Dec. 16, Young, London, again wrote to Hay. "I note in *The Times* that your people have made 'Owen Denny' Consul General in Shaghae. This, means, of course, O. N. Denny, now at Tientsin. I want to congratulate you on the appointment. We have no better man in our service.—I have seen more of China and Japan, than any American now living except Gen. Grant. I mean by this, that I was brought into close

and friendly relations with all the leading men in China and Japan.—I came away profoundly convinced that we had no diplomacy worth half as much, for our own interests,
as what opened to us in these two nations. We have thrown away many chances by our
bad appointments, and I never heard Gen Grant grieve over anything so much, as over
what he learned in China, As he said in his Shanghae speech he wished he had known
ten years ago what he knew now.—These statesmen are all—I do not know an exception,—anxious to throw themselves into the arms of the U. S. They dread Russia and
England.—We are the only power whose ~~views~~ wishes would be respected by them, the
only power that ~~they~~ European nations would fear.—And a wise, firm, friendly policy
would make America dominant from Singapore to Hakodadi.—The three points where
we want strong men are Bangkok, Yokahama, & Peking,—beyond all things Peking.—I
spoke of this to Mr Evarts & the President. It was as much the desire to do this as anything else that carried me to Wn—You will find Gen. Grant very earnest on the subject.
I could bore your life out on this theme if I had no pity for you.—Peking is the most important place in the gift of the President, for the good that can be done. Burlingame saw
this, and if he had lived he would have changed the face of Asiatic politics. . . ." ALS, *ibid.*
On Dec. 4, President Rutherford B. Hayes had nominated Owen N. Denny as consul
gen., Shanghai. See letter to Adolph E. Borie, June 6, 1879.

    1. On Dec. 26, in Philadelphia, USG met Hayes at the home of John Welsh. On
Dec. 27, Saturday, Hayes wrote to Lucy Webb Hayes. "A most agreeable talk with
General Grant for two hours alone. He looks well and is in excellent spirits. He will go
to Washington today, and *said he would call on you*—probably Monday, but if Sunday,
the ushers will of course admit him." Charles Richard Williams, ed., *Diary and Let-
ters of Rutherford Birchard Hayes* (Columbus, 1922–26), III, 583. See Ari Hoogenboom,
Rutherford B. Hayes: Warrior & President (Lawrence, Kan., 1995), p. 416; letter to Elihu
B. Washburne, Feb. 2, 1880.

To James B. Campbell

Galena, Ill.
Dec. 2d /79

JAS. B. CAMPBELL, ESQ;
DEAR SIR.

    I have your letter of the 28th of Nov. and note contents. I have
no Autograph of Mr. Lincoln save those attached to commissions.

    The address officials of Japan would give their Emperor I can
not give you, but anything addressed to the Minister of Foreign
Affairs, for the Emperor, Tokeo, Japan, would reach him.

Very Truly
U. S. GRANT

ALS (facsimile), eBay, May 18, 2003.

To Hamilton Fish, Jr.

———

Galena, Ill.
Dec. 2d 79

Hon. Hamilton Fish, Jr.
My Dear sir

I have your letter of the 28th of Nov. suggesting that the 26th or 29th of Dec.—probably the latter—would be convenient days to have me go to New York. The 29th will suit me quite well. But since I wrote to you last[1] an invitation has been sent to me to accept a special car to Key West, Fla. & passage from there to Havana, to leave New York, Phila or Washington about the 26th or 27th of Dec. If I accept this I will not go to New York before my return next spring. On the whole I think it is better to defer going until that time.

If anything should detain me so as to make it necessary to go to New York I will inform you as soon as I am made aware of it.

Please remember Mrs. Grant & me kindly to the Governor & Mrs. Fish.

Very Truly Yours
U. S. Grant

ALS, ICarbS. On Dec. 6, 1879, Hamilton Fish, Jr., New York City, wrote to USG, Chicago. "Your kind letter of the 27th ult. gave reason to hope that the Legislative Committee might have the honor to expect you in New-York about the 24th inst., and I accordingly convened the committee this morning. In the meantime, your letter of Dec. 2, in which you intimate that your acceptance of the special car to Key West will not allow you to visit New-York until your return from the West Indies next Spring, reached me, and was read to the committee. The committee desire above all things to consult your convenience, and are anxious to perform the agreeable duty devolved upon them by the Legislature. The members reside in different portions of the State, and some notice would be necessary to bring them together. We shall, therefore, suppose that your visit to New-York is deferred. Should your arrangements, however, undergo a change, I have to request, on behalf of the committee, such notification (if possible, by telegraph,) as will be convenient to you, and will afford sufficient time to make all the necessary preparations for your visit to New-York." *New York Times*, Dec. 7, 1879. On Dec. 5, a correspondent in Philadelphia had quoted from a "private letter received to-day from Gen. Grant." "I expect to get to New-York a day or two before Christmas, and will remain there a day or two after. . . . I have an offer of a special train to Florida and a steamer thence to Havana, which I think I shall accept, but this will depend upon other matters when I reach Philadelphia." *Ibid.*, Dec. 6, 1879.

On Dec. 6, a report stated that USG had accepted an invitation from John P. Newman to preside over a meeting to promote a world's fair in New York City for 1883. USG "replied by letter, the greater part of which was personal to Dr. Newman. He wrote that he took a great interest in the work undertaken by the World's Fair Committee, and would do all in his power to aid in making it a success. . . . He only asked that the World's Fair Committee should consult with the legislative committee as to time." *New York Tribune*, Dec. 6, 1879. See Remarks, [*Jan. 14, 1881*].

On Dec. 1, Mayor James Howell of Brooklyn had written to USG. "Intelligence has been communicated of your intention to visit the City of New-York some time during the present month, and that the authorities of that City purpose on that occasion to afford to its citizens an opportunity to give expression to their cordial respect toward you. I have the honor to ask you (provided it can be found convenient) to extend your visit to the City of Brooklyn, in order that our people may enjoy in an informal way a like opportunity of offering you their respects." *New York Times*, Dec. 10, 1879. On Dec. 6, Frederick Dent Grant, Chicago, wrote to Howell. "Gen. Grant directs me to write and thank you for your kind invitation to visit Brooklyn, but will be unable to do so this Winter." *Ibid.* On the same day, Frederick Grant wrote to John F. Henry, New York City. "I am directed by my father to say that it will be impossible for him to visit New York and Brooklyn this winter. He thanks you very much for your invitation." *New York Herald*, Dec. 10, 1879. On Dec. 10, USG, Columbus, Ind., wrote to Mayor Henry J. Yates of Newark. "I feel that I cannot make further engagements until after my arrival in Philadelphia. It is my desire to leave for Cuba at as early a day as possible." *Ibid.*, Dec. 11, 1879.

1. At about this time, USG wrote to [*Fish, Jr.*]. "P. S. I was glad to receive the Governors welcome letter during my stay in San Francisco. I was kept so busy while there that I could not answer any of the congratulatory letters I received, but I should have answered his.—Please present Mrs. Grants and my best regards to the Governor and Mrs. Fish. We shall hope to to see much of them when we get to the city." ALS (undated fragment), USGA.

To John R. Goodrich

———

GALENA, Ill., Dec. 2. [*1879*]—JOHN R. GOODRICH, President Merchants' Association, Milwaukee—*Dear Sir:* I am in receipt of the very kind invitation of the chamber of commerce and Merchants' association of your city to have me visit it on my return to the United States in May or June next, and to be the guest of the people during my stay. It will give me great pleasure to accept this invitation if I am so situated at the time as to be able to. I hope to return to Galena about the 1st of May next, and if so will be able to allow the citizens of Milwaukee to fix their own time for my visit, not later than about the 10th of June. Thanking the citizens of Milwaukee for their very kind invitation, I am, very sincerely, yours,

U. S. GRANT.

Chicago Times, Dec. 6, 1879. On Nov. 26, 1879, Mayor John Black of Milwaukee and other civic leaders, including John R. Goodrich, wholesale grocer, met to invite USG to visit the city in June, 1880. "A committee of six was appointed to tender the invitation and it was understood that efforts would be made to have the soldiers' reunion occur at the time of the reception." *Milwaukee Sentinel*, Nov. 27, 1879.

On Dec. 31, 1879, Dexter N. Kasson, Milwaukee, telegraphed to USG care of Edward F. Beale, Washington, D. C. "The soldiers of Wisconsin, and Merchants Association and Chamber of Commerce of this City desire to unite in tendering to you a reception in the City of Milwaukee, and in order that the soldiers of the State may be advised of the time we respectfully desire you to fix the date on which you will make the visit, if you can conveniently do so. . . . If General Grant has left Washington will General Beale please forward." Copy (telegram sent), WHi. On the same day, Ulysses S. Grant, Jr., Washington, D. C., telegraphed to Kasson. "Genl Grant has started for Florida telegram forwarded by mail" Telegram received (at 3:11 P.M.), *ibid.* On Jan. 4, 1880, Frederick Dent Grant, Fernandina, Fla., wrote to Kasson. "Your telegrame to Genl Grant dated Dec 31 just received. Genl Grant directs me to say that he will not be in the north west for so long atime that it is impossible for him to make any engagements now for that time. He will return to Galena about the middle of next May if you will communicate with him then & it is possible for him to go to Milwaukee he it will afford him great pleasure to meet the old soldiers there" ALS, *ibid.* On Jan. 6, Grant, Jr., New York City, telegraphed to Kasson. "Telegram addressed to Jacksonville with request to forward would reach General Grant" Telegram received, *ibid.* On the same day, Kasson telegraphed to USG, Jacksonville, Fla. "The soldiers of Wisconsin have decided to hold a reunion during the summer of 1880 and desire to unite with our Merchants Association and Chamber of Commerce in tendering you a reception during the reunion. In order that the soldiers of the State may be advised of the time we respectfully request you to fix the date on which you will make the visit, if you can conveniently do so. We intend to go into camp for one week" Copy (telegram sent), *ibid.* On Jan. 12, Grant, Jr., Brooklyn, telegraphed to Kasson. "General is not likely to be back before middle may" Telegram received (at 6:20 P.M.), *ibid.* See *Milwaukee Sentinel*, Dec. 31, 1879, Jan. 9, 14, 1880; letter to Roscoe Conkling, June 10, 1880.

Speech

[*Chicago, Dec. 4, 1879*]

I am glad to receive the ministers of the various denominations of Christians here this morning. I thank you for this cordial welcome. I am not able to respond to the words that I have heard, for they were entirely unexpected to me. But I can say that I have always believed, and now believe, that nations as well as individuals, that act on other principles than those of right and justice, receive punishment. The great conflict which we have gone through with, and to which you have referred, was a punishment for national sins that had to come sooner or later in some shape, and probably in blood. But, fortunately, it ended by leaving us a nation, and one that will last many generations, and that will work out finally all that is wrong in it now. I thank you for your kind words.

Chicago Times, Dec. 5, 1879. Edward P. Goodwin, First Congregational Church, introduced USG to Chicago clergy gathered at the home of Frederick Dent Grant. Before the speeches, USG "conversed freely" with Ezra M. Boring, Methodist elder. "Both were boys in Georgetown, O., together. . . . Mrs. Boring and Gen. Grant went to school together, recited in the same classes, and have often slided down hill together on the same hand-sled. The general said in his conversation, on yesterday, to Elder Boring, that Georgetown was a place which united many extremes. It had some of the most ardent supporters of the union during the war, and some of its most bitter foes. The Methodist minister there used to preach the worst kind of treason, and there was hardly a time during the struggle when Jeff Davis would not have received more votes for the presidency than Mr. Lincoln." *Ibid.* After the reception, USG spoke at length with Goodwin and several others about Japan and China. *Ibid.* See *Chicago Tribune*, Dec. 5, 1879.

On Dec. 6, 1879, USG planted an elm tree in South Park, Chicago. "Mr. Commissioner: I perform the task which has been allotted to me with great pleasure, and hope that in my future visit to your magnificent park I may see the tree which I am now about to plant growing and flourishing, and that in its growth it may be symbolical of the growth and prosperity of your magnificent city." *Chicago Inter-Ocean*, Dec. 8, 1879.

Also on Dec. 6, President J. W. Doane of the Chicago Commercial Club introduced USG during a banquet at the Grand Pacific Hotel. USG replied. "Mr. President, and Gentlemen of the Chicago Commercial Club and Guests: The allusions of your president to myself have been very gratifying on the whole; and the assurances that he has held out to me, that if I would settle among you, that I can receive the unanimous vote of this club for its presidency, is the most tempting offer that I have had yet. I have read of numerous places having been cut out for me before; but this is the only one that I have had any assurance of. But in this case, even, I am somewhat embarrassed. My understanding, before coming here this evening, was that to become a member of this club a man had to represent some industry or other—some one of the great industries which have made our country so great and so prosperous. And I am at a loss really to know where I should come in. I do see here one or two of the 'ring' that have been referred to—that Galena ring—who, I believe, have the honor of being enrolled as members of this club. How they got in is equally puzzling to me. Gentlemen, I thank you very heartily for the honor you have done me, not only in this kind offer you have made to locate me in the honorable and responsible place, but for the way you have received me on the whole." *Chicago Times*, Dec. 7, 1879. Those in attendance with Galena roots included Elihu B. Washburne, J. Russell Jones, and Henry Corwith. Other speakers included Horace Porter.

To Daniel Ammen

CHICAGO, ILLINOIS, Dec. 5th, 1879.

MY DEAR ADMIRAL,—

I have received all of your letters, and noted their contents. Pierrepont has also written me in connection with Canal matters. He probably informed you of my answer. I have not heard whether I am to expect Mr. De Franco here or not. I rather hope now I will not; my time will be so taken up with engagements from this until Tuesday morning [1]—when I leave here—that I fear I should be able to give him little time. However, if he comes I will manage to see him. I presume nothing can be done this winter to prevent my carrying out my plan of visiting Cuba and Mexico. The charter for a canal, and subscriptions can be raised without my presence. These obtained, a thorough survey of the route, and estimates of labor and costs, are the next things. I agree with you that a thorough survey of the Panama route should be made at the same time. If it should be the best route, it should be adopted. If it is not, it will be worth while to have the fact demonstrated, to stop all . . . at first. One million seems to me enough to commence the surveys with. The government, too, should furnish facilities from the navy,—in vessels, etc.,—to reduce the cost of surveys very materially.

I think now I will not go to New York before my return in the spring. This will give me time for work, if any should be necessary, in Philadelphia, before my departure. . . .

P. S.—Since writing this, I have received yours of the 3d of December, hence retain your draft of incorporation.

Daniel Ammen, *The Old Navy and the New* (Philadelphia, 1891), pp. 549–50. Ellipses represent text lost by a clipped signature.

On Dec. 8, 1879, Thomas J. Sizer, Buffalo, wrote to USG. "I write you on the subject of a ship-canal across the American isthmus; not because I am ignorant of the interest which, as president, you manifested in the subject, nor because I doubt your superior opportunities, your inclination, or your ability, to understand it; but only because, having made both the subject of canals and that of republican government studies for years, I am strongly impressed by the conviction that this is a critical moment for this great enterprise, especially as it relates to our country, and because, also, I consider patriotism and republicanism your dominant characteristics, and that you, personally, may, perhaps, now hold the key to the destiny of our country, as it may be greatly affected by this subject. A ship-canal across from the Atlantic to the Pacific can be made and will be made. *Where*, and *how*, are the only questions. That the Nicaragua route is the most practicable according to all past engineering experiments, I do not doubt. . . . No private company, however chartered, or patronized, or guaranteed, should be permitted to set itself down as the keeper of a toll-gate between the two great oceans of the world. The civilized nations of the world ought not to permit it. This nation ought not to permit it, even if all others consent. It has probably made a mistake in setting up the monopolies in the way of rail-roads which cross the continent. It would have saved money and lands and would far more have benefitted the people, if it had built the roads, itself. . . . I see that the minister of Nicaragua to this country, Senor De Franco, is said to have declared, in a late interview, that his countrymen are so enthusiastically in favor of opening a ship-canal there, that if they thought there was no other way of carrying it out, they would demand annexation to the United States. As a merely physical problem I have expressed myself in favor of the shortest and level canal, instead; and I think that this shortest one is the one which ought to be opened by the nations, or by this nation: but so strong is my conviction that national and republican principles are, and should be kept, paramount, and that the canal should not be a private monopoly, that I would adopt and nationalize the Nicaragua route and prohibit and prevent the DeLesseps plan entirely, rather than to acquiesce in the monopoly, and all which that implies. I forbear to more than suggest how much good there would be, in uniting our whole people, now, in a great, beneficient, and glorious *national* enterprise of this kind. Please excuse this letter. I have not intended to be uncivilly presuming; and I close, with the expression of one other conviction, namely: that you can do more for this particular cause, in other ways and capacities, as well as more for your country, and its renown, in all time, than you can by becoming the president of any ship canal *company*." ALS, USG 3. See letter to Elihu B. Washburne, Dec. 22, 1879.

1. Dec. 9.

Speech

[*Louisville, Dec. 10, 1879*]

MR. MAYOR AND CITIZENS OF LOUISVILLE, KENTUCKY—It is with great gratification that I am with you here to-day. I feel honored by the reception which you have tendered to me, as I do by the receptions which I have received at the hands of our American citizens at every place where it has been my fortune to stop since my return from abroad. The receptions which I have received in foreign countries, as you have remarked, have never been extended to any American citizen; they have been a mark of the great respect in which our country—our nation—is now held by the nations abroad. The study of those countries has only made me return to my own, and value it more highly. As I have on frequent occasions since my return remarked, all persons visiting abroad as I have done, and seeing these countries for themselves, return to America better satisfied with their own country. There is in many countries abroad all freedom to the citizens, practically all freedom to the citizens that we enjoy here, but the resources of those countries have either been exhausted partially or developed to their utmost capacity. With us, we have resources which are in their infancy, and, with a united people, we must be happy, and we must grow in importance in our own estimation and in the estimation of the outside world. Gentlemen, again I thank you for the reception you have extended to me.

Louisville Courier-Journal, Dec. 11, 1879. USG spoke after a welcoming address by Mayor John G. Baxter.

On Dec. 10, 1879, at Louisville, Mayor Thomas A. Kercheval of Nashville invited USG to attend "a celebration on the 24th of April next, the anniversary of the centennial of Nashville." USG replied. "I will be very glad to accept, if I can, but I am now on my way to Cuba and Mexico, and I don't expect to be back in time. If I can go I will be very glad to." *Louisville Commercial*, Dec. 11, 1879.

Also on Dec. 10, USG spoke. "I am very much obliged to the colored citizens of Louisville for their words, and express the hope with them that all the rights of citizenship may be enjoyed by them as it is guaranteed to them already by the law and constitutional amendments; and I think the day is not far distant when, without any embarrassment whatever, they will, by common consent, enjoy unmolested and freely every right to judge conscientiously of the suffrages that they want to exercise wherever they will live, and, in all respects, to be free and equally independent before the law." *Louisville Courier-Journal*, Dec. 11, 1879. On the same day, Walter C. Whitaker, former col., 6th Ky., and brig. gen., introduced USG to Union veterans. In reply, USG noted: ". . . While there is a bond of friendship between those who are united, we are glad to welcome all those who were on the other side, only asking them to be like ourselves, good and true citizens, friends of the nation, and ready to stand up with us if we should ever have a foreign war; fighting under one flag, for one cause—American unity and greatness." *Ibid.* Prior to USG's visit, "ex-Confederate soldiers of Louisville and vicinity," led by Basil W. Duke, met and resolved "that we, as citizens hereby, without any political significance whatever, extend to this distinguished invited guest of the city our courteous and hospitable greeting." *Ibid.*, Dec. 10, 1879.

On Dec. 2, USG, Galena, had telegraphed to Henry Watterson, *Louisville Courier-Journal*. "The hour, named for your dinner, acceptable" Telegram received (at 11:10 A.M.), DLC-Henry Watterson. An invitation to a Dec. 10 dinner is *ibid.* Invitations to a reception to be held in USG's honor at the Galt House on the same day are in Western Kentucky University, Bowling Green, Ky., and DLC-William M. Evarts. Probably before Dec., USG received an invitation to visit Louisville schools from the board of trustees. D, Smithsonian Institution.

On Nov. 3, Mayor Samuel Jacobs of Logansport, Ind., and Henry C. Thornton had written to USG inviting him to stop on his way from Chicago to Indianapolis.

DS, USG 3. On Dec. 9, Jacobs welcomed USG in a speech that was interrupted by the collapse of the reviewing stand. USG made a brief speech in reply and later remarked. "That was a non-partisan platform. It might have been very well for one party, but you see both parties got on and it broke down." *Chicago Tribune*, Dec. 10, 1879. On the same day, at Indianapolis, Frederick Knefler, former col. 79th Ind. and bvt. brig. gen., introduced USG at the Grand Hotel. USG responded. "I thank you, General. I feel most grateful to the citizens of Indiana and to the citizens of Indianapolis, to the old soldiers whom I meet here, for the hearty welcome which I receive. . . ." *Indianapolis Journal*, Dec. 10, 1879. En route from Indianapolis to Louisville, USG spoke to a reporter about his private car. "It is the finest car in the world. It belongs to Mr. George Pullman. He built it for his own use, and according to his own design. . . ." USG shook hands with well-wishers when the train stopped in a village. "I frequently have had my hand held by persons inadvertently, until it was painful. Often, as I have stood on the platform, my hand has been held until the cars were moving at such a rate that to save myself from falling I have been obliged to pull the person behind the hand up on the platform. But that is nothing." *Cincinnati Commercial*, Dec. 12, 1879.

Speech

[*Cincinnati, Dec. 11, 1879*]

Mr. Mayor—It is with great gratification that I return once again to my native State, and I am further gratified to be received by the citizens of this city and of this State, as I have been here by you and the people of Cincinnati. If I were in the habit of public speaking I could better give expression to the thoughts that fill my mind at this time, but not being accustomed to public speaking, I will extend my heartfelt thanks to the citizens of Cincinnati and Ohio for this greeting, through you, and will add what I have had to say on frequent occasions since my return to my own country, that my travels have all only served to strengthen my love of country. By comparison and by contrast our country stands out in a better light than when you see it alone. My receptions abroad have been highly gratifying to me personally, and very gratifying as a recognition of this great land. But the comparison I speak of is between a new country, full of resources, not fully developed, and older countries that have been occupied for so many centuries that the resources in some cases are exhausted and in others developed to their fullest capacity. A traveler may enjoy his passage through them hugely, because he can see the treasured riches of antiquity there, but if he had to earn money there to support him, he would wish to have himself back again to this grand, free country. Again, Mr. Mayor, I thank you and the people of Cincinnati.

Cincinnati Commercial, Dec. 12, 1879. Mayor Charles Jacob, Jr., introduced USG to a large crowd at Cincinnati's Music Hall. Earlier on Dec. 11, 1879, USG responded to a welcoming speech by Benjamin Eggleston. "I feel, citizens of Cincinnati and State of Ohio, very grateful for the welcome you have given me. The language of the address of welcome which I have just heard forces from me this recognition. I am proud of this greatest distinction that I have the title of an American citizen, which is the proudest title that could be allowed to any man. It has been my fortune to serve the State and Nation, and I am grateful to its soldiers who went with me and enabled me to render such services as I may have been enabled to render. Again I thank you for the cordiality of this welcome tendered me by the citizens of Cincinnati." *Ibid.* Later, at a dinner hosted by Washington McLean, USG responded to a toast by Samuel F. Hunt. "GENTLEMEN OF CINCINNATI—Like all of you, I have listened to all the eloquent words which have just been uttered, and I have not heard one, except so far as applied to myself individually, that I do not subscribe to and indorse in the fullest sense. If the eloquent speaker and myself have ever disagreed in politics I do not know why it has been, unless it's simply that we have voted opposite tickets. Our views certainly have coincided exactly. I thank you for listening to the words which you have heard so eloquently spoken by the gentleman who spoke last and for the greetings which you give me here." *Ibid.*

On Oct. 28, Robert M. Moore and six others, George H. Thomas Post No. 13, Grand Army of the Republic, Cincinnati, had written to USG "inviting you to a welcome to this, your old home, so near the spot where your boyhood days were passed. . . ." *Ibid.*, Oct. 30, 1879. On Nov. 1, Moore *et al.* telegraphed to USG. "The citizens and soldiers of this city have joined in a request for you to visit our city, your old home. A formal invitation has been mailed to you at Omaha, in care of the postmaster, who will deliver it to you on your arrival there. Please advise us by telegraph." *Ibid.*, Nov. 5, 1879. On the same day, USG, Columbus, Neb., telegraphed to Moore *et al.* "I expect to spend a day in Cincinnati when on my way East. I can not say now when that will be, but will endeavor to inform you in time. I accept your invitation then with pleasure." *Ibid.*

On Dec. 12, a delegation of the Evangelical Ministerial Alliance, led by Frank S. Fitch, praised USG's opposition to public funding for sectarian schools, his mediation between China and Japan, and his support for Christian missionaries. USG replied. "GENTLEMEN OF THE ALLIANCE—I feel very much obliged for your kind words and for this reception. I have but very few minutes to remain, for the arrangements are made for me to leave on the train. The train leaves at 11 o'clock, so that I can add no more, gentlemen, than that I am very grateful to you for the expressions of your resolution and the words you have just read." *Ibid.*, Dec. 13, 1879.

On [*Nov. 2*], USG had telegraphed to Governor Richard M. Bishop of Ohio, William Dennison, *et al.* "I will pass through Columbus on my way East, which will probably be some time in December." *Columbus Dispatch*, Nov. 3, 1879. In a letter received Nov. 25, USG wrote to David W. Caldwell, general manager, Pittsburgh, Cincinnati, and St. Louis Railroad, "that he will leave Cincinnati early on the morning of December 12, stopping a few hours in Columbus and arriving in Pittsburgh the same night.

The letter states that the General would have written sooner had his plans been definitely formed. . . . Ex-Governor Dennison has written to General Grant asking him to
change his plans so as to remain in the city until 12 o'clock, midnight, giving as the
reason the evening reception to be tendered him." *Ibid.*, Nov. 25, 1879. On the same day,
Bishop *et al.* telegraphed to USG, Galena. "Report says you will stop here but three
hours. Arrangements are all made and published for you to be here from one o'clock
until ten at night. Any change will greatly disappoint the public. We urge that you
give us the time desired. You can leave here Saturday morning and reach Pittsburgh
in five hours. Please answer by telegraph giving us from about noon until 10 P. M."
Ibid., Nov. 26, 1879. USG replied. "It was my expectation to be in Columbus Friday
afternoon late and to go to Pittsburgh Saturday." *Ibid.* On [*Nov. 27*], USG again telegraphed. "I will reach Columbus Friday, early in the afternoon, December 12th, and
will attend the evening entertainment with Mrs. Grant. Will start early Saturday, in
the private car. I will be entirely at the command of the Committee during our stay at
Columbus." *Ibid.*, Nov. 28, 1879.

On Dec. 12, en route from Cincinnati, USG stopped at Xenia, Ohio, and made a
brief speech to local officials and children from the Soldiers' Orphans' Home. Between
Xenia and Columbus, USG spoke to reporters about his travel plans and declined to
discuss a third term. "He, however, had a few words to say about the stopping of the
coining of silver. He said, 'Well, I don't think the Secretary of the Treasury should be
forced into coining two millions per month. There is no good in coining it if you can't
put it into circulation among the people. I don't think they want to accumulate it in the
Treasury beyond the capacity of the vaults to hold it.' In answer to the question as to
what should be done with greenbacks, he said: 'Well, let the people work and get as
many of them as possible and keep them as good as gold.'" *Ibid.*, Dec. 12, 1879. At Columbus, Mayor Gilbert G. Collins welcomed USG, who replied. "I thank the citizens of
Columbus and the State of Ohio for the cordial greeting I am receiving at their hands.
Ohio has been, from its first admission into the Union, an energetic, growing and prosperous State. I am very glad to hear of the additional prosperity which has come upon
the State in the last few years, and to know that the prosperity is becoming general
throughout the country. If we can have it extend over the whole of this broad land, it
will go far towards diminishing the political asperity that has kept us, at least, I think,
uncertain as to our future. Nothing has a greater tendency to produce conservatism
and good citizenship than general and diffused prosperity. I hope that what Columbus
has been experiencing in the few years that you have spoken of, may extend to every
foot of our great country. Nothing else is wanted but unity of sentiment among our
people to perpetuate what we are now, the greatest and best country for a man to live
in. Mr. Mayor, I thank the citizens of Columbus for this pleasant greeting." *Ibid.*, Dec.
12, 1879. Later, USG responded to a toast by George W. Manypenny during an evening banquet. "COLONEL, GENTLEMEN OF COLUMBUS: I am very glad that I go away from
here at 12 o'clock tonight, and go out of the State of Ohio without encountering any
more demonstrations which call me out to make speeches. I left Cincinnati—almost
at the other end from where I shall go out of the State—this morning, having met
two or three delegations, all of which made speeches, to which I responded in a very
few words. On the road we happened to stop once long enough to enable a gentleman,
whom I afterward learned was not the Mayor of the city, but somebody who could talk,
and who made a very excellent speech, and I made one. And I was permitted to occupy
the platform at your depot and make a lengthy and exhaustive mental effort, and when
I came into your Capitol I had to make another, and I am happy to say that I was so

fortunate as not to catch a reporter, and so, of course, that will not appear. Now, gentlemen, it would be mere repetition for me to say how thankful I am for the honor with which I have been received, not only in Columbus, but in every place I have been in my native State, as well as every place I have been since I returned to America." *Ibid.*, Dec. 13, 1879.

Speech

———

[*Pittsburgh, Dec. 13, 1879*]

GENTLEMEN—This being Saturday night it would hardly be legitimate to keep open longer than 12 o'clock. I supposed the time that each one would occupy would not be over seven minutes. In this instance, however, we have had two speeches that have occupied thirteen and a half minutes, and it gives me just about the time—a half minute—that it generally takes me to say what I have on my mind. My powers of speech never were good, but my knowledge of mathematics is excellent. I have figured this down to a nicety, and now I have just half a minute, and the more time I can spend in the way I am talking the less I will have to say. My friend Mr Moore[1] has pleasantly alluded to the way in which I let an able-bodied man, who wasn't carrying arms on our side, to escape to the North. Why, sir, I was down there just for that purpose—to get them up North, and when we could not get them up any other way we were sending them up under guard, and furnishing rations for them. We were always glad to get able-bodied men away from that section up North that had money enough to pay their way and support themselves, and not require the services of a good able-bodied soldier to guard them and keep them there. I remember when Mr. Moore went up North, and was glad to get him there, as I knew he would stay. Mr. President, hasn't my time about expired?[2]

Well, I assure you that I will finish before this cigar goes out, and I will do so by simply thanking you for the kind words I have heard here this evening; and I feel highly gratified that I am called upon so early in the evening, because now I can sit here and see all of you punished and enjoy it.

Pittsburgh Commercial Gazette, Dec. 15, 1879. USG spoke during a banquet at the Monongahela House.

Earlier on Dec. 13, 1879, USG addressed a delegation of the Pittsburgh Chamber of Commerce at the Monongahela House. "One of the most gratifying sights to my eyes on my arrival in my own country was the evidence of the revival of the business of the country on a permanent, firm and substantial basis—on a basis of money which was not fluctuating in value from day to day. It was my firm belief years ago that there would be no permanent prosperity for the country and for the whole people until we had a dollar which represented something that was in turn represented by the labor of the people. I have to meet so many Chambers of Commerce and other boards, soldiers and others, and have to say a few words three or four times a day, perhaps, and it is not my habit to talk much. I cannot do it with fluency and ease, as I could with a pen, on a subject of this kind, and you will therefore excuse me. I return you my thanks for your cordial welcome." *New York Tribune*, Dec. 14, 1879.

On the same day, USG spoke at Library Hall. "It is a source of great gratification to me that my course has been approved. It is a somewhat remarkable fact that during the years of my absence I have not known a day's sickness, although I have been in every latitude. It is also a source of gratification and acknowledgment that an invisible Power protected me on my journey." USG also favorably contrasted opportunity in the U.S. with that in Europe. "Here is a soil and extent of territory capable of accommodating 500,000,000 people without crowding. This is a source of great gratification, and should make our people more patriotic and love their country better." *New York Herald*, Dec. 14, 1879.

Also on Dec. 13, USG addressed a delegation of school principals. "GENTLEMEN— There is no interest in your city or in the land that I feel as deep an interest in and desire to see fostered as I do the free public school system. Ignorance is the only thing that upholds monarchy, and it was that in particular that was the cause of our civil war. I would have education diffused all over the land, and then our country would never be in danger. I only regret that there is so much ignorance in our country as there is. In glancing over some statistics the other day, I was greatly surprised at the number of uneducated persons there are. I am in favor of compulsory education, and that each State should enact laws compelling the attendance of every child at the proper age at some institution of learning. Of course the general government could not pass laws to this end, but by the sale of public lands and the proceeds set aside for educational purposes, could indirectly, if not directly, further the school facilities in every State. Gentlemen, I hope your efforts will be imitated all over the land, and will soon see a general attendance of the rising generation in every portion of our country. Gentlemen, I thank you for your kind attention and the courtesy that has been shown me in your great city." *Pittsburgh Commercial Gazette*, Dec. 15, 1879.

Augustus C. Hoyer then addressed USG on behalf of "the Grant Club of Western Pennsylvania, . . . they are absolutely and unqualifiedly for General U. S. Grant for next President of this nation." USG replied. "CITIZENS OF WESTERN PENNSYLVANIA:—I appreciate highly your kindly welcome and thank you for the kindness shown me on every hand. Of course you are a political organization, and with that I have nothing to do The gentleman has nominated a man for whom I have never voted and never will. I again thank you for your cordial welcome." *Ibid.* In Nov., William T. Lindsay had written to USG and members of the Pittsburgh Grant Club. "You have been elected a member of said club. Inclosed you will find a printed copy of the constitution and by-laws. There will be a meeting of the club on Thursday, the 20th inst., at 7:30 P. M. Business of great importance will be considered. Please acknowledge on inclosed postal the receipt of this notice and signify your acceptance of terms of membership." *Washington Post*, Nov. 25, 1879. On Nov. 21, USG, Galena, wrote to Lindsay. "The Grant club preamble is so personal to myself that I think good taste requires that I should decline membership, which has been so kindly voted, but I may be able to meet some of the members during my proposed visit to Pittsburg." *Ibid.* Members paid $10 to further USG's reelection.

On Dec. 14, Sunday, a reporter asked USG if he had attended church. "Yes, sir. I went to Christ Church on Penn avenue, and got there rather late, but that needs an explanation. On my way to this city from Ohio, I was approached by several committees, who invited me to attend services at Christ church. I consented to do so, and waited Sunday morning until eleven o'clock, but no committee called. I started out with a boy to find my way to the church, and meeting General Kane we went to Christ Church together." USG also spoke about his busy schedule. "I have been closely pressed at times, and had a hard time to get to bed last night so many people were brought into my room to be introduced. I had to have the door locked at last on the outside before I could get to bed." *Pittsburgh Commercial Gazette*, Dec. 15, 1879.

A Dec. 15 resolution applauded USG's refusal "to take any stimulant at the close of the procession, and the dignified example he set at the ban[q]uet on Saturday evening, when he inverted his wine glasses and refused, with a few other gentleme[n] to partake of any intoxicating beverage—thereby endorsing the request of the W. C. T. U. of Allegheny." *Ibid.*, Dec. 16, 1879.

On Dec. 15, Governor Henry M. Hoyt of Pa. and Mayor John D. Patterson of Harrisburg welcomed USG before a crowd gathered in front of the Executive Mansion. USG replied. "GOVERNOR: I thank you for your cordial welcome, and through you I also thank the Mayor and people of Harrisburg, and of Pennsylvania, for the reception given me to day at the capital of your State. Since I left Philadelphia for my journeys abroad, and since I landed at San Francisco, to travel across the continent of North America, I have received no more cordial welcome than that given me by the people of Harrisburg. My reception abroad was full of honor, which I attributed to the reputation of my country and the grandeur of its institutions, not to any deservings of my own. I again thank you, Governor, for your cordial greeting." *Harrisburg Telegraph*, Dec. 15, 1879. Later, USG addressed veterans at a Grand Army of the Republic fair. "Comrades—I thank you for your kindly greeting on this occasion, and know that your welcome is sincere." *Ibid.*, Dec. 16, 1879.

On Nov. 21, USG, Galena, had written to Pa. Representative Joseph R. Souder. "I am just in receipt of your letter of the 15th of November, informing me of the courteous resolutions of the Legislature of the State of Pennsylvania, tendering me her hospitalities, and inquiring when and by what route I expect to go there. My present expectation is to go from Columbus, Ohio, to Pittsburg, on Saturday, the 13th of December, and to remain there over Sunday. On the 15th to go to Harrisburg, stay over night and reach Philadelphia on the 16th, at such hour as may be agreeable to the citizens of that city." *Philadelphia Public Ledger*, Nov. 26, 1879. Souder later described protocol disputes during USG's visit. *Philadelphia Press*, Dec. 22, 1879.

1. Toastmaster William D. Moore, a minister turned lawyer, introduced USG. A former resident of Port Gibson, Miss., Moore witnessed fighting on May 1, 1863, after which his son and other local boys were detained by Federal troops. ". . . In such misery as you can imagine, I applied, through a friend, to Gov. Yates, and making myself known to him—Masonically and otherwise—he app[e]aled to General Grant,

who instantly ordered their release. They had been informed upon by the negroes; they were always traitors—(to the Confederacy). My wife and children were enveloped in the strife of the pursuing and retreating armies more than they could possibly have been in the town, and in her anxiety and terror she sent a note to Gen. Grant, begging that she might return with her children to the town. This is [h]is answer: *Mrs. E. B. Moore.* DEAR MADAM—You are at liberty to return to Port Gibson whenever you wish; women and children are non-combatants—we do not make war upon them. U. S. GRANT." After Vicksburg fell, Moore sought to return to Pittsburgh, but Maj. Gen. James B. McPherson refused. "I went to General Grant's headquarters at the lower end of the town and, I suppose, by virtue of my being a college professor, which I then was, speedy access was obtained to his pres[e]nce. I stated my case, he turned to his desk, handed me a cigar and in a few moments handed me this note: 'The bearer, Mr. Moore, is permitted to go up the river to Cairo with his family and baggage, and any government boat going up is authorized and directed to receive him on board and convey him to his destination. U. S. GRANT. General Commanding.' I was astonished that he should send an able bodied man up North, but I remember no moment of my life in which I have felt so thankful and glad. . . ." *Pittsburgh Commercial Gazette*, Dec. 15, 1879.

    2. John H. Ricketson answered USG. "No; I think you've got about one quarter of a minute yet." *Ibid.*

Speech

——————

[*Philadelphia, Dec. 19, 1879*]

    Mr. President and gentlemen of the Commercial Exchange:— Your President, in the welcoming address he has just delivered, does me a great deal more honor than I feel to be my deserts. But it is only in keeping with the reception that I have received at the hands of Philadelphians of all classes—the commercial classes, the soldiers, ex-soldiers and all the citizens. It makes me feel very grateful to Philadelphians to be always so welcomed by them.

    In the remarks that have been made about the extension of our commerce, my visit abroad has enabled me to see how I think our trade might be very much increased with the East. In Europe it is already taken care of, and I know of no change that can be made to increase it any more rapidly than it is being increased. The merchants of our country have their correspondents all over Europe, and understand exactly what they are to do to increase their trade in that quarter; but in the East, America is beginning to be known, and is beginning to be appreciated. It has now a history which all of the Eastern nations are beginning to study and read. And with a little change, and with a more positive American policy in the East, our trade there can be very much increased, and is increasing; but we are badly represented, and must continue to be until a new policy is adopted of at least fixing the duties of our Consuls. They are sent to the East with salaries affixed which will not support respectably even a single man, let alone a man with a family, and he is forbidden to engage in private business. The clamor that would be raised against any American Consul engaging in business or interesting himself in business, if it were reported at home would brand him as an unworthy citizen of the United States, and a man not to be trusted or associated with. The policy of the European powers is entirely different. Their Consuls are really business agents to increase the commerce and trade of their respective countries. There are few of these ports at which such a salary is fixed as will enable the President to appoint a competent Consul, as the salary is regulated by fees, which in many instances amount to but a few hundred dollars. Yet in many places the fees might be increased until they would become very large. At all such places our Consul Generals are compelled to appoint some one to act as American Consuls—in almost every instance it is some European merchant who is a trader there, but not interested in extending the commerce of the United States, but on the contrary interested in suppressing it and keeping it out of that country. The remedy for this in my judgment would be for Congress to authorize the Consuls in the East to be agents for manufacturing and commercial firms of the United States and act for them, and to say to the Chambers of Commerce of the United States, as I said to the religious societies of the country in appointing Indian agents, if you will suggest men whom you are willing to trust with your business, let them be appointed and let them act as American agents for the merchants and manufacturers and commercial interests. In addition to the fees they receive they can earn such a percentage as would enable the Government to get able, energetic men, such as we are willing should represent us as American citizens abroad.

Gentlemen, I had no idea of saying this when I came here—I am almost sorry that I did say it. All I intended to say was to thank you for the reception you have accorded me.

Philadelphia Public Ledger, Dec. 20, 1879. USG responded to an address by John T. Bailey, president, Philadelphia Commercial Exchange. Mayor William S. Stokley of Philadelphia called USG a "very observant visitor. He has seen what is necessary for the country to do both at home and abroad, and if he is ever again called to act officially you can see how much better he will be fitted to act than ever before." *Ibid.* On Dec. 20, 1879, a correspondent reported from Washington, D. C. "Gen. Grant, in conversation with your correspondent a few days ago, mentioned very fully his views on the Consular and Diplomatic service, and said that a revision of the Consular system could be made at once. In speaking of the Consulates in Europe he said that the condition of the service, and, in some instances, the status of the incumbents, were not a matter of so much importance as they were near home and were subject to local laws and the surveilance of diplomatic representatives, but the Oriental Consulates as usual were officered by men who failed to appreciate the importance and duties of their positions, and taking advantage of the extraordinary authority vested in the consular office in pagan countries seemed to subordinate personal interests and opportunity to the honor of the country and the welfare of American interests. He found a degree of responsibility which amazed him, and in the exercise of judicial functions by the Consuls in the now Christian countries of Asia such an utter disregard for judicial forms and the dispensation of justice that the whole system was a subject of severe comment among officers and subjects of foreign nationalities, not to speak of the oppressions they heaped upon American citizens. He attributed this, in a great measure, to the manner in which selection for these offices are made, in which influence outweighs a lack of fitness. The compensation being inadequate, he said, doubtless prevented the Government from securing a higher class of fitness. The consular officers of foreign governments, he said, were liberally compensated and were surrounded by a proper staff of assistants where trade was important. They were also educated for the duties, and advanced in rank for meritorious service that they contributed under the auspices of their governments to the extension of commerce and advancement of trade and influence. . . . Gen. Grant could hardly find terms in which to express his admiration of the American Minister, Mr. Bingham, and was exceedingly gratified to learn the high estimation in which he is held by the Government of Japan; that he inaugurated an entire change in the diplomatic relations of the people to other nations; that heretofore foreign diplomatic representatives treated the Government more as a dependency than as an equal as a nation. This attitude, through the position assumed by Mr. Bingham, has been revolutionized, and Japan occupies her proper position in the list of nations. In speaking of Mr. Seward, the United States Minister to China, he said that it was unfortunate that he had placed himself in a position which destroyed his usefulness, and that the report of the condition of affairs at the Consulate General at Shanghai in 1870, and the subsequent investigation by Congress, had exposed a state of things which had lost him the consideration which a Minister of the United States should enjoy from the Government to which he is accredited." *St. Louis Globe-Democrat*, Dec. 21, 1879. For the congressional investigation of George F. Seward, see *HRC*, 45-3-117, 45-3-134.

On Dec. 15, USG had addressed city councilmen escorting him from Harrisburg, Pa., to Philadelphia. "Gentlemen of Philadelphia:—With a lively recollection of my departure from Philadelphia two years and seven months ago, I return again with equal pleasure. In my absence I have visited all of the countries of Europe, every capital, and most of those of Asia, together with a little of Africa. I have been nowhere that I could be willing to change for a residence in my own country, for anything or for any position that those countries could offer me. But I would not disparage any of them, because I have received the utmost kindness from them, and the very best of feeling has been manifested towards our great country. I will be ready to start with you back to Philadelphia at 6 o'clock to-morrow or at any hour that may be designated for our departure. I have no doubt that from my past experience, I will have to meet with several committees to whom I will have to say a few words. I shall do no more at present than to express my gratitude to the people of Philadelphia for the feeling manifested towards me and mine, and what I believe to be a sincere and genuine friendship for me—more than I deserved." *Philadelphia Public Ledger,* Dec. 16, 1879. On Dec. 16, Mayor Stokley welcomed USG to Philadelphia. USG replied. "Thank you, Mr. Mayor, and the good citizens of Philadelphia. It has always been a home to me since I first became acquainted with the citizens of Philadelphia, and I return to it with great pleasure." *Ibid.*, Dec. 17, 1879. On Nov. 25, a city council committee, planning the Dec. 16 reception, had determined "that there is and will be no distinction as to race, religion, color, political belief, or anything else in this reception." *Ibid.*, Nov. 26, 1879. For George H. Stuart's recollection of an early USG visit to the city, see *Philadelphia Times,* Dec. 16, 1879.

On Sept. 11, James L. Claghorn, Union League of Philadelphia, had telegraphed and written to USG, San Francisco, inviting him to a reception. Telegram received (at 4:00 P.M.) and ALS, DLC-USG, IB. On Oct. 4, John Russell Young, San Francisco, wrote to Claghorn. "General Grant requests me to acknowledge your kind invitation on behalf of the Union League, and to say that he cannot now say when he will be able to visit Philadelphia; but that when he does so nothing will afford him more pleasure than to visit the Union League and accept the courtesy you so kindly offer him. He thanks you very much for your letter." *Philadelphia Press,* Oct. 14, 1879. On Oct. 21, USG, San Francisco, wrote to [Claghorn]. "It is not my present purpose to go further east than Chicago before late in December. The exact date I cannot now fix, but I will inform you or Mr. Borie, who I understand is chairman of the committee, through whom the invitation was sent, at the earliest practicable date." *Philadelphia Public Ledger,* Nov. 7, 1879. On Nov. 22, Edwin H. Fitler, finance committee, wrote to Union League members soliciting a $10 contribution for the Dec. 23 reception. D, Union League of Philadelphia, Philadelphia, Pa. Related papers are *ibid.*

On Dec. 17, USG spoke at Carpenters' Hall. "Gentlemen of the Carpenters' Company, of the present day, it is with much pleasure that I hear your kind welcome spoken and accept the address which I see before me. I shall preserve it and hand it down to my children for preservation. I shall regard it as of great value, and one that will grow in estimation as time passes, and as long as our Republic lasts—which, it is hoped, and of which I think we have the assurance now, will be as long as time lasts." *Philadelphia Public Ledger,* Dec. 18, 1879. Walter Allison and two others signed the address. DS, Smithsonian Institution. On Dec. 8, Allison *et al.* had written to invite USG to this reception. DS (six signatures), USG 3. See *PUSG,* 25, 207.

Also on Dec. 17, John W. Forney presented a delegation of "the First Defenders, of Pottsville," Pa. vols. who arrived in Washington, D. C., on April 18, 1861, and were quartered in the Capitol. The Pa. troops preceded the 6th Mass., delayed by a riot in Baltimore on April 19. USG addressed the veterans. "It has always been an impression with me—I don't know how I got it, perhaps it was because I have seen so much in the papers—that the Sixth Massachusetts was the first regiment which found its way to Washington on the breaking out of the Rebellion, in answer to the first call for defenders of the national Union. I am very glad, indeed, to know the truth of history in that regard, and I am sure, as Col. Forney has said, if we never had as loyal a Congress as while you gentlemen occupied the hall of the House of Representatives, that there have been times since, at all events, when there has not been so loyal a Congress, and I hope that the time is not very distant when we will have all our members in that body representatives of the National idea and the idea of Unionism and integrity of the Union, which all of you fought so gallantly to maintain. At all events I hope that the spirit which carried you to Washington on the occasion referred to will be so thoroughly imbued in the hearts and minds of the great majority of people that any who attempt to again lower the flag of the Union will find, not only a single regiment, but a sufficient number of regiments to crush in the bud any attempt at national degradation. I am very glad to have seen these gentlemen this morning." *Philadelphia Public Ledger,* Dec. 18, 1879. Henry L. Cake, former col., 25th and 96th Pa., replied. "We thank you from our hearts for those words, and all we ask is—give us Grant and let us have peace." *Ibid.* USG chatted with the delegation. Forney said. "I have seen some of the General's writing that was rather hard to decipher." USG replied. "No, no; that's where you are wrong. In all my letters, and I write nearly every one myself, the trouble is that I make each letter so plain that people find out when I misspell a word or make any other mistake." *Ibid.*

On Dec. 18, Governor Henry M. Hoyt of Pa. introduced USG to veterans gathered at the Academy of Music. USG replied. "Governor Hoyt and comrades of the Grand Army of the Republic, It is a matter of very deep regret with me that I had not thought of something or prepared something to say in response to the welcome which I am receiving here at your hands this evening, but really since my arrival here I have not had the time, and before that I scarcely thought of it. But I can say to you all that in the two years and seven months since I left this city to make a circuit of the globe I have visited every capital in Europe and most of the Eastern nations, but there has not been a country which I have visited in that circuit where I have not found some of our members. In crossing our own land from the Pacific to the Atlantic side, there is scarcely a new settlement, a cattle range, or collection of pioneers, that they are not composed almost entirely of veterans of the late war. It calls to my mind the fact that, while wars are to be deplored, and unjust wars always to be avoided, yet they are not unmixed evil. The boy who is brought up at his country home, or his village home, or his city home, without any exciting cause, is apt to remain there and follow the pursuit of his parent, and not develop beyond it, and, in the majority of cases, not come up to it. But, being carried away in the great struggle, and, particularly, one where so much principle is involved as in our late conflict, it brings to his view a wider field than he contemplated at his home, and although in his field service he longs for the home he left behind him, yet when he gets there he finds that disappointment, and has struck out for new fields, and has developed the vast domains which are given to us for our keeping— for the thousands of liberty-seeking people. The ex-soldier has become the pioneer, not only of our own land, but has extended our commerce and trade and knowledge of us and our institutions to all other lands, and when brighter days dawn upon other nations, particularly those nations of the East, America will step in for her share of the trade, which will be opened, and through the exertions of the ex-soldier, the comrade, veterans, and I might say members of the Grand Army of the Republic. Comrades, having been compelled, as often as I have been since my arrival in San Francisco, to utter a few words, not only to ex-soldiers but to all other classes of citizens of our great country, and always speaking without any preparation, I have necessarily been obliged to repeat, possibly not in the same words, but the same ideas. But the one thing I want to impress is that we have a country to be proud of, to fight for and die for, if necessary. While many of the countries of Europe give practical protection and freedom to the citizen, yet there is no European country that compares in its resources, particularly its undeveloped resources, with our own. There is no country where the young and energetic man can, by his own labor and his own industry, ingenuity and frugality, acquire competency as he can in America. A trip abroad and a study of the institutions and difficulties of a poor man making his way in the world is all that is necessary to make us better and happier citizens with our lot here. Comrades, I thank you for the very cordial welcome you have given me, and I regret that I have not been prepared better to say better what I would like to say to you." *Ibid.*, Dec. 19, 1879.

On Dec. 20, USG addressed public school students at the Academy of Music. "I am too hoarse to-day to be heard far, but I hope I will be able to be heard by those who are near me. I merely wish to state my appreciation of the public school system as one of the safeguards of the Republic. Pennsylvania has been more fortunate in the progress of education than most of the other States, but everywhere the progress is apparent, and the more the progress is continued, the less danger there will be to the institutions of the Republic. For this I have no doubt that thanks are due to the Educational Board of the State and city for the advantages which they have prepared, and I hope that the results of your earnest efforts will extend beyond your own bounds to those of all the States of the Union. When illiteracy is banished, the danger to our free institutions will be practically removed." *Ibid.*, Dec. 22, 1879. A printed program is in USG 3.

Also on Dec. 20, USG attended a banquet at St. George's Hall. "All I have to say to you is good night, and thank you for the courtesy that I have always received in this good city of Philadelphia. Good night." *Philadelphia Public Ledger*, Dec. 22, 1879.

On Dec. 22, USG addressed Girard College officials. "Mr. President—The death of Mr. Girard, and his will was probably one of the best known incidents in our country; I think it was printed in every country newspaper throughout America. I myself was a boy at the time, but I remember it. I read it in our village paper, and perhaps remembered the substance of it better at that day than now. Those colossal fortunes were not as common as they are to-day, and where possessed by one individual it was more universally known of than at the present time, and when such a man in those days died and gave any of his property for charitable purposes it was noted all over the country. I remember how magnificent his donation to this institution was regarded at the time; and it met with general approval, as did also the fact that it was to be entirely non-sectarian in its objects. Perhaps it was criticised by some as being a little too extreme in that direction, but the object was certainly a right one in having the institution free for the admission of orphans without doing prejudice to the religious views or sentiments of whatever families they might have still remaining. I believe it is entirely for whole orphans? I have heard, from time to time, of the benefits that have been conferred and of the standing some of the students that have been turned out of this institution have taken. Some of them occupy high official positions, and others have made their way in the world, acquiring a competency, and, what is more important, a good standing and name from the neighbors in the community in which they reside. I wish for the College every possible success and long endurance." *Ibid.*, Dec. 23, 1879. Henry M. Phillips, president, Board of City Trusts, answered USG's question. "No, those deprived of fathers." *Ibid.* USG later addressed students in the college chapel. "Boys of Girard College: I know, in after years, you will appreciate the advantages which this institution will give you. If you only appreciate now, as I hope you do, the advantages, and avail yourselves of the opportunities offered you, you will, all of you, be prepared to go out into the world, when of the proper age, to make a fair record for yourselves, and a good living, and be honorable and respectable citizens of the United States. You are fortunate in having a country where every opportunity is afforded you of reaching any position in it. There is no position whatever under this free Government to which you are not all of you eligible. It will depend upon yourselves, and you have now as fair an opportunity to begin life as the most favored children in the land. I have heard good accounts from many gone forth from this institution, and I hope the example set by them will be followed by all of you. I am very glad to see you here to-day, looking so contented and happy, and with such marks of good health." *Ibid.* USG shared an anecdote with reporters. "If I had been prepared to say anything, I should have remarked that a few years after the death of Mr. Girard, in the spring of 1839, I was passing through Philadelphia for the first time, and one of the first things which I did was to inquire the way out to Girard College, which was being built, and then walked out here, and saw them hauling big stones, now in this building, with immense teams, which were matters of curiosity to me, a boy from the West, with ten or twelve horses strung out in a single line, and with no line on any except the wheel-horse. Since that I have visited the institution but once, and that was a few years ago, when I found it in successful operation, turning out boys with a fair common school education to enter the battle of life." *Ibid.* See *PUSG*, 19, 102.

To Levi P. Morton

[*Dec. 22–26, 1879*]

Please keep this strictly private, except from Beale, until I go to Washington. I have now determined to go to Washington on Saturday to remain over until the following Tuesday, but do not want it generally understood. Tell Beale not to have any dinner parties unless he chooses to ask in socially a few persons for Monday evening, and not to ask them until after I get there.

U. S. G.

P. S. I have concluded to address this to Beale to hand ~~to~~ you when he sees you.

AL, DLC-Decatur House Papers. On Saturday, Dec. 27, 1879, USG, Philadelphia, telegraphed to Edward F. Beale, Washington, D. C. "Party of five arrive by limited express today Sheridan and Col Grant on Monday" Telegram received, *ibid.* On Dec. 26, USG had telegraphed to U.S. Representative Levi P. Morton of N. Y. "I leave it to Gen'l Beale whether to make Engagement for Me at Dinner Monday or Not—" Telegram received (at 8:06 P.M.), *ibid.* For USG's visit and Morton's dinner on Dec. 29, see *Washington Post*, Dec. 27, 29–31, 1879; *Washington Evening Star*, Dec. 29, 1879. Secretary of

State William M. Evarts, Chief Justice Morrison R. Waite, and Daniel Ammen were among the dinner guests.

On Dec. 28, Gen. William T. Sherman wrote to "Dear Genl," presumably Beale. "I am to dine with Genl & Mrs Grant at Mr Camerons this Evig—but will also accept your kind invitation for lunch, though I had supposed the Genl wanted his Sunday for rest—" ALS, DLC-Decatur House Papers.

To Elihu B. Washburne

Phila Pa
Dec. 22d /79

MY DEAR MR. WASHBURNE,

Since my arrival here I have scarsely had time to read my mail much less answer it. The people of Phila have shewn a cordiality unsurpassed, but they have kept me so constantly going that I have not been able to see what the papers say about it. But I suppose it is all reported. I have determined to leave here for the south on Saturday next.[1] I hope you can go along. I rather expect Sheridan and Fred. and their wives.[2] But this is not yet certain. We will remain in Washington over Sunday & Monday, so our start will really be from there on Tuesday the 30th.

I have seen Mr. de Franch. I did not look at his letters because I had not the time, and I knew what they contained from persons who did see them. They amount substantially to a promise of funds for the construction of a canal if all the conditions are right. I expressed my interest in the enterprise, and the interest I had taken in it for a good many years, and my willingness to aid it all I could so long as it seemed to be in honest hands, but that I could give no promise of further connection with it than my good offices until a proper concession was obtained, the money subscribed and every preliminary aranged to insure the completion of the work, and then I would determine whether I would take a more active part. After all other preliminaries are arranged it will take an entire working season in the tropics to determine positively whether the undertaking is entirely practicable or not.[3]

If you do not go south with us I will write you again from Fla.

Mrs. Grant joins me in kindest regards to Mrs. Washburne & all the family.

Yours Truly

U. S. Grant

ALS, IHi.

1. Dec. 27, 1879.
2. On Nov. 30, Lt. Gen. Philip H. Sheridan, Chicago, wrote to Gen. William T. Sherman. ". . . Genl Grant wants me to go with him to Cuba & Mexico leaving him at the latter city as I do not wish to stay longer than ~~six~~ five weeks while he wants to stay until Spring. It is doubtful however if I will go—. . ." AL, DLC-William T. Sherman.
3. On Dec. 17, a correspondent reported from Philadelphia that USG and Daniel Ammen discussed the Nicaragua canal project. Ammen later said that USG would accept the presidency of a canal co. if certain conditions were met. "He will make it the crowning work of his life." *New York Herald*, Dec. 18, 1879. For doubts concerning Ammen's optimism, see *New York Times*, Dec. 19, 1879. A Washington, D. C., newspaper reported that in "a recent conversation with a gentleman of this city," USG had recounted his early interest in an interoceanic canal, and reaffirmed his support for the Nicaraguan route, provided "that the act of incorporation should be granted by the Congress of the United States." *Washington Evening Star*, Dec. 20, 1879. On Dec. 20, a correspondent interviewed Aniceto G. Menocal, civil engineer, U.S. Navy, about his recent meeting with USG. ". . . I have no objection to your saying that General Grant leads the project to establish the Nicaragua Canal Company. He is not waiting for capital or promises; he is to-day the most active of the promoters of the enterprise, and I presume it is not saying too much to say that General Grant is waiting for others; they are not waiting for him. . . ." *New York Herald*, Dec. 21, 1879. On Dec. 21, a correspondent in New York City questioned Thomas de Franco, Nicaraguan envoy, concerning the canal initiative and his discussions with USG at Philadelphia. "I enjoyed not only one but many interviews with him. Yesterday I had an interview with him, lasting two hours. . . . He has been in favor of the enterprise for a long time, and has been largely [*i*]nstrumental in securing public interest in it. . . . Mr. Menocal has said all there is to say at present. The enterprise is one the people of this country should be proud of, take an interest in and aid in every way they can. . . ." *Ibid.*, Dec. 22, 1879. See letters to Daniel Ammen, Nov. 16, 1879, Feb. 8, 1880; *CR*, 46-2, 12–15; *New York Herald*, Dec. 11, 19–20, 1879; *Philadelphia Times*, Dec. 18–20, 1879; Daniel Ammen, "Recollections and Letters of Grant," *North American Review*, CXLI, cccxlviii (Nov., 1885), 425–26.

To Adolph E. Borie

Dec. 23d /79

My Dear Mr. Borie,

Mrs Drexel you & I make three of the party. It makes no difference which of the gentlemen named makes the fourth.—I go to

Jersey City in the morning but will return in the afternoon in time to take an early dinner at the hotel, and will be at your house by seven.

Very Truly yours

U. S. GRANT

ALS, PHi.

On Dec. 17, 1879, Hannah Simpson Grant greeted a reporter at the Jersey City home of her daughter, Virginia Grant Corbin. "I was just reading about General Grant's reception in Philadelphia. What a time they are making over him." Hannah Grant said she had not seen USG since his return, "and I wonder what his plans are. He is not to have a formal reception in New York, I know, but he promised to come here before his departure for the South. How does he look? He must be tired. . . . The General was always a good traveler. He possessed that characteristic from his boyhood, and I do not think he would ever tire of it." Told that USG had not alluded to a possible presidential nomination, Hannah Grant replied: "It would be unlike him if he did. The General is not in the habit of giving himself up to conjectures. When a question arises he decides it, and I do not think that he has given any thought to the possibility of his being nominated again." *Philadelphia Press,* Dec. 19, 1879.

On Dec. 18, William D. Simpson, cousin and boyhood companion of USG, spoke at his home in Havre de Grace, Md. ". . . Hiram took after his mother's people; he looked like them. When he was a boy he was a little stoop-shouldered, as nearly all the Simpsons are. I remember how he looked—a short, stout boy, plain in his appearance. He never was much of a talker and used to stay at home a great deal, but he had more determination than any boy I ever saw. If he once set about a thing he would move heaven and earth to accomplish his purpose. Sometimes the boys would get after the rats which had their holes under the old stables and buildings about; well, when the scheme was once on foot 'Hi' would go further than anybody else to get those rats out. He would stay there and work after many of the others had given up, and he would persist until the stable was nearly torn down but he'd get the rats out. Once the boys got into a fight over something, I forget what, and there was a big fellow, named Slifer, who threatened to lick a boy a good deal smaller than himself. Grant was there, but he hadn't much to do with it until this Slifer began to put his threats into execution. Grant was standing by, but at this he stepped forward, rolled up his sleeves, and told Slifer that he shouldn't fight that little fellow; that if there was any fighting to be done he could fight him. 'I'll take the licking,' said Grant, and he looked as if he would, too, and that put an end to the quarrel, for Slifer backed out. . . . I have heard his father talk and laugh about him many a time. The old gentleman thought his son was a remarkable boy. Once he sent him with the team away out into the woods for some logs. He didn't expect that Hiram could do much with the logs, for they were huge, heavy timber that a strong man could hardly manage. But after awhile the boy brought the team with the logs back home. He had accomplished the task, but no doubt he thought his father had imposed upon him and had not treated him with justice, for when he came into the house he could not keep the tears back. I don't know what his father's idea was in sending him on such an errand. Maybe he thought it would develop the boy's self-reliance. Jesse was evidently proud of what 'Hi' had done, for he often told the story and would laugh about it. Grant was a peculiar boy, and if, when he undertook something, an accident occurred, or it became impossible for him to accomplish the end he desired, he was apt to cry—not in a babyish kind of way at not being able to get what he wanted, but as if his pride were wounded. He worked about the tannery, and sometimes he did a little work in a clay-pipe factory. . . ." *Ibid.*, Dec. 20, 1879.

To John F. Long

————

Dec. 25th /79

MY DEAR JUDGE,

Since leaving Galena for the East I have been so run that I have had no time to write letters. But I feel that I must drop a line to you before my departure for Cuba & Mexico, and to say how sorry I am ~~at~~to ~~y~~hear of your suffering. I sincerely hope that the warm weather of spring will bring you out all right again.

Present your Grand daughter, Nellie Grant, a silver cup from Nellie Grant Sartoris at my expense, and take it out of my funds.

On my return from Mexico in the Spring I shall stop for some days in St. Louis. If there seems to be a chance then to lease my farm in lots of from five to twenty acres—to suit tenants—for a period of ten years, for market garden purposes, I will lease it out and hold the property for the benefit of my children. Otherwise I shall sell as soon as I can realize anything like its value.

If Gen. Harney would meet me in Havana about the 1st of Feb.y and go with me to Mexico I think he would enjoy the trip and be set back in years to about forty-five, or ten years. The General I suppose admits to fifty-five now.[1]

Present Mrs. Grant's and my kindest regards to Mrs. Long & all your family.

Yours Truly
U. S. GRANT

ALS, MoSHi.

1. William S. Harney was born on Aug. 22, 1800.

To Frank T. Weldon

———

Philadelphia Pa
Dec. 25th 1879.

FRANK T. WELDON, ESQ.
MY DEAR SIR:

On this day, recognized as a Holiday by all Christendom, I acknowledge the receipt of the beautiful table,—fac-simile of the center table on which Gen. Lee & myself signed the terms of the formers surrender at Appomattox Court-House, Va—made of gold, and the still more highly appreciated expression with which it is accompanyed, printed on satin. Both will have a sacred place among the souviniers which I hope to preserve through life, and then to transmit to my children as heirlooms to be preserved by them as equally sacred.

Very Truly Yours
U. S. GRANT

ALS, Catherine Barnes Autographs, Philadelphia, Pa. See *Philadelphia Inquirer,* Dec. 16, 1879; William H. Allen, *The American Civil War Book and Grant Album* (Boston and New York, 1894).

Speech

———

[*Philadelphia, Dec. 26, 1879*]

My views on the subject of universal peace and the resort to the conflict of arms have been well known, having been made public in an official way. Although educated and brought up a soldier, and having probably been in as many battles as any one, certainly as many as most people could have been, yet there was never a time or a day when it was not my desire that some just and fair way should be established for settling difficulties, instead of bringing innocent persons into the conflict and thus withdrawing from productive labor, abled-bodied men who, in a large majority of cases, have no particular interest in the subject for which they are contending.

I look forward for a day when there will be a Court established, that shall be recognized by all nations, which will take into consideration all questions of difference between nations, and settle by arbitration or decision of such court, those questions, instead of keeping up large standing armies as in Europe, although we are not troubled, ourselves, in that way.

In the course of my travels, from what I have seen, I am constrained to believe, however, that the day is yet distant when such a result may be hoped for. The differences between some European powers are such at the present time that if one was to reduce its armament it would be in danger from those who are stronger. This is the gravest objection.

The Eastern question is one which it will be a long time before the nations interested will consent to arbitrate. The European powers have to look abroad, beyond their own continent, for trade and support. They each and all of them are looking, more or less, to the East. Each nation is jealous of the advance made by all the others in that direction in the acquisition of territory or establishment of commercial relations.

I do not think, however, that this should be any cause for abatement on the part of the Universal Peace Society. What they look forward to is a great reform, and such reforms are never accomplished in a day. I only wish it was susceptible of speedy solution, but, as I remarked, I do not think it is.

It has been a pleasure to meet with you as the representatives of the Peace Association.

Voice of Peace, VI, 11 (Feb., 1880), 163. USG responded to an address by Alfred H. Love, president, Universal Peace Union, during a reception at the Continental Hotel. Love described USG's "eminent civil services for peace" and sought his support for an international court of arbitration. He concluded: "We would esteem it a favor if you would inform us whether you found more of a peace than a war feeling abroad among the Governments and the governed, and whether you think there is not good reason to hope that some general system of disarmament could be adopted, and that a tribunal of arbitration could be established between some, if not all nations, wherein all difficulties could be settled. We are grateful for this opportunity, and in your contemplated journey we desire your continued health and safety, and may we not hope from the past, that you will do still more for peace, and make war, and indeed the military system, so unpopular, that there may be developed a higher civilization and a grander republican idea of reliance upon reason and the Christian principles of peace rather than the barbarous custom of deadly force." *Ibid.* After USG spoke, the Peace Union presented him with a crayon portrait of Lucretia Mott, who was too ill to attend. USG responded: "I receive this picture with very great pleasure. The life and history of Lucretia Mott are well known in this country as well as abroad. I have had the pleasure of meeting her, and I appreciate her devotion to the cause of peace very highly." *Ibid.* Earlier, George W. Childs had told Love that USG "would feel it a great favor to have Lucretia Mott present & he would treat her very kindly that he wants to meet the peace friends & feels a great interest in the cause" Alfred H. Love diary, Dec. 18, 1879, Swarthmore College Peace Collection, Swarthmore, Pa. See letter to Alfred H. Love, Nov. 26, 1879.

Also on Dec. 26, 1879, USG addressed a delegation of Methodist ministers. "There was no doubt about the loyalty of the Methodist Church in the North, and there was no doubt of its disloyalty in the South. What is true of the loyalty of the Methodist Church in the North might be said in regard to the churches of the other denominations, with not perhaps the same unanimity—enough, however, to save them. I thank you for the words you have spoken." *New York Herald*, Dec. 27, 1879; variant text, *Philadelphia Public Ledger*, Dec. 27, 1879.

To Adam Badeau

Philadelphia Pa
Dec. 27th /79

My Dear Badeau:

I have now been in Phila nearly two weeks and have been kept so busy all the time that I have not been able to glance over the morning papers even except two or thre times. The trip from Chicago here has been a very fatiguing one though very gratifying. No doubt you have seen fuller accounts of it than I would give if I was going to describe it. The reception at Louisville however astonished me. Notwithstanding a heavy rain storm when I reached there, and ancle deep mud mud in the streets, the way was packed with people throughout the whole line marked out for the prosession. The windows were crowded with ladies & children waving their handkerchiefs, and the houses all decorated with stars & stripes. The people seemed very cordial & enthusiastic. The reception here has been simply overwhelming.—To-day I start for Cuba & Mexico. Sheridan & wife, Fred & his wife & Kittie Felt, Mrs. Grant & I make up the party. We will stop over in Washington until the 30th. We go to Fla. by rail and cross over to Havana from there.

In the two last chapters of your book I have seen nothing to critizcise. Your chapter on Stanton is the best pen picture of a historical character I ever read. I venture to predict that it will be so considered by critics when it comes before the public. The fact is I think the whole book will rank among the most truthful, and best written, histories ever presented to the public. It will be criticised of course by friends of some Generals who do not rank in your estimation as they do in their own, and by personal enemies. But you will find on the whole favorable criticisms.[1]

I expect to be back in Galena as soon as the weather gets pleasant in the spring, and to remain there until time to go to Long Branch. I will then have the summer to arrange for a permanent home and occupation. It may be the Canal in which case I will live in New York City. It must be occupation or a country home. My means will not admit of a city home without employment to suppliment them.

All my family join in kindest regards to you.

Very Truly yours
U. S. GRANT

ALS, Munson-Williams-Proctor Institute, Utica, N. Y.

1. On Feb. 10, 1880, Gen. William T. Sherman wrote at length to Adam Badeau, consul gen., London. ". . . I have many original private letters from Genl. Grant, which never have seen the light of publicity, but may at some future time, and these might militate against your recorded facts or judgment. I will show them to you *only*, because their publication at this time would throw on Genl. Grant the onus of criticism, which I have long borne as to Genl. Thomas and others. You doubtless have seen the almost fulsome praise of me officially and personally by the General in his published conversations with Jno. Russell Young in his 'Tour around the world'. I understand these conversations are to form part of Volume 2. of Young's book but now ar[e] i[ss]ued only in pamphlet form. In one of these Genl. Grant describes the effect on himself of H. V. Boynton's garbled extracts and comments on my Memoirs—the pain it gave him for three weeks and until he had time to read the Memoirs himself, when he had to admit that the Memoirs were true, just to my comrades and himself, and just such a Book as I ought to have written &c &c. As soon as this reached the public, Boynton felt he had been caught in a lie, and in a conspiracy 'to write Sherman down' (which by the way is a trade), he forthwith rushed to his Paper, the Cincinnati Gazette, and published a three column article going to show that he had derived the facts and opinions, which he had published from Genl. Grant himself, or his immediate surroundings, quoting several confidential letters of Genl. Babcock, which partially sustained his position. . . ." Copy, DLC-William T. Sherman. On Feb. 14, John Russell Young, London, wrote to Sherman. ". . . I cannot conceive how Gen. Boynton should welcome the controversy he forces upon you, unless upon the theory that in any such quarrel he can lose noth-

ing.—I saw in an idle way, all that was written on both sides of the question, even some articles of that brilliant vagabond and Bohemian Donn Piatt. Piatt charged Gen. Grant and myself with being 'rogues,' because I made the General deny any knowledge of Boynton's book, while Piatt said Grant had read the proof.—It seemed to me that there was nothing that even mischief or malice could construe into a difference between Gen. Grant and yourself.—Gen. Grant's story, as I wrote it, seemed to me, not only very natural but very beautiful, one of the prettiest things I had ever heard, as a mere matter of art.—I heard him tell it a dozen of times, during the two years when I was as close to him as I ~~was~~ ever was to ~~his~~ my father, when I was a member of his family.— When I wrote it out, he read it over, corrected it in proof and gave me permission to print. On that point I may as well say, that I never printed a line, purporting to repeat General Grant's words, that he did not revise. I should as soon have thought of picking his pocket as taking the liberty of quoting him without his permission. In fact I left out of print and have among my papers a great many things which Gen Grant said were true, 'but I had not better print, at least now.'—I keep them for his memoirs, which I hope to write should I, as in the course of nature, I may, survive him.—As I was about to say before I went off on this digression,—I see no real reason for any breach ~~of~~ in the narrative between what Gen Grant says, and what Gen Boynton says.—The trouble is, Boynton assumes motives, assumes that you were conspiring to rob Gen. Grant of his laurels. What Gen. Grant meant to say, what I tried to report him as saying,— what I have heard him say ~~a hundred~~ many times, was that he did not approve ~~to the~~ of the march to the sea, until Hood had been destroyed. He thought ~~that~~ Hood's army remaining intact in your rear the weak point of the movement,—and the fact that you had made the march and taken what seemed to him a terrible, and what might have been a fatal risk entitled ~~you~~ you to the glory and honor of the feat.—I remember his saying,—I am not sure whether it is printed or not,—that under the circumstances, (his strong feeling about Hood I mean,) he would never have consented to any one but yourself, and Sheridan perhaps,—taking the army into Georgia. That is to say, he would never have approved such a movement on the part of Thomas, or Schofield or Logan. I think I made this clear in my conversations. If I did not, I failed to report Gen Grant correctly, fr I know what was in his mind.—I knew all about the letter to you, & to Conkling—I am not sure which. If Gen. Grant had had a copy of that letter I would have coaxed him to let me print it. I think you should print it now. It would confirm the truth of the narrative beyond ~~a~~ question. I have heard Gen. Grant speak of the war, when you and he were concerned—I cannot say how many times.—It was always very beautiful to hear him on this theme.—I mean by this, that it was then, that Gen. Grant showed, what the world does not accept, the affectionate and loyal nature of the man.— You must not object to my saying that I have a great love for Gen Grant. It has been my fortune to know well, familiarly in many cases most of the great men in America since Lincoln's time. No man, for instance, knew Stanton better, and I saw the womanly side of that stern, hard, rugged imperious, unjust temperament. This experience makes me cynical about men, or at least in my judgments of men.—But Grant always seemed so loyal, so high-minded, so pure-minded, so great and so simple, that I look upon him as the first of our race & time; second only to Washington, *if* second.—This quality never appeared so strongly as when you became the subject of his conversation—He had a great love for Sheridan. But Sheridan was always as a foster-son, you seemed to be as a brother. I shall never forget when he came into my room at our palace of Enrio-kwan, in Tokio, one morning very early, I only half dressed,—and said 'Read this letter from Sherman.'—It was the long letter you wrote him about the Presidency, where you spoke about the cruel position in which Destiny seemed to be forcing you—John Sherman and Ulysses S. Grant as possible rivals in a Republican convention. You will, I am sure remember the letter. He was very much affected. The tears seemed to be in his eyes,—certainly he spoke like a man under deep emotion: 'People may wonder' he said 'why I love Sherman. How could I help loving Sherman. And he has always been the same during the thirty five years I have known him. He was so at West Point.'—. . ." ALS, *ibid*. See Sherman to Young, Feb. 24, 1880, *ibid*.; *PUSG*, 27, 16–20; letter to William T. Sherman, May 29, 1879; letter to Henry M. Cist, Oct. 21, 1879; *Washington Post*, Feb. 19, 1880; *Young*, II, 290–94.

Speech

[*Fernandina, Fla., Jan. 5, 1880*]

GENERAL DAVIS AND CITIZENS OF FLORIDA: It affords me great pleasure to visit this State, which I never entered until yesterday. I have visited every one except this before. I have been much pleased since I crossed the Potomac River at the cordiality which I have met everywhere, I believe, as sincere as it has been warm, I am glad to see it.[1] In my tour around the world what I have seen has only made me more of a lover of my own country—from Florida to Maine, the whole of it. The poorest part of this country is superior to any of foreign lands, and if the people could only travel abroad and study the hardship and suffering in every other country, every citizen of the republic would be better satisfied under this government, where all can be happy. In the report alluded to that I made in 1866,[2] I reported what I found to be the case, as I believed. I believed the citizens of the Southern States were ready to accept the situation. That it was not quite so, I believe, was not their fault. I believe that I have seen causes that have induced what we may call sectional issues, but I shall not state in public what I think they were, because they do not exist now, and that the interest of one part of the country is the same as each other part. I think we shall go on in harmony now, and if we do, the Union need fear no extremes at home or abroad. Gentlemen, I thank you.

Chicago Inter-Ocean, Jan. 6, 1880. USG spoke after William G. M. Davis, former brig. gen., C.S. Army. Another group then addressed USG. "On behalf of the members of John Brown Union Lodge, No. 20, I. O. G. T., we tender you welcome. We are glad to learn from reliable public sources that you are a friend to the temperance cause, and trust you will give to us your word of encouragement, that at our next regular meeting we may convey the same to those of our order who were not able to be present here with us to-day. General Grant, the black men are not unmindful of the great good you rendered in the darkest days of the race's history, when there was but one real peril that threatened our nation's glory, slavery. Your victories gave the proclamation emancipating our race effectiveness. Thus the only actual danger to our country was removed." In reply, USG "spoke briefly, not alluding to the political phase of the address but expressing hope in the future of their order, saying that he thought intoxicating liquors the chief cause of poverty and crime." *Ibid.*

On Jan. 7, USG addressed a Jacksonville banquet. ". . . I never wanted anything for myself that I was not willing to accord to any other citizen as long as he obeyed the laws and upheld the nation. I believe we are now on a basis of fraternal peace and concord, and we shall move on to peace and prosperity greater than ever known in this land, or possible in any other. We are in our infancy now, but we are stronger than any other in the world, and will be so as long as we are true to ourselves, and remain one and indivisible." *Ibid.*, Jan. 8, 1880.

On Jan. 8, USG and party, including reporter Byron Andrews and illustrator Frank H. Taylor, left Jacksonville for a six-day excursion up the St. Johns and Oklawaha rivers, stopping at Palatka, Ocala, and Tocoi, and ending at St. Augustine. See *ibid.*, Jan. 22, 24, 1880; *Philadelphia Times*, Jan. 19, 1880; *Harper's Weekly*, Feb. 7, 14, 21, 1880; Nancy L. Gustke, *The Special Artist in American Culture: A Biography of Frank Hamilton Taylor (1846–1927)* (New York, 1995), pp. 51–62, 68–73, 108–9.

1. On Dec. 28, 1879, USG, Washington, D. C., had telegraphed to Wilberforce Daniel. "Thanks for the invitation of the citizens of Augusta. I will not probably be able to stop longer than the train may be detained in your city." *Chicago Inter-Ocean*, Dec. 29, 1879. USG visited Augusta, Ga., on Dec. 31.

Also on Dec. 31, during a brief stop at Columbia, S. C., Mayor William B. Stanley had tendered to USG "the hospitalities of the capital." USG responded: "Mr. Mayor, I thank you for your kind invitation. It would afford me great pleasure to accept the kindly proffered hospitality of the good people of Columbia, thus afforded me without regard to party, but my engagements are such that I am denied this pleasure. You will please return my sincere thanks to the Common Council and the people of Columbia for their hospitable invitation." *New York Herald*, Jan. 1, 1880. Afterward, in USG's private car, "it was remarked that Mayor Stanley, who was a Confederate soldier, and whose splendid residence perished in burning Columbia, and the General had been comrades in Mexico. To this the ex-President replied:—'Captain, we were under the same flag then, and in future wars, if they ever come, we shall stand under the same flag together again.'" *Ibid.*

On Jan. 1, 1880, USG spoke at Beaufort, S. C. "It has afforded me great pleasure to pay a visit to the town of Beaufort. It is a place that has occupied a conspicuous place in the history of our country for the past twenty years and it is to be hoped that it is a place where the best of the newly enfranchised race are to be developed. I hope that they will become worthy and capable citizens. I thank the people for the manner in which I have been welcomed here." *Chicago Inter-Ocean*, Jan. 2, 1880. An impromptu reception featured white and black military companies, the latter organized by Robert Smalls. See *ibid.*, Jan. 9, 1880.

On Dec. 31, Wednesday, USG, Charlotte, N. C., had telegraphed to Frank E. Rebarer, clerk of council, Savannah. "I take pleasure in acknowledging the courtesy of the

City Council of Savannah. I expect to reach Savannah to-morrow evening or the next day, and remain until Saturday afternoon." *Savannah Morning News*, Jan. 1, 1880. See *ibid.*, Jan. 2, 1880. On Jan. 2, "the Savannah Volunteer Guards Band" serenaded USG at his hotel. USG responded, "stating his appreciation of the compliment, and of the courtesy that had been extended him in Savannah, and regretting that his stay was not longer, as he would like to see more of the city and the citizens." *Ibid.*, Jan. 3, 1880. On Jan. 3, the party boarded a steamer for Fernandina. See *ibid.*, Jan. 5, 1880.

    2. See *PUSG*, 15, 434–37.

To George W. Childs

————

[*St. Augustine, Fla., Jan. 18, 1880*]

Please say to General Patterson—you probably know he contemplates accompanying us to the city of Mexico—that a week after our arrival in Cuba I expect to sail on a naval vessel to the principal West India islands, Yucatan, etc.[,] to bring up at Vera Cruz about the 15th or 16th of February. If he is in Havana to take the New York steamer which leaves Havana February 12th he will meet me in Vera Cruz. If I should not go all the way on a naval vessel, but return from my excursion to Havana, I shall take the steamer on the 12th of February.[1]

I am very much pleased with Florida. It has a great future before it. A peninsula extending out from a great continent like ours, affording an unlimited demand for all the semi-tropical productions it can supply, there is scarcely a limit to its resources. It is capable of supplying all the oranges, lemons, pine-apples and other semi-tropical fruits used in the United States, the one hundred million dollars of sugar now imported, materials for rope, bagging, coarse matting, &c., any quantity of good pine, spruce and live oak timber, rice, &c. It has an area greater than New York, Massachusetts and Connecticut combined, with deposits of fertilizers under it and about it sufficient for many generations. It only wants people and enterprise, both of which it is rapidly obtaining. Florida today affords the best opening in the world for young men of small means and great industry. The next thing wanted here is the establishment of moderate sized sugar mills over the country, to purchase

all the cane small farmers will raise and send to them. I will probably have more to say on this subject when I get back home.

Very truly yours,

U. S. Grant.

Philadelphia Public Ledger, Jan. 27, 1880. The two paragraphs appeared separately in
the same issue, the first identified as to George W. Childs, the second (with closing)
as "Extract from private letter." The date is conjectured from the second paragraph by
comparing it to the letter to Elihu B. Washburne, Jan. 18, 1880.

1. "General Patterson said last evening that he intends, his health permitting, to
leave on the steamer which sails on the 12th of February for Vera Cruz, and will stop at
Havana. . . ." *Philadelphia Public Ledger*, Jan. 27, 1880.

To Ellen Grant Sartoris

St. Augustine, Fla.
Jan.y 18th /80

My Dear Daughter:

The papers announce that Algie is in New York City, or was
over a week ago. But as we hear nothing more about it I do not
credit the report. We have had a most enjoyable trip through the
south. The people have shewn the same sort of enthusiasm they
did in the North. We have now been in Florida two weeks. The
weather is like spring in Washington. The oranges are in full blast,
the gardens are teaming with strawberries, cucumbers, mellons
and almost all kinds of vegitables. This is becoming a great resort
for invalids and people who wish to avoid the rigors of a Northern
Winter.

We sail from Cedar Keys for Havana on the 20th. After re-
maing there a week or ten days we expect to take a Naval Vessels &
visit most of the important West India Islands. About the 15th of
Feb.y we will reach Vera Cruz and go on up to the City of Mexico
to remain until about the 1st of Apl. Write to us there directing
your letter to the care of the U. S. Consul General. We will stop in
Colorado on our way back and remain until the weather is pleasant in Galena, say about the 10th of May.—I wrote you a letter

from Galena asking you, Algie & the little boy & girl to come over and spend the summer with us at Long Branch. I also extended a special invitation for your father-in-law to come. Did you get the letter?—Your Ma has directed Buck to send you a check for fifty pounds (£50) as a Christmas present.

Fred & Ida, Gen. & Mrs. Sheridan, & Kitty Felt are with us, and will remain at least until we get to Denver, probably all but Gen. & Mrs. Sheridan until we go to Galena.

I wish you would write often. Your Ma is always anxious to hear from you. Your Ma thought you might want to get something pretty so she sent you the £50. She asks me to say this and also how much she wishes you were with us.—Next summer we will have Ida & Julia with us, and a part of the time Fred. Buck & Jesse will spend a good part of their time with us also so that if you & the children come we will have all our treasures together.

With love to all,

yours affectionately
U. S. GRANT

ALS, ICHi.

To Elihu B. Washburne

St. Augustine, Fla.
Jan. 18th /80

MY DEAR MR. WASHBURNE:

I wrote you a hasty letter from Phila but do not know whether you received it. Our trip through the south has been so far without an incident to mar the pleasure of it. All the way from Washington the people of all classes and colors were at the stations to meet the train and to extend invitations for myself and party to stop and accept their hospitalities. The business boom has reached the south and the people are begining to feel much better contented in consequence. I am very much pleased with Florida. The winter climate is perfection, and, I am told by Northern men settled here

that the summers are not near so hot here as in the North, though
of longer continuance. This state has a great future before it.[1] It has
the capacity to raise all the sugar and semi tropical fruits the whole
country needs besides supplying vast amounts of timber, early vegitables, rice, material for paper, rope, baging, coarse matting &c.
It affords the best opening to be found in any country for young
men of little means but full of energy, industry and patience. The
impetus already given will supply in a few years all the semi tropical fruits required by the country. What is now wanted is the establishment of moderate sugar mills over the country to buy all the
sugar cane small farmers will furnish. The state is underlayed and
has around it deposites of valuable fertilizers sufficient for many
generations. If you do not join me in Cuba I hope you will come
here to spend March & Apl. I do not doubt but you would receive
much benefit from the visit.

I will sail from Cedar Keys for Havana on the 20th.[2] The sec.
of the Navy has placed at Havana a vessel at my command. I think
I shall make an excursion to Hayti, St Domingo, Porto Rico & Ja-
maica, and swing around by Yucatan so as to reach Vera Cruz about
the 15th of Feb.y. When I return it will be by the way of Galveston &
Denver. At the latter place, and in Colorado generally, I expect to
stop until the weather is pleasant in Galena, say about the 10th of
May. I shall be very much pleased to meet you in Havana and have
you go on the trip to the West Indies if you are sailor enough to
enjoy the trip.

With kindest regards of Mrs. Grant & myself to you, Mrs. W.
and all the family, I am,

Very Truly

U. S. GRANT

ALS, IHi. See James P. Jones, ed., "Grant Forecasts the Future of Florida," *Florida
Historical Quarterly*, XXIX, 1 (July, 1960), 52–54.

1. On Jan. 14, 1880, USG spoke at St. Augustine, after a welcoming address from
Mayor George S. Greeno. "Mr. Mayor, I thank you for your kind welcome. I have seen
something of your State and am greatly pleased with it. Florida is the oldest settled State,
but really the youngest in development. From what I have seen I am convinced that it
will in time produce more than any other State—that is, from its soil. It cannot of course
be expected to equal in manufactures and commerce many of the Northern States. The

soil products of some of our Northern States are enormous, but I feel sure, although it may appear to be an exaggerated statement, that in time your sugar and semi-tropical fruits will exceed in value the products of any other State in the Union. Again I thank you for your kindly expressions of welcome." *New York Tribune,* Jan. 20, 1880.

2. On Jan. 21, USG spoke at Key West. "I heartily thank the colored citizens of Key West for their cordial welcome. I trust that they will ever appreciate the new rights bestowed upon them and attend well to the duties entailed upon them, to society and their country by these privileges. In this way you will disarm any unfriendly critics and live to enjoy the greatness and beneficence of our country and participate in its progress." *Ibid.,* Jan. 30, 1880. Cuban refugees also welcomed USG. "General Grant said, in reply, that the Cubans, or any other refugees in this country, would always find a free home with us. He trusted they would prosper in their adopted country and never desire to leave it." *Ibid.*

To Jesse Root Grant, Jr.

———

Havana, Cuba,
Jan.y 23d 1880.

DEAR JESSE:

Your ma was very much pleased to receive your letter, which she did on our arrival here yesterday. We were received at the landing by the principle Officials of the island and city, and conducted to the Governmt Palace where we are quartered in great magnificence Next week we expect to take one of our Naval Vessels and isit a few others of the West India Island and return here in time for the steamer which passes about the 12th of Feb.y for Vera Cruz. We will return in April by Galveston to Colorado where we will remain until May. You and Buck must write to us, to this place, on receipt of this. After that to the City of Mexico.

We were both glad to hear you had started out so well. I hope it will continue and improve as time passes. What have you heard from your Arizona Mines? Buck I hope has been fortunate enough to invest some for me where it will do well. I would like to make enough to get me a house in Washington . . . terrific earthquakes here last night, the first it is said they have ever had in Havana. It frightened the people very much and your Ma & Ida were sorry they had enlisted for the journey. I have not heard that any harm was done in the city. . . .

AL (signature clipped), Barry Bernstein, Randolph, Mass. For USG's visit to Cuba, see
Chicago Inter-Ocean, Jan. 23, 24, Feb. 9, 12, 14, 21, 1880; *Philadelphia Times*, Feb. 13, 24,
1880; *Harper's Weekly*, Feb. 28, March 6, 1880.
　　On Jan. 23, 1880, USG received a congratulatory message from King Alfonso XII
of Spain. *Chicago Inter-Ocean*, Jan. 24, 1880. On Jan. 24, citizens of Havana presented
USG with an address. D (in Spanish), Smithsonian Institution.

To Julius A. Skilton

Havana, Cuba,
Feb.y 2d 1880

DR. JULIUS A. SKILTON,
U. S. CONSUL, MEXICO,
DEAR DR.

　　Your favor of the 24th of Jan.y inquiring the time of my arrival
in Vera Cruz is just received. I have taken passage on the Steamer
Alexandra which will leave Havana about the 13th of this month.
My party consists of self & Mrs. Grant, with two young ladies,
Gen. & Mrs. Sheridan, Col. & Mrs. Grant—My son & wife—and
General Paterson of Philadelphia, an old gentleman of 87 or 89
years who will remain in the City of Mexico but a few days. He
will be of my party however as long as he remains. It is very kind
in the Mexican authorities to fix up a house for me and I appreciate
the compliment. I hope I may have an opportunity of returning the
compliment in part some day.

　　With many thanks for your kind interest, I am Dr.

Very Truly yours
U. S. GRANT

ALS, Boston Public Library, Boston, Mass. Born in 1833 in Troy, N. Y., Julius A.
Skilton trained as a physician, served as a surgeon during the war, and moved to Mexico City, where he served as consul and consul gen. (1869–1878). See *PUSG*, 19, 421.
On March 1, 1880, John W. Foster, U.S. minister, Mexico City, wrote to Skilton. ". . .
What led you to address me your first letter of the 16th ultimo was that at a meeting
of the American residents of the City of Mexico, on the 11th ultimo, to ma[ke] arrangements for a proper reception to General Gran[t,] of which meeting I was made
chairman and empo[w]ered by it to nominate a general committee of a[r]rangements,
in selecting said committee I did n[ot] see proper to include you as a member of it. I
am at a loss to know why you have a greater caus[e] of complaint for this omission than

the othe[r] thirty or more persons who where present at said meeting and who, like you, were not placed on the committee. Feeling aggrieved by my omission, you sen[t] a gentleman to me to ask me if I intentionally omitte[d] to place you on the committee, to which I promptly [res]ponded that I did so intentionally; and when aske[d] why I did so, I replied that I did not consider yo[u] a proper person to represent the American residents [*of*] Mexico. . . . based upon certain supposed charges against your conduct during your consular career in this country. . . ." Copy, DNA, RG 59, Diplomatic Despatches, Mexico.

On July 1, 1879, Foster had written to USG. "Noticing your expected early arrival at San Francisco, I wish to recall to your attention a desire you expressed to me before the close of your last Presidential term, that when out of office you might be able to make a visit to Mexico. I earnestly hope that you may now find it convenient to carry out that desire. I beg to extend to you in my own name and that of all our countrymen resident in this Republic a hearty and pressing invitation, and I can assure you of a most cordial reception on the part of the Mexican government and the authorities and people generally. By the time you shall have made a short visit in the Pacific States, the season will be the most favorable of the entire year for a trip to Mexico, crossing the country from the Pacific to the Gulf coast. I send this letter through my late Secretary of Legation, Mr. Richardson, who is well acquainted with the country and can give you valuable information as to the routes, climate &c. With my congratulations on your safe return to your native land, after so long and distinguished an absence, . . ." ALS, DLC-USG, IB. "Minister Foster has received a letter from Gen. Grant, dated Dec. 21st informing him that he will carry out his long cherished desire, and visit Mexico, and may be expected to arrive during the first week in February, next." *The Two Republics,* Jan. 11, 1880.

To Elihu B. Washburne

——

Havana, Cuba,
Feb.y 2d 1880,

My Dear Mr. Washburne,

Your letter of the 25th of Jan.y is just received. The same mail brings New York papers of the 29th by which I see you were in that city at that time. Your letter directed to me in Washington City was received there but I neglected to mention it.—I see by the papers the same that you mention about Sherman. I predict that it will do him no good, and as far as it may effect me I care nothing about it. All that I want is that the Government rule should remain in the hands of those who saved the Union until all the questions growing out of the war are forever settled. I would much rather any one of many I could mention should be President than that I should have it. On that subject I stand just as I told you in Chicago. I shall not gratify my enemies by declining what has not been offered. I am not a candidate for any thing, and if the Chicago convention nominates a candidate that can be elected it will gratify me, and the gratification will be greater if it should be some one other than myself. In confidence I will tell you I should feel sorry if it should be John Sherman. Blain I would like to see elected, but I fear the party could not elect him. He would create inthusiasm, but he would have opposition in his own party that might loose him some Northern states that the republicans should carry.

My reception here has been more than cordial by both officials and the people. The weather is sultry, just such as we run from at home in the Dog Days. If this winter is a sample Fla. is a much better winter resort.

Please present Mrs. Grant's and my best regards to Mrs. Washburne and your family, with the same to yourself. I shall be pleased to hear from you in the City of Mexico.

Very Truly yours

U. S. GRANT

ALS, IHi. On Feb. 11, 1880, Elihu B. Washburne, Chicago, wrote to USG. "You see I am home again and I have this moment received Your esteemed letter of the 2d instant. I wrote you quite fully from N. Y. as to the State of things and there has been no particular change. The Blaine men seem to have taken courage from the action of Pennsylvania, but I cannot see from what stand point. They made a stubborn fight and were *beaten.* They have now commenced an aggressive campaign everywhere and are exceedingly boast-full. In this State they have commenced a regular campaign and one of the tricks is to take a 'census' of the votes in particular localities and of course, their man always comes out ahead. They are attempting to arouse the prejudice of the Germans and asserting all the time that you cannot get the German vote, while *he* can. I profess to know as much about the Germans as any one, and I think I have told you that you would get as many German votes as any republican candidate, and perhaps more. John Sherman may be regarded as practically out of the fight. He is not sure of all of Ohio, and he will get no other votes than those manipulated for him from the Southern States. His utter weakness surprises even his enemies. While the party and the country fully understand your position touching the Presidency, your friends have launched your name as a candidate and do not intend to be beaten. There is a great effort made to weaken you by putting afloat all kinds of canards and they have had a certain effect by bewildering your friends. 1st That you would not accept any nomination. 2d That you would not receive any nomination unless tendered unanimously. 3d That you had written home that you would not—accept any nomination. Upon consultation with Mr. Jones, of the Times, it was thought best to have the enclosed appear and then telegraphed over the Country, as has been done. It is believed that the statement will be accepted as correct. I wrote you that Logan had been bitten by the 'Black Horse,' implying that you might be beaten, or out of the way. I am now assured that he denies it. I am in a friendly correspondence with him and I hope he will act cordially and in good faith with me. He is a power in the State. I must tell you frankly what we have to meet and what is doing us more damage than all else combined. Indeed, if it were not for that there would practically be no serious opposition. It is the senseless, dishonest and fraudulent cry of the 'Third Term'. Of course the copperheads howl over it, and now the opposition of our own party is howling still louder and it is humiliating to acknowledge with a good deal of effect. This constant dinging has prejudiced a greater number of people than you could imagine. I meet so many republicans and who have been great friend of yours, who talk thus: 'I like Grant, have always voted for him, would now be glad to do anything for him, but am unalterably opposed to a third term. I hold to the example of Washington, and if we depart from it, particularly in the case of a Military man, he might through the patronage of the Government perpetuate himself in office. If we elect Grant again he may so strengthen himself that he may hold on for life.' It is no use to argue with such a man and tell him how dishonest the third term cry is—that it is no third term in any honest sense, and that every evil ascribed to a third term has been cured by the intervention of a term. He answers me one term more & it means indefinite terms. I feel, and all your real friends feel, that we should have some help in this matter to take the sting out of this sort of argument. I take it that if you should again be elected President you would have no desire to serve more than one term more under any possible circumstances, and I submit whether that cannot be said by you in a letter to some friend, who can make it public. But you understand these matters so well, that I would not presume to advise, or scarcely to suggest. Yet I venture to jot down on another page as to what I think would do good & for you to give such consideration as you see fit, feeling that I have but one motive, and that is to act for the best with the lights before me. Pray dont think I have the least pride of opinion and believe I should defer to your ~~better~~ better judgment. . . . It seems to me that you might properly write that you have seen in the home newspapers the progress of the campaign which seems to have opened for the Republican nomination for President and had observed that your name had been used & that the Penn. delegates had been instructed to support your nomination. If you should address a letter to me you could say that I have been made aware of the position which you have always held on the subject—that you have in no wise changed and that you have never had part nor lot, either directly or indirectly in any movement touching your nomination by the Republican party. [Nothing could be more admirable than what you say in your letter to me] 'That all my interest centres in this, that the Government should remain in the hands of those who served it until all the questions growing out of the war are forever settled. I would much prefer to see many, whom I can mention, President for the coming term than to be President myself. No one knows better than ~~myself~~ yourself that I have never sought positions for myself, either in the military or civil service, and was never a candidate for anything. Should the Chicago Convention nominate a candidate, as it unquestionably will, who can be elected, it would be far more gratifying to me than if the nomination should fall upon myself.' And I should add that whatever services you had rendered the country were not in the hope of office, but in vindication of a holy cause, involving the salvation of the Union and the happiness and prosperity of a great people for all coming times. That your services have received the highest honor which a free people could bestow and that any suggestion that you are seeking any-thing further is unjust to you. [Now as to the third term business, which is by far the most important of all & doing us more damage than everything else put together. I wish you could find something to say that would help us.] Perhaps you could get at it by saying that you have seen in the press a discussion of the Third Term and your can-didacy in connection therewith, all of which is also unjust to you as you have never been a candidate for *any term*. That you had expressed your views on the third term in a letter to Gen.l White of Pa. in May 18765. That you could never see the danger of a third term which had been so vividly depicted by many good & patriotic men. I find 'that the idea that any man could reelect himself President or even renominate himself is preposterous. It is a reflection upon the intelligence and patriotism of the people to suppose such a thing possible.' But whatever may be the argument or the reason on the subject of third consecutive term, the sentiment of the people undoubtedly is to hold to the example of Washington and the traditions of the country. There might be a well grounded fear that by being too long in power, and strengthening himself by the use of the vast patronage of the Government and controlling political organizations a Presi-dent *might* perpetuate himself in office. While such a state of things might seem impos-sible in a country so free intelligent and enlightened as ours, yet such a sentiment, in-spired by a feeling of true patriotism, must be heeded. And if in the future of our country it should so happen, as it probably never will happen, that after a man had served for two terms as President, and should after the invention of one term, be elected a third time, he should in deference to the public opinion on this subject, have it clearly understood that he would not under any circumstances or conditions whatever be a candidate for another election. It is with the utmost diffidence that I make this suggestion. You may think it better to say nothing, or if anything, different from this. Of course you must use your own better judgment. I only want to tell you how that shoe is pinching us. I am on general principles against writing political letters, but there are occasions which demand such letters. It is for you to judge in this instance. No person on earth knows of my writing you and after reading may destroy. I find your letter to Harry White also despatched from N. Y." AL (initialed, brackets in orig-inal), USG 3. "A near personal and political friend of ex-President GRANT, who doubt-less knows whereof he speaks, authorizes the following as a correct statement of the General's position with reference to the Presidency. He says: Gen. GRANT is not now, nor has he ever been, a candidate for Presidential nomination. But, should the Republi-can National Convention nominate him in the same manner as any other candidate would be nominated, he would deem it his duty to the country and the party to accept. Traveling abroad, he was a stranger to the contest now going on for the Presidential nomination, and has written no letters on the subject to any person, and all assertions to the contrary are without foundation in fact." *New York Times*, Feb. 10, 1880. See *PUSG*, 26, 132–34.

On Oct. 27, 1879, James M. Comly had written to President Rutherford B. Hayes. "Personal . . . At San Francisco General Grant sent for me one night at 12 o'clock, and kept me (part of the time very uneasily, for I thought it was surely too much of a tax on him) until 2 a. m. He talked in the most interesting manner of his entire trip—but it is not of that I want to write, just now. I asked him frankly and in the most direct and unequivocal English at my command, whether he would be willing under any cir-cumstances to allow his name to be brought out for a third Term—telling him his communication could be as confident[ial] as he desired, if he wished me to say noth-ing on the subject. He responded with the utmost frankness, without any injunction at secrecy, but (as I understood) with a wish to avoid any public mention or discussion. He said, substantially—(I think I give his exact language)—'I do not want to run again. I would rather somebody else would be nominated. I do not think I am needed for a candidate. I would rather they would take somebody else.' He mentioned some names which he said were good strong names and good Republicans. Spoke very cordially of Sherman first—Blaine, and yourself. Said he was sorry you had such an an objection to a second term. I think he referred to a reported interview with you in Chicago, which came by telegraph about that day, covering that point. After one or two more expressions in a general way, he said, 'I would not turn my hand over, either way,' (making the motion with his hand.) He then began again talking about his trip. The conversation changed my opinion entirely as to Grant's candidacy—his willingness I mean. I am convinced that he will not decline a [nom]ination, if tendered with full acquiescence of leading Republicans. One thing has made this conversation seem of sufficient interest to justify the space it has occupied—and that is the following: Before I went in (with Grant's valet, whom he sent for me,) John Russell Young said that Grant was going to send for me after the crowd was gone, and he said, very urgently—'The General has not told anybody about the third Term business yet. He has been asked by a good many, and he looks straight before him and simply refuses to reply at all. I know he will tell you, if you ask him.' I expressed the astonishment I felt at such an assertion, but Young repeated, 'I know what I am talking about—you ask him—he will tell you all about it.' The next morning, Young was passing to the carriages with the party, as I stood in the Court of the Hotel, and he ran out from them to say 'That it was as I told you, wasn't it?' Of course I am not quite foolish enough to suppose that General Grant talked to me for any reason personal to myself. I think I was expected to write to you about it—and have accordingly done so—though I shall treat the conversation as otherwise strictly confidential for the present, until otherwise advised at least. . . ." Typescript, OHi.

On Dec. 29, Washburne, Chicago, wrote to John A. Logan. ". . . I have had long talks with the most prominent and influential Germans here. While they say that Grant is not a particular favorite that the Republican Germans will all vote for him as against the rebel and copperhead candidate. It is idle to talk of Sherman—he has no strength anywhere.—with Grant out of the way the Convention would be Blaine without a question, in my mind. But I think it will be so overwhelming for Grant that Blaine will get out of the road. . . ." ALS, DLC-John A. Logan. On Jan. 16, 17, 20, and 25, 1880, Washburne wrote to Logan. "I want you to tell me, in a word, if there be anything in all the talk they are making at Washington and in Ohio about an 'Anti-Grant' boom. It looks a little as if J. S. were mending his fences in Ohio. . . . There is undoubtedly a concerted effort making to detach the Germans from Grant, but I am satisfied they will swing into line when the time come" "*Strictly private*. . . . Last night the chairman of the Ohio Republican State committee come here to see me. He is an enthusiastic Grant man and wanted to talk with me about the situation. He says the Sherman men are making herculean efforts and that he very much fears they will carry the four delegates at large. But the other delegates are elected by the districts and that the Grant men will contest in all the districts and certainly carry some of them. He is down on Sherman and the Hayes crowd. Charley Foster, Garfield and others are bellowing for Sherman. He is evidently alarmed a little at 'the Sherman boom.' The enclosed will shew you the fraud they are practicing on the public in order to influence public opinion. One gratifying thing, he says the talk they are making all the time about the Germans not voting for Grant is all humbug—that the Ohio Germans (Republican) will vote for Grant and that there will be no doubt about his carrying the State."

"*Private* . . . There is no doubt a Sherman boom is to be worked up here by the proconsul and the custom house gang generally, who seriously think there is a chance to capture the State. Then there is a Blaine boom. The two will hunt in couples—'anything to beat Grant.' There are indications that we cannot afford to ignore. . . ." "You are quite right the 'enemies are at work.' The Sherman men scruple at nothing and the last dodge, which I today denounced, is that you have dropped Grant and are going for Sherman & Hawley in consideration of the patronage. I hear of agents going over the whole State in S's interests. It, therefore, behooves all the General's friends to be active and awake, though I cannot consider there is any reasonable fear that we cannot carry the State overwhelmingly in the convention. The stuff they write you about me is simply absurd and untrue. I have never under any circumstances held but one language— that being for Grant first, last and all the time—that having very often thought that if he should be out of the way, (which he will not be) I might be a candidate, would simply prove me false. Under no conditions would I be a candidate for President, and I should only run for Governor to help the boom along here.—I am watching the progress of events as to what we ought to do in the General's interest, and have made no determination as to what I ought to do about the Governorship There can be no antagonism between us. . . ." ALS, *ibid.* On Feb. 10, Washburne again wrote to Logan. "*strictly private* . . . From what I have seen here I confess I do not like the outlook. They have started an Anti Grant boom and its *apparent* strength would surprise you. A good many of your great number of friends are in it, as well as some of my very small number of friends. There are things going on in quarters little dreamed of. Fore warned is to be forearmed. It now looks to me as if all the exertions of Genl Grants' true and unselfish friends would be needed to carry our State for him in the National Convention. No one can regret as much as I do the suggestion which continues to be made that I may come in if Grant be out of the way. It implies a want of good faith in me towards the General. Whoever pretends to be for him, and has an afterthought for himself is of no value to him, for the logic is, if he think he may be a candidate under certain circumstances, he will act in such a manner as to bring the circumstances about. It would have been with the greatest reluctance that I would have taken the field for Governor, and only in the hope that my candidacy that my candidacy might have smoothed the way for the General, especially with the Germans. I have no earthly desire for the position. In looking over the field and seeing the great number of candidates who would have to be antagonized, I think I can do more, by being entirely foot loose, which is in accordance with my inclination. I shall not, therefore, permit the use of my name. . . ." ALS, *ibid.* See John Sherman to William H. Smith, Jan. 26, 1880, InHi; Allan Peskin, *Garfield* (Kent, Ohio, 1978), pp. 452–60.

In Feb., at Gainesville, Ga., a reporter asked James Longstreet whom he preferred for president. "First and foremost, General Grant, . . . There are Southern States which one Republican and one alone can carry, and that one is General Grant—North Carolina, Louisiana, Georgia. . . . Yes, it is possible for Grant to carry Georgia. Why not? Almost half the population of the State are negroes, every man of them Republicans at heart. . . . They have begun organizing clubs in this State already; clubs composed exclusively of negroes, manipulated by no white politicians; and the sentiment of these clubs seems to be that the negroes shall act independently for Grant, regardless of the efforts of politicians to gain their proxies to the nominating convention. The negroes of Georgia are a unit for Grant; but for Sherman or Blaine there will be no such enthusiasm, and their nomination would enable the Democrats of Georgia again to control the negro vote. . . ." *Chicago Inter-Ocean,* Feb. 20, 1880.

To John Russell Young
———

~~C~~Havana, Cuba
Feb.y 2d 1880.

My Dear Commodore:

I received four letters, with some enclosures, from you just before leaving Fla. for which I am much obliged. We have now been ten days in Cuba. The weather has been oppressive, just such as we run from in the U. S. in July & August.[1] The reception by the authorities & people has been as warm as the climate The Acting Capt. Gen.—in the absence of Gen. Blanco[2] who we met in Barcilona—met us on the steamer when we entered the harbor and conducted us to the Govt. Palace where we have been Masters of the establishment, much after the style in Tokio, ever since. General Blanco left two of his Aides to see that nothing should be wanted, and a number of carriages for our use. Our excursions are by special trains, with officers to accompany us, and escorts of Cavalry, headed by the Governor of the province we may be in, on leaving the trains for the points to be visited. It is all very kind, but it is at the same time doubtful wheather it is just the best way to see the country.—On the 13th we take our departure for Mexico. I understand the authorities there have fitted up a house for us. This will be very pleasant unless things have changed very much since I was there. At that time there was not a public place in the country where a traveler could be comfortable except in private houses. The accommodations in Victoria, Spain, would be luxury compared to them.—You have probably noticed that we stopped about two weeks in Florida? I have changed my notions materially about that state. It has now but little over 200.000 people, with an area greater than New York, Massachusetts & Connecticut combined, and a capacity to produce all the sugar, semi-tropical fruits, rice & tobacco we now import, besides furnishing much lumber, early vegitables &c. It is just begining to take a start, and I predict that the census of 1890 will show it to be one of the richest states in the Union per capita of its inhabitants instead of the very poorest, as it was according to the census of /70. We will always be pleased to hear from you, and regret that you are not along. I am very glad to be out of the United States at this time. At a distance I can read the papers and feel as indifferent as to results—so far as they relate to individual aspirations—as the woman did who witnessed the encounter between her husband and ~~the~~ a bear. Mrs. Grant says this is a slander on the woman.

With kind regards of all the party,

Yours Truly,

U. S. GRANT

J. R. YOUNG, ESQ.

ALS, DLC-John Russell Young.

On Jan. 1, 1880, George W. Childs, Philadelphia, wrote to John Russell Young. "Your kind note of Dec. 12. came just an hour or two before your friend Genl. Grant ~~before~~was leaving the city. He seemed much gratified in getting his letter, with the London Times article, and read both very attentively, and I also let him read your letter to me. He said he would read them over again in the train, and try to write to you from Washington, if he could possibly get a moment. He always speaks of you in the warmest terms, and I know appreciates you most highly, as you deserve. He said he wished you could have accompanied him to Cuba and Mexico. Mrs. Grant told me to be sure and give her kindest remembrances to you, and say she enjoyed your company very much. I wish I could tell you all the kind things Genl. & Mrs. Grant say of you. The Grant reception here was truly grand. Nothing like it has ever been seen on this Continent. Cook is glad you like his despatches. Mr. Borie speaks in the most affectionate terms of you. He is not well. A. J. D. is much better and leaves for Europe with his family on Mondy 12th, so you will no doubt see him. He has always been a good friend of yours. Fred. Grant has been staying a few days with me. When your book is completed, it should then have a much increased sale. Take good care of your self, and always remember you have many friends in America, chief among them is yours sincerely" ALS, *ibid.*

1. On Jan. 27, touring Havana's Morro Castle with USG, "General Sheridan remarked that this was just the kind of weather people ran away from at home in summer, and now in winter they come down here to find it." *Chicago Inter-Ocean*, Feb. 9, 1880.

2. Ramon Blanco, appointed capt. gen. of Cuba in April, 1879.

To Ellen Grant Sartoris

Havana, Cuba,

Feb.y 7th 1880

MY DEAR DAUGHTER:

In a few days now we start for Mexico. We have had a delightful time here though the weather has been too warm. It has been about the same it is in Washington in July & August. In Mexico, though four degrees further south, it will be much cooler owing to the great altitude. I wish you and Algy were with us. But you will be all next Summer. I expect little Algie and I to have a good time fishing, driving fast horses, playing in the sand &c. He will probably be able to throw me down as Jesse used to do before he got to big and clumsy.—You will probably hear before this reaches you that Mr. Borie died two days ago.[1] I have heard none of the particulars; only a dispatch announcing the fact.

I presume you hear from Buck & Jesse. They are both at work on their own account and I hope doing well. But just how they are doing I do not know. Probably Algy can tell you better.—Will Mr. Sartoris, Sr. make us a visit? He would enjoy a summer in the United States I know.—We have visited several places of interest since our arrival on this island. One to the celebrated hot springs and a large tobacco pl and sugar plantation towards the Western part of the island, and one to Matansas, east of here. We have had about fifty miles experience traveling in Volantes, the two wheeled vehicles of this country.[2] To-morrow commences the three days carnival common in exclusively Catholic countries.

All send love and kisses to you and the children. Write to us directed to the care of the United States Minister, City of Mexico.

yours affectionately
U. S. Grant

Ida you know is with us. She is a great favorite with every one we meet, and as much so with your Ma as ever. She and Fred. and Gen. & Mrs. Sheridan sends love also. Your Ma sends kisses to you and the little ones.

ALS, ICHi.

1. On Feb. 7, 1880, USG, Havana, telegraphed to Elizabeth M. Borie, Philadelphia. "Mrs Grant and I condole with you over the loss of your beloved husband one of our best of friends & of Philadelphias noblest and most highly respected citizens many an honest tear will be shed over the memory of one so universally beloved" Telegram received, PHi. On Feb. 12, George W. Childs wrote to John Russell Young. "I know how sad you were to hear of the death of your dear good friend, Mr. Borie. He appreciated you and took so much pleasure in speaking of you. Such friends are not easily replaced. I have forwarded all your letters to Gen. Grant; and he very much regretted

you could not accompany him to Cuba and Mexico. Your book is much quoted, and grows in interest." John Russell Young, *Men and Memories: Personal Reminiscences* (New York, 1901), II, 294. In his will, Adolph E. Borie left USG $10,000. *Philadelphia Times*, Feb. 11, 1880. Borie also bequeathed to Orville E. Babcock an annual sum of $1,200 until the total reached $5,000, "including one thousand dollars I have paid him in the year 1876, . . ." *Ibid.*, Feb. 15, 1880.

    2. Accompanying the Grant party, journalists Byron Andrews and Frank H. Taylor described the volante in the *Chicago Inter-Ocean* and *Philadelphia Times*, Feb. 9, 1880. See also *Julia Grant*, p. 313.

To Daniel Ammen

HAVANA, CUBA, February 8th, 1880.

MY DEAR ADMIRAL,—

When I last wrote you I neglected to say that I received the *North American Review* containing your article on the Lesseps[1] canal. I had read the article while in Florida, together with some criticisms on it, characterizing it as more personal than argumentative. I could not see, for the life of me, that the criticisms had any foundation. Now that Congress has taken the matter up,[2] there is more reason to hope that something may be done towards the solution of an Inter-Oceanic canal. Eads writes me in favor of his ship-railroad project,[3] predicting for it success and a hasty completion when once commenced. Of course the route for such a road would be Tehuantepec. I never like to predict that a thing can't be done; but it seems to me that a ship with full cargo making a long land-voyage might prove unseaworthy when she got in the water again.

We leave here for Mexico when the steamer Alexandra—which sailed from New York yesterday—passes here. It is not my expectation to reach Galena before about the middle of May, nor the Eastern States until time to occupy my Long Branch house,—say about the first of July.

The authorities here have been extremely hospitable, as have been the people also. Last night there was a beautiful fancy ball[4] given to us by one of our citizens. but Mrs. Grant and I could not have it in our hearts to go, having just heard of the death of my dear old friend, associate in the Cabinet, and travelling-companion,

Mr. Borie. I knew he was weak, but hoped he had many years before him.

Mrs. Grant sends her love to Mrs. Ammen, Mrs. Atocha, and the children. With best regards to all of them,

Yours truly,

U. S. GRANT.

Daniel Ammen, *The Old Navy and the New* (Philadelphia, 1891), p. 550. See *ibid.*, pp. 477–79; *Chicago Inter-Ocean*, Jan. 9, 1880; letter to Daniel Ammen, June 22, 1880. Ammen's article, "M. de Lesseps and His Canal," appeared in the *North American Review*, CXXX, CCLXXIX (Feb., 1880), 130–46.

1. Born in 1805, Ferdinand de Lesseps left a career as a French diplomat to direct the successful completion of the Suez Canal (1854–69). In 1879, after a Paris conference selected Panama over Nicaragua and Mexico as the best route for a canal, de Lesseps agreed to lead the effort. See de Lesseps, "The Interoceanic Canal," *ibid.*, CCLXXXIII (Jan., 1880), 1–15; letter to Nathan Appleton, Jan. 1, 1881.
    2. See *HMD*, 46-3-16.
    3. See letter to James B. Eads, Jan. 13, 1882.
    4. See *Chicago Inter-Ocean*, Feb. 20, 1880.

To Alfred H. Isaacson

HAVANA, Cuba, Feb. 15, 1880.

TO THE HONORABLE A. H. ISAACSON, ACTING MAYOR OF NEW ORLEANS:

DEAR SIR—I have the honor and pleasure to acknowledge the receipt of your letter of the fourth of February, transmitting a copy of the resolution of the council of the city of New Orleans, inviting me to visit the city on my return from Mexico to the United States.

It would afford me pleasure to accept this invitation, but my route home from Mexico is so uncertain that I reluctantly decline. If the facilities of travel are sufficiently good to warrant it, I expect to cross over to the Pacific and to return by the way of San Francisco.[1] If they are not, I am desirous of returning home through Texas to enable me to visit some old places which were familiar to me before the Mexican war. With sincere thanks to the council of

New Orleans and your honor for your cordial invitation, I am, very respectfully, your obedient servant,

U. S. Grant.

New Orleans Times, Feb. 22, 1880. Born in 1833 in Philadelphia, former clerk, La. House of Representatives, Alfred H. Isaacson served as New Orleans administrator of finance. See Speech, [*March 31, 1880*].

1. On March 2, 1880, USG telegraphed to Secretary of the Navy Richard W. Thompson, from Mexico. "Will not be able to reach the Pacific Coast to accept services of vessel from there." Telegram received (at 9:05 p.m.), InFtwL.

Speech

[*Vera Cruz, Mexico, Feb. 18, 1880*]

General Teran, I am very glad to come to Mexico and to land at Vera Cruz. It has long been a wish of mine to come to this country, and I am pleased to find it at the moment of my arrival at peace with all the world. I hope that the relations between the United States and Mexico will grow closer every day. The development of this country will be a great advantage to the United States. Many Americans are watching with interest your progress, and manifesting a lively satisfaction in your progress. No one can be more gratified than myself at your improvement. I thank you for the marked cordiality and kindness with which I have been greeted.

Chicago Inter-Ocean, Feb. 27, 1880. Governor Luis Mier y Terán of Vera Cruz welcomed USG. "General Grant, the people of Vera Cruz are highly pleased at your arrival on the Mexican shores, and offer to you their fraternal hospitalities. This people desired your coming, as it wished the arrival of an old friend it remembers, and will always recollect with gratefulness your sympathy for this country, and the distinguished services you rendered Mexico on a very momentous occasion. We have always been bound to you, General Grant, with ties of friendship and good-will, and by a community of political principles. We have admired you when you contributed in such a controlling way with your victorious hand to break the chains of slavery and to maintain the national Union in your country, and when you ruled as a free and sincere republican the destinies of your great and enlightened nation. The State and city of Vera Cruz open their doors to you, rejoiced to-day on your arrival in Mexico. We wish that your stay in our country may be pleasant to you. Vera Cruz is proud that she is the first Mexican city which welcomes such a distinguished guest, such a great soldier and patriot." *Ibid.*

On Feb. 15, 1880, a newspaper reported. "Gen. Ignacio Mejia, ex-Minister of War and Mr. Matias Romero, ex-Minister of the Treasury, have been appointed a committee to receive Gen. Grant and party at Vera Cruz. . . ." *The Two Republics,* Feb. 15, 1880. On Feb. 18, aboard the *City of Alexandria,* Matías Romero welcomed USG to Mexico. "Gen. Grant responded, in substance, as follows: I am greatly obliged to the President of Mexico for having directed his congratulations upon my arrival, through you whom I have known in the service of Mexico under circumstance very difficult in our several countries. For a long time I have desired to visit Mexico and I am greatly gratified at having realized this desire. I believe that the progress and prosperity of Mexico is as earnestly desidered by my countrymen as by your own; and as one of them I entertain the most ardent desires for the aggrandisement of this beautiful country." *Ibid.,* Feb. 29, 1880. See *Philadelphia Times,* Feb. 29, 1880; Alberto Maria Carreño, ed., *Archivo Del General Porfirio Diaz: Memorias y Documentos* (Mexico City, 1947–61), XXX, 171–76, 179–80.

On [*Feb. 17*], Governor Simon Sarla of Tabasco had written to USG. "Not being able to have the honor of offering you my personal respects in your transit by this State, it is very pleasing to do it by the present sending you my friendly welcome, and wishing that your trip to our republic may be for the future the source of well-being for our respective nations, which now and ever must be united with the bonds of sympathy and fraternity. In the name of the State of Tabasco, whose future is under my care, I felicitate your Excellency most cordially for your arrival in our country." *Chicago Inter-Ocean,* Feb. 27, 1880.

On Feb. 19, USG, Orizaba, telegraphed to Sebastian Camacho *et al.* "Your telegram of this date extending a welcome to me, my family and persons who accompany me, was received in the moment that I was leaving Vera Cruz. I tender to you and the authorities my cordial thanks for the hospitable welcome with which I have been receceived in all parts in this interesting country." *The Two Republics,* Feb. 22, 1880.

To George W. Childs

————

City of Mexico
Feb.y 26th 1880.

My Dear Mr. Childs.

I received your letter, marked "Important" at night the second day before leaving Havana. My mail was very large, more than I got through reading that night. The following day I had an engagement to visit a model plantation in the interior of the island. On our way back the train ran over a cow and was thrown from the track. This detained us all night in the cars without a place to lay down. On our return to the city we only had time to get ready and board the steamer for Vera Cruz. We will be back in the United States about the 22d of March by which time public opinion will be sufficiently developed for me to determine my duty.

There is no part of the world where we have enjoyed our visit more than in Mexico. The climate is perfection, the scenery unsurpassed and the people as clever and hospitable as it is possible for them to be. The country is exceedingly productive both agriculturally and in minerals. From its latitude vegitation is perpetual. By its varied altitude every product from those of the torid to the frigid zone is possible. Although a mountainous country the plains run in such a way as to make the building of rail and other roads much easyer than in our eastern states. From the City of Mexico to the Rio Grande a road could be graded with as little labor as through an equal distance in Iowa. The people are not so much of an obsticle to the developement of the great resources of the country as is the bad name given to them abroad. With proper encouragement for a time, the introduction of foreign capital and enterprise to put the people on their feet Mexico would become a rich country, a good neighbor, and the two Republics would profit by the contact. Mexico could produce all the tropical & semi-tropical products we now import, and take from us Machinery of all sorts, agricultural impliments, and every variety of manufactured articles we make.

Give our kindest regards to Mrs. Childs, Miss Lizzie and to all our Phila friends.

Yours Truly

U. S. GRANT

ALS, DLC-USG.

USG reached Mexico City on Feb. 22, 1880. On Feb. 23, USG and Lt. Gen. Philip H. Sheridan called on President Porfirio Díaz at the national palace. On Feb. 24, visiting Molino del Rey, USG described events during the Mexican War. See *Philadelphia Times*, March 9, 13, 14, 1880.

On Feb. 26, David H. Strother, consul gen., Mexico City, welcomed USG to a banquet given by Americans resident in Mexico. USG replied. "Citizens of the United States and neigbors of Mexico: I am very glad to meet you here and see the good feeling that exists between men of the two greatest Republics on this continent. I hope that it may be emblematical of the perpetual peace that may exist between us. I trust that we may always be a benefit to each other as we may well be. I think I speak the sentiments of the great mass of my own people when I say that we only wish prosperity to this country and that Mexico may improve, as she is capable of doing, and grow great; that she may become our rival and move along, side by side with us. We have no jealousy, but are willing to be taught as well as to teach." *The Two Republics*, March 7, 1880. See Cecil D. Eby, Jr., "'Porte Crayon' Meets General Grant," *Journal of the Illinois State Historical Society*, LII, 2 (Spring, 1959), 235–36.

To Vicente Riva Palacio et al.

MEXICO, March 17, 1880.

MESSERS. V. RIVA PALACIO,[1] E. G. GILLOW,[2] M. ROMERO, I. MEJIA[3]
AND OTHERS:

GENTLEMEN:

I have your letter of yesterday's date setting forth a project for
organizing to build railroads in the Republic of Mexico, to the end
that cheap transportation may be afforded to carry the vast products of which this country is capable, to the Gulf of Mexico, to the
Pacific and to the United States; and setting forth the vast advange
such roads would be to both Republics, particularly to the roads in
the United States, coming to the border of Mexico; and asking my
cooperation in securing such aid as may be necessary to carry out
this laudable project.

The natural resources of Mexico warrant the execution of your
project. My visit to this country convinces me that the people are
sober, industrious and frugal, and that with employment the pe-
riodical disturbances which have heretofore afflcted the country,
would wholly disappear. The building of the projected roads would
employ many thousands of heads of families, it would open fields
for the production of food which would find a home market; for
the production of sugar, coffee, tobacco and many other articles
valuable in commerce make mines that are now practically inaccessible valuable, thus affording abundant employment for all who
chose to labor, and open fields for millions yet to come. To my own
country it would be of inestimable value. Mexico could furnish all
those articles which we now import from tropical countries, and
which take but little from us in return but specie, and take advantage of our necessities, to fill their treasuries by charging export
duties upon all we take from them. These roads would bring the
two Republics in easy, quick and healthy communication, at all
seasons of the year, would lead us to know each other better, to
appreciate each other more highly, and strengthen the bands of
friendship. Each Nation would become interested in the progress

of the other, and both would be benefited by whatever advanced either.

I wish for your project every success. Anything I can do to advance it, I will do. There is no doubt in my mind but that the great roads of the Northern Republic, now pressing upon your borders so closely, will find it to their interest to penetrate this vast and rich empire, if they can do so on fair terms and with assurances of protection. That these conditions can, and will be, secured by Mexico, I fully believe. I will lend the project my aid in every way possible, both as an American citizens, wishing the greatest good to my own country, and as a friend to Mexico, desiring her advancement in wealth and prosperity,

Very Trully Your Obedient servant.
U. S. GRANT.

The Two Republics, March 28, 1880. On March 16, 1880, Vicente Riva Palacio *et al.*, Mexico City, wrote to USG. "Believing the Mexicans who sign this letter that the principal need of their country is the construction of railroads, which will facilitate the extraccion to proper markets, of their products, without the heavy charges for freight to which they are now subjected; and that the said roads, once built, the general condition of the country will improve considerably, its elements of wealth will be developed and that disturbances and insecurity caused in a great measure by the public need and the want of occupation for the people, will cease with the of prosperity and abundance in the country, we have to-day decided to organize Mexican companies which will undertake at once to obtain the proper grants from the Federal government, for the construction of railroads, which will place us in easy and cheap communication amongst ourselves with both seas and with the markets of the United States. In attempting this enterprize we do not have in view the personal advantages which might result from its success, but the great benefits that our country will derive from its realization. We believe that after ourselves, none will be more interested in the construction of railroads in Mexico than the United States, both because the Mexican railroads will increase the business of the North American lines which are coming to our frontier, and because by the increase of the traffic between the two Republics which will be the necessary consequence of the construction of the said lines, the United States could buy from us some of the tropical fruits, as sugar, coffee and tobacco which they now purchase principally from Cuba and Brazil, paying for them in specie, which to us they could pay in manufactures which they produce under good conditions and which we need from abroad, and now buy principally, from European nations. Wishing therefore, that the business men of the United States, and specially the railroad corporations will cooperate with us in the construction of railroads, in Mexico, and to the connexion of the lines of the two Republics, we take the liberty to address ourselves to you, General, to beg of you should you find no objection to be kind enough to represent to the classes in the United States to which may interest this matter, how much both nations will gain with the increase of their commerce, and how certainly this important object will be attained, by the construction of railroads in Mexico. We flatter ourselves, General, with the hope that you will lend to the cause of material progress and aggrandizement of our country, which will be obtained with the rapid construction on large scale of railroads in Mexico, services as efficient and desinterested as those you rendered to the cause of its independence and autonomy." *Ibid.* See letter to Matías Romero, April 13, 1880.

On March 22, "ON BOARD THE STEAMER CITY OF MEXICO," Byron Andrews reported. ". . . The General concluded his sight-seeing in Mexico practically by two excursions out of the city. The first was to San Angel, the cotton mills at Tlalpan, and the fields over which Scott's army maneuvered during the battles outside the gates of the [C]ity of Mexico. At 9 o'clock the ever-industrious Romero was on hand, and we were away. The cars are drawn by mules. They went at a run, and were changed every few minutes. A guard of Federal cavalry followed, raising the dust in clouds under their horses' hoofs. A ride of an hour brought us to San Antonio, near Cherubusco, about nine miles south of the city. Here there was a short halt, and Mr. Romero, General Mejia, and the rest alighted for a few minutes, while the car was lifted from the track to allow the other to pass. 'Right here among these haciendas,' said General Grant, 'my command lay all day waiting for the battle of Contreras to be fought. By staying here we threatened the enemy and kept him from drawing off reinforcements for the real fight, which was over there,' pointing to the west, 'at the foot of the mountain. When they were defeated at Contreras the enemy made no stand to speak of, so that we had pretty easy work at Cherubusco. Near here Phil Kearney lost his arm, and it was lucky for him that he did, for he was galloping after the retreating enemy, right up to the gates, and if that fortunate shot had not taken off his arm he would have lost his life, and his entire command would no doubt have been butchered, being shot from the housetops. Kearney was always a brave man—as brave and gallant a fellow as ever lived. Too rash—still of great ability and a patriot.' Someone asked if Kearney was not much like Custer. 'Yes,' continued the General, 'he was like Custer in personal gallantry and valor, but he had more ability. Custer was not a very level-headed man, while Kearney was of good ability. He was killed at Chantilly Creek, in our own war. He was not like Fitz John Porter, who hesitated to make an attack. Kearney would attack anything, and instead of disobeying orders to fight it would have been the other way. He feared nothing, and was always ready.'. . ." *Chicago Inter-Ocean*, April 3, 1880. In an undated note, USG replied to a request. "Not being in the habit of collecting autographs, nor even of retaing letters received, I cannot inform you where to look for autographs of Gen.s Kearney & Mead." ANS (facsimile), HCA Auctions, May 17, 2001, no. 369.

1. Born in Mexico City in 1832, grandson of Mexican Independence hero Vicente Guerrero, Riva Palacio was himself a hero in the war against French intervention, resumed a career as a writer and politician, and served as public works minister under Porfirio Díaz.

2. Born in Puebla in 1841, educated in Europe, Eulogio G. Gillow was ordained a priest in 1865 and served as personal secretary to Pope Pius IX. Returning to Mexico, Gillow worked to attract U.S. investors to Mexico.

3. Born in Oaxaca in 1814, Ignacio Mejía pursued a career as a politician and soldier and rose to gen. in the war against French intervention.

Speech

[*Galveston, Tex., March 24, 1880*]

Gentlemen of Galveston: I am very much obliged to one and all of you for the very kind reception which I have received at your hands, and at the hands of all the citizens of this city, and I assure you that it affords me very great pleasure to be here on this occasion, and to see so many of you. It was my fortune more than a third of a century ago, to visit Texas as a second lieutenant and to have been one of those who went into the conflict which was to settle the boundary of Texas. I am glad to come back now on this occasion to behold a territory which is an empire in itself, and larger than some of the empires of Europe. I wish for the people of Texas as I do for the people of the entire south, that they may go on developing their resources and become great and powerful, and in their prosperity forget, (as the worthy mayor has expressed it) that there is a boundary between the north and the south. I am sure we will all be happier and much more prosperous when the day comes that there will be no sectional feeling. Let any American, who can, travel abroad as I have done, and with the opportunities of witnessing what is there to be seen that I have had and he will return to America a better American and a better citizen than he was when he went away. He will return more in love with his own country. Far be it from me to find fault with any of the European governments. I was well received at their hands on every side, by every nation in Europe; but with their dense populations and their worn-out soil, it takes a great deal of government to enable the people to get from the soil a bare subsistence. Here we have a rich virgin soil, with room enough for all of us to expand and live with the use of very little government. I do hope that we long may be able to get along happily and contentedly, without being too much governed. Gentlemen, I will not detain you any longer. I return my thanks again for the cordial reception which I have received at your hands.

Galveston News, March 25, 1880. Mayor Charles H. Leonard of Galveston spoke at a banquet held in USG's honor. ". . . If the great and good men throughout the United

States, both north and south, would follow the example that Gen. Grant has set by his visit to this city, the people would cease to think that there is such a thing as a political line dividing the north and the south, and would once more learn how to be a happy and united people. . . ." *Ibid.*

On March 19, 1880, USG and party (including Byron Andrews, *Chicago Inter-Ocean*) left Vera Cruz, Mexico, aboard the *City of Mexico*. Andrews later reported. "We were away at sunset, and no sooner had the steamer stood out upon the Gulf than a most terrific sea was encountered, and a norther set in with a vengeance. Nearly all the passengers were deadly sick and very much frightened. Mrs. Grant was about the only lady who stood the ordeal with any degree of comfort. . . ." *Chicago Inter-Ocean,* March 24, 1880. On March 23, the *City of Mexico* reached Galveston. USG responded to Leonard's welcome at the wharf. "Thank you, sir. We are tired, yet feel rejoiced at again reaching home. I am glad to be in Texas, though I have been here before and know it to be a great country. Thank you, Mr. Leonard, for your forbearance." *Ibid.* Asked later about his "narrow escape from shipwreck," USG "answered that he had had the pleasure of reading his obituary in a Democratic paper, and commenting on it seemed rather pleased that his actions were attributed at least to honest motives." *New Orleans Democrat,* April 7, 1880.

On March 25, USG visited cotton presses and the cotton exchange, then "drove out to the Barnes institute, (colored), conducted by Mrs. J. E. Cuney, with Col. W. H. Sinclair." Willie Whales addressed USG on behalf of the students. ". . . We have often looked with grateful emotions at your picture hanging there, where it has hung for the past ten years, but we never expected to behold your distinguished person. We rejoice that the institution of slavery has crumbled into fine dust, and, though it long retarded our growth, and doomed us to be the most disesteemed people of America, yet we cherish no harsh feelings toward those who upheld it, and this they well know. . . ." *Ibid.* USG responded. "Teachers and children, I am very glad to meet you, and hope that you will become good citizens and educated men and women. I am glad to see that the colored children of Galveston have the opportunity of becoming useful citizens, and hope that you will improve it by obtaining a common school education, and that the white children will do likewise. If you do not improve the opportunity it is your own fault. Allow me to thank you for your kind reception and the attention you have given me." *Galveston News,* March 26, 1880.

On Dec. 8, 1879, Leon Blum and 104 others, Galveston, had written to USG. "Learning of your contemplated visit to Cuba and Mexico, the citizens of Galveston beg to extend to you a cordial invitation to visit their island city at such time as your arrangements will allow and you may be pleased to designate. . . ." *Ibid.*, Dec. 14, 1879.

On March 29, 1880, USG spoke at Pillot's Opera House, Houston. "Ladies and gentlemen, it is not necessary to make a speech, but it has been set apart for me to receive you between 6 and 8 o'clock in the parlors of the hotel, and I shall be happy to see all of you who may choose to call." *Chicago Inter-Ocean,* March 30, 1880. Later, USG addressed a banquet. "GENTLEMEN OF HOUSTON: I am very glad to respond to the sentiments we have just heard. I only regret I cannot in such language as I would like. In regard to the receptions that have been given me in all parts of the globe there are none which have gone nearer my heart than those which I received from my own people, and none nearer than when they come from a section with which we were so lately antagonized. I cordially indorse the sentiments uttered by the gentlemen. We are now a happy, united people, and it would take a power stronger than any single nation to separate us. We are stronger than any other one nation, and would be united, and have more people, both North and South, who would know more this time about what they were fighting for, than any other power could muster. But we want no more use for armed forces. We have in this great nation only a standing army of 20,000, while Europe is supporting about 10,000,000. We will never come to that, I hope. We do not want to fight among ourselves, and no one wants to fight us. In your State of Texas, with a population greater than Massachusetts, you have a territory sufficient to support the whole United States, and could produce enough to feed the whole of the people. Yet we have other States which I hope will also develop and become prosperous. My wish is, that all of us, whatever State we belong to, will aid in making it great and prosperous. Gentlemen, I thank you." *Ibid.*

To Elihu B. Washburne

Galveston, Texas, March 25th *1880*.

MY DEAR MR. WASHBURNE;

Your letter of the 11th of Feb.y only reached Mexico by the last mail but one before my departure. I was away from the City of Mexico at the time, on an excursion to the Rio Del Monte Silver Mines,[1] and did not return until after the departure of the Steamer bringing it. Yours of the 26th of Feb.y was taken by the Steamer on which I returned. There was no opportunity of answering either therefore earlyer—or so that you could receive it earlyer,—than by writing from here.[2]

In regard to your suggestion that I should authorize some one to say that in no event would I consent to ever being a candidate again after 1880, I think any statement from me would be misconstrued and would only serve as a handle for my enemies. Such a statement might well be made after the nomination, if I am nominated in such a way as to accept. It is a matter of supreme indifference to me whether I am or not. There are many persons I would prefer should have the office to myself. I owe so much to the Union men of the country that if they think my chances are better for election than ~~that~~ for other probable candidates, in case I should decline, that I can not decline if the nomination is tendered without seeking on my part.

Mexico shows many signs of progress since I was there thirty-two years ago. Rail-roads are pushing out slowly from the capital and with every advance greater prosperity & employment for the poor follows. I think it should be the policy of our government now to cultivate the strongest feelings of friendship between the peoples of the two Republics. Soon we will have rail road connection between the two countries and our people will begin to mix and become better acquainted. Mexico can, and will, raise all the tropical & semi-tropical products which we now buy from countries that take nothing from us in exchange, except sterling exchange, and will take from us in return the products of our manufactures. Americans are begining now to work their mines. Soon they will be cultivating their sugar, coffee & tobacco plantations, running their factories, doing their banking, &c.—I go to San Antonio for a day or two, thence to New Orleans and up the River to Memphis. I will probably run over to Hot Springs from the latter to absorb time until the weather in Galena gets pleasant. I do not care to get there before the 1st of May.

> Very Truly yours
> U. S. GRANT

ALS, IHi. Written on stationery of the Tremont House. On Feb. 26, 1880, Elihu B. Washburne, Chicago, wrote to USG. "We have corded them up in this State. A full blown plot was developed about two weeks ago, on the part of the Blaine men, to capture this State. It was an unseen hand, but nerved by the money of Jay Gould. It was determined to make the first dash at the meeting of the Republican State Committee yesterday. The meeting was for the purpose of fixing the time of holding the State Convention, and that is always made the occasion of a gathering of prominent Republicans from all parts of the State, who are expected to express the Sentiment of the people. The interest aroused was extraordinary and there were a thousand republicans present and there could not been more interest and excitement manifested at a State Convention. The consequence was that the Blaine bladder was punctured and it turned out that there was nothing but *wind.* Blaine sent out Steve Hurlbut, (who is spending the winter in Washington) to manage his case. It takes a man for whom you have done the most to be your worst enemy. But all was of no avail. The sentiment was overwhelming for you. You had friends from unexpected quarters. E. C. Larned a north-side man, a man of high character influence and ability who went for Greeley in '72, made a very strong speech for you. I have no time to tell you of all the meanness of the Blaine men *but,* but it is now of no consequence. Illinois will follow N. Y. & Pa. and I am more confirmed than ever of what I have always told you—that you will be nominated by acclamation. Sherman has never had a show and now Blaine's dish is cooked. I have this morning a letter from a leading Tennessee Republican who says: 'This State will be overwhelmingly for Grant and the delegation to Chicago will be instructed for him.' You will have every Southern State not manipulated by Sherman. Indiana has not come up, as we had a right to suppose, but it makes no difference. Logan has worked nobly in this State. The loyal people of the north are more aroused than since the war. They see the impending danger. The attempt of the rebels to steal Maine, and now to steal Minnesota, by unseating my brother, elected by 3000 majority, shows the animus. A Copperhead congressman in Washington the other night proclaimed that the democrats would inaugerate their President, *whether elected or not*. They now try to explain it away by saying he was *tight*. In vino veritas. I hope you are all having a good time revelling in the Halls of the Montezumas, but if you do not like Mexico better than I did, you will not remain long. We all join in the kindest regards to yourself and party." AL (initialed), USG 3. See letter to Elihu B. Washburne, Feb. 2, 1880.

On Feb. 24, Tuesday, and April 8, Washburne wrote to U.S. Senator John A. Logan of Ill. ". . . It wont do for me to be thrusting myself too constantly before the public as the champion of Grant. It will produce disgust and reaction. By my private conversation, by my private correspondence, by what I have authorized to be stated in the papers, every intelligent man knows where I stand, and it is only the other side that professes to be in the dark. And I do not lose courage at all these boomerangs. Our old Chief will go through and you will find all these chaps who are now howling the loudest were *original Grant men*. You say what I am talking all the time. It is Grant or Blaine The natural absurdity of all this talk about me becomes intensified in view of that fact. Mark what I say: *my name will not be mentioned at the Convention* as it is not now seriously considered by anybody. But I must close for the mail and will write you again after the 'jamboree' to-morrow." "I received your letter of the 31st ult. the day after I wrote you. There is no doubt but the Jay Gould fellows have been getting the drop on us in this State, but it is not too late to retrieve ourselves. Shepard has undoubtedly written you what is now being done and we shall give them the hot end of the poker from this time out. We shall have a big Grant meeting here next week which will be the key note. I have had Fred telegraph his father to make no more engagements and come into the State as soon as possible. He has also written him, to which I added my endorsement, explaining the propriety of his coming up thro' the State from Cairo, and we have sent the letter by a special messenger who started to-night. The general wants to come here for a few days before he goes to Galena. Then we shall try and have him go out in a special train to G. stopping at all the principal points, Marengo, Belvidere, Rockford, Freeport, &c. and I shall try and get him invited, after he gets home, to visit, Dixon, Sterling, Morrison, Mt. Carroll and other places in my old district. We dont intend they shall get away with us. I have a letter from the General since his arrival and they must not lay the flattering unction to their souls that he will withdraw. I shall try and get a special train to bring him up from Cairo, so he can stop where he pleases & as long as he pleases.—After the General gets home I shall advise him to remain there until after the Convention, only leaving to go to the neighboring Counties on invitation of citizens of all parties. Just write when you have any suggestions to make." AL (initialed) and ALS, DLC-John A. Logan. See also Washburne to Logan, April 10, 1880, *ibid.*

On April 19, Secretary of the Treasury John Sherman wrote to William H. Smith, Chicago. ". . . Your conversation with Logan was a very interesting one, but the best thing to say to him is that, while I have the warmest personal feeling for Gen Grant; I still think his nomination would be fatal to us in the election, and, therefore, I ought not to take any position as between him and Blaine. . . ." LS, InHi. On April 24, Albert Hawley, Chicago, wrote to Sherman. "I have Just returned from an extended trip Through this State and it is quite plain that the delegation will be devided between Grant & Blaine, with a very bitter feeling. there will be an attempt on the part of

Grants friends to controle their part of the convention for Washburn. Now in my Judgment if your friends would See the deligates at once and let them know what the program is on the part of the *managers* all of the Blaine & Some of the Grant men might be
Secured for you. . . . P S I am a member of the Union Vet Club and know all the Soldiers
in the State there are many opposed to 3d term." ALS, *ibid.*

On April 30, Washburne wrote to Logan. ". . . The General is now here feeling
first rate, calm as a summer moring and feeling fully assured of success, the same as we
all feel. From accepted results, so far, it appears impossible that his nomination can fail.
I think now, as I always have, *by acclamation.* . . ." ALS, DLC-John A. Logan.

1. On March 4–8, USG had visited the mining region of Pachuca and Real del
Monte north of Mexico City. See Speech, [*Nov. 11, 1880*]; *The Two Republics*, March
14, 1880; Cecil D. Eby, Jr., "'Porte Crayon' Meets General Grant," *Journal of the Illinois
State Historical Society*, LII, 2 (Spring, 1959), 239–42.

2. On [*March*] 23, USG, Galveston, telegraphed to Washburne. "Just arrived
will return to Galena via Neworleans & Mississippi river to Cairo probably early in
April. Your letters of eleventh & twenty sixth March recd too late for any mail leaving Mexico before the steamer on which I Came" Telegram received, DLC-Elihu B.
Washburne.

Speech

———

[*New Orleans, March 31, 1880*]

GENERAL AND CITIZENS OF NEW ORLEANS—After an absence of
a great many years from your State I am happy to return to it and
very proud of the reception I am receiving at your hands, and very
glad that it is given by your citizens irrespective of former relations.
The scenes of war are now passed; we are a united people. I believe
that if this country should unfortunately become involved in war
we will all wear the same uniform and fight under the same flag. I
hope for New Orleans and this section the prosperity it deserves.
What benefits this city benefits the adjoining section. This State is
capable of producing millions of dollars worth of sugar more than
at present. I rejoice with you in the prosperity you have. I am glad
to hear that this city has been so much benefited by the improvements at the mouth of the river.[1] What helps you helps a large section of our country, and the entire Mississippi Valley in fact. I wish
New Orleans and the entire South increased and long continued
prosperity, believing and knowing that it is the best cure for disor-

ders and sectional animosities. Industrious people are always happy and contented. Again let me thank you, Mr. Chairman and friends, for this kind reception, and, in conclusion, I hope that the blue and the gray may never again be arrayed against each other. The past is gone. Again I thank you.

New York Herald, April 1, 1880. USG spoke at the St. Charles Hotel in response to a welcoming address by Cyrus Bussey, president, New Orleans Chamber of Commerce, and former col., 3rd Iowa Cav.

On March 25, 1880, a newspaper reported. "We have been permitted to use the following telegram from Gen. Grant to a gentleman of this city: GALVESTON, March 24.—Will visit San Antonio, and not reach New Orleans until Wednesday, 31st of March. U. S. GRANT." *New Orleans Picayune*, March 25, 1880.

On March 31, USG attended a banquet given by Albert Baldwin, president of the Royal Host. "During its progress Baldwin announced that the General had been elected a member of the Royal Host and the title Duke of America conferred upon him. The General was immediately decorated with the Order of St. Rex by Judge George H. Braughn, Lord High Chamberlain, . . ." *Chicago Tribune*, April 2, 1880. USG spoke. "LADIES AND GENTLEMEN: I thank you very much for this kind reception, and for the compliment which the Rex Association has just paid me. For, pronounced republican as I am, it would, under ordinary circumstances, hardly be proper for me to accept the distinction which you have just conferred upon me, especially as I have been frequently charged with an attempt to seize upon a higher title. But, as I said before, under such circumstances, and appreciating the objects of your worthy organization, I accept the title of Duke, and thank you again for the compliment paid and kind reception extended me." *Ibid.* See Reid Mitchell, *All on a Mardi Gras Day: Episodes in the History of New Orleans Carnival* (Cambridge, Mass., 1995), pp. 82–88.

On April 1, USG held a reception at the St. Charles Hotel during which "members of the Washington Artillery, were introduced by Gen. Owen, who remarked that they were two veterans of the Washington Artillery who had worked the guns at Shiloh, and were also members of the detachment that fired the salute to welcome him, (Gen. Grant.) The latter said he preferred the latter demonstration, 'for at Shiloh, General,' he continued, 'your men put shot in their guns.'" *New Orleans Picayune*, April 2, 1880. At the same reception, USG greeted a delegation of lawmakers. "*Gentlemen of the Joint Committee*—I feel very grateful to the members of the Legislature of Louisiana for the courtesy extended in the passage of and presentation to me of this resolution through you. Some time ago I was stationed two years in this State, and visited this city four or five times. I have long been anxious to revisit Louisiana and New Orleans, and I feel as if I had returned to an old home. The kindness that I have met from every quarter since I arrived in your beautiful city has been most bountiful. I again thank you, as the representatives of the General Assembly, for the courtesy shown me by this resolution." *Ibid.* On March 30, the La. Senate had voted 19–14 against a resolution of welcome to USG passed by the La. House of Representatives. La. Senator Robert L. Luckett spoke. "I am sorry that this resolution has come up before the Senate. I respect Gen. Grant as I respect bravery and stubbornness of purpose, but I can never forget that he foisted on us the bayonet rule and kept down the prosperity of this State until we were on the verge of abject poverty. I can never forget when I and others were carried out of this building, the legal representatives of this people, and I do not feel like extending welcome to a candidate for the Presidency of the United States, who, in that capacity, will, no doubt, extend the same rule over us." *New Orleans Democrat*, March 31, 1880. La. Senator Theodore S. Fontenot "said he would vote 'no,' because he could not show a good face to one whom he did not like." *Ibid.* Upon reconsideration, the resolution passed 18–13. Copy (largely illegible), Smithsonian Institution. See *PUSG*, 26, 3–35.

On April 2, USG addressed the La. House of Representatives. *"Mr. Speaker and Gentlemen of the Legislature of Louisiana*—It is rather an unusual thing for me to attempt to say anything in public halls, particularly in legislative halls. But I am delighted to be here and to hear such generous sentiments as were uttered by your worthy Speaker, because they are my own. I have always felt that differences between a common people, after they have once been settled, should remain so forever. I am sure that I rejoice as much as any member of this Legislature at anything that goes to make up the prosperity of Louisiana and of the entire South. We are members of a united and contented family. I believe that no one nation or all the nations combined could separate us. In other words, gentlemen, should such an attempt be made, I believe that among the bravest defenders of the Union would be found the men before me. I rejoice with you in the prosperity of your State, knowing as I do that whatever benefits one portion of the country will also benefit the entire country. Gentlemen, I thank you for this very cordial reception, and I am not only grateful for it, but for all the kind attentions shown me since my arrival here." *New Orleans Democrat*, April 3, 1880. USG also spoke to the La. Senate. "Gentlemen of the Senate, I am very happy to meet you here. I have just visited the other branch of the Legislature. I expressed to them my thanks, and I wish to express to you my thanks for this reception." *Ibid.*

On April 5, USG "visited the Wesley Chapel on Liberty street. This is the principal church of the colored people of the Methodist persuasion. A very large crowd of colored people had assembled in the church and on the surrounding streets. The interior of the edifice was handsomely decorated. Rev. Emperor Williams received Gen. Grant with a few remarks, and an address was then delivered by Rev. Dr. Hartzell." *New Orleans Picayune*, April 6, 1880. USG spoke. *"Fellow-Citizens*—Those who expect to hear anything like an address from me will be very much disappointed. It has never been my habit to make speeches. I was fifty-five years of age before I ever attempted to respond to any address, and I have never extended any remarks beyond a few sentences. I can say to you, however, that I am very glad to meet you here this morning. I am very glad to hear the remarks that have just been made by Dr. Hartzell as to the extent of the work of this church in the Southern States. I hope the work which has been commenced to secure the Gospel and the spelling-book to every class will be continued, so all denominations and individuals, white and black, may have these blessings. The South has been the home of the colored man, and I hope he will always be permitted to live peaceably in the South, freely, and that the right to work out his own fortunes without molestation, to the best of his ability, will not be denied. Of course, I would not deny to the colored man any right to change his location, but I want him to have the privilege to stay where the climate suits him, with the right to go where he can do best, if he wants to. I am very much obliged for your attention." *Ibid.*

Later on April 5, USG addressed a banquet at the St. Charles Hotel. "Gentlemen: I was very much in hopes that your magnificent treatment of me since I have come upon the soil of Louisiana lately would have exhausted itself before this. While I cannot talk my thanks, I assure you I can appreciate all that you have done. I thank you. I shall carry away from Louisiana the most pleasant recollections of the State and the people. I think that every one here to-night is interested in the common welfare of our common country. I think that any public-spirited citizen is interested in the welfare of every portion of this country. I hope that our commerce, of which the commerce of this city is so great a portion, will go on increasing every day. It is well known that the more the people of the South produce the more oats and Galena potatoes you will want to buy. Prosperity which will be felt in Portland, Maine, will be felt in Portland, Oregon; and the success of business in New-York will be attended by a growth of business in your city. I hope that the result will be no divided county, North, South, East, or West, and that we may all join hands and be proud that we belong to and are members of one great country, and that we may always be reciprocal in our common interests and common feelings. We have the most favored country on earth. I have visited them all, and we have better climate, soil, and products here than I have seen anywhere else. We have only the present to do with. The future will prepare for the future. If we carry out these plain thoughts, we will do the best that can be done." _New York Times_, April 11, 1880. "The assemblage was in every respect a representative one. There were members of the clergy, medical profession, the bar, Federal, State and city officials, the press and leading merchants. There were present about one hundred and fifty persons. . . ." _New Orleans Picayune_, April 6, 1880. On March 24, USG, Galveston, had telegraphed to Joseph H. Oglesby, president, La. National Bank, concerning this banquet. "I will be in New Orleans during all the first week in April, and accept your invitation for any day which does not interfere with any day in the programme arranged by the city authorities." _New Orleans Times_, March 25, 1880.

On April 7, USG visited Straight University, where President Walter S. Alexander introduced him. "Our hearts most joyous and grateful welcome greets your coming to this in[f]ant university. Chartered by the State of Louisiana in 1869, this institution will attain in June its eleventh birthday. In these years it has assisted in the education of 3000 young men and women of Louisiana and the adjoining States of Texas, Mississippi and Florida. The young people are here taught to 'Love God, their country and liberty'—to strive after the highest type of manhood and womanhood, and to become good citizens of this State and the republic. Those for whom I speak to-day would hardly forgive me, did I not express their sense of obligation and gratitude for your friendship toward their race when they most greatly needed it in the dawning of their new life as citizens, and in their struggle for equal rights before the law. . . ." _Ibid._, April 8, 1880. USG replied. "It is a good sign to see such a university as this attended by colored people who were for so long deprived of any such advantage. Those who have gone before you had no such advantages. But by the gift of these institutions, these here are taking the first great step towards improving the advantages guaranteed to them by the constitution. Great advantages are given these people by the provisions of the constitution and the amendments, and the colored people are coming to improve them. The privilege of emigration is permitted and allowed to any people. But other things being equal, every one is happiest in passing his life in the locality where he was born. So that I am glad to see you improving these opportunities. I hope everything for the colored people, and may you make freedom a blessing to yourselves. Gentlemen, I thank you for your kindness." _Ibid._

On the same day, USG spoke at a reception given by the Colored Men's Protective Union at the home of Pinckney B. S. Pinchback. "FELLOW-CITIZENS—I am very glad to meet you all here to-day, and I thank you for the kind things you have said to me. I believe that the colored people are reaping the benefits every day of a common school education. They need a good education to make them discharge properly and intelligently the duties of citizenship. I have noticed lately that there is a disposition on the part of every one, of all political parties, to accord to the colored man all the rights guaranteed him by the constitution and the amendments. I hope the colored man will be allowed to live peaceably in the South, for I think the South is better suited to him than any other place, and I hope that the right to work out his own fortune will not be denied him. Of course, I would not deny him the right to emigrate, or to change his place of living if he wants to, but I want him to have the right to stay where the climate suits him, with the privilege to go where he thinks he can do the best for himself. I thank you all for your kind attention." *New Orleans Louisianian*, April 10, 1880. William H. Green, secretary, had addressed USG "In behalf of the Colored Men's Protective Union, and of the benevolent and social organizations of this City and State." DS (10 signatures, undated), Smithsonian Institution. *New Orleans Louisianian*, April 10, 1880. See James Haskins, *Pinckney Benton Stewart Pinchback* (New York, 1973), pp. 245–46.

On April 8, "officers of the Federal army and navy of the late war gave a complimentary banquet at Moreau's" to USG. "Major Rouse sat at the head of the table with Gen. Grant upon his right and Gen. Harney upon his left." *New Orleans Times*, April 9, 1880. USG spoke. "Gentlemen—I wish this part of the entertainment had come earlier, so that I might be through now and be enjoying your punishment. Your chairman has honored me in his address far beyond what I deserve. I did the best I could, but the man who bore the musket was as worthy of credit as he who directed their course. I had your support and that of hundreds of thousands of others, to whom is due the praise. As to the result, I think we all agree now, even those who fought against us, that the war ended in the best way for all, both North and South, of the whole nation. If those who fought against us for the separation of this nation had succeeded, we should have been disgraced in the eyes of the entire world. The honor that has been done to me abroad come to me because we were a great united nation, and was a recognition of our greatness as such. I believe now, that with the exception of questions of tariff and finance, upon which there will always be differences, that we shall progress as a unit until we are regarded abroad as we now regard ourselves—the first nation on the earth; first in a military point of view, first in intelligence, first in wealth and first in setting a good example to all who love liberty. While we fought for what we thought was right and think so now and more every day, we do it, we must admit, from a selfish point of view, for we know that we are greater and more prosperous as one than we would be if divided. I hope you will all be happy in your adopted home, and find the same cordiality here as in the locality from which you started as soldiers. I thank you for the honor." *Ibid.*

1. See *PUSG*, 26, 255–58.

Speech

[*Mobile, April 9, 1880*]

MR. CHAIRMAN AND GENTLEMEN—I shall not detain you by any lengthy remarks, and could not, perhaps, if I were to attempt it; but I have been now a little over two weeks in the Southern States, and

I have been so well received and so much entertained that I have been saying something everywhere, and it is getting a little monotonous, for it is pretty hard to say anything now without repeating, and this is a country where we have telegraphs and post-roads and the rapid mails, and we are a people who read; and what I have said from San Antonio to this city, has probably been read by you, and if so, all that I have to say in regard to this section of the country has been read by you and I hope approved. At all events, I shall only repeat a little of the substance of what I have had to say before, and that is, that I am delighted to see that there is so much good feeling existing between this section and the section from which I come. I believe it is to be lasting, and that this is what is to be hoped, over the whole country.[1] We have a country to be proud of, and it applies to all of us equally, and I hope to see the most generous and lively competition between every section of this entire country, each one striving to develop the resources of its own section, and enjoin the development of all other sections. I am very much obliged and very glad of the opportunity of visiting your city.

Mobile Register, April 10, 1880. USG responded to a toast during a banquet hosted by the Mobile Cotton Exchange. Earlier, after receptions by civic leaders at the Manassas Club and by "the colored people in the United States Court-room at the Custom-house," USG took a carriage ride "through the city and down the bay shell road to Magnolia race course, where, to the admiring eye of the General was shown the magnificent 'pet of the turf,' Kimball." *Ibid.* See William Warren Rogers, Jr., "'The Past is Gone' Ulysses S. Grant Visits Mobile," *Gulf Coast Historical Review,* 5, 1 (Fall, 1989), 7–19.

On March 31, 1880, Lyman C. Dorgan and three others, Mobile, wrote to USG, New Orleans. "We have the honor to represent the Mobile Cotton Exchange, which, as a body, authorizes us to extend to your honorable self and party an invitation to visit the Port of Mobile, and we trust that you will find it agreeable and convenient to comply with the request." LS, USG 3. On April 2, Friday, Dorgan led a delegation that called on USG, who responded: "Gentlemen, I thank you kindly for the invitation to visit Mobile. It has long been my desire to do so. I find that my engagements here ending with a visit to the jetties, will keep me very busy until late Thursday night; therefore, I cannot visit your city before Friday night. If that will be agreeable, I shall feel honored in accepting your hospitality on that occasion." *Mobile Register,* April 3, 1880. On the same day, "the colored citizens of the Port of Mobile, in mass meeting assembled," resolved to welcome USG. "An invitation was sent that night by telegraph to Gen. Grant, and a reply was received from him accepting the invitation." *Ibid.,* April 6, 1880. USG left New Orleans on the morning of April 9. "The party sat in the parlor car, and conversation was general. In answer to a question as to the nationality of his servant, Gen. Grant said he was from Japan, and was above the ordinary class. He was traveling with him principally to become intimately acquainted with the English language and with the manners and customs of our country; he would then return to Japan, and could no doubt rise to be a person of some consequence. The Japanese stand very high in the General's estimation; they have adopted largely the American customs; English is taught in all the higher schools, and our text-books are standard. . . . He then compared China with Japan, and drew a picture of Chinese life which Kearney would indorse to the letter. He has a high admiration for their courage a quality not usually accorded them in dime novels or even in history, but in his opinion there are no braver people on the face of the earth, being fatalists they are necessarily so. . . ." *New Orleans Democrat*, April 11, 1880.

USG returned to New Orleans on April 10. "Upon the arrival of Gen. Grant in our city, Theo. Lilienthal, proprietor of the celebrated art studio on Canal street, remembered that just after the fall of Vicksburg he took the General's picture. The negative was unearthed and a fine likeness, by the Lambert process, was soon produced, neatly framed in velvet, and presented to Mrs. Grant by the noted artist. Immediately upon the General's return from Mobile, yesterday, he called upon Mr. Lilienthal and was shown by him to the operating-room and seated before the instrument, which resembles somewhat a sixty-four pounder. The General remarked that this was not the first time that he had placed himself in range of Lilienthal's batteries, and hoped the result produced on this occasion would be as gratifying and the picture as admirable as the one taken seventeen years ago." *Ibid.*

1. On March 22, Jones M. Withers, former C.S.A. maj. gen. and Mobile mayor, had written at length to the *New York Times*. ". . . It will prove the grand crowning act of his eventful life for Gen. Grant to call up his countrymen from the low level of sectional animosity and party strife to his own high level of pure patriotism and true statesmanship, and reconcile them to the kindly feelings and fraternal relations which can alone accomplish Mr. Lincoln's 'paramount object'—a Union restored in spirit as well as fact. . . ." *New York Times*, March 29, 1880. In response, the *Mobile Register* editorialized. ". . . Unless our people have eaten of the insane root and lost their reason, Grantism can have no foothold at the South. We have not yet become dogs to lick the hand that smites us." *Mobile Register*, April 2, 1880.

Speech

[*Vicksburg, April 12, 1880*]

GENTLEMEN AND CITIZENS OF VICKSBURG: It is with unfeigned pleasure that I come to this historic city, and am received in such a manner as I have been to-day. I confess that I feel great satisfaction upon my safe arrival here at the time just referred to by the gentleman. I am glad that the conflict is over, never again to be resumed, and that it left us united. I know that nothing can again array the blue against the gray. This fact is proven by the citizens coming here to-day, white and colored together. It is a happy evidence of the termination of a feeling equally unfortunate for the South and the whole country. I agree with the gentleman who just spoke, that it is to be hoped and desired that the capital, virtue, and energy of the North may be united with the capital, virtue, and energy of the South, and that there may be no more difference between the North and South, sect or color. I believe that the day of general prosperity is dawning, and that the next few years will do more than the last fifteen has accomplished to make us one united people.

Chicago Inter-Ocean, April 13, 1880. William H. McCardle, former Miss. col. and AG, welcomed USG. ". . . There was a time when your presence here was less welcome than it is to-day. You were then with a large retinue of your friends, anxious to make a visit to this city, and those of us who were then present were equally anxious that you should forego that pleasure. . . ." *Ibid.* Hannibal C. Carter also addressed USG "in behalf of the colored citizens." *Ibid.*

On April 2, 1880, USG spoke in New Orleans. "Gentlemen of the Vicksburg delegation—I thank you for inviting me to come to your city. I cannot promise you that I will stay very long. My stay in New Orleans will be much longer than I thought it would be when I first came here. To-morrow week I shall take the boat, and can only remain in Vicksburg so long as the captain can be induced to let her lie at the wharves. I am glad to go to Vicksburg through the front door; once, you know, I was forced to come in through the back door." *New Orleans Times*, April 3, 1880. On April 3, Saturday, a "sub-committee of colored men" invited USG to visit Miss. USG replied that "he would be in Vicksburg on Monday week, and would expressly request the committee to meet him again." *Ibid.*, April 4, 1880.

On Oct. 1, 1879, Charles A. Hobbs, former sgt., 99th Ill., "& for the last ten years Pastor Baptist Ch. Mason City, Ills.," Danville, Ill., had written to USG. "May I not hope that the presumption of this note of enquiry will be forgotten in your invariable kindness to those who have 'carried the musket,' and aimed, where you said it—straight toward the foe?—In the name of a soldier then, unknown indeed, yet once a soldier under your command, I venture to state what I greatly wish to know. I hope soon to publish a Poem entitled 'Vicksburg', of some length, & upon which I have spent much time, and it has been my one desire to give to it at least the merit of historical exactness. I have consulted many authorities,—especially—'Badeau,' but one point of some importance to *my* purpose, remains uncertain. I know of no one who can solve it but yourself. It is said that Gen. Johnston intended to charge *your* lines from without, the 7th of July, & sent a messenger to Pemberton, to do the same from within, of course on the same day. It is also said that the messenger he sent was captured by *you*, and that *you* had determined to charge again, on the 6th—Now, did that captured messenger have any thing to do with it; or did you learn at all at that time of Johnston's definite plan? Or—again—did you decide to charge again the City upon 6th July, independent of all such things? If, in the multiplicity of the claims upon you, & from a kindness upon which *my* claim is nothing, you yet can assist me in this matter, the favor, be assured, will be most highly appreciated. . . . P. S. I enclose the particular part of Poem which I would like to correct, if need be, to make accurate history." ALS, DLC-USG, IB. See C. A. Hobbs, *Vicksburg. A Poem.* (Chicago, 1880).

Speech

[*Memphis, April 13, 1880*]

MR. CHAIRMAN AND CITIZENS OF MEMPHIS—The reception I have received here at your hands could not be otherwise than gratifying to me. It is pleasant to hear such words here to-day and throughout the southern States. The feeling growing up since the war gives evidence of prosperity and happiness. I assure my friends of the south that there has never been a day when I did not feel as much interest in their prosperity as they did themselves. I always felt kindly for this section of our country. I never saw stronger evidence that the bitterness of feeling was dying away than at present. I am pleased to see the people of all sections scattered over this land, and on friendly relations. A better understanding between the sections of country is the best cure we can possibly have for past differences, and such an understanding will bring about prosperity. I thank you, Mr. Chairman and fellow-citizens, for your welcome.

Memphis Appeal, April 14, 1880. Josiah Patterson, Memphis lawyer and former col., 5th Ala. Cav., welcomed USG at a ceremony in Court Square, following a procession from the Peabody Hotel. ". . . If . . . you had not interposed the influence of your great example to prevent men who never felt the shock of battle from turning loose upon a defenseless people the terrors of the law and the sword, the south would have been for generations yet to come the Poland of America, and to-day her sons would be in open resistance or prostrate beneath the tread of a standing army. But, sir, we are under brighter skies. . . ." *Ibid.*

On April 5, 1880, David T. Porter and John M. Keating telegraphed to USG, New Orleans. "The undersigned, in behalf of the citizens of Memphis without distinction of party, cordially invite you to accept the hospitalities of the city so long as you can so-journ with us. When will you be here? Please answer." *Ibid.*, April 6, 1880. On April 7, the *Appeal* published a letter from Minor Meriwether criticizing plans to welcome and honor USG. Subsequent correspondence in favor of honoring USG included a letter from James Phelan (April 9), answered by Avery Meriwether (April 10). On April 13, the *Appeal* editorialized. ". . . We are, let us hope, upon the threshold of the new era when all trace of the bloody contest will be blotted out . . . We will entertain General Grant as our guest, and by another generous, hospitable act, hasten forward the day when only the greatest of the achievements of both north and south, a common heritage, will be remembered or recalled." *Ibid.*, April 13, 1880.

On April 13, a delegation boarded USG's train upon arrival from Vicksburg. Porter greeted USG and thanked the people of the U.S. "for their princely charity that flowed in upon us from every quarter, through three epidemics in such unabated and grateful measure, as to mitigate, as much as might be, the terrors of that frightful pestilence that devastated our fair city and filled our hearts with woe." *Ibid.*

On the same day, Benjamin K. Sampson welcomed USG at the Beale Street Baptist Church. ". . . That memorable sentence so kindly expressed by yourself—'Where I go they can come'—finds a grateful response in our hearts, when we remember that it evidences a constancy to and a sympathy for a people who so much need the amenities and good will of the nation. As colored men, we represent more than a million of producers who by their contributions to home production and mechanical industry have furnished a measure of the means for the intercourse of all nations. These you have encouraged, and in the administration of public duties they recognized your endeavor to preserve the advantages of peace and protect the rights of every citizen. . . ." *Memphies Daily, April 14, 1886.* USG replied. "FELLOW-CITIZENS—I wish it was in my power to respond as eloquently as the address has been delivered. But speaking is not in my line of business, although, since I arrived on southern soil, I have tried it, having had to make four or five speeches a day; but it did not take much time to read them after they were printed. It is a matter of great satisfaction to me to hear this address from a colored citizen. I recognize the fact that your work affects a large part of the commerce of the world. From your work in the cultivation of the soil I find a large percentage of per capita which makes our commerce on the seas. I hope you get your reward from this commerce. I hope, for one and all, that you receive all the rights and privileges of all the amendments given by our constitution. I hope that every colored citizen will have discretion to accept the advantages offered them. The white people of this country should be gratified that four million colored people have made rapid advancement so far, and I hope that only a short time will elapse when every right and privilege under the constitution will be granted to all of you." *Ibid.* USG and party then "drove out Beale street, amid enthusiastic cheering, to LeMoyne (colored) institute, on Orleans street, where he was met by Prof. A. J. Steele, the principal of the school, and was shown into the library, where he was introduced to the teachers. Arriving at the school-room, where some fifty pupils were assembled and a large number of other colored citizens, a song of greeting was rendered by the choir. When all had been seated, Prof. Steele stated to the school that General Grant needed no introduction. He thought that one of the reasons why he was so well received in Memphis today was owing to the fact that, while in this city years ago, he had selected Colonel Eaton to take charge of the educational interests of the colored people, and when he became President, he had appointed Colonel Eaton to a high position at the head of education in the government. He was requested to state that General Grant declined to make a speech that evening; but, if any one wished to take him by the hand, they could pass around the room and do so as they went by the stand. He then asked the choir to sing a hymn entitled *Winter Will Soon Be Over,* as General Grant would be glad to hear it. . . ." *Ibid.*

Also on April 13, USG attended a banquet at the Peabody Hotel. "I have no doubt but that every one present can make a longer, better speech than I can. I know that there are several editors here, who have written longer editorials than they will write for the morning papers, if they only report what I say. Now, I have no doubt you considered it an act of kindness to call upon me to respond to this sentiment tonight, and I am glad you called upon me so early, for then it will soon be over, and I shall be glad to sit and smoke and enjoy the misery of those who are to follow. Yes, gentlemen, I thank you for the kindness intended, and forgive you for the harm you have done me." *Chicago Inter-Ocean,* April 14, 1880. See *Memphis Appeal,* April 14, 1880.

To Matías Romero

—

MEMPHIS, TENN. Apl. 13th, 1880.

HON. M. ROMERO.

DEAR SIR: . . .

I have found much opportunity of talking with iuflential business and railroad people about our relations with Mexico; the importance of close friendly and commmercial relations between the two republics; connecting roads and steamship lines ect., and found every one with whom I talked appreciative of the subject. There is no doubt in my mind but that if Mexico will give the proper encouragement the most important roads in the contry will be taken hold of by capitalists who have the means and energy to build them in the shortest possible time—and that without the enormous subsidies Mexico has been giving heretofore to such enterprises—and that within a less period. Then passengers will be able to take the cars in New York city for the city of Mexico direct, time six or seven days. No one can estimate the immense benefit to both nations. Mexico will be able to furnish the United States alone with two hundred millions dollars worth a year of her tropical and semitropical products which she has to import now, and can produce an indefinite amount beside for markets elsewhere the revenues of the State can be raised from sixteen or eighteen to eighty millions annually, without being one half the burden upon production felt now in the absence of transportation for her surplus.

I confess that much may depend upon the result of your approaching presidential election.[1] If that goes off quietly, and the President elect, who ever he may be, is quietly and peacebly inaugurated, I feel that the future of the country may be regarded as secured. I most sincerely hope for this result, and in this belief I express the views of 99. per cent of my countrymen. . . .

I will write when I have anything of interest to communicate, and will always be glad to hear from you.

Very truly yours,
U. S. GRANT.

The Two Republics (ellipses in original), Sept. 5, 1880.

On April 6, 1880, during a trip from New Orleans to the mouth of the Mississippi River, USG spoke about railroad development in Mexico. ". . . They have nothing, except this road from Vera Cruz to Mexico, and little spurs that run out from the City of Mexico twenty or thirty miles. The road from Vera Cruz is a splendid road, and you are treated to magnifcent scenery going over it. . . . Two hundred and sixty miles—that is, if it went in a straight line. It is well ballasted; we have not a better road in our country. It was built by Englishmen, the Mexican Government giving a subsidy that nearly built it. And the funny part of it is, they would not allow them to commence in any place but the City of Mexico to build it—that is, 259 or 260 miles off. They commenced at the city of Mexico to build it down to Vera Cruz, and they had to haul every rail and every tie out to the City of Mexico for making the start, and then drag them on the line of the road from there down. Yet that road pays on its enormous cost. . . . Well, the working classes, if they can get twenty-five cents a day, are in clover. Then, you see, their families will raise a little patch of corn, and they will live almost exclusively on the tortilla, which they make from the corn product. They have laborers there where they are grading the railroads that get 25 to 40 cents a day in silver. Their families will make tortilla, which is cooked by their wives at home. It is made of corn which is soaked in lye, and then it is worked down into a paste between two stones, very thin. They make cakes of it, and eight or ten pounds of corn in this way will keep a man a week. They raise that; the luxuries they do not have. When they work around the house they will raise a few tomatoes and a few chickens and beans. But these they have only as luxuries. . . . After you get up to an elevation of 6,500 feet they make and drink 'pulka,' [*pulque*] produced from the megna [*maguey*] plant. They drink an enormous sight of it. It is healthy, and about the color of milk, and if you are a little accustomed to it it is quite palatable and very refreshing. You can buy it for about two cents a gallon. They are a very temperate eating and drinking class. There is an enormous amount of this preparation drank because everybody drinks it. It is very profitable to raise at two cents a gallon. It is much like cocoanut milk, except in drinking you can feel a very slight sense of exhilaration. . . . There has been a very strong prejudice against us ever since our war, when we took so much of their territory. But they recollect and put down to our credit the fact that when we were there we treated them well. We disturbed none of them in their homes, and we bought all our supplies and forage from them, and we paid for it, although we were there as invading enemies. They say the French, when there, made us respectable. . . . Now, for instance, there was a Catholic priest, one of the most energetic men in the whole country, and who is to-day doing more than any other one man to develop it. He wears his clerical dress and performs his functions of a priest occasionally, but he is a very large planter, and his father was before him. They are a rich family, and use all our American agricultural implements, too. He was telling me that he was a boy when we were in Mexico—that is, the American army—but when we advanced through Puebla down in the hills between the edge of the valley and Puebla, he and his father had a large amount of wheat, and as we were getting toward Puebla, he thought it a good thing to get as far from the invader as possible, so he took the wheat to Molino del Rey, quite near to the City of Mexico. But we were on our road to Mexico and Molino del Rey was one of the first places we went to. We hadn't any too many provisions, and we first took all the wheat there was in that mill to feed our animals and to send to the mill to be ground for our men. He said after we got into the City of Mexico and got settled down there, his father ventured up to see General Scott to see if there was any possible chance for getting anything for it. He went in to see Scott, and the General heard his story, and asked him if there was any

other wheat there besides his, and he said yes, there were other parties who had some there, but his was the bulk of it. 'Well, now,' said General Scott, 'you go off and ascertain just exactly what wheat there was in that mill, and who owns it, and come back and see me again, bringing a statement of it.' He did so, and he says Scott sat down and wrote an order on the Quartermaster to pay so much, and his father got $100,000 in American gold when he never expected a cent. Now all those things are recollected, and they come up to our credit, and never are better in mind than when contrasted with the doings of the French. So, if we would give them some assurance, and if there was a general public expression here that we did not want any more territory, and that we were desirous of establishing friendly relations between this country and Mexico, and close commercial relations, and would be glad to see their prosperity and to help them in it, we would have plenty of friends in the Mexican Government.... Any young man can go there now and do well, if he will. I should say let him go to Oajaca, and he will make a fortune if he will just be a little patient and steady. In the first place, you can buy a piece of land about six sections, two miles and six-tenths square, of the best sugar and coffee land, in the world for $500, and can hire laborers for 25 cents a day. A man with $1,000 or $2,000 could buy one of those big tracts of land and hire men to commence putting it in. In doing the planting he ought to generally commence planting coffee and sugar, and, when he has done that, watch the market and keep a little store where he can buy sugar and coffee—(we can buy sugar for a cent a pound there)—buy all the sugar and all the coffee that comes in, and pay the money for it; they will take the money for what they bring in, first, but the poor people would not carry a cent away; and he could build up a big trade in his store. I speak of Oajaca, as that is only about twenty-five miles from the Pacific coast, where there is a harbor, and where steamers already stop once a month. He could thus ship direct to San Francisco, or he could ship by Panama for the Eastern market that way.... There is a big opening both for individuals and for the country. It is a thing we've got to look to, as we are importing an enormous amount of the articles which Mexico could furnish us, and which we could get by an exchange of commodities. Even Havana, right on our coast, doesn't buy anything from us; if we want to sell her flour, she has to send to Spain to get our flour. President Diaz is the best soldier they have, and his energy has kept the country quiet during his four years. He would be elected without opposition if he were eligible. And the hope is that a man may succeed him who is on good terms with Diaz, and Diaz will support him and preserve quiet in the country. At the end of the term of his successor Diaz will unquestionably be re-elected unanimously, and if it should turn out that way I think the difficulties of the country will be solved...."
Chicago Inter-Ocean, May 4, 1880. See *New Orleans Democrat*, April 7, 1880; letter to Vicente Riva Palacio *et al.*, March 17, 1880, note 2; letter to Porfirio Díaz, May 21, 1880.

1. Manuel González won elections held in June and July and replaced Porfirio Díaz as president on Dec. 1.

Speech

[*Little Rock, April 15, 1880*]

GENTLEMEN, MAYOR OF THE CITY OF LITTLE ROCK AND CITIZENS OF THE STATE OF ARKANSAS—I come here at the invitation of your mayo[r] and citizens[.] On first landing on the soil of your State, at every stopping pl[a]ce on the road, the people from the country flocked around and greeted me. I saw by their greeting that the feelings of the past were gone. You have a great State and a great future, and nothing will advance your prospects as much as an enti[r]e absence of sectionalism. I have noticed in my travels that sectionalism is passing away and the coun[t]ries of the world are returning to that broad field of liberality, which is progress. You have a soil that will make you a great State and a latitude that will enable you to produce a vast amount of one of the staples of the world, namely, cotton. You have not enough people, but I have no doubt that the resources of your State will attract inhabitants; that all new comers may be received as I have been to-day, and that they will make good citizens of Arkansas and aid in developing the country is my wish.

Memphis Appeal, April 16, 1880. Mayor John C. Fletcher of Little Rock and Governor William R. Miller of Ark. spoke briefly before USG.

    Also on April 15, 1880, USG addressed a banquet in Concordia Hall. "Mr. Presi-dent and Gentlemen: The toast, 'The United States of America; forever United,' is one that persons accustomed to speaking might talk on all night, but I am not accustomed to talking; those who write might write on it all night. It is one that I am satisfied that all who are here hope to see; that all whom I met in my travels are united on. Believing, that is, that the United States should be forever united. The advantages we can be to each other as a united people are manifest to everybody. We can avoid many heavy expenses, we do not have to keep two standing armies, we do not require a long line of custom houses, to say nothing about the rivalries and jealousies of two countries of the same people on the same continent. All foreigners find a welcome here. We make them American citizens. After we receive them, it is but one generation until they are Americans. Our people are better than those of any other nation, I think, because we have a mixture of blood of all the better nations of the earth. I believe you are all with me, and that you all hope that all the questions likely to divide us are settled, and that all animosities are passing away rapidly. But I will not dwell. I see there are fifteen toasts, with music after each. It will be to-morrow morning when we get through if we all take as much time as the subjects admit of. I thank you, and will say no more." *The Daily Graphic* (New York), April 26, 1880.

    On April 12, a committee had met to plan USG's reception in Little Rock. "Early in the morning a telegram came from General Grant expressing a desire to leave here during the day of the fifteenth, to which the committee replied so emphatically expressing the great disappointment which would ensue unless General Grant remained during the entire day and evening, that they were gratified during the day by receiving a telegram from him as follows: 'I will remain over fifteenth.'" *Arkansas Gazette*, April 13, 1880. USG and party traveled from Memphis to Little Rock on Wednesday, April 14. "The following telegram received by Col. Roots, yesterday, will show Gen. Grant's line of march after leaving here. The telegram is dated at Blackfish, a station on the Memphis and Little Rock railway: 'I expect to remain in Cairo Friday afternoon and night. Saturday go to Bloomington via Illinois Central, remain there until Monday and then go to Galena.'" *Ibid.*, April 15, 1880. At Little Rock, a reporter asked USG if this was his first visit to the city. "'Yes. I was never in the state before, only along the Missis-sippi river.' 'You find Little Rock quite an active town?' 'Yes,' and as the crowd surged below, and as there arose a murmuring as of a far off sea, the general added: 'It seems as though it would be a good time to take the sensus.'" *Ibid.*

Speech

———

[*Cairo, April 16, 1880*]

When last I was with you, my friends, your little city was a camp of bristling bayonets. You are now in the full enjoyment of the pursuits of peace, a thrifty, promising little city.

Of late I have traveled over a considerable bit of the south, have visited many parts of several states, and everywhere I saw the same signs of devotion to the restored Union I see here to-day. I met men who had held high positions in the rebel army, men who served in the confederate congress and legislatures and men occupying high social and official positions among their fellow citizens, and one and all of them expressed themselves satisfied with the results, and in no wise felt inclined to attempt to disturb them. I believe that these men spoke the truth, and I hope they represent the masses. I have reason for believing in their honesty, and that we have now a permanen[t] Union and one that will last forever. Everywhere I saw due respect shown for the old flag, and heard a willingness expressed on all sides, to heartily and patriotically unite with the North in defending it against any assaults from abroad, let them come from whatever quarter they may. But I have already said more than I expected to say on this occasion, having been led thereto by the remarks of the gentlemen who have preceded me. I will now close by thanking you for your very kind reception.

Cairo Bulletin, April 17, 1880. USG responded to a lengthy address by Judge William H. Green and a welcome by Mayor Napoleon B. Thistlewood of Cairo. *Ibid.*

On April 12, 1880, USG, Vicksburg, telegraphed to Thistlewood and Samuel S. Taylor. "I accept with pleasure invitation of citizens and corporation to visit Cairo. Will arrive there from Little Rock fifteenth or sixteenth, and remain over night. Will telegraph exact day from Little Rock." *Ibid.*, April 13, 1880. On the same day, USG telegraphed to Thistlewood. "Will remain in Cairo night of sixteenth." *Ibid.*

On April 15, Benjamin H. Campbell, St. Louis, wrote to Orville E. Babcock. "I re-turned here this morning—from Memphis, I arrived thre same day—Genl Grant came, of course, found it dificult to get an interview with him, He of course did not expect to find me there—& when I was taken to his room by J. Y. Scammen of Chicago, the Genl was surprised to see me—found, him Mrs Grant Miss Felt Mr Scammen in the private Room—was recived very cordially by the Genl & Mrs Grant after the *compliments* of *season* I took the Genl one side & told him where I was from & for what purpose I had called on him at the earnest request of his *true* friends Logan & Cameron—he heard me all through & listened as he always does very attentivly, & appeared to realise the importance of his early arrival in our state & his immediate arrival at his home in Galena—he was under contract—to go to Little Rock—& could not get out of it as a committee was there in waiting for him—Tho, he *declined* to go to *Hot Springs* & will leave Little Rock to night & be at Cairo to morrow & will go—direct from there to Galena by Illinois Central—He will find a delegation there to accompany him through the state—just what his friends wanted—& will have its effect in the right direction—Both He & Mrs Grant are looking very well & of course, verry solicitous for the future—The Genl is well posted of what is going on & appears to be well-pleased—I had a very short interview but said all I wanted to—& had an engagement with Mrs Grant after Tea to call on her & Miss Felt—but did not see Mrs Grant—She sent me word, not knowing I would leave the next morning at 6. o clock—her eyes were troubling her very much—Tho she knew what I came for & fully appreciated the interest her friends were taking for her husband—I asked the Genl—If he would remain at, home for *some time* as his friends desired he said yes—only he would have to run over after a while for a few days to Chicago have some dentisty perform on his teeth—he has lost one of his front teeth—I told him that must effect his *speech making* he laughfed—his tour through the South has been very satisfactory & is doing him much good—. . ." ALS, ICN.

On April 17, USG spoke at Cobden and later repeated his remarks at Du Quoin, Ill. "General Grant said he was glad to be in his own State once more. He was tired of traveling and was really homesick. He felt though that one foot was already within his own home since he crossed the river into Illinois." *Chicago Inter-Ocean*, April 19, 1880. On the same day, USG spoke at Centralia, Ill. "LADIES AND GENTLEMEN—I thank you for this reception. I had hoped to reach your city by noon, but was detained by accident on the road, so that my stay with you must be necessarily brief. Reference has been made to the service I am said to have rendered to my country. I am sure I could not have succeeded in doing what I am credited with without the aid of the soldiers, many of whom are before me. To them all honor is due. We have no standing army, and I am glad of it. I have had opportunity in the last three years to see much of standing armies, and I know what they are. In our country every man is a sovereign, and when necessary every man is a soldier; I again thank you for this ovation, and hope the time may come in the future when I can visit you again and have longer to stay." *St. Louis Globe-Democrat*, April 18, 1880. An excursion train carrying passengers back from greeting USG at Cairo had derailed at Elkville, Ill., delaying USG's train by several hours.

Also on April 17, USG spoke at Bloomington, Ill. "LADIES AND GENTLEMEN: It is alike pleasing for me to be thus welcomed by those who have always been upon the same side with me, and those who recently were not. It may be appropriate on this occasion to refer to my trip through the Southern States, and to what I have seen while traveling. I have been gratified at my reception in all the recently rebellious states. I passed from Philadelphia to Florida on my way to Havana, and on my return came via Texas from Mexico, thus passing through all the rebellious States, and it will be agreeable to all to know that hospitality was tendered me at every city through which I passed, and accepted in nearly all of them by me. The same decorations were seen in every State that are seen here to-night. The Union flag floated over us everywhere, and the eyes of the people of those States are as familiar with its colors as yours, and look upon it as guaranteeing to all the rights and privileges of a free people without regard to race color or previous condition of servitude. In most of the States upon the reception committees, side by side, were men that wore the blue and men that wore the gray, and reception addresses were made in part by those who wore the blue and those who wore the gray. We have no reason to doubt that those who wore the gray will fulfill all they have promised in loyalty to the flag and the Nation. After travelling nearly three years in foreign lands, and comparing their condition and institutions with those of the United States, I am sure that we all ought to be good and loyal citizens. Ladies and gentlemen of Bloomington I thank you." *Bloomington Pantagraph*, April 19, 1880. USG spoke at the Ashley House, after addresses by Judge John M. Scott, Ill. Supreme Court, and Gus A. Hill, "the well known colored orator of Bloomington." *Ibid*. Earlier, at the depot, USG greeted the crowd. "Ladies and gentleman, I am glad to meet you, but as I expect to remain in your city until 11 o'clock Monday morning, I hope I will have the pleasure of seeing you all personally." *Ibid*. On April 15, Thursday, USG, Little Rock, had telegraphed to the *Pantagraph*. "I will leave for Bloomington on Saturday morning, and will stay over Sunday. Can not say what hour will arrive." *Ibid.*, April 16, 1880.

On April 18, USG spoke at the Soldiers' Orphans' Home in Normal, Ill. "CHILDREN: I am sorry that some one was not called upon who could have done better in speaking to you. It is a matter of pleasure to me to speak to and to see the orphans of our Union soldiers so well provided for. It is a duty we owe to the children of the men who fought for and preserved the nation. I have no doubt you will all avail yourselves of the advantages that are given you, and will endeavor to become good and worthy citizens of the Republic for which your fathers fought and bled and died. Wishing you all prosperity and success in life, I will say again that I am glad to see you." *Ibid.*, April 19, 1880.

On April 17, Saturday, Mayor David W. Lamme of El Paso, Ill., had telegraphed to USG, Decatur, Ill. "The City Council invites you to stop a short time at El Paso. If agreeable to you a committee will meet you at Bloomington Monday morning and return on your special train." *Chicago Inter-Ocean*, April 20, 1880. On the same day, USG telegraphed to Lamme. "Will pass through El Paso Monday." *Ibid*. On April 19, USG, Bloomington, again telegraphed to Lamme. "Will be in El Paso at 11:30 o'clock this morning." *Ibid*.

To Chester C. Cole

Galena, Ill.
Apl. 21st 1880,

MY DEAR JUDGE;

Your very kind invitation to me to visit Des Moines reached me while in New Orleans. I did not answer it then because I did not know what to say. I receive so many invitations to visit various parts of the country that I must necessarily decline many. I expect however to visit the Rocky Mountains this summer and will endeavor to pass Des Moines either going or coming.

When I can fix the time I will inform you.

Mrs Grant joins me in best regards to Mrs. Cole and all the members of your family.

Faithfully yours
U. S. GRANT

JUDGE C. C. COLE

ALS, IaHa. Born in 1824 in N. Y., Chester C. Cole graduated Harvard Law School in 1848, practiced in Ky., and settled in Iowa, where he helped found a law school and served on the supreme court.

On July 12, 1879, Cole, Des Moines, wrote to USG, San Francisco. "I had the pleasure of meeting Ex-Secy. Borie on his return home through here, three weeks ago to-day, and of travelling with him a half day. From him I learned where to address you. Myself and family desire to extend to you & suite a most cordial invitation to visit us here, on your way home. We shall be more than pleased to meet and entertain you. I suppose, from what Mr. Borie told me, that you have had but limited opportunities to keep fully posted upon our political affairs. In my judgment, you will, in 1880, be again called upon, as you were in 1868, to sacrifice your personal preferences to the manifest demands of the People & of patriotic duty, to accept the nomination of the Republican party and again resume the charge of the Government as its Chief Executive. With you in the Presidential Chair, the people of the Southern States will yield an obedience to law and duty, which they would not under any other; and as I think, a majority of them would, in their hearts and by their ballots, gladly welcome your return, because of the relief from their present unrest it would afford & the assurance of peace and order it would bring. Your election would be more nearly unanimous than of any predecessor. My family join me in kindest regards to you, Mrs. G., Col. Fred and wife. . . . P. S. Sent original of above to you at Yokohoma, China." LS, DLC-USG, IB. In [*Oct.*], USG, Portland, Ore., telegraphed to Cole. "Having accepted passage by CB & S Road will have to defer visit to DesMoines until after return to Galena" Telegram received, IaHa.

To Stephen T. Logan,[1] Shelby M. Cullom, and others

Galena, Ill.
Apl. 21st 1880.

HON S. T. LOGAN,[1] GOVR CULLOM,[2] & OTHERS;
GENTLEMEN:

Your letter of the 17th of this month conveying a kind invitation to me to visit the Capital of the State, the city from which I started nineteen years ago as Colonel of the 21st Regt. Ill. Vols.— now veterans,—was duly presented to me by the Governor of the State. I take pleasure in accepting your invitation but cannot just now fix the exact date when I can be there. It will however probably be early in next month. As soon as I can determine exactly the date I will inform some one of the signers of the invitation of it.

I appreciate this invitation more coming as it does from the citizens of the Capital of the State "without distinction of party," and recognizing too the propriety of re-visiting the home of the Martyr to whom the Nation owes so much—and to whom I was personally so much indebted for constant support, through all detraction, though an entire stranger to him except officially.

Later I came to know President Lincoln intimately, and my appreciation of his great ability, noble & generous nature, and forgiving disposition increased with acquaintance.

> With great respect,
> your obt. svt.
> U. S. GRANT

ALS, IHi. On April 17, 1880, Stephen T. Logan *et al.*, Springfield, Ill., wrote to USG, Galena. ". . . Permit us to suggest that your travels would hardly be complete witho[u]t including in your circuit of the world the late home of the Great Man with whose fame your own is so indissolubly connected; the city too which first witnessed the humble beginning of your own great career as a military leader. Requesting an early reply, . . ." *Illinois State Journal*, April 23, 1880.

On April 23, "Rev. Edw'd Anderson, President of the Union Veterans' Union, received a letter to-day from Gen. Grant, acknowledging the receipt of the invitation of the society and other invitations from citizens, to visit Quincy, the letter having been written on the supposition that he was going home by way of the river. He closes by saying that it is possible he may yet visit Quincy. Efforts will be made to have him come to Quincy when he visits Springfield." *St. Louis Globe-Democrat*, April 24, 1880.

1. Born in 1800 in Ky., Stephen T. Logan moved to Ill. in 1832, served as Ill. judge and representative, and practiced law with Abraham Lincoln.

2. Born in 1829, Shelby M. Cullom settled in Springfield, practiced law, served in the Ill. House and in Congress, and was elected governor in 1876.

To George W. Childs

Galena, Ill.
Apl. 23d 1880

MY DEAR MR. CHILDS:

We have now all been at home long enough to feel rested. Our last trip was quite as interesting as almost any portion of that round the world. I hope before many years to see the two Republics, Mexico & the United States, bound together by continuous lines of rail-roads, bonds of friendship, commerce and mutual confidence. When all this takes place I expect to hear of you taking a foreign trip, and not before knowing your antipathy to the Sea. Mexico can furnish any climate desired any day of the year and will be the most visited country in the world perhaps, except France, by travelers. As ~~I~~ we expect to spend five or six weeks in the Rocky Mountains this Summer we will not go to Long Branch. I have written to Mr. Brown[1] that he might rent my cottage.

Please present my kindest regards to Mrs. Childs & Miss Lizzie, Mr. Drexel & family, and to all my Phila friends, in all of which Mrs. Grant joins me.

Very Truly yours
U. S. GRANT

ALS, James S. Copley Library, La Jolla, Calif.

1. Probably Lewis B. Brown, a Long Branch developer. See *PUSG*, 23, 133.

To Gen. William T. Sherman

Galena, Ill.
Apl. 26th 1880

GEN. W. T. SHERMAN
COMD.G U. S. ARMY
WASHINGTON, D. C.
MY DEAR GENERAL:

I unite with Gen. Sheridan in suggesting—requesting if you please—the appointment of a Judg Advocate of the Army instead of a Recorder for the Warren court of Enquiry.

Of course neither General Sheridan or myself can appear as prossecutors, or even as defendants, before the court, so that to employ council to meet the eminent lawyer employed by Gen. Warren would be manifestly in bad taste. I would suggest Major Gardner because I know him better than any other officer of the Department except the head.

Very Truly Yours

U. S. GRANT

ALS, DLC-William T. Sherman. On April 24, 1880, Lt. Gen. Philip H. Sheridan wrote to Gen. William T. Sherman. "After a consultation with Mr. Robert Lincoln, a lawyer of good ability in reference to the Warren Court of Inquiry, he addressed me the enclosed communication which I submit to you with this note. I have no status before the court, nor has General Grant; although both of us are greatly interested in the conclusions it may arrive at. It would not be agreeable to, nor proper for, me to appear there as a prosecutor of General Warren, even if the Court would grant me that privilege, and I therefore respectfully request that a Judge Advocate such as Major Gardner or Major Barr,—either of whom I feel confident would fully develope both sides of the case, be substituted for the present recorder. Col. Langdon is a most excellent officer, but he is not a lawyer, and it is no reflection on him for me to say, I doubt his ability to meet a man in the legal field, of the legal acumen of Mr. Stickney. . . . " LS (press), DLC-Philip H. Sheridan. On June 14, Lt. Col. Michael V. Sheridan, Chicago, wrote to Maj. Asa B. Gardiner. "The General starts to-day for the meeting of the Army of the Potomac at Burlington Vermont. He desires me to write you relative to subpoena-ing General Grant and wants to know your judgment in regard to it. He feels that General Grant should be called but of course rests the matter on your judgment. I think he should be called also and as Warren desires to reflect on him too it seems to me that Court ought to call him even if no one else did, still the whole matter is with you and if convenient I would like to hear from you about it by the time the General returns the last of the week." Copy (press), *ibid.* Related papers are *ibid.* See Testimony, [*Oct. 23, 1880*].

To William Breeden et al.

———

GALENA, ILLS, April 26. [*1880*]

WILLIAM BREEDEN AND OTHERS:

GENTLEMEN:—I have your kind invitation to visit Santa some time during the summer.

It is my expectation to go to Colorado about the latter part of June, to be absent from here some five or six weeks. During my absence, I hope to see a little of New Mexico and I will of course, take in the capital, the ancient city, of which I have heard a good deal. Without seeing Santa Fe, I should have not seen anything of New Mexico.

I accept therefore, your kind invitation with great pleasure, and I will let some one of your committee know the date as soon as it is determined upon.

Very Truly Yours,

U. S. GRANT.

Weekly New Mexican (Santa Fé), May 3, 1880. Born in Ky., William Breeden served New Mexico Territory as supreme court clerk, attorney gen., U.S. commissioner, and delegate to the 1876 and 1880 Republican National Conventions. On April 20, 1880, Breeden and ten others, Santa Fé, wrote to USG, Galena. "At a meeting of the citizens of Santa Fe, irrespective of party, the undersigned were appointed a committee to extend to you an invitation to visit the Ancient City of 'Holy Faith,' at such time as you may name, as we understand that you contemplate coming west at an early day. The committee feel assured from their knowledge of the people of this Territory and their universal esteem for you, that a hearty welcome will be extended you at this their capital. They would not hope or expect to approach in any design, the magnificent receptions which have been extended to you as the greatest of living generals and statesmen by many of the potentates and people of the great cities of the world whom and where you have visited in your recent extensive travels, but our citizens will extend to you a welcome second to none in earnestness and cordiality should you offer them the opportunity by coming among them. The committee enclose a printed notice of the meeting held here on the 15 inst. and in pursuance thereof extend to you a cordial and earnest invitation to to visit us, and should you be able to do so, please advise us at your earliest convenience of the time when we may expect you." *Ibid.*, April 26, 1880. See letter to Adam Badeau, July 28, 1880, note 1.

Speech

———

[*Galena, April 27, 1880*]

FELLOW CITIZENS: This pleasant visit, though entirely unexpected, is none the less welcome. I thank you for the kindness, expressed through your speaker, Mr. McClellan.[1] I cannot complain of the treatment I have received from the world, since I came to Galena twenty years ago. I have had many honors bestowed upon me, and I have also been abused, perhaps, more than any other man, yet the ill treatment I have received has been more than compensated for by the expressio[n]s of esteem and friendship I have received from friends such as are assembled here to-night, who have always vindicated me. I thank you again for this visit. I am sorry that my house is not large enough to comfortably accommodate you all, but

I should be pleased to have you all come in. You will find standing room if not sitting room.

Galena Gazette, April 28, 1880. "Yesterday being General Grant's 58th birthday, he was the recipient of an entirely informal and impromptu congratulatory visit last evening from a large number of his fellow citizens, who arrived at the house about half-past 9 o'clock. . . ." *Ibid.* On April 27, 1880, Hamilton Fish, New York City, wrote to USG. "I hope that you do not object to have it remembered that this is your Birth-day, & that you will accept my cordial congratulations, on its return, & my best wishes that there may be many, *very many* happy returns of the day in store for you. Your very kind note to Hamilton, shews you at Galena, with the expectation of remaining there for some time—Well—in that case there will be many pilgrims to that City during the coming Summer—for although your journeying may be suspended, I imagine that you are to the object of very many a journey, for some time to come—but this bears upon a point which I do not wish you to notice. I want only to tender the congratulations above expressed, & the further congratulations upon your safe reaching the End of your long, & most journey which must have so many delightful & gratifying recollections, for Mrs Grant & yourself—My wife desires to be most cordially, & affectionately remembered to Mrs Grant & to you. She is not strong & has never recovered entirely from the very severe illness which she experienced about a year ago—& recently we have been called upon to mourn the loss of two of our grandsons—Hamiltons wedding tomorrow is to be quite quiet & private, Miss Mann having recently lost her Father, & our own family, being also in mourning—. . . P S—If you wish a case of Port wine, which was sent here, for you, shortly after you left, forwarded, let me know—It is safe in my wine Cellar, & can remain there as long as you wish." ALS (press), DLC-Hamilton Fish.

1. Born in 1823 in N. Y., Robert H. McClellan moved to Galena in 1850, prospered as a lawyer and banker, and served in the Ill. House and Senate.

Speech

[*Springfield, Ill., May 5, 1880*]

GENERAL PALMER, GOVERNOR CULLOM, CITIZENS OF SPRING-FIELD AND ILLINOIS: After an absence from my country of nearly three years, in which I have made a circuit of the globe, it has seemed to me fitting and proper that I should come to this city, from which I first started in the memorable struggle in which I first became acquainted with so many citizens of this State. I assure you it is with great pleasure that I see you here to-day, and I thank you for the hearty welcome which has greeted me here. In all my travels I can say to the citizens here before me that none

have a country, a climate, a fertility of soil to surpass just what
we have around this capital of the State of Illinois, and if all of
you could see as I have seen other countries, other people, and the
struggle for life and existence there, it would make each one, if possible, a better citizen of his own country, and he certainly would
feel that he had nothing to complain of here. Our Union, as General Palmer has said, has cost us a great struggle to preserve, and
I see before me here many of those who went to the field with me,
determined that it should not perish, and if they had seen what
I have, they would feel certainly as well satisfied that what they
fought for then was worth even more than the price we paid for
our present Union. In my travels through our own country, I am
happy to say that I thought I saw signs of returning prosperity in
the section that we were lately in conflict with, and with prosperity
a returning love to the flag that floats on this side of the platform.
That is what we desire certainly; that there shall be no sectional
feeling, that there should be a substantial, solid, Union feeling in
every section of the country; and, no matter what the public position of parties nineteen years ago, they should all feel that now
they have a common interest in the country, and are protected
by the same flag, and, if necessary, should fight for it too. Gentlemen, I don't know that it is necessary for me to say any more.
I return thanks again, and give you an opportunity to get out of
the sun.

Chicago Inter-Ocean, May 6, 1880. John M. Palmer, *Personal Recollections of John M. Palmer: The Story of an Earnest Life* (Cincinnati, 1901), pp. 436–37. John M. Palmer introduced USG to a crowd outside the state capitol. See *ibid.*, pp. 432–35; *Illinois State Journal*, May 5, 6, 1880.

On April 28, 1880, USG traveled from Galena to Chicago, stopping for three hours at Rockford, where he addressed a crowd. ". . . I am indeed surprised to find, so near my own home, a place of so large manufacturing interests, and so much wealth; I have known much of your city by reputation, but have never before had an oppor-tunity of riding about the streets and viewing the prosperity. You have manufactur-ing interests here of which a city of three times the size might well be proud, and ere another decade I hope that such may be the case, and that I may again have the privi-lege of greeting you, and taking each and all by the hand." *Rockford Gazette*, April 28, 1880.

On May 4, en route from Chicago to Springfield, Ill., USG spoke briefly at Pon-tiac and at Lincoln. See Newton Bateman *et al.*, eds., *Historical Encyclopedia of Illinois and History of Livingston County* (Chicago, 1909), II, 730; *Illinois State Journal*, May 5, 1880.

Elihu B. Washburne accompanied USG to Springfield. On May 4 and 5, the *St. Louis Globe-Democrat* had accused Washburne of plotting his own candidacy while avowing support for USG. On May 5, USG commented on these allegations. "I am very sorry to see this, and especially if my friends had anything to do with it. Mr. Washburne is my friend. He has always been a very warm and sincere friend to me, and was such at a time when his friendship was so valuable that, no matter what happens, I can never forget it nor cease to remember it with gratitude." *Chicago Inter-Ocean*, May 6, 1880. On the same day, USG attended a reception at the state capitol. In his memoirs, Governor Shelby M. Cullom of Ill. accused Washburne of avoiding this reception for political reasons. "His conduct in the evening was still more remarkable. I had arranged a reception to General and Mrs. Grant and Mr. Washburne at the Executive Mansion that same evening, but Mr. Washburne gave some excuse which he claimed necessitated his presence in the East, and departed—. . ." Cullom, *Fifty Years of Public Service: Personal Recollections of Shelby M. Cullom, Senior United States Senator from Illinois* (Chicago, 1911), p. 171. See also Augustus L. Chetlain, *Recollections of Seventy Years* (Galena, 1899), pp. 179–85. On May 14, Washburne, Portland, Maine, wrote "*To the Editor of the New-York Times:* My position in regard to the candidacy for President, and my relations to Gen. Grant's nomination, are not changed in any respect whatever. All reports sent out by certain parties in Chicago, asserting or suggesting duplicity toward Gen. Grant, are utterly and absolutely false, and known to be so by their authors. I left Chicago some 10 days ago. All combinations alleged to have been made in that city by my friends and those of other candidates have been entered into without my knowledge or approbation. I have been confined to my room here for nearly a week by serious illness, and shall return home as soon as I am able to travel and have attended to the business which brought me to this State." *New York Times*, May 15, 1880.

During USG's visit to Springfield, Wiley Crafton wrote "To the Editor: In the year 1861, when Gen. Grant was appointed Drill Master at Camp Yates, he came to my stable, in company with Governor Yates, and they together made arrangements for livery for the General (then Captain). The General was furnished with a horse and buggy—for the use of which he paid periodically, or nightly, as it was returned. He liked the horse, and he gave directions to reserve that particular animal for his use. The General was, at that time, employed by the State authorities as a Drill Master of recruits at Camp Yates, and when he left I had no notice of relinquishment of his claim upon his right to use the animal, and I continued to hold the horse subject to his order. There was left a bill of $15 which accrued upon the animal while he stood in the stable subject to Captain Grant's orders, at the time he left Springfield. That bill of *fifteen dollars* I yesterday put into the hands of an agent, for collection, and I understand that he, without authority, collected an additional amount for interest for nineteen years. I did not authorize the agent to make any such collection, and he retained all the amount above the said $15. I believe the State should have paid my bill, and I did not authorize the said agent to ask of any Justice of the Peace the issuance of any process or papers in the matter as against Gen. Grant." *Illinois State Journal*, May 6, 1880. Charles Cannon had presented USG with a bill for $32.10. "Gov. Cullom, knowing the class of cattle represented by the parties, protested against the outrage, but Gen. Grant, saying he had paid thousands of dollars of just such claims, paid the bill." *Ibid.* See *ibid.*, May 7, 1880; *PUSG*, 21, 398.

To Daniel Ammen

——

GALENA, ILLINOIS, May 8th, 1880.

MY DEAR AMMEN,—

I have your letter of May the 4th, and received duly all your letters. I received probably about the time you did the proceedings of the Board of Trade of San Francisco on the subject of an inter-oceanic canal, and read it with great interest.[1] I was going to send it to you, but supposed from your known interest in the undertaking that you would likely receive it without my sending.

I shall not go East, unless something changes my mind, before breaking up here for the winter,—say about the 1st of December. My mind is not made up yet where to spend the winter, but probably in Washington and Florida.

My visit to Mexico was the pleasantest in all my travels, except possibly to Japan, and of the greatest interest to me. I feel that we may help both countries and help ourselves at the same time. Mexico is ripe now for improvements that will develop her great resources. If we do not take advantage of it and establish friendly and commercial relations, worth millions annually to each country, it will be our own fault. It takes me six to ten hours a day to read and answer my correspondence; otherwise I would prepare, with some care, articles on both Japan and Mexico. But I lack the time and the industry. Has Beale returned? Mrs. Grant has had several letters from Emily, but he had not returned at last accounts.

Please present Mrs. Grant's and my kindest regards to Mrs. Atocha, Mrs. Ammen, and the children.

Yours very truly,

U. S. GRANT.

Daniel Ammen, *The Old Navy and the New* (Philadelphia, 1891), pp. 550–51.

1. On Feb. 2, 1880, the San Francisco Board of Trade appointed a committee of five "to consider the question of an inter-oceanic canal in its bearings on the Pacific coast, and to investigate, from a commercial standpoint, which projected route should meet the approval of San Francisco merchants." The Board of Trade of San Francisco, *Report of Special Committee on Inter-Oceanic Canal* (San Francisco, 1880), p. 3. The report favored the Nicaragua over the Panama route.

To Fenwick Y. Hedley

Galena Ill.
May 8th 1880

F. Y. HEDLEY, SEC. U. V. CLUB,
DEAR SIR:

On my return here from an absence of over a week I found your letter of the 29th of Apl. asking for something from me to be read on the occasion of the Decoration of the Union Soldiers graves on the 29th of this month. It would be hard for me to express the sentiments I feel towards the soldiers who maintained the Union at the risk of their lives, and particularly those who sacrificed their live. It is fitting that their memory should be kept green in the memory of their living comrades, and in the memory of their descendents as long as time lasts. Nothing can conduce to this end more effectually than the beautiful custom of Decorating the graves of the patriotic dead every recurring May.

Yours sincerely
U. S. GRANT

ALS (facsimile), *Memorial Day Message from General Ulysses Simpson Grant* (n. p., [1922]). Born in England in 1844, former 1st lt., 32nd Ill., Fenwick Y. Hedley edited the *Bunker Hill* (Ill.) *Gazette* and served as postmaster. See *New York Times*, June 14, 1897, Jan. 9, 1924.

To Robert T. Van Horn

Galena, Ill.
May 8th 1880.

COL. R. T. VAN HORN, & OTHERS
GENTLEMEN;

Your letter of the 23d of Apl. asking me to appoint a day when I can be in Kansas City must have reached here after my departure for Chicago ten days ago. At all events I only found it on my return a couple of days since.

It is my expectation to leave here about the last of June for the Rocky Mountains. I can then go by Kansas City, and stop over for the time you specify. If this is not to late for the exercises contemplated I will be at Kansas City at any time you may arrange for from the 28th of June to the 3d of July. If this does not suit I beg you will not put the citizens of Kansas City to any inconvenience on my account.

Very Truly Yours

U. S. GRANT

ALS, University of Missouri-Kansas City, Kansas City, Mo. Born in Pa. in 1824, trained in law and journalism, Robert T. Van Horn settled in Kansas City, Mo., in 1855, and served as lt. col., 25th Mo., postmaster, mayor, state senator, and U.S. Representative (1865–71). On Dec. 8, 1875, USG nominated Van Horn as collector of Internal Revenue, 6th District, Mo. On May 26, 1880, USG wrote to Van Horn. "The party with me on my proposed visit to Kansas City will consist of Mrs. Grant, Miss McKennan, possibly one of my sons, and Mr. W. W. Smith, a friend and relative of mine. I would prefer going through DesMoines, Iowa, if convenient, and either route from here to that point. I am not specially particular however as to route." ALS, *ibid.* See Speech, [*July 2, 1880*].

On Oct. 8, 1879, Mayor George M. Shelley, C. P. Prescott, and Van Horn had telegraphed to USG, San Francisco. "Will you pass through Kansas City our people want to greet you please answer" Telegram received (at 3:00 P.M.), DLC-USG, IB.

On May 9, 1880, USG wrote to an unknown person. ". . . I do not expect to go east before the latter part of Nov. having determined to spend part of the summer in the Rocky mountains . . ." Carnegie Book Shop Inc., Catalogue No. 364 [1978], no. 172.

On May 24, USG wrote to Arthur C. Stewart, Louisiana, Mo. "I should like exceedingly to be able to accept your invitation, and to see Mrs. Stewart again who I believe I have not met since before I went to West Point." Craig W. Ross, [1972], no. 95. On Dec. 6, 1869, USG had nominated Stewart as collector of Internal Revenue, 4th District, Mo. See *PUSG*, 15, 520–21.

To John F. H. Claiborne

Galena, Ill.

May 11th 1880

J. T. H. CLAIBORNE, ESQ.

MY DEAR SIR:

I take pleasure in acknowledging the receipt of your letter of the 6th of May, just received, with its enclosure, Ex Governor Brown's [1] letter to you. I have read both with great pleasure, and thinking you may want the Governors letter return it herewith.

I know Govr Brown, of course, by reputation, as most people do from his long and distinguished public career, and have heard frequently since my last return to the United states of his earnest desire for a cessation of the miserable sectional strife that has now been kept us so long to the detriment of the whole country, and particularly of the South. People rarely reflect that it is now two years longer since the close of the rebellion than it was from the close of the Mexican war to the opening of the rebellion. Many thousands of voters of to-day were in their nurses arms when the rebellion commenced. They should not be made to fight over the battles of the past. It is time we had a Nation in which all could feel an interest and a pride. I wish we had more Governor Browns as I understand him and believe him.

> Very Truly yours
> U. S. GRANT

ALS, Boston University, Boston, Mass. John F. H. Claiborne had served as U.S. Representative from Miss. (1835–38) and wrote a history of Miss.

　1. Probably Albert G. Brown, former Miss. governor (1844–48), and Claiborne's correspondent and political ally. See James Byrne Ranck, *Albert Gallatin Brown: Radical Southern Nationalist* (New York, 1937), pp. 286–91.

To Edward F. Beale

———

> Galena, Ill.
> May 16th 1880.

MY DEAR GEN. BEALE:

I was glad to receive your letter of the 27th of Apl. I should have written to you from Mexico, but I knew you had gone to California, did not know your address there, and expected your return to Washington before this.—My last trip was quite as pleasant as any that preceded it. Mexico has made no great strides since we were there as young men. But it is just preparing for rapid developement. With a peaceable Presidential election this summer, and quiet inauguration following, Mexico will be able to invite foreign capital to build her roads, develope her sugar, coffee, tobacco and mines, and build up a commerce commensurate with her great natural resources. Now

that we have roads going to her very borders they should form connections with a whole net work in that country. We are now paying two hundred millions a year, in sterling exchange, for tropical &
semi-tropical products which ᵐMexico could furnish, and would receive largely in exchange, the products of our soil & manufacturies.

The campaign east of the Mountains has been unprecedented.
The democratic papers need not bother their heads for matter to
fill up their campaign documents. All they need to do will be to re-
publish what the republican papers have said about the candidates
whos nomination they opposed. But I hope the election will come
out right.

Buck returned two weeks ago. Jesse we hear nothing from. Ere
this I hope he is at your house.

I forget to mention that I did not go to Honolulu because I found
that it would be impossible to get to the Pacific from Mexico with
any comfort with ladies and all the interminable baggage they carry.

With kindest regards of Mrs. Grant & myself,

Yours Truly

U. S. GRANT

ALS, DLC-Decatur House Papers.

To *William W. Smith*

————

Galena, Ill.
May 17th 1880

DEAR SMITH:

About the 25th of June Mrs. Grant & I expect to leave here for
Colorado. Mrs. Grant will stop at Colorado Springs while I expect
to go to Leadville and through the mining regions as far as New
Mexico, possibly taking from two to three weeks from the Springs
before returning. Possibly Buck may be able to go with me. I write
now to ask if you would not like to go? If so we would be delighted
to have you.

I am kept very busy here since my return with the mails. But I
pay no attention to political letters. I am not half as much interested

in that matter as my friends seem to be, nor a tenth as much as my enemies. I can submit without loss of rest to the verdict no matter what it may be.

Write and let me know if you think you can go with me. You should arrange your affairs so as to be absent from Washington at least five weeks if you go.

All are well and desire to be remembered.

yours Truly

U. S. GRANT

ALS, Washington County Historical Society, Washington, Pa.

To John Thompson

————

Galena, Ill.
May 18th 1880.

MY DEAR MR. THOMPSON;

On Monday next[1] Mr. Ryan[2] & myself go to Dubuque by the noon train, to return by the 9 pm train. I will see you there if you are in the City and will fix the time when Mrs. Grant & I can accept yours & Mrs Thompsons kind invitation to go over and spend the night.[3]

Very Truly yours

U. S. GRANT

We will dine with Mr. Wm Ryan.

U. S. G.

ALS, Clarke Historical Library, Central Michigan University, Mount Pleasant, Mich. Born in N. Y. in 1821, John Thompson settled in Dubuque in 1857, traded in leather goods and served as mayor. He married Mary Marshall in 1843. See *PUSG*, 15, 302.

On Dec. 1, 1879, William Vandever welcomed USG to Dubuque. USG replied. "GENERAL: I thank the citizens of Dubuque and yourself for the kind welcome which you have extended to me. I shall not attempt to make any remarks further than to say that I most heartily thank you. After an absence of two and a half years I have returned to our country appreciating it more highly than ever." *Chicago Times*, Dec. 2, 1879. USG spent the day as Thompson's guest.

1. May 24, 1880. See *Dubuque Herald*, May 25, 1880.
2. Brothers James M. and William Ryan operated meat packing plants in Galena and Dubuque, respectively.

3. USG and Julia Dent Grant spent the night of May 31 as guests of the Thompsons. "General Grant remained up until a late hour after the party, to hear news from Chicago, which was furnished at his request from the HERALD office. . . ." *Ibid.*, June 1, 1880.

To King Chulalongkorn

—————

Galena, Ill,
May 19th 1880.

HIS MAJESTY KING OF SIAM,

I take pleasure in presenting Gen. John A. Halderman,[1] who goes to Bankok as United States Consul to your country. General Halderman I feel sure will give great satisfaction to your Majesty and your people. He will have no other object than to preserve the the most friendly relations between his own country & countrymen and the goverment & people of Siam. I am sure if Your Majesty should want to consult or advise with him in relation to any matters that might come up you could do so with full assurance of sincere and honest desire on his part to be entirely just and fair towards Siam. While enjoying the hospitalities of your Majesty I thought I saw where impositions had been practiced upon Siam which I do not believe Gen. Halderman would be guilty of, and I know his country would not approve of.[2]

Since my return to the United States I have been a further traveler beyond the borders of my own country. I have had a most delightful visit to Cuba & Mexico.

I regreted to learn that you had abandoned the idea of visiting the United States this year. Hope you will come yet even if it should be at a later day.

With assurances of my high regards, I am,

very sincerely,
your obt. svt
U. S. GRANT

ALS, Smithsonian Institution. On Aug. 20, 1880, King Chulalongkorn of Siam endorsed this letter. "Given to General Halderman at his request" ES, *ibid.*

1. Born in 1833 in Ky., John A. Halderman studied law, moved to Kan. in 1854, and served as maj., 1st Kan., Leavenworth mayor, and Kan. representative and senator. See *Transactions of the Kansas State Historical Society*, VIII (1903–4), 331.

2. See *Young*, II, 252–53.

To Porfirio Díaz

Galena Ill.
May 21st 1880

HIS EXCELLENCY P. DIAZ
PRESIDENT REPUBLIC OF MEXICO.
MY DEAR MR PRESIDENT,

During my late and very pleasant visit to the Republic of Mexico presided over by you so ably I had the honor of several conversations with you, at your solicitation, on the subject of a Mexican and International railroad system as a means of developing the great resources of your country, and of establishing brotherly and commercial relations between the two countries. You will probably remember that I then stated that whenever either of the great railroad corporations now pressing towards the borders of Mexico should apply for a concession to build roads in the country, the concession might be granted with full assurance that whatever was undertaken by them would find the means to accomplish, and their work would be completed in the shortest practicable time.

Among the corporations mentioned by me was the Southern Pacific road, now being built along the 32nd N latitude. I am now asked by Mr C. P. Huntington[1] one of the capitalists building said road for a letter to some influential person connected with your government, endorsing their ability to carry out whatever they agree to.

I give this letter cheerfully, and would be delighted if it should contribute in any degree to the consummation of what I believe of the utmost importance to Mexico, and of great benefit to the United States, the connection of the two republics by a thorough railroad system, such as the United States and the Dominion of Canada now have.

With assurances of high personal regard

> I am
>
> very respectfully
>
> Your obt servant
>
> U. S. GRANT

Copy, Syracuse University, Syracuse, N. Y. Alberto Maria Carreño, ed., *Archivo Del General Porfirio Diaz: Memorias y Documentos* (Mexico City, 1947–61), XXX, 257. On June 8, President Porfirio Díaz of Mexico wrote to USG acknowledging this letter. *Ibid.*, p. 258.

    1. See following letter.

To Collis P. Huntington

———

> Galena Ill
>
> May 21st 1880

C. R. HUNTINGTON, ESQ.

DEAR SIR:

Since enclosing a letter to you this am, addressed to President Diaz, I have written another to Mr. Romero, on the same subject, and took the liberty of enclosing yours. I informed him of the letter addressed to the President, and further fortified it, hoping to contribute to a work which I look upon as so important to the commerce of this country, & to the wellfare of Mexico. With facilities of transportation Mexico is capable of producing all the tropical & semi-tropical products we now import, and pay for mostly in sterling exchange, and would take in return the products of our manufactures. I sincerely hope arrangements may be made so satisfactory as to induce U. S. capital to build the required roads in Mexico.

> Very Truly yours
>
> U. S. GRANT

ALS, Syracuse University, Syracuse, N. Y. Born in 1821 in Conn., Collis P. Huntington prospered as a Calif. hardware merchant, then turned to railroad promotion, help-
ing to build and operate the Central Pacific, Southern Pacific, and the Chesapeake
and Ohio.

To John A. Logan

Galena Ill.
May 25th 1880

MY DEAR GEN. LOGAN:

At the close of the Springfield convention I received a number
of dispatches from different deligates announcing the result, and
among them one from you. It never occurred to me that any answer was required or expected. I made no reply to any of them.
This morning I read in the Times a paragraph saying that no reply
had yet been made by me to your dispatch. I am not influenced by
what the Times says about me, but it brought to my mind the possibility that I should have recognized in some way the action of my
friends in the convention, and especially of yourself & the Chairman. I assure you that there was no intentional neglect on my part,
and that I appreciate the action of my friends in the convention as
highly probably as if more demonstrative about it.

Sincerely Yours
U. S. GRANT

ALS, DLC-John A. Logan. On May 21, 1880, Green B. Raum, Springfield, Ill., telegraphed to USG, Galena. "The Republican Convention of Illinois, now in session, have
directed me to send greeting to you, with an earnest assurance that its 42 delegates
will give their united support for the nomination of Gen. U. S. Grant for the Presidency
of the United States in the National Convention. I take great pleasure in discharging
this duty." *Illinois State Journal*, May 22, 1880. See *Chicago Times*, May 24, 1880; Raum,
History of Illinois Republicanism . . . (Chicago, 1900), pp. 157–63.

On May 15, Secretary of the Treasury John Sherman had written to William H.
Smith, Chicago. "Confidential . . . I have kept a careful lookout on matters in Chicago
and have heard from several sources of the strong disposition on the part of Grant's
followers to come to my assistance, but within a day they seem to have taken hope
again and propose to make the contest to the end. At the same time the friends of Mr.
Blaine have been much more polite and considerate. It seems to me the logic of these
events is the defeat of both Grant and Blaine. . . ." LS, InHi.

To John W. Forney

———

Galena, Ill.
May 26th 1880

My Dear Col. Forney:

I have had your letter of the 20th for several days and have delayed answering because I did not know exactly what to say. On mature reflection, and without a soul knowing from me that I have received such a letter, I would say not to make any change in your paper without feeling at least that it will not entail any pecuniary loss. I heartily wish you were back in controll of your old paper, The Press, but that I suppose impossible. You have, I have no doubt, friends much better to advise about the pecuniary prospects in case of change of the form of your paper than me. I hope they will give you advice that will lead to your success. The Progress has given me an able and dignified support which I appreciate, and which has been copied into the press of the country with good effect.

Thanking you for the past, and hoping to deserve your good opinion in the future, I am,

Very Truly yours
U. S. Grant

ALS (facsimile), USGA. After selling *The Press* in 1877, John W. Forney established *The Progress* in 1878; in June, 1880, he aligned the weekly with the Democratic Party. See *Chicago Inter-Ocean*, June 5, 1880; James Thompson Sheep, "John W. Forney— Stormy Petrel of American Journalism," Ph.D. Dissertation, University of Pittsburgh, 1959, pp. 114–21.

To John H. Hauser

———

Galena, Ill.
May 26th 1880

J. H. Hauser Sec. &c.
Dear Sir:

I have written to Col. Grant,[1] who makes th[e] arrangements for my trip to Milwaukee, that I wish to go on Friday[2] of the week of the soldiers meeting, to Green Bay, to leave the latter place for Galena on the followin[g] Monday. That I would like to stop at Fond du Lac³ for an hour or two—the time is not so important if I do not have to stay over the day—either going or coming if the arrangement can be made without inconvenience to the road. If this arrangement can be made I shall be very glad to meet the Veteran Club of Fond du Lac.

Very Truly yours

U. S. GRANT

ALS, Richard Norton Smith, West Branch, Iowa. John H. Hauser, Fond du Lac lawyer, had served as capt., 40th Wis.

On May 17, 1880, USG, Galena, wrote to Charles S. Hamilton. ". . . It is my expectation to go to Chicago either Saturday or Monday before starting for Milwaukee; to go with Sheridan . . . by special train . . . This gives practically three days . . . I stay with you, and in regard to the manner of proceeding from the cars to your house, only remember the less delay and the less parade the better I will be pleased . . ." R. M. Smythe & Co., Inc., Sale No. 99, Oct. 23, 1991, no. 149.

On [*April 20*], USG "wrote a letter to Marshalltown declining to visit that place on the 30th of May to attend a reunion of the First Regiment of Iowa Veterans. He has an engagement some where else at the time." *Dubuque Herald*, April 27, 1880. Also in April, USG wrote to [*Delos*] Phillips, as reported from Kalamazoo, "regarding the reception tendered him here in May by the Soldiers' and Sailors' Association of Southwestern Michigan, that he will have to defer his anticipated visit, but hopes to see Michigan ere long. He resided in this State two years." *Chicago Inter-Ocean*, April 28, 1880. Probably about the same time, USG declined an invitation to another veterans' gathering at Burlington, Vt., on June 16. "I am sorry not to be able to meet my old comrades of the Army of the Potomac on so interesting an occasion as I know they will have, but I must forego the pleasure this time, hoping they will have many more meetings of the same sort, some of which I may be able to attend." *The Society of the Army of the Potomac. Report of the Eleventh Annual Re-Union, . . .* (New York, 1880), p. 79.

1. On May 24, Lt. Gen. Philip H. Sheridan, Chicago, telegraphed to USG. "Your telegram rcd No hurry about Fred" ADfS and copy, DLC-Philip H. Sheridan.

2. June 11.

3. USG visited Fond du Lac on June 14 and responded to a welcoming address. "His remarks we were unable to take in detail, as he spoke very low and feelingly. He said that he was pleased to have visited the city, and he could appreciate the welcome afforded. Also that the American nation failed to estimate its own importance, and that it was esteemed by foreign nations much more than it appreciated itself." *Fond du Lac Commonwealth*, June 19, 1880.

To John Russell Young

[Galena, May 26, 1880]

DEAR YOUNG.

The enclosed dispatch has been laying here for two days. Expecting you here I have not opened until just now, and thinking it may be important to you send it. Mrs. Grant & I have been hoping to see you here for several days. The four or five last letters I received from you from Europe announced your early departure for the U. S. and all I received after your arrival in the country announced your early departure for the West. This kept me from writing to you as I otherwise would have done. I hope we will see you out here soon.

yours Truly

U. S. GRANT

ALS (undated, envelope postmarked Galena, May 26), DLC-John Russell Young. USG addressed John Russell Young at the Palmer House, Chicago. Young arrived at Galena on the evening of May 26, 1880, and left on May 28. On June 4, Young, Cheyenne, Wyoming Territory, wrote to John Hay, asst. secretary of state. "I meant to have written you from Galena as I had promised, but I was very busy while there, and this is the only pause in the whirl. My visit to Galena was very pleasant. I was the General's only guest and we knocked about the country together like a pair of boys on a holiday. I never saw him better or in better form. He was indifferent about the nomination, and said there was only one consideration that prevented his withdrawing his name absolutely, and that was the belief that he could be the means of ending the 'miserable sectional strifes' between the North and South.—I gave him your message, & he was very much pleased with it, and asked me to remember him to you Assurances of kindness from the present administration have been so rare that yours was grateful. Gen Grant took a deep interest in the Chinese question and wants the mission to be a success. I told him of the President's offer of the Secretaryship, and how sorry I was I could not go.—But a Secretary would be a kind of courier—would have no voice in the embassy, and I did not see that I could do any good.—Grant's influence in the negotiation would be ~~worth~~ incalculable.—. . . It looks as if Grant were beaten. If not Grant I hope it will be Blaine. If we cannot have one thing, let us have the other.—It would be the crowning end of the campaign of slander.—. . ." ALS, RPB. Young told a reporter that USG "has some very original views about a future American policy connected with China and Japan. The European nations have all, in their turn, been picking at those Oriental powers which confront us on the other side of the Pacific. I think that Grant has some idea that the western nation ought to extend at least its moral support to those useful people and make them feel that their nearest Christian neighbor is the best worth their consideration and trade." *Chicago Times*, May 28, 1880.

To James M. Comly

————

Galena, Ill.
May 29th 1880.

MY DEAR GEN. COMLY;

Your very welcome letter of the 12th of Apl. come duly to hand. I regret as much as any one can my inability to visit Honolulu. There were four ladies in my party visiting Mexico. You know ladies do not travel with handbags, but quite the contrary, with trunks and some of them big enough to camp in in a pinch. When we got to Mexico we found that it would take six or seven days on horseback, besides the distance that could be made in coaches, with pack animals for the baggage,—before we could reach Acapulco. We were then in the midst of the dry season, and the dust was worked up as deep as the mud was ever seen in Ohio when you & I were boys. Under all these circumstances I was forced to give up a visit that I had looked forward to with much pleasure.

Please convey to the King my disappointment at not being able to accept his kind invitation, and my hope that I will yet have that pleasure. Also my thanks for the cordiality of his invitation.

At this writing the Klans are marshaling in Chicago to determine upon the destiny of the Nation. There has never been a campaign in which so much feeling has been exhibited within any party. What is to be the result, or final effect, I do not pretend to predict. I only hope that the nation may not be the sufferer.

Very Truly yours
U. S. GRANT

ALS, Blumhaven Library and Gallery, Philadelphia, Pa. Born in 1832 in Ohio, James M. Comly practiced law in Columbus, served under Rutherford B. Hayes in the 23rd Ohio, and rose to bvt. brig. gen. After the war, Comly edited the *Ohio State Journal* and served as Columbus postmaster under USG and minister to Hawaii under Hayes.

To George W. Childs

Galena, Ill.
May 30th 1880.

My Dear Mr. Childs:

I was very glad to receive your letter. I knew Gen. Patterson was my friend, but I was just as glad to hear his defense of me. I hope to see him in the fall just as well and robust as when we last met. We would like to go on to Long Branch very much. But our house would require a good deal of repairs and refurnishing and Mrs. Grant is tired and does not feel like attending to it. Next Spring we will have all that attended to before time to go go on there. Then too we have felt anxious to spend a little time in Colorado. Mrs. Grant has been there twice before, and I oftener, but then we were always in a hurry, stopping no place for any time. This time we expect to remain quietly at Manitou Spring and take excursions from there occasionally to points of interest. I think you and Mrs. Childs ~~with~~ would find a visit there very agreeable. The traveling is easy, and the scenery surpasses any thing in Switzerland. The hotels are good and there are no finer or more refined people to be found anywhere than in Colorado.

I received a letter from Mr. Drexel just before he sailed for Europe but have not answered him yet. I will write to him within a few days. Give our love to him and his family, and also to Mrs. Childs & Miss Lizzie.

Yours Truly
U. S. Grant

ALS, Haverford College Library, Haverford, Pa. A newspaper editorialized: "An item has been going the rounds of the press asserting that Geo. W. Childs, of the Philadelphia *Ledger*, had stated that General Grant would order his name withdrawn from the contest at the National Convention in Chicago. Neither Geo. W. Childs nor any one else has authority for making such an assertion. . . ." *Galena Gazette*, May 24, 1880.

To Hiram S. Town

———

Galena, Ill.
June 2d 1880.

H. S. Town, Esq.

Dear Sir

I return from Green Bay to Galena on the 14th of this month and will have but little time to stop by the way. I have received a similar invitation to yours from Fon du Lac and replied substantially that I was not familiar with the route from Green Bay to this place, but that if it lead by their city, or it could be reached without in[convenience to] the railroad co. I would stop for hour or two with pleasure, but will want to get back home without material delay. I mus[t] make the same answer to your kind invitation. If Ripon on the route I will be very glad to meet the Veteran Club, and any other citizens who choose to call for a short time.

Very Truly yours
U. S. Grant

ALS, Paul Simon, Makanda, Ill. Hiram S. Town served as 1st lt., 1st Wis. Cav. On June 23, 1870, USG nominated Town as postmaster, Ripon, Wis.

To Frederick Dent Grant

———

Galena, Ill.
June 8th 1880.

Dear Fred.

I received a letter from Gen. Porter this am saying that Senator Conkling would like to see me after the convention adjourns. Say to Porter or Conkling, or both, that if a committee, or any members of the convention contemplate coming here I will wait to meet them. If they do not I have an engagement to go to Milwaukee and will go by Chicago, remaining over long enough to see the Senator and any others who desire to see me.

The reported interview in a ~~d~~Dubuque paper did not take place. I have had no interview with any one. I have expressed my high admiration of Senator Edmunds and my choice of him above all others when names are before the Convention. It is possible that some one connected with the paper in Dubuque may have heard this or heard of it. My preference is most unquestionably for Edmunds above all others named. There are several persons not named who I would have an equal or possibly greater preference for.

If a committee is coming over here do not forget to send a caterer,—with supplies—as directed in my previous letter.

Yours Affectionately

U. S. GRANT

Your ma says she has not heard from you for so long she is getting quite concerned.

Tell Julia we are nearly sick to see her.

ALS, DLC-Roscoe Conkling. Frederick Dent Grant, Chicago, endorsed this letter to "Dear Senator," probably U.S. Senator Roscoe Conkling of N. Y. "I forward this to you thinking you would like to see it. I thank you for your magnificent fight & I think the republican party will be sorry before november that they did'nt do as you wanted them to do" AES (undated), *ibid.* On June 8, 1880, Republican delegates at Chicago nominated U.S. Representative James A. Garfield of Ohio as the party's presidential candidate on the thirty-sixth ballot, breaking a deadlock between USG and U.S. Senator James G. Blaine of Maine. Jesse Root Grant, Jr., later claimed that USG rejected a deal, brokered by U.S. Senator John A. Logan of Ill., to reappoint John Sherman as secretary of the treasury in return for his pledged delegates. See Jesse R. Grant, *In the Days of My Father General Grant* (New York, 1925), p. 329.

To Roscoe Conkling

MILWAUKEE, WIS., June 10, 1880.

MY DEAR SENATOR CONKLING:

I hoped to see you in Chicago yesterday morning on my way here, but was informed on my arrival there that you had left for Washington the night before. Just before starting, however, I heard that you had delayed your departure until the morning, and were still therefore in the city. But as a special train was then awaiting me, and a small party going with me from Chicago, and it was about the time you would probably be starting, I was disappointed in the opportunity of thanking you in person for your magnificent and generous support during and before the Convention. I feel very grateful to you and the three hundred and odd who stood with you through your week's labors. Individually, I am much relieved at the result, having grown weary of constant abuse—always disagreeable, and doubly so when it comes from former professed friends. I have no presentiment as to what is likely to be the result of the labors of the Convention, or the result of the election which is to follow, but I hope for the best to the country.

Mrs. Grant asks me to present her kindest regards to you and to Mrs. Conkling.

Very truly yours,
U. S. GRANT.

Alfred R. Conkling, *The Life and Letters of Roscoe Conkling* . . . (New York, 1889), pp. 608–9. On June 26, 1880, U.S. Senator Roscoe Conkling of N. Y., Elton, wrote to USG. "*Private.* . . . Ever since receiving your valued Letter from Milwaukie I have sought a quiet hour to write you. The fates have been against me and now on reaching home I am compelled to take train to keep a professional engagement. It were idle to tell you of my disappointment at Chicago. The blunder is monumental. Your nomination would have saved the House at a time when the House is hardly less important than the Presidency itself; would have saved the Senate, and would have broken up the Solid South. Now House & Senate are I fear lost beyond hope, and what is to become of the Electoral ticket seems full of doubt. If the Republicans of the Country believe that success at the polls means four years more of Hayes, they will not give heart to the canvass. Had you been nominated, the Election would have 'whistled itself.' When we meet I shall have something to tell you which had I time perhaps would be hardly worth your reading. Mrs. Conkling sends kindest regards to Mrs Grant & to you. I join in them all . . ." ALS, USG 3.

On June 9, Charles C. Tompkins, Chicago, wrote to the editor. "THE INTER OCEAN of this date contains the names of those who are entitled to honorable mention, as belonging to the 'roll of honor,' who, from first to last, stood true to General U. S. Grant and to the best interests of the Republican party.' My name was spelled incorrectly, and, as I am proud to belong to the gallant 306, I respectfully request that the error in spelling the name may be corrected. I wish to be on record as a Grant man, first, last and all the time. For four years I endeavored to serve the Southern Confederacy as a Confederate soldier, but, since the collapse of the lost cause, I have, in my feeble way, used every honorable effort to advance the interests of Republicanism in my native State—Virginia. . . ." *Chicago Inter-Ocean*, June 14, 1880. USG's first cousin, Tompkins was the son of Rachel Grant and William Tompkins.

Also on June 9, Alexander K. McClure reported USG's arrival in Chicago from Galena. "General Grant quietly stepped into the Palmer House at 10 o'clock this morning, and I never saw him look more gentle or composed. He came unheralded, at least

to the multitude, and witnessed with complacency the profuse floral and bunting decorations of the Palmer rotunda and lobbies, which were intended to celebrate his nomination. He chatted pleasantly in passing his acquaintances, walked leisurely to the
ladies' parlor, and the outer doors closed against all when he entered. In half an hour
he stepped out in the same unostentatious manner, and the faces of Cameron, Logan
and Storrs were visible as the lieutenants with whom he had been in conference. What
transpired in that brief council of war will probably never be known to the public, but
after Grant had hurried off to the Milwaukee train both Cameron and Logan said publicly that Grant would be nominated without opposition in 1884." *Philadelphia Times*,
June 10, 1880.

On the same day, at a Milwaukee veterans' reunion, a reporter asked USG about
the convention. "I am very greatly obliged to my friends, who stood by me so nobly."
As for Conkling, "I wish he had been nominated," but "he refused it. It was not his
object or wish. He was not a candidate and wouldn't consent to be." U.S. Representative James A. Garfield of Ohio also refused, "but in a way that did not bind him. . . .
He is a good man. Garfield has always been right." Garfield had little strength in the
south. "There is, of course, 'Old Virginia,' where there is a chance for the Republicans
to make a combination with the Ma[h]one men and carry the State, but he cannot very
well expect any other." USG expected the Democrats to nominate Horatio Seymour. "I
have been backing against the others singly, and I am almost ready to back him against
the field. At present, Hancock has no show whatever, though of course he may win it."
Milwaukee Sentinel, June 10, 1880.

On June 10, USG spoke briefly at a Loyal Legion lunch given by the Wisconsin
Commandery to the Illinois Commandery. *Ibid.*, June 11, 1880. USG, Lt. Gen. Philip H.
Sheridan, and fifteen others gave their hosts a signed memorial. *Ibid.* Later, USG addressed veterans. ". . . It has been a great pleasure in this my third visit to Milwaukee,
to have had the opportunity of meeting so many of my old comrades in arms. I am very
glad to see you all well and find the country in a happy and prosperous condition. . . ."
Evening Wisconsin (Milwaukee), June 11, 1880.

On June 15, Thomas Speed and four others, Louisville, wrote to USG. "We having earnestly desired your nomination beg leave to express to you our feelings of regret that a result which in our judgment would have been of inestimable benefit to
the country was prevented We believe it was the desire of a very great majority of
the republicans in the United States that you should have been elected to the next
Presidency. We feel that there was a wide spread sentiment that in this way pacification and good feeling between the North and the South would have been thoroughly
accomplished. We sincerely regret that the majority of the convention at Chicago were
from one cause and another induced to reason differently. We assure you Sir that while
you can cheerfully abide the result personally, we are extremely sorry the country has
failed to call to the chief Magistracy her most distinguished citizen, who could have
done far more than any other in the interests of harmony and prosperity With assurances of our highest esteem and confidence and regard, . . ." LS, USG 3.

Also on June 15, John Russell Young, San Francisco, wrote to John Hay, asst. secretary of state. ". . . I was sorry for some reasons that Grant's name was mentioned in
the canvass. I am not sorry now,—although of course the defeat was to be regretted. It
makes Grant much more of a political figure than before,—so strong in himself alone
that it required all that the railroads, the lobby, the saints, the Treasury, and the ablest
men in Congress could do to beat him.—Nothing was clearer than that his friends had
the convention. It was taken from him by methods which seem to me to make political

action as a party impossible.—It would have been difficult for any friend of Grant to vote for Blaine, & maintain his self respect. It will be hard enough for them to vote for Garfield.—The course of the anti-Grant men since the nomination does Garfield no good.—But I will not bore you with politics. I could have had some enthusiasm for Grant or Evarts, or even Washburne. Garfield strikes me somehow as a joke. Arthur is not so well known, but is I think a man of more ability." ALS, RPB.

On June 26, Orville E. Babcock, Washington, D. C., wrote to Garfield, Mentor, Ohio. "I was not in the city when you returned from Chicago (having been called to Kansas to see a sick brother returned only last night) or should have called in person to extend my congratulations—You know and appreciate my desire to have my old chief Genl Grant, nominated. His name aside no nomination no nomination could have afforded me the satisfaction yours does. . . ." LS, DLC-James A. Garfield.

On July 1, William Johnston, Cincinnati, wrote to USG. "By the journals I see you are still importuned by your friends on the subject of Presidency. I have as good a right to be heard as any of them. I spent as much time, labor and brains, in proportion to what I had, as any of them, to promote your former elections and support your administration, and am ready to do the same thing again should you be a candidate; a service I would be loath, at my time of life, to promise any other man in America. But from the high position you hold in the world, I should regret to see you descend into the arena of politics. No man ever served his country more faithfully; and no man was ever rewarded more worthily. None was ever worse abused, or better vindicated; and now, standing on the highest round of the climax, I do not see how you can take another step without treading on emptiness, perhaps failing. There are thousands of honest men who love and admire you, who consider the example of Washington, Jefferson, Madison, Monroe and Jackson, equivalent to a constitutional inhibition to a third term; and the fact that a term has intervened makes no substantial difference. I should consider the country entirely safe in your hands a hundred years, if you should live and retain your faculties so long; but the example of one who has won the admiration of the world could scarcely fail to be pleaded on behalf of bad, ambitious, and dangerous men hereafter It must be remembered also, that there are already in the field several prominent candidates, to whose ambition the one-term pledge of Mr. Hayes opened the door at the very commencement of his administration Each one of these has an army of smaller politicians eagerly at work, who will make common cause against you, like so many sparrow-hawks on the back of an eagle, crying as I have already heard them cry, 'Third term me ans Presidency for life.' There is another fiend lurking in your pathway, . . . the envy of men who have been less successful, or whose merits have been less appreciated. This feeling is irrepressible so long as a rival's name dwells on the lip of applause. The Greek, who was tired of hearing of Aristides, the Just, is still alive, and thinks, as one of our editors expresses it, 'There is too much Grant.' There is another consideration which I beg leave to impress upon you. You have seen enough of the world to appreciate the influence of American freedom and progress on the people of the old world. You stand at this time, and I hope will in all times to come, as a representative man—an incarnation so to speak, of American freedom and progress. If you should allow your name to go before the convention, and be rejected, you are something more or less than human, if you do not feel that you have been treated with ingratitude, and the admiration of your friends at home, and the friends of our country abroad would be sadly chilled; and if you should be nominated by the convention, and rejected by the people, it will retard the progress of free principles in the old world a hundred years. Thus far you have drunk of the cup of power without intoxication, and now to pass it voluntarily from your lips would be grander victory than the siege of Vicksburg or the battle of the Wilderness." *Marion Weekly Star* (Ohio), Jan. 20, 1912 (ellipsis in original).

On July 6, Hamilton Fish wrote to Israel Washburn, Portland, Maine. "I have delayed too long an acknowledgment of your letter of 12th ult—I have been much engaged with some builders—but among the causes of delay has been my disappointment on the defeat of my Old Chief, & my good friend—His nomination would, I think, have ensured the success of our ticket, & with his election would have ended the *Sectional* division of parties, & the 'solidity' of the South—The Country needs a division of political parties, on *national* issues not by geographical lines—Had Genl Grant been nominated the Democrats would not have nominated Hancock, who, while a good & gallant soldier, would not have been set up against the *great* Soldier—our opponents have gained an appeal to the *Soldier* Element & in some sense to the loyal feeling of the Community—I have a very high regard for Genl Garfield, he is a *very* able, & a very upright man—*infinitely* the superior to Hancock, in every thing requisite for the duties of the parties to which they are nominated—But I see no enthusiasm of response to the nomination—A defensive, a non-agressive campaign, will, I fear, be an unfortunate one to the Republicans—but still I *hope*—& rely upon the justice, & the merits of our Cause—National Nominating Conventions, (me judice) are a farce—more than a farce—Contrivance—Clap-trap, & temporary furor, (not to call it 'insanity') takes the place of judgment, deliberation, & discretion—The old 'Congressional Caucus,' deliberated—& it was the deliberation of men *fairly* deemed to represent the majority of their Constituents—Our modern Conventions are composed of a large number, who after all, are chosen or designated by half a dozen or a dozen men." ALS (press), DLC-Hamilton Fish.

On July 12, Col. Thomas L. Crittenden, New York City, wrote to USG. ". . . The Chicago Convention broke the tie that bound me to the Republican party, when it ignored the wishes of the people and permitted the politicians to select a Candidate not asked for by any State. The Cincinati Convention by ignoring the politician[s] and heeding the wishes of the people, conformed to what I think a fundamental principle in free Government. And when they nominated a gentleman of honor, a very distinguished Officer of the Army, and an undoubted union man, they just about came to the politics of an old line whig. With profound admiration and friendship" ALS, USG 3.

On Oct. 4, David K. Hitchcock, Boston, wrote to USG. "I need not tell you how disappointed I am at the result of the Chicago Convention. It is the nations loss. However, we will in *1884* place you at the head of the government. The treachery and the ingratitude of a few has endeared you to the whole people who have experienced your patriotic and invaluable services, which will never be forgotten. I suggested to the Printer and wrote the inclosed circular so that those delegates and their constituents may have a keepsake or memento of what they so nobly did at the convention I enclose also the remarks of a dear friend who is and always was one of your most earnest and grateful admirers." ALS, *ibid.*

On May 28, 1897, George S. Boutwell, Boston, wrote to Frederick Dent Grant, New York City. "You will of course recall the fact that John Russell Young some months ago, made a public statement in which he declared that he brought from Galena to Chicago during the session of the Republican Convention of 1880, a letter from General Grant in which he gave specific directions to Conkling, Cameron and Boutwell to withdraw his name as a candidate from the Convention. Some months ago I had some correspondence with A. R. Conkling, and also with yourself in regard to the contents of the letter written by General Grant. Mr. A. R. Conkling sent me a copy of a portion of a letter which, as he advised me, he had received from you. A copy of that extract I herewith enclose. As one of the friends of General Grant and as one of the persons to whom bad faith was imputed by Mr. Young, it is my purpose to place the matter before the public with such evidence as I can command, for the purpose of showing the character of the letter. My daughter has a letter written by me to her during ªthe session of the Convention in which I stated that General Grant had placed the matter of his candidacy in the hands of Conkling, Logan, Cameron and myself, with entire freedom to act as we thought wise under circumstances as they might appear from time to time. I wish to obtain from you such a statement as you are willing to make with the understanding that whenever the case shall be presented to the public, your letter may be used. I presume that the extract which I received through A. R. Conkling is accurate, but I should prefer a letter over your signature and in such a form as you may see fit to give to it. Aside from actual evidence tending to show that Young's statement is erroneous, I cannot believe that General Grant would have recognized as a friend either one of the persons named, if his explicit instructions for the withdrawal of his name had been made by him and disregarded by them." TLS, *ibid.* The enclosure is *ibid.* On May 30, Grant wrote to Boutwell. "I received yesterday your letter of May 28th, in which you ask me what I remember about a letter which my father, General Grant, wrote to his four leading friends, during the session of the Republican National Convention at Chicago in 1880. With reference to this matter my recollection is, that Mr. John Russell Young, who had been visiting my father in Galena brought from him a large sealed envelope which he delivered to me, at my home in Chicago, with directions from my father that I should read the letter contained therein, and then see that it was received safely by his four friends, Senators Conkling, Boutwell, Cameron and Logan. The substance of General Grant's letter was, that the personal feeling of the partisans of the leading Candidates had become so bitter that it might seem advisable for the good of the Republican party to select as their Candidate some one whose name had not been prominently before the Convention, and that he therefore wrote to those who represented his interest in the Convention, to say that it would be quite satisfactory to him, if they would confer with those who represented the interest of Mr Blaine, and decided to have both his name and Mr Blaine's withdrawn from before the Convention. I delivered in person this letter from my father, to Senator Conkling—What disposition he made of it I do not know." ALS, *ibid.* On June 1, Boutwell wrote to Grant. "I am much obliged to you for your letter of May 30. All of those whose names have been mentioned by Mr. Young, who are living, and those who bear the names or have inherited the blood of those are not living, are interested in the correction of the error into which Mr. Young has fallen." ALS, *ibid.*

To Julia Dent Grant

———

June 15th 1880.

DEAR JULIA:

I am sorry you are sick. We can go home to-morrow as well as any other day. But do you not think we had better remain over one day longer?—No dispatches received yet from New York. Probably Buck will not receive the dispatch sent last night until this morning. If he did he could not answer until he could see Harry Honoré[1] this am, say eleven o'clock.—I have had my tooth pulled.—Saw Maj. Lydecker[2] who says Tilly[3] got off friday.[4] He placed her in charge of the conductor—fast train—who said they would be due in Wheeling next Morning—Saturday—at 8 am.—I have to go to the Dentist between 2 & 3 this pm to have another tooth set in the plate to take the place of the one pulled.

Yours

U. S. G.

ALS, DLC-USG. On June 17, 1880, USG and Julia Dent Grant returned to Galena from Chicago.

1. Henry H. Honoré, Jr., brother of Ida Honoré Grant. On Jan. 9, a correspondent had reported from New York City. "H. H. Honore, Jr., brother-in-law of Fred Grant, and Jesse R. Grant, son of the General, having formed a copartnership in the general produce business, under the style of Honore & Grant, they were both formally admitted yesterday to membership in the Produce Exchange." *Milwaukee Sentinel*, Jan. 10, 1880. Ulysses S. Grant, Jr., later sued Honoré, Jr., over financial obligations. See *New York Times*, June 30, 1882.

2. Maj. Garrett J. Lydecker, USMA 1864, supervised harbor improvements at Chicago.

3. Matilda McKennan, of Washington, Pa., had accompanied USG and Julia Grant to Cuba and Mexico.

4. June 11.

To Elizabeth M. Borie

Galena, Ill.

June 18th 1880.

My Dear Mrs. Borie:

On the 1st of July Mrs. Grant & I start for Colorado. We will go to Manitou Springs first, and make that place our head quarters as long as we remain[.] From there we will visit all points of interest reache[d] by rail-road, and return home whenever we get tired,—in three weeks, six or more as may be. Mrs. Grant has suggested that you might feel like accompanying us, and if so we will be most delighted to have you. If you conclude to go with us come directly here as soon as you please and make us a little visit before starting. In this way I know you can spend a pleasant summer, and I think you will find the mountain air delightful, and possibly beneficial.

With kindest regards of Mrs. Grant & myself to you and all the family.

Very Truly yours
U. S. GRANT

ALS, PHi.

To Dexter N. Kasson

———

Galena Ill.
June 21st 1880.

CAPT. D. W. KASSON,
MY DEAR CAPT.

Your letter of the 16th was duly received. I assure you that I had a most pleasant and agreeable visit to Milwaukee, one that I shall always remember with pleasure. I do not see how I could have been more cordially received and entertained. Please give yourself no concern on that subject. I perfectly understand that you were officially engaged during the entire reunion.

Very Truly yours
U. S. GRANT

ALS, WHi. Born in 1840 in N. Y., Dexter N. Kasson served as 1st lt., 24th Wis., deputy provost marshal gen. under Maj. Gen. George H. Thomas, and deputy pension agent, Milwaukee. See letter to Dexter N. Kasson, Feb. 27, 1881.

To Leonard F. Parker

———

Galena, Ill.
June 21st 1880.

PROF. L. F. PARKER,
STATE UNIVERSITY OF IOWA:
MY DEAR SIR:

Your letter of the 15th, requesting the manuscript of my remarks made at the Veteran reunion at Desmoines in 1875, was duly

received. I would gladly comply with your request if I knew where
the paper was to be found. I have not got even a copy of my remarks at hand or I would rewrite and send to you.

Thanking you for the estimate placed upon a few thoughts so
hastily put into words, I am,

Very Truly yours

U. S. Grant

ALS, State Historical Society of Iowa, Iowa City, Iowa. Born in 1825 in N. Y., Leonard
F. Parker graduated from Oberlin College (1851), served as Iowa representative (1868–
70), and taught Greek and history at Grinnell College and the University of Iowa. See
PUSG, 26, 342–51; Parker, "President Grant's Des Moines Address," *Annals of Iowa*,
Third Series, III, 3 (Oct., 1897), 179–92.

To Matías Romero

Galena, Illinois, June 21st, 1880.

My dear Mr. Romero.

Your letter of 17th May, came duly to hand. . . . I do not doubt
now but the work will go on with great rapidity, and that Mexico
will commence upon a remarkable development and prosperity.
If I could go East and attend to interesting the proper parties in
the enterprise. I believe I could form a Syndicate that could build
a complete system of roads over the country, all at once, and on
terms less oppressive to the government of Mexico that she will
necessarily have to submit to, having each road built by separate
corporations. Without going into detail, my idea is that the subsidy
might be given in government bonds, bearing 6 per cent interest,
accompanied by a free banking system; these bonds being the basis
upon which the paper money would be secured, the government
making them legal tender in payment of debts to government and
individuals, the banking and railroad companies, taking a share of
the responsibility of keeping the notes at par with silver, until the
government credit was made good by the very development of the
resources of the country which the roads would bring about.

Mexico could in few years furnish us $200,000,000 worth of
the products of her soil; she would take in return a large part of the
products of our country's manufactures. But if Mexico can retain at

home her precious metals, she will be rich enough, without drawing from abroad.

I repeat what I have said before, if Mexico gets through her present Presidential struggle, and inauguration without strife, I feel that her future is secured.

The two republics can be of great mutual benefit.

You are at liberty to show anything I write to you to the President or any one you choose. You ask also if you are at liberty to publish extracts. Of course you may do as you please with anything I write you.

Very truly yours,
U. S. GRANT.

The Two Republics (ellipsis in original), Sept. 5, 1880.

To John Thompson

———

June 21st 1880,

MY DEAR MR. THOMPSON,

Your letter of the 18th come no doubt in due time. But like most unsystematic persons I have my table littered up with papers and unanswered letters all the time, and yours with several others got under some that had been opened and read and I only discovered them a little while ago. I telegraphed at once on seeing your letter that I have an engagement to go out of town to-morrow. Mrs. Grant will go with me probably, if the day is not to warm. But we will be at home the balance of the week, and next week, and will be glad to see you, Mrs & Miss Thompson, and the ladies with you any day you may designate. Our sleeping accomodations are limited or we would be glad to have you stay over night. They are sufficient for your own family but no more.

With best regards of Mrs. Grant and myself to Mrs. & Miss Thompson,

yours Truly
U. S. GRANT

ALS, Central Michigan University, Mount Pleasant, Mich. "Mr. and Mrs. John Thompson and daughter Ella, with their guests, . . . of Dubuque, paid General and Mrs. Grant a visit yesterday afternoon, and took dinner at 5 o'clock with the distinguished couple, departing for home on the 6:28 train." *Galena Gazette*, June 26, 1880.

To Daniel Ammen

GALENA, Ill., June 22, 1880.

MY DEAR AMMEN: Your dispatch informing me of the departure of Capt. Phelps for Europe came after I had left here for Milwaukee. I wrote at once a letter for the Captain, directed to Gen. Hayes,[1] our Minister to France, but intended for general use. I sent it to the care of our Consul at Liverpool, thinking that was where you said I should direct any letter for him. Since, I have found in my pocket your dispatch, and see that I have made a mistake. I hope he will receive it on arrival. My letter was probably in time for the steamer of last Saturday week.[2]

To-day I received a letter from Seligman, inclosing a cablegram from de Lesseps offering me the Presidency of the Panama Canal (New-York Presidency) with the same salary he is to receive, namely 125,000f. per annum. The letter also says that the Seligmans with some other bank or banks[3] that they can associate with them will have the business of receiving the American subscriptions for performing the work. I telegraphed back my non-acceptance and wrote giving my reasons.

I gave the work that had been done in the way of surveys, what had been proved by these surveys, &c., and that while I would like to have my name associated with the successful completion of a ship channel between the two oceans, I was not willing to connect it with a failure and when I believe subscribers would lose all they put in.

I start on the 1st of July for Colorado and New-Mexico to be gone several weeks. Yours truly,

U. S. GRANT.

New York Times, Feb. 15, 1888. See letter to Daniel Ammen, Oct. 17, 1880; Lindley Miller Keasbey, *The Nicaragua Canal and the Monroe Doctrine* (New York, 1896), pp. 364–66.

1. Edward F. Noyes served as minister to France.
2. June 12, 1880.
3. See *ibid.*, p. 378.

To Adam Badeau

June 23d 1880.

My Dear Badeau;

Your letter of the 19th is just received. I will be very glad to see you before your return to England. I will not be going east however before the latter part of November. In one week I will be starting west and may remain about six weeks. I may get tired in three weeks and return here. In any event I expect to get back before the end of August.

I Since writing the above I have read the admiral chapter which accompanied your letter. There is no criticism to make upon it. If you want it returned write or telegraph me. Supposing you have a copy I do not return it with this.—I am glad you are getting on so well with your book. Hope to see it out before you return to England. It will not probably have so great a sale, at once, as would have had the result at Chicago been what many thought it would be. But it will have a long run, finding a market long after you and I are gone.

Tell Porter that I received his letter, and Seligmans. I answered Seligman both by telegraph & letter, declining his offer. Seligman will no doubt allow him to see my letter.

We are all well here and Mrs. Grant & Jesse, who is here for a day or two, join me in kindest regards.

Very Truly yours
U. S. Grant

ALS, Munson-Williams-Proctor Institute, Utica, N. Y.

To Thomas Nast

————

Galena, Ill.
June 26th 1880

MY DEAR MR. NAST;

I have your letter of the 23d. You had better devower the proposed lunch and get another ready some time in Nov. I start next
thursday[1] for the Rocky Mountains and may remain absent all
summer. At all events I have no intention of going east until after
the Nov. election.—As you say I am "out of the Wilderness" and feel
very much relieved thereat. But I do'nt see how you are there?—I
would like very much to see you, but unless you take a run to Colorado, or come out here after my return, I do not see how that is to
be before fall. If you come here bring Mrs. Nast with you. Mrs.
Grant & I would be glad to see you both. Give her and the children
my love. Mrs. Grant would return hers but she is not yet up.

Very Truly yours
U. S. GRANT

ALS (facsimile), University Archives, May 1995, no. 65.

On Dec. 23, 1879, USG, signing as "Mrs. U. S. Grant," had written to Thomas
Nast. "Many thanks for your photograph, just rec'd. The likeness is perfect and should
go in Harper's." ALS (facsimile), RWA Inc. Auction Catalog, March 21–22, 1998, no.
1504.

1. July 1, 1880.

To William C. Whitney

————

Galena, Ill,
June 26th 1880

COL. W. C. WHITNEY,
DEAR COL.

It will be impossible for me to accept your kind invitation to
visit Cawker. My party will be large and arrangements are already

complete to take us through to Los Vegas, N. M. leaving Leavenworth Monday, the 5th of July.

With thanks for the cordiality of your invitation, I am

Very Truly yours

U. S. Grant

ALS, KHi. William C. Whitney, former capt., 11th U.S. Colored Troops, owned a hotel
in Cawker City, Kan.

To Ellen Grant Sartoris

———

Galena Ill.

June 27th 1880

Dear Daughter:

I received your nice long letter a day or two ago. We were all
delighted to hear that you are all well and enjoying your self. If little Algie is such a bother to his pa send him over to us and we will
bring him up *"And* away he will go." I am very sorry you are not all
here now to go with us. On the 1st of July we start for the Rocky
Mountains to be gone during the hot weather. Fred is out on the
Rio Grande, and Ida & Julia, Will Smith and probably Buck will
be with us. That country is now so intersected with rail-roads that
all the fine scenery can be visited without any difficulty. It exceeds
Switzerland in grandure and immensity.—Buck & Fred have been
with us a little this summer, but not together, and last Jesse. Jesse
just left here a few days ago. He was just on his return from Arizona
and Northern Mexico, where he had been for about three months
looking after mines. Jesse has quite a large interest in mines and
one of them has developed very rich. You know I presume that he is
in business in New York City? He is doing quite well too.

I felt no disappointment at the result of the Chicago convention. In fact I felt much relieved. The most unscrupulous means had
been resorted to by the friends of other candidates—no doubt by
their advice—and even then a good majority of the delegates chosen were for me. But means were resorted to to displace them and

give a small majority for all the other candidates combined.[1] Had I been nominated there would have been the most violent campaign even known in our country made against me. This I have avoided.

Next summer we will be at Long Branch and then we will expect you. It may be that we will get a house in Washington for the winter. If we should could not you, Algie & the children come over as soon as the fact is ascertained that we do?

All send much love to you, Algie & the children.

Yours Affectionately
U. S. GRANT

Give my respects to Mr. Sartoris, Sr. and say that I am sorry he is not with us to take this summer trip.

U. S. G.

ALS, ICHi.

1. Defeat of the unit rule, under which delegations from Ill. and other states had by tradition voted unanimously, thwarted USG's chances at the Republican National Convention. See Green B. Raum, *History of Illinois Republicanism* . . . (Chicago, 1900), pp. 164–75.

To George W. Childs

June 30th 1880

MY DEAR MR. CHILDS:

Inclosed I send you a letter received from Mr. Stephens—our Minster to Sweden & Norway,—and Bill of Lading of a little purchase made by Mrs. Grant when we were in Stockholm. The letter will explain how Mr. S. happened to send to your care. I hope it wo'nt give you too much trouble to receive the articles. We will be leaving here to-morrow and will not probably return before the end of August so I do not know where to direct these articles to be sent. If they are in your way Buck can take them to his quarters in New York City.

Mrs. Grant wants me to thank Mrs. Childs for her invitation to have us visit you this Summer, but to say that it will be cold weather, probably after the election in Nov. before we go east. We will then visit our Phila friends of course before going into winter quarters.

With kindest regards of Mrs Grant & myself to you all, I am,

Very Truly yours

U. S. GRANT

ALS, Richard G. Mannion, Norcross, Ga.

To Thomas P. Robb

—————

June 30th 1880

DEAR SIR

I have received no cablegram making inquiries of the nature you suggest, and as I leave here tomorrow morning early probably will not. Should I be called on, I would not—could not—say anything detrimental to you, but as the object is to indorse you in matter involving large pecuniary responsibility, I would have to decline saying anything, because I have always regarded an Endorsement in such cases as morally binding me as bondsman I return Mr Palmers letter thinking you may desire to retain it. I hope the Enterprise you are about to engage in may prove profitable to you and to those who invest in it

very truly yours

U S. GRANT

COL T P. ROBB

Copy, IHi. Written on stationery of the Anglo-American Land and Claim Association, Chicago. Thomas P. Robb served as a director of the Chicago, Texas and Mexican Central Railway Co., chartered on Sept. 16, 1880. See *PUSG*, 23, 23–32.

Speech

—————

[*Merriam, Kan., July 2, 1880*]

Gov. St. John and Citizens of Kansas:—I have been taken a little by surprise, though I [d]o not know that it makes any very great difference to me, as I am not in the habit of speaking to any great extent. I feel under many obligations to such citizens of Kansas as are here present, and to the million that have been spoken of by your worthy governor, for their respect and esteem. I assure you that to a soldier there is nothing so gratifying as to have the good will and the respect of the people whom he has served, or tried to serve. In the positions that I have been, both military and civil, it has been my effort to render the very best service in my power for the whole people, and, as Gov. St. John has said, without respect to race, color, previous condition or political affiliation.

I am not aware of having committed an act in my life, or of having said a word, which was intended to affect my own standing one way or the other; and certainly not in a political way. I have indeed belonged to one of the great political parties of the country, because, on the whole, I believe it is much nearer right than the other. But I claim to have as much good feeling and friendship for the party opposed to me as for the party which has heretofore conferred honors upon me. I have always believed that what was best for the [en]tire country was going to help both political parties in the end, for we are citizens in common of one great nation, and the greatest nation that the sun shines on today.

This young state which I visit today I have frequently visited before, and I have seen it grow up from having but one delegate in congress till it has now three, and entitled, probably, to seven. Congratulating you upon the growth of your state, the intelligence of its people and its bright prospective future, I thank you for the welcome you have so generously accorded me.

Kansas City Journal, July 3, 1880. USG spoke at a new excursion park developed by the Kansas City, Fort Scott, and Gulf Railroad. See Kendall Bailes, *From Hunting Ground to Suburb: A History of Merriam, Kansas* (Merriam, Kan., 1956), pp. 24–25.

   Later on July 2, 1880, USG addressed a banquet. "Gentlemen of Kansas City: I can set you a very good example, I think, to be followed at this late hour of the night, or early hour in the morning, and that will be in making a speech that is very short, an example that, if followed by the other gentlemen who follow me, will permit us to get home before morning. I thank you very heartily for the kind reception which I have received from my first entrance into this growing and prosperous city. This is the first time that I have been upon the bluffs, except once at night for a few moments, although I have passed through here on the cars frequently. In going over your city today, I see evidence of its recent growth and very rapid development, and I predict for Kansas

City a very bright and prosperous future, and I propose to you, gentlemen, the growth and prosperity of Kansas City." *Kansas City Journal,* July 3, 1880. See *ibid.,* July 4, 1880; William H. Wilson, ed., "The Diary of a Kansas City Merchant 1874–1880," *Missouri Historical Society Bulletin,* XIX, 3 (April, 1963), 258–59.

On July 1, William D. Sanders had welcomed USG during a stop at Jacksonville, Ill. ". . . Our little city which rejoices in the honor of this brief visit from the world's great general, is not likely to forget that on this very anniversary week in July 1861, there marched through its streets the 21st Regiment of Illinois Volunteers commanded by a modest colon[e]l bearing a commission from our own dear Yates, the grandest of the grand war governors . . ." *Jacksonville Journal,* July 2, 1880. USG replied. "LADIES AND GENTLEMEN OF JACKSONVILLE: I thank you most heartily for this impromptu reception. I am glad to meet so many of your citizens on this occasion, and trust that I shall be enabled to see many of you again. Since my passage through this pleasant city in 1861, nineteen years have intervened, and I trust that so long a period may not transpire before I shall have the pleasure of visiting it again, for, in that case, I should, by that time, be an old man. There is no time now for extended remarks, and all I wish to say is that the speaker who has addressed us on this occasion should ascribe as much honor to others, and to many among you, as to myself. It was absolutely impossible for any one man to accomplish all that was done in the eventful years referred to on this occasion. To the brave soldiers who bore the brunt of the conflict is due more credit than to their leaders. Again thanking you for your kind attention and hospitality, I will resume my seat." *Ibid.* See *The United States Biographical Dictionary . . . Illinois Volume* (Chicago, 1876), pp. 332–33; John H. Krenkel, ed., *Serving the Republic—Richard Yates . . . An Autobiography* (Danville, Ill., 1968), pp. 47–50.

On July 3, USG traveled from Kansas City to Fort Leavenworth, Kan. Interviewed aboard the train, USG asked several questions about local railroads. The reporter asked him if he tired of public ceremonies. "Oh, no; I rather enjoy them if I could only get sleep enough." *Leavenworth Times,* July 4, 1880. On July 4, USG held a reception at the office of Brig. Gen. John Pope at Fort Leavenworth, Kan. "During his conversation with the gentlemen present the General spoke of his visit to Japan. He said he had no trouble whatever with the people, as everywhere he found native Japanese who speak the English language fluently, the government having introduced the language into the public schools. He says that in the interior Districts of the country in almost every school precinct young people may be found who have never been away from home, and yet speak English in a manner that would be no discredit to Lindlay Murray. . . . In Siam, as in other places, he found the English language the principal foreign language taught in the schools. He thought, he said, that when he started he should need a supply of French, but found by experience that good English is the better language for a trip around the world. He thinks English is sure to be the common language for all nations and that the more progressive countries, seeing this, are teaching it in their schools. . . . He says the Mexicans love manufacturing and all the mechanical arts, and that the reputation they have gained as being thieves is utterly without foundation, there being some it is true, he said, who have become marauders through necessity. He is of the opinion that if a healthy trade system between Mexico and the United States could be perfected, that Mexico would improve so much in twenty years that it would not seem to be the same country." *Ibid.,* July 6, 1880.

On July 5, USG spoke at Emporia, Kan. "LADIES AND GENTLEMEN OF EMPORIA:— There are more of you here than I can possibly make hear me if I was to do my utmost to make myself heard. I assure you that it is very gratifying to me to see so many

American people out here where but a few years since the buffalo and the wild Indians occupied the territory, and it is gratifying to me also that this country which when I first saw it constituted and was supposed to be a part of a desert which the farmer never could cultivate, has been so prosperous. In our whole beautiful country we have none that looks to be more productive than the very land I see around me here. I wish for all of you continued prosperity in your new homes; may they continue productive in all industries. I like Kansas. I like the Kansas people; they implanted in our soil the principles of universal liberty. If all the population of our country, was like the population of Kansas, our noble institutions would have nothing to fear. You were born in the struggle for freedom, when civil war overran our land. If all our people will be like the people of noble Kansas we can always be a free nation. Gentlemen, I thank you." *Emporia Journal*, July 10, 1880. After this speech, USG addressed the crowd. "Ladies and Gentlemen:—If I had more time I would be very glad to meet all of you and shake hands with you, but I am traveling on a special train. We arrived here an hour and a half late and cannot spend the time here we would like to and intended to spend. We have to go on and get out of the way of the regular trains." *Ibid.*

To Adam Badeau

Manitau Springs, Col.
July 28th 1880.

Dear Badeau;

Your letter of the 18th of July, with chapter enclosed, only reached me on the 26th, at Leadville. I have read the chapter over carefully and see nothing to critizise. In your letter you say that you sent me the first part of "Fort Fisher" some weeks ago, before the receipt of my letter. The last I have received from you, before your letter of the 18th was the chapter which I approved in my letter from Galena.

I think now I will be in New York City soon after my return to Galena. The probabilities are that I shall make my home there. But this is not entirely certain. I am obliged to do something to suppliment my means to live upon and I have very favorable offers there. Fortunately none of my children are a tax upon me. If they were we would all have to retire to the farm and work that.

I have been looking at the mines in New Mexico and in this state and flatter myself that I have obtained something of an insight into the resources of the two—the state & territory—and a large insight in the way mines are managed.[1] Without going into details I would not buy stock in any mine in the country, when the stock is throw[n] upon the market, any more that? I would buy lottery tickets. The mines are producing largely, bu[t] those quoted pay no dividends to the stockholders unless it is to put up the price of the stocks so the know[ing] ones can sell out. Porter & Co. have a magnificent mine manag[ed] by a thoroughly competant and hones[t] man. It is so opened that they will get out all there is in it in the most economical manner, and the dividends will be regular, subject to no visisitudes except strikes, epidemics or earthquakes. I go on Saturday[2] to the Gunnison and probably from there to the San Juan region. That visit over I will have seen a large part of the Mining region

My family are all well. Buck is with m[e] and Fred. is on his way between Santa Fe & here. The climate of this place is perfect. While you are sweltering in New York cloth clothing is comfortable here. All desire to be remembered to you.

Yours Truly
U. S. Grant

ALS, Munson-Williams-Proctor Institute, Utica, N. Y.

1. On July 7, 1880, USG spoke at Las Vegas, New Mexico Territory. "Ladies and Gentlemen of Las Vegas and New Mexico. Although I have visited all the States and most of the Territories, this is my first visit to New Mexico. It affords me great pleasure [t]o visit you and meet you. Before I leave the Territory I hope to see more of this country, of which I have read and heard so much. I wish you prosperity and advancement, and I hope you will succeed in building up a State which will be an honor to yourselves and an honor to the nation. I hope the natives may succeed beyond their expectations, as also the 'carpet-baggers.' I thank you, ladies and gentlemen, for the cordial reception of to-day." *Denver Tribune*, July 8, 1880.

Also on July 7, Mayor Martin W. Bremen of Silver City, New Mexico Territory, telegraphed to USG. "On behalf of the people of Silver City I tender to you a cordial invitation to visit our town that we may have an opportunity of expressing to you personally something of the great esteem in which you are held by the people of Grant county." *Weekly New Mexican* (Santa Fé), July 12, 1880. On [*July 8*], USG telegraphed to Bremen. "Accept my thanks for your kind invitation, and say to the citizens of Silver City that it would give me the greatest pleasure to visit your city but it will be impossible at this time for me to do so owing to previous engagements." *Ibid.*

On July 8, USG spoke at Santa Fé. ". . . I am glad to have come to Santa Fé, and I am pleased to have met with so many of those whom I have known in both private life and on the battle-field. I wish to them and to the city which has so kindly tendered me this tribute of respect, all the honor and greatness which in the future could possibly accrue to them, and which I am confident is only the due of this progressive capital of New-Mexico and its citizens." *New York Times*, July 18, 1880. On July 21, USG, Manitou Springs, Colo., wrote to Henry M. Atkinson "that his party would leave the Springs for Leadville on the next day, but that the ladies would return to the Springs while he would proceed to the Gunnison and other portions of the country. He was particular in his inquiries after persons whom he met in Santa Fe and desired General Atkinson to thank everybody for their attention which made the visit to this city so pleasant." *Weekly New Mexican* (Santa Fé), July 30, 1880.

On July 9, USG, Santa Fé, had written to Alexander M. Stetson, Hotel Glenarm, Denver. "I shall probably remain in this Territory a week yet and then go to Manitou. From the latter place I expect to visit Leadville and the mines further away, thence to Denver." *Denver Tribune*, July 13, 1880.

On July 16, at Trinidad, Colo., USG "said that it afforded him great pleasure to make this his first visit to the State of Colorado and the fourth to the Territory. On his first visit there were no railroads touching, but he even then (in 1868) formed a favorable opinion of Colorado, and looked forward to its early admission as a State. He was fortunate enough to sign the bill creating it a State, and he was proud to say that his representations had induced members of Congress to vote for its admission. Many members believed it had not the requisite population, nor resources sufficient to sustain the population necessary to entitle it to a representation in Congress. But it not only had the population, but was capable agriculturally of supporting ten times the number, to say nothing of the mineral resources, which, though yet in their infancy, had assumed proportions equaled in no other State in the Union. The State had already advanced more than he predicted, and he hoped for its continued prosperity. The next decade, he said, will see Colorado second to no other State in wealth and population, and he was glad that it was during his administration that it should become one of the constellation." USG continued. "All parties, without regard to political feeling, now feel, and in the future will feel more than ever, that we have a future that every man will fight for. I had a high opinion of my own country and people before I went abroad. Since my return that opinion is enhanced. In no other country is there the absolute freedom that exists here, and nothing can be grander, no title prouder than that of American sovereign and citizen." *Denver Tribune*, July 23, 1880.

On July 17, on the train between Pueblo and Colorado Springs, USG agreed with Joseph G. Brown, *Denver Tribune* reporter and C.S. Army veteran, that the war had ended for the best. "Yes, and through all the war it was my constant thought that the defeat of the Confederacy would be as much a benefit, and even more, to the South than it would be to the Union. The victory of the South, if such a thing were possible, would have been a personal disaster to the Southern people." Brown added, "With the view, I suppose, that only the slaveholders and large land owners would have thrived?" USG replied. "Exactly. Such men would have become the nabobs of the land, with both political and money power in their own hands, and the poorer classes would naturally have resorted to other fields of industry." Brown said, "As it is, they are scattered all over the land." USG concluded. "And I have no doubt they have done much better for themselves." Brown asked USG about the presidential campaign. "I can say without hesitation that I will give Garfield my most earnest and hearty support. I am a Republican. There is no reason why any Republican should hesitate to define his position, or not vote for Garfield. I know him to be a man of talent, thoroughly accomplished, and an upright man. I have nothing against General Hancock. But Garfield is the man for the office. A certain correspondent had reported a conversation that had never occurred, in which he stated that I complained that Conkling and Logan had deceived me. I never saw the correspondent or traveled with him. Have had no letter to or from Conkling or Logan up to the time of the Convention and did not see Conkling till after the Convention since my return to America, and I can say frankly, that of all men they are the last I could find fault with, and I feel to-day, more proud of the support of the 312 that stood by me till the last than I would have been, for my own peace of mind if I had received the nomination by any unfair means." *Ibid.*, July 18, 1880. Brown recalled this interview in a 1927 memorandum. D, Denver Public Library, Denver, Colo. On arrival at Colorado Springs, USG spoke. *"Ladies and gentlemen of Colorado Springs:* I thank you kindly for this reception tendered to me. It has been five years since I last visited your city, and I see marked improvements on every side. The increase of your population and that of the whole state is the most wonderful of all. I imagine I see before me here more people than existed south of Denver five years ago. Again thanking you all for the compliments extended, I bid you good day." *Rocky Mountain News* (Denver), July 18, 1880.

On July 21, USG, Manitou Springs, Colo., telegraphed to Drake DeKay, AG, "Boys in Blue," New York City. "Publish order telegraphed. In my opinion the best interests of the whole country, North and South, demand the success of the ticket headed by Garfield and Arthur." *New York Herald*, July 25, 1880. On July 22, DeKay published orders in USG's name. "GENERAL ORDERS NO. 1. I. The member for each State of the National Committee of the Union Veterans' Union will at once proceed to organize the 'Boys in Blue' in their respective States to promote the election of Garfield and Arthur. II. The organizations of 'Boys in Blue' will report to the Department commanders in their respective States." *Ibid.*

On July 25, USG wrote to Archibald J. Sampson, former Colo. attorney gen., and four others. *"Gentlemen*—Your kind letter of the 21st of July, conveying an invitation to me to visit Silver Cliff as the guest of the citizens of that flourishing mining camp, was only received last evening. I regret that I cannot accept on this occasion, but I hope at a later day—probably not on this visit to Colorado—to visit Silver Cliff, and to meet the great body of citizens engaged in developing the rich resources of that quarter of Colorado." *Denver Tribune*, Aug. 3, 1880.

2. July 31.

To Jesse Root Grant, Jr.

Manitou Springs, Col.
July 30th 1880.

DEAR JESSE:

I am to lazy to write what you asked me in your last letter. If I was busily employed in an official capacity I might find time to give you my ideas on political economy, the influence of the press, &c. &c. but having nothing to do I am enjoying it very much, and it consumes all my time. You had better leave the subject alone for the present, and devote your time to your business and to your correspondence with the young lady you wrote to your ma about. Your ma says she approves highly of your attachment if the young lady is deserving. We do'nt intend to publish in the papers what you say, nor what we think about the matter however until we know more about it our selves.[1]

Since we come to this place I have been to Leadville[2] and examined every thing there to my own satisfaction. I have made up my mind that I would no more buy mining stocks upon the market than I would buy lottery tickets. One is about as uncertain as the other. That there are good mines at Leadville, well and economically managed, there is no doubt. But the shares are not to be purchased upon the stock board.—Buck arrived here last sunday[3] and went to Leadville yesterday. He meets me to-morrow evening at South Arkansas, thirty miles east of Leadville, to go with me to the Gunnison.[4] I have been expecting Fred. for a week, but his is in New Mexico detained by washouts on the rail-road. He may be here this evening, and if he is I want him to go along.[5]

We will be in New York late in Sept. and we may remain there. I have partially accepted the Presidency of the San Pedro & Cañion del Agua Co.[6] I have examined the property and have no doubt of its great richness in placer and fissure gold, and easily worked copper for an indefinite length of time. There is also a large amount of timber on the property, and coal in abundance. The property is not, as I understand, in the hands of speculators, but is owned by rich Boston men who have furnished all the capital necessary for working the copper and gold, and will not sell until they are assured of its capacity to pay dividends on the stock. At all events I do not accept the Presidency except on that assurance. You need not mention this matter, but when the statement is made, that I will probably go to New York [to] live you need not deny it.

Your Ma wants you to write to her often and tell her all about the young lady you hinted about. She will remain here during our absence and for some days after my return.

All send love.

yours affectionately
U. S. GRANT

ALS, Chapman Grant, Escondido, Calif.

1. See letter to Ellen Grant Sartoris, Sept. 3, 1880.

2. On July 20, 1880, USG, Manitou Springs, twice telegraphed to Amos P. Curry, Leadville, Colo. "I will be in Leadville on Thursday, July 22." "I authorized acceptance of soldiers invitations several days ago. Party about six. Will remain until Monday." *Leadville Democrat*, July 21, 1880. On July 24, USG spoke to Leadville veterans about meeting "old soldiers" throughout his foreign travels "and said that although wars were generally injurious to any countries involved, still he believed that the restless spirit inculcated by the life of a soldier, which had taken men from the workshop, the plow and the counting house, and destroyed in a great measure their strict attachment to home, had been the means of causing much of this exodus to the great west, and more especially to Colorado, thereby developing our great mineral and agricultural resources more rapidly and fully than would otherwise have been done. That no soldier who had given the best years of his life to the service of his country, would ever again possess the same physical vigor or youthful energy to enable him to pass again through a similar ordeal, and it was but just that the same soil for which they risked their lives should yield to them sufficient remuneration to enable them to rest the balance of their years in comfort, and he hoped every soldier in this state would find that fortune here, which he so well deserved." *Leadville Weekly Herald*, July 31, 1880. At a banquet held the same day, USG praised Leadville and repeated his wish "that those persons who had come in search of wealth would not be disappointed, and would become prosperous." *Ibid.*

3. July 25.

4. On July 30, Ulysses S. Grant, Jr., Leadville, wrote to Charles H. Rogers. ". . . Tomorrow father is coming up from Manitou and I will join him at So Arkansas, from which place with a few friends we will travel through Gunnison, Roaring Forks & Dolores Countries. It will be a hard trip I expect but father is never tired of travelling and of seeing new countries. . . ." ALS, DLC-USG. On Aug. 2, USG visited Saguache, en route to Gunnison, and responded to a reporter who criticized "some of his Colorado appointments" as president. "I started out with the idea of appointing only *bona fide* residents of the Territories to fill the federal offices, but in a short time I found that whenever there was an appointment to be made, there were two or more applicants, each with about the same amount of backing, and that each faction was making a war upon the other. The strife was so great that I was led to believe that if either was appointed, great inharmony would be the result, so finally I concluded to take only strangers for positions in the Territories." *Saguache Chronicle*, Aug. 6, 1880.

5. On July 31, Lt. Gen. Philip H. Sheridan, Chicago, had telegraphed to USG, Pueblo, Colo. "Telegram received. Fred Can go with you for Ten days." ADfS and copy, DLC-Philip H. Sheridan.

6. See letter to Edward F. Beale, Sept. 3, 1880.

To Chicago Advance

———

[*July, 1880*]

You probably have seen that I denied the canard started by the New York *Truth* the very day it was started. I have nothing to say against Gen. Hancock. I have known him forty years. His personal, official, and military record is good. The record of the party which has put him in nomination is bad.

Yours Truly,

U. S. GRANT.

Advance (Chicago), July 8, 1880. See *ibid.*, July 1, 1880; *New York Times*, June 26, 1880.

To Julia Dent Grant

Parlin's Station,
August 4th 1880.

DEAR JULIA:

This is the first opportunity I have had to write. From South Arkansas we took teams and visited first a new Mining camp on Kelly's Creek.[1] There are about one thousand people at the camp, but as yet not a single log cabin. The prospect looks fine, and Mr. Watson,[2] Gov. Routts partner and superintendent, stopped off to locate, if he could, some mines for the Govr himself, Fred, & I, in equal parts. He is an old miner and thinks the prospect the finest he has seen anywhere in the state.—We are now within twelve miles of Gunnison where we will find Fred. We have now driven about one hundred & fifty miles over the mountains with a private-hired-team. I think we will get back to Manitou Springs Sunday evening.[3] I enjoy this trip very much aside from the prospect it gives of something to live upon in the future. Love and kisses for you, Ida & Julia.

Yours Affectionately

U. S. GRANT

ALS, DLC-USG.

1. USG toured mining camps along Kerber Creek, site of recent gold and silver discoveries. See *New York Times*, Aug. 16, 1880; Perry Eberhart, *Guide to the Colorado Ghost Towns and Mining Camps* (Chicago, 1969), pp. 419–21.

On Aug. 7, 1880, USG visited Irwin, Colo., and inspected local mines. "While riding alongside the creek which empties into the lake, the General was informed that it was known as S-n o' a B---h creek, when he suggested it be changed to Carl Schurz creek. We inferred from the General's remark that he thought the suggestion if acted upon would not materially change the name of the creek, but only put it in low Dutch. The name of the creek was accordingly changed to S-n o' a B---h or Carl Schurz creek." *Elk Mountain Pilot* (Irwin, Colo.), Aug. 12, 1880.

2. Joseph W. Watson managed Leadville's Morning Star mine, part of a group of mines he owned with former Colo. governor John L. Routt.

3. Aug. 8.

To James A. Garfield

————

Gunnison, Colorado
August 5th 1880

MY DEAR GENERAL:

On my arrival here last evening I found your very welcome letter of the 26th of July. As I leave again in a few minuets I have only time to reply to that portion of your letter which asks a reply. I shall be very glad to see you on my return east either at my home in Galena, or any place where I may be traveling. I expect to leave Colorado for home about the first week in Sept. I have promised, or partially promised, to attend the state Fair at Madison, Wis. on the 6th & 7th of Sept. and two other fairs following soon after, in Rockford and Sterling, Ill. Probably about the 20th of Sept. I shall be going east, to New York and Boston. Should we not meet before that could you not join me some place in Ohio, or further west, and go east with me as far as might be convenient to you?

I feel a very deep interest in the success of the republican ticket, and have never failed to say a word in favor of the party, and its candidates, when I felt that I [co]uld do any good. I shall not fail in the future.

With assurances of my most hearty wishes for your success in the coming campaign, I am,

Very Truly Yours
U. S. GRANT

ALS, DLC-James A. Garfield. On July 26, 1880, U.S. Representative James A. Garfield of Ohio wrote to USG. "I have read with satis[faction] and deep gratitude the kind things you have said of me in connection with the pending campaign I neither sought nor desired the nomination at Chicago, but since it came to me I am anxious to do my whole duty to the party and the country. Certainly no American is so well able, by an experience wholly unequalled in our history as you, to aid in bringing our people into harmony and ensuring the success of our party. I write to express the hope that I may have the pleasure of seeing you at as early a day as will suit your convenience. If agreeable to you please let me know when you will be coming this way and enable me to meet you either he[re] at my home, where you will be most welcome, ~~or at~~ or at any other ~~place~~ point which will suit your convenience. . . . P. S. Mrs Garfield joins me in cordially inviting you and Mrs Grant to visit us at any time" ALS (press), *ibid.* A note dated Aug. 5, Gunnison, Colo., indicating USG's willingness to accept Garfield's invitation, is *ibid.*

On July 19, Garfield, Mentor, Ohio, had written to President Rutherford B. Hayes. ". . . I want to ask you if you have any knowledge of Grants attitude—I learn from what appears to be a trustworthy source, that he intends to visit me on his return from the west—and that he will take hold cordially in the work of the campaign If this be so, it may put some New York people into a strait betwixt two courses—. . ." ALS, InHi.

On Aug. 18, George Milmine, Toledo, telegraphed to USG, Denver. "You are cordially invited to meet Genl Garfield at the Anual Tri State Fair of Ohio Indian[a] and Michigan at Toledo Sept 15th to 17 inclusive. Can you be presen[t]" Telegram sent, DLC-James A. Garfield. On the same day, USG replied. "It will be impossible for me to be in Toledo sept seventeen[th] (17)" Telegram received, *ibid.*

On Aug. 24, Garfield telegraphed to USG, Denver. "Will you attend the reunion of the Army of the Cumberland at Toledo Sept 22nd Please answer" Copy, *ibid.* On [*Aug.*] 26, USG, Galena, telegraphed to Garfield. "Not likely I will be in Toledo Sept twenty second. Will be going east late in Sept and if at that time will stop at Toledo" Telegram received (at 1:48 P.M.), *ibid.* On Sept. 18, USG wrote to John W. Fuller. "I do not think it possible for me to be in Toledo at Reunion. I regret it very much, but my engagements will not admit of my doing so." *Society of the Army of the Cumberland Twelfth Reunion, Toledo, Ohio, 1880* (Cincinnati, 1881), p. 96.

On Aug. 26, Frederick Dent Grant, Galena, had written to Joseph A. Howells, chairman, Republican Central Committee, Ashtabula County, Ohio. "Genl Grant directs me to write and answer yours of Aug 23 and say that it will be impossible for him to be in Jefferson during the month of Oct as he goes East in Sept & will not return this fall" ALS, OFH. See Howells to Garfield, Aug. 28, 1880, DLC-James A. Garfield.

On Aug. 28, John Meharg, Ravenna, Ohio, wrote to USG for "prominent citizens" of Portage County. "we take great pleasure in joining the Portage County Agricultural Society in their invitation to you to attend the Annual Fair in Sept prox. and the acceptance by you of this invitation will be considerd a memorable honor. as Ravenna was once the home of your honored father we shall esteem it a high privilege to welcome his illustrious Son among us if but for a day We may be pardoned for alluding to the fact that Gen Garfield was a citizen of Portage County when he entred the Union Army and has resided with us most of the years of his public life. Coming here therefor you come among admiring friends than whom none have more rejoiced at the fadeless renown your patriotic services have bestowed upon the whole american Nation Allow us to suggest that a visit from you at this time will incidentally, be of inestimable value in a direction, which we know is held in the highest esteem by you Anticipating a favorable acceptance . . ." Copy, *ibid.* On the same day, Meharg wrote to Garfield that he intended to present this invitation to USG. ". . . I will Say to him that should *he* wish to visit Ravenna that you would be glad to go with him . . ." ALS, *ibid.*

On Aug. 30, Julia Dent Grant, Galena, wrote to Lucretia R. Garfield. "I regret to say in reply to the very polite invitation received from you a few days since That when we leave here for the East Genl Grant proposes to go directly through Genl Grant hopes however to meet Genl Garfield on his way East. After thanking you Mrs Garfield for your kind thoughtfulness, Let me add the hope that all your most sanguine anticipations may be realized." ALS, DLC-Lucretia R. Garfield.

To Matías Romero

———

Manitou Springs Colorado
August 10th 1880

My dear Mr Romero

This will introduce to you Genl: A. T. A. Torbert formerly of the regular army, and a Major General in the late rebellion under Sheridan. Since the war Genl: Torbert left the army, and has represented this Govt as Minister to one of the Central American States; as Consul General to Cuba, and also as Consul General to France.

He visits Mexico to represent a scheme for building rail roads and making other internal national improvements in Mexico by the Government itself, which looks to me practical and feasable.

I have looked over the plan carefully, but have not had time to consider it sufficiently to pronounce a positive judgement. But it is so much in the direction of what I hinted in a letter I wrote you in June, which I did deliberate on, that I think well of it.

It has the advantage over the plan that I had thought of in this, that it leaves the property when completed in the hands of the Government of Mexico, while mine contemplated a foreign ownership.

I feel as you know a sincere interest in the progress of Mexico, both as a friend of the country, and as an American desiring the progress of my own country. We are now consumers of about 200.000.000 of tropical and semi-tropical products produced by countries collecting export duties, and which take nothing in exchange to speak of, but gold. Mexico with facilities for transportation, could furnish the whole of this, with much more.

With close commercial relations between the two countries, a warm friendship would spring up, both would grow stronger and prove a protection to Republicanism

With kind regards to all the people from whom I received so much kindness during my recent visit—I am

Very Truly yours

U. S. Grant

Copy (facsimile), DLC-Matías Romero. On Sept. 8, 1880, Albert G. Buzby, Mexican Internal Improvement Syndicate, Philadelphia, wrote to Matías Romero. "With this I send you copy of the letter from Genl: Grant to yourself, which was to have been delivered in person by our Genl: Torbert, who was as you are doubtless informed, lost on the unfortunate str: Vera Cruz: Mr Owen having been spared, he will again sail for Mexico on the next str: succeeding this. . . ." ALS (facsimile), *ibid.* On Sept. 5, Sunday, Albert K. Owen had written to Romero. ". . . The General had a four page letter to you from Gen. Grant in behalf of our mission to the Mexican people. The original is lost; besides this important manuscripts, maps, etc. I have, however, telegraphed to our office in Philadelphia and have asked them to communicate with you by the Steamer of Wednesday, inclosing copy of Gen. Grants letter. This sad affair will interrupt me in coming to you as early as I had hoped; *but* my purpose is more than ever with the true interests of your people; and I hope to sail in the steamer which follows this letter—reorganized to carry out all that I have previously suggested—Please make my regards to President Diaz and to the true friends of Mexico and assure them that my life has been spared I trust, that I may assist them to better the physical condition of their countrymen. . . . I expect to reach New York Thursday. I mail this from Charleston: S. C—" ALS (facsimile), *ibid.*

On July 29, Owen, Chester, Pa., had written to Romero. "Many thanks for your favor of July 15th. It came this A. m. and I will take it with me to show Gen. Grant. We were already to start this noon, but Gen. Torbert had a telegram from Gen. Grant saying that he would be on the Gunnison River on an excursion for a week dating from yesterday so we concluded not to go until tomorrow noon—and then meet the General at Denver on his return. We will make all possible dispatch to get back in time to take the Steamer from New York August 11th—but if we should fail in this we will telegraph you as to our success with Gen. Grant and as to his co-operation. We feel that those whom we associate with the *Syndicate* will give it a character which will guarantee success, and yourself and your friends will give your own country confidence that an earnest and an intelligent effort is going to be made for the permanent progress of their country. This will go via New Orleans, and will arrive I expect about the time manuscripts sent by us to you via yesterday's steamer from New York. Please make our efforts known to the President and be assured that I, at least, will be in Mexico during August. . . ." ALS (facsimile), *ibid.* On Aug. 5, Thursday, Owen, Denver, again wrote to Romero. "Gen. Torbert and I reached this State Monday afternoon; but have been unable to get a dispatch to Gen. Grant as he is in the mountains. He is expected in, however, to-morrow. There is a suite of rooms taken for himself and family at this hotel, but whether he is to come here and have his family join him, or is first to go to them at Manitou is not certain. Gen. Torbert has gone to Manitou, to-day, to see Mrs. Grant and to telegraph the General if he can be found. Calculating that it may be Sunday or

Monday before we can have the desired talk with Gen. Grant, it occurs to me that the probabilities are that I will be too late in reaching New York to take the steamer of the 11th inst.; but Gen. Torbert and I will come in the next, and will have then had time to perfect the details of our *Syndicate.* . . . Gen. Torbert has just returned from Manitou. He learned from Mrs. Grant that the General from last accounts will either be in to-day or on Tuesday; i. e. that if he only went as far as the Gunnison District he would be back at once, but if he went to the San Juan District, Tuesday, would be as early as he could join her at Manitou. Gen Torbert and I will go to Manitou Saturday and there await Gen. Grant. If he approves of our plans then we can associate the best of his friends to give character to our *Syndicate* and thus will we be in the best possible position to assist Mexico to ma[ke her] credit good and to complete her internal improvements without delay." ALS (facsimile), *ibid.*

On Nov. 22, [Owen] wrote to USG. "If a plan for railroad construction and management can be suggested which will be more remunerative than the present system to those concerned in its accomplishment, and which at the same time, can be made to harmonize with the interests of the public it certainly deserves the attention of Gen. Grant and Mr. Romero at this time. An inward conviction that such a plan is possible urges me to make a brief outline of long studied thoughts upon this subject, with the earnest hope that the Mexican people may be hastily given the advantages of the most approved railroads. Railroads built with credits based upon interest-bearing securities cost, at least, twice as much as they would if they were built with money not borrowed upon such obligations. A nation which permits railroads to be built by foreigners and with credits based upon interest-bearing securities placed among a people not its own, permits an absenteeism of the most ruinous character: particularly would this be the case with Mexico, which in the absence of diversified home industries must be classed as a primative country, . . ." AL (incomplete facsimile), *ibid.* See *Calendar,* May 29, 1875; David M. Pletcher, *Rails, Mines, and Progress: Seven American Promoters in Mexico, 1867–1911* (Ithaca, N. Y., 1958), pp. 106–15.

To Emory W. Adams

Manitou Springs, Col., Aug. 12. [*1880*]

E. W. Adams, Esq.:

Dear Sir: I have your letter inviting me to attend the emancipation celebration to be held at Findlay, Ohio. You must accept my regrets, as I have already more engagements for the month of September than I will be able to keep. Fully sympathizing with the colored people of the United States in their efforts to become worthy citizens of a Republic that, theoretically, knows no difference of race, color, or previous condition of its electors, and hoping that the day is not far distant when the word "practically" may be substituted for the word "theoretically," I am, very truly, yours,

U. S. GRANT.

New York Times, Sept. 25, 1880. See Emory W. Adams to James A. Garfield, July 21, 1880, DLC-James A. Garfield.

To Adam Badeau

—————

Manitou Springs, Col.
Aug. 12th 1880.

MY DEAR GENERAL:

I returned here day before yesterday and found a mail awaiting me which has required all my spare time until now just to read. In it I find your two letters, and the first part of the chapter on Fort Fisher. I have read it carefully and do not see how a word can be changed. All that you say that exception can be take to is supported by quotations, or citation to, orders and letters of instruction of the time.

I have been away from here for ten days visiting parts of Colorado I had never seen before. The trip was a very hard one though full of interest. I am satisfied this state has a great destiny before it. The new regions that I visited will shew greater mineral resources than all that has been heretofore discovered in the state beside considerable agricultural resources. But I will see you in September, when I shall be in New York, and then I can tell you more than I can write. When I go to New York it will be determined whether I accept the Presidency of the Mining Co. to which I have been elected. One thing is certain: I must do something to suppliment my income or continue to live in Galena or on a farm. I have not got the means to live in a city.

With kindest regards of Mrs. Grant, Fred. & Buck—the latter has just left—I am as ever,

yours Truly
U. S. GRANT

P. S. I do not return the chapter on F. F. supposing you have a du-
plicate as Sherman's men had of all the R. R. tunnels the rebels
destroyed.

ALS, Munson-Williams-Proctor Institute, Utica, N. Y.

To John A. Logan

Manitou Springs, Col.
Aug. 12th 1880

MY DEAR GENERAL LOGAN;

I left this place two weeks ago for an extended tour through
San Louis Park and the Gunnison country and hence have only
just received your letter of the 28th of July. I will be going east the
latter part of Sept. and will gladly attend any meeting intended
to further the sucsess of the ticket headed by Garfield & Arthur.
I agree with you that it will not do to be beaten now. We should
never be beaten until every man who counts, or represents those
who count, in the innumeration to give representation in the Electoral College can cast his vote just as he pleases, and can have it
counted just as he cast it.[1]

Please present Mrs. Grants & my kindest regards to Mrs
Logan.

yours Truly
U. S. GRANT

ALS, DLC-John A. Logan.

On Aug. 12, 1880, USG, Manitou Springs, Colo., wrote to Stephen W. Dorsey,
secretary, Republican National Committee, concerning a meeting in New York City
on Sept. 5. "It will be impossible for me to attend at that date, as I will hardly be home
before Sept. 5, and besides, I must go East the latter part of the month, and do not care
to make two trips so near together. But you have my full sympathy in support of the
ticket headed by Garfield and Arthur. I have lost no opportunity in saying what I could
in private conversation—or rather in conversation—in behalf of the ticket, and shall
not." *New York Times*, Aug. 19, 1880.

1. On Aug. 31, Henry A. Mumaw, Mennonite printer, Elkhart, Ind., wrote to USG,
Galena. "Will you please send me a short motto—a rule of life with autograph? Awaiting a favorable reply, . . ." ALS (facsimile), Profiles in History, Catalog 36 (Winter, 2003),

no. 30. USG endorsed this letter. "Vote the Republican ticket until every man in the Nation, entitled to a vote, can cast just one vote, at each election, for which party he pleases, without fear or molestation, and have it honestly counted, and you will feel conscious of having done your duty as a citizen." AES (facsimile, undated), *ibid.*

To Maj. Joseph W. Wham

Hotel Glenarm,
Denver, Colo. Aug. 22, 1880.

Dear Major Wham:

Although I shall return home by way of Cheyenne,[1] three days earlier than I expected when you were here, I regret that I shall not be able to stop. My youngest son leaves New York city on Tuesday[2] for the Pacific coast, on important business, and wants to meet me before going[.] For this purpose I give up my trip to Idaho Springs and go directly to Galena.

I am very much obliged to you and the officers at Fort D. A. Russell for your kind invitation, and regret that I cannot [acc]ept.

Yours, truly,

U. S. Grant.

Cheyenne Leader, Aug. 24, 1880.

On May 7, 1867, U.S. Representative John A. Logan of Ill., Carbondale, wrote to USG. "I would most earnestly request you to recommend, Joseph. W. Wham. of your old reg't. was ~~L~~first Lt. of Co G. 21st Ills—regt. was a good officer and soldier is a worthy young man, and desires a position in the regular army. I would be very much pleased could his request be granted, he has on file in the War office the best of credentials from the Gov. and adjt. Genl & others of this state, Genl Palmer among them I would be glad to hear what can be done in this case." ALS, DNA, RG 94, ACP, 1278 1877. On May 13, USG endorsed this letter. "Respectfully forwarded to the Secretary of War in connection with previous papers. Lt. Wham has already been recommended for a 2d Lt'cy of Infantry by me, and the recommendation is now renewed." ES, *ibid.* Wham was appointed 2nd lt. as of May 22. On Sept. 22, Wham, Indianola, Tex., wrote to USG. "In looking over the Army Register for 1866 I see that Illinois has but one appointment in each of the Q. M. and C. S. Depts and being personally aquainted with Gov. Oglesby, Genl Logan, Genl Hanie and numerous other prominent men in that State, and having served for Four Years and Nine Months in your old Regiment (21st Ills) I would Most Respectfully ask if there is a vacancy in either of the above Depts, and if so, would you be kind enough to retain it, until I can forward a recommendation. I know that I can produce as good a recommendation as any man from the State of Illinois. If you will excuse this presumtion and reply you will render me under eternal obligations." Copy, *ibid.*

On Dec. 23, 1875, Warren E. McMackin, Salem, Ill., wrote to USG. "I have known J. W. Wham, who will hand you this, since boy hood; he enjoys the full confidence of this community where he was raised, and where he enlisted in your old Regiment when a boy. He is now, and has, at all times, been a firm friend of you, and your Administration. and I am satisfied that any Trust confided to him will be faithfully kept" LS, *ibid.*, Correspondence, USMA. See *PUSG*, 20, 221; *ibid.*, 22, 427.

1. On Aug. 23, 1880, Monday, USG spoke at Cheyenne. "I fear my voice will not reach you. I had intended to have left Denver on Thursday and so to have remained over a day here, and thus have had an opportunity of seeing you. But I am compelled to go east to-day. Next year, however, I expect to come west and pass here, and then I trust I shall have an opportunity of seeing more of you." *Cheyenne Leader*, Aug. 24, 1880.
2. Aug. 24.

To George W. Ballou

——

Denver, Colo. Aug. 22d *1880.*

GEO. WM BALLOU, ESQ.

MY DEAR SIR:

I leave here for Galena to-morrow. The letter you advised me of, by telegraph, has not ~~yet~~ reached me, thouh it may yet do so before I leave. If it does not it will follow me to Galena.

I enclose you some papers which reached me a few days ago, by mail. Every valuable claim in New Mexico, particularly those held under Spanish Grants, will be embarrassed by lawsuits of some sort, and they will give a gooddeal of trouble even if fictitious and only intended to blackmail. I know, of course, nothing of the merits of this, but send it to you for such action as you may think it merits.

Very Truly yours

U. S. GRANT

ALS, CtY. Written on stationery of the Hotel Glenarm. "Mr. George Wm. Ballou, a leading New York banker, was in Galena yesterday, and dined last evening, at the residence of General Grant. Mr. Ballou is one of the heaviest stockholders in the San Pedro Mining Company." *Galena Gazette*, Sept. 3, 1880. See letter to Edward F. Beale, Sept. 3, 1880; *New York Times*, May 1, 1929.

On Aug. 16, 1880, USG arrived in Denver, rode horseback in a procession from the depot to the hotel, then spoke from the balcony. "Ladies and Gentlemen: I will just introduce to you Governor Routt, who is present here. Governor Routt has just been making speeches all over the State, and I know he likes nothing better than talking to large crowds." *Denver Tribune*, Aug. 17, 1880. Former Colo. governor John L. Routt replied. "The General has been telling yarns on me all over the mountains. I am satisfied that if you will wait till to-morrow and give him time to prepare himself he will make you a splendid speech." *Ibid.* On Aug. 17, USG spoke at a banquet. "The general alluded to his former visits to this city, but more particularly to the one in 1868, when Denver was small, and the then territory, weak. But he was firmly convinced at that time that the people had the elements and the territory the resources to create a great and magnificent state, an opinion which never faltered. Alluding to the trips he has recently made in the mountains and among the mines, the General expressed pleasure at the evidences of prosperity and intelligence of the people." *Denver Weekly Times*, Aug. 25, 1880.

On Aug. 21, Mayor John A. Ellet of Boulder introduced USG at a reception at Boettcher's Hall. USG replied. "I hardly know how to thank you for your reception and the kind words of your Mayor. I have often met larger numbers of people than are assembled here this morning, and more beligerant looking crowds, but never felt greater trepidation, though I know you have no intention of hurting me. I thank you for your presence here, and trust it will not be the last occurrence of my visiting you here in Boulder. This is my fourth visit to Colorado, and, if my health favors me, I hope to visit the State and this section of the country oftener than heretofore. . . ." *Boulder News and Courier*, Aug. 27, 1880. Later, at a banquet at Brainard's Hotel, USG responded to the toast "Our Country." ". . . The toast allotted me is a large one, for our country is large and cannot be enlarged upon in a speech of this kind. It can only be fully appreciated after having visited other countries. It has been my fortune, as you are all aware, to visit almost all the countries under the sun, making a complete circuit of the whole globe, but all that I have seen in my travels would not make one America. There is much to see, much to learn, and much to admire in Europe, but after all there is no single country as good as ours, none affording so many facilities for the working people to make a comfortable living. For me to say what these resources are would be but to repeat what you all know and are aware of. We have agricultural and mineral resources such as no other country has, and our working people have perfect freedom of speech and action. Few of this class of people in other countries feel themselves safe or secure in leaving their homes or the place where they were raised. Now, I know that there are gentlemen here as fond of talking as I am of getting out of it so I will not take up any more of your time." *Ibid.* On July 24, Ellet, former lt. col., Mississippi Marine Brigade, had written to USG, Leadville. "The citizens of the Town of Boulder, being desirous of attesting their appreciation of your invaluable services to your country, have instructed me, through their Board of Trustees, to tender you an informal reception at such time, in the near future as you may be pleased to designate. While we do not aspire to rival the great commercial centers in the splendors of an ovation in your honor, we beg to assure you that we yield to none in our admiration for your character and acchievements, and we most earnestly hope that we may have the pleasure of taking you by the hand, and giving you an old-fashioned western welcome." ALS, USG 3. On July 26, USG wrote to Ellet. "Your dispatch of this date, tendering me a reception on the part of the citizens of Boulder, is received. Although I have made frequent visits to the Territory and State of Colorado, it has never been my fortune to visit Boulder, and I intended from the start to do so on this occasion. I can not now fix the date exactly when I can be there, but it will be within a few days after my arrival in Denver. That will be somewhere between the 5th and 10th of August. Thanking you and the citizens of Boulder for the cordiality of your invitation, . . ." *Boulder News and Courier*, July 30, 1880.

To William F. Vilas

Denver, Colo. Aug. 22d *1880.*

My Dear Gen. Vilas

I am in receipt of your kind letter of the 16th of this month conveying an invitation for Mrs Grant & myself to be your guests during our proposed visit to Madison, on the occasion of the state Fair. I expect to be there at that time, and think Mrs. Grant may be also, though she has not fully determined upon it. For my self I accept your invitation, if the committee sending the invitation to me to visit the Fair, have not made other arrangements. General Bryant[1] can inform you on this subject no doubt, and I will do just as he says about the matter.

No matter where I stay I am much obliged to you and Mrs. Vilas for your kind invitation.

Very Truly yours
U. S. Grant

ALS, WHi. A prominent Madison, Wis., lawyer, William F. Vilas served as lt. col., 23rd Wis., law professor, and delegate to the Democratic National Convention in 1876 and 1880. USG stayed with Vilas during the state fair in Sept., 1880. See Speech, [*Sept. 7, 1880*].

On Aug. 3, a newspaper had reported. "A letter from General Grant, dated at Leadville, July 26th, brings assurance that he will be with us during two days of the Fair, unless some unforeseen event occurs to prevent his coming." *Wisconsin State Journal*, Aug. 3, 1880.

1. Born in 1832 in Vt., George E. Bryant settled in Madison, practiced law, and served as col., 12th Wis., county judge, Wis. senator, Wis. q. m. gen., and secretary, Wis. agricultural society. On Oct. 9, 1878, Lucius Fairchild, consul gen., Paris, wrote to Bryant. "I have given General Grant your invitation to attend the Wisconsin State Agricultural Society's Fair, next year. The General desires me to thank your Society for the invitation, and to say that he cannot now promise to attend, but he hopes to be able to do so." *Ibid.*, Aug. 30, 1880.

Speech

[*Galena, Aug. 27, 1880*]

Ladies and Gentlemen: I did not intend to speak when I came here to-night. I am very much like Judge Orton.[1] I have never made

a Republican speech in my life, or any kind of a political speech. I
am sure it would require some time and much preparation to make
one of any length. I can go a little farther than Judge Orton and
say that I never voted a Republican Presidential ticket in my life,
and but one Democratic ticket, and that was many years ago, when
I was quite a young man. I have less to answer for on this score
therefore, than the Judge. But I will pledge you my word here to-
night, that if I am spared, although I shall be some distance from
you in November next, I shall return to Galena to cast a Republican
vote[2] for President of the United States; and I hope that the city of
Galena will cast a Republican vote—such as it never cast before.

Galena Gazette, Aug. 28, 1880. USG spoke in Turner Hall at a meeting of the Garfield
and Arthur Club.

1. "Judge Philo A Orton, of Darlington, Wis., who has enlisted under the Garfield banner, after a service of twenty years in the ranks of Democracy, has occupied
many positions of trust and honor in the party that he has now deserted. He has been
the Democratic candidate for Attorney-General of the State, the candidate for Congress in the Third District, a Presidential Elector, and a member of the Democratic
State Central Committee." *Ibid.*, July 19, 1880.

2. See letter to Madison Y. Johnson, Sept. 24, 1880; letter to William R. Rowley,
Dec. 12, 1880.

To Chester A. Arthur

———

GALENA, Ill., Aug. 28, 1880.

My Dear Gen. Arthur:

I am just in receipt of your letter of day before yesterday, asking me to be present and to preside at a meeting of Republicans to
be held in New-York City on the 17th of September, at which Senator Conkling will speak. I need not tell you how gladly I would
accept the invitation if I could be there at the time specified. But I
cannot. I have accepted invitations to attend soldiers' reunions in
the West, and State and county fairs, covering the time to about
the 23d of September. Then, too, when I go East, I do not want
to return here before next Spring—excepting one day, the 2d of
November, without my family, to cast a vote for Garfield and Arthur. I hope you may have a rousing meeting that will awaken the

people to the importance of keeping control of the Government in the hands of the Republican Party, until we can have two national parties, every member of which can cast their ballots as judgment dictates, without fear of molestation or ostracism, and have them honestly counted; parties not differing in opinion as to whether we are a nation, but as to policy to secure the greatest good to the greatest number of its citizens. Sincerely believing that the Democratic Party, as now constituted and controlled, is not a fit party to trust with the control of the general Government, I believe it to the interest of all sections, South as well as North, that the Republican Party should succeed in November. Very truly yours,

U. S. GRANT.

Gen. C. A. ARTHUR, New-York City.

New York Times, Sept. 18, 1880. See *ibid.*, Sept. 12, 1880. On Sept. 17, 1880, USG's letter was read to a rally at the Academy of Music in New York City. On Aug. 28, USG, Galena, had telegraphed to Chester A. Arthur, New York City. "I will not be able to visit NewYork earlier than Sept twenty eighth. Letter by mail." Telegram received, DLC-Chester A. Arthur.

To John L. Routt

GALENA, Illinois, August 29, 1880.

My Dear Governor Routt:

We arrived here last Thursday evening[1] all well, without fatigue and without dust, rain having preceded us all the way. Mrs. Grant has made up her mind not to leave Galena again until we break up for the winter. I must go, however, nearly continually to attend State and county fairs, soldiers reunions, political meetings, etc. The Republicans seem to feel great confidence in carrying New York and Indiana. If they do, we are safe, and another four years will probably see the breaking up of the Democratic party and the organization of two national parties exercising the franchise freely, without fear, in all sections alike.

Yours truly,

U. S. GRANT.

Denver Tribune, Sept. 3, 1880. Former capt., 94th Ill., and q. m., John L. Routt served during USG's presidency as marshal, Southern District, Ill., and territorial and state governor, Colo.

1. Aug. 26, 1880.

To Marshall Jewell

Galena, Ill.
Aug. 31st 1880.

MY DEAR MR. JEWELL:

I would gladly accept the invitation to attend, and preside at, the meeting in New York City to be addressed by Senator Conkling if I could. But, as I have advised Gn. Arthur, I have accepted invitations here covering the time when the New York meeting takes place. Beside when I go east I do not expect to return here, only for a day to vote, until next spring, and do not wish to make two trips to the east this season. I am to be in Boston on the 6th of Oct. and do no expect to leave here until just in time to reach there by that date, allowing two or three days for delay in New York City.

Very Truly yours
U. S. GRANT

ALS, InFtWL. Marshall Jewell served as chairman, Republican National Committee.

To John M. Stull

Galena, Ill.
Aug. 31st 1880

JOHN M. STULL, ESQ.
DEAR SIR:

I have your letter of the 25th inst. inviting to preside at a political meeting to be held in Warren in Sept. and for me to fix the day when I can be there. I wish I could accept the call, but I can not. I go east in time to be in Boston on the 6th of Oct. and to stop two or three days in New York City, but I cannot stop very well before reaching the latter place.

You will know the reason—why I do not care to stop—later, but I do not wish to state it now. The reason is not political however, but on the contrary quite domestic. There is nothing honorable and proper I would not do to secure the success of the Republican National ticket at the approaching election.

Very Truly yours

U. S. GRANT

ALS, USG 3. See letter to Chester A. Arthur, Sept. 13, 1880; letter to John M. Stull, Sept. 23, 1880. Born in 1823 in Trumbull County, Ohio, John M. Stull worked as a blacksmith, taught school, studied law, settled in Warren, and served as mayor (1858) and Republican county chairman.

On Sept. 2, 1880, U.S. Senator Roscoe Conkling of N. Y., Utica, wrote to Stull, Warren. "*Personal.* . . . Many thanks for your cordial letter. It will give me great pleasure, whenever I can do so, to meet the Republicans of your District. So many things however, political and others, must have my attention within the next two months that I dare not promise myself the privelege you offer. I may be able to get somewhat out of our own State, but I do not feel safe now in making any appointments abroad, much as I should like to do so." LS, John W. Barkley, Cleveland, Ohio.

To Edward F. Beale

———

Galena, Ill.

Sept. 3d 1880.

MY DEAR GEN. BEALE;

Your very kind letter advising against my accepting the position assigned me by the papers with the San Pedro Mining Co. was duly received. I had examined the property and really believe it to be the most valuable piece of mining property now known. I had the offer of the Presidency of the Co. with a good salary, and a part ownership, on favorable terms, with an assurance that the stock would not be put upon the market, nor any of it sold. With these conditions I thought I would accept, but fortunately declined to do so until I should go to New York City in the fall. Soon I saw some of the property was being sold it apparently having enhanced in value in the estimation of some people as soon as my connection with it was published, and the temptation being to great for some of them to withstand. I at once wrote casting much doubt about my having anything to do with it. Later learning of at least one person who had purchased on the assurance that I had, or would undoubtedly accepted the charge, I wrote positively declining to have any thing to do with it.

Your letter stated that you would go to Washington in a short time. I address this to you there therefore. We will leave here for the east in less than a month, not to return before next spring. Where we will spend the winter is not yet determined, but probably a good deal of it will be in Washington City. That is where I prefer to make my principle home, but circumstances may compell me to locate elswhere. There are two subjects I wish particularly to promote, if in my power—the construction of an Inter-Oceanic Canal, and the building of rail-roads in Mexico to connect with ours—and these subjects may possibly fix my location without referrence to my preferences.—Mrs. Grant & I will certainly meet you and Mrs. Beale during the fall or winter, either in New York or Washington, or both.

With the best regards of Mrs. Grant & I to you and all your family, I am,

Very Truly yours
U. S. GRANT

ALS, DLC-Decatur House Papers. Interviewed in Boston on Sept. 18, 1880, George W. Ballou reportedly produced a letter of acceptance written by USG after San Pedro Mining Co. directors elected him president on July 24. Ballou said that USG corresponded frequently on business matters in the ensuing month, then wrote a letter "declining the presidency of the company—in brief, backing out from the whole enterprise. It was not a complete surprise to me, however. In truth, I had received some intimation that great pressure was being brought to bear upon the General to prevent his permanent connection with our company, and his own letters from time to time contained some evidence that this state of things probably existed. However, I believed that he would eventually 'stick,' and in this belief I was confirmed by some of the General's most intimate friends, who, I may say, were very desirous that he should do so. The reasons given were these, as far as I understood the matter:—In the first place, as I have said, great pressure was brought to bear upon the General by his political friends and associates, who insisted that his political position would be compromised by his connection with such a business enterprise. Then, it is said other business connections were offered, some of them presenting a tempting allurement. Indeed the General has always had great faith in possible business operations to be established in Mexico and a strong inclination to become connected with such. Probably all these causes combined to produce the result." *New York Herald*, Sept. 19, 1880. See letter to George W. Ballou, Aug. 22, 1880; *Rocky Mountain News* (Denver), Aug. 17, 1880; *Chicago Tribune*, Oct. 8, 1880.

To Ellen Grant Sartoris

————

Galena, Ill.

Sept. 3d 1880,

MY DEAR DAUGHTER;

Your Ma & I have each received nice long letters from you since our return from the mountains, a week since. The summer in the states east of the mountains has been about the hottest ever known. But where we have been we have felt no warm weather. Your ma took a good rest while we were in New Mexico & Colorado, making no excursions from our stopping places—Santo Fe, Manitou Springs & Denver—except our trip to Leadville, and short excursions in the neighborhood. I was traveling about a good deal and so saw much of the mountains, valleys and new mining discoveries. I am sure Mr Sartoris would have enjoyed the trip exceedingly.— Jesse has been with us several days. He leaves Chicago to-day for San Francisco and will be married on the 21st of this month.[1] He will return by here to stop three or four days when we will all go east together as far as New York city. Jesse will then probably go to England for a short visit. I suppose he cannot remain away long on account of his business. Buck is in Arazona but will be at the wedding, and probably return with Jesse. The papers have been proclaiming for nearly a year that Buck was engaged, but he does not admit it and I do not know whether it is true or not.

When we leave here it will be for the winter. I do not know certainly where we will stay, but we will remain in New York City for some time, and it may be that I will make such arrangements as to make that my permanent home. Where ever we are we will expect to have you all make us a visit. Your Ma & I send much love to you, Algie and the children. You must write often to your Ma or me.

Yours Affectionately

U. S. GRANT

Your Ma is engaged in making a dress for your little girl. You must not anticipate much for she is doing it herself. It will no doubt be finished before the quilt which she commenced before we were engaged, and probably before the little girl is grown.

ALS, ICHi.

1. Jesse Root Grant, Jr., married Elizabeth Chapman, the daughter of Sarah Armstrong and William S. Chapman, a San Francisco merchant known for "bold and gigantic operations in real estate." *New York Times*, Sept. 23, 1880.

To Colostin D. Myers

————

Galena, Ill.
Sept. 5th 1880.

C. D. MYERS, ESQ.
DEAR SIR:

I have your letter of yesterday inviting me to be present at the Republican meeting, which is to be held in Bloomington on the 21st inst. I would like very much to be there not only to hear the speeches which will be made on that occasion, but to meet so many of the citizens of McLean Co. who I know will be present. But I have accepted invitations which will take up all the time from now until my departure for the Winter.

Very Truly yours
U. S. GRANT

ALS, McLean County Historical Society, Bloomington, Ill. Born in Ohio in 1847, Colostin D. Myers served in the 140th Ohio, graduated from the National Normal School in Lebanon, Ohio (1872), earned a law degree from the University of Michigan (1874), and settled in Bloomington, Ill., where he practiced law and chaired the Republican county committee.

To Horace Porter

————

Galena, Ill.
Sept. 5th 1880.

DEAR GENERAL;

I received your letter in due time, but as I have so many letters to write every day I did not hasten to answer it. You have no doubt seen that I have given Garfield & Arthur every support in my power. It requires no argument with me, and I think it should not with any man having an interest in the welfare of the nation, to shew that it would be a most dangerous experiment to turn over the controll of the country to the party that tried to destroy it, and particularly while they will not tolerate a free ballot where they hold controll. I have written to General Garfield that I would like to meet him when I go east, and have him travel with me through Ohio, or as much of the way as he can spare time for.

Jesse you know is to be married in San Francisco on the 21st of this month. He will start immediately for Chicago. Mrs. Grant & I will join him there and all go east together, starting from there I think on thursday the 30th May I ask you if you can secure for us, on that occasion, a special car? Fred. & wife will probably be with us. I do not care what road we go by, but would prefer avoiding the large cities as much as possible. Mrs. Grant & I will not be able to accept your kind invitation to visit you at Long Branch, I go to Boston directly from New York, and will not be back to the latter city before the 10th of Oct. This will bring it to late to visit Long Branch.

With kindest regards of Mrs Grant & myself to Mrs. Porter and the boys, I am,

> Yours Very Truly
> U. S. GRANT

ALS, Horace Porter Mende, Zurich, Switzerland.

Speech

———

[*Madison, Wis., Sept. 7, 1880*]

MR. SECRETARY, OLD COMRADES, AND LADIES AND GENTLEMEN:—In 1850, I visited Wisconsin, and have not been within your beautiful State since.[1] And when I was here before, I did not come to Madison, so that this is my first visit to your Capital, which is so far-famed for its beauty and many attractions; and I assure you that it meets all my expectations; I only wish I could stay longer and see more of this fair city. The people of Wisconsin are to be sincerely congratulated upon their wealth and prosperity, as evidenced in this magnificent display of industrial and agricultural products. As General BRYANT has remarked, it is indeed a most fitting thing that the beautiful grounds now occupied by this assemblage should have been transformed from a soldiers' camp to the uses of an agricultural association—it is a symbol of beating the spears of war into the plowshares of peace. I hope that these grounds may never again be the scene of warlike preparations, never again be used for military purposes; and may the young men and boys before me, and these fine-appearing militiamen, never be called upon to witness the scenes of strife which these old veterans have gone through.

Mr. Secretary, I again thank you for this cordial reception, and shall be happy to grasp my brother veterans and you all by the hand.

Wisconsin State Journal, Sept. 8, 1880. George E. Bryant, secretary, Wis. agricultural society, introduced USG to a crowd at "old Camp Randall, the gathering place,—where a hundred thousand of the youth and manhood of loyal Wisconsin fitted for the fray!" *Ibid.* USG attended the state fair Sept. 6–8, 1880.

1. USG made his first recorded visit to Wis. in 1860, on business. See *PUSG*, 1, 358–59. USG made other visits prior to June, 1880, when he attended a veterans' reunion at Milwaukee, then traveled to Fond du Lac and Green Bay.

To Edwards Pierrepont

Galena, Ill.
Sept. 10th 1880.

MY DEAR JUDGE:

I have your letter of the 7th inst. written from the White Mountains, inviting Mrs. Grant & I to be your guests during our proposed visit to New York City.

The invitation is very kind and I appreciate it, but when I go Fred. and his wife and Jesse with his bride will be of the party, to many for any private house. Also, Mrs. Grant and I expect to remain in New York City most of the fall and Winter, and expect therefore to take up sort of permanent quarters. Jesse will sail—or expects to—very soon for Europe on a short tour.

Thanking you and Mrs. Pierrepont for your kind invitation, in which Mrs Grant joins me, I am

> Very Truly yours
> U. S. GRANT

JUDGE EDWARDS PIE[RRE]PONT

ALS, DLC–USG.

To Alphonso Taft

———

> Galena Ill.
> Sept. 10th 1880

MY DEAR JUDGE TAFT;

On my return yesterday from an absence of a few days I found your letter of the 5th inst. I would be delighted to meet you here at any time to confer on the subject of your letter. Next week I will be absent most of the time; but tuesday and wednesday I will be at Rockford,[1] near Chicago, where I could meet you. If I knew you would be here after that I would stay at home.

It would take a long letter to give you my recollections of Hancocks civil command in La. & Texas, the motive for sending him there, the cause of his leaving and &c. and then some of the particulars would have to be verified by referrence to official documents in the War Dept. If you meet me I will give you all the facts I know, and the means of getting the facts indisputably. There is nothing easier in my mind than to show that the celebrated Order No 40 was an order to defeat the Civil law—the Acts of Congress which the Military are bound by duty and by oath of office to carry out—by the use of the Military.

With kindest regards of Mrs. Grant and myself to Mrs. Taft, I am,

> Very Truly yours
> U. S. GRANT

ALS, NjP. On Sept. 18, 1880, Alphonso Taft, Oberlin, Ohio, wrote to U.S. Representative James A. Garfield of Ohio. "I saw Genl G. & Genl Sheridan & got a good deal of insight into the subject we were talking of. The sense of the matter is that H. allowed himself to be made an instrument in the hands of Johnson, to defeat the Acts of Congress, and to accomplish the purposes of the confederates, & this at a heavy cost of life to the colored population of La. & Texas. I have telegraphed to Col H. C. Corbin to get if possible, the correspondence (telegraphic) between Generals Grant & Hancock, which ended in H. asking to be relieved. It was a trying time, and Grant & Sheridan bore themselves splendidly. I think I can prepared a condensed statement of that part of H's career which may be of some use. . . ." ALS, DLC-James A. Garfield.

On Sept. 21, Charles H. Fowler, Methodist official, Galena, wrote [to his wife]. "I have just returned [f]rom a protracted call upon Gen. Grant. I went with Brother Cramb, Grant's pastor. When we were introduced into his library we found him at [h]is desk writing. He rose, and calling my name [s]aid, 'I have not seen you since we met at Chaut[a]uqua, Sunday School Assembly.' He was very free and full of talk. He talked about the political situation, [c]anvassing the country and the men with great [f]reedom." *Cincinnati Gazette*, Oct. 5, 1880. James O. Cramb was a Methodist pastor in Galena. Fowler's account of his conversation with USG began with his regret that USG had not won the Republican nomination, "not for your [c]omfort or fame, but for the country." USG responded. "Not for my comfort, I am glad to be released from [t]he care. There were three reasons why I would [h]ave accepted the nomination: First—On account of the character of the men [w]ho urged it. I esteem their respect and confidence [m]ore than the nomination. Second—I believe I could have broken up the [s]olid South. Many life long Democrats in the South had given the strongest assurances of their cordial support, believing that I could deliver them from the evils of a solid South. Florida is a Republican State, if they had a fair chance. The Republicans are so distributed that they can secure a fair count, except in the northwest corner of the State, where the negroes are chiefly centered, and where the society is like Georgia—is really a part of Georgia. While I would have received probably but 200 or 300 more votes from the State than Garfield will receive, those few are so located as to secure a fair count in that northwest corner. These are the substantial reasons. Third—There is another partial reason. I believe that I could have induced, from my knowledge of our consulates, the enactment of certain laws touching our commerce that would have given us control of much desirable commerce—for instance, in Mexico—instead of dealing with people who use only slave labor, and receive little or nothing but [s]terling in exchange. . . . I have known [*Winfield S. Hancock*] for forty years. He is a weak, vain man. He is the most selfish man I know. He could never endure to have anyone else receive any credit. Though he received all the mention from his superiors he deserved, and often more, he was always displeased that he was not praised more, and that anyone else was mentioned at all. He is the most selfish man I know. He was a very good corps commander. He was ambitious, and had courage and a fine presence; but he is vain, selfish, weak, and easily flattered. He can not bear to hear anyone else praised, but can take any amount of flattery. Down to 1864 he seemed like a man ambitious to do his duty as an officer. But in 1864, when McClellan was nominated, Hancock received one vote, and that greatly excited and changed him. He was so delighted that he smiled all over. You could not even sit behind him without seeing him smile. He smiled all over. It crazed him. Before that we got on well. After that he would hardly speak to me. I was working to enforce the laws of Congress, and he was working for the Presidency. Perhaps he thought I did not praise him enough, but any way he hardly spoke to me. It was on my nomination that he was made a Brigadier General in the regular army. When I was made General, Stanton told me it was a compliment to me, and that I could name the men to fill the vacancies in Lieutenant Generalship and Major Generalship caused by my promotion. I nominated him for the vacant Major Generalship in the regular army. He acknowledged it manfully. He was a very fair corps commander, but was never thought of for any great place. When the Army of the Potomac was hunting for a commander, it took almost everybody—even came over into the West for officers—but no one ever even suggested Hancock for the place. After he received that vote in 1864 he had 'the bee in his bonnet,' and shaped everything to gain Democratic and Southern favor. He has watched, and planned, and waited, till at last he has received the Democratic nomination. . . . He is crazy to be President. He is ambitious, vain, and weak. [*The South*] will easily control him. . . . I will give you the true inner history of Order No. 40. Congress was striving to prevent Andrew Johnson from undoing the reconstruction laws. Whenever Congress passed a law Johnson bent his energies to defeat its enforcement, and would find pretexts to dodge round it. Then Congress would pass another law to hedge him up there. So it went on till Congress had taken from him all control of the Generals commanding the seven districts of the South, except the power to recall them and appoint others in their places. These commanders could remove any civil officer of any grade, Judge or Governor. When I was made General, and they were determining my powers and duties, they gave the General, by accident, I think, or without seeing all it involved, coordinate power with these district commanders, and as I was senior it gave me authority. Gen. Sheridan was sent to the Department of Louisiana, covering Louisiana and Texas. He is very shrewd and very able. If he is in charge of any field, and there is anything he ought to know in that field, he is sure to know it. He is as able and vigilant an officer as the country has, or as any country has. He kept his eyes open, learning rapidly the men who were not worthy to occupy their places, and discovering competent and worthy men to put in their places. He had a good list and a black list, a list of unworthy officers, ready to change them in an hour when the time should come. He consulted with me privately about it, and did nothing rashly. The Legislature of Louisiana passed a law authorizing the issue of $7,000,000 of *leeve* bonds, ostensibly for the levee. They conditioned their sale on their bringing to the State not less than 80 per cent. of their face. The Governor and three Commissioners were to place the bonds on the market. But they soon found that the bonds would not bring more than 40 per cent. To avoid the law they invented the plan of borrowing money and using the bonds as collateral. They could borrow about 34 or 35 per cent. of the face of the bonds. Just at this juncture, to prevent these men from defrauding the State, Gen. Sheridan took off the heads of the Governor and Commissioners so quick that they did not know what ailed them, and appointed good men in their places. For some reason the removed men were very anxious to be reappointed. They employed Reverdy Johnson and another lawyer to work for them, agreeing to pay them $250,000 if they were reinstated. This is a great deal of money for four men to pay for positions, unless there is some special gain in the case. Reverdy Johnson came to me, but I was so stupid and stubborn that I could not be induced to reappoint them. He then went to Andrew Johnson and made his case and Andrew Johnson sent for me, and asked me to reinstate those men. I refused to do so. He said, 'Reinstate them even if it is only for one day. I will promise that they will resign.' I thought Johnson might not know of the motive why they were so anxious to be reinstated, and thinking I would do him a great service in keeping him from a great blunder, I told him that 'one hour would do those men as well as one day,' and I unfolded their intent. But Johnson insisted on their being reinstated. I refused, and excused myself.

Johnson then removed Gen. Sheridan and appointed Gen. Hancock. He called Hancock to Washington to instruct him in defeating the laws of Congress concerning reconstruction. As soon as I learned that Hancock was in town, I called at his hotel instead of sending for him. I wanted to see him privately in his own room. I found him in his room, perhaps before he had his breakfast. I said, 'General, you and I are soldiers; army officers. We have life positions; we serve under successive administrations without regard to party. It is our duty to enforce the laws of Congress. We are not responsible for the wisdom of the laws. Congress bears that responsibility; we simply enforce them.' He said, 'Well, I am opposed to nigger domination.' I said, 'General, it is not a question of nigger domination. Four millions of ex-slaves, without education or property can hardly dominate 30,000,000 of whites with all the education and property. It is a question of doing our sworn duty?' He said, 'Well I'm opposed to nigger domination.' I saw that my only chance to influence him was by the remnant of authority left in my hands. He was determined to please the Democratic party and the South. He went South and removed the Governor and Commissioners that Gen. Sheridan had appointed. I instantly telegraphed him not to appoint to office any men who had been removed, and to give me his reasons by mail for removing the men. He telegraphed in a long reply costing the Government $250, his reasons. I telegraphed him that the reasons were not sufficient; to send me by mail other reasons. He again telegraphed about the same points, only not quite so long, costing only $150. He telegraphed that if he could not have freedom to act, his usefulness would be destroyed, and that he would have to ask to be relieved. I telegraphed him to revoke his order. He asked Johnson to relieve him, as no one else could. That is the inner history and spirit of his celebrated Order No. 40. This order resulted in the loss of many lives. I know of cases. I can give them. The names and dates are within reach, so that no Democrat can dispute them. Two brothers, ex-Confederate soldiers in Texas, took up for the outraged negroes and Unionists in their neighborhood. They believed in fair play and free speech. They were soon threatened, soon condemned, and the order given among their neighbors for their death. They had to flee in the night. They found an old horse worth about $10 and mounted him and rode as far as they could out of their neighborhood. Then by hiding by day and traveling by night they finally got over into Mexico and to safety. After a long time, when they thought the matter had passed over, they returned to another part of Texas, away from the thoroughfares, hoping to be let alone. Their presence became known, and an order for their arrest on the charge of horse stealing was issued. They fled to the military camp and asked to be put in the guard house. An ex-rebel lawyer took up their case, made out the appeal to Gen. Hancock, asking that they might be tried by the military authorities and not returned, as they could not have a fair trial where they were charged, nor any trial; that the writ simply meant to murder them. This was sent to Hancock under his Order No. 40. He referred it to the Governor of Texas. The Governor ordered their return. They were taken from the guard house and returned. They were put in a dungeon, a tight log house, and before court day, after much abuse and suffering, they met death. A band of masked men surrounded the jail and burned it, watching against their escape. They were burned alive. This is some of the fruit of Order No. 40. There are more cases that are abundantly proven. His statement that the civil authorities are supreme is a truth admitted by all in time of established peace. But I can demonstrate, as the facts I have mentioned show, that he did not subject the military power to the civil, but that he used his military power to overthrow the civil. . . . We must elect Garfield. He is a great man. He has but few intellectual peers in public life. He is every way worthy[.]" Fowler asked, "What if Hancock should be elected?" USG replied. "Then the North would submit quietly and watch closely. As soon as things began to go wrong, every Northern legislature would be convened and compel their representatives to resign or resist the solid South. . . . I expect to witness the most gigantic frauds in Indiana and New York City. Pretext will be sought for throwing out States or parts of States. If the election is thus thrown into the House, then Washburn, of Minnesota, will be thrown out. They are determined to seize the government, regardless of cost. I hope that many Democrats who will not change will take the alarm and stay at home. . . . I regard [*Roscoe Conkling*] as the greatest mind in public life, or that has been in public life since the beginning of the government. He has the advantage of having been trained from his very infancy. He had a father of unusual ability, who early taught him to reason, and corrected his errors. He has grown to great proportions. I did not get acquainted with him while I was General of the Army. I was in Washington four years and met him, but did not know him. You know some men chill you by their presence. You feel like keeping yourself in reserve when they are near you. Others draw you out. They warm and cheer you. You immediately cheer up, and you are glad of their presence. When I came to know Conkling, he was always welcome. His external bearing is only external. He has true greatness and simplicity." *Ibid.* On Sept. 21, USG wrote to Fowler. "I have no objection to your noting down anything I said to-day for future reference, but as I told substantially the same thing to a Republican speaker, who is to address the voters of several States during the canvass, I would prefer what I said should not go out as an interview until he brings it out. This is due to him." *Ibid.*, Oct. 12, 1880. For a summary of a similar, earlier interview with Governor William E. Smith of Wis., see *Galena Gazette*, Sept. 11, 1880. Maj. Gen. Winfield S. Hancock had issued Special Orders No. 40 upon assuming command in New Orleans, Nov. 29, 1867. USG conflated two separate episodes in his account of Hancock's order. See *Cincinnati Gazette*, Oct. 8, 1880; *PUSG*, 17, 185–86, 468–69; *ibid.*, 18, 39–44, 175–82; Johnson, *Papers*, 12, 307–8, 373–78; Joseph G. Dawson III, *Army Generals and Reconstruction: Louisiana, 1862–1877* (Baton Rouge, 1982), pp. 50–58, 69–74; David M. Jordan, *Winfield Scott Hancock: A Soldier's Life* (Bloomington, Ind., 1988), pp. 203–5, 210–11, 289–90.

On Oct. 5, 1880, USG spoke to a reporter in Chicago. "The reported interview, though it is in most respects correct, contains also many mistakes, and makes me say things in a way not intended, and use some language that I did not employ. The facts are these: Dr. Fowler called at my house in company with Mr. Cramb to pay his respects, and the conversation turned upon politics. I talked freely, without suspecting for a moment that the conversation was ever to be published. Sometime afterward, Dr. Fowler, on whose mind the conversation had made some impression, wrote to me, saying he desired to publish it if I did not object. I replied, saying I would rather this would not be done until one of our speakers, who had the same facts, and was verifying them from the files of the War Department, had made them public; that as he was preparing the facts carefully it would hardly be fair to anticipate him. That might imply permission to Dr. Fowler to publish his report of the conversation when the speaker alluded to had made the speech. I have not noticed that he has yet made it, but he probably has, or Dr. Fowler would not have published this article. . . . It is inaccurate in many respects. He reports me for instance as follows: 'Down to 1864 he (Hancock) seemed like a man ambitious to do his duty as an officer. But in 1864, when McClellan was nominated, Hancock received one vote, and that greatly excited and changed him. He was so delighted that he smiled all over. It crazed him. Before that we got on well. After that he would hardly speak to me. I was working to enforce the laws of Congress, and he was working for the Presidency. Perhaps he thought I did not praise him enough; but, any way, he hardly spoke to me.' I said substantially that up to 1864 I didn't suppose Hancock had a thought of the Presidency; but at the Democratic Convention of that year he got a vote (not *one* vote, as Dr. Fowler has it; which makes me imply that he got the support of but one delegate), and from that time he had had the Presidential bee in his bonnet. When I met him afterward his smile was so broad that you could almost see it when his back was turned. I do not know that I said he thought I did not praise him enough, though possibly that may be the fact. Hancock is a man who likes to hear himself praised, and sometimes complained that he was not complimented highly enough. . . . I stated to Dr. Fowler that Hancock was promoted to be a Brigadier and a Major General in the regular army on my recommendation. I recommended him and Sheridan at the same time. Hancock's appointment was made at once, but Sheridan's was delayed for a time. One of Hancock's promotions was made after the war, and I think it was after the Chicago convention that he was made a Brigadier. When I recommended him for Major General, he had been very cold toward me, and hadn't spoken to me for a long time. I never knew what was the matter, unless he thought I had not consulted him in making his assignments to duty. When promoted, however, he wrote a manly letter to me in which he said substantially that he believed he was entirely indebted to me for it, though he had thought I was not willing to do him justice. This convinced him that he had been mistaken. He was made a Major General when I was made General. . . . [*Fowler*] does not get hold of the points about order No. 40 correctly. By the various reconstruction acts Congress, for consistency's sake, I suppose, stripped me of all authority over the district commanders in their civil duties except in the matter of the appointment and removal of civil officers in the reconstructed States. As I was senior my authority was superior to others. Dr. Fowler quotes me as saying that the Louisiana Legislature passed a law authorizing the issue of $7,000,000 of levee bonds. This I may have said, but if I did it was a mistake, the amount being $4,000,000. In regard to the statement also that the Louisiana Commissioners agreed to pay Reverdy Johnson and other lawyers $250,000, I stated what I understood, and not a fact within my own personal knowledge. The next paragraph of Dr. Fowler's report is wide of the mark. I am made to say, 'He (Johnson) called Hancock to Washington to instruct him in defeating the laws of Congress.' I, of course, do not know why Johnson called Hancock. I could only surmise. I know Hancock came. A mistake also occurs in the following paragraph, wherein I am made to say: 'He (Hancock) went South and removed the government and commissioners that Governor Sheridan had appointed. I instantly telegraphed not to appoint to office any men who had been removed, and give his reasons by mail for removing the men.' When Hancock went South I published an order prohibiting him from appointing anybody to office who had been removed by his predecessor. This, I suppose, he did not like, but my object was to prevent the possibility of the men being put in place who had arranged for the negotiation of those bonds, even for one hour. I had intended to tell Hancock all about it as I had Johnson, but seeing during my interview with him that he was not disposed to listen to my advice, I did not tell him. After he had been down South some time he made a pretty clean sweep of the officers who had been appointed by General Sheridan. I then telegraphed him to suspend his orders of removals and report to me by mail. (There was an order existing, if I remember aright, prohibiting the use of the telegraph when the mail could be employed.) He replied in a very long dispatch, costing, if I remember correctly, about $250. I informed him I was not satisfied, but if he had any further reasons to communicate to do so by mail. He again replied by telegraph, but gave nothing new, saying simply that his usefulness would be destroyed if he was not left free to act, and that unless he was left free to act he should ask to be relieved. [*I*] ordered him to revoke his order making removals and to make no more. He then asked to be relieved, and I relieved him. I always regarded his mere declaration in order No. 40. that the military should be subordinate to the civil power, as something that everybody accepted and nobody disputed. As officers, we were sworn to obey our superiors. Congress was our superior, and had made the laws, and these laws made the military subordinate. We were acting under them. But his order, or his construction of his order, made the laws subordinate to his own opinions." The reporter asked whether Fowler had correctly described USG's feelings about the Chicago convention. "Well, correct in substance, but expressed as I would hardly express it. I said that no man felt more relieved at the final result at the Chicago convention than myself. I would have declined to permit the use of my name had it not been for the character of the men who were urging it, but I did not think it would be fair toward them to do so. It is also true, as stated by Dr. Fowler, that I believed I could break up the solid South and bring about a state of affairs where the two great parties would be national parties. I also thought that my visits abroad and my study of the questions of commerce and trade would enable me to materially advance the interests of this country in a commercial sense. Particularly did I think this to be the case with Mexico, which country raises all the tropical products that we use in the United States and is ready to take in exchange our own products, while in the case of many other nations of whom we buy we are unable to give anything in exchange except sterling exchange." *Chicago Inter-Ocean*, Oct. 6, 1880. On Aug. 11, 1864, USG had recommended the promotion of Winfield S. Hancock to brig. gen. Hancock was formally nominated and confirmed in Jan., 1865, to date from Aug. 12, 1864. Democrats met Aug. 29–31 in Chicago. See *PUSG*, 11, 400, 427.

On Oct. 6, 1880, a correspondent reported from Cincinnati. ". . . The attempt of the Democrats to break the force of the interview, by denying its genuineness, falls to the ground when it is known that Gen. Grant related the same things to ex-Attorney-General Taft, who has been making use of them in his speeches in the Ohio campaign. Judge Taft visited Gen. Grant a few days before Dr. Fowler, . . ." *New York Times*, Oct. 7, 1880. On Oct. 7, a correspondent reported from New York City. "It appears, from inquiries made at Governor's Island to-day by newspaper reporters, that Gen. Hancock has sent a telegram to Gen. Grant asking him to affirm or deny the statements made in the interview with the Rev. Charles H. Fowler, . . ." *Chicago Tribune*, Oct. 8, 1880.

1. USG and Taft attended the Winnebago County Fair at Rockford, Ill., on Wednesday, Sept. 15. USG addressed the crowd. "I am taken entirely by surprise at being introduced in a manner that would indicate that I am expected to make a speech. I had supposed that I was invited here to look at the products of this section of our state. I am much better as a spectator than as a speaker. I can look at a horse-race as well as any many? you ever saw. I had no idea of seeing such a number here after the storm. I am pleased to be with you and anticipate much pleasure and a more favorable day to-morrow." *Rockford Register*, Sept. 16, 1880. In the evening, USG and Taft attended a Republican rally. On Sept. 16, USG again spoke at the fair. "I was introduced on this platform yesterday and was not aware that I would be expected to say anything here to-day. I spent this forenoon here and noticed your agricultural exposition, your products and manufactures. It affords me great pleasure to see my adopted state making so much progress. As was suggested by the speaker yesterday, Illinois is the first state in the Union in agricultural products. I am glad to see you all here and will not take up the time with any remarks, as there are gentlemen here who are more accustomed to speaking. I will bid you good-bye." *Ibid.*, Sept. 17, 1880.

To Edward F. Beale

———

Galena, Ill.
Sept. 12th 1880.

MY DEAR GEN. BEALE:

Your letter of the 8th is just received. I saw some days ago the parigraph which you enclose me. I do not recollect just what I did write you, but I know I did not say all this slip contains because at no time have I expected to be in Washington during Sept. or the 1st of Oct. I will leave Chicago on the 30th inst. for the east, and after a few days visit to Boston, expect to return to New York City and to spend the fall and winter there and in wWashington. Mrs. Grant & I, or I alone, will accept the kind hospitalities tendered by Mrs. Beale and you when we visit Washington to secure quarters for our more permanent stay. But when this will be I can not now tell, probably not before Dec. some time.—I wrote to you soon after receiving your last letter and directed it to your house in Washington. I hope you received it.

Please present Mrs. Grants and my kindest regards to Mrs. Beale and Miss Emily. Mrs. Grant received a letter from Miss Emily a short time since. Neither hers nor yours indicate that my last letter to you had been rec'd.

Very Truly yours
U. S. GRANT

ALS, DLC-Decatur House Papers.

To John M. Farquhar

———

GALENA, Ill., Sept. 12, 1880.

Major John M. Farquhar:

DEAR MAJOR: I regret that I will not be able to accept the invitation of the Erie County (N. Y.) Veteran Club to be with them about the 1st of October. I should like very much to accept, because

I want to contribute all I can to the success of the Republican cause in November. But I leave here—or Chicago—on the 30th inst. for New-York City. After stopping there a few days I go—by invitation accepted some time since—to Boston, to remain until the 10th of October. After that I must attend to some business for myself, and cannot say when I will be able to accept any invitation which would take me away from where I may be staying. With many regrets that I cannot be with the Erie County veterans in their demonstration of love for the cause for which they fought, I am, very truly yours,

U. S. Grant.

New York Times, Sept. 18, 1880. Born in 1832 in Scotland, John M. Farquhar settled as a boy in Buffalo, where he became an editor and publisher. For his action as sgt. maj., 89th Ill., at Murfreesboro, Tenn., Farquhar was awarded the Congressional Medal of Honor.

To Chester A. Arthur

Galena Ill,
Sept. 13th 1880

My Dear General Arthur;

After answering your dispatch requesting me to preside at a meeting in Northern Ohio, to be addressed by Senator Conkling, some time before Sept. 28th I concluded to break any other engagement that might conflict, and go at any time you might fix, and intended to send you a dispatch the following morning to that effect. During the night—after 12—I received your second dispatch saying it would be inconvenient to fix a date so late as the 28th and asking if I could not go at an earlyer date, and return to Ill. before my final departure for the east. I replied to that dispatch just as I intended to telegraph if it had not been received. I fear from your dispatch of this date, informing me that Gen. Garfield had been requested to fix place of meeting, with date either the 28th or 29th Sept. that my dispatch—second dispatch—has not been received. I

beg that you will have the date of the meeting fixed so as to sub-
serve the best interests of the cause, and not consider me atall. In
fact I would rather go any time after this week, and before the 28th
of Sept. than at the latter date. I could then attend the meeting,
return to Chicago and go through to New York with my family all
the way, and by any route. But whatever may be done I will con-
form to.

Very Truly yours
U. S. GRANT

ALS, DLC-Chester A. Arthur. On Sept. 13, 1880, Chester A. Arthur telegraphed to
USG. "I have telegraphed General Garfield to have meeting arranged at such place in
Northern Ohio, as deemed best on the 28th or 29th September & that you will preside
and Senator Conkling will speak. Will telegraph you as soon as I hear further" Copy,
ibid.

On Sept. 10, USG, Galena, had telegraphed to Arthur. "I leave Chicago for the
East Sept thirtieth I might go a day or two earlier for purpose named in your dispatch
and leave my family to meet me at place named do not make the meeting earlier than
twenty eighth" Telegram received (at 5:56 P.M.), *ibid.* On Sept. 11, USG telegraphed
twice to Arthur. "Arrange for meeting in ohio any day best suiteding your other appointments and I will be there" "Will write tomorrow and answer" Telegrams received, *ibid.* On Sept. 13, USG again telegraphed to Arthur. "You are at liberty to name
any day from now to first October for meeting & I will be present I so telegraphed in
aswer to your last despatch" Telegram received, *ibid.*

On Sept. 13, USG telegraphed to John M. Stull, Warren, Ohio. "I meet Senator
Conkling in Ohio at any time this month arranged by National Committee" Telegram
received (at 3:40 P.M.), John W. Barkley, Cleveland, Ohio. Also on Sept. 13, U.S. Representative James A. Garfield of Ohio, Mentor, telegraphed to Stull and Harmon Austin.
"I have intended to have the Grant Conkling meeting at Warren but the Senator will
not speak out of doors—I am very sorry" Telegram received, *ibid.* On Sept. 14, Garfield
telegraphed twice to Stull. "Announce wigwam mass meeting for Grant and Conkling Tuesday afternoon Sept twenty eighth Gen Arthur authorizes it Have written"
"If you build wigwam for great Audience Grant will preside and Conkling will speak
Tuesday twenty eighth Answer" Telegrams received (at 8:00 A.M. and 5:00 P.M.), *ibid.*
On Sept. 15, Arthur, New York City, wrote to Stull. ". . . I have been engaged for several days in arranging for the Mass Meeting in Ohio, at which Senator Conkling will
speak, General Grant preside and General Garfield be present. As you will doubtless
learn before this reaches you, the Meeting has been arranged for the 28th inst. In response to your kind invitation to visit Warren, I can only say at this time that it would
give me great pleasure to attend the Meeting, but I cannot now tell if it will be possible
for me to do so. . . ." LS, *ibid.* On Sept. 17, Arthur telegraphed to Stull. "I would invite
other speakers for outside meetings I have no particular suggestion to make—I would
invite General Logan certainly E. A. Storrs of Chicago and W O Bradley of Lancaster
Kentucky would be good speaker Thanking you for your cordial invitation I fear that
the duties I have undertaken as chairman of our state committee will prevent my being
present" Telegram received, *ibid.*

To James A. Garfield

Galena, Ill.
Sept. 19th 1880.

DEAR GENERAL GARFIELD:

On my return yesterday from visiting some Fairs in this state I found your letter of the 15th inst. inviting me to spend the night of the 27th at your home. I would be glad to do so, but that is the day we expect Jesse & his bride to arrive in Chicago. Mrs. Grant & I expect to meet him there, and I will go to Ohio—Warren—by the night train.

The news from Maine seem to have improved since your letter was written. I hope however the republicans will fire no guns until the returns are in from the last town, and they know exactly what they are rejoicing over.[1] "He laughs best who laughs last."

Very Truly yours
U. S. GRANT

ALS, DLC-James A. Garfield. On Sept. 15, 1880, U.S. Representative James A. Garfield of Ohio telegraphed to Chester A. Arthur, New York City. "Please arrange that Gen Grant, Senator Conkling and yourself spend the night of Sept 27th at my house— Answer" ALS (press, telegram sent), *ibid.* On Sept. 20, Garfield, Mentor, Ohio, wrote to Worthy S. Streator, Cleveland. "Yours of the 18th is received. I have not yet heard from General Grant. I wrote him inviting him to spend the night of the 27th with me here. If he does that I think he will take a special train which the Lake shore people have tendered him from here by way of Ashtabula. If he is not able to come then he will doubtless go out to Warren from Cleveland. As soon as I know the situation definitely I will at once let you know" ALS (facsimile), Alexander Autographs, Oct. 21, 2000, no. 260. On Sept. 22, Arthur drafted a note to USG concerning Garfield's invitation. ADf, DLC-Chester A. Arthur.

On Sept. 21, USG, Galena, had telegraphed to Marshall Jewell, chairman, Republican National Committee. "While I shall do all in my power to aid the Republican cause, I cannot now engage to attend any meeting. I will be in New-York about the 10th of October, and after visiting Boston expect to be there through the Fall. Until about the 20th of October my time is now all engaged." *New York Times*, Sept. 23, 1880. On Sept. 24, USG telegraphed to the *Cleveland Herald*: "I have had no idea at any time of breaking my engagement to be in Warren on the 28th. Dispatch to Gov. Jewell is misquoted or has been sent wrong." *Ibid.*, Sept. 25, 1880.

1. Republicans narrowly lost the Maine governorship in a Sept. 13 election. See Allan Peskin, *Garfield: A Biography* (Kent, Ohio, 1978), p. 492.

To Herbert E. Hill

Galena Ill.
Sept. 19th /80

MY DEAR MR. HILL;

I was very sorry to have to disappoint you by not keeping my engagement to meet the Middlsex Club at the date I had fixed myself. But the fact is my old regiment, the 21st Ill. Vols. has been trying for a number of years before I left the country to have a reunion of the surviving members at which I should be present. Immediately on my return, last fall, they reniewed their invitation and I made a positive engagement—as positive as I dared when the time was so far ahead—to be present. On my return from Mexico the invitation was repeated and unconditionally accepted. When I fixed the date for meeting the Middlesex Club I was under the impression that the reunion was to be the latter part of this month, and knew no better until the papers published the fact that I was to be in Boston on the 6th of Oct. This attracted the attention of the old soldiers and they sent a Committee to see me at once to know if I was going to disappoint them again. They said their invitations had been sent to members of the regiment who had emigrated to other states and Territories, and many of them from a distance had signified their intention to be present on the occasion of this reunion. Under these circumstances I felt compelled to send the dispatch I did. I hope it will be accepted as satisfactory, although I can hardly forgive myself for not knowing what I was doing when authorizing you to fix the time of my being in Boston betwe[en] certain dates.

Very Truly yours
U. S. GRANT

ALS (facsimile), USGA. Born in 1845 in Mass., former corporal, 8th Vt., Herbert E. Hill prospered in the cotton business and served as secretary of Boston's Middlesex Club. See Speech, [*Oct. 13, 1880*].

On June 30, 1880, USG accepted an invitation to the Middlesex Club. Coins & Currency Inc., Philadelphia, Public Auction Sale, April 21, 1972, no. 51.

To John F. Long

———

Galena, Ill,
Sept. 19th /80

MY DEAR JUDGE LONG;

I received your letter enclosing check for $700 00 just as I was about leaving to attend some of our County fairs, and have had no earlyer opportunity of acknowledging it.

I have postponed the time of my departure for the east one week. But this will not give me any time to visit St Louis. I stay to give myself the opportunity of attending a reunion of my old regiment, the 21st Ill. Vols.

With kind regards to all your family,

Very Truly yours
U. S. GRANT

ALS, MoSHi.

To John Ramsey

———

Galena Ill.
Sept. 19th /80

GEN. JOHN RAMSAY;
DEAR GENERAL:

Having been absent from home for several days until yesterday I could not answer your letter of the 15 inst. earlyer. I have been compelled to postpone my trip east for one week so that I will not be in New York city much, if any, before the 20th of Oct. to remain any time. Any meeting you have therefore had better be without referance to my presence. If you have one and I am where I can attend, I will do so with pleasure. But for some days after my arrival in New York City I will probably be very busy.

With hopes that New Jersey will roll up a republican majority in Nov. for Garfield & Arthur that will demonstrate unmistakably that they do not want the democracy to take controll of this Government—Nation—until they learn that voters are free men, entitled to cast their ballots as they please, and have them counted as cast, I am,

Very Truly Yours
U. S. Grant

ALS, Gilder Lehrman Collection, NHi. Active in Jersey City politics, John Ramsey had commanded the 8th N. J. See *New York Times*, Feb. 12, 1901.

On Sept. 11, 1880, USG wrote to Ramsey. "I have your letter of the 6th inst. inviting me to be present at a grand rally of the Republicans of New-Jersey at some time after my arrival in New-York. I will be there about the 2d of October, to stay only for a few days, but will return on the 10th to remain for an indefinite period. If you should have your meeting after the latter date, at any time that may suit you best, I would attend with great pleasure." *Ibid.*, Sept. 15, 1880.

To J. Ambler Smith

[*Galena, Sept. 19, 1880*][1]

Dear Sir: I just returned yesterday from a visit to some of our country fairs and found your letter of the 13th inst. inviting me to spend a few days in Virginia. I will not be able to do so, but if the effect would be what you predict—to add materially to the Garfield and Arthur ticket—I would make great sacrifices to accomplish that result. I don't think there are many friends of mine who will fail to support the ticket, unless it is where (and because) they think their vote can do no possible good. In Virginia they should not think this. Hoping for the best results in your State, I am very truly yours,

U. S. Grant.

New York Times, Oct. 22, 1880; *Chicago Tribune*, Oct. 26, 1880. A prominent Va. Republican, J. Ambler Smith served one term in Congress (1873–75).

1. The opening resembles letters written on Sept. 19, 1880.

To Adam Badeau

Galena, Ill,
Sept. 20th /80

My Dear Badeau:

I have just read your last chapter furnished me. It is admirable. You have not written one better, nor one more interesting.

I am glad you have put so distictly before your readers the vexatious delays of Thomas & Canby. They were both excellent men; but ~~they~~ possessed fatal defects to being successful directors or excecutors of great military movements, unless on the defensive. You give true history in regard to them, and furnish the proof as you go along. While I would not wish to detract from any one I think history should record the truth.—I read this chapter out loud to Mrs. Grant. She wants me to say that she was much interested. I have been compelled to delay my departure to the east[1] one week to enable me to keep an engagement to meet my old regiment at a reunion, which I had promised last fall to do, but had forgotten the date of the meeting when I arranged to start on the last of this month. I shall hope to meet you then and would like to have you go on to Boston with me for four or five days if it would not interfere with your book too much. Tell Porter of my delay.

  With kind regards of Mrs. Grant & myself;

Yours Truly
U. S. GRANT

ALS, Munson-Williams-Proctor Institute, Utica, N. Y.

  1. On Sept. 21, 1880, USG, Galena, wrote to James R. Myers. "I do not know what route I will be going east by. My departure from Chicago will be on Oct. 8th. If by Peru I will [sto]p over as long as the train is willing to stop, but my party will be so large that I can not lay over one train." ALS (facsimile), eBay, Feb. 26, 2000.

To John M. Stull

———

Galena Ill.
Sept. 23d 1880

JOHN M. STULL; ESQ.
DEAR SIR:

  I will remain in Chicago[1] until 5 15 pm Monday, the 27th inst. to meet my son and his bride, who are expected from California that day, and then start by the Lake Shore R. R. for Warren, reaching there, as I understand, about 10 am, the 28th On the 29th I want to return to Chicago having other engagements in this state before my departure for the east. I will probably remain in Warren the night of the 28th and return by the day train.

Very Truly yours
U. S. GRANT

ALS, USG 3.

On Sept. 22, 1880, U.S. Senator John A. Logan of Ill., Murphysboro, wrote to John M. Stull. "I am better today and will certainly come to Warren on the 28th if I do not have another attack of sickness." ALS, John W. Barkley, Cleveland, Ohio. On the same day, U.S. Senator Roscoe Conkling of N. Y., Utica, wrote to Stull. "*Personal.* . . . Just at home I have your several letters. I understand that I am to be at Warren to speak at a day time meeting next Tuesday. I shall be there in time, but by what route or at what hour, I cannot say. I prefer to come quietly in my own way making no trouble for anybody." LS, *ibid.*

1. On Sept. 21, Lt. Gen. Philip H. Sheridan telegraphed to USG. "I have only a moment to telegraph you before starting for Toledo for the Army of the Cumberland that Mrs Sheridan & myself will expct you to Come to our house. to & Mrs Grant to stay with us during your visit to chicago—I will try & go with you to Decatur." ADfS and copy, DLC-Philip H. Sheridan.

To Madison Y. Johnson

Galena, Ill., Sept. 24th 188.0

MY DEAR MR. JOHNSON,

I have been anxious to see you for several days As I leave to morrow morning, and may not meet you, I leave this with Gen. Rowley who please say yes or no to as you may decide. You know it is said that once, a man of accredited veracity, asserted that his horse was seventeen feet high. Of course it was understood that he meant hands. But being a man of firmness as well as veracity he stuck to it that the horse was seventeen feet high though it was through inadvertency that he had said so. It would have been cruelty to have had every man coming along to have enquired of him enquiring how tall his horse was, and make him repeat his falsehood In the same way some men have, in a passion, or in an excitement, have announced that they would never vote other than a democratic ticket, Their consciences, in their cooler moments,

might might trouble them for their rash determination. But their
firmness keeps them to their rash resolution. In such cases it is humane to relieve such persons from the performance of the humiliating act, without a violation of their pledge. Now I want to vote
the republican ticket as a conscientious duty. I will have to travel
a thousand miles, and retrace my steps, to do so. Now what I propose is to pair off with you at the approaching election. Will you do
it. You will oblige me very much if you say yes.

yours very Truly

U. S. GRANT

P. S. This agreement is not to deprive you of the privilage of
voting for such republicans on the general ticket as you may desire
to vote for.

U S. G.

ALS (facsimile), ICHi and Galena Historical Society, Galena, Ill. On Sept. 25, 1880,
Johnson, Galena, wrote to USG. "I was to unwell to pay my respects to you before you
left, and take this method, through our mutual friend Genl Rowley, to answer your
note. That man you speak of, 'of accredited veracity, that asserted his horse was 17
feet high, and stuck to it, simply because he said so inadvertently,' proves his firmness,
at the expense of his veracity, and it establishes another fact, that when he finds he is
wrong, he has not the courage, to correct his mistake as it would be an impeachment
of his firmness, that he is unwilling to make. Now if he had deliberately thought of
the matters, he would not have subjected himself to the cruelty of being compelled to
repe[at] his falsehood, and as he chooses to maintain his firmness at the expense of
his veracity and courage, I think it would not be cruelty, but a just punishment to him
for his falsehood Let me give you an Example of firmness and courage that should be
imitated, and point out the difference 'A distinguished General said he would fight it
out on that line, if it took all Summer' now by sticking too it, he proved his firmness,
his veracity and courage, but no one, at the expense of the other traits of character.
Allow me to assure you my dear General, If there is any man, I would pair with, it is
yourself—but I remember when you were President, you voted next after me. You then
told me, you killed my vote, and I said nothing Short of a Presidents vote would do it.
That was an illustration of the glorious system of our Government, that the President,
and a plain citizen were on an Equality, both Sovereigns in the discharge of a conscien-
cious duty. now I want that Example presented to the world again, of an Ex President,
who has had more attention shown him, than any man that Ever lived, to relegate his
greatness, and take upon himself the duty of a plain citizen again, And I am perhaps
a little Selfish in my refusal to pair with you, for I know, that no duty imposed on
you, will be unperformed, and that will enable me, to See your genial face again on
Election day—As to the County Ticket, I am free to make the pair with you with the
agreement, it is not to deprive you of voting for any Democrat on the ticket, or me
from voting for any Republican on their Ticket" ALS (facsimile), *ibid.* See *PUSG*, 17,
319–20.

To William L. Robinson

Galena, Ill.
Sept. 24th /80

DEAR SIR:

I regret that I will not be able to accept your courtious invitation of the 22d inst. to visit the Exposition now being held in Cincinnati. My engagements will keep me in this state until the 8th of October, too late for the exposition. I then must go directly through to New York City[1] and Boston. I thank you very kindly for the invitation.

Very Truly Yours
U. S. GRANT

WM L. ROBINSON, CHMN &C.

ALS (facsimile), eBay, Feb., 2006. Cincinnati held its eighth annual industrial exposition from Sept. 8 to Oct. 9, 1880.

1. On Oct. 4, Thursday, USG, Chicago, wrote to Hitchcock & Darling, Fifth Avenue Hotel, New York City. "I leave here on Friday for New York City, via Fort Wayne & Pittsburg road, and will reach Jersey City the afternoon of Saturday. . . . As I will be in Decatur, Ill., until about midnight, I may not reach Chicago in time for the morning train. In this case I will . . . reach New York City early Monday. I will telegraph. . . . Besides Mrs. Grant & myself, Jim [*Jesse*] Grant & bride will be with the party. . . ." Christie's Sale 7086, June 1990, no. 68.

Speech

[*Warren, Ohio, Sept. 28, 1880*]

LADIES AND GENTLEMEN: I hope we may be able to have quiet and order here. It is not important so far as anything that I will have to say to you is concerned, because I shall not be able to make many of you hear, but the next speaker[1] is one whom I know you will all be glad to hear, and you can do so by keeping quiet and orderly. Not being accustomed to speaking publicly, I have drawn off a few words that I will say in advance of the gentleman who is to follow me. In view of the known character and ability of the speaker who is to

address you to-day, and his long public career and association with
the leading statesmen of this country for the past 20 years, it would
not be becoming in me to detain you with many remarks of my own.
But it may be proper for me to account to you, on the first occasion
of my presiding at political meetings, for the faith that is in me.

I am a Republican as the two great political parties are now
divided, because the Republican Party is a national party seeking
the greatest good for the greatest number of citizens. There is not a
precinct in this vast Nation where a Democrat cannot cast his ballot and have it counted as cast. No matter what the prominence of
the opposite party, he can proclaim his political opinions, even if he
is only one among a thousand, without fear and without proscrip-
tion on account of his opinions. There are 14 States and localities in
some other States where Republicans have not this privilege. This is
one reason why I am a Republican. But I am a Republican for many
other reasons. The Republican Party assures protection to life and
property, the public credit, and the payment of the debts of the Government, State, county, or municipality, so far as it can control. The
Democratic Party does not promise this: if it does, it has broken its
promises to the extent of hundreds of millions, as many Northern
Democrats can testify to their sorrow. I am Republican as between
the existing parties because it fosters the production of the field and
farm and of manufactories, and it encourages the general education
of the poor as well as the rich. The Democratic party discourages
all these when in absolute power. The Republican Party is a party
of progress and of liberality toward its opponents. It encourages
the poor to strive to better their condition, the ignorant to educate
their children, to enable them to compete successfully with their
more fortunate associates, and, in fine, it secures an entire equality
before the law of every citizen, no matter what his race, nationality,
or previous condition. It tolerates no privileged class. Every one has
the opportunity to make himself all he is capable of.

Ladies and gentlemen, do you believe this can be truthfully said
in the greater part of 14 of the States of this Union to-day which
the Democratic Party control absolutely? The Republican Party is
a party of principles, the same principles prevailing wherever it has

a foothold. The Democratic Party is united in but one thing, and that is in getting control of the Government in all its branches[.] It is for internal improvement at the expense of the Government in one section and against this in another. It favors repudiation of solemn obligations in one section and honest payment of its debts in another, where public opinion will not tolerate any other view. It favors fiat money in one place and good money in another. Finally, it favors the pooling of all issues not favored by the Republicans to the end that it may secure the one principle upon which the party is a most harmonious unit, namely: getting control of the Government in all its branches. I have been in some part of every State lately in rebellion within the last year. I was most hospitably received at every place where I stopped. My receptions were not by the Union class alone, but by all classes without distinction. I had a free talk with many who were against me in the war and who have been against the Republican Party ever since. They were in all instances reasonable men, judged by what they said. I believed then and I believe now that they sincerely want a break-up in this "solid South" political condition. They see that it is to their pecuniary interest as well as to their happiness that there should be harmony and confidence between all sections. They want to break away from the slavery which binds them to a party name. They want a pretext that enough of them can unite upon to make it respectable. Once started the solid South will go as Kukluism did before, as is so admirably told by Judge Tourgee[2] in his "Fool's Errand." When the break comes, those who start it will be astonished to find how many of their friends have been in favor of it for a long time, and have only been waiting to see some one take the lead. This desirable solution can only be attained by the defeat and continued defeat of the Democratic Party as now constituted.

New York Times, Sept. 29, 1880. USG spoke before a crowd estimated at 12,000 at a Republican rally in Warren, Ohio. "The speech was delivered in a very low tone of voice, and was heard by only a few." *Ibid.*

   1. U.S. Senator Roscoe Conkling of N. Y.
   2. Born in 1838 in Ohio, Albion W. Tourgee served as 1st lt., 105th Ohio, moved to N. C., won election as superior court judge, and fought the Ku Klux Klan. He based his first novel, *A Fool's Errand* (1879), on experiences in N. C.

Calendar

1878, OCT. 15.   Joshua K. Brown, president, Soldiers' and Sailors' National Reunion, and seven others, Cambridge, Ohio, to USG. "The Sixth Annual National Reunion of Soldiers and Sailors of the late war will be held at Cambridge Ohio on the 26th 27th 28th & 29th days of August 1879, and hearing of your proposed return to the United States some time during the coming Spring, we take this early oportunity of addressing you hoping you can make it convenient to honor the occasion with your presence. Designing to make this Re-union, in fact, one of National importance, we have selected yourself and Genl Joseph E Johnson to act in the capacity of Field Marshals. We therefore beg that you will not disappoint the high expectation of thousands of your old comrades who have an earnest desire to again see among them, the man who so often led them to victory. With a hope that you will grant us an early and favorable reply, . . ."—DS, DLC-John Russell Young. On Dec. 17, Ulysses S. Grant, Jr., New York City, wrote to Gen. William T. Sherman. "Father, in his last letter, said that he had received an invitation to be present at some Army Reunion in Ohio in August next, that he took but little note of the contents at the first reading, as he put it aside to reread and answer and that he had been unable to find it since. As he was unable to remember the names and date he has been unable to answer, and now requests that you will let the Society know that he expects to be in the United States next year in time to accept the invitation, and that in that case he ~~promises~~ will be pleased to be present at the Reunion. Trusting that I make my father's wishes plain and that it is not troubling you too much . . ."—ALS, DLC-William T. Sherman. USG was still overseas at the time of this reunion, which attracted prominent politicians, including U.S. Representatives James A. Garfield and Thomas Ewing of Ohio. See *Cambridge* (Ohio) *Jeffersonian*, Oct. 3, 1878, Sept. 4, 1879; *Chicago Tribune*, Aug. 27–29, 1879; Harry James Brown and Frederick D. Williams, eds., *The Diary of James A. Garfield* (East Lansing, Mich., 1967–81), IV, 281.

[*1878, Nov.*].   To Augustus S. Worthington from Paris directing that a private suit for damages be contested in court.—*New York Herald*, Dec. 6, 1878. On Dec. 5, a correspondent reported from Washington, D. C. "In the summer of 1874 it was reported to the detectives of this city by President Grant that he was pursued constantly by a large and muscular Irishman, and confronted unexpectedly and threateningly by him during his daily walks; that he was not only spoken to by the man, but most frequently the latter would stand and glare at him as he passed; that on some occasions the man would demand, in a very resolute manner, payment of a large sum of money, which he claimed General Grant owed him; . . . The matter progressed until constant repetition became unendurable, and the General provided himself with a large and heavy cane, as he believed that he would sooner or later be assaulted. This man turned out to be Thomas Biggins, a man of some property, who carried on the business of a grocer and a retailer of liquor at a place a short distance west of the Executive Mansion. He was a man of good habits and peaceful disposition ordinarily, and of Herculean physical proportions. Biggins was a widower, and dressed richly and in good taste, and it was suggested that his peculiar conduct was the result of mental aberration. . . ."—*Ibid.* Temporarily committed to an insane asylum, Thomas Biggins filed suit against USG for false imprisonment. The case concluded in USG's favor when counsel for Biggins acknowledged that his client's testimony lacked merit. See *New York Times,* March 21–22, 1877, Jan. 11, 1879; *New York Tribune,* May 8, 1878; *Washington Evening Star,* Jan. 9–10, 1879; *New York Herald,* Jan. 10, 1879; *Washington Post,* Jan. 11, 1879.

1879, JAN. 12.   To W. H. Ince, from Paris. "On my return from a very pleasant visit to Ireland, a few days since, I found in my pocket your letter of the 4th of Jan.y requesting an Autograph and photograph. I take pleasure in complying with your request."—ALS, ICHi.

1879, FEB. 20.   Secretary of State William M. Evarts to Gen. William T. Sherman, Jacksonville, Fla. "I have the pleasure to acknowledge the receipt of the letter from General Grant of 21st ultimo, bearing your endorsement of the 13th instant, with reference to granting a leave of absence for six months, to Mr. Moran, the Chargé at Lisbon, and to assure you in reply that considering the ill health of Mr. Moran and his public services, I should be glad to accede as far as possible to the request, did the law permit me to do so, and in case it could be done without detriment to the service. But the law in regard of leaves of absence gives me no discretion enabling me to comply with Mr. Moran's wishes; and he has been so informed. Regretting the untoward circumstance, in this case, . . ."—LS, DLC-William T. Sherman.

1879, SEPT. 19.   Governor John P. St. John of Kan. to USG, San Francisco. "The Shawnee county Agricultural Fair will open at this place October the 1st, and continue for five days, and at the request of the directors I take great pleasure in inviting you to be present at least one day during the time above mentioned, assuring you as I do that should you honor the Capital city of our state with a visit that we will try to make it pleasat for you, Allow me also to add, there is no state in the union in proportion to population that has as many stalwart Grant men as has Kansas, and we desire the opportunity to give you a receptin of which our state may have reason to be proud, and you never have reason to regret, Now my dear General, do Kansas the honor to to visit us, Won'tyou? If you can possibly come, will you notify me by telegraph?"—TLS, DLC-USG, IB.

1879, SEPT.   Tully T. Young, Walker Landing, Calif., to USG, San Francisco. "I fear you may not grant me an audience, being an entire stranger to you. So beg leave to call your kind attention to a brief introductory, and the following statement—hope I dont intrude—which I hope you will carefully read. I am the son of the late Dr Jno. W Young—a native of Brown County—Ohio, and write in regard to him. Your father, and his were intimate friends—Jesse Grant & Thomas Young—both lived in adjoining Counties in Ohio, and were well acquainted. This introductory is written with the hope of you taking a deeper interest in the following statement. I herewith enclose a (copy) letter of one, addressed and forwarded to E B. French Auditor of War Claims—I believe—Washington D. C. by my father Jno. W Young M. D. asking for information concerning an application, forwarded to Washington, regarding four (4) months back pay—due—for services rendered &c, and the same approved by Col Burk, and Med Director Warden of Gen Grants Staff. See enclosed copy of letter forwarded to E. B. French, which explains itself. There is about Eight Hundred Dollars ($800) due my father for services rendered and interest on same from time payment became due. *This* Sir: *should* be paid! . . ."—ALS, DLC-John Russell Young.

1879, OCT. 9.   To President Rutherford B. Hayes, from San Francisco. "I cordially recommend to your consideration for appointment from civil life to the U. S. Army, Lincoln D. Wright. Mr. Wright was educated at Harvard University an is a nephew of Gen. Joseph Dana Webster (deceased) who served under me at Fort Donelson and who was for a time a member of my staff."—eBay, Nov. 16, 1999. No appointment followed.

1879, OCT. 14.   To Gen. William T. Sherman, from Portland, Ore. "Please say to President Would take it as personal favor if he would appoint Edwd H Brooks to the army"—Telegram received, DNA, RG 94, ACP, 6177 1879. On Oct. 15, Wednesday, Sherman telegraphed to USG. "Despatch received, and I will submit it in person to the President who is expected back from Ohio on Saturday—Think he is committed to make no more Civilian appointments until after the next West Point Class"—ALS (telegram sent, at 10:20 A.M.), *ibid.* On Oct. 21, Sherman telegraphed to USG, San Francisco. "The President has appointed Brooks."—ALS (telegram sent), *ibid.*, RG 107, Telegrams Collected (Bound). Edward H. Brooke was appointed 2nd lt. as of Nov. 28, 1879.

1879, Nov. 25.   To Thomas B. Hughlett, from Galena. "I find that I have so many letters to write to-day that I will not be able to go out to Mr. Rawlins place."—ALS, MH. See *PUSG*, 2, 117.

1879, Nov. 25.   To James W. Thynne, secretary, Caledonian Society of St. Louis, from Galena. "I regret that I cannot accept the invitation of the Caledonia Club for dinner on Dec. 1st /79. It will not be possible for me to visit St. Louis before next spring otherwise I would gladly accept."—ALS (facsimile), Alexander Autographs, Inc., Feb. 4, 1997, no. 829. See *St. Louis Globe-Dispatch*, Dec. 2, 1879.

1879, Nov. 27.   To Charles A. Getty, Amboy, Ill., from Galena. "I have received your letter of the 26, and Platform of the National Encampment O. C. D., and read both. I am my own Secretary at present, and have so many letters to write daily, that I can only say, that your platform is *sound*, according to my judgment, *in every plank*."—Broadside, ICarbS. Getty, former private, 18th N. Y., served as AG, "Our Country's Defenders," whose twelve-point platform promoted the interests of Union veterans.

1880, May 2.   To U.S. Senator Roscoe Conkling of N. Y., from "New York."
"I am in receipt of your last letter, and have very considerately weighed the
matter in all its bearings. The tribute you pay my services to the country, I
appreciate, but at the same time I fear you overestimate my services and un-
derestimate the indulgence of our country. There have been exigencies that
warranted a second term, but I do not believe that the best interests or the
country's good ever demanded a third term, or ever will. I had my doubts
even as to the advisability of a second term, and you know that I have so
expressed myself to you in our confidential talks. This is a big country, full
of brainy and ambitious men who can serve the country eminently well as its
President, and I sincerely question the policy of thwarting their noble ambition. In a republic, cosmopolitan like ours, a man's fame is too frequently
dependent upon the status of public sentiment. Fame in this country ebbs and
flows. To-day you are the peer; to-morrow you may be submerged beneath
the wave of adverse sentiment. This is another reason why the noble ambition
to be President should not be restricted to one man. I feel that our country
has amply repaid me for all my services by the honors it has bestowed upon
me, and I feel that to be a candidate or accept the nomination for a third term
would be ingratitude and would eventually affect me with the people who
have loved me, and whom I love. I am still of the opinion that I should speak
to the country, that I should break the silence in a letter declining emphatically to accept a nomination for a third term. I appreciate your efforts, your
friendship and loyalty, but I fear that your zealousness for me is an error, not
of heart but of mind. Knowing that with all your nobleness you have a highly
sensitive nature, and knowing your antipathy to the Maine statesman, I have
always refrained from speaking of him to you, but I now feel that I should
speak on that matter and plainly. This estrangement between you two, unless checked, must prove a mutual disadvantage. It will hurt Mr. Conkling. It
will hurt Mr. Blaine. It will be a stumbling block in the way of the ambitions
of both. I believe that could the differences existing be amicably adjusted the
nomination, this year, would go to one, leaving the honor four years hence
more than a probability for the other. It is not only necessary for the good of
each that an amicable adjustment be reached, but for the good of the party;
and more, for the good of the country. I fear that the presentation of my
name at the convention would not only assist in the defeat of Mr. Blaine,
but seriously effect your future, besides warping my career. Even should I be
nominated, it could only come after a spirited contest in which much bitterness would be injected; and then I doubt if I could be elected, as I seriously
doubt whether any man can ever again be elected even for a second term,
unless perchance there should arise some extraordinary emergency, which
now appears improbable, even in the dim future. I am aware that this matter
has gone on to an extent where an announcement from me refusing to accept
would be looked upon, by some, as cowardice. But would it not be far better
to be considered a coward than a usurper? I also appreciate your position, as
you say, 'the final and supreme effort of your life for supremacy,' yet in the
face of all, I still believe that my name should not be presented. And further,
I believe that your anxiety about the effect an announcement from me would

have on your future is in error. I trust you will consider gravely and carefully my wishes. I am generous enough to suffer myself rather than to have
my friends suffer, if I am convinced that any act of mine would cause them to
suffer. Awaiting your reply before acting, . . ."—*Columbus Dispatch*, May 20,
1892. See *ibid.*, May 23, 24, 26, 28, June 2, 1892.

The *Chicago Inter-Ocean* editorialized concerning this letter. "The above
comes to THE INTER OCEAN from its correspondent at Columbus, Ohio, and
is printed as one of the curiosities of this peculiar campaign. *It is doubt[l]ess a
fake and a fraud.* Its object is apparent. Those who concocted it were evidently
willing to malign some of our most honored and revered dead to forward
certain secret conspiracies *for controlling the convention at Minneapolis.* To any
one who can read between the lines the object is evident. . . . The words of
the pretended letter sound in no way like Grant's words, and every statement
made is contradicted by the statements of those who were nearest to Grant
in those days, and are contradicted by the public and private interviews with
Grant after the famous campaign of 1880." ". . . It is evidently the product
of some misguided man who knows how to write and who wanted to injure
the chances of President Harrison for renomination and if possible bring
Mr. Blaine to the front. . . ."—*Chicago Inter-Ocean*, May 21, 28, 1892. Ulysses S.
Grant, Jr., said he knew nothing about this letter. "But it doesn't sound a bit
like father, . . . Father wasn't given to talking about his 'generosity' in the
way this letter makes him speak. Then, again, the phraseology isn't his. The
letter is altogether too long for father to have written it. Had he addressed a
communication on such a subject to Senator Conkling, or any one else who
might have been as intimate a friend as was Senator Conkling, he would have
said what he had to say in a few words—two or three paragraphs, or, possibly,
sentences, at the outside. . . ."—*New York Times*, May 22, 1892. On May 23,
1892, Julia Dent Grant, New York City, said: "I am sure General Grant never
wrote the letter in question. He was in New York only for a few days after
he left the White House, when Mr. Hayes was inaugurated, when he, or we,
sailed for our trip around the globe. He did not return here until long after
Garfield was nominated, and at that time a grand reception was given him at
the Fifth Avenue Hotel. General Grant came then to assist in the canvass for
Garfield, and accompanied Mr. Conkling on one or more tours. It was said
they did great service for the party. I am certain this letter is not the General's, for I know he was not opposed to a second term, and I know he was
not opposed to a third term as the alleged letter pretends, or he would never
have allowed his name to be used. I have received too many letters from him
to recognize this as one of his handwriting. Even had it been dated from Galena I would have doubted it in consequence for it does not sound like him.
It is too long and too effusive. Although General Grant did not want a third
term he was not opposed to it. I made up my mind that it is a safe rule to
have terms of office in case the President proves obnoxious, but if you have a
good one why not keep him in office?"—*Chicago Inter-Ocean*, May 24, 1892.
On April 28, 1880, USG had left Galena for Chicago, where he remained until May 4. See *Julia Grant*, pp. 321–22; George S. Boutwell, *Reminiscences of
Sixty Years in Public Affairs* (New York, 1902), II, 267–272.

1880, MAY 10.   To John Wesley Hooper, Lake View, Ill., from Galena. "I
have rec'd and read the poem which you wrote and forwarded to me. Of
course I can make no comment on it further than to say it is complimentary to me, probably more so than I deserve."—ALS (facsimile), eBay, April,
2007. On April 11, 1884, USG, Washington, D. C., wrote to Hooper. "Yours
of 22nd ult. was duly received. I have no profile likeness of myself. There are
engravings of that sort existing, but I have none of them."—LS (facsimile),
ibid. See *Chicago Tribune,* Dec. 3, 1898, Jan. 19, 1899.

1880, MAY 14.   USG endorsement, from Galena. "I remember the sickness
of Surgeon Allen as described within distinctly and was cognizant of his services during the early part of the rebellion. I know nothing of the immediate cause of his death, however . . . I know he was an earnest and efficient
worker in the War and came near dying from disease contracted during the
War."—*The Collector,* No. 821 [n. d.], F-10. See *Chicago Inter-Ocean,* June 3,
1880; *PUSG,* 7, 404.

1880, MAY 29.   To Henry A. Brown, from Galena. "Your favor of the 22d of
May, and the documents covering your analyses of the Sugar Tariff question,
come duly to hand. I have not had time to examine them but will preserve
them for refference. Thanking you for your kindness, . . ."—ALS, ViU. See
Henry A. Brown, *Revised Analyses on the Sugar Question . . .* (Saxonville, Mass.,
1879), and his other publications on the same topic.

1880, JUNE 7.   Alexander J. D. Thurston, Seymour, Ind., to USG. "Will you
allow an ex rebel colonel to express to you his honest admiration of your
character and bearing in this contest through which you are passing. When
war is made upon one by his political associates, of the character made upon
you at the present time, by the *politicians* of your party, it is enough to make
one foreswear all party affiliations   Do you believe the Democrats of the
South if they had a chance to elect Jefferson Davis, Genl Joseph E. Johnson
or Robert E. Lee (if living) to the presidency, would stab them with gigantic
lies, as the *politicians* have endeavored to stab you in Chicago. We can not
honor our officers with presidencies and high national honors, but we teach
the Northern great men their duty to their noble officers by our magnificent
fidelity to our own survivors and remembrance of our honored dead. Please
forgive me General, I could not with hold my admiration of yourself, while
you are being slaughtered by beings you have politically created,—that is if
they could slaughter you."—ALS, USG 3. See Johnson, *Papers,* 4, 384.

1880, JUNE 25.   USG check. "The National Bank of Galena please pay to
the order of Chas. Gossage & Co. Chicago, Ill. Four Hundred, Sixty Four
(464) dollars Eighty-two cents & charge, $464 82/100"—ADS (facsimile),
R. M. Smythe & Co., Inc., Sale No. 225, Nov. 14, 2002, no. 356.

1880, AUG. 31.   Horace H. Walpole, Syracuse, N. Y., to USG. "Again I tres-
pass upon your valuable time, to thank you for your Characteristic, Kindly

letter to me & the surviving members of my late command, the 122d N. Y. Vols. It was read to the '*Boys*' at their reunion, August 28th inst. & such a Cheer & shout as went up from their throats is rarely heard among citizens of equal numbers. Our 122d men, are most of them facsimiles of the glorious *306* at Chicago dear Genl, & it useless to endeavor to more fully express our abiding affection for you & yours. Trusting that OUR DAY may some time come, to see your face & form among us, & that your life may be prolonged many, many years beyond the allotted age of man, full of health and 'that peace which passeth all understanding.'"—ALS, USG 3.

1880, SEPT. 2. To unknown addressee, from Galena. "Your letter of the 24th of August came duly to hand several days ago. I find it before me and do not know whether it has been answered or not. For fear it has not I answer it now, accepting the honor conferred by electing me an honorary member of your Club, suggesting however for the consideration of yourself and associates whether it would not be better to change the name to 'The Garfield and Arthur Club.'"—David Battan Autographs, Catalogue 7, [1970], no. 49.

1880, SEPT. 19. To Philip A. Hoyne, secretary, Union League of America, Chicago, from Galena. "On my return yesterday from visiting some Fairs in this state, I found your letter of the 15th inst. notifying me of my election as honorary member of the Chicago Club of the Union League of America. Please present my thanks to the Club for the compliment which I accept with pleasure"—ALS (facsimile), *Union League Men and Events*, XXXVI, 1 (Jan., 1960), 2.

1880, SEPT. 25. USG announcement. "The Union Veteran Soldiers and Sailors of the United States will meet in Convention at Indianapolis, Indiana, on Thursday the 7th day of October, 1880."—D (issued by Drake DeKay), DLC-James A. Garfield. USG did not attend the Union Veterans' Union gathering in Indianapolis. See *New York Herald*, Oct. 9, 1880.

On Oct. 11, Monday, USG attended a Boys in Blue demonstration in New York City. On Oct. 13, Horace Porter, New York City, wrote to U.S. Representative James A. Garfield of Ohio. ". . . No description you have seen can give you any idea of the magnitude and effect of the all-night review we gave to Gen. Grant Monday. I trotted out my war horse once more, and organized and commanded a Division of just 20.000 men. We had 58000 on paper, and about 49000 actually in line The route was magnificently decorated and illuminated. Gen. Grant, like the good soul he is, sat and stood on the platform from 10 P. M. till 4 A. M. when the last organization passed I am certain it created a profound impression upon a large class here who do not read or think much, but who are easily impressed with a show of power and numbers. Gen. Grant keeps up his admirable, logical talks in private and public, and continues to do no end of good. He strikes fire every time. . . ."—ALS, DLC-James A. Garfield. See *New York Herald*, Oct. 12, 1880.

Index

All letters written by USG of which the text was available for use in this volume are indexed under the names of the recipients. The dates of these letters are included in the index as an indication of the existence of text. Abbreviations used in the index are explained on pp. xix–xxiv. Individual regts. are indexed under the names of the states in which they originated.